国际环境法

INTERNATIONAL ENVIRONMENTAL LAW

[法] 皮埃尔·玛丽·杜普（Pierre-Marie Dupuy）
[英] 豪尔赫·E.维努阿莱斯（Jorge E. Viñuales） ◎著

胡斌 马亮 ◎译 秦天宝 ◎审校

中国社会科学出版社

CAMBRIDGE

图字：01-2021-6131 号

图书在版编目（CIP）数据

国际环境法／（法）皮埃尔·玛丽·杜普，（英）豪尔赫·E. 维努阿莱斯著；胡斌，马亮译.—北京：中国社会科学出版社，2021.11

书名原文：International Environmental Law

ISBN 978-7-5203-9034-7

Ⅰ.①国⋯ Ⅱ.①皮⋯ ②豪⋯ ③胡⋯ ④马⋯ Ⅲ.①国际环境法学 Ⅳ.①D996.9

中国版本图书馆 CIP 数据核字（2021）第 179904 号

Colonial Policy and Practice：International Environmental Law was originally published by Cambridge University Press

ⓒ Cambridge University Press［2018］

出 版 人	赵剑英
责任编辑	梁剑琴
责任校对	李　莉
责任印制	郝美娜
出　　版	中国社会科学出版社
社　　址	北京鼓楼西大街甲 158 号
邮　　编	100720
网　　址	http：//www.csspw.cn
发 行 部	010-84083685
门 市 部	010-84029450
经　　销	新华书店及其他书店
印　　刷	北京君升印刷有限公司
装　　订	廊坊市广阳区广增装订厂
版　　次	2021 年 11 月第 1 版
印　　次	2021 年 11 月第 1 次印刷
开　　本	710×1000　1/16
印　　张	40.5
字　　数	688 千字
定　　价	158.00 元

凡购买中国社会科学出版社图书，如有质量问题请与本社营销中心联系调换
电话：010-84083683
版权所有　侵权必究

This is a Simplified-Chinese translation edition of the following title published by Cambridge University Press:

International Environmental Law

ISBN 978-1-108-43811-7

© Cambridge University Press 2018

This Simplified-Chinese translation edition for the People's Republic of China (excluding Hong Kong, Macau and Taiwan) is published by arrangement with the Press Syndicate of the University of Cambridge, Cambridge, United Kingdom.

© Cambridge University Press and China Social Sciences Press 2021

This Simplified-Chinese translation edition is authorized for sale in the People's Republic of China (excluding Hong Kong, Macau and Taiwan) only. Unauthorised export of this Simplified-Chinese translation edition is a violation of the Copyright Act. No part of this publication may be reproduced or distributed by any means, or stored in a database or retrieval system, without the prior written permission of Cambridge University Press and China Social Sciences Press.

Copies of this book sold without a Cambridge University Press sticker on the cover are unauthorized and illegal.

本书封面贴有 Cambridge University Press 防伪标签，无标签者不得销售。

第二版序言

> 地球就像橙子那样蓝
> L'Amour la Poésie（1929）Paul Eluard
> ——《爱情与诗歌》（1929）保尔·艾吕雅

　　写书是核对与收集经验和记忆的一种方式，而这些经验和记忆正是作者想要坚持的。在本书第二版原稿的检查即将完成之际，两位作者来到了意大利托斯卡纳区，并对最后细节做出了微调。托斯卡纳区的小山为这一序言的撰写提供了一个惬意的环境。

　　关于本书最重要的目的，我们可以重述我们为第一版撰写的序言。努力提供一个关于国际环境法的精确的、概念清晰的、技术严格的描述，将其作为国际法的必要部分，仍然是第二版的核心目的。第一版出版以来，国际环境法迎来了大量规范上的发展，其中有些进展显得足够突出，例如，"可持续发展目标"（Sustainable Development Goals，SDGs）和关于气候变化的《巴黎协定》（Paris Agreement）的通过，以至于可以用"以前"和"以后"来严格区分，因此有必要出版第二版。同时，每隔三年至五年的定期更新，也是我们当初撰写本书时的设想，其目的就是紧跟国际环境法的飞速发展步伐。

　　第二版反映了截至 2017 年 5 月的进展。笔者更新了所有的章节，有些还进行了重大的重写。除了可持续发展目标和《巴黎协定》，另外一些重大的补充包含了最近几年司法判决的实质内容，它们有助于增强对国际环境法基本原则及其在某些条约 [例如《联合国海洋法公约》（UNCLOS）] 中的应用的理解，还有《蒙特利尔议定书》之《基加利修订案》（Kigali Amendment to the Montreal Protocol）的制定，当前围绕国家管辖范围外生物多样性问题的谈判，国际法对淡水的延伸应对、国际法委员会（International Law Commission）针对大气以及与军事冲突相关的环境问题所开展的工作，在大量相关案例的基础上，对人权与环境之间关系的深入探讨，以及将环境因素融入投资、贸易和知识产权法之中这一当前趋势。

  总而言之，第二版所涉及的进展说明了国际环境法在国际法律实践中的成长和真实的展现。当前，国际法律工作者的知识体系和培训中的一个主要短板就是他们对国际环境法这一学科的生疏。国际环境法有可能并最终将成为一个主流学科。这也使我们有理由去期望，将来环境将交到更好的人手中。期望可以变为一个记忆，这也是本书作者的一个希望，正如他们漫步在托斯卡纳区山中时所一直想要坚守的。

第一版序言

> 如何保持美永不消逝，是否在某地存在一个我们不知道的碗、胸针、辫子、支架、花边、门闩、窗钩或钥匙？
>
> ——《灰色回声与金色回声》，杰拉德·曼利·霍普金斯

本书试图解决我们在国际环境法的教学与实践中遇到的两个主要难题。

第一个难题是一个实质性问题，它来源于这一学科本身所具备的令人生畏的范围和多样性。在初学者看来，国际环境法给人的印象与国际法的其他领域都不相同，它具有分散性、模糊、异国风味等特点。在国际环境法的标签下，汇集的主题涵盖了湿地、鲸鱼、遗传资源的保护和核能、臭氧层消耗或有害废物管理。这些主题的每一个都可自成体系。但是，自20世纪70年代以来，（人们）一直试图努力将它们纳入一个单一的学科，这么多年来，该学科还是需要高强度的系统化。本书是我们为这些努力所做出的一份贡献。本书所讨论的内容是基于国际环境法这一概念，它在本书中得以精确地阐释。我们将涉及环境保护的国际法看作国际法的一个分支和一个方面。作为一个分支，国际环境法是基于预防（环境危害的预防）和平衡（不同关切和利益相关者之间的平衡）的理念，本书第一编的第三章所探讨的数个原则和概念就是通过法律形式对这两种理念进行了阐释。随后，本书第二编通过分析相关条约的框架，第三编通过分析条约的实施方法来具体说明这些原则和概念。通过这样一种金字塔结构，即从理念到原则和概念，再到条约及其行政法，笔者用概念性描绘的方法清晰地表述了国际环境法所涵盖的不同内容。但是，涉及环境保护的国际法并不能被一个分支的条条框框所局限。环境保护不应被看作一项单独范围内的活动，而应被当作一个目标，需要人类其他一切活动的参与，只有这

样，才能实现环保的目的。站在这一高度看，涉及环境保护的国际法并不缺乏国际公法所必需的一切形式，只不过它的重点是给环境因素适当的考量。本书第四编进一步发展了这一观点，特别强调了环境保护对人权、战时法、诉诸战争权、裁军法、外商投资法、国际贸易法和知识产权的影响。把国际环境法当作一个分支和一个方面来学习，我们的目的是表明这一领域的学习具有一些独具一格的特点，它不能仅仅被局限于一个分支。

第二个难题属于教学法上的问题，也与前文的第一个难题密切相关。面对如此多样和宽泛的规范、条约以及法律上有关联的条约，一个对本领域不熟悉的初学者，无论是学生、实务工作者还是研究人员，很容易被击垮。国际环境法的特殊性确实给入门造成了较大的障碍。这一领域的不同主题都还在持续不断地演进，这也增加了障碍的难度，因此，需要课本和实践教材频繁地进行更新，所涉及的内容也是海量的。为了应对这一挑战，现有的少数几本综合性著作也涵盖了这一领域的全部内容，从范围和体量来看，它们也几乎可以被认定是严格意义上的论述。但是，仍然有必要针对这一主题开展更具体的研究，目的是让读者了解不同的主题，阐明每个主题在金字塔结构中的定位，并特别强调相关规范制度中最重要的专业内容。这就是本书所遵循的方法。本书尝试绘制这样一个路线图，即对这一领域的了解从完全陌生进化到现有条约和其他次级法律资源所阐述的复杂知识，它提供了一个基本的方法，希望能够充当一个指南针的作用，为后续更深的探究指明方向。

在从事本书的撰写时，我们在剑桥和日内瓦与几代学生的相处经历给了我们很大的鼓励，他们正是通过这一概念分析和技术分析相结合的方法来接触国际环境法的。他们中的许多人后来都成为研究者或实务工作者，非常感谢他们与我们分享了他们在工作中运用这一教学方法的经验。因此，本书不仅浓缩了老师的经验，还在一定程度上浓缩了学生的经验。另外，几代优秀的教学和研究助理也对这一漫长而耐心的习作过程贡献良多。特别要诚挚感谢 Stephanie Chuffart、Maria de la Colina、Martina Kunz、Magnus Jesko Langer、Jason Rudall、Pablo Sandonato de Leon，他们在 2009—2014 年为本书的筹备做出了重大贡献。当然，本书可能出现的错漏的责任仅由作者本人负责。

最后，我们还想补充说明一点，本书的撰写是一件乐事。两个作者对国际环境法的内容、方法和总体理解心有灵犀，都认为其是国际法的一个领域和一个方面，其对国际法的演化的影响也在日益增加。

　　本书所描述的保护环境的大量尝试见证了国际社会为了"挽留消逝中的美丽"所做的努力。这些努力很重要，但是并不充分。将爱美之心进行道德说教也可能会导致对其最终结果的完全漠视，那些不切实际的期望和战略就是如此虚伪。建立明晰的环境法规并明文规定优先事项，应当是落实从法规到实践，并实现真实的环境保护的唯一现实方法。霍普金斯的动人诗歌是一个针对美丽的消逝、老化和衰退的温和而浓烈的抗争。我们不可避免地会自动丧失青春之美，但是，这种必然性不应发生在我们的环境之美上。

中文版序言

看到我们的国际环境法教程的中文版即将出版,我们感到非常高兴。本书由武汉大学环境法研究所胡斌博士领导的团队进行翻译,它将被用于武汉大学这样一个在中国领先的环境法研究中心以及广大华语区科研机构的教学工作。

我们非常感谢武汉大学环境法研究所,特别是所长秦天宝教授、胡斌博士带领的翻译团队以及武汉大学所做的这项工作,它让我们的研究和教学能够在中国得到更大的普及。国际环境法的重要性无以复加。它可能是当今国际法中最关键的领域,也是一个关键手段,以便促使人类进行转变并确定一个发展轨迹以避免气候变化和环境退化的最坏后果。

年轻一代及我们的后代在这一转变进程中发挥着至关重要的作用。为了提供一个简明的、概念清晰、技术严谨的陈述,我们做出了多年的努力,自始至终都是为了帮助我们的后代有能力做出必要的抉择。

皮埃尔·玛丽·杜普(Pierre-Marie Dupuy)
豪尔赫·E. 维努阿莱斯(Jorge E. Viñuales)
2021 年 6 月 21 日

译者序

本书的翻译起源于英国剑桥大学豪尔赫·E. 维努阿莱斯（Jorge E. Viñuales）教授在2019年4月对武汉大学法学院的访问。我本人对剑桥大学有着一种特殊的情愫，在大学时最喜欢的诗歌就是徐志摩的《再别康桥》，在2017年9月曾经在剑桥大学小驻，并写了一篇散文——《康桥若只如初见》。因此，我便主动联系豪尔赫·E. 维努阿莱斯教授并陪其在武汉大学游览。在漫步交谈中，得知他和日内瓦高级国际关系及发展研究院的皮埃尔·玛丽·杜普（Pierre-Marie Dupuy）教授合著的第二版《国际环境法》刚刚由剑桥大学出版社出版，我便提出将其翻译成中文，豪尔赫·E. 维努阿莱斯教授欣然应允。

皮埃尔·玛丽·杜普教授和豪尔赫·E. 维努阿莱斯教授都是国际环境法领域的权威专家，翻译他们的宏编巨著也让我有了一次系统学习国际环境法的机会。本书的序言和前七章由我翻译，第八章以后由马亮博士翻译并由我修订，最终由我统稿并经秦天宝教授审校。本书涉及环境法、国际法、法理学等诸多部门法，在翻译的过程中，得到了秦天宝教授和张万洪教授等学者的诸多帮助，在此一并致谢。中国社会科学出版社的责任编辑梁剑琴博士为本书的出版付出了辛勤的努力，她精益求精的审稿和一丝不苟的工作态度对保证本书的高质量助力良多。

因为繁杂的行政工作的束缚，我只有在暑假和寒假才有精力开展翻译工作。主要的翻译工作是在2020年1—4月完成的。这也是源于历史的巧合。2020年1月中旬我和母亲去海南度假，因为新冠肺炎疫情而滞留到4月中旬才回到湖北，这才使我有了整整三个月的时间专心致志地进行翻译。这三个月也是我和母亲朝夕相处的三个月，仿佛又回到了自己的中学时代，我在课桌上埋头苦读，母亲精心照料着我的生活起居。自从上大学以后就再也没有这种体验，以后永远也不会再有了。忽有故人心上过，回首山河已是秋。树欲静而风不止，子欲养而亲不待。母亲一直以我为荣，这本译著也寄托着我对她的深深怀念。

　　此刻我正带着女儿在恩施大峡谷避暑，她即将进入高中，面临着紧张的三年苦读。希望她在多年之后也能回忆起这段时光，正如我回忆我的母亲。

胡　斌
2021 年 7 月 30 日于恩施

缩略词

AB——Appellate Body of the WTO Dispute Settlement Body
世界贸易组织争端解决机构中的上诉机构

African Commission——African Commission of Human and Peoples' Rights
非洲人权和人民权利委员会

African Court——African Court of Human and Peoples' Rights
非洲人权和民族权法院

APEC——Asia Pacific Economic Co-operation
亚太区经济合作组织

ASMA——Antarctic Specially Managed Areas
南极特别管理区

ASPA——Antarctic Specially Protected Areas
南极特别保护区

ATCM——Antarctic Treaty Consultative Meeting
南极条约协商会议

ATS——Antarctic Treaty System
南极条约体系

BAT——Best Available Technology
最佳可得技术

BCH——Biosafety Clearing House
生物安全资料交换所

BIT——Bilateral Investment Treaty
单边投资条约

CBD——Convention on Biological Diversity
生物多样性公约

CBDR——Common But Differentiated Responsibility
共同但有区别的责任

CDM——Clean Development Mechanism
清洁发展机制

CESCR——UN Committee on Economic, Social and Cultural Rights
联合国经济、社会与文化权利委员会

CFR——United States Code of Federal Regulations
美国联邦法规

CMP——Conference of the Parties acting as the Meeting of the Parties
充当缔约方会议的缔约方大会

COP（COPs）——Conference（s）of the Parties
缔约方大会

CRF——Common Reporting Format
通用报告格式

CSD——Commission for Sustainable Development
可持续发展委员会

ECOSOC——UN Economic and Social Council
联合国经济及社会理事会

ECtHR——European Court of Human Rights
欧洲人权法院

EEZ——Exclusive Economic Zone
专属经济区

EGS——Environmental Goods and Services
环境商品和服务

EIA——Environmental Impact Assessment
环境影响评价

EMEP——European Monitoring and Evaluation Programme
欧洲监测和评估项目网络

EPA——United States Environmental Protection Agency
美国环保署

ETIS——Elephant Trade Information System
大象贸易信息系统

FAO——UN Food and Agriculture Organization
联合国粮农组织

FTA——Free Trade Agreement
自由贸易协定

GA（or UNGA）——United Nations General Assembly
联合国大会

GAOR——UN General Assembly Official Records
联合国大会官方记录

GAW——Global Atmosphere Watch
全球大气观测

GDP——Gross Domestic Product
国内生产总值

GEF——Global Environmental Facility
全球环境基金

GMA——Global Mercury Assessment
全球汞评估

GMO——Genetically Modified Organism
转基因生物

HRC——UN Human Rights Committee
联合国人权委员会

IAEA——International Atomic Energy Agency
国际原子能机构

ICEF——International Court of the Environment Foundation
环境基金国际法院

ICJ——International Court of Justice
国际法院

ICommHR——InterAmerican Commission on Human Rights
美洲人权委员会

ICSID——International Centre for Settlement of Investment Disputes
国际投资争端解决中心

ICtHR——Inter-American Court of Human Rights
美洲人权法院

IDI——Institut de Droit International
国际法研究院

IIA（s）——International Investment Agreement（s）
国际投资协定

IISD——International Institute for Sustainable Development
国际可持续发展研究院

ILA——International Law Association
国际法协会

ILC——International Law Commission
（联合国）国际法委员会

ILM——International Legal Materials
《国际法律资料》

IMO——International Maritime Organization
国际海事组织

INC——Intergovernmental Negotiation Committee
政府间谈判委员会

IOMC——Inter-organization Programme for the Sound Management of Chemicals
化学品无害管理组织间方案

IPCC——International Panel on Climate Change
政府间气候变化专门委员会

IPR——Intellectual Property Rights
知识产权

ITLOS——International Tribunal for the Law of the Sea
国际海洋法法庭

IUCN——International Union for the Conservation of Nature
世界自然保护联盟

LMO——Living Modified Organism
改性活生物体

MDG——Millennium Development Goal
千年发展目标

MEA（s）——Multilateral Environmental Agreement（s）

多边环境协定

MIKE——Monitoring the Illegal Killing of Elephants
大象非法捕杀监测（组织）

NAFO——Northwest Atlantic Fisheries Organization
西北大西洋渔业组织

NCP——Non-Compliance Procedures
不遵约程序

NGO——Non-Governmental Organization
非政府组织

NIR——National Inventory Report
国家库存报告

OAS——Organization of American States
美洲国家组织

OECD——Organisation for Economic Co-operation and Development
经济合作与发展组织

OHCHR——Office of the High Commissioner for Human Rights
联合国人权事务高级专员办公室

PCA——Permanent Court of Arbitration
常设仲裁法院

PES——Payment for Ecosystem Services
生态系统服务付费

PIC——Prior Informed Consent
事先知情同意

POP——Persistent Organic Pollutants
持久性有机污染物

PPP——Public-Private Partnership
公共和私营部门伙伴关系

REDD——Reduced Emissions from Deforestation and Forest Degradation
通过减少砍伐森林和减缓森林退化而降低温室气体排放

RFMO——Regional Fisheries Management Organization
区域渔业管理组织

RIAA——Reports of International Arbitral Awards

国际仲裁裁决报告

SAICM——Strategic Approach to International Chemicals Management
国际化学品管理战略方针

SC（or UNSC）——United Nations Security Council
联合国安理会

SDG——Sustainable Development Goals
可持续发展目标

SFDI——Société Française pour le Droit International
法国国际法学会

SGRP——System-wide Genetic Resources Programme of the Treaty on Plant Genetic Resources
《植物遗传资源条约》的整套遗传资源项目

TFDD——www.transboundarywaters.orst.edu
跨界淡水资源争端数据库

TOMAs——Tropospheric Ozone Management Areas
对流层臭氧区域

TWC——Reports of Trials of War Criminals
战争犯罪审判报告

UN——United Nations
联合国

UNCC——United Nations Compensation Commission
联合国赔偿委员会

UNCCD——United Nations Convention to Combat
《联合国防治荒漠化公约》

UNCED——United Nations Conference on Environment and Development
联合国环境与发展大会

UNCITRAL——United Nations Commission on International Trade Law
联合国国际贸易法委员会

UNCTAD——United Nations Commission on Trade and Development
联合国贸易与发展委员会

UNDESA——United Nations Department of Economic and Social Affairs
联合国经济和社会事务部

UNDP——United Nations Development Programme
联合国开发规划署

UNECE——United Nations Economic Commission for Europe
联合国欧洲经济委员会

UNEP——United Nations Environment Programme
联合国环境规划署

UNFCCC——United Nations Framework Convention on Climate Change
《联合国气候变化框架公约》

UNHCR——United Nations High Commissioner for Refugees
联合国难民署

UNTS——United Nations Treaty Series
联合国条约集

VOC——Volatile Organic Compound
挥发性有机化合物

WMO——World Meteorological Organization
世界气象组织

WTO——World Trade Organization
世界贸易组织

WWF——World Wildlife Fund
世界自然基金会

案例清单

常设国际法院/国际法院

Armed Activities on the Territory of the Congo (Democratic Republic of the Congo v. Uganda), Judgment, ICJ Reports 2005, p. 168. 7, 421

Case relating to the territorial jurisdiction of the International Commission on the River Oder, PCIJ Series A No. 23, Judgment (10 September 1929), p. 130

Certain Activities Carried Out by Nicaragua in the Border Area (Costa Rica v. Nicaragua), Provisional Measures, Order of 8 March 2011, ICJ Reports 2011, p. 6. 40, 75, 426

Certain Activities Carried Out by Nicaragua in the Border Area (Costa Rica v. Nicaragua), Construction of aroad in Costa Rica along the river San Juan (Nicaragua v. Costa Rica), Judgment of 16 December 2015 (ICJ), p. 116. 306, 426

Certain Phosphate Lands in Nauru (Nauru v. Australia), Preliminary Objections, Judgment, ICJ Reports 1992, p. 240. 302

CorfuChannel case (United Kingdom v. Albania), Judgment, ICJ Reports 1949, p. 4. 5. 5, 63, 64

Fisheries case (United Kingdom v. Norway), Judgment, ICJ Reports 1951, p. 108

Fisheries Jurisdiction case (UK v. Iceland), Decision on Jurisdiction, ICJ Reports 1974, p. 3. 75

Fisheries Jurisdiction (Federal Republic of Germany v. Iceland), Merits, Judgment, ICJ Reports 1974, p. 175. 109

Fisheries Jurisdiction (Spain v. Canada), Judgment, ICJ Reports 1998,

p. 432. 112, 211

Gabčíkovo – Nagymaros Project (Hungary v. Slovakia), Judgment, ICJ Reports1997, p. 7. 40, 60, 129, 149, 302

Legal Consequences of the Construction of a Wall in the Occupied Palestinian Territory, Advisory Opinion, ICJ Reports 2004, p. 136. 421

Legality of the Threat or Use of Nuclear Weapons, Advisory Opinion, ICJ Reports 1996, p. 226. 30, 60, 149, 295, 411

Legality of the Use by a State of Nuclear Weapons in Armed Conflict, AdvisoryOpinion, ICJ Reports 1996, p. 66. 302

North Sea Continental Shelf Case, Judgment, ICJ Reports 1969, p. 3. 75

Nuclear Tests (Australia v. France), Request for the Indication of Interim Measures of Protection, Order (22 June 1973), ICJ Reports 1973, p. 99. 65, 75

Nuclear Tests (New Zealand v. France), Request for the Indication of Interim Measures of Protection, Order (22 June 1973), ICJ Reports 1973, p. 135. 65

Oil Platforms case (Islamic Republic of Iran v. United States of America), ICJ Reports 2003, p. 161. 306, 427, 476

Preah Vihear case (Cambodia v. Thailand), Judgment, ICJ Reports 1962, p. 6. 229

Pulp Mills on the River Uruguay (Argentinav. Uruguay), ProvisionalMeasures, Order (13 July 2006), ICJ Reports 2006, p. 113. 40

Pulp Mills on the River Uruguay (Argentina v. Uruguay), Judgment, ICJ Reports 2010, p. 14. 64, 115, 149, 191, 306

Questions relating to the Obligation to Prosecute or Extradite (Belgium v. Senegal), Judgment, ICJ Reports 2012, p. 422. 53, 317

Request for Interpretation of the Judgment of 15 June 1962 in the Caseconcerning the Temple of Preah Vihear (Cambodia v. Thailand), Judgment, ICJ Reports 2013, p. 281. 229

Whaling in the Antarctic (Australia v. Japan: New Zealand intervening), Judgment, ICJ Reports 2014, p. 226. 53, 213, 317

国际海洋法法庭以及与《联合国海洋法公约》相关的仲裁庭

Arctic Sunrise Arbitration (The Netherlands v. Russia), Award on the Merits (24 August 2015). 111

Dispute Concerning Delimitation of the Maritime Boundary between Ghanaand Côte d'Ivoire in the Atlantic Ocean (Ghana/Côte d'Ivoire), ITLOS Case No. 23, Order of 25 April 2015. 54, 67, 112, 305, 315, 377

Inthe matter of the Chagos Marine Protected Area Arbitration before an Arbitral Tribunal constituted under Annex VII of the United Nations Conventionon the Lawof the Sea (Mauritius v. UK), Award (18 March 2015). 30, 111

Inthe matter of the South China Sea Arbitration before an Arbitral Tribunalconstituted under Annex VII of the United Nations Convention on the Law of the Sea (Republic of the Philippines v. People's Republic of China), PCA Case No. 2013-19, Award (12 July 2016). 54, 61, 112, 314

MOX Plant case (Ireland v. United Kingdom), Provisional Measures, ITLOS Case No. 10, Order (3 December 2001). p. 64. 73, 305

Request for an Advisory Opinion Submitted by the Sub-Regional Fisheries Commission (SRFC), Advisory Opinion of 2 April 2015, ITLOS Case No. 21. 54, 67, 112, 191, 209, 305

Responsibilities and Obligations of States sponsoring Persons and Entities with respect to Activities in the Area, ITLOS (Seabed Disputes Chamber) Case No. 17, Advisory Opinion (1 February 2011), p. 60. 69, 115, 191, 305

Southern Bluefin Tuna Cases (New Zealand v. Japan; Australia v. Japan), Provisional Measures, ITLOS Case Nos. 3 and 4 (27 August 1999), p. 64. 73, 75, 305

世界贸易组织争端解决机构

Argentina-Measures Relating to Trade in Goods and Services, AB Report (14 April 2016), WT/DS453/AB/R. 482

Brazil-Measures Affecting Imports of Retreaded Tyres, AB Report (3 December 2007), WT/DS332/AB/R. 485

Canada-Certain Measures Affecting the Renewable Energy Generation Sector, Panel Report (19 December 2012), WT/DS412/R. 480

Canada-Measures Relating to the Feed in Tariff Program, AB Report (6 May 2013), WT/DS412/AB/R and WT/DS426/AB/R. 480

China-Measures Related to the Exportation of Various Raw Materials, Panel Reports (5 July 2011), WT/DS394/R; WT/DS395/R; WT/DS398/R. 307, 476

China-Measures Relating to the Exportation of Rare Earths, Tungsten, and Molybdenum, AB Report (7 August 2014), WT/DS431/AB/R, WT/DS432/AB/R, and WT/DS433/AB/R. 485

European Communities-Measures Affecting Asbestos and Products Containing Asbestos, AB Report (12 March 2001), WT/DS135/AB/R. 484

European Communities-Measures Affecting the Approval and Marketing of Biotech Products, Panel Report, (29 September 2006), WT/DS291/R, WT/DS292/R, WT/DS293/R. 70, 307, 476

European Communities-Measures Concerning Meat and Meat Products (Hormones), AB Report (16 January 1998) WT/DS26/AB/R, WT/DS48/AB/R. 70, 307, 488

European Communities-Measures Prohibiting the Importation and Marketing of Seal Products, AB Report (22 May 2014), WT/DS400/AB/R, WT/DS401/AB/R. 485

European Union-Anti - Dumping Measures on Biodiesel from Indonesia. Request for consultations by Indonesia (17 June 2014), WT/DS480/1, G/L/1071, G/ADP/D104/1. 480

European Union and certain Member States-Certain Measures Affecting Renewable Energy Generation Sector. Request for Consultations by China (7 November 2012), WT/DS452/1, G/L/1008, G/SCM/D95/1, G/TRIMS/D/34. 480

European Union and certain Member States-Certain Measures on theImportation and Marketing of Biodiesel and Measures Supporting the Biodiesel Industry. Request for consultations by Argentina (23 May 2013), WT/DS459/1, G/L/1027, G/SCM/D97/1, G/TRIMS/D/36, G/TBT/D/44. 480

India-Certain Measures relating to Solar Cells and Solar Modules-Report of the Appellate Body, WT/DS456/AB/R (16 September 2016). 308, 480

Mexico-Tax Measures on Soft Drinks and Other Beverages, AB Report (6 March 2006), WT/DS308/AB/R. 482

United States-Import Prohibition of Certain Shrimp and Certain Products Containing Shrimp, AB Report (12 October 1998), WT/DS58/AB/R. 307, 475

United States-Measures Concerning the Importation, Marketing and Sale of Tuna and Tuna Products, AB Report (16 May 2012), WT/DS381/AB/R. 489

United States-Restrictions on Imports of Tuna, Panel Report, (3 September 1991), DS21/R-39 S/155. 473

United States-Standards for Reformulated and Conventional Gasoline, AB Report (29 April 1996), WT/DS2/AB/R. 479

国家（或被合并的国家）间其他的仲裁

In the Matter of an Arbitration before a Tribunal constituted in accordance with Article 5 of the Arbitration Agreement between the Government of Sudan and the Sudan People's Liberation Movement/Army on Delimiting Abyei Area, Final Award (22 July 2009), available at: www.pca-cpa.org. 446

In the matter of the Indus Waters Kishenganga Arbitration before the Court of Arbitration constituted in accordance with the Indus Waters Treaty 1960 between the Government of India and the Government of Pakistan signed on 19 September 1960 (Islamic Republic of Pakistan v. Republic of India), PCA, Partial Award (18 February 2013). 69, 115, 314

In the matter of the Indus Waters Kishenganga Arbitration before the Court of Arbitration constituted in accordance with the Indus Waters Treaty 1960 between the Government of India and the Government of Pakistan signed on 19 September 1960 (Islamic Republic of Pakistan v. Republic of India), PCA, Final Award (20 December 2014). 134

Bering Sea Fur Seals Arbitration, Award (15 August 1893), RIAA, Vol. XXVIII, p. 263. 4

Iron Rhine (Ijzeren Rijn) Railway Arbitration (Belgium/Netherlands),

RIAA, Vol. XXVII (2005), p. 25. 93

Lake Lanoux Arbitration (Spain/France), RIAA, Vol. XII (1957), p. 281. 5, 75, 130, 133

Trail Smelter Arbitration, RIAA, Vol. III (1941), p. 1905. 5, 61, 63, 149

厄立特里亚和埃塞俄比亚边界委员会

Final Award-Pensions: Eritrea's Claims 15, 19 & 23 (19 December 2005), RIAA, Vol. XXVI (2005), p. 471. 424

联合国赔偿委员会

Report and Recommendation made by the Panel of Commissioners appointed to Review the Well Blowout Control Claim (WBC Claim), UN Doc. S/AC. 26/1996/5/Annex, 18 December 1996. 438

Report and Recommendation made by the Panel of Commissioners concerning the First Installment of F4 Claims, UN Doc. S/AC. 26/2001/16, 22 June2001. 30

Report and Recommendation made by the Panel of Commissioners concerning the Second Installment of F4 Claims, UN Doc. S/AC. 26/2002/26, 3 October 2002. 30

Report and Recommendation made by the Panel of Commissioners concerning the Third Installment of F4 Claims, UN Doc. S/AC. 26/2003/31, 18 December2003. 30

Report and Recommendation made by the Panel of Commissioners concerning the Fourth Installment of F4 Claims, part I, UN Doc. S/AC. 26/2004/16, 9 December 2004, part II UN Doc. S/AC. 26/2004/17, 9 December 2004. 31

Report and Recommendation made by the Panel of Commissioners concerning the Fifth Installment of F4 Claims, UN Doc. S/AC. 26/2005/10, 30 June 2005. 31

投资争端

Adel AHamadi Al Tamimi v. Sultanate of Oman, ICSID Case No. ARB/

11/33, Award (3 November 2015). 309, 465

Chemtura Corporation (formerly Crompton Corporation) v. Government of Canada, UNCITRAL, Award (2 August 2010). 308, 464

Compañía del Desarrollo de Santa Elena SA v. Republic of Costa Rica, ICSID Case No. ARB/96/1, Award (17 February 2000). 308, 462

Gold Reserve Inc. v. Bolivarian Republic of Venezuela, ICSID Case No. ARB (AF) /09/1, A ward (22 September 2014). 465

Grand River Enterprises Six Nations, Ltd and others v. United States of America NAFTA Arbitration (UNCITRAL Rules), Award (12 January 2011). 395

Kuwait v. American Independent Oil Company (AMINOIL), Arbitral Award (24 March 1982), 21 ILM 1982. 7

LG&E v. Argentine Republic, ICSID Case No. ARB/02/1, Decision on Liability (13 October 2006). 465

Libyan American Oil Company (LIAMCO) v. TheGovernment of the Libyan Arab Republic, Arbitral Award (12 April 1977), 20 ILM 1981. 7

Marion Unglaube v. Republic of Costa Rica, ICSID Case No. ARB/08/1 and Reinhard Unglaube v. Republic of Costa Rica, ICSID Case No. ARB/09/20, Award (16 May 2012). 309, 465

Mesa Power Group LLC v. Government of Canada, NAFTA (UNCITRAL) Arbitration, Notice of Arbitration (4 October 2011). 398

Metalclad Corp. v. United Mexican States, ICSID Case No. ARB (AF) /97/1, Award (25 August 2000). 308, 462

Parkerings – Compagniet AS v. Republic of Lithuania, ICSID Case No. ARB/05/8, Award (11 September 2007). 309, 464

Perenco Ecuador Ltd v. The Republic of Ecuador and Empresa Estatal Petróleosdel Ecuador (Petroecuador), ICSID Case No. ARB/08/6, Interim Decision on the Environmental Counterclaim (11 August 2015). 465

Plama Consortium Ltd. v. Republic of Bulgaria, ICSID Case No. ARB/03/24, Award (27 August 2008). 309, 464

S. D. Myers Inc. v. Canada, NAFTA Arbitration (UNCITRAL Rules), Partial Award (13 November 2000). 277, 462

Southern Pacific Properties (Middle East) Limited (SPP) v. Arab Republic of Egypt, ICSID Case No. ARB/84/3, Award (20 May 1992). 228, 462

Suez, Sociedad General de Aguas de Barcelona SA and Inter Aguas Servicios Integrales del Agua SA v. The Argentine Republic, ICSID Case No. ARB/03/17, Decision on Liability (31 July 2010). 309, 465

Suez, Sociedad General de Aguas de Barcelona SA and Vivendi Universal SA v. The Argentine Republic, ICSID Case No. ARB/03/19, Decision on Liability (31 July 2010). 309, 465

Técnicas Medioambientales Tecmed S. A. v. United Mexican States, ICSID Case No. ARB (AF) /00/2, Award (29 May 2003). 308, 462

Texaco Overseas Petroleum Company and California Asiatic Oil Company v. The Government of the Libyan Arab Republic, Arbitral Award (19 January 1977), 17 ILM 1978. 7

William Ralph Clayton, William Richard Clayton, Douglas Clayton, Daniel Clayton, and Bilcon of Delaware, Inc. v. Government of Canada, NAFTA (UNCITRAL), Award (17 March 2015). 309, 465

Windstream Energy LLC v. Government of Canada, NAFTA (UNCITRAL), Notice of Arbitration (28 January 2013). 298

欧洲人权法院

Apanasewicz v. Poland, ECtHR Application No. 6854/07, Judgment (3 May 2011). 370

Atanasov v. Bulgaria, ECtHR Application No. 12853/03, Judgment (12 December 2010). 370

Athanassoglou and others v. Switzerland, ECtHR Application No. 27644/95, Judgment (6 April 2000). 388

Aydin and others v. Turkey, ECtHR Application No. 40806/07, Decision (15 May 2012). 392

Balmer-Schafroth and others v. Switzerland, ECtHR ApplicationNo. 22110/93, Judgment (26 August 1997). 390

Brincat and others v. Malta, ECtHR Applications Nos. 60908/11, 62110/

11, 62129/11, 62312/11 and 62338/11, Judgment (24 July 2014). 305, 370

Brosset-Triboulet and others v. France, ECtHR Application No. 34078/02, Judgment (29 March 2010). 370, 403

Budayeva and others v. Russia, ECtHR Application Nos. 15339/02, 21166/02, 20058/02, 11673/02 and 15343/02, Judgment (29 September 2008). 370

Chisv. Romania, ECtHR Application No. 55396/07, Decision (admissibility) (9 September 2014). 370

Costel Popa v. Romania, ECtHR Application Nos. 47558/10, Judgment (26 April 2016). 370

Depalle v. France, ECtHR Application No. 34044/02, Judgment (29 March 2010). 370, 403

Di Sarno and others v. Italy, ECtHR Application No. 30765/08, Judgment (10 January 2012). 305

Elefteriadis v. Romania, ECtHR Application No. 38427/05, Judgment (25 January 2011). 365

Fadeyeva v. Russia, ECtHR Application Nos. 55723/00, Judgment (30 November 2005). 370

Fägerskiöld v. Sweden, ECtHR Application No. 37664/04, Decision as to Admissibility (26 February 2008). 389

Florea v. Romania, ECtHR Application No. 37186/03, Judgment (14 September 2010). 365

Grimkovskaya v. Ukraine, ECtHR Application No. 38182/03, Judgment (21 July 2011). 305

Guerra and others v. Italy, ECtHR Application No. 116/1996/735/932, Judgment (19 February 1998). 370

Hatton and others v. United Kingdom, ECtHR Application No. 36022/97, Judgment (8 July 2003). 369

Kolyadenko and others v. Russia, ECtHR Applications Nos. 17423/05, 20534/05, 20678/05, 23263/05, 24283/05 and 35673/05, Judgment (28 February 2012). 370

Kyrtatos v. Greece, ECtHR Application No. 41666/98, Judgment (22 May2003). 387

L'Erablière A. S. B. L. v. Belgium, ECtHR Application No. 49230/07, Judgment (24 February 2009). 370

Loizidou v. Turkey (Preliminary Objections), ECtHR Application No. 15318/89, Judgment (23 May 1995). 366

Lopez-Ostra v. Spain, ECtHR Application No. 16798/90, Judgment (9 December 1994). 369

Okyay and others v. Turkey, ECtHR Application No. 36220/97, Judgment (12 October 2005). 370

Oneryildiz v. Turkey, ECtHR Application No. 48939/99, Judgment (30 November 2004). 370

Özel and others v. Turkey, ECtHR Applications Nos. 14350/05, 15245/05, and16051/05, Judgment (17 November 2015). 370

Powell and Rayner v. United Kingdom, ECtHR Application No. 9310/81, Judgment (21 February 1990). 369

Smaltini v. Italy, ECtHR Application No. 43961/09, Decision (admissibility) (24 March 2015). 370

Taskin and others v. Turkey, ECtHR Application No. 46117/99, Judgment (10 November 2004, Final 30 March 2005). 88, 305, 370

Tătar v. Romania, ECtHR Application No. 67021/01, Judgment (27 January 2009, Final 6July 2009). 73, 88, 305, 370

Turgut v. Turkey, ECtHR Application No. 1411/03, Judgment-Merits (8 July 2008), Judgment-Just Satisfaction (13 October 2009). 370

Vides Aizsardzibas Klubs v. Latvia, ECtHR Application No. 57829/00, Judgment (27 May 2004). 370

Vilnes and others v. Norway, ECtHR Application No. 52806/09, Judgment (5 December 2013). 370

美洲人权法院

Afro-Descendant Communities Displaced from the Cacarica River Basin (Operation Genesis) v. Colombia, ICtHR Ser. C No. 270, Preliminary Objections, Merits, Reparations, and Costs, Judgment (20 November 2013). 372

Case of the Kuna Indigenous People of Madungandíand the Emberá Indigenous People of Bayano and their members v. Panama, ICtHR Series C No. 284 (Preliminary Objections, Merits, Reparations and Costs), Judgment (14 October 2014). 372

Indigenous Community Yakye Axa v. Paraguay, ICtHR Series C No. 125 (17 June 2005). 372, 373

Indigenous People Kichwa of Sarayaku v. Ecuador, ICtHR Series C No. 245, Judgment-Merits and Compensation (27 June 2012). 372

Kaliña and Lokono Peoples v. Suriname, ICtHR Case No. 12.639 (Merits, Reparations and Costs), Judgment (25 November 2015). 373, 402

Kawas-Fernandez v. Honduras, ICtHR Series C No. 196, Judgment-Merits, Reparation and Costs (3 April 2009). 377

Mayagna (Sumo) Awas Tingni Community v. Nicaragua, ICtHR Series C No. 79, Judgment (31 August 2001). 89, 371

(The) Right to Information on Consular Assistance in the Framework of the Guarantees of the Due Process of Law, ICtHR Advisory Opinion OC-16/99, Series A No. 16 (1 October 1999). 366

Saramaka People v. Suriname, ICtHR Series C No. 172, Judgment (28 November 2007). 372

Sawhoyamaxa Indigenous Community v. Paraguay, ICtHR Series C No. 146 (29 March 2006). 372, 403

美洲人权委员会

Ana Miran Romero and others, ICommHR Precautionary Measure No. 589/15 (24 November 2015). 360

Children and Adolescents of the Communities of Uribia, Manaure, Riohachaand Maicao of the Wayuu People, in the Department of the Guajira, Colombia, IComm HR Precautionary Measure No. 51/15 (11 December 2015). 377

Community of La Oroya v. Peru, ICommHR Petition 1473/06, Report on Admissibility 76/09 (5 August 2009). 371

Community of San Mateo de Huanchor and its Members v. Peru, IComm HR Petition 504/03, Report No. 69/04 (15 October 2004). 371

Kevin Donaldo Ramirez and Family, IComm HR, Precautionary Measure No. 460-15 (28 September 2015). 360

Maya Indigenous Community of the Toledo District v. Belize, IComm HR Case12. 053, Report (12 October 2004). 371

Metropolitan Nature Reserve v. Panama, Case IComm HR Case 11. 533, Report No. 88/03, OEA/Ser. L/V/II. 118 Doc. 70 rev. 2 at 524 (2003). 388

U'wa People v. Colombia, IComm HR Case11. 754, Reporton Admissibility 33/15 (22 July 2015). 371

Yanomani Indians v. Brazil, IComm HR Case 7615, Decision (5 March 1985). 371

非洲人权和民族委员会、非洲人权和人民法院

African Commission on Human and Peoples' Rights v. Kenya, Order on-Provisional Measures, African Court Application No. 006/2012 (15 March 2013). 402

African Commission on Human and Peoples' Rights v. Kenya, Judgment, African Court Application No. 006/2012 (27 May 2017). 374

Centre for Minority Rights Development (Kenya) and Minority Rights Group International on behalf of Endorois Welfare Council v. Kenya, African Commission Application No. 276/2003. 374

Social and Economic Rights Action Center and the Center for Economic and Social Rights v. Nigeria, ACHPR Communication 155/96, 15th Activity Report of the Acomm HRP (2001-2002). 373, 446

The Nubian Community in Kenya v. The Republic of Kenya, African Commission Application No. 317/06 (30 May 2016). 374

西非国家经济共同体法院

SERAP v. Federal Republic of Nigeria, ECOWAS Court of Justice, Judgment No. ECW/CCJ/JUD/18/12 (14 December 2012). 373

国际刑事法庭

Final Report to the Prosecutor (International Criminal Tribunal for the Former Yugoslavia) by the Committee Established to Review the NATO Bombing Campaign against the Federal Republic of Yugoslavia, 13 June 2000. 415

High Command Case (USv. Von Leeb), 11 TWC 462 (1950). 419

Hostage Case (USv. List), 11 TWC 759 (1950). 419

Prosecutor v. Ante Gotovina et al., ICTY Trial Chamber, Judgment (Volume IIof II), Case No. IT-06-90-T (15 April 2011). 420

Prosecutorv. Vlastimirorđević, ICTY Trial Chamber, Judgment, Case No. IT-05-87/1-T (23 February 2011). 420

Prosecutor v. Emmanuel Rukundo, ICTR Trial Chamber, Judgment, Case No. ICTR-2001-70-T (27 February 2009). 420

Prosecutor v. Germain Katanga, ICTR Trial Chamber, Judgment Pursuant to Article 74 of the Statute, Case No. ICC - 01/04 - 01/07 (7 March 2014). 420

Prosecutor v. Charles Ghankay Taylor, Special Tribunal for Sierra Leone, Trial Chamber, Judgment, SCSL-03-01-T (18 May 2012). 420

The Prosecutor v. Ahmad Al Faqi Al Mahdi, ICC Trial Chamber VIII, ICC-01/12-01/15-171, Judgment and Sentence (27 September 2016). 420

欧洲共同体法院

Air Transport Association of America and others v. Secretary of State for Energyand Climate Change, CJEU Case C-366/10 (21 December 2011). 463

Artegodan GmbH and others v. Commission, CFI Case T - 74/00, Decision (26 November 2002), ECR II-4945. 70

Gowan Comércio Internacional eServiços Lda v. Ministero della Salute, CJEUCase C-77/09, Judgment (22 December 2010). 73

International Association of Independent Tanker Owners (Intertanko) and others v. Secretary of State for Transport, ECJ (Grand Chamber), CaseC - 308/06, Judgment (3 June 2008). 111

Pfizer Animal Health SA v. Council, CFI Case T-13/99, Judgment (11 September 2002). 73

人权委员会

Apirana Mahuika and others v. New Zealand, HRC Communication No. 547/93 (27 October 2000). 368

Bernard Ominayak and the Lubicon Lake Band v. Canada, HRC Communication No. 167/1984 (26 March 1990). 367

Bordes et Temeharo v. France, HRC Communication No. 645/1995 (22 July 1996). 367

Brun v. France, HRC Communication No. 1453/2006 (18 October 2006). 367

Diergaardt v. Namibia, HRC Communication No. 760/1997 (6 September 2000). 368

E. H. P. v. Canada, HRC Communication No. 67/1980 (27 October 1982). 89, 367

Ilmari Länsman and others v. Finland, HRC Communication No. 511/1992 (8 November 1995). 368

Jouni E. Länsman and others v. Finland, HRC Communication No. 671/1995 (30 October 1996). 368

Kitok v. Sweden, HRC Complaint 197/1985 (27 July 1988). 367, 402

Poma Poma v. Peru, HRC Communication No. 1457/2006 (27 March 2009). 368

国内案例法

Born Free USA v. Norton, 278 F. Supp 2d 5 (DDC 2003). 215Erika, Cour de Cassation, Chambre criminelle, Arrêt No. 3439 (25 September 2012). 323

Kelsey Cascadia Rose Juliana et al. v. United States of America et al., US District Court of Oregon (Eugene Division), Case No. 6: 15-cv-01517-TC, Opinionand Order (10 November 2016). 396

Netherlands Crown Decision (in Dutch) in the case lodged by the Competent Authority for the Island of Bonaire on the annulment of two of its decisions onthe Lac Wetland by the Governor of the Netherlands Antilles, 11 September

2007, Staatsblad 2007, p. 347. 228, 463

Oposa andothers v. Factoran, Jr, and others, Supreme Court of the Philippines, Decision (30 June 1993). 89

Petition to the Commission on Human Rights of the Philippines requesting for Investigation of the Responsibility of the Carbon Majors for Human Rights Violations or Threats of Violations Resulting from the Impacts of Climate Change, submitted by Greenpeace Southeast Asia etal. (22 September 2015). 396

Richardson v. Forestry Commission [1988] HCA 10, (1988) 164 CLR 261. 228 Specific Instance regarding the World Wide Fund for Nature International (WWF) submitted by Survival International Charitable Trust, OECD Guidelines-National Contact Point of Switzerland, Initial Assessment (20 December 2016). 402

Urgenda Foundation v. State of Netherlands, Hague District Court, C/09/456689/HA ZA 13-1396 Judgment (24 June 2015) (translation). 396

不遵约委员会的决议

Aarhus Compliance Committee, BelarusACCC/C/2009/44, ECE/MP. PP/C. 1/2011/6/Add. 1 (19 September 2011). 384

Aarhus Compliance Committee, Belgium ACCC/2005/11, ECE/MP. PP/C. 1/2006/4/Add. 2 (28 July 2006). 386

Aarhus Compliance Committee, Croatia ACCC/C/2012/66, ECE/MP. PP/C. 1/2014/4 (13 January 2014). 384

Aarhus Compliance Committee, Czech Republic ACCC/C/2010/50, ECE/MP. PP/C. 1/2012/11 (2 October 2012). 384

Aarhus Compliance Committee, Czech Republic ACCC/C/2012/70, ECE/MP. PP/C. 1/2014/9 (4 June 2014). 384

Aarhus Compliance Committee, European Community ACCC/C/2007/21, ECE/MP. PP/C. 1/2009/2/Add. 1 (11 December 2009). 382

Aarhus Compliance Committee, Kazakhstan ACCC/C/2004/2, ECE/MP. PP/C. 1/2005/2/Add. 2 (14 March 2005). 382

Aarhus Compliance Committee, Kazakhstan ACCC/C/2004/6, ECE/MP. PP/C. 1/2006/4/Add. 1 (28 July 2006). 385

Aarhus Compliance Committee, Moldova ACCC/C/2008/30, ECE/MP. PP/C. 1/2009/6/Add. 3 (8 February 2011). 382

Aarhus Compliance Committee, Spain ACCC/C/2008/24, ECE/MP. PP/C. 1/2009/8/Add. 1 (30 September 2010). 384

Aarhus Compliance Committee, United Kingdom ACCC/C/2008/27, ECE/MP. PP/C. 1/2010/6/Add. 2 (November 2010). 385

Aarhus Compliance Committee, United Kingdom ACCC/C/2010/53, ECE/MP. PP/C. 1/2013/3 (11 January 2013). 382

Aarhus Compliance Committee, United Kingdom ACCC/C/2010/45 andACCC/C/2011/60, ECE/MP. PP/C. 1/2013/12 (23 October 2013). 384

Kyoto Protocol Compliance Committee, Final Decision: Croatia, CC-2009-1-8/Croatia/EB (19 February 2010). 51, 347

Kyoto Protocol Compliance Committee, Final Decision: Greece, CC-2007-1-8/Greece/EB (17 April 2008). 51, 347

Kyoto Protocol Compliance Committee, Final Decision: Greece, CC-2007-1-13/Greece/EB (13 November 2008). 347

条约和文件清单

日期	全称	缩写	页数
20 March 1883	Paris Convention for the Protection of Industrial Property, available at: www.wipo.org.		492
30 June 1885	Treaty concerning the Regulation of Salmon Fishery in the Rhine River Basin, available at: www.ecolex.org (TRE-000072).		5
29 July 1899	Hague Declaration (IV, 2) concerning Asphyxiating Gases, 187 CTS 453.		429
19 March 1902	Convention for the Protection of Birds Usefulto Agriculture, B7p. 902:22.		5
21 May 1906	Treaty between the United States of America and Mexico concerning the Equitable Distribution of the Waters of the Rio Grande, 34 Stat. 2953.		7
18 October 1907	Convention (No. IV) respecting the Laws and Customs of War on Landand its Annex: Regulations concerning the Laws and Customs of War on Land, 205CTS 277.	Hague Convention IV	418, 429
7 July 1911	Convention between the United States, Great Britain, Japan and Russiaproviding for the Preservation and Protection of Fur Seals, 37Stat. 1542.	Fur Seals Convention	5, 202
9 December 1923	Convention relating to the Development of Hydraulic Power Affecting More than One State, 36 LNTS 77.		127
17 June 1925	Protocol for the Prohibition of the Use in War of Asphyxiating, Poisonousor Other Gases, and of Bacteriological Methods of Warfare, 94 LNTS 65.	1925 Geneva Protocol	428, 429, 431

续表

日期	全称	缩写	页数
8 November 1927	Convention for the Abolition of Import and Export Prohibitions and Restrictions, 97 LNTS 391.		473
24 September 1931	Convention for the Regulation of Whaling, available at: www.ecolex.org (TRE-000073).		5, 201
12 October 1940	Convention on Nature Protection and Wild Life Preservation in the Western Hemisphere, 56Stat. 1354, TS 981.	Western Hemisphere Convention	203
3 February 1944	Treaty between the United States of America and Mexico relating to theutilization of the Watersof the Colorado and Tijuana Rivers and of the Rio Grande, 3 UNTS 314.	1944 Water Utilisation Treaty	7
26 June 1945	Charter of the United Nations, 1 UNTS XVI.		34
16 October 1945	Constitution of the Food and Agriculture Organization of the United Nations, 12UST 980.		33
2 December 1946	International Conventionfor the Regulation of Whaling with Schedule of Whaling Regulations, 161UNTS 361.	Whaling Convention	5, 88, 202
11 October 1947	Convention of the World Meteorological Organization, 77UNTS 143.		33
6 March 1948	Convention of the International Maritime Organization, 289UNTS 4.		33
24 March 1948	Havana Charter for anInternational Trade Organization, UN Doc. E/Conf. 2178.	Havana Charter	473
2 May 1948	American Declaration on the Rights and Duties of Man, adopted by the Ninth International Conference of American States, Bogotá, Colombia	American Declaration	371
18 August 1948	Convention Concerning the Regime of Navigation on the Danube, available at: www.ecolex.org(TRE-000555).		6
12 August 1949	Geneva Convention Relative to the Treatment of Prisoners of War, 75UNTS 31.	III Geneva Convention	379
12 August 1949	Geneva Convention Relative to the Treatment of Civilian Persons in Time of War, 75 UNTS 287.	IV Geneva Convention	31, 379, 419

续表

日期	全称	缩写	页数
8 April 1950	Protocol to Establish a Tripartite Standing Commission on Polluted Waters, available at: www.ecolex.org(TRE-000493).		6
4 November 1950	Convention for the Protection of Human Rights and Fundamental Freedoms, 4 November 1950, 213 UNTS 221.	ECHR	305, 365, 366
20 March 1952	Protocol to the Conventionfor the Protection of Human Rights and Fundamental Freedoms, ETS 9.	Protocol I	308
12 May 1954	International Convention for the Prevention of Pollution of the Sea by Oil, 327 UNTS 3.	OILPOL	118
17 September 1955	Convention Concerning the Regulation of Lake Luganoand its Additional Protocol, 291 UNTS 218.		6
26 October 1956, asamended on 28 December 1989	Statute of the Atomic Energy Agency, availableat: www.iaea.org.		281
1 December 1959	The Antarctic Treaty, 402 UNTS 71.	Antarctic Treaty	84, 126, 138, 230, 434
29 July 1960	Convention on Third Party Liability in the Field of Nuclear Energy, 956UNTS 251.	Paris Convention	318
27 October 1960	Agreement on the Protection of Lake Constance against Pollution, available at: www.ecolex.org(TRE-000464).		6
19 September 1960	Indus Water Treaty(India/Pakistan), 419 UNTS 126.	Indus Water Treaty	134
16 November 1962	Agreement between Franceand Switzerland on the Protection of Lake Geneva, 1974 UNTS 54.		6
14 December 1962	"Permanent Sovereigntyover Natural Resources", UN Doc. A/RES/1803/XVII	Resolution 1803	7, 40, 64, 137
31 January 1963	Convention Supplementary to the Paris Convention of 29 July 1960 on Third Party Liability in the Fieldof Nuclear Energy, 1041 UNTS 358.	Brussels Supplementary Convention	318, 321

续表

日期	全称	缩写	页数
29 April 1963	Agreement Concerning the International Commission for the Protection of the Rhineagainst Pollution, avail able at: www. ecolex. org(TRE-000484).		6
21 May 1963	Convention on Civil Liability for Nuclear Damage, 1063 UNTS 265, as subsequently amended by the Protocol to amend the Vienna Conventionon Civil Liability for Nuclear Damage, 12September 1997, 2241UNTS 302.	ViennaConvention	318
5 August 1963	Treaty Banning Nuclear Weapons Tests in the Atmosphere, in Outer Space and under Water, 480 UNTS 43.	PNTB	434
13 December 1963	"Declaration of Legal Principles Governing the Activities of States in the Exploration and Use of Outer Space", UN Doc. A/18/1962.	Outer Space Declaration	95
22 November 1965	"Consolidation of the Special Fund and the Expanded Programme of Technical Assistance in a United Nations Development Programme", UN Doc. Resolution 2029 (XX).		34
20 August 1966	Helsinki Rules on the Usesof the Waters of International Rivers; adopted by the International Law Association at its 52nd conference, Helsinki.		41, 74, 127
16 December 1966	International Covenant on Civil and Political Rights, 999 UNTS 171.	ICCPR	86, 366
16 December 1966	International Covenant on Economic, Social and Cultural Rights, 993 UNTS 3.	ICESCR	366
27 January 1967	Treaty on Principles Governing the Activities of States in the Exploration and Use of Outer Space, including the Moon and Other Celestial Bodies, 610UNTS 205.	Outer Space Treaty	84, 434
14 February 1967	Treaty for the Prohibition of Nuclear Weaponsin Latin America, 634 UNTS 281.	Treaty of Tlatelcoco	433
14 February 1967	Additional Protocol I to the Treaty for the Prohibition of Nuclear Weapons in Latin America, 634UNTS 360.		433
14 February 1967	Additional Protocol II to the Treaty for the Prohibition of Nuclear Weapons in Latin America, 634UNTS 364.		434

续表

日期	全称	缩写	页数
1 July 1968	Treaty on the Non-Proliferation of Nuclear Weapons, 729 UNTS 161.	NPT	280, 434
15 September 1968 (revised on 11 July 2003)	African Convention on the Conservation of Natureand Natural Resources, 1001 UNTS 3.	African Conservation Convention	203, 425
3 December 1968	"Problems of the Human Environment", UN Doc. 2398/XXIII.		9
23 May 1969	Vienna Convention on the Law of Treaties, 1155 UNTS 331.	VCLT	171, 277, 304, 422, 476
10 September 1969	Convention Governing the Specific Aspects of Refugee Problems in Africa, 1001 UNTS 45.		442
22 November 1969	American Convention on Human Rights, 1144 UNTS 123.	ACHR	366
29 November 1969	International Conventionrelating to Intervention on the High Seas in cases of Oil Pollution Casualties, availableat: www.ecolex.org (TRE-000111)	Intervention Convention	120
19 June 1970	Patent Cooperation Treaty, 1160 UNTS 231.	PCT	492
19 June 1970	Patent Law Treaty, 39 ILM 1047.		498
26 October 1970	"Declaration on Principles of International Law con cerning Friendly Relations and Cooperation among States in accordance withthe Charter of the United Nations", Res. 2625(XXV).		74
17 December 1970	"Declaration of Principles Governing the Seabed and the Ocean Floor, and the Subsoil There of, Beyond the Limits of National Jurisdiction", Res. 2749(XXV).	Seabed Declaration	85
2 February 1971	Convention on Wetlands of International Importanceespecially as Waterfowl Habitat, 996 UNTS 245.	Ramsar Convention	12, 48, 202, 297, 332, 425, 456

日期	全称	缩写	页数
11 February 1971	Treaty on the Prohibition of the Emplacement of Nuclear Weapons and Other Weapons of Mass Destruction on the Sea-Bed and the Ocean Floor and in the Subsoil Thereof, 955 UNTS 115.		434
17 December 1971	Convention Relating to Third Party Liability in the Field of Maritime Carriage of Nuclear Material, 944 UNTS 255.		319
20 December 1971	"Development and Environment", UN Doc. 2849(XXVI).		9, 24
29 March 1972	Convention on International Liability for Damage Caused by Space Objects, 961 UNTS 187.		49, 311
10 April 1972	Convention on the Prohibition of the Development, Production and Stockpiling of Bacteriological (Biological) and Toxin Weapons and on their Destruction, 1015 UNTS 163.	BWC	428
1 June 1972	Convention for the Conservation of Antarctic Seals, signed in London, 1080 UNTS 175.	CCAS or Antarctic Seals Convention	126, 230
16 June 1972	"Declaration of the United Nations Conference on the Human Environment", Stockholm, UN Doc. A/CONF 48/14/Rev. 1, pp. 2ff.	Stockholm Declaration	9, 29, 88, 358
16 June 1972	"Action Plan for the Human Environment", UN Doc. A/CONF 48/14, pp. 10–62.		9
16 November 1972	Convention for the Protection of the World Cultural and Natural Heritage, 1037 UNTS 151.	WHC	12, 45, 97, 202, 332, 425
15 December 1972	"Institutional and Financial Arrangements for International Environmental Cooperation", UN Doc. A/RES/2997/XXVII.		9, 34
29 December 1972 (modified on 7 November 1996)	Convention for the Prevention of Marine Pollution by Dumping of Wastes and Other Matter, as modified by the Protocol of 7 November 1996, 1046 UNTS 120.	London Convention	12, 59, 121

续表

日期	全称	缩写	页数
3 March 1973	Convention on International Trade in Endangered Species of Wild Fauna and Flora, 983 UNTS 243.	CITES	12, 202, 218, 295, 346, 423, 476
2 November 1973 (modified on 17 February 1978)	International Convention for the Prevention of Pollution from Ships, as modified by the Protocol of 1978 relating thereto, 1340 UNTS 184.	MARPOL 73/78 or MARPOL	12, 118
19 February 1974	Nordic Convention on the Protection of the Environment, available in English at: www.ecolex.org(TRE-000491).	Nordic Convention	151
1 May 1974	"Declaration on the Establishment of a New International Economic Order", Res. 3201(S-VI).		84
26 February 1975	Statute of the River Uruguay (Argentina/Uruguay), 1295 UNTS 340.		134
16 February 1976	Protocol for the Prevention and Elimination of Pollution of the Mediterranean Sea by Dumping from Ships and Aircraft, available at: www.ecolex.org (TRE-001285).		125
12 June 1976	Convention on the Conservation of Nature in the South Pacific, available at: www.ecolex.org(TRE-000540).	Apia Convention	203
10 December 1976	Convention for the Prohibition of Military or other Hostile Use of Environmental Modification Techniques, 1108 UNTS 151.	ENMOD Convention	412
8 June 1977	Protocol Additional to the Geneva Conventions of 12 August 1949, and Relating to the Protection of Victims of International Armed Conflicts, 1125 UNTS 3.	Additional Protocol I	379, 412
8 June 1977	Protocol Additional to the Geneva Conventions of 12 August 1949, and relating to the Protection of Victims of Non-International Armed Conflicts (Protocol II), 1125 UNTS 609.	Additional Protocol II	379
24 April 1978	Regional Convention for Cooperation on the Protection of the Marine Environment from Pollution, available at: www.ecolex.org (TRE-000537).	Kuwait Convention	124

续表

日期	全称	缩写	页数
24 October 1978	Convention on Future Multilateral Cooperation on Northwest Atlantic Fisheries, available at: www. nafo. int	NAFO	208
23 June 1979	Convention on the Conservation of Migratory Species of Wild Animals, 1651 UNTS 333.	CMS	12, 423, 456
19 September 1979	Convention on the Conservation of European Wildlife and Natural Habitats, ETS No. 104.	Bern Convention	203
13 November 1979	Convention on Long–Range Transboundary Air Pollution, 1302 UNTS 217.	LRTAP Convention	48, 74, 148, 252, 350
18 December 1979	Convention on the Elimination of All Forms of Discrimination against Women, 1249 UNTS 13.	CEDAW	379
18 December 1979	Agreement Governing the Activities of States on the Moon and Other Celestial Bodies, 1363 UNTS 3.	Moon Treaty	96
3 March 1980	Convention on the Physical Protection of Nuclear Material, 1458 UNTS 125		281
17 May 1980	Protocol of the Protection of the Mediterranean Seaagainst Pollution from Land–Based Sources, available at: www. ecolex. org(TRE-000544).		125
20 May 1980	Convention for the Conservation of Antarctic Marine Living Resources, 1329 UNTS 47.	CCAMLR	126, 203, 230
23 March 1981	Convention for Co-operation in the Protection and Development of the Marine and Coastal Environment of the Westand Central African Region, available at: www. ecolex. org(TRE-000547).	Abidjan Convention	124
23 March 1981	Protocol Concerning Cooperation in Combating Pollution in Cases of Emergency, available at: www. ecolex. org (TRE-000548).		125
27 June 1981	African Charter on Humanand Peoples' Rights, 21ILM 58(1982).	African Charter	366

日期	全称	缩写	页数
12 November 1981	Convention Concerning the Protection of the Marine Environment and Coastal Area of the South East Pacific, available on www. eco lex. org(TRE-000741).	Lima Convention	124
12 November 1981	Agreement on Regional Cooperation in Combating Pollution of the South-East Pacific by Hydrocarbons or Other Harmful Substances in Cases of Emergency, available at: www. ecolex. org (TRE-000742).		125
14 February 1982	Regional Convention for the Conservation of the Marine Environment of the Red Sea and Gulf of Aden, available at: www. ecolex.org(TRE-000743).	Jeddah Convention	124
14 February 1982	Protocol concerning Regional Cooperation in Combating Pollution by Oil and Other Harmful Substances in Cases of Emergency (Red Sea and Gulf of Aden), availableat: www.ecolex.org(TRE-000745).		125
30 April 1982	HRC, General Comment No. 6: Article 6 (Right to Life), UNDoc. HRI/GEN/1/Rev. 9(Vol. 1).		364
27 August 1982	Report of the Governing Council on its Session of a Special Character(10-18May 1982), UN Doc. A/RES/37/219, Annex II.	Nairobi Declaration	12
28 October 1982	World Charter for Nature, UN Doc. A/RES/37/7.	World Charter for Nature	12, 29, 203
10 December 1982	United Nations Conventionon the Law of the Sea, 1833 UNTS 396.	UNCLOS	12, 30, 59, 107, 147, 207, 295, 476
24 March 1983	Convention for the Protection and Development of the Marine Environment of the Wider Caribbean Region, available at: www. ecolex. org(TRE-000763).	Cartagena Convention	124

续表

日期	全称	缩写	页数
24 March 1983	Protocol Concerning Cooperation in Combating Oil Spills in the Wider Caribbean Region, available at: www.ecolex.org (TRE-000764).		125
22 July 1983	Protocol for the Protection of the South-East Atlanticagainst Pollution from Land-based Sources, available at: www.ecolex.org (TRE-000768).		125
22 July 1983	Supplementary Protocol on the Agreement on Regional Cooperation in Combating Pollution of the South-East Pacific by Hydrocarbons or Other Harmful Substances in Cases of Emergency, available at: www.ecolex.org lex.org(TRE-000769).		125
19 December 1983	"Process of Preparation of the Environmental Perspective to the Year 2000 and Beyond", UNDoc. A/RES/38/161.		13
28 September 1984	Protocol to the 1979 Convention on Long-Range Transboundary Air Pollution on the Long-term Financing of the Cooperative Programme for Monitoring and Evaluation of the Long-Range Transport of Air Pollutants in Europe (EMEP), 1491 UNTS 167.	EMEP Protocol	45, 153
22 November 1984	Cartagena Declaration on Refugees, Annual Report of the Inter-American Commission on Human Rights, OAS Doc. OEA/Ser.L/V/II.66/doc. 10, Rev.1.		442
22 March 1985	Vienna Convention for the Protection of the Ozone Layer, 1513 UNTS 293.	Ozone Convention	12, 159, 276, 301
21 June 1985	Convention for the Protection, Managementand Development of the Marine and Coastal Region of East Africa, available at: www.ecolex.org(TRE-000821).	Nairobi Convention	124
21 June 1985	Protocol Concerning Cooperation in Combating Marine Pollution in Cases of Emergency in the Eastern African Region, availableat: www.ecolex.org (TRE-000825).		125
8 July 1985	Protocol on the Reductionof Sulphur Emissions or their Transboundary Fluxes, 1480 UNTS 215.	Sulphur Protocol I	154, 296

续表

日期	全称	缩写	页数
9 July 1985	ASEAN Agreement on the Conservation of Natureand Natural Resources, 15EPL 64.	Kuala Lumpur Agreement	203
6 August 1985	South Pacific Nuclear Free Zone Treaty, 1445UNTS 177.	Treaty of Rarotonga	434
28 November 1985	International Code of Conduct on the Distribution and Use of Pesticides, adopted by the FAO Conference in Resolution 10/85.		48
26 September 1986	Convention on Early Notification of a Nuclear Accident, 1439UNTS 275.	Convention on Early Notification	74, 252
26 September 1986	Conventionon Assistancein Case of a Nuclear Accident or Radiological Emergency, 1457UNTS 133.	Convention on Assistance	252
1986	Seoul Complementary Rules, adopted at the 62 nd Conference of theILA(1986).	Seoul Rules	127
25 November 1986	Convention for the Protection of Natural Resources and Environment of the South Pacific Region, availableat: www.ecolex.org (TRE-000892).	Noumea Convention	124
25 November 1986	Protocol for the Prevention of Pollution of the South Pacific Region by Dumping, available at: www.ecolex.org (TRE-000893).		126
1 December 1986	Protocol 2 to the South Pacific Nuclear Free Zone Treaty, 1971 UNTS 475.		434
10 March 1987	Report of the World Commission on Environment and Development, "Our Common Future".	Brundtl and Report	13, 410
7 July 1987	Report on the Right to Adequate Food as a Human Right. A Final Report presented by the Rapporteur Asbjorn Eide, UN Doc. E/CN. 4/Sub. 2/19878/23.		363
16 September 1987	Montreal Protocol on Substances that Deplete the Ozone Layer, 1522UNTS 28.	Montreal Protocol	2, 44, 71, 159, 251, 295, 330, 423, 480

续表

日期	全称	缩写	页数
27 September 1988	Joint Protocol Relating to the Application of the Vienna Convention and the Paris Convention, 1672 UNTS 293.	Joint Protocol	318
31 October 1988	Protocol concerning the Control of Emissions of Nitrogen Oxides or their Transboundary Fluxes, 28ILM 214.	NOx Protocol	154
16 November 1988	Additional Protocol to the American Convention on Human Rightsin the Areaof Economic, Social and Cultural Rights, OAS Treaty Series No. 69.	Protocol of San Salvador	366
22 March 1989	Basel Convention on the Control of Transboundary Movements of Hazardous Wastes and their Disposal, 1673 UNTS 57.	Basel Convention	12, 74, 252, 295, 332, 423, 480
25 May 1989	London Guidelines for the Exchange of Informationon Chemicals in International Trade, Decision 15/30 of the UNEP Governing Council.		48
29 May 1989	Protocol concerning Marine Pollution resulting from Exploration and Exploitation of the Continental Shelf(ROPME Sea Area), available at: www. eco lex. org (TRE-001128).		125
27 June 1989	Convention(No. 169) concerning Indigenous and Tribal Peoples in Independent Countries, 28 ILM 1382(1989).	ILO Convention 169	76
21 September 1989	Protocol for the Conservation and Management of Protected Marine and Coastal Areasof the South East Pacific, available at: www. eco lex. org(TRE-001085).		125
20 November 1989	Convention on the Rights of the Child, 1577 UNTS 3.	CRC	377
22 December 1989	"United Nations Conferenceon Environment and Development", UN Doc. A/RES/44/228.		13
18 January 1990	Protocol Concerning Specially Protected Areaand Wildlife (SPAW), available at: www. ecolex. org(TRE-001040).		126

续表

日期	全称	缩写	页数
21 February 1990	Kuwait Protocol on the Protection of the Marine Environment against Pollution from Land-based Sources, available at: www.ecolex.org(TRE-001129).		124
12 September 1990	Treaty on the Final Settlement with Respect to Germany, 1696UNTS 115.		434
30 November 1990	International Convention on Oil Pollution Preparedness, Response and Cooperation, available at: www.ecolex.org (TRE-001109).	OPRC Conventio	120
30 January 1991	Bamako Convention on the Ban on the Import into Africa and the Control of Transboundary Movement and Management of Hazardous Wastes within Africa, 30 ILM 773.	Bamako Convention	71, 252
25 February 1991	Convention on Environmental Impact Assessment in a Transboundary Context, 1989 UNTS 309.	Espoo Convention	48, 268, 350, 384
13 March 1991	Agreement between the Government of Canada and the Government of the United States of America on Air Quality, available at: www.epa.gov/usc a/agreement.html.	Air Quality Agreement	149
19 March 1991	International Convention for the Protection of New Varieties of Plants of December 2, 1961, as revised at Geneva on 10 November 1972, 23 October 1978 and 19 March 1991, available at: www.ecolex.org (TRE-001119).	UPOV Convention	241, 497
4 October 1991	Protocol on Environmental Protection to the Antarctic Treaty, 30 ILM1455.	Madrid Protocol	30, 78, 95, 126, 203
18 November 1991	Protocol concerning the Control of Emissions of Volatile Organic Compounds or their Transboundary Fluxes, 31ILM 573.	VOC Protocol	154
17 March 1992	Convention on the Transboundary Effects of Industrial Accidents, 2105 UNTS 457.	Convention on Industrial Accidents	74, 252
18 March 1992	Convention on the Protection and Use of Transboundary Watercourses and International Lakes, 1936UNTS 269.	UNECE Water Convention or Helsinki Convention	71, 127

续表

日期	全称	缩写	页数
9 April 1992	Convention on the Protection of the Marine Environment of the Baltic Sea Area, available at: www. eco lex. org (TRE-001153).		126
21 April 1992	Convention on the Protection of the Black Sea against Pollution, available at: www. ecolex. org(TRE-001149).	Bucharest Convention	124
21 April 1992	Protocol on Cooperation in Combating Pollution of the Black Sea Marine Environment by Oil and other Harmful Substancesin Emergency Situations, available at: www. ecolex. org(TRE-001391).		125
21 April 1992	Protocol on the Protectionof the Marine Environment of the Black Sea against Pollution by Dumping of Waste, available at: www. eco lex. org(TRE-001393).		125
21 April 1992	Protocol on the Protection of the Marine Environment of the Black Sea against Pollution from Land-based Sources, available at: www. ecolex. org(TRE-001392).		125
9 May 1992	United Nations Framework Convention on Climate Change, 1771 UNTS 107.	UNFCCC	14, 31, 60, 175, 297, 334, 423
5 June 1992	Convention on Biological Diversity, 1760 UNTS 79.	CBD	14, 33, 59, 203, 295, 423, 497
13 June 1992	"Rio Declaration on Environment and Development", UN Doc. A/CONF. 151/26. Rev.1.	Rio Declaration	13, 29, 59, 265, 364, 440, 474
13 June 1992	Report of the United Nations Conference on Environment and Development, A/CONF. 151/26/Rev. 1(Vol. 1), Resolution 1, Annex 2: Agenda 21.	Agenda 21	14, 16, 123, 256, 455

日期	全称	缩写	页数
14 August 1992	"Non-legally Binding Authoritative Statementof Principles for a Global Consensus on the Management, Conservation and Sustainable Developmentof All Types of Forests", UN Doc. A/CONF/151/26 (Vol. III).	Forest Principles	14, 41
17 September 1992	North American Agreementon Environmental Cooperation, 32 ILM1519.	NAAEC	473
22 September 1992	Convention for the Protection of the Marine Environment of the North-East Atlantic, 2354UNTS 67.	OSPAR Convention	71, 126, 301
25 November 1992	Terms of Reference for the Multilateral Fund, UNEP/OzL. Pro. 4/15.		167, 330, 333
27 November 1992	Protocol amending the International Conventionon Civil Liability for Oil Pollution Damage, available at: www.eco lex.org (TRE-001 177).	CLC/92	318, 320
27 November 1992	Protocol to Amend the International Conventionon the Establishment of an International Fund for Compensation for Oil Pollution Damage, available at: www.ecolex.org(TRE-001 176).	FUND/92	318, 321
17 December 1992	North American Free Trade Agreement, 32 ILM 296.	NAFTA	308, 473
13 January 1993	Convention on the Prohibiti on of the Development, Production, Stockpiling and Use of Chemical Weapons and on their Destruction, 1974UNTS 45.	CWC	431
19 January 1993	"Institutional arrangements to follow up the United Nations Conference on Environment and Development", UN Doc. A/RES/47/191.		14, 34
21 June 1993	Convention on Civil Liability for Damage Resulting from Activities Dangerous to the Environment, availableat: www.ecolex.org (TRE-001 166).	Lugano Convention	319
24 November 1993	Agreement to Promote Compliance with International Conservation and Management Measuresby Vessels on the High Seas, 2221 UNTS 91	Compliance Agreement	207
15 April 1994	Agreement establishing the World Trade Organization, 1867UNTS 154.	Marrakesh Agreement	473

续表

日期	全称	缩写	页数
15 April 1994	Agreement on Sanitary and Phytosanitary Measures, 1867 UNTS 493.	SPS Agreement	72, 307, 488
15 April 1994	Agreement on Subsidies and Countervailing Measures, 1867 UNTS 14.	SCM Agreement	481
15 April 1994	Agreement on Trade-Related Aspects of Intellectual Property Rights, 1869 UNTS 299.	TRIPS Agreement	241, 492
14 June 1994	Protocol to the LRTAP Convention on Further Reduction of Sulphur Emissions, 2030 UNTS 122.	Sulphur Protocol II	154, 296
17 June 1994	Convention on Nuclear Safety, 1963 UNTS 293.	Convention on Nuclear Safety	252
17 June 1994	United Nations Conventionto Combat Desertificationin those Countries Experiencing Serious Drought and/or Desertification, Particularly in Africa, UNDoc. A/AC. 241/15/Rev. 7(1994), 33 ILM 1328.	UNCCD	14, 74, 205, 440
29 June 1994	The Convention on Cooperation for the Protection and Sustainable Use of the River Danube, IER35:0251.	Danube Convention	71, 134
6 July 1994	Human Rights and the Environment. Finalreport presented by Mrs Fatma Zohra Ksentini, Special Rapporteur, UNDoc. E/CN. 4/Sub. 2/1994/9.	Ksentini Report	362
14 October 1994	Protocol for the Protection of the Mediterranean Sea against Pollution Resulting from Exploration and Exploitation of the Continental Shelf and the Seabed and its Subsoil, available at: www. ecolex. org (TRE-001206).		125
2 June 1995	The Berlin Mandate: Review of paragraphs (a) and (b) of paragraph 2 of Article 4 of the Convention to Determine if they are Adequate, Plans for a Protocol and Follow-up Decisions, Decision 1/CP. 1, doc. FCCC/CP/1995/7/Add. 1.	Berlin Mandate	175, 298
10 June 1995	Protocol Concerning Specially Protected Areasand Biological Diversityin the Mediterranean, available at: www. ecolex. org (TRE-001220).		125

续表

日期	全称	缩写	页数
10 June 1995	Convention for the Protection of the Mediterranean Seaagainst Pollution, 16 February 1976, asamended and laterbecoming the Conventionfor the Protection of the Marine Environment and the Mediterrane an Coastal Environment, available at: www.ecolex.org (TRE-001284).	Barcelona Convention	124
4 August 1995	Agreement for the Implementation of the Provisions of the United Nations Convention on the Law of the Sea of 10 December 1982 relating to the Conservation and Management of Straddling Fish Stocks and Highly Migratory Fish Stocks, S. Treaty Doc. No. 104-24, 2167UNTS 3.	Straddling Fish Stocks Agreement	14, 71, 112, 207, 208
31 October 1995	Code of Conduct for Responsible Fisheries, available at: www.fao.org		207
3 May 1996	International Conventionon Liability and Compensation for Damage in Connection-with the Carriage of Hazardous and Noxious Substances, amended by the Protocol of 30 April 2010, available at: www.ecolex.org(TRE-001 245).	HNS Convention 2010	319
1 October 1996	Protocol on the Prevention of Pollution of the Mediterranean Sea by Transboundary Movements of Hazardous Wastes and their Disposal(Hazardous Wastes Protocol), available at: www.ecolex.org (TRE-001334).		126
21 May 1997	United Nations Convention on the Law of the Non-Navigational Uses of International Watercourses, 36ILM 700.	UN Convention on Watercourses	41, 64, 128
28 June 1997	"Programme for the Further Implementation of Agenda 21", UN Doc. A/S/19-2, Annex.		17
5 September 1997	Joint Convention on the Safety of Spent Fuel Management and on the Safety of Radioactive Waste Management, available at: www.eco lex.org(TRE-001273).	Joint Convention	252
12 September 1997	Convention on Supplementary Compensation for Nuclear Damage, IAEAINFCIRC/567.	Complementary Vienna Convention	318

续表

日期	全称	缩写	页数
11 December 1997	Kyoto Protocol to the United Nations Framework Conventionon Climate Change, Kyoto, 2303 UNTS 148.	Kyoto Protocol	31, 60, 85, 175, 251, 295, 338
11 February 1998	Guiding Principles on Internal Displacement, UN Doc. E/CN. 4/1998/53/Add. 2 (1998), Annex.		444
17 March 1998	Protocol on the Control of Marine Transboundary Movements and Disposal of Hazardous Wastes and Other Wastes (ROPME Sea Area), available at: www. ecolex. org (TRE-001298).		126
24 June 1998	Protocol on Persistent Organic Pollutants to the LRTAP Convention, 2230 UNTS 79.	POP Protocol	154, 262, 308
24 June 1998	Protocol on Heavy Metals to the LRTAP Convention, 2237 UNTS 4.	Heavy Metals Protocol or HM Protocol	154, 252
25 June 1998	Convention on Access to Information, Public Participation in Decision-making and Access to Justice in Environmental Matters, 2161 UNTS 447.	Aarhus Convention	87, 269, 305, 345, 364
10 September 1998	Rotterdam Convention onthe Prior Informed Consent Procedure for Certain Hazardous Chemicals and Pesticidesin International Trade, 2244 UNTS 337.	PIC Convention	48, 74, 252, 295, 423, 475
1999	IBRD, Amended and Restated Instrument Establishing the Prototype Carbon Fund, Resolution No. 99-1.	PCF Instrument	338
12 April 1999	Convention on th eProtection of the Rhine, available at: www. ecolex. org (TRE-001307)		134
12 May 1999	General Comment No 12: The Right to Adequate Food, UN Doc. E/C. 12/1999/5.		364
17 June 1999	Protocol on Water and Health to the 1992 Convention on the Protection and Use of Transboundary Watercourses and International Lakes, 2331UNTS 202.	Protocol on Waterand Health	128, 345, 381

续表

日期	全称	缩写	页数
30 November 1999	Protocol to the 1979 Convention on Long-Range Transboundary Air Pollution on the Reduction of Acidification, Eutrophication and Ground-Level Ozone, Document of the Economic and Social Council EB. AIR/1999/1.	Gothenburg Protocol	154, 252
10 December 1999	Basel Protocol on Liability and Compensation for Damage resulting from Transboundary Movements of Hazardous Wastes and their Disposal, available at: www.ecolex.org(TRE-001341).	Basel Protocol	45, 319
29 January 2000	Cartagena Protocol on Biosafety to the Convention on Biological Diversity, 39 ILM 1027(2000).	Biosafety Protocol	71, 202, 345, 475
15 March 2000	Protocol on Preparedness, Response and Cooperation to Pollution Incidents by Hazardous and Noxious Substances, available at: www.ecolex.org(TRE-002482).	Protocol HNSOPRC	120
13 September 2000	"Millennium Declaration", UN Doc. A/RES/55/2.	Millennium Declaration	19, 29
15 November 2000	UN Convention against Transnational Organized Crime, 2225 UNTS 209.	UNCTOC	219
23 March 2001	International Convention on Civil Liability for Oil Pollution Damage, available at: www.ecolex.org(TRE-001377).	BUNKERS 2001	318
22 May 2001	Stockholm Convention on Persistent Organic Pollutants, 40 ILM 532.	POP Convention	33, 71, 157, 252, 295, 400, 423, 475
5 October 2001	International Convention on the Control of Harmful Anti-fouling Systems on Ships, available at: www.ecolex.org (TRE-001394).	AFS Convention	119
3 November 2001	International Treaty on Plant Genetic Resources for Food and Agriculture, 2400 UNTS 379.	Treaty on Plant Genetic Resources or ITPGR	242, 475
20 November 2001	WTO Ministerial Conference Fourth Session, Ministerial Declaration, WT/MIN(01)/DEC/1.	Doha Declaration	473

日期	全称	缩写	页数
12 December 2001	Draft Articles on the Prevention of Transboundary Harmfrom Hazardous Activities, GA Res. 56/82, UN Doc. A/RES/56/82.	ILC Prevention Articles	64, 313
12 December 2001	Responsibility of States forInternationally Wrongful Acts, GA Res. 56/83, UNDoc. A/RES/56/83.	ILC Articles	293
25 January 2002	Protocol Concerning Cooperation in Preventing Pollutionfrom Ships and, in Cases of Emergency, Combating Pollution of the Mediterranean Sea, available at: www. eco lex. org(TRE-001402).		125
6 April 2002	ILA New Delhi Declarationof Principles of International Law Relating to Sustainable Development.		83
21 May 2002	Decision of the Councilconcerning the revision of Decision (92) 39/FINALon the Control of Transboundary Movements of Wastesdestined for Recovery Operations, C(2001)107/FINAL.	OECD Wastes Decision	27
10 June 2002	ASEAN Agreement on Transboundary Haze Pollution, available in English at: www. eco lex. org(TRE-001344).		148
14 June 2002	Black Sea Biodiversity and Landscape Conservation Protocol, available at: www. ecolex. org(TRE-154497).		126
4 September 2002	"Political Declaration", Report of World Summiton Sustainable Development in Johannesburg(SouthAfrica), 26 August to 4 September 2002. UN Doc. A/CONF. 199/20, p. 1, 2002.	Political declaration	18, 91, 256
4 September 2002	"Implementati on Plan", Report of the World Summit on Sustainable Development at Johannesburg (South Africa), 26 August- 4 September 2002. UN Doc. A/CONF. 199/20.	Implementationplan	18
26 November 2002	Committee on Economic, Social and Cultural Rights, General Comment No. 15 (2002), The Rightto Water(Articles 11 and 12 of the International Covenant on Economic, Social and CulturalRights), UN ESCOR Doc. E/C. 12/2002/11.	GC 15	378

续表

日期	全称	缩写	页数
16 May 2003	Protocol to the International Convention on the Establishment of anInternational Fund for Compensation for Oil Pollution, available at: www.ecolex.org (TRE-001401).	FUND/2003	318
21 May 2003	Protocol on Civil Liability and Compensation for Damage Caused by the Transboundary Effects of Industrial Accidents on Transboundary Waters, Doc. ECE/MP.WAT/11-ECE/CP.TEIA/9.	Kiev Protocol	318
13 October 2003	Directive 2003/87/EC of the European Parliament and of the Council of 13 October 2003 establishing a scheme for greenhousegas emission allowancetrading within the Community and amending Council Directive 96/61/E, OJ L 0087, 25 June2009 (consolidatedversion).	ETS Directive	457
4 November 2003	Framework Convention for the Protection of the Marine Environment in the Caspian Sea, availableat: www.ecolex.org (TRE-001396).	Tehran Convention	126
16 February 2004	International Convention for the Control and Management of Ships' Ballast Water and Sediments, available at: www.ecolex.org(TRE-001412).		119
30 April 2004	Directive 2004/35/CE of the European Parliament and Council of 21 April 2004 on environmental liability with regard to the prevention and remedying of environmental damage, OJ L 143/56.		324
21 August 2004	Berlin Rules on Water Resources, adopted at the71st Conference of theILA(2004).	Berlin Rules	127
20 October 2005	Convention on the Protection and Promotion of the Diversity of Cultural Expressions, 2440 UNTS 311.		475
8 September 2006	Treaty on a Nuclear-Weapon-Free Zone in Central Asia, 2212 UNTS 257.	Treaty of Semipalatinsk	434
22 November 2006	Framework Convention on Environmental Protection for Sustainable Development in Central Asia, available in Englishat: www.ecolex.org(TRE-143806).		151

续表

日期	全称	缩写	页数
4 December 2006	Draft Principles on the Allocation of Loss in the Case of Transboundary Harm arising out of Hazardous Activities, GA Res. 61/36, UN Doc. A/RES/61/36.	ILC Principles	66, 313
29 May 2007	Regulation (EC) No.1907/2006 of the European Parliament and of the Council of 18 December 2006 concerning the Registration, Evaluation, Authorisation and Restriction of Chemicals (REACH), establishing an European Chemicals Agency, amending Directive 1999/45/EC andrepealing Council Regulation (EEC) No.793/93 and Commission Regulation (EC) No.1488/94 aswellas Council Directive76/769/EECand Commission Directives91/155/EEC, 93/105/ECand 2000/21/EC, OJL136/3.	REACH Regulation	255
2007	UNEP, Strategic Approach to International Chemicals Management. SAIC Mtexts and resolutions of the International Conferenceon Chemicals Management, 2007, available at: www.unece.org	SAICM	253, 257
13 September 2007	"United Nations Declarationon the Rights of Indigenous Peoples", UNDoc. A/RES/61/295, annex.	UNDRIP	76, 393
13 December 2007	Treaty on the Functioning of the European Union, OJC 83, 30 March 2010.	TFEU	71
7 March 2008	SADC Regional Policy Framework on Air Pollution, available at: www.unep.org		151
14 March 2008	Bali Plan of Action, Decision1/CP.13, doc. FCCC/CP/2007/6/Add.1.	Bali Mandate	175
30 May 2008	Convention on Cluster Munitions, 2688 UNTS 39.	CCM	431
23 October 2008	Eastern Africa Regional Framework Agreementon Air Pollution, available at: www.unep.org		151
11 December 2008	"Draft Articles on the Law of Transboundary Aquifers", GA Res. 63/124, UN Doc. A/RES/63/124.	ILC Aquifers Draft	128
15 January 2009	Report of the Office of the United Nations High Commissioner for Human Rights on the Relationship between Climate Changeand Human Rights, UNDoc. A/HRC/10/61.		188, 395, 441

续表

日期	全称	缩写	页数
22 July 2009	West and Central Africa Regional Framework Agreement on Air Pollution, available at: www. unep. org.		152, 446
14 August 2009	United Nations High Commissioner for Refugees, Climate Change, Natural Disasters and Human Displacement: A UNHCRPerspective.	UNHCR Report	441
23 October 2009	African Union Conventionfor the Protection and Assistance of Internally Displaced Persons in Africa, 49 ILM 86.	Kampala Convention	444
22 November 2009	Agreement on Port State Measures to Prevent, Deter and Eliminate Illegal, Unreported and Unregulated Fishing, [2010] ATNIF 41.	Agreement on Port State Measures	207
26 February 2010	Decision SS. XI/5, Part A "Guidelines on Developing National Legislation on Access to Information, Public Participation in Decision-Making and Access to Justice in Environmental Matters", Doc GCSS. XI/11	Bali Guidelines	87, 364
30 March 2010	Copenhagen Accord, UN Doc. FCCC/CP/2009/L. 7.	Copenhagen Accord	40, 175
31 March 2010	"Implementation of Agenda 21, the Programme for the Further Implementation of Agenda 21 and the outcomes of the World Summit on Sustainable Development", UN Doc. A/RES/64/236.	Enabling resolution	19
28 July 2010	"The Human Right to Waterand Sanitation", UN Doc. A/64/L. 63/Rev. 1.		380
24 September 2010	"Human Rights and Accessto Safe Drinking Waterand Sanitation", A/HRC/15/L. 14.		380
16 October 2010	The Nagoya-Kuala Lumpur Supplementary Protocol on Liability and Redress to the Cartagena Protocol on Biosafety, available at: bch.cbd.int/protocol/NKL_text. shtml		240, 319
29 October 2010	Nagoya Protocol on Accessto Genetic Resources and the Fair and Equitable Sharing of the Benefits Arising from their Utilization to the Convention on Biological Diversity, available at: www. cbd. int/abs/doc/protocol/nagoya-protocol-en. pdf.	ABS Protocol or Nagoya Protocol	76, 202, 475

续表

日期	全称	缩写	页数
15 March 2011	"The Cancun Agreements: Outcome of the Work of the Ad Hoc Working Group on Long-term Cooperative Actionunder the Convention", Decision 1/CP. 16, doc. FCCC/CP/2010/7/Add. 1.	Cancun Agreements or Decision 1/CP. 16	175, 342, 443
15 March 2011	The Cancun Agreements: Outcome of the Work of the Ad Hoc Working Group on Further Commitments for AnnexI Parties under the Kyoto Protocol at its 15 th session, Decision 1/CMP. 6, doc. FCCC/KP/CMP/2010/12/Add. 1.	Cancun Agreements	175
15 March 2011	The Cancun Agreements: Land Use, Land-use Change and Forestry, Decision 2/CMP. 6, doc. FCCC/KP/CMP/2010/12/Add. 1.	Cancun Agreements	175
October 2011	"Instrument for the Establishment of the Restructured Global Environment Facility".	GEF Instrument	336
9 December 2011	Draft Articles on the Effects of Armed Conflict on Treaties, GA Res. 66/99, UN Doc. A/RES/66/99.	2011 ILC Draft Articles	423
16 December 2011	Office of the High Commissioner on Human Rights ("OHCHR"), Analytical Study on the Relationship between Human Rights and the Environment, UNDoc. A//HRC/19/34.	OHCHR Analytical Study	358
15 March 2012	Establishment of an Ad Hoc Working Group on the Durban Platform for Enhanced Action, Decision 1/CP. 17, Doc. FCCC/CP/2011/9/Add. 1, 2.	Durban Platform	176, 179
15 March 2012	Establishment of the Green Climate Fund, Decision3/CP. 17, Doc. FCCC/CP/2011/9/Add. 1, Annex: Governing instrument for the Green Climate Fund.	GCF Instrument	178, 334
15 March 2012	Outcome of the Work of the Ad Hoc Working Groupon Long-term Cooperative Actionunder the Convention, Decision 2/CP. 17, Doc. FCCC/CP/@011/9/Add. 1.		175, 179
2012	UNCTAD, World Investment Report. Towards a New Generation of Investment Policies(2012), Chapter IV(Investment Policy Framework for Sustainable Development).	IPFSD	459, 470

续表

日期	全称	缩写	页数
24 July 2012	Directive 2012/18/EU of the European Parliament and Council of 4 July 2012 on the control of major-accident hazards involving dangerous substances, amending and subsequently repealing Council Directive 96/82/EC, OJL197/1 24 July 2012.	Seveso II	257
11 September 2012	"The Future We Want", UNDoc. A/Res/66/288.		11, 34, 245, 400
19 November 2012	ASEAN Human Rights Declaration, available at: www.asean.org.		377
10 October 2013	Minamata Convention on Mercury, available at: www.mercuryconvention.org (last visited on 15 January 2014).	Minamata Convention	252, 401, 428
18 March 2015	Sendai Framework for Disaster Risk Reduction 2015-2030, available at: www.unisdr.org (last visited on 8 April 2017).	Sendai Framework	269
15 July 2015	'Tackling illicit trafficking in wildlife", UN Doc. A/69/L.80.		219
27 July 2015	"Addis Ababa Action Agenda of the Third International Conference on Financing for Development (Addis Ababa Action Agenda)", UNGA Resolution 69/313, UN Doc. A/RES/69/313, Annex.	Addis Ababa Action Agenda	22, 460
21 October 2015	Resolution 70/1, "Transforming our World: The 2030 Agenda for Sustainable Development", UN Doc. A/RES/70/1.	2030 Agenda	21, 22, 118, 149, 207, 258, 380, 455
12 December 2015	"Adoption of the Paris Agreement", 1/CP.21, FCCC//CP/2015/L.9/Rev.1, Annex.	Paris Agreement	38, 60, 184, 316, 334, 395, 443
17 December 2015	Resolution 70/169, "The human rights to safe drinking water and sanitation", UN Doc. A/RES/70/169.		380

续表

日期	全称	缩写	页数
16 June 2016	American Declaration on the Rights of Indigenous Peoples, OAS AG/RES. 2888 (XLVI-0/16), p.167.		393
6 October 2016	ICAO Assembly, Resolution 22/2 "Consolidated statement of continuing ICAO policies and practices relating to environmental protection – Global Market – Based Measure (GMBM) scheme", Doc. ICAO/A/39-WP/530.	CORSIA Resolution	196
14 October 2016	Decision XXVIII/1, "Furtheramendment of the Montreal Protocol", NEP/OzL. Pro. 28/CRP/10; Decision XXVIII/2; "Decision related to theamendment phasing down hydrofluorocarbons", UNEP/OzL. Pro. 28/CRP/10.	Kigali Amendment	168
April 2017	Preliminary Document on the Regional Agreementon Access to Information, Participation and Justicein Environmental Mattersin Latin America and the Caribbean, available at: http//repositorio.cepal.org (visitted on 17 April 2017).	ECLAC Draft	364
7 July 2017	Treaty on the Prohibition of Nuclear Weapons, UNDoc. A/CONF. 229/2017/L. 3/Rev. 1.	TPNW	429

目 录

第一编 基 础

第一章 国际环境法的出现和发展 …………………………………（3）
  第一节 导言 …………………………………………………………（3）
  第二节 先例 …………………………………………………………（4）
  第三节 自然资源永久主权 …………………………………………（7）
  第四节 1972年斯德哥尔摩人类环境会议 …………………………（9）
  第五节 环境与发展里约大会 ……………………………………（14）
  第六节 可持续发展世界首脑会议 ………………………………（19）
  第七节 里约峰会（2012年）………………………………………（22）
  第八节 《2030年可持续发展议程》（2015年）和全球环境
        治理的未来 …………………………………………………（24）
    部分参考文献 ……………………………………………………（28）

第二章 国际环境法的主要特点 ……………………………………（32）
  第一节 导言 ………………………………………………………（32）
  第二节 "环境"作为一个法律客体 ………………………………（33）
    一 概述 …………………………………………………………（33）
    二 科学层面 ……………………………………………………（33）
    三 法律层面 ……………………………………………………（34）
    四 操作层面 ……………………………………………………（37）
  第三节 主要行为体 ………………………………………………（37）
    一 从挑战到架构 ………………………………………………（37）
    二 国际架构和行为体 …………………………………………（38）
    三 跨国环境治理 ………………………………………………（42）

第四节 国际环境法的渊源 …………………………………(45)
     一 条约的大量出现 ………………………………………(46)
     二 软法的作用 ……………………………………………(47)
     三 授权立法 ………………………………………………(49)
   第五节 国际环境法的履行 …………………………………(50)
     一 概述 ……………………………………………………(50)
     二 刺激机制 ………………………………………………(51)
     三 管理科学不确定性 ……………………………………(54)
     四 不遵约的管理 …………………………………………(58)
   第六节 国际环境法中的法律环境 …………………………(59)
     部分参考文献 ……………………………………………(63)

第三章 国际环境法的原则 ……………………………………(68)
   第一节 导论 …………………………………………………(68)
   第二节 不同的分析方法 ……………………………………(68)
   第三节 国际环境法中的预防 ………………………………(73)
     一 引论 ……………………………………………………(73)
     二 无害原则 ………………………………………………(74)
     三 损害预防原则 …………………………………………(77)
     四 国际法中的风险预防 …………………………………(81)
     五 合作、通知、协商 ……………………………………(86)
     六 事先知情同意 …………………………………………(89)
     七 环境影响评价 …………………………………………(91)
   第四节 国际环境法中的平衡 ………………………………(94)
     一 体现平衡观念的原则 …………………………………(94)
     二 表述平衡观念的概念 …………………………………(105)
   第五节 从原则到规制 ………………………………………(115)
     部分参考文献 ……………………………………………(116)

第二编 实体规制

第四章 大洋、海洋和淡水 ……………………………………(125)
   第一节 引论 …………………………………………………(125)

第二节　海洋环境的国际规制 ……………………………… (126)
　　一　针对海洋地区的环境管辖权 ……………………… (126)
　　二　海洋环境保护概览 ………………………………… (132)
　　三　污染源的规制 ……………………………………… (137)
　　四　区域海洋环境的保护 ……………………………… (145)
第三节　淡水资源的国际规制 ……………………………… (148)
　　一　规制框架 …………………………………………… (148)
　　二　国际水道 …………………………………………… (150)
　　三　跨界含水层 ………………………………………… (157)
　　四　冰冻淡水资源 ……………………………………… (160)
　　部分参考文献 …………………………………………… (164)

第五章　大气保护 ……………………………………………… (173)
第一节　导论 ………………………………………………… (173)
第二节　"本地"越界空气污染 …………………………… (175)
第三节　远程越界空气污染 ………………………………… (177)
　　一　制度的起源 ………………………………………… (177)
　　二　《远程越界空气污染公约》 ……………………… (178)
　　三　《远程越界空气污染公约》之议定书 …………… (180)
第四节　臭氧层的保护 ……………………………………… (186)
　　一　制度的起源 ………………………………………… (186)
　　二　1985年《维也纳公约》 …………………………… (188)
　　三　1987年《蒙特利尔议定书》 ……………………… (190)
　　四　2016年《基加利修正案》 ………………………… (198)
第五节　气候变化 …………………………………………… (201)
　　一　问题概述 …………………………………………… (201)
　　二　体制的两大支柱 …………………………………… (203)
　　三　《联合国气候变化框架公约》 …………………… (207)
　　四　1997年《京都议定书》 …………………………… (210)
　　五　2015年《巴黎协定》 ……………………………… (215)
　　部分参考文献 …………………………………………… (230)

第六章　物种、生态系统和生物多样性 …………………… (237)
第一节　导论 ………………………………………………… (237)

第二节 规制方法 …………………………………………… (239)
第三节 物种的保护 ………………………………………… (242)
　一 开发的规制：渔业 …………………………………… (242)
　二 贸易的规制：《濒危野生动植物种国际贸易公约》 …… (249)
第四节 空间的保护（地点、栖息地、生态系统）………… (257)
　一 "自上而下"的规制和"自下而上"的规制 ………… (257)
　二 自上而下的方法：建立保护地 ……………………… (258)
　三 自下而上的方法：《联合国防治荒漠化公约》……… (272)
第五节 生物多样性的保护 ………………………………… (274)
　一 一个复杂的规制客体 ………………………………… (274)
　二 生物多样性的规制 …………………………………… (275)
　三 转基因生物的规制 …………………………………… (278)
　四 遗传资源的获取和惠益分享 ………………………… (281)
　五 国家管辖范围外的生物多样性 ……………………… (286)
　部分参考文献 ……………………………………………… (289)

第七章　危险物质和活动 ………………………………… (295)
第一节 导论 ………………………………………………… (295)
第二节 国际规制框架的客体和结构 ……………………… (297)
第三节 制定一个全球规制框架的努力 …………………… (300)
　一 政治原动力 …………………………………………… (300)
　二 主要成果：《联合国化学品全球统一分类和标签制度》和
　　　《国际化学品管理战略方针》………………………… (302)
第四节 特定物质和活动的规制 …………………………… (305)
　一 受规制的客体和技术 ………………………………… (305)
　二 生产和使用的规制 …………………………………… (307)
　三 贸易的规制：《事先知情同意公约》………………… (316)
　四 废物的规制：《巴塞尔公约》………………………… (320)
　五 综合方法 ……………………………………………… (325)
　部分参考文献 ……………………………………………… (334)

第三编　履行

第八章　履行：传统方法 ………………………………………（343）
第一节　导论 …………………………………………………（343）
第二节　监测和报告 …………………………………………（344）
　　一　义务类型 ………………………………………………（344）
　　二　机制的类型 ……………………………………………（346）
第三节　争端解决及法律后果 ………………………………（349）
　　一　前言 ……………………………………………………（349）
　　二　国际环境裁判 …………………………………………（350）
　　三　环境损害的后果 ………………………………………（361）
　　部分参考文献 ………………………………………………（377）

第九章　履行：新方法 …………………………………………（383）
第一节　导论 …………………………………………………（383）
第二节　促进遵约的手段 ……………………………………（384）
　　一　手段类型 ………………………………………………（384）
　　二　面向援助的手段 ………………………………………（385）
　　三　以效率为导向的手段 …………………………………（399）
第三节　管理不遵约的手段 …………………………………（400）
　　一　不遵约程序 ……………………………………………（400）
　　二　不遵约程序的法律依据及其影响 ……………………（403）
　　三　不遵约程序的启动 ……………………………………（405）
　　四　不遵约程序机构的组成 ………………………………（407）
　　五　不遵约程序采取的措施 ………………………………（408）
　　部分参考文献 ………………………………………………（409）

第四编　作为一种视角的国际环境法

第十章　人权和环境 ……………………………………………（417）
第一节　导论 …………………………………………………（417）
第二节　人权与环境保护之间的关系 ………………………（418）

第三节 协同效应 …… (422)
- 一 两个关键问题 …… (422)
- 二 确定含有环境内容的人权条款 …… (423)
- 三 人权文件中环境保护的范围 …… (450)

第四节 冲突 …… (464)
部分参考文献 …… (469)

第十一章 国际安全的环境维度 …… (478)

第一节 导论 …… (478)

第二节 环境和战时法 …… (479)
- 一 环境和武装冲突 …… (479)
- 二 诉诸战争的环境维度 …… (507)

第三节 国际法上的环境安全 …… (510)
- 一 避免因环境引发冲突 …… (510)
- 二 环境引发的流离失所 …… (512)
- 三 后冲突场景下的环境安全 …… (518)

部分参考文献 …… (520)

第十二章 环境保护与国际经济法 …… (526)

第一节 导论 …… (526)

第二节 国际法中的外国投资和环境 …… (527)
- 一 概览 …… (527)
- 二 协同 …… (528)
- 三 冲突 …… (536)

第三节 环境保护与国际贸易法 …… (547)
- 一 概述 …… (547)
- 二 协同效应 …… (550)
- 三 冲突 …… (555)

第四节 环境保护与知识产权 …… (568)
- 一 概述 …… (568)
- 二 协同效应 …… (569)
- 三 冲突 …… (572)

部分参考文献 …… (577)

图表列表

图 1-1　斯德哥尔摩会议（1972 年）···（10）
图 1-2　里约会议（1992 年）···（16）
图 1-3　约翰内斯堡峰会（2002 年）···（20）
图 1-4　可持续发展蛇形图···（27）
图 2-1　环境组织的类型···（42）
图 2-2　应对科学不确定性的法律手段··（55）
图 3-1　国际环境法的原则和概念···（72）
图 4-1　《联合国海洋法公约》下管辖权的分布·······································（128）
图 4-2　《联合国海洋法公约》环境框架概览···（133）
图 4-3　淡水资源及其国际规制···（149）
图 5-1　《蒙特利尔议定书》——承诺的结构（氟氯化碳）·························（192）
图 5-2　《蒙特利尔议定书》的维度··（197）
图 5-3　气候变化体制的两大支柱··（207）
图 5-4　《巴黎协定》的结构···（219）
图 6-1　广义规制方法···（242）
图 6-2　《濒危野生动植物种国际贸易公约》以及名录方法·······················（250）
图 6-3　《拉姆萨公约》的基本结构··（263）
图 6-4　《世界遗产公约》的基本结构···（269）
图 7-1　危险物质/行为的国际规制框架···（299）
图 7-2　《持久性有机污染物公约》的基本结构····································（308）
图 7-3　《事先知情同意公约》的基本结构··（318）
图 7-4　《巴塞尔公约》的基本结构···（323）
图 8-1　遵约程序的各阶段··（344）
图 8-2　国际环境法法庭··（351）

图 9-1	遵约流程的"软肋"	……………………………	(384)
图 9-2	财政援助手段	……………………………………	(386)
图 9-3	部分不遵约程序（NCPs）概述	…………………	(402)
图 10-1	"一般性"权利的环境维度	……………………	(429)
图 10-2	具体环境权概览	………………………………	(437)
图 10-3	基本的因果关系求证	…………………………	(461)
图 12-1	贸易与环境关系的法律问题	……………………	(550)
表 5-1	大气污染规制手段	……………………………	(186)
表 5-2	《基加利修正案》	……………………………	(199)
表 6-1	《濒危野生动植物种国际贸易公约》许可制度	………	(252)
表 6-2	《生物多样性公约》的基本结构	…………………	(276)
表 8-1	法律后果的类型	………………………………	(363)
表 10-1	人权与环境保护之间的关系	……………………	(421)
表 11-1	武装冲突中环境保护的法律方法	…………………	(481)
表 12-1	处理投资与环境关联的判例法方法	………………	(540)

第一编 基 础

第一章 国际环境法的出现和发展

第一节 导言

关于环境问题的国际法规并不是一个近期才出现的现象。早在 19 世纪和 20 世纪早期，就已经出现了类似今天国际环境法的数个先例。而现代国际环境法的显著特点是关注对环境本身的保护（根本上是为了人类的目的但不只是把它当作有用的资源）以及为达此目标而制定的复杂的法律措施。

本章的目的是详细介绍构成了现代国际环境法骨架部分的主要进展。[1] 我们不想详述这些进展的历史细节，[2] 我们也不打算针对导致这些进展的多重原因进行一个综合分析。但是，我们仍将会讨论一些关键的进展，这些进展共同构成了一个总体趋势。从 19 世纪晚期到 20 世纪 70 年代初期，环境问题的管理从一个保守型或一个资源型的逻辑转变为更加综合型的逻辑；而环境保护也越来越受到重视，其原因是多种多样的，既包括资源保护和自然保护，也涉及污染、人口过剩或环境安全。自 20 世纪 70 年代以来，保护环境的必要性就逐渐成为国际日程中最为紧迫的政策问题之一。然而，与此同时，晚近独立国家和其他一些发展中国家也在努

---

[1] For a more detailed introduction see L. K. Caldwell, *International Environmental Policy, From the Twentieth to the Twenty-First Century* (Durham: Duke University Press, 3rd edn, 1996).

[2] 两项杰出的研究，一项是采取长远视角，将早期的环境保护论和殖民主义结合起来，另一项聚焦于第二次世界大战后国际层面保守运动的兴起。参见 R. H. Grove, *Green Imperialism. Colonial Expansion, Tropical Island Edens and the Origins of Environmentalism, 1600-1860* (Cambridge University Press, 1996); S. Macekura, *Of Limits and Growth. The Rise of International Sustainable Development in the Twentieth Century* (Cambridge University Press, 2015)。

力确保环境管理不会成为他们追求自认为合适的发展政策的"紧箍咒"。

总而言之，本章所讨论的趋势如果用图的形式表现出来，就是一根在经济发展和环境保护之间摇摆不定的线条。在过去的十年，对发展的考量得到了增强，特别是在2002年约翰内斯堡峰会、2012年里约峰会以及最近的2015年通过的《2030年可持续发展议程》[确定了17个可持续发展目标（Sustainable Development Goals，SDGs）]后，实际的实施已经启动。我们应当注意的是，"环境—发展方程式"当前需要进行重大的重新校准，以便实现（经济）发展/增长和环境保护之间的一个适当平衡。

第二节 先例

对环境问题进行国际管理的最初方法是围绕三个核心事项进行的，即调整特定资源开发、跨界污染和共享水道利用的规则。为了说明这些事项，借用三个典型案例会很有帮助，它们也经常被当作现代国际环境法的先例而被引用。[3]

第一个案例是"（美国诉英国）白令海海豹仲裁案"，[4] 这个案例显示了不同国家对共同资源的竞争性开发所导致的难题。美国在1867年获取了阿拉斯加以后就采取了一系列步骤，针对白令海的航行活动建立了排他性的管辖。美国海军禁止英国船舶在白令海航行。美国、英国和俄国之间协商数年未果，后来依据1892年2月29日的一项条约，这一问题被提交仲裁。在仲裁庭审中，美国的核心观点是，美国享有该地区的主权（以前归俄国所有）；有趣的是，美国还主张即使海豹处于美国领海范围之外，它也拥有权利和义务来保护海豹。后一主张是基于美国政府法律顾问提出的一个理念，即美国被赋予了防止过度开发海豹的义务，而英国船舶的航行则对此造成了威胁。仲裁庭在1893年8月15日做出的裁决中否决了美国的主张并支持了英国。值得指出的是，美国的第二项主张的目的

---

[3] For a selection of early environmental cases, see C. A. R. Robb (ed.), *International Environmental Law Reports*, Vol. 1, Early Decisions (Cambridge University Press, 1998).

[4] *Bering Sea Fur Seals Arbitration*, Award (15 August 1893), RIAA, Vol. XXVIII, pp. 263-276 ("*Fur Seals* Arbitration").

并不是保护这一物种本身,而是保护其经济开发。因此,海豹仲裁案很好地展示了那个时代的精神,尽管美国的主张也是一种创新。这样的一种考量也成为这一时期达成的数项动物物种保护条约的基础。[5]

第二个重要的案例是"(美国诉加拿大)特雷尔冶炼厂仲裁案"。[6]这一案例展示了传统环境管理在本质上的跨界特性,它对国际环境法的发展造成了深远的影响。[7] 美国抗议位于加拿大领土上的一个冶炼厂排放的二氧化硫对其邻近的美国华盛顿州的农作物和土地造成了危害。依据1935年4月15日的一项条约,这一问题被提交仲裁。仲裁庭在1941年3月11日做出了裁决,并得出了一个著名的结论,即依据国际法的基本原则,

> 如果已发生后果严重的情况,而损害又是证据确凿的话,任何国家没有权利这样地利用或允许利用它的领土,以致其烟雾在他国领土或对他国领土上的财产和生命造成损害。[8]

这一基本原则后来在国际法院就"(英国诉阿尔巴尼亚)科孚海峡案"[9]的判决中再次得以确认,并对国际法委员会有关合法行为导致危害后果的责任承担问题的工作造成了深远影响。[10] 本章稍后也会谈及,这一原则的现代版本在今天已经成为国际环境法的一个核心组成部分。

---

  5 See, e.g.: Treaty concerning the Regulation of Salmon Fishery in the Rhine River Basin, 30 June 1885, available at: www.ecolex.org (TRE - 000072); Convention for the Protection of Birds Useful to Agriculture, 19 March 1902, available at: www.ecolex.org (TRE-000067); Convention between the United States, Great Britain, Japan and Russia Providing for the Preservation and Protection of the Fur Seals, 7 July 1911, 37 Stat. 1542; Convention for the Regulation of Whaling, 24 September 1931, available at: www.ecolex.org (TRE - 000073); International Convention for the Regulation of Whaling, 2 December 1946, 161 UNTS 361.

  6 Trail Smelter Arbitration, RIAA, vol. III, pp. 1905-1982 ("Trail Smelter Arbitration").

  7 See J. E. Viñuales, "The Contribution of the International Court of Justice to the Development of International Environmental Law" (2008) 32 Fordham International Law Journal 232.

  8 Trail Smelter Arbitration, supra footnote 6, p. 1965.

  9 Corfu Channel Case, Decision of 9 April 1949, ICJ Reports 1949, p. 22 ("Corfu Channel Case").

  10 See infra Chapter 11.

第三个案例是"(西班牙诉法国)拉努湖仲裁案"[11],这一案例展示了传统环境管理的另一个领域,即共享水道的使用问题。法国采取了一些措施,使得拉努湖一个支流的水流改道。西班牙认为,这些措施影响了流入西班牙的水流量(通过卡罗河流入),因此违法了国际法。在其1957年11月16日做出的裁决中,仲裁庭驳回了这一诉求,并指出:

> 西班牙政府致力于建立与现行实证国际法类似的内容。它所展示的一些原则与现在讨论的问题其实并无关联。如果有一个原则禁止上游国家改变河流的水流并对下游国家造成危害,那么这一原则并不适用于当前的案件,因为仲裁庭认为法国的方案并不会改变卡罗河的水流。国际河流的产业利用导致了各种利益的冲突,事实上,各国对这些利益的重要性非常了解,也认识到有必要用双方妥协的方式来调整这些利益。实现利益的妥协的唯一方式就是在一个日益全面的基础上达成协议。[12]

在那个时代(当今也是如此)通过缔结条约的方式来确定共享水道的利用是一个普遍现象。[13] 其中有些条约仅仅包含了数条防止水污染的规定,而其他的条约则主要关注共享水道问题。[14]

---

11 *Lake Lanoux Arbitration* (*Spain/France*), Award, (16 November 1957), RIAA Vol. XII, pp. 281ff ("*Lake Lanoux Arbitration*").

12 *Lake Lanoux Arbitration* (*Spain/France*), Award, (16 November 1957), RIAA Vol. XII, pp. 281ff ("*Lake Lanoux Arbitration*"), para. 13.

13 See, e. g.: Treaty between the United States of America and Mexico Concerning the Equitable Distribution of the Waters of the Rio Grande, 21 May 1906, 34 Stat. 2953; Treaty between the United States of America and Mexico Relating to the Utilization of the Waters of the Colorado and Tijuana Rivers and of the Rio Grande, 3 February 1944, 3 UNTS 314; Convention Concerning the Regime of Navigation on the Danube, 18 August 1948, available at: www.eco lex.org (TRE-000555); Convention Concerning the Regulation of Lake Lugano and its Additional Protocol, 17 September 1955, 291 UNTS 218.

14 See e. g.: Protocol to Establish a Tripartite Standing Commission on Polluted Waters, 8 April 1950, available at: www.ecolex.org (TRE-000493); Agreement on the Protection of Lake Constance Against Pollution, 27 October 1960, available at: www.ecolex.org (TRE-000464); Agreement between France and Switzerland on the Protection of Lake Geneva, 16 November 1962, 1974 UNTS 54; Agreement Concerning the International Commission for the Protection of the Rhine against Pollution, 29 April 1963, available at: www.ecolex.org (TRE-000484).

这三个里程碑式的案例揭示了 20 世纪 60 年代之前相关事务（现今这些事务归属于环境范畴）国际管制的方法。需要强调指出的是，总体上看，这些方法主要是促进特定物种或资源的经济开发。后文将会谈及，这一理念在 20 世纪 60 年代早期依然流行。

第三节　自然资源永久主权

长期以来，对特定资源或地区的保护都是与国家主权这一概念密不可分的。公海、国家主权或其殖民者及军管政府以外的区域是例外，很少受到国际法的调整，直到 20 世纪后半叶。

伴随着去殖民化进程的兴起，新独立的国家特别重视它们对其自然资源所拥有的权利，并将其看作实现政治独立和经济独立的前提条件。正如一位著名的评论员所说：

> 通过旗帜鲜明地运用主权原则（这里使用的是政治含义）来利用和自由处置自然资源，其目的是强调主权与自决权之间永久而无形的联系，主权不仅是自决权的政治实现（例如独立）的一个法律保障，同时也是自决权能在经济领域得以实施的永久保证。[15]

在许多方面，也许还是似是而非，自然资源永久主权原则是现代环境规制的基石。直到 20 世纪 70 年代，新独立国家运用这一原则的目的仅仅是以经济开发的视角来保护资源。但是，在后续的数十年中，这一原则与无害原则建立了联系，后来被概括为预防原则的起源，本书第三章将会谈及。

就当前目标而言，最终结果比这一原则在历史演进中的兴衰更为重要，[16] 联合国大会于 1962 年 12 月 14 日通过了《关于自然资源永久主权

15　G. Abi-Saab, "La souveraineté permanente sur les ressources naturelles", in M. Bedjaoui (ed.), *Droit International: Bilan et Perspectives* (Paris: Pedone, 1989), pp. 638-661, at 639-640 (our translation).

16　See N. Schrijver, *Sovereignty over Natural Resources. Balancing Rights and Duties* (Cambridge University Press, 1997), pp. 36-76.

的1803号决议》。[17] 这一里程碑式的决议，通常被认为是一种国际习惯法的表述，[18] 在其第一段指出：

> 人民和国家对其自然财富和资源的永久主权应当是为他们国家的发展和人民的福祉服务而行使。
>
> 自然资源主权的主要特点是它的永久性。主权实际上是规则，它的适用限制是"除非有必要在空间和时间上对其加以限制"。[19]

根据这一决议起草者们的设想，本决议也有适用限制，即与外国投资者签署的自然资源开发协议可能引发的问题。但是，从20世纪60年代晚期开始，另一个种类的适用限制开始出现，即早期的环境规制所带来的限制。这个背景大概可以解释发展中国家对工业化国家在环境保护领域发起的第一次重要运动的怀疑。[20] 事实上，正如后文所述，基于开发目的的资源管理和环境保护这两者之间的紧张关系一直以来都是国际环境法的一个重要特征。[21]

---

[17] "Permanent Sovereignty over Natural Resources"，14 December 1962, UN Doc. A/RES/1803/XVII,（"Resolution 1803"）.

[18] Abi-Saab, supra footnote 15, p. 644; *Texaco Overseas Petroleum Company and California Asiatic Oil Company* v. *The Government of the Libyan Arab Republic*, Arbitral Award（19 January 1977）, 17 ILM 1978, para. 87; *Libyan American Oil Company（LIAMCO）* v. *The Government of the Libyan Arab Republic*, Arbitral Award（12 April 1977）, 20 ILM 1981, p. 103; *Kuwait* v. *American Independent Oil Company（AMINOIL）*, Arbitral Award（24 March 1982）, 21 ILM 1982, para. 1803; *Armed Activities on the Territory of the Congo（Democratic Republic of the Congo* v. *Uganda）*, Judgment（19 December 2005）, ICJ Reports 2005, p. 168, paras. 244-245.

[19] Abi-Saab, supra footnote 15, p. 645（our translation）.

[20] Schrijver, supra footnote 16, at pp. 231-250.

[21] 这种紧张关系的法律层面随着时间不断演变，有两个回顾性研究值得参考，参见 S. Alam, S. Atapattu, C. Gonzalez, J. Razzaque（eds.）, *International Environmental Law and the Global South*（Cambridge University Press, 2016）; C. Brighton, "Unlikely Bedfellows: The Evolution of the Relationship between Environmental Protection and Development"（2017）66 *International and Comparative Law Quarterly* 209。

第四节　1972年斯德哥尔摩人类环境会议

20世纪60年代，数个环境问题引起了国际社会的高度关注并使人们意识到必须采取行动。[22]

1962年，蕾切尔·卡逊发表了她的划时代著作《寂静的春天》，[23] 强调指出了杀虫剂对环境造成的副作用，认为它们更贴切的名称应当是灭微生物剂。本书是一系列重要出版物的第一本著作，它们关注的都是人类活动对环境造成的负面影响，例如，肯尼思·博尔丁的《即将到来的太空船地球的经济学》，[24] 麦克斯·尼科尔森的《环境革命》[25] 或者巴里·康芒纳的《封闭的循环》。[26] 与此相类似，梅多斯的报告《增长的极限》[27] 所提出的惊人后果，都为罗马俱乐部的成立做了铺垫，它们也为吸引大众关注环境问题做出了贡献。[28] 其他数个事件也加剧了这种紧迫感，例如利比里亚油轮"托里·坎荣"号在英国海岸搁浅，以及日本一个村庄的水俣病对居民的毒害（它是由一个石油化工厂的汞泄漏造成的）。

在此背景下，国际社会启动了许多尝试。例如，在1968年12月，联合国大会通过了题为"人类环境的问题"并召开一次关于人类环境的联

---

[22] 关于推动环境运动的主要科学贡献，参见 J. Grinevald, *La Biosphère de l'Anthropocène. Climat et Pétrole, la Double Menace. Repères Transdiciplinaires* (1824–2007) (Geneva: Georg, 2007), pp. 115ff. On the immediate origins of the Stockholm Conference (although with a markedly US perspective) and the cleavages underpinning the "environmental movement" see Macekura, supra footnote 2, chapter 3。

[23] R. Carson, *Silent Spring* (Boston: Houghton Mifflin, 1962)。

[24] K. E. Boulding, "The Economics of the Coming Spaceship Earth", in H. Jarrett (ed.), *Environmental Quality in a Growing Economy* (Baltimore: Johns Hopkins University Press, 1966), pp. 3–14.

[25] M. Nicholson, *The Environmental Revolution: A Guide for the New Masters of the World* (London: Hodder & Stoughton, 1969).

[26] B. Commoner, *The Closing Circle: Nature, Man, and Technology* (New York: Alfred Knopf, 1971).

[27] D. H. Meadows, D. L. Meadows, J. Randers and W. W. Behrens III, *The Limits to Growth* (New York: Universe Books, 1972).

[28] See R. Guha, *Environmentalism: A Global History* (New York: Longman, 2000); A. Dobson, *Green Political Thought* (New York: Routledge, 4th edn, 2007).

合国会议的 2398 号决议[29]。本次会议于 1972 年 6 月 5—16 日在瑞典斯德哥尔摩召开，通常被当作现代国际环境法起源的时间节点。偶然的是，在本次会议即将召开之际，巴西提议的一项决议获得通过，它强调了经济发展和环境保护之间的紧张关系。[30] 这一决议关注的问题是环境政策对贫穷国家的发展可能带来的负面影响，它重申了国际合作的主要目标是将独立的经济和社会发展置于首要地位，并确保人类的福祉、自由和世界安全。[31]

一百多个国家的代表团和主要国际组织的代表参加了斯德哥尔摩会议。数百个非政府组织通过一种当今绝大多数环境会议所采取的方式集结在会议周围，有些甚至还参加了会议。协商达成了三项主要成果，即一份《人类环境宣言》，[32] 通常称为《斯德哥尔摩宣言》，一项《人类环境行动计划》，[33] 以及随后不久成立的联合国环境规划署（United Nations Environment Programme or UNEP）。[34] 图 1-1 概括了这些成果。

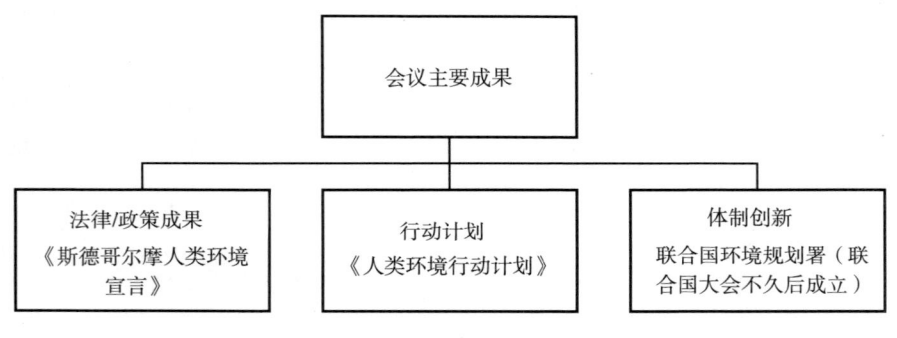

```
                  ┌──────────────┐
                  │  会议主要成果  │
                  └──────┬───────┘
         ┌───────────────┼───────────────┐
  ┌──────┴──────┐ ┌──────┴──────┐ ┌──────┴──────┐
  │ 法律/政策成果 │ │   行动计划   │ │   体制创新   │
  │《斯德哥尔摩   │ │《人类环境    │ │ 联合国环境规划│
  │ 人类环境宣言》│ │  行动计划》  │ │ 署（联合国大会│
  │              │ │              │ │ 不久后成立） │
  └──────────────┘ └──────────────┘ └──────────────┘
```

图 1-1　斯德哥尔摩会议（1972 年）

---

[29] "Problems of the Human Environment", 3 December 1968, UN Doc. 2398 (XXIII).

[30] "Development and Environment", 20 December 1971, UN Doc. 2849 (XXVI). 关于斯德哥尔摩会议筹备阶段所出现的发展与环境之间紧张关系的苗头，参见 K. Mickelson, "The Stockholm Conference and the Creation of the South-North Divide in International Environmental Law and Policy", in S. Alam et al, Supra Supra *Footnote* 21, pp. 109-129。

[31] "Development and Environment", supra footnote 30, para. 11.

[32] "Declaration of the United Nations Conference on the Human Environment", Stockholm, 16 June 1972, UN Doc. A/CONF 48/14/Rev. 1, pp. 2ff ("Stockholm Declaration").

[33] "Action Plan for the Human Environment", 16 June 1972, UN Doc. A/CONF 48/14, pp. 10-62.

[34] "Institutional and Financial Arrangements for International Environmental Cooperation", 15 December 1972, UN Doc. A/RES/2997/XXVII ("Resolution 2997").

这些成果的重要意义是不言而喻的。《斯德哥尔摩宣言》包含了一个序言和26条基本原则。针对这项重要的文书，已经有了大量的研究成果。[35] 为了当前的需要，我们有必要强调它的某些主要主题。宣言的第1条原则确定"在一种能够过着尊严和幸福的生活的环境中，享有适当生活条件"是一项基本人权。

这一原则所引发的争论一直持续到今天，主要是围绕健康环境权是否存在以及它的范围和可能的方式。后文的第十章也会谈及，这一项权利现在已经体现在许多国内和国际制度中。从更广的角度来看，这一原则是将环境保护全部努力的出发点放在人类中心主义；换言之，环境保护对人类非常重要。宣言的第2—26条原则的主要内容大体上可以分为三个部分，即国际环境法这一领域的定义（第2—7条）、指导本领域工作的实质性原则的声明、一些特定的实施方式。第一部分包括对地球上自然资源的保护，包含空气、水、土地、植物和动物以及自然生态系统的代表性样本（第2条），环境保护的国际合作（第24条），还有最重要的——环境危害的预防（第21条）。后者对我们的主题非常重要，因为它概括了环境保护的三个支柱，即国家对其自然资源享有永久主权，但是有义务确保在其领土管辖或控制范围内的活动不得对其他国家的环境或国家管辖外的区域造成危害。随后，《斯德哥尔摩宣言》还涉及履行的问题，特别关注了发展中国家的情况以及它们的具体需求。在数个场合，宣言提及了经济发展与环境保护的关系问题，这一问题在斯德哥尔摩会议筹备中的争论也很激烈。宣言回顾了经济发展的重要性在于确保获取一个健康的环境（第8条）或者应对一些特定的环境问题（第9条和第10条）。它还强调有必要为发展中国家提供技术和财政援助（第12条），另外，意义重大的是，它还针对国内环境政策对经济发展可能造成的负面影响发出了警示（第11条）。

斯德哥尔摩会议的另外两项成果都与环境政策的实施密切相关。大会通过的《人类环境行动计划》包含了109条建议，主要是围绕三个基本主轴，即环境影响评价、环境管理和环境支持措施。在这一文件所涉及的

---

[35] See A. Kiss anc D. Sicault, "La Conférence des Nations Unies sur l'environnement (Stockholm, 5-16 June 1972)" (1972) 18 *Annuaire Français de Droit International* 603; L. B. Sohn, "The Stockholm Declaration on the Human Environment" (1973) 14 *Harvard International Law Journal* 423.

多个主题中，第 4 条建议是将联合国环境事务的协调工作授权给一个单独机构。依据此项建议，联合国大会通过了第 2997 号决议，成立了联合国环境规划署。[36] 直到 2012 年，这一联合国的附属机构由一个由 58 个会员国组成的理事会来进行管理，它们由联合国大会根据地区分布选举产生，每期任期三年。[37]

2012 年，联合国环境规划署理事会的成员扩充到联合国大会的所有成员。在 2016 年联合国环境规划署更名为联合国环境署，它的日常管理被授权给一个位于肯尼亚内罗毕的秘书处，由一个执行主任领导，目前是挪威人埃里克·索尔海姆。建立联合国环境规划署的初衷主要是监督斯德哥尔摩规划的实施，包括第 2997 号决议第三部分所计划的环境基金的管理。从宏观上说，它的任务是促进环境事务的国际合作，包括规范的编撰。在过去这些年，联合国环境规划署的最具影响力的工作有可能就是大量的立法，特别是在著名的穆斯塔法·托尔巴（Mostafa K. Tolba）担任执行主任的任期内（1975—1992 年）。

斯德哥尔摩会议的影响是深远的，可以从三个层面对其进行评价。[38] 在国内层面，会议为数个国家建立部长级机构来应对环境问题提供了推动力。[39] 在区域层面，欧共体正是在这个时候开始制定环境立法。在国际层面，斯德哥尔摩会议不仅成功地引起了联合国对环境问题的关注，[40] 而且

36　See supra footnote 34.

37　在 2012 年 6 月召开的里约+20 峰会上，决定在联合国环境规划署的理事会中吸收全体会员国，参见"The Future We Want", 11 September 2012, UN Doc. A/Res/66/288, para. 88（a）("The Future We Want")。

38　See P. Galizzi, "From Stockholm to New York, via Rio and Johannesburg: Has the Environment Lost its Way on the Global Agenda?"（2005/2006）29 *Fordham International Law Journal*, 952, at 966-967.

39　See H. Selin and B. -O. Linner, "The Quest for Global Sustainability: International Efforts on Linking Environment and Development", *CID Graduate Student and Postdoctoral Fellow Working Paper No.* 5, January 2005, at p. 35.

40　第 2997 号决议第 2—3 段表达了如下认知：意识到采取行动保护和改善环境的责任主要在于各国政府，在国家和区域层面实施的效率更高，同时也意识到有些环境问题能造成广泛而重大的国际影响，因此必须归属于联合国体制内。See R. Gardner, "Can the UN Lead the Environmental Parade?"（1970）64 *American Journal of International Law* 211.

第一章 国际环境法的出现和发展　　　　　　　　　　　　　13

还为大量协议的达成提供了动力。[41] 这些协议的领域涉及栖息地和场所的保护、[42] 濒危物种贸易、[43] 海洋污染[44]或迁徙物种的保护。[45] 随后还有一些其他的文书在20世纪80年代得以制定，例如联合国大会于1982年10月28日通过的《第37/7号决议》（《世界自然宪章》），[46] 以及最重要的、在1982年12月10日获得通过的《联合国海洋法公约》，[47] 它用了一整个部分（第7部分）和多个其他条款来专门规定海洋环境的保护和保存。[48] 值得关注的是，从80年代开始，环境条约的签订从可见的环境问题（第一代），例如污染和物种保护，逐步转变为更加复杂的环境问题。这一趋势的主要例证有1985年《保护臭氧层维也纳公约》[49] 及其1987年《蒙特利尔议定书》[50]，以及1989年《控制危险废料越境转移及其处置巴塞尔公约》[51] 的通过。

41　See A. O. Adede, "The Treaty System from Stockholm (1972) to Rio de Janeiro (1992)" (1995) 13 *Pace Environmental Law Review* 33.

42　Convention on Wetlands of International Importance especially as Waterfowl Habitat, 2 February 1971, 996 UNTS 245 ("Ramsar Convention"); Convention Concerning the Protection of the World Cultural and Natural Heritage, 16 November 1972, 1037 UNTS 151 ("WHC").

43　Convention on International Trade in Endangered Species of Wild Fauna and Flora, 3 March 1973, 993 UNTS 243 ("CITES").

44　Convention on the Prevention of Marine Pollution by Dumping of Wastes and Other Matter, 29 December 1972 ("London Convention"), subsequently modified by the Protocol of 7 November 1996 to the Convention of 1972 on the Prevention of Marine Pollution by Dumping of Wastes and Other Matter, 7 November 1996, 1046 UNTS 120 ("London Protocol"); International Convention for the Prevention of Pollution from Ships, 2 November 1973, amended by the Protocol of 17 February 1978, 1340 UNTS 184 ("MARPOL 73/78").

45　Convention on the Conservation of Migratory Species of Wild Animals, 23 June 1979, 1651 UNTS 333.

46　World Charter for Nature, 28 October 1982, UN Doc. A/RES/37/7 ("World Charter for Nature").

47　United Nations Convention on the Law of the Sea, 10 December 1982, 1833 UNTS 396 ("UNCLOS").

48　See our analysis *Infra* at Chapter 4.

49　Vienna Convention on the Protection of the Ozone Layer, 22 March 1985, 1513 UNTS 293.

50　Montreal Protocol on Substances that Deplete the Ozone Layer, 16 September 1987, 1522 UNTS 28 ("Montreal Protocol").

51　Basel Convention on the Control of Transboundary Movements of Hazardous Wastes and their Disposal, 22 March 1989, 1573 UNTS 57 ("Basel Convention").

除了以上这些重要的进展，斯德哥尔摩会议的建议对特定环境变量所产生的影响还是要远低于期望值。有鉴于此，联合国决定重新评估全球环境治理问题，并计划于 1992 年在巴西里约热内卢召开另一次重要会议。

第五节　环境与发展里约大会

斯德哥尔摩会议十年以后，联合国环境规划署理事会开会讨论斯德哥尔摩会议建议的实施情况。这次会议的结果是在 1982 年 5 月 18 日通过了《内罗毕宣言》[52]，在这个宣言中，理事会重申了《斯德哥尔摩宣言》的基本原则（第一段），同时也承认斯德哥尔摩会议通过的行动计划的实施还不够充分（第二段）。这些结论得到了联合国大会的支持，联合国大会因此决定建立一个专门的委员会来研究 2000 年及以后的环境保护的前景。[53] 这一委员会的主席格罗·哈莱姆·布伦特兰发布了一份影响深远的报告——《我们共同的未来》，[54] 因此这个委员会通常被称为布伦特兰委员会。这一报告介绍了"可持续发展"的概念，在第二章的介绍中将可持续发展定义为：

> 既能满足当代人的需要，又不对后代人满足其需要的能力构成危害的发展。[55]

联合国大会高度认可《布伦特兰报告》，不久之后决定召开第二次会议，这次会议的主题不是人类环境，而是环境与发展之间的关系。[56] 自斯

---

[52] Report of the Governing Council on its Session of a Special Character (10–18 May 1982), 27 August 1982, UN Doc. A/RES/37/219, Annex II ("Nairobi Declaration").

[53] "Process of Preparation of the Environmental Perspective to the Year 2000 and Beyond", 19 December 1983, UN Doc. A/RES/38/161.

[54] Report of the World Commission on Environment and Development, "Our Common Future", 10 March 1987 ("Brundtland Report").

[55] Ibid., para. 49.

[56] "United Nations Conference on Environment and Development", 22 December 1989, UN Doc. A/RES/44/228.

德哥尔摩会议的筹备阶段以来，如何调和发展与环境保护的关系，实际上可能一直是国际环境治理面临的主要挑战。

联合国环境与发展大会，通常被称为"地球峰会"或"里约会议"，于 1992 年 6 月 1—15 日在巴西里约热内卢召开。[57] 176 个国家的代表团（大部分是由国家元首或政府首脑出席）以及国际组织、非政府组织和私营机构参加了本次大会。会议的协商达成了五项主要成果，分别是《环境与发展里约宣言》、[58] 一项宏大的远期行动计划《21 世纪议程》、[59] 两个开放签署的全球公约（分别聚焦气候变化[60]和生物多样性[61]）、可持续发展委员会的成立（归属于联合国经济和社会理事会）、[62] 一个不具法律约束力的权威声明（《关于所有类型森林的管理、保存和可持续开发的无法律约束力的全球协商一致意见权威性原则声明》）。[63] 另外，里约会议增强了区域的凝聚力，1994 年，由非洲提议通过了一项防治荒漠化的多边公约，[64] 同时也促成在 1995 年签署了一项关于高度洄游和跨界鱼类种群

---

[57] On the conference, see A. Kiss and S. Doumbé-Bille, "La Conférence des Nations Unies sur l'environnement et le développement（Rio de Janeiro, 3-14 juin 1992）"（1992）38 *Annuaire Francais de Droit International* 823; L. A. Kimball and W. Boyd, "International Institutional Arrangements for Environment and Development: a Post-Rio Assessment"（1992）1 *Review of Community and International Environmental Law* 295; M. Pallamaerts, "International Environmental Law from Stockholm to Rio: Back to the Future"（1992）1 *Review of Community and International Environmental Law* 254; P. H. Sand, "International Environmental Law After Rio"（1993）4 *European Journal of International Law* 377.

[58] "Rio Declaration on Environment and Development", 13 June 1992, UN Doc. A/CONF. 151/26. Rev. 1（"Rio Declaration"）.

[59] Report of the United Nations Conference on Environment and Development, A/CONF. 151/26/Rev. 1（Vol. 1）, Resolution 1, Annex 2: Agenda 21（"Agenda 21"）.

[60] United Nations Framework Convention on Climate Change, 9 May 1992, 1771 UNTS 107（"UNFCCC"）. 这一条约实际上是在里约会议之前达成的，但还是被当成了里约会议的遗产的一部分，因为它的结论受到了地球峰会的支持。

[61] Convention on Biological Diversity, 5 June 1992, 1760 UNTS 79（"CBD"）.

[62] "Institutional Arrangements to follow up the United Nations Conference on Environment and Development", 22 December 1992, UN Doc. A/RES/47/191.

[63] "Non-legally Binding Authoritative Statement of Principles for a Global Consensus on the Management, Conservation and Sustainable Development of All Types of Forests", 14 August 1992, UN Doc. A/CONF/151/26（Vol. III）（"Forest Principles"）.

[64] United Nations Convention to Combat Desertification in Countries Experiencing Serious Drought and/or Desertification, Particularly in Africa, 17 June 1994, 1954 UNTS 3（"UNCCD"）.

的协议。⁶⁵ 图 1-2 概括了这些成果。

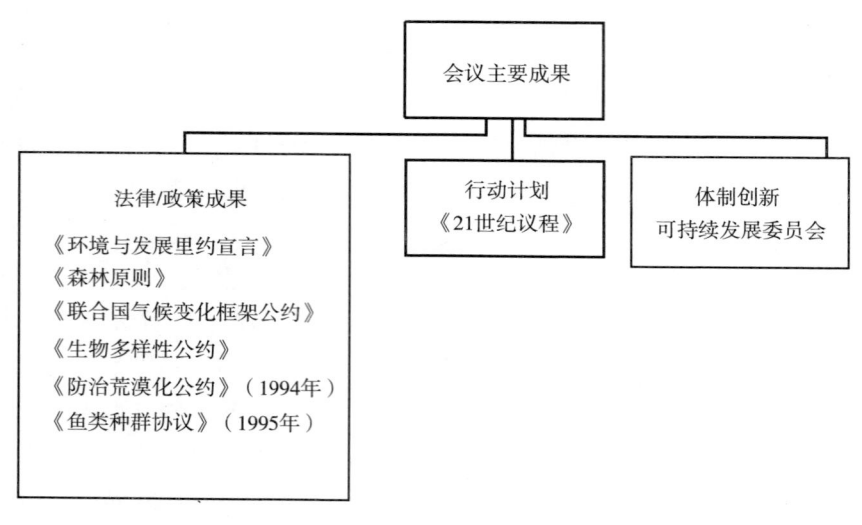

```
                        会议主要成果
            ┌───────────────┼───────────────┐
    法律/政策成果          行动计划          体制创新
    《环境与发展里约宣言》   《21世纪议程》      可持续发展委员会
    《森林原则》
    《联合国气候变化框架公约》
    《生物多样性公约》
    《防治荒漠化公约》（1994年）
    《鱼类种群协议》（1995年）
```

图 1-2　里约会议（1992 年）

本书第二编将会谈及在里约会议上开放签署的两个条约。在这里主要分析的是《里约宣言》《21 世纪议程》和可持续发展委员会。从法律的视角来看，《里约宣言》是这三项成果中最重要的一项，也是涵盖国际环境法全领域的最具代表性的文件。它包含了一个简短的序言和 27 条基本原则。⁶⁶ 从《斯德哥尔摩宣言》发布后，重心就由环境保护逐步转向环境保护与日益凸显的发展问题之间的关系，发展问题与共产主义意识形态也失去了关联。回顾往事，《里约宣言》在相互竞争的环境与发展两者之间实现了一个公平的平衡。许多原则（例如第 3 条、第 5 条、第 6 条、第 7—9 条、第 12 条、第 13 条、第 20—23 条）都表现出了较明显的发展腔调。但是，《里约宣言》同时还提供了被最广泛接受的国际环境法主要原则的构想，包括预防原则（第 2 条）、代际公平原则（第 3 条）、公众参与原则（第 10 条）、跨界和全球事务合作原则（第 18 条和第 19 条，还

65　Agreement for the Implementation of the Provisions of the United Nations Convention on the Law of the Sea of 10 December 1982 Relating to the Conservation and Management of Straddling Fish Stocks and High Migratory Fish Stocks, 4 August 1995, 2167 UNTS 3.

66　On this instrument see J. E. Viñuales (ed.), *The Rio Declaration on Environment and Development. A Commentary* (Oxford University Press, 2015), Preliminary study.

有第 7 条和第 27 条)、风险预防原则（第 15 条）、环境影响评价原则（第 17 条）以及污染者付费原则（第 16 条）。《里约宣言》还触及环境事务中的个人权利问题。第 1 条原则规定人类"享有以与自然和谐的方式过健康而富有成果的生活的权利"，这样的表述不如《斯德哥尔摩宣言》那样直截了当。在当时看起来似乎是一种倒退，人权与环境保护之间的关系从那时起变得日益重要，以至于掩盖了 20 世纪 90 年代所表现出的担心。此外，《里约宣言》还在第 10 条原则中明文表述了所谓"环境民主"的主要构成内容。这一原则指出：

> 每个人应有适当的途径获得有关公共机构掌握的环境问题的信息，其中包括有害物质和活动的信息……而且应有机会参加决策过程。

第 10 条原则还规定：

> 应提供采用司法和行政程序的有效途径，其中包括赔偿和补救措施。

最后，《里约宣言》还提到了履行的问题，第 8 条原则指出：

> 尤其需要"减少和消除不能持续的生产和消费模式并倡导适当的人口政策"。

第 9 条原则鼓励技术转让，第 10 条原则确保民间团体的参与，第 12 条原则避免利用环境作为借口来限制贸易，第 13 条原则针对环境危害赔偿来制定国家和国际手段，第 14 条原则防止危险废物转移到发展中国家。

里约会议所制定的履行战略具体体现在目标远大的《21 世纪议程》之中，[67] 它包括一个序言和 47 个章节，共计数百页，分为四个主要部分

---

[67] See N. A. Robinson (ed.), *Agenda 21: Earth's Action Plan Annotated* (New York: Oceana Publications, 1993).

（第一部分：社会和经济方面；第二部分：保存和管理资源以促进发展；第三部分：加强各主要群组的作用；第四部分：履行手段）。当然，我们在此无法详述这一冗长的文本。但是我们足以看出发展的问题贯穿于这一文本的始终。序言的前两段就为发展问题定调，指出：

> 可持续发展全球伙伴关系必须建立在对环境与发展问题采取均衡的、综合的处理办法的基础之上。[68]

我们在文本全文中都可以发现这一重点，特别是在第一部分社会和经济方面中。《21世纪议程》第39章通过表述这一领域将来的条约谈判所应遵循的指导原则，从法律的视角进一步阐释了这一整体性政策：

> 进一步制定关于可持续发展的国际法，并应特别关注环境问题与发展问题的精致平衡；必须澄清和加强现有环境领域的国际文本或协议与相关环境和社会经济协议或文本的关系，并考虑到发展中国家的特别需要。[69]

《21世纪议程》这一文件的主要目的是指导整体性措施的履行，它在各个不同领域的实际效果参差不齐，也许是因为它所设定的目标太过于宏大。但是，它提供了一个非常有用的宏图，描绘出了环境政策无比宽泛和多样的适用领域，例如大洋和海洋的保护（第17章）和水资源的保护（第18章），化学品和废物的管理（第19—22章），生态系统的保护（第11—13章和第15章），土地资源的规划和管理（第10章和第14章），甚至还有生物技术的管理（第16章）。《21世纪议程》还是2015年通过的可持续发展目标（SDGs，后文将会谈及）的一个重要前身，相比联合国千年发展目标（2000 Millennium Development Goals, MDGs）而言，《21世纪议程》对其内容的贡献更大。

里约会议还促成联合国经济和社会理事会（ECOSOC）建立了一个

68　Rio Declaration, supra footnote 58, paras. 1.1 and 1.2.

69　Agenda 21, supra footnote 59, para. 39.1.

新的机构，即可持续发展委员会（Commission for Sustainable Development, CSD）。[70] 虽然可持续发展委员会已经被一个高级别政治论坛所取代，但是它 20 年的运行经历还是值得一些评价。它由 53 个联合国会员国组成，由联合国经济和社会理事会根据地区分布选举产生，每届任期三年。它的职权主要是监督《21 世纪议程》、《里约宣言》和《约翰内斯堡计划》（后文会谈及）的履行。随着时间的变迁，可持续发展委员会重构了这一宽泛的职权范围，主要聚焦于考察各国针对《21 世纪议程》所提建议的履行报告，以及这一领域内制度性合作的指导原则的进展情况。1993—2003年，可持续发展委员会全面评估了《21 世纪议程》的各项构件。2003年，它制订了一项跨年度计划，分为 7 个周期（履行循环），每两年一个周期，每个周期关注其职权范围内的一个特定方面的问题。[71] 最早的三个周期关注的问题分别是水管理和人类定居（2004—2005 年）、能源发展和大气保护（2006—2007 年）以及广义的土地资源管理（2008—2009 年）。在其运行的最后几年，可持续发展委员会关注的问题是交通、资源开采、化学品和废物管理以及生产和消费方式。

第六节 可持续发展世界首脑会议

里约会议已经成为全球环境治理历史上的一个里程碑，以至于我们把在它之后召开的会议称为"里约后 5 年"或"里约后 10 年"，最近的一个会议是"里约后 20 年峰会"。实际上，现在的观点是，里约会议并非 20 年前斯德哥尔摩会议的重复，它本身已经成为一个奠基的时刻。如果斯德哥尔摩代表了现代国际环境法的诞生，那么里约则是代表了它的成年。当今，全球环境治理仍然是按照里约会议制定的广义原则来运行，直到 2002 年在约翰内斯堡举办的可持续发展世界首脑会议上，焦点才由规

---

70 依据 1992 年 12 月 22 日的第 A/RES. 47/191 号决议，联合国大会根据《21 世纪议程》第 38 章的建议，要求联合国经济和社会理事会成立可持续发展委员会，同时规定这一机构的职权范围。联合国经济和社会理事会通过 1993 年 2 月 12 日的第 1993/207 号决议正式成立了可持续发展委员会。

71 Future programme, organisation and methods of work of the Commission on Sustainable Development: Annex. Programme of Work of the Commission on Sustainable Development, 25 July 2003, UN Doc. E/2003/29 and E/2003/L. 32.

范的制定转变为履行。

1997年,联合国大会针对里约建议的履行情况召开了一个特别会议,并得出一个结论,即虽然里约会议对规范的制定做出了贡献,但是环境本身还是继续在恶化。[72] 换言之,现在的主要挑战应当是前些年通过的建议和标准的实际履行。在此背景下,2000年12月,联合国大会决定在南非约翰内斯堡组织第三次重要会议。[73] 在会议筹备过程中,挑选了数个优先问题作为重点,相比环境保护而言,更加关注发展的问题。这一关注重点后来被称为WEHAB议程,指的是水和卫生、能源、健康、农业生产力和生物多样性。

约翰内斯堡大会,通常也称为可持续发展世界首脑会议或约翰内斯堡峰会,于2002年8—9月召开。与前文谈及的两个会议相似,约翰内斯堡峰会的成果也可以按照图1-3的方式分为三个主要种类。

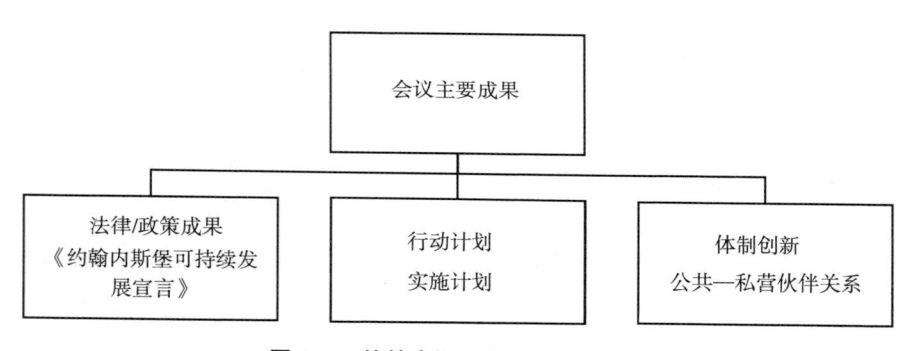

```
                会议主要成果
      ┌──────────────┼──────────────┐
  法律/政策成果        行动计划          体制创新
 《约翰内斯堡可持续     实施计划        公共—私营伙伴关系
    发展宣言》
```

图1-3 约翰内斯堡峰会(2002年)

从第一类来看,这次峰会的贡献相当一般。代表团通过了一份包含37个段落的政治宣言,即《约翰内斯堡可持续发展宣言》,对国际环境法的规范制定几乎没有补充。[74] 该宣言最重要的部分是它强调发展的社会方

---

[72] GA Resolution S/19-2, 28 June 1997, Annex, "Programme for the Further Implementation of Agenda 21", para. 9. See also UNEP, *Global Environment Outlook*, 1997.

[73] See "Ten-year Review of Progress Achieved in the Implementation of the Outcome of the United Nations Conference on Environment and Development", 20 December 2000, UN Doc. A/RES/55/199.

[74] Resolution 1: "Political declaration", 4 September 2002, Report of World Summit on Sustainable Development in Johannesburg (South Africa), 26 August to 4 September 2002, UN Doc. A/CONF.199/20, p. 1, 2002 ("Political Declaration").

面也是可持续发展的有机组成部分:

> 为此,我们担负起一项共同的责任,即在地方、国家、区域和全球各个层面来促进和加强经济、社会发展和环境保护这几个相互依存、相互增强的可持续发展支柱。[75]

事实上,这一宣言明确指向了履行问题。[76] 它特别在第 27 段提到了私营部门的作用,指出:

> 私营部门,包括大小公司,在从事合法活动时,有义务为发展公平和可持续的社区和社会做出贡献。

在约翰内斯堡通过的履行计划也针对私营部门的参与做出了进一步阐释。[77] 计划分为 11 个章节,主要领域包括 WEHAB 议程(消除贫困、可持续消费/生产、自然资源管理、健康等),区域行动(聚焦非洲、亚洲和拉丁美洲)以及可持续发展的制度框架。

后面的章节将可持续发展委员会的视野拓展到多部门合作伙伴关系的监督。[78] 多部门合作伙伴关系这一问题贯穿于这一文件的始终,仅以履行计划的几个章节为例,伙伴关系与消除贫困、[79] 改变不可持续的生产/消费方式、[80] 自然资源管理[81]或经济全球化[82]等问题密切相关。这些伙伴关系反映了约翰内斯堡峰会的精髓,被认为是实现千年发展目标(联合国大会在 2000 年通过)的一种方式。[83] 多年以来,数百个伙伴关系得以建立,

---

75　Ibid., paras. 5 and 18.
76　See, notably, Ibid., paras. 34-37.
77　Report of the World Summit on Sustainable Development at Johannesburg (South Africa), 26 August-4 September 2002, UN Doc. A/CONF.199/20 ("Implementation Plan").
78　Ibid., para. 145.
79　Ibid., paras. 7 (j) and 9 (g).
80　Ibid., para. 20 (t).
81　Ibid., para. 25 (g) and 43 (a).
82　Ibid., para. 49.
83　"Millennium Declaration", 13 September 2000, UN Doc. A/RES/55/2.

主要集中于水、能源和教育等领域。从地区分布的视角来看，这些伙伴关系大部分都是全球范围的，其余的那些也都是区域性或次区域性的。但是，这种对公共—私营伙伴关系的倚重是否对实践产生了有意义的影响，目前还不清楚。[84] 另外，2002 年，可持续发展委员会被一个高级别政治论坛所替代，它的职权范围也发生了改变，[85] 这也是一整套旨在加强履行措施的一部分。

第七节　里约峰会（2012 年）

2000 年，千年发展目标的通过又一次引起了公众对可持续发展问题的关注。虽然千年峰会的重心很明显是经济和社会发展，但是它通过提及里约会议的成果，也重点强调了尊重自然和保护我们共同的环境。[86] 因此，千年发展目标在其第七个目标指出，有必要确保环境的可持续性，并进一步明确了四个目标，其中两个与环境密切相关（使可持续发展政策成为主流并扭转环境资源损失；减少生物多样性丧失），另外两个关注的则是社会发展（提升水和卫生的获取；改善贫民窟居民的生活）。[87]

自 2000 年以来，联合国大会召集了数次会议来评估千年发展目标的履行进展。鉴于在环境保护领域（特别是与气候变化减缓和生物多样性丧失相关联的领域）所取得的进展乏善可陈，同时巴西也提议主办另一次全球大会，联合国大会最终决定 2012 年在里约热内卢召集一次新的峰会。[88] 根据授权的决议，"里约后 20 年峰会"的目标是：

> 确保针对可持续发展的新的政治承诺，针对主要峰会有关可持续

---

[84] See P. Glasbergen, F. Biermann and A. Mol（eds.）, *Partnerships, Governance and Sustainable Development. Reflections on Theory and Practice*（Cheltenham: Edward Elgar, 2007）.

[85] See B. H. Desai, B. K. Sidhu, "Quest for International Environmental Institutions: Transition to CSD to HLPF", in S. Alam et al, supra footnote 21, pp. 152–168.

[86] See Millennium Declaration, supra footnote 83, paras. 6 and 21–23.

[87] See www.un.org/millenniumgoals/environ.shtml（accessed on 17 December 2012）.

[88] "Implementation of Agenda 21, the Programme for the Further Implementation of Agenda 21 and the outcomes of the World Summit on Sustainable Development", 31 March 2010, UN Doc. A/RES/64/236, para. 20（"Enabling Resolution"）.

发展的成果履行的进展和不足进行评估,应对新的和新兴的挑战。[89]

另外,这一决议还明确指出了会议筹备期间应当讨论和完善的两个核心主题:可持续发展和消除贫困背景下的绿色经济以及可持续发展体制框架。[90]

这次峰会的筹备过程没有引起太多关注,因为大量媒体的注意力都集中于2009年12月召开的哥本哈根气候大会以及会议失败后导致的幻灭。此外,这次峰会所设定的主题过于宽泛,还细分成了7个"优先领域"(好工作、能源、可持续城市、食品安全和可持续农业、水、海洋及灾害救济)和16个"议题"(涉及贸易、科学、技术、人口动态等),这就导致讨论无法聚焦。峰会的成果文件《我们需要的未来》,再次确认了约翰内斯堡峰会首创的转变,即转向履行和发展关切。这次会议加强了联合国环境规划署,将其改为联合国环境署,特别是将其理事会扩展到联合国大会的全体会员并给予其一项更大的预算,[91] 除此之外,这一文件的主要贡献就是提出要努力实现"可测量"的进展。事实上,这次峰会的三个主要成就的核心就是"可测量":(1) 呼吁为2015年后议程制定可持续发展目标,[92] 最终在2015年9月获得通过;(2) 由一个高层次政治论坛对这些目标进行定期评估,[93] 采用的是"自愿的国家评估"这一体制;[94] (3) 呼吁为提升国内生产总值提出更广泛的促进措施,在文件起草时这

---

89 "Implementation of Agenda 21, the Programme for the Further Implementation of Agenda 21 and the outcomes of the World Summit on Sustainable Development", 31 March 2010, UN Doc. A/RES/64/236, para. 20 (a).

90 "Implementation of Agenda 21, the Programme for the Further Implementation of Agenda 21 and the outcomes of the World Summit on Sustainable Development", 31 March 2010, UN Doc. A/RES/64/236, para. 20 (a) infine.

91 The Future We Want, supra footnote 37, para. 88.

92 The Future We Want, supra footnote 37, paras. 245-251.

93 The Future We Want, supra footnote 37, para. 85 (e).

94 See *Critical Milestones Towards Coherent, Efficient and Inclusive Follow-up and Review at the Global Level. Report of the Secretary General*, 15 January 2016, UN doc A/70/684, Annex (common voluntary reporting guidelines). 2016年,有22个发达国家和发展中国家作为第一批参与了第一次的报告行动,按照日程是在每年的7月举行。

一工作仍在进行。⁹⁵ 后文将会谈及，先前被逐步设计的可持续发展目标现在已经成为一份重要文件的核心部分，它将指导近期到中期的全球环境治理，这份文件被称为《2030年可持续发展议程》(*2030 Agenda for Sustainable Development*)。

第八节 《2030年可持续发展议程》（2015年）和全球环境治理的未来

紧接着里约峰会（2012年）的成果，两个谈判进程得以启动，其目的是设计可持续发展目标和一个更广的2015年后的议程，各种团体包括民间团体都广泛参与了谈判。⁹⁶ 这些进程在2015年9月达到了顶峰，联合国大会通过了一份名为《改变我们的世界：2030年可持续发展议程》(《2030年议程》)的文件。⁹⁷《2030年议程》由四个主要部分组成：(1) 一个简短的序言；(2) 一个宣言；(3) 一套可持续发展目标（包含17个目标）；(4) 一套针对履行的观察报告（通过履行手段和评估制度）。

序言陈述了《2030年议程》的核心内容，它与《里约宣言》所述的高度相似，一个由和平和伙伴关系（合作）构成的总体框架，追求的目标是社会发展（人类）、环境保护（星球）以及经济增长和发展（繁荣）。

宣言进一步指明了这些核心内容。意义重大的是，在"我们共享的原则和承诺"这一部分，宣言强调了国际法的作用⁹⁸和《里约宣言》原则（提到两次）的作用，特别是共同但有区别的责任原则（common but dif-

---

95　The Future We Want, supra footnote 37, para. 38.

96　On the two tracks see P. Chasek et al, "Getting to 2030: Negotiating the Post-2015 Sustainable Development Agenda" (2016) 25/1 *Review of European, Comparative and International Environmental Law* 5.

97　See Resolution 70/1, "Transforming our World: The 2030 Agenda for Sustainable Development", 21 October 2015, UN doc A/RES/70/1. The discussion of this instrument relies on J. E. Viñuales, Foreign Investment and the Environment in International Law: Current Trends", in K. Miles (ed.), Research Handbook on Environment and Investment Law (Cheltenham: Edward Elgar, forthcoming 2018), chapter. 2.

98　2030 Agenda, supra footnote 97, Declaration, para 10.

ferentiated responsibilities principle）。[99] 宣言提供了《2030 年议程》主要构成部分的背景资料，即可持续发展目标。[100]

总体上有 17 个可持续发展目标，其中 16 个是实质性目标，[101] 而最后一个即第 17 个目标关注的则是履行问题。[102] 每个可持续发展目标又被分解为多个具体目标，总计有 169 个目标。一个由 27 个国家组成的工作组（意味着更多自下而上的参与）设计了 230 个指标对这些目标轮流进行评测。这些指标在 2016 年 3 月获得了联合国统计委员会的通过。广义来讲，可持续发展目标有五个主要特征：

（1）它们是整体性的和不可分割的，因此不能按照它们在文本中出现的先后顺序对其进行等级划分；（2）它们是基于国家层面的，这样就意味着，虽然承认全球、区域和次区域的努力的重要性，它们还是将核心的责任放置在国家层面；（3）它们事关所有国家而不仅仅限于发展中国家（这一点与千年发展目标差别很大），因此，"发展"在这里被理解为"繁荣"或者发展和成长；（4）它们强调了各国处于不同的发展阶段，因此有必要区别对待；（5）它们产生于一个非常包容的、开放的进程（与起草千年发展目标时的自上而下的方法大相径庭）。

最后，《2030 年议程》特别提出了履行的手段，包括财政、技术转让和履行评估。针对后两项还规定了制度应对，一个是技术便利机制

99　2030 Agenda, supra footnote 97, Declaration, para. 12.
100　有关可持续发展目标的国际法律方面，参见 the special issue of the *Review of European, Comparative & International Environmental Law*, Vol. 25, issue 1, April 2016, devoted to "The SDGs and International Environmental Law", with contributions from（Chasek et al, Kim, Lode et al, Spijkers, Orellana, Persson et al）。
101　可持续目标的简短版本可以作如下表述：（1）没有贫困；（2）零饥饿；（3）好的健康和福利；（4）高质量教育；（5）性别平等；（6）清洁的水和卫生；（7）负担得起的、清洁的能源；（8）好工作和经济增长；（9）工业、创新和基础设施；（10）减少不平等；（11）可持续城市和社区；（12）负责任的消费和生产；（13）气候行动；（14）水下生物；（15）陆上生物；（16）和平、工作和强力的体系。
102　第 17 个可持续发展目标（针对目标的伙伴关系）。

(Technology Facilitation Mechanism),[103] 另一个是履行评估制度（可以体现 2012 年里约峰会上建立的高层次政治论坛的特点）。[104] 财政手段则与 2015 年早期通过的一项文件有着很大关联，文件名称是《亚的斯亚贝巴行动议程》（Addis Ababa Action Agenda），它源自第三次国际发展筹资大会（Third International Conference on Financing for Development）。[105] 针对《亚的斯亚贝巴行动议程》，《2030 年议程》包含了一个明确的回顾，因此前者也被认为是《2030 年可持续发展议程》的一个有机组成部分"。[106]

要想判断《2030 年议程》能否将世界引入可持续发展的道路，现在还为时过早。因为它包含的事项太过繁杂而导致中心的缺失，现在已经受到批评，即使如此，议程还是为国际和国内层面的改变提供了重大的推动力。政府、国际组织、私营部门和民间团体正在将可持续发展目标融入他们的行动当中，虽然现在还不清楚这种对政策的认同是否蕴含了实质性转变抑或只是规划上的转变。另外，虽然议程强调了可持续发展目标的整体性特点，并无等级划分，但是，人们还是会很容易注意到这样一个事实，即前 10 个可持续发展目标的重心是社会经济发展，而气候变化、海洋环境和生物多样性则被放在后面。

从 2012 年里约峰会以后，社会和经济发展就不再是可持续发展的一个首要目标，[107] 而是变成了主要挑战。

正如成果文件所述，"消除贫困是当今世界面临的最大的全球挑战，它也是可持续发展必不可少的一个要求"。[108] 《2030 年议程》中的可持续发展目标确认了这一转变，它把消除贫困放在 17 个目标的第一个加以明确。毫无疑问的是，消除贫困是一项迫切需求。我们需要认真评估的是可

---

[103] 2030 Agenda, supra footnote 97, Means of Implementation and the Global Partnership, para. 70.

[104] 2030 Agenda, supra footnote 97, Follow up and Review, paras. 82-90.

[105] *Addis Ababa Action Agenda of the Third International Conference on Financing for Development* (Addis Ababa Action Agenda), UNGA Resolution 69/313, 27 July 2015, UN Doc A/RES/69/313, Annex.

[106] 2030 Agenda, supra footnote 97, Means of implementation and the Global Partnership, para. 62.

[107] See e. g. : Political Declaration, supra footnote 74, para. 11; Enabling Resolution, supra footnote 88, preamble, para. 12.

[108] The Future We Want, supra footnote 37, para. 2.

持续发展的各个支柱之间所表现出的明显的等级划分。在此背景下，我们可以回想一下 1971 年第 2849 号决议的措辞，它是发展中国家对环境关切持怀疑态度的早期表述之一。这一决议的最后一段重申，将独立的经济和社会发展置于首要位置并把它当作国际合作主要的、最重要的目标符合人类的福祉和世界的和平与安全。[109] 图 1-4 概括了环境—发展这一方程式自 20 世纪 60 年代以来的历史轨迹。[110]

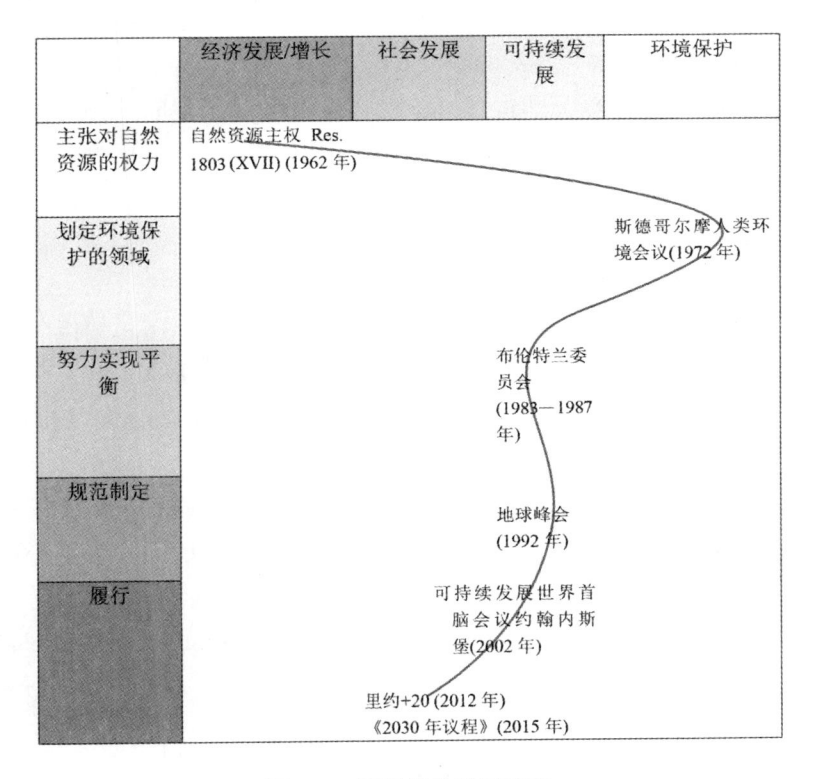

	经济发展/增长	社会发展	可持续发展	环境保护
主张对自然资源的权力	自然资源主权 Res. 1803 (XVII) (1962 年)			
划定环境保护的领域				斯德哥尔摩人类环境会议(1972 年)
努力实现平衡			布伦特兰委员会 (1983—1987 年)	
规范制定			地球峰会 (1992 年)	
履行			可持续发展世界首脑会议约翰内斯堡(2002 年)	
		里约+20 (2012 年) 《2030 年议程》(2015 年)		

图 1-4 可持续发展蛇形图

可持续发展正在逐渐褪色。当然，我们也不能回到起点。本章所展示的重要里程碑表明，与 50 年前相比，环境关切在当今国际和国家政策议程中出现的频率大幅增加。然而，环境—发展这一方程式至今还是饱受实

---

109 Development and Environment, supra footnote 30, para. 11.

110 Source：J. E. Viñuales, "The Rise and Fall of Sustainable Development" (2013) 22 *Review of Community and International Environmental Law* 3.

施问题的困扰。虽然广义的可持续发展概念给出了暂时的答案，但是我们还是需要新思维来超越这一答案。这可能是当前国际环境法最重要的理论前沿问题。

部分参考文献

［1］Abi-Saab, G., "La souveraineté permanente sur les ressources naturelles", in M. Bedjaoui (ed.), *Droit International: Bilan et Perspectives* (Paris: Pedone, 1989), pp. 638-661.

［2］Adede, A. O., "The Treaty System from Stockholm (1972) to Rio de Janeiro (1992)" (1995) 13 *Pace Environmental Law Review* 33.

［3］Alam, S., S. Atapattu, C. Gonzalez and J. Razzaque (eds.), *International Environmental Law and the Global South* (Cambridge University Press, 2016).

［4］Boer, B., "The Globalisation of Environmental Law: The Role of the United Nations" (1995) 20 *Melbourne University Law Review* 101.

［5］Boisson de Chazournes, L., "Environmental Treaties in Time" (2009) 39 *Environmental Policy and Law* 293.

［6］Bratspies, R. and R. Miller (eds.), *Transboundary Harm in International Law: Lessons from the Trail Smelter Arbitration* (Cambridge University Press, 2006).

［7］Brighton, C., "Unlikely Bedfellows: The Evolution of the Relationship between Environmental Protection and Development" (2017) 66 *International and Comparative Law Quarterly* 209.

［8］Brown Weiss, E., "The Evolution of International Environmental Law" (2011) 54 *Japanese Yearbook of International Law* 1.

［9］Brunnée, J., "The Stockholm Declaration and the Structure and Processes of International Environmental Law", in A. Chircop (ed.), *The Future of Ocean Regime-building: Essays in Tribute to Douglas M. Johnston* (Leiden: Martinus Nijhoff, 2009), pp. 41-62.

［10］Caldwell, L. K., *International Environmental Policy. From the Twentieth to the Twenty-First Century* (Durham: Duke University Press, 3rd edn, 1996).

[11] Chasek, P., L. M. Wagner, F. Leone, A. -M. Lebada and N. Risse, "Getting to 2030: Negotiating the Post-2015 Sustainable Development Agenda" (2016) 25/1 *Review of European, Comparative and International Environmental Law* 5.

[12] Dobson, A., *Green Political Thought* (New York: Routledge, 4th edn, 2007).

[13] Driesen, D., "Thirty Years of International Environmental Law: A Retrospective and Plea for Reinvigoration" (2003) 30 *Syracuse Journal of International Law and Commerce* 353.

[14] Dupuy, P. -M., "Où en est le droit international de l'environnement à la fin du siècle?" (2007) *Revue Générale de Droit International Public* 873.

[15] Ellis, J., "Unilateral Exercises of Public Authority: Addressing Issues of Fairness in Teck v. Pakootas" (2012) 25 *Leiden Journal of International Law* 397.

[16] Galizzi, P., "From Stockholm to New York, via Rio and Johannesburg: Has the Environment Lost its Way on the Global Agenda?" (2005/2006) 29 *Fordham International Law Journal* 952.

[17] Grove, R. H., *Green Imperialism. Colonial Expansion, Tropical Island Edens and the Origins of Environmentalism, 1600-1860* (Cambridge University Press, 1996).

[18] Kennet, K., "The Stockholm Conference on the Human Environment" (1972) 48 *International Affairs* 33.

[19] Kim, R. E., "The Nexus between International Law and the Sustainable Development Goals" (2016) 25 *Review of European, Comparative and International Environmental Law* 15.

[20] Kiss, A., "Dix ans après Stockholm-une décennie de droit international de l'environnement" (1982) 28 *Annuaire Français de Droit International* 784-93.

[21] Kiss, A. and S. Doumbé-Bille, "La Conférence des Nations Unies sur l'environnement et le développement (Rio de Janeiro, 3-14 juin 1992)" (1992) 38 *Annuaire Français de Droit International* 823.

[22] Kiss, A. and D. Sicault, "La Conférence des Nations Unies sur

l'environnement (Stockholm, 5 – 16 juin 1972)" (1972) 18 *Annuaire français de droit international* 603.

[23] Macekura, S., *Of Limits and Growth. The Rise of International Sustainable Development in the Twentieth Century* (Cambridge University Press, 2015).

[24] Maljean-Dubois, S., "Environnement, développement durable et droit international. De Rio à Johannesbourg: et au – delà?" (2002) 48 *Annuaire français de droit international* 592.

"The making of international law challenging environmental protection", in S. Maljean-Dubois and Y. Kerbrat (eds.), *The Transformation of International Environmental Law* (Oxford: Hart Publishing, 2011), pp. 25–54.

[25] Pallamaerts, M., "International Environmental Law from Stockholm to Rio: Back to the Future" (1992) 1 *Review of European Community and International Environmental Law* 254.

[26] Rajamani, L., "From Stockholm to Johannesburg: The Anatomy of Dissonance in the International Environmental Dialogue" (2003) 12 *Review of European Community and International Environmental Law* 23.

[27] Robinson, N. A., *Agenda 21: Earth's Action Plan Annotated* (New York/London: Oceana Publications, 1993).

[28] Sand, P. H., "International Environmental Law After Rio" (1993) 4 *European Journal of International Law* 377.

"The Evolution of International Environmental Law", in D. Bodansky, J. Brunnée and E. Hey (eds.), *The Oxford Handbook of International Environmental Law* (Oxford University Press, 2007), pp. 31–43.

[29] Sands, P. "The environment, community and international law" (1989) 30 *Harvard International Law Journal* 393.

"International Environmental Law Ten Years On" (1999) 8*Review of European Community and International Environmental Law* 239.

[30] Schachter, O., "The Emergence of International Environmental Law" (1991) 44 *Journal of International Affairs* 457.

[31] Schrijver, N., *Sovereignty over Natural Resources. Balancing Rights and Duties* (Cambridge University Press, 1997).

[32] Selin, H. and B. -O. Linner, "The Quest for Global Sustainability: International Efforts on Linking Environment and Development", *CID Graduate Student and Postdoctoral Fellow Working Paper No.* 5, January 2005.

[33] Sohn, L. B., "The Stockholm Declaration on the Human Environment" (1973) 14 *Harvard International Law Journal* 423.

[34] Viñuales, J. E., "The Contribution of the International Court of Justice to the Development of International Environmental Law" (2008) 32 *Fordham International Law Journal* 232.

"The Rise and Fall of Sustainable Development" (2013) 22*Review of European Community and International Environmental Law* 3.

"The Rio Declaration on Environment and Development. Preliminary Study", in J. E. Viñuales (ed.), *The Rio Declaration on Environment and Development. A Commentary* (Oxford University Press, 2015).

第二章 国际环境法的主要特点

第一节 导言

在前面一章，我们研究了形塑国际环境法发展的各个里程碑。在探讨这一领域国际法的技术方面之前，有必要研究一下它最显著的特点。在当前阶段，对这些特点进行评论可以起到三个作用。第一，为了勾画出国际环境法的轮廓，就有必要明确它的具体客体，也就是环境。第二，通过对主要多边环境协定（Multilateral Environmental Agreements，MEAs）的比较研究，系统展示其呈现出来的多个显著特征，有助于我们理解条约的运行，正如语法有助于我们加深对一门语言的理解。第三，国际环境法的特点为我们提供了大量信息，揭示了其作为一个法律和社会现象的动态性以及未来的演变趋势。

换言之，无论是从理论研究的角度（将国际环境法作为一门学科来界定）还是从实践的角度（了解它的渊源、方法和运行），了解国际环境法的主要特点都是有用的。关于理论方面，国际环境法作为一门学科的相对统一在一定程度上是源自它的客体——环境以及那些支撑绝大多数环境条约的共同基本原则，这些原则是最重要的。在本章中，我们将分析对一个如环境这般宽泛、多面的现实进行概念化的过程中遇到的困难（本章第二节），对统一的原则的研究则放在第三章。在国际环境法的实践方面，它的显著特点诸如它的主要主体（本章第三节）、渊源（本章第四节）和管理手段（本章第五节）在很大程度上可以被当作这一部门法对其一直以来所面对的政治、经济和科学挑战的回应。本章的最后一个部分（本章第六节）聚焦于国际环境法在国际法律秩序中的位置。

第二节 "环境"作为一个法律客体

一 概述

当我们尝试去了解国际环境法的客体时,涌现出的第一问题是,"环境"这一术语指的是否是一个单一的实体,它是否具备一个具体的法律或实践含义。"环境"这一术语流行于科学、政治和媒体话语中,但是它的含义仍然不太清楚。当谈及"时间"这一概念时,奥古斯丁曾经说过,当我们不再被要求对其做一个定义时,我们就知道了它的含义,"环境"这一术语一方面很简单,可以凭直觉来理解,另一方面又很难,需要精确地加以界定。为了当前的目的,我们有必要从三个层面对其做一个特征描述。

二 科学层面

首先,"环境"这一术语可以从科学层面来刻画它的特征,更具体地说,是用生态学的方法,相关著作对它的特点给出了不同的解说。

从广义来讲,环境的定义是"围绕着一个空间实体的任何东西,无生命的或者是活着的"。[1] 20世纪70年代的广义概念还包含了人这一要素,将其作为操控力量。[2] 当今,这一术语的平衡已经摆脱了单纯以人类为中心,而是以一个"有机体"(包括了人类)为轴心来运转。根据《牛津生态学词典》,"环境"是:

---

[1] F. Ramade, *Dictionnaire Encyclopédique de L'écologie et des Sciences de L'environnement* (Paris: Dunod, 2002), p. 279 (our translation).

[2] 在20世纪初期,"环境"这一术语被当作"地理"的同义词来使用(E. Reclus, *L' Homme et la Terre*, 6 vols. (Paris: Librairie Universelle, 1905). See Y. Veyret, "Environnement', in Y. Veyret (ed.), *Dictionnaire de L'environnement* (Paris: Armand Colin, 2007), p. 133)。在20世纪晚期,生态学开始从地理学中区分出来,生态学的重点是生态的分析,但是生态学和地理学之间的人的位置是一个非常重要的问题,贯穿了整个20世纪。将生态学当作一门科学进行研究的早期成果包括: W. C. Allee, O. Park, A. E. Emerson, T. Park and K. P. Schmidt, *Principles of Animal Ecology* (Philadelphia: Saunders, 1949); E. P. Odum, *Fundamentals of Ecology* (Philadelphia: Saunders, 1st edn. 1953, 2nd edn. 1959, 3rd edn. 1971). On the history of ecology, see J.-P. Deleage, *Histoire de L'écologie: une Science de L'homme et de la Nature* (Paris: La Découverte, 1991)。

一个有机物所生活的外部条件的完整范围,包括物理的和生态的。环境包括社会的、文化的以及经济和政治的(对人类而言)关切,更多时候它的特征被理解为土壤、气候和食物供给。[3]

这一广义和平衡的概念在今天仍然流行,在"生态系统方法"的根源中也可以发现它的存在,而多边环境协定越来越多地在运用"生态系统方法"。[4] 但是,这一科学概念看起来似乎太过宽泛,以至于无法确定国际环境法作为一门理论学科的研究领域。人类环境的社会、文化、经济和政治方面实际上已经包含了国际法的整个领域。对环境的科学定性强调了环境保护有必要采取一种平衡的方法,因为环境不仅被定义为围绕在人类周围的状况(一种"人类中心主义"观点),还被定义为那些围绕在任何其他有机物周围的东西(一种"生态中心主义"观点)。

三 法律层面

我们同样会问,国际法是否对"环境"这一术语的一个或多个含义赋予了特定的法律后果。这一问题的答案必须到一系列多种多样的法律手段中去寻求。

第一种方法,我们可以回顾第一章谈到的国际环境法的奠基文件。但是它们并不是完全令人满意的,因为这些方法都没有对"环境"这一术语做出具体定性。不过,它们还是提供了一些有用的见解。例如,《斯德哥尔摩宣言》的序言就提到了人类环境的两个构成部分:"自然的和人造的,对人类幸福和享受基本人权以及生命权至关重要的。"[5] 它还进一步提及"地球上的各种自然资源,包括空气、水、土地、植物和动物以及其他各自然生态系统中有代表性的种群"。[6] 后来的《世界自然宪章》(*World Charter for Nature*)、《里约宣言》(*Rio Declaration*)和《千年宣

---

[3] M. Allaby, *Oxford Dictionary of Ecology* (Oxford University Press, 3rd edn, 2005), at 154.

[4] 有关生态系统方法成为一种法律框架的起源,参见 V. De Lucia, "Competing Narratives and Complex Genealogies: The Ecosystem Approach in International Environmental Law" (2015) 27 *Journal of Environmental Law* 91。

[5] Declaration of the United Nations Conference on the Human Environment, Stockholm, 16 June 1972, UN Doc. A/CONF 48/14/Rev. 1 ("Stockholm Declaration"), preamble, para. 1.

[6] Ibid., Principle 2.

言》(Millennium Declaration)的文本,针对《斯德哥尔摩宣言》对环境的特性描述几乎没有增加内容。[7] 因此,我们可以得出结论,这一方法就其本身而论是不够充分的。

第二种可能的方法是参考国际上的法院和法庭的裁决,特别是国际法院的裁决。在其关于核武器合法性的咨询意见中,国际法院指出:

> 环境不是一个抽象的概念,它代表了人类的生存空间、生活质量和健康,包括未出生的人类。[8]

如果不探究这一意见的用意何在,还是不足以给出"环境"这一术语的法律内涵的。

第三种方法是在一个特定的规范性文本(例如一个条约或者一个规范)中寻求对"环境"这一术语的定义。例如,在查戈斯岛案中,[9] 英国尝试限制仲裁庭的管辖权限,主张海洋保护区(Marine Protected Area,MPA)不能被定性为《联合国海洋法公约》第297条第1款第3点所规定的一项"海洋环境的保护和保存措施",[10] 因为它包含了"对专属经济区内的生物资源行使国家主权"这一行为,所以根据公约第297条第3款第1点之规定,应当排除仲裁庭的管辖权。仲裁庭驳回了英国的主张,因为它发现海洋保护区是被当作一个"环境关切"来定性的。[11] 如此一来,"环境"或"环境的"这一术语就有了特定的法律内涵。但是,这种方法

---

[7] 《世界自然宪章》在其序言中指出,"人类是自然的一部分,生命有赖于自然系统的功能维持不坠,以保证能源和养料的供应",它还指出,有必要维持"基本的生态过程和生命维持系统,以及生命形式的多种多样"。《世界自然宪章》,1982年10月28日,UN Doc. A/RES/37/7。《里约宣言》在其第7条原则也提及"地球生态系统的健康和完整",《里约宣言》,1992年6月13日,UN Doc. A/CONF. 151/26。《千年宣言》在其第6段提到"尊重自然"和"所有生命物种和自然资源的管理",《千年宣言》,2000年9月13日,UN Doc. A/RES. 55/2。

[8] *Legality of the Threat or Use of Nuclear Weapons*, Advisory Opinion, ICJ Reports 1996, para. 29 ("*Legality of Nuclear Weapons*").

[9] *In the Matter of the Chagos Marine Protected Area Arbitration Before an Arbitral Tribunal constituted under Annex VII of the United Nations Convention on the Law of the Sea* (*Mauritius v. UK*), Award (18 March 2015).

[10] United Nations Convention on the Law of the Sea, 10 December 1982, 1833 UNTS 397 ("UNCLOS").

[11] *Chagos Island*, supra footnote 9, para. 291.

最大的长处也恰恰是其主要的短处。这种方法可以明确某一术语在一个特定条约语境下的含义，但是这一含义通常也只限于这一语境。例如，在南极条约体制中对环境的定义，[12] 一旦脱离南极这一特定语境，就几乎没有法律关联性。同样地，在涉及石油泄漏的民事责任制度语境下，环境危害一词中"环境"的定义[13]，以及在1949年《日内瓦公约第一议定书》（Protocol I to the 1949 Geneva Conventions）在谈及环境危害时对"环境"的定义，[14] 并不能简单地概括为它们排除了自然或人造环境的特定成分，[15] 这也是《斯德哥尔摩宣言》的准则所规定的。[16] 甚至还有一个更广义的定性，例如《联合国气候变化框架公约》（UNFCCC）第1条第1款之规定，[17] 但是，在缺乏一个法律关系［例如公约与《京都议定书》（Kyoto

---

[12] 参见《南极海洋生物资源保护公约》，1980年5月20日，33 UST 3476，在第1条将其范围定义为"本公约适用于南纬60°以南地区的南极海洋生物资源以及这一纬度和南极辐合带（南极辐合带构成了南极海洋生态系统的一部分）之间地区的南极海洋生物资源……南极海洋生态系统指的是南极海洋生物资源相互之间以及与它们的物理环境之间的各种关系"。与此相类似，《南极条约之环境保护议定书》，1991年10月4日，30 ILM 1455（1991年）在第3条第1款定义其范围时借鉴了南极条约所规定的地区（南纬60°以南）并明确将那一地区的环境定义为"南极环境和互相依赖、关联的生态系统以及南极的固有价值，包括它的荒野和美学价值及其在当地开展科学研究的价值，特别是那些对理解全球环境至关重要的研究"。See P. Birnie, A. Boyle and C. Redgwell, *International Law and the Environment* (Oxford University Press, 2009), p. 6.

[13] See infra Chapter 8.

[14] See infra Chapter 11.

[15] See United Nations Compensation Commission, *Report and Recommendation made by the Panel of Commissioners concerning the F4 claims*, 22 June 2001, UN Doc. S/AC. 26/2001/16, (first instalment); 3 October 2002, S/AC. 26/2002/26 (second instalment); 18 December 2003, S/AC. 26/2003/31 (third instalment); 9 December 2004, S/AC. 26/2004/16 (fourth instalment, part I); 9 December 2004, S/AC. 26/2004/17 (fourth instalment part II), and 30 June 2005, S/AC. 26/2005/10 (fifth instalment). J.-C. Martin, "The United Nations Compensation Commission Practice with Regards to Environmental Claims", in S. Maljean-Dubois and Y. Kerbrat (eds.), *The Transformation of International Environmental Law* (Oxford: Hart, 2011), pp. 251-267.

[16] Stockholm Declaration, supra footnote 5, preamble, para. 1. In addition, international humanitarian law protects civilian objects. See, notably, The (IV) Geneva Convention Relative to the Protection of Civilian Persons in Time of War, 12 August 1949, 75 UNTS 287, Art. 33.

[17] 《联合国气候变化框架公约》第1条第1款将"气候变化的不利影响"定义为"气候变化所造成的自然环境或生物区系的变化，这些变化对自然的和管理下的生态系统的组成、复原力或生产力，或对社会经济系统的运作，或对人类的健康和福利产生重大的有害影响"，《联合国气候变化框架公约》，1992年5月9日，1771 UNTS 107.

Protocol)[18] 之间的关系] 的情况下，不能将这一定性借用至其他条约的语境当中。

四 操作层面

最后，如果完全从操作层面考虑，"环境"这一术语的含义可以从"国际环境法"所涵盖的整套文书中获取。当然，从理论角度来看，这一种方法是不太让人满意的，因为它是一种逻辑上的循环。但是，在实践中，它又非常实用，特别是它为国际环境法这样一门学科提供了一个结构性综述，并可用于专业研究或教育的目的。实际上，它帮助组建了这一学科的主要内容，而且它这种方式有助于将这些内容当作一个整体来理解。

例如，在前文对"环境"定性时所提及的物理的（空气、水、土地）、生物的（物种，包括人类、栖息地、生态系统和生物多样性）和文化的（人类生存和审美方面的考量）这些组成部分就可以被分门别类地纳入实体规制的不同类别或领域。这就是我们所采用的方法。在本书的后续部分，我们将聚焦于国际环境法这一完整"大陆"的四个"次大陆"：[19]（1）海洋环境和淡水；[20]（2）大气保护；[21]（3）物种、生态系统和生物多样性；[22]（4）危险物质和活动的规制。[23]

以上其实就是对国际环境法所要研究内容的特性描述，现在我们开始介绍这一实体法的主要特征。

第三节　主要行为体

一　从挑战到架构

想要了解究竟是哪些主要行为体塑造了国际环境法的活力，我们有必

18　Protocol to the United Nations Framework Convention on Climate Change, Kyoto, 11 December 1997, 2303 UNTS 148（"Kyoto Protocol"）, Art. 1.

19　See D. Bodansky, J. Brunnée and E. Hay（eds.）, *The Oxford Handbook of International Environmental Law*（Oxford University Press, 2007）, part III.

20　See our analysis infra Chapter 4.

21　See infra Chapter 5.

22　See infra Chapter 6.

23　See infra Chapter 7.

要回顾一下这一学科自 20 世纪 60 年代的现代起源以来所面临的挑战。这些挑战可以被分为两大类。

第一类包含了国际层面的政治难题,主要是因为:(1) 发展中国家把国际环境法看作富裕国家的一个奢侈品或者限制其发展的一个紧箍咒,甚至是发达国家用来限制发展中国家贸易的一种保护主义手段;(2) 不同国家间的战略竞争;[24] (3) 为了应对跨界或全球环境问题,必须开展合作并协调努力。

第二类指的是国内难题,主要原因在于:(1) 那些受到环境规制不利影响的各个经济利益集团拥有足够的手段组织在一起并对政府在各种环境问题上的立场施加影响;(2) 环境规制的一些更广义的内涵,例如它可能导致的竞争劣势,以及外包和失业的风险,无论是因为正当或不正当的原因,它们通常都会与环境规则的制定扯上关系。[25]

为了应对这两种挑战,国际环境法形成了两个本质上可以被归纳为"组织性的"特点,因为它们反映了全球环境治理主要主体的组织建设。[26] 解决第一种难题的答案在于创立多个国际组织(或者某些已有组织的重新定位)来促进环境事务中的国家合作(本章第三节第二部分)。而第二种难题的解决办法则是鼓励民间团体去抵消经济利益集团的影响并广泛参与环境规范的履行(本章第二节第三部分)。

二 国际架构和行为体

在国家之间的关系中,信任和效率问题,是通过创立新的国际组织或者重新定位或扩张已有组织来解决的。在这里我们并不打算详述国际组织的理论,[27]

---

[24] 美国参议院拒绝通过《京都议定书》的原因通常被归根于这样一个事实,即美国的一些战略竞争者,没有被要求达到足够数量的减排目标。See especially "Getting Warmer", *The Economist*, 3 December 2009.

[25] See Ibid.

[26] See generally J. G. Speth and P. Haas, *Global Environmental Governance* (Washington DC: Island Press, 2006).

[27] See M. Virally, *L'organisation Mondiale* (Paris: Armand Colin, 1972); H. G. Schermers and N. M. Blokker, *International Institutional Law* (Leiden: Martinus Nijhoff, 5th edn, 2011).

也不会详述它们在国际关系中的作用。[28] 我们只是探讨那些在全球环境治理中比较活跃的国际组织的种类划分。

根据国际组织的创建方式和它们的职权范围,广义来看,可以将其划分为四类。第一类,可能也是最常见的一类,包含那些通过"组织条约"创建的国际组织,这类组织的作用范围和主要机构都由"组织条约"做出明确规定。涉及环境事务的著名组织包括世界气象组织(WMO)、[29] 联合国粮农组织(FAO)[30] 和国际海事组织(IMO)。[31] 这些组织的基本功能是协调各国在某一特定领域的规范制定合作,它们通常会为条约谈判或者标准制定提供一个框架。

第二类组织是第一类的变异,两者的主要区别在于,原有条约并未打算为了某一特定领域的目的去创建一个新的组织,而是计划规制一个具体的问题,于是就成立机构来管理条约的进展。举例来讲,绝大多数多边环境协定(MEAs)都建立了类似于缔约方大会(COP)和秘书处的机构。[32] 第二类组织的例证包括《巴塞尔公约》《联合国气候变化框架公约》《生物多样性公约》《防治荒漠化公约》和《斯德哥尔摩公约》所建立的缔约方大会和秘书处。[33] 这些机构的作用是通过组织定期谈判来促进某一特定制度的发展,这些谈判通常会导致新的和更多的具体条约,或者引入大量

---

28 See P. Haas, R. O. Keohane and M. A. Levy (eds.), *Institutions for the Earth*: *Sources of Effective International Environmental Protection* (Cambridge MA: MIT Press, 1993); Speth and Haas, supra footnote 26.

29 Convention of the World Meteorological Organization, 11 October 1947, 77 UNTS 143.

30 Constitution of the Food and Agriculture Organization of the United Nations, 16 October 1945, 12 UST 980.

31 Convention of the International Maritime Organization, 6 March 1948, 289 UNTS 4.

32 See J. M. Lavieille (ed.), *Conventions de Protection de L'environnement, Secrétariats, Conférences des Parties, Comités d'Experts* (Limoges: PULIM, 1999); B. H. Desai, *Multilateral Environmental Agreements. Legal Status of the Secretariats* (Cambridge University Press, 2010).

33 Basel Convention on the Control of Transboundary Movements of Hazardous Wastes and their Disposal, 22 March 1989, 1673 UNTS 57 ("Basel Convention"), Art. 15; UNFCCC, supra footnote 17, Art. 7; Convention on Biological Diversity, 5 June 1992, 1760 UNTS 79 ("CBD"), Art. 23; United Nations Convention on Action Against Desertification in Countries Experiencing Serious Drought and/or Desertification, Particularly in Africa, 14 October 1994, 1954 UNTS 3 ("UNCCD"), Art. 22; Stockholm Convention on Persistent Organic Pollutants, 22 May 2001, 2256 UNTS 119 ("POP Convention"), Art. 19.

的其他法律制度（典型的就是进一步明确原有条约所规定的权利内容和范围的缔约方大会决议）。

第三类组织，即某一条约的一个主要机构所建立的辅助机构，它可以被看作前两类组织的副产品。例如，联合国大会作为联合国的重要机构之一，[34] 就建立了几个辅助机构，其中有两个在环境事务中非常重要，即联合国环境规划署（United Nations Environment Programme，UNEP）[35]［在2016年更名为联合国环境署（UN Environment）］和联合国开发规划署（United Nations Development Programme，UNDP）。[36] 本书将频繁提及这些辅助机构的活动。在当前阶段，则只需强调联合国环境署对国际环境法的发展起到了某种"创业者"和"催化剂"的作用，[37] 而联合国开发规划署则是聚焦于项目的实施，其中某些项目包含有环境的部分。第三个例证是可持续发展委员会，它是由联合国另一个重要组织——联合国经济及社会理事会（UN Economic and Social Council）建立的。[38] 后来，根据2012年里约峰会的成果文件，可持续发展委员会已经被一个高级别政治论坛所取代。[39] 缔约方大会也有权力来建立辅助机构。例如，作为《京都议定书》的缔约方会议（MOP），《联合国气候变化框架公约》缔约方大会（COP）就建立了机构来管理议定书第6条和第12条规定的灵活机制。[40] 在有些情况下，辅助机构也可以参与到一个新的组织的创立中。例如，在1991年，联合国环境规划署和联合国开发规划署就联合世界银行（World Bank），创立了全球环境基金（Global Environmental Facility，GEF），它于

---

[34] Charter of the United Nations, 26 June 1945, 1 UNTS XVI, Art.7.1.

[35] "Institutional and Financial Arrangements for International Environmental Cooperation", 15 December 1972, UN Doc. A/Res/2997/XXVII ("Resolution 2997").

[36] "Consolidation of the Special Fund and the Expanded Programme of Technical Assistance in a United Nations Development Programme", 22 November 1965, UN Doc. Resolution 2029 (XX).

[37] On the role of UNEP see M. Ivanova, "UNEP in Global Environmental Governance: Design, Leadership, Location" (2010) 10 *Global Environmental Politics* 30.

[38] "Institutional Arrangements to follow up the United Nations Conference on Environment and Development", 22 December 1992, UN Doc. A/Res/47/191.

[39] "The Future We Want", 11 September 2012, UN Doc. A/Res/66/288, para. 84.

[40] See Doc. FCCC/KP/CMP/2005/8/Add.2, Decisions 3/CMP.1 and 9/CMP.1.

1994 年成为一个独立组织。[41] 这一变化发生的大部分原因是来自发展中国家的压力，目的是限制世界银行（也就是发达国家）对全球环境基金的资金分配的影响力。

第四类组织的特点比较明显，即它们是相对非正式的，因为它们不是基于某个条约或者某个组织的一个决议，而是为各国（有时是其他一些实体）之间的讨论提供一个交流平台。因此，它们的组织构成会随着所要讨论的事项而相应地得以扩大。例如，七国集团峰会，汇集了德国、加拿大、美国、法国、意大利、日本和英国的国家元首或政府首脑，有时候就会被扩大以便将某些国家（例如南非、巴西、中国、印度或墨西哥）也当作合作伙伴吸收进来。[42] 另一个与七国集团峰会相关联的论坛，即"主要经济体论坛"，最初于 2009 年 7 月召集了 16 个国家（包括欧盟），这些国家排放了绝大部分的温室气体，[43] 后来，这一论坛逐步发展为一个真正的主要"经济体"（不再是主要"排放者"）论坛。除了这些论坛，还有一些针对某些事项（例如气候合作[44]或化学品管理[45]）的对话，它们会包含各种利益相关方，目的是在正式谈判之前提前清除障碍。图 2-1 概括了前文列举说明的四种组织类型。

这一简短的审视凸显了全球环境治理的一个重要特征，即它的去中心化，更具体地讲，是它的治理架构的散乱分布。针对这样一个分散性布局，一个著名的环境法学家称其为"条约拥堵"。[46] 实际上，虽然有过几

---

[41] See Instrument for the Establishment of the Restructured Global Environmental Facility (October 2011). The text of the "Instrument" is reproduced at 9-41 of the 2011 publication.

[42] 2008 年八国集团峰会，北海道，日本东京，2007 年 7 月 7—9 日（当时，俄罗斯是该组织一员，因此称为八国集团峰会。2014 年，因为克里米亚问题，俄罗斯被排除出了该组织）。

[43] Declaration of the Leaders of the Major Economies Forum on Energy and Climate, see www.g8italia2009.it/static/G8_ Allegato/MEF_ Declarationl.pdf（3 February 2012）.

[44] See J. E. Viñuales, "Du bon dosage du droit international: Les négociations climatiques en perspective"（2010）56 *Annuaire Français de Droit International* 437ss.

[45] 参见后文第七章关于"国际化学品安全性论坛"和"化学品无害管理组织间方案"的讨论。

[46] See E. Brown Weiss, "International Environmental Law: Contemporary Issues and the Emergence of a New World Order"（1995）81 *Georgetown Law Journal* 675.

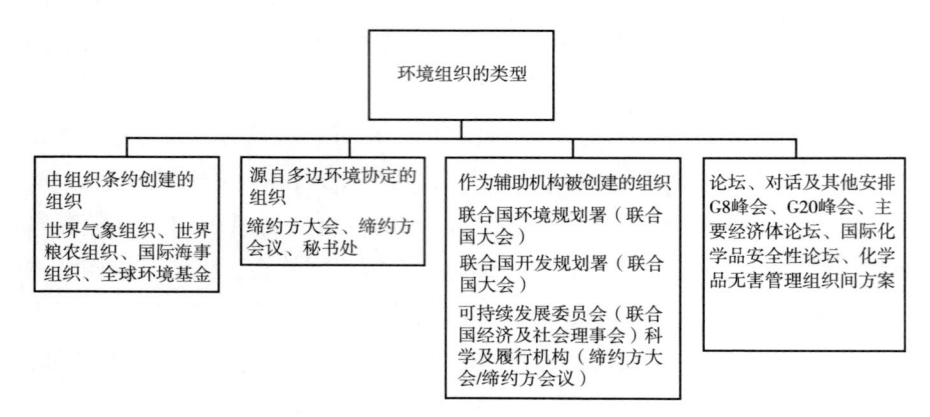

```
┌─────────────────┐
│   环境组织的类型  │
└─────────────────┘
         │
┌────────┼────────┬────────────────┬──────────────┐
│        │        │                │              │
由组织条约创建的   源自多边环境协定的  作为辅助机构被创建的    论坛、对话及其他安排
组织              组织              组织                 G8峰会、G20峰会、主
世界气象组织、世界  缔约方大会、缔约方  联合国环境规划署（联合  要经济体论坛、国际化
粮农组织、国际海事  会议、秘书处       国大会）             学品安全性论坛、化学
组织、全球环境基金                   联合国开发规划署（联合  品无害管理组织间方案
                                   国大会）
                                   可持续发展委员会（联合
                                   国经济及社会理事会）科
                                   学及履行机构（缔约方大
                                   会/缔约方会议）
```

图 2-1　环境组织的类型

次尝试，但是目前还没有产生一个"世界环境组织"，[47] 不像有些领域（例如国际贸易或全球卫生问题）已经有了专门组织。这些活跃在环境事务中的各种组织的作用主要是协调各国在此领域的工作，尽可能地避免重复工作并促进资源的高效利用。全球环境治理的分散性还远远超出了政府间组织的范畴，后文将继续讨论。

三　跨国环境治理

除了前文讨论过的四种组织，私营部门组织和其他民间团体组织也对国际环境法的形成和发展发挥了一个非常重要的作用。[48] 毫不夸张地说，除了人权这一领域之外，[49] 其他所有领域的公众参与程度都不如环境保护。另外，次国家实体，例如城市和地区，也在环境治理中发挥了越来越大的作用，它们被当作国家政府所采取行动的延伸或在国家层面的行

---

[47] See F. Biermann and S. Bauer (eds.), *A World Environmental Organization*: *Solution or Threat for Effective International Environmental Governance* (Aldershot: Ashgate, 2005); B. Desai, *International Environmental Governance*: *Towards UNEPO* (Leiden: Nijhoff, 2014).

[48] See A. Pomade, *La Société Civile et le Droit de L'environnement. Contribution à la Réflexion sur les Théories des Sources du Droit et de la Validité* (Paris: LGDJ, 2010).

[49] See e.g. C. Welch (ed.), *NGOs and Human Rights*: *Promise and Performance* (Philadelphia: University of Pennsylvania Press, 2001).

动缺位下的一种替代品。在气候变化治理方面，这一现象表现得特别明显。[50]

民间团体的参与对抵消经济利益集团的影响非常重要，因为国家干预和消费习惯通常并不能有效解决经济利益集团的环境外部性（externalities）问题。以下这些环保组织，例如塞拉俱乐部（Sierra Club）、绿色和平（Greenpeace）、地球之友（Friends of the Earth）、自然保护（Nature Conservancy）、保护国际（Conservation International）、环境与发展国际研究院（International Institute for Environment and Development）、世界资源研究院（World Resources Institute）、可持续发展国际研究院（International Institute for Sustainable Development）、世界自然基金会（World Wildlife Fund, WWF）或世界自然保护联盟（International Union for the Conservation of Nature, IUCN），[51] 只是蓬勃发展的大量环保组织的几个杰出代表，这些组织积极活跃于国家或国际层面，它们做出了实实在在的努力，以便提升公众对环境恶化的认识并引导公众压力。[52] 实际上，这些组织发挥的主要功能可以被划分为四大类：[53]（1）开发有关环境保护的研究和资源；（2）展示民间团体的利益诉求；（3）为履行提供帮助；（4）引导公众压力。当然，在实施这些功能时，办法都是千差万别的。例如，世界自然基金会支持发布的一份报告就极大地推动了《关于持久性有机污染物的斯德哥尔摩公约》的制定。[54] 另一个例证是世界自然保护联盟在开发生态服务付费机制（例如生物多样性的保存库、温室气体排放库）中发挥的作用。[55] 最后，民间团体组织的干预可以对某一事件的处理产生重大影响，例如布兰特史帕尔储油平台事件中，壳牌公司想要下沉一个在北海上的石油平台，

50　See H. Bulkeley et al, *Transnational Climate Change Governance*（Cambridge University Press, 2014）.

51　世界自然保护联盟是一个混合型组织，它包含了政府间组织。

52　On the role of NGOs, see A. K. Lindblom, *Non‐Governmental Organisations in International Law*（Cambridge University Press, 2006）.

53　Three of these functions are identified by D. Hunter, J. Salzman and D. Zaelke, *International Environmental Law and Policy*（New York: Foundation Press, 2007）, Chapter 5.

54　For a list of detailed examples, see Ibid., pp. 255-267.

55　IUCN UNFCCC Newsletter; Reducing Emissions from Deforestation and Forest Degradation, 09/09, available at: cmsdata.iucn.org/downloads/unfccc_ newsletter_ _september_ 09.pdf（last visited 3 February 2012）.

绿色和平组织通过引导公众压力反对这种拆除方式，对此进行了干预并成功予以阻止。[56]

民间团体和私营部门之间的关系，或者私营部门和环境保护之间的关系，就要复杂得多。实际上，缺失了私营部门的合作甚或是推动，环境保护就很难得以实现，在 2002 年约翰内斯堡峰会上尤其如此。私营部门与以下内容关系重大：(1) 项目资助；(2) 技术转让；(3) 环境治理。因此，挑战不仅仅是限制私营部门的活动（例如公司社会责任法或者追责机制[57]），还必须引导私营部门对环保项目的兴趣。要达此目的，一种办法是建立公共—私营伙伴关系（Public-Private Partnerships，PPPs）。[58] 公共—私营伙伴关系在某些事务中表现比较积极，例如可再生能源、水净化或者废物处理，以及在引导资金投入环保项目方面。私营部门的作用一直是被热议的问题，特别是有关气候变化减缓和适应的项目资助。[59]

一般来看，气候变化治理一直以来都是一个充满了试验和创新的领域。传统更重视国家间关系的国际环境法只是最近才开始注重跨国环境治理和法律的作用，[60] 而气候变化则是一个特别重要的领域。[61] 在此背景下，

56　On the ambiguous results of the intervention of Greenpeace, see Hunter et al., supra footnote 53, pp. 827–829.

57　OECD Guidelines for Multinational Enterprises: revised in 2000, 11 September 2000, Doc. DAFFE/IME/WPG (2000) 9; Tripartite Declaration of Principles Concerning Multinational Enterprises and Social Policy, International Labour Organization, 2006; The Ten Principles of the Global Compact, and more particularly Principles 7 to 9, available at: www.unglobalcom pact.org/aboutthegc/thetenprinciples/index.html (last visited 3 February 2012). See E. Morgera, *Corporate Accountability in International Environmental Law* (Oxford University Press, 2009).

58　See P. Glasbergen, F. Biermann and A. Mol (eds.), *Partnerships, Governance and Sustainable Development. Reflections on Theory and Practice* (Cheltenham: Edward Elgar, 2007).

59　See P.-M. Dupuy and J.E. Viñuales (eds.), *Harnessing Foreign Investment to Promote Environmental Protection: Incentives and Safeguards* (Cambridge University Press, 2013); R. Stewart, B. Kingsbury and B. Rudyk, *Climate Finance: Regulatory and Funding Strategies for Climate Change and Global Development* (New York University Press, 2009).

60　2012 年，聚焦跨国环境法（Transnational Environmental Law）的一个新的学术杂志正式发布，由 T. Etty 和 V. Heyvaert 担任联合主编。第一期的数篇文章介绍了研究领域并强调了其重要性（作者是 Etty/Heyvaert, Carlarne/Farber, Lin/Scott, Shaffer/Bodansky, Fisher, Yang, Kheng Lian, Kysar, Krämer, Lee, Gunningham, Streck, Brown Weiss, Gillespie, Sand, and Kotzé 等人）。

61　See Bulkeley et al, supra footnote 50.

为了解决环境问题，次国家主体例如城市和地区的网络，以及包含私营部门和民间团体的网络都得以发展壮大，例如国内层面的有美国九个州组成的"地区温室气体倡议"（the Regional Greenhouse Gas Initiative），[62] 国际层面的有美国加利福尼亚州和加拿大魁北克省在碳排放交易机制上的关联，[63] 以及C40网络的发展，它汇集了80多个大城市来协调气候变化行动。[64] 这一领域是极其广阔的，即使仅限于气候变化治理。2014年，在秘鲁利马举行的《联合国气候变化框架公约》第20次缔约方大会上，一个名为"气候行动非国家行动者地带"的平台得以建立，它包含了无数个跨国层面的应对气候变化的行动倡议。[65] 正是因为观察到这一重要趋势，在巴黎召开的第21次缔约方大会通过的《巴黎协定》设有一个专门的部分来谈"非缔约方利益相关者"。[66] 这些主体和网络的参与也对公法与国际法提出了一些法律上的难题（例如权力的下放、缔约权、协议的法律性质等），特别是当行为发生在当事国政府无力或者不想采取行动的背景之下。[67] 在此，这些问题只能一笔带过。为了当前的目的，重要的问题是跨国环境治理日益增长的作用以及它所造成的法律挑战。

第四节 国际环境法的渊源

国际环境法面临的挑战不仅影响到它的组织特征的塑造，也对环境规范的产生过程造成了影响。不同国家利益的交缠、环境谈判的制度化需要以及非国家主体在环境规范制定和履行中的重要作用，都影响了国际环境法的渊源。然而，除非我们将另一个挑战也考虑在内，否则就无法理解这种影响。这一挑战就是必须应对科学和技术进步问题，而它对环境规制的

62　On the RGGI see：https：//www.rggi.org/（visited on 27 March 2017）.

63　从2008年项目启动开始，加利福尼亚州和魁北克省的总量控制和排放交易制度于2013年正式建立关联，并于2014年举办了它们的首次碳单位拍卖会。

64　On this network see：http：//www.c40.org/about（visited on 27 March 2017）.

65　On this platform see：http：//climateaction.unfccc.int/（visited on 27 March 2017）.

66　"Adoption of the Paris Agreement"，1/CP.21，12 December 2015，FCCC//CP/2015/L.9/Rev.1，section V.

67　For a case-study see M. Finck，"Above and Below the Surface：The Status of Sub-National Authorities in EU Climate Change Regulation"（2014）26 *Journal of Environmental Law* 443.

影响要大于它对所有其他国际法分支的影响。

那些创立国际法的传统方法如何在环境这一背景下运作，这一问题确实受到了这些挑战的重大影响。这一影响根植于国际环境法的三个重大特征：（1）大量的条约成为国际环境法的一个渊源；（2）软法文件的大量使用；[68]（3）环境领域的派生法或行政法（以多边环境协定缔约方大会制定的决议的形式）的日益发展。

一 条约的大量出现

可能是因为国际习惯法近期才开始流行，所以它对国际环境法的作用还是有限的，但是它的重要性不应被低估。[69] 除了一些原则例如无害（当今一般理解为谨慎注意）、预防、合作（通知及协商），或者国际水道的合理和公平利用（一般由跨界污染或共有自然资源引起），[70] 以及最新的开展环境影响评价的要求，[71] 习惯才刚刚开始在具体的环境问题中得以显现。[72]

与之相反，自20世纪70年代《斯德哥尔摩宣言》通过以来，条约所发挥的作用就稳步增加。在第一章我们已经介绍了国际环境法的历史进程，在后续章节中我们将详细分析那些最重要的环境条约。在此，我们只是简要探讨在国际法这一领域出现如此繁多的条约的成因。

第一，环境问题是相对新颖的，导致的结果就是，早先的传统规范无法有效地应对它们。理所当然的是，新的问题需要新的规范，因为原有规

---

[68] See P.-M. Dupuy, "Soft Law and the International Law of the Environment" (1990/1991) 12 *Michigan Journal of International Law* 420.

[69] See P.-M. Dupuy, "Formation of Customary International Law and General Principles" in Bodansky et al., supra footnote 19, p. 450.

[70] See P.-M. Dupuy, "Overview of the Existing Customary Legal Regime Regarding International Pollution" in D. Magraw (ed.), *International Law and Pollution* (Philadelphia: University of Pennsylvania Press, 1991), pp. 61–89; J. E. Viñuales, "The Contribution of the International Court of Justice to the Development of International Environmental Law: A Contemporary Assessment" (2008) 32 *Fordham International Law Journal* 232.

[71] See infra Chapter 3.

[72] For a statement of the current state of customary international law with respect to environmental protection see J. E. Viñuales, "La Protección Ambiental en el Derecho Internacional Consuetudinario" (2017) 69/2 *Revista Española de Derecho Internacional* 71.

范的制定是为了一个不同的目的,新规范更适应它所要调整的客体。第二,环境问题是没有边界的,同时对它们的科学认知也是与时俱进的。因此,它们的规制也就涉及大量的制度和程序方面的内容,而条约法能更好地处理这一问题。第三,针对那些有可能阻碍它们经济发展的措施,发展中国家都不太情愿,这也就可以解释条约的吸引力,它允许在发达国家和发展中国家之间存在一定程度的差异化。对环境规制的感知不同也可以在一定程度上解释为何在此领域不具约束力的"软法"更具吸引力。

二 软法的作用

自其现代起源以来,软法就对国际环境法的发展起到了一个主要作用。[73] 1972年的《斯德哥尔摩宣言》和1992年的《里约宣言》这两个被称为国际环境法奠基性文件的文本,就是属于软法文件。我们还可以举出许多其他的例证,从1962年《关于自然资源永久主权的1803号决议》[74]到1982年通过的《世界自然宪章》,[75] 以及1992年里约峰会上通过的《森林宣言》,[76] 2009年12月的关于气候变化的《哥本哈根协议》。[77]

为了理解这些文件的运作,有必要介绍一下文件及其内容的一个传统划分方法。采用"软"这一形容词来描述一种文件的法律地位的目的就是强调这一文件不具有法律约束力,不论它的内容如何。但是,文件的具体内容,在某些其他情况下,也有可能具有法律约束力。在国际环境法中,这一现象最显著的例证就是《斯德哥尔摩宣言》(第21条原则)和《里约宣言》(第2条原则)都体现出的预防原则。当前被认为是国际环境法基石的这一原则,是不具有法律约束力的,因为它在大量软法文件(包括上面提及的两个宣言)中出现,但是它本质上还是习惯法,国际法

---

[73] See Dupuy, supra footnote 68.

[74] "Permanent Sovereignty Over Natural Resources", 14 December 1964, UN Doc. Resolution 1803 (XVII).

[75] World Charter for Nature, supra footnote 7.

[76] "Non-Legally Binding Authoritative Statement of Principles for a Global Consensus on the Management, Conservation and Sustainable Development of All Types of Forests", 14 August 1992, UN Doc. A/CONF/151/26 (Vol. III) ("Forests Principles").

[77] Copenhagen Accord, 19 December 2009, UN Doc. FCCC/CP/2009/L. 7.

院（International Court of Justice，ICJ）在多个场合对此予以承认。[78] 国际法院是基于这些软法文件的表述方式来判定这一原则的习惯法属性。这些文件本身、连同制定它们的会议和机构作为新的国际规范的催化剂发挥了重要的规范性作用。从这一角度，我们可以将那些有能力代表国家的组织（例如政府间组织或国际会议的全体大会）和那些通过制定各种文件以便影响国家的组织区分开来。联合国大会或者环境与发展里约大会属于第一类，而国际法协会（International Law Association，ILA）、国际法研究院（Institut de Droit International，IDI）以及国际法委员会（International Law Commission，ILC），它们都包含了独立专家，就属于第二类。

无论是直接充当具有法律约束力的规范的创立者，还是间接影响其他组织负责制定的法律文书，这些组织的规范性作用都不应被低估。谈及第一种作用，我们可以举例说明，世界自然保护联盟在 1963 年制定的一项决议后来就成为《濒危野生动植物种国际贸易公约》的基础。谈及第二种作用，国际法协会于 1966 年制定的《赫尔辛基规则》[79] 对国际法委员会后续工作的影响就是一个很好的例证，后来，在联合国大会的支持下，它也促成了一个条约的谈判和制定。[80]

需要补充说明的是，即使软法的内容并不具备法律约束力，它们仍然还是有可能拥有影响力的。例如，许多金融中介机构，比如世界银行、国际金融公司（International Finance Corporation）、区域开发银行甚至私营放款人，都采用了环境和可持续性标准，这些标准因为会影响资金的支出，

78　*Legality of Nuclear Weapons*, supra n. 7, para. 29; *Gabčíkovo‑Nagymaros Project* (*Hungary* v. *Slovakia*), Judgment, ICJ Reports 1997, p. 7 ("*Gabčíkovo‑Nagymaros Project*"), para. 53; *Pulp Mills on the River Uruguay* (*Argentina* v. *Uruguay*), Provisional Measures, Order (13 July 2006), ICJ Reports 2006, p. 113, para. 72 ("*Pulp Mills*"); *Certain activities carried out by Nicaragua in the Border Area* (*Costa Rica* v. *Nicaragua*), *Construction of a road in Costa Rica along the river San Juan* (*Nicaragua* v. *Costa Rica*), Judgment of 16 December 2015 (ICJ), para. 104.

79　Helsinki Rules on the Uses of the Waters of International Rivers; adopted by the International Law Association at its 52nd conference, Helsinki, 20 August 1966, International Law Association, *Report of the Fifty‑second Conference*, London, 1967, p. 56.

80　See United Nations Convention on the Law of the Non‑Navigational Uses of International Watercourses, 21 May 1997, 36 ILM 700. 这一公约于 2014 年生效，它的部分规定被看作国际习惯法的一个声明。See L. Caflisch, "La convention du 21 mai 1997 sur l'utilisation des cours d'eau internationaux à des fins autres que la navigation" (1997) 43 *Annuaire Français de Droit International* 751, at 770.

所以具有重要的权威性。[81]

三 授权立法

法语术语"授权立法"（droit dérivé）指的是某一条约授权的机构所制定的法律法规。在环境背景下，它指的是某些政府间组织（例如联合国大会或安全理事会，更具体地说，例如多边环境协定所建立的缔约方大会和缔约方会议）制定的法律。术语"授权"表明，这些机构所制定的决议、建议和决定（法规）的法律效力有赖于组织条约的缔约国授权给它们的规范性权力。正如软法一样，这些法规严格说来并不能算是国际法的一个正式渊源，而只有组织条约才是。[82] 然而，在国际标准的制定上，它们依然是一个非常重要的手段。[83]

在国际环境法中，这些法规主要采用的形式是缔约方大会（或缔约方会议）针对各种主题所制定的决议，例如：[84]（1）内部规则（程序、行政或财政规则）；（2）旨在履行多边环境协定所引发的义务的法规；（3）外部法规（涉及履约、与其他条约的合作等事项，或者细化各种标准，以便指导各国和其他主体的行为）。举例说明将会有助于阐明这些法规的不同类型。

第一类例证来自1987年《蒙特利尔议定书》（Montreal Protocol）第2条第9款之规定，根据一项决议，允许对那些受规制物质的臭氧消耗潜力做出调整，这项决议由缔约方会议采取特定多数票的方式通过，并对所有缔约方具有约束力（第2条第9款）。第二类例证来自《联合国气候变化框架公约》缔约方大会的一系列决议，即所谓的《马拉喀什协议》（Marrakesh Accords）（后来由《京都议定书》缔约方会议批准），这些决议负责管理议定书规定的三种"灵活机制"的具体工作，即联合履约（joint

---

81　See B. J. Richardson, *Socially Responsible Investment Law* (Oxford University Press, 2008).

82　即使授权允许该机构有权通过具有法律约束力的法规，这些法规仍然不能算是国际法的一个正式渊源。例如根据《联合国海洋法公约》第11部分建立的国际海底管理局所通过的规则和法规。see J. Harrison, *Making the Law of the Sea* (Cambridge University Press, 2011), at 122-123), as the "formal" source remains the treaty.

83　See J. Brunnée, "COPing with Consent: Law-making under Multilateral Environmental Agreements" (2002) 15 *Leiden Journal of International Law* 1.

84　See G. Ulfstein, "Treaty Bodies" in Bodansky et al., supra footnote 19, pp. 880-888.

implementation）、[85] 清洁发展机制（clean development mechanism）[86] 和排放交易（emissions trading）。[87] 第三类例证涉及某些履行机制的架构，即数个多边环境协定框架制定的所谓"不遵约程序"。[88] 我们将在本章第五节第四部分讨论这些机制，同时在第九章对其进行概括。

鉴于授权立法所管理的事项是相当重要的，毫不夸张地说，这些法规对多边环境协定的运作起到了关键性作用。

第五节 国际环境法的履行

一 概述

国际环境法的履行具有许多显著的特征，因此有必要在本节的概述中对其加以说明。为了应对履行过程中的挑战（这些挑战来自经济利益集团、政治和战略考量的阻力，或者对不断发展的科学和技术进步的持续适应能力），国际社会已经制定了多种措施。[89]

---

[85] Decision 2/CMP.1, FCCC/KP/CMP/2005/8/Add.1（"Decision 15/CP.7"）; Decision 9/CMP.1, FCCC/KP/CMP/2005/8/Add.2（"Decision 16/CP.7"）; Decision 10/CMP.1, FCCC/KP/CMP/2005/8/Add.2; Decision 2/CMP.2, FCCC/KP/CMP/2006/10/Add.1; Decision 3/CMP.2, FCCC/KP/CMP/2006/10/Add.1; Decision 3/CMP.3, FCCC/KP/CMP/2007/9/Add.1; Decision 5/CMP.4, FCCC/KP/CMP/2008/11/Add.1.

[86] See Decision 2/CMP.1, FCCC/KP/CMP/2005/8/Add.1（"Decision 15/CP.7"）; Decision 3/CMP.1, FCCC/KP/CMP/2005/8/Add.1（"Decision 17/CP.7"）; Decision 4/CMP.1, FCCC/KP/CMP/2005/8/Add.1（"Decision 21/CP.8 and 18/CP.9"）; Decision 5/CMP.1, FCCC/KP/CMP/2005/8/Add.1（"Decision 19/CP.9"）; Decision 6/CMP.1, FCCC/KP/CMP/2005/8/Add.1（"Decision 14/CP.10"）; Decision 7/CMP.1, FCCC/KP/CMP/2005/8/Add.1; Decision 8/CMP.1, FCCC/KP/CMP/2005/8/Add.1; Decision 1/CMP.2, FCCC/KP/CMP/2006/10/Add.1; Decision 2/CMP.3, FCCC/KP/CMP/2007/9/Add.1; Decision 9/CMP.3, FCCC/KP/CMP/2007/9/Add.1; Decision 2/CMP.4, FCCC/KP/CMP/2008/11/Add.1.

[87] See M. Wara, "Measuring the Clean Development Mechanism's Performance and Potential"（2008）55 *UCLA Law Review* 1759.

[88] See T. Treves et al. (eds.), *Non-Compliance Procedures and Mechanisms and the Effectiveness of International Environmental Agreements* (The Hague: TMC Asser Press, 2009).

[89] See J. E. Viñuales, "Legal Techniques for Dealing with Scientific Uncertainty in Environmental Law"（2010）43 *Vanderbilt Journal of Transnational Law* 437.

面对这些困难，国际法履行所采用的传统机制（例如，将某一特定行为定性为违约并确定其法律后果），[90] 并不适合用来管理那些由于国家（财政或技术）能力欠缺而造成无法遵守某项规范所导致的不遵约。正是基于这一观点，才产生了一种新方法来实现国际法的履约，[91] 它将履约当作一个进程，必须通过多种非对抗性手段来进行管理，例如财政和技术援助，或者降低传统争端解决机制中的对抗性。在此部分，我们将概括介绍那些有助于促进履约和"管理"不遵约的可行手段。第九章将会有一个更加详细的分析。

二 刺激机制

环境标准方面的刺激机制有两个主要目标，即提升效率（通过减少遵约成本）并弥补某些国家在技术和财政上的能力欠缺（通过援助机制）。对效率的追求通常是发达国家的关注重点，而发展中国家主要感兴趣的则是技术和财政援助。

谈及提升效率的手段，我们在《京都议定书》《巴黎协定》以及《蒙特利尔议定书》（灵活机制的萌芽）中可以找到的灵活机制就是很好的例证。[92] 为了更好地理解这些机制是如何降低遵守环境标准的成本，我们可以对它们进行更细致的观察。根据《京都议定书》第 3 条之规定，《联合国气候变化框架公约》附录一所列举的国家必须在 2008—2012 年和修订开始生效的 2013—2020 年将它们温室气体的平均排放水平在 1990 年（基准年）的基础上降低一定的百分比（由议定书的附录二规定）。为了遵守此项义务，各国应当采取国家层面和国际层面的措施。谈及国际层面的措施，议定书的第 17 条建立了一个排放交易机制，允许附录二中的国家（或位于那些国家的公司）采取更有效率的方式来履行他们的义务。效率

---

[90] See infra Chapter 8.

[91] See A. Chayes and A. Handler Chayes, *The New Sovereignty: Compliance with International Regulatory Agreements* (Cambridge MA: Harvard University Press, 1995); E. Brown Weiss and H. K. Jacobson (eds.), *Engaging Countries: Strengthening Compliance with International Environmental Accords* (Cambridge MA: MIT Press, 1998).

[92] See Arts. 2.5 (transfers of production) and 2.8 (a) (mechanism known as the "bubble") of the Montreal Protocol on Substances that Deplete the Ozone Layer, 16 September 1987, 1522 UNTS 3 ("Montreal Protocol").

的提升来自这样一个事实,即根据各国或各公司的具体情况,一吨二氧化碳(或者另一种受规制温室气体之等量)排放的价值是存在差异的。这种差异来自各国或者公司的生产过程的不同,或者来自更清洁技术的使用所导致的各国或各公司的不同费用,或者来自各国能源结构的不同。与此一脉相承的是,《巴黎协定》第 6 条第 3 款旨在通过促进不同国家或次国家主体的总量控制和排放交易这两种制度的关联来提升效率。这种关联通过允许那些用于遵守一种制度的碳单位也被另一种制度承认(并用于遵约)的方式,提升了效率。这也为通过更广泛的贸易机会来提升效率提供了可能,[93] 虽然现实并非如此简单。[94]

  《京都议定书》第 6 条和第 12 条,以及《巴黎协定》第 6 条第 4 款都设计了其他基于项目的灵活机制。我们将在第五章探讨它们的运作,但是,现在还是有必要对《京都议定书》第 12 条规定的"清洁发展机制"做一个简短的说明,关于这一点已经有了重要的过往经验。清洁发展机制允许工业化国家(议定书附件二国家)资助发展中国家的减排项目,经过一个验证程序后,可以获取一个与实际减排相等的碳信用额(carbon credits)(经核证的温室气体减排量 CERs),也就是这一项目所实现的排放量和该项目缺位下的排放量两者之间的差额。这些碳信用额可以为工业化国家提供一定的效率提升幅度。在发展中国家实现这样的减排确实要比在发达国家采用其他方式减排(例如采用环境税、排放总量控制或技术要求)更加便宜,而且提升的空间也更大。[95] 同时,作为这些项目运营地的发展中国家也收获了资金和技术支持,这也可以当作援助的一种形式。

  上段最后一句将我们的讨论转向援助机制。数个多边环境协定承认某些成员国的特殊状况,特别是承认它们需要援助来完成它们的义务。例

---

[93] See J. Jaffe, M. Ranson and R. Stavins, "Linking tradable permit systems: A key element of emerging international climate policy architecture" (2010) 36 *Ecology Law Quarterly* 789.

[94] See J. F. Green, "Don't link carbon markets!" (2017) 543/7646 *Nature* 484 (highlighting the complexities involved in a carbon market managed by different competing authorities rather than a single entity).

[95] M. A. Toman, R. D. Morganstern and J. Anderson, "The Economics of 'When' Flexibility in the Design of Greenhouse Gas Abatement Policies" in *Resources for the Future Discussion Paper* 99-38-REV, 2-3, 1999 年分析了这一机制带来的经济方面的效率提升。

如，《巴塞尔公约》第 4 条第 2 款[96]要求缔约国必须尽可能地在其领土内建立足够的废物处置设施，以便实现对有害废物的"环境友好型"管理。但是，为了满足这一要求，必须要有一定程度的技术进步。就这一点而言，第 14 条第 1 款构想了建立区域和次区域财政[97]和技术转让机制。[98] 与此相类似，在《濒危野生动植物种国际贸易公约》中，专门建立了一项基金用于资助技术援助活动。[99] 这两个例证只是多边环境协定这一普遍特点的冰山一角。[100]

近年来，财政和技术援助这一问题在气候谈判中受到了持续的关注。绿色气候基金在韩国得以建立，目的是资助气候变化减缓措施以及对气候变化的适应措施。在经历了一个漫长的建立过程以后，它开始在 2016 年年底分配资金，它很有可能成为气候相关项目的国际资助的一个非常重要的来源。在此之前，多边气候资金的主要来源仍然是全球环境基金。全球环境基金同时还是其他一些多边环境协定的金融工具，例如《生物多样性公约》（CBD）、《持久性有机污染物公约》（POP Convention）或《联

---

[96] Basel Convention, supra footnote 33.

[97] 后来建立了一个技术援助基金，采取自愿捐赠的形式。基金被称为"帮助发展中国家和其他需要技术援助的国家实施《巴塞尔公约》关于有害废物的越境转移管理及其处置的信托基金"。See "Enlargement of the Scope of the Technical Cooperation Trust Fund", Decision V/32, Conference of Parties, 5th meeting, *Report of the Fifth Meeting of the Conference of the Parties to the Basel Convention*, Annex, 10 December 1999, UN Doc. UNEP/CHW. 5/29, p. 57.

[98] See *Basel Convention Regional and Coordinating Centres* brochure prepared by the Secretariat of the Convention, available at: www.basel.int (last visited 3 February 2014).

[99] Technical Cooperation, Resolution of the Conference of Parties, Third Session, New Delhi (India), 25 February-8 March 1981, CITES Conf 3.4.

[100] See, in particular: Protocol to the 1979 Convention on Long - range Transboundary Air Pollution, on the Long-term Financing of the Cooperative Programme for Monitoring and Evaluation of the Long-range Transmission of Air Pollutants in Europe ("EMEP"), 28 September 1984, 1491 UNTS 167, the Small Grants Fund of the Ramsar Convention (SGF), www.ramsar.org/SGF/ (last visited 3 February 2014); Multilateral Fund on the Implementation of Montreal Protocol (better known by its acronym "MFMP"), 29 June 1990, UN Doc. UNEP/OzL. Pro. 2/3; World Heritage Fund, Convention for the Protection of the World Cultural and Natural Heritage, 16 November 1972, 1037 UNTS 151, Art. 15ff. On this subject, see L. Boisson de Chazournes, "Technical and Financial Assistance" in Bodansky et al., supra footnote 19, pp. 945-973.

合国防治荒漠化公约》（UNCCD）。[101] 另外，区域开发银行[102]和许多市场机制也会提供环境资金，包括清洁发展机制以及通过减少砍伐森林和减缓森林退化而降低温室气体排放（REDD），后者的法律基础来自《巴黎协定》第5条第2款。

三 管理科学不确定性

前面探讨的一些手段对于应对环境制度面临的一个主要挑战也很重要，这个挑战就是科学和技术的变化。[103]

为了便于理解这些手段，有必要区分环境制度在制定过程中的四个主要步骤。[104] 第一步涉及明确某一具体环境问题（即使这一问题存在着重大的科学不确定性），以及倡议制定一项法律制度来管理这一问题。第二步聚焦于制度的设计。在选择制度的组成部分和设计制度框架时，非常重要的一点是必须将应对科学和技术变化的需求考虑在内。第三步涉及的是实施所设计的环境制度。随着时间的推移，这一制度有可能不得不去应对各种渠道的"制度压力"，原因可能是条约的政治或经济基础抑或是针对这一问题的科学认识发生了变化。第四步也就是最后一步，涉及的是在修复环境危害（指这一制度没有能力预防的危害）过程中的科学不确定性问题。这种区分是一种单纯的层次分析方法，也许并不一定能对某项环境制度的生命周期做出一个精确的描述。另外，有些手段也有可能在多个步骤中会用到。即便如此，这种区分对明确那些步骤还是有用的，每一个步骤都有一个特定的手段与之相对应，换言之，有助于理解在某个关键节点应当采取何种最有用的手段。

图2-2[105] 将制度制定的四个步骤与那些旨在管理风险和不确定性的各种手段联系在一起。在第一步，风险预防"方法"或"原则"是一个强

---

[101] Instrument for the Establishment of the Restructured Global Environmental Facility, GEF, October 2011, pp. 7-41, Art. I (6), available at: www.thegef.org (last visited 3 February 2014).

[102] 非洲开发银行和非洲开发基金、亚洲开发银行和亚洲开发基金、美洲开发银行及其特别运行基金。

[103] See Viñuales, supra footnote 89.

[104] See H. Breitmeier, O. R. Young and M. Zurn, *Analyzing International Environmental Regimes: From Case Study to Database* (Cambridge MA: MIT Press, 2007).

[105] Source: Viñuales, supra footnote 89, p. 448.

第一步：倡议	（1）风险预防分析
第二步：设计	（2）框架—议定书方法
	（3）科学咨询机构
第三步：实施	（4）条约机构的立法工作
	（5）遵约的管理办法
	（6）事先知情同意
	（7）环境影响评价和监测
第四步：修复	（8）临时措施
	（9）证据
	（10）促成的责任

图 2-2 应对科学不确定性的法律手段

有力的手段，它可以推动某一特定环境问题的规制。[106] 在第三章中我们将会审视这一手段的法律方面。在此我们仅需要指出，风险预防这一手段的主要目标就是鼓励对某一环境问题采取行动，即使从科学的视角来看，人们对这一问题知之甚少。这一手段早期最著名的成功案例就是臭氧制度（即 1985 年《保护臭氧层维也纳公约》（*Vienna Convention on the Protection of the Ozone Layer of 1985*）和最重要的 1987 年《蒙特利尔议定书》）的制订。实际上，《蒙特利尔议定书》所规定的淘汰义务的严苛与 1987 年晚期仍然流行的科学不确定性（有关平流层臭氧消耗的成因）形成了鲜明的对比。[107]

第一步中的科学不确定性可能会对制度的特征产生重大影响，而这些特征将在第二步进行谈判并在最终的条约中得以体现。在科学不确定性背景下制定的制度必须有能力整合与这一环境问题相关的科学认识的变化。一个通常的方法是达成框架条约，并安排一个制度结构以便为后续通过更多具体义务提供便利，一般是采取议定书的形式。[108]《维也纳公约》（框

---

[106] See A. Trouwborst, *Evolution and Status of the Precautionary Principle in International Law* (Dordrecht: Kluwer, 2002).

[107] 参加《蒙特利尔议定书》协商的美国首席外交官的一本著作强调了这一观点。See R. E. Benedick, *Ozone Diplomacy* (Cambridge MA: Harvard University Press, 1998).

[108] See on this subject: A. Kiss, "Les traités-cadre: une technique juridique caractéristique du droit international de l'environnement" (1993) 39 *Annuaire Français de Droit International* 792.

架)和《蒙特利尔议定书》(具体义务)就是这种方法的最佳例证。其他一些著名的例证还包括《远程越界空气污染公约》框架下制定的多个议定书,[109]《联合国气候变化框架公约》及其《京都议定书》,《生物多样性公约》及其后来制定的两个进一步明确《生物多样性公约》相关规定的议定书(2000 年关于生物安全的议定书,2010 年关于获取和惠益分享的议定书)。无论新旧条约,[110] 环境条约另一个重要的设计特点是建立了辅助性科学机构,目的是帮助制度来适应最新的科学和技术数据。[111] 在某些情况下,科学机构被授权针对新物质列入清单这一问题向缔约方大会提出建议,例如《持久性有机污染物公约》就是如此。[112]

第三步,也就是制度的实施,它包含了多个手段。特别值得一提的是授权立法(droit dérivé)以及财政和技术援助的规定,这两点在前文都已经讨论过。另外,部分条约还设立了"事先知情同意"(prior informed consent)这一制度,目的是确保危险物质和活动只会发往那些愿意并有能力正确处置的国家。[113] 与此一脉相承的是,还有大量的条约要求开展环境影响评价,目的是明确某项工程可能对环境造成的影响。[114] 这一要求同

---

[109] Convention on Long-range Transboundary Air Pollution, 13 November 1979, 1302 UNTS 217 ("LRTAP Convention")。这些议定书涉及长期资助欧洲空气污染物远程转移的监测和评估的合作项目,减少硫黄排放与氧化氮和挥发性有机化合物,进一步减少硫黄排放和对流层中的持久性有机污染物、重金属、酸化和富营养化。

[110] See e. g. Convention on Wetlands of International Importance, especially as Waterfowl Habitat, 2 February 1971, 996 UNTS 245 ("Ramsar Convention") and Resolution 5.5 (1993) of the Ramsar COP.

[111] See e. g. the role of the EMEP in the LRTAP Convention, supra footnote 109, Art. 9.

[112] See POP Convention, supra footnote 33, Art. 8.

[113] International Code of Conduct on the Distribution and Use of Pesticides, adopted by the FAO Conference in Resolution 10/85, 28 November 1985; London Guidelines for the Exchange of Information on Chemicals in International Trade, Decision 15/30 of the UNEP Governing Council of 25 May 1989; Rotterdam Convention on the Prior Informed Consent Procedure for Certain Hazardous Chemicals and Pesticides in International Trade, 10 September 1998, 2244 UNTS 337 ("PIC Convention"). See P. Barrios, "The Rotterdam Convention on Hazardous Chemicals: A Meaningful Step towards Environmental Protection?" (2004) 16 *Georgetown International Environmental Law Review* 679.

[114] Convention on Environmental Impact Assessment in a Transboundary Context, 25 February 1991, 1989 UNTS 309. See N. Craik, *The International Law of Environmental Impact Assessment* (Cambridge University Press, 2008).

样也来自国际习惯法,虽然它的具体轮廓还有待明确。[115]

最后,在涉及环境危害的修复时,科学不确定性也有可能造成某些困难。为了应对第四步的科学不确定性,几种手段也应运而生,包括诉讼程序中的一些程序性工具和一大批特有的义务制度。复杂的生态过程(即一系列的行为关联在一起并导致环境危害的发生)所导致的科学不确定性可以通过将举证责任转移到被告的方式来解决,也可以通过放宽证据的适用标准[116]以及通过为法院和法庭提供更便捷的专家支持来解决。[117] 但是,即使原告免除了举证责任,案件中的行为人也有可能表明他已经采取了所有合理措施来预防危害,因此他在主观上没有过错,在客观上也没有违反某项义务,或者说是无法证明他的行为和危害结果之间的因果关系的。在当前科技水平下,要想明确这种因果关系可能是比较困难的甚至是不可能的。举例来说,有些要素之间的因果关系是相当清楚的,例如温室气体排放、气候变化和气候变化造成的不利影响,但是,某个工厂的具体排放和某个社区受到的具体伤害之间的因果联系就不是那么清楚了。我们可以建立一个多层次制度而非通过证据手段来处理这种不确定性,这一制度聚焦于修复那些由某些具有一定程度风险的活动所造成的危害。"促成的"责任制度可以分为不同的等级。无须证明过错或者违约(严格责任)可以被当作一种可行方法来处理某些种类的科学不确定性。其他一些种类的科学不确定性,则可以通过建立一个修复框架来处理,这一框架适用于某一受规制行为所造成的任何危害(即使无法完全确立两者间的因果联系)。严格责任制度属于国际法的特例。因为除了空间物体造成的危害,[118] 在国际法中国家是没有此类严格责任的。在我们提及严格责任制度时,[119] 通常

---

[115] See infra Chapter 3.

[116] On the difficulties of evidence, see C. Foster, *Science and the Precautionary Principle in International Courts and Tribunals* (Cambridge University Press, 2011).

[117] On the recourse to experts, see L. Savadogo, "Le recours des juridictions internationales à des experts" (2004) 50 *Annuaire Français de Droit International* 231.

[118] See Convention on International Liability for Damage Caused by Space Objects, 29 March 1972, 961 UNTS 187, Art. 2.

[119] See A. Kiss and D. Shelton, "Strict Liability in International Environmental Law", in T. M. Ndiaye and R. Wolfrum (eds.), *Liber Amicorum Judge Thomas A. Mensah* (Leiden: Martinus Nijhoff, 2007), pp. 1131–1151.

它是指一种民事责任,责任主体一般指的是那些从事某种受规制行为(或者受益于这种行为)的经济运营者(例如油罐车或核能设施的所有者)。涉及气候变化的不利影响所造成的"损失和伤害"的谈判本应形成一个类似于石油污染危害管理的制度。但是,《巴黎协定》第8条(关于损失和伤害)生效的前提条件是缔约方大会通过协定时决议中的一段话,即缔约方"同意协定的第8条并不涉及任何责任或赔偿或者为其提供依据"。[120]

四 不遵约的管理

第三种手段涉及的是对不遵约的管理。[121] 必须把"不遵约"这一概念同"违约"区分开来。虽然这两个概念有一定程度的重叠,但是不遵约的外延更广,因为它不仅包含明确的"违约",还包含了那些只是暂时没有遵守环境义务的行为,以及非实质的违约(例如单纯的程序性违约),甚至是那些预示可能违约的一些缺陷(例如,如果一个合成行为的某些前期步骤结合在一起,可能会导致违约)。另外,"不遵约"这一概念有可能避免"违约"所蕴含的负面内涵。它用一个标准将"不遵守"定性为一种偏差,而这种偏差必须受到控制和管理直到被修正。

在此背景下,我们就更能容易理解"不遵约程序"的独有特征了。首先,不遵约程序的引发不仅可以由别国或者条约的秘书处(正如其他对抗性机制)来提起,还可以由不遵约国本身来提起。[122] 其次,诉讼程序的证据和程序正当性标准并不适用于不遵约程序。[123] 再次,不遵约程序的首要目标并不是为了制止、修复或者处罚某项违约行为,而是为了管理这一自愿或非自愿的偏差行为。因此,最终结果往往是一个技术或财政上的

---

[120] See Decision 1/CP. 21, supra footnote 66, para. 52.

[121] See E. Milano, "The Outcomes of the Procedure and their Legal Effects" in Treves et al., supra footnote 88, pp. 407–418.

[122] See F. Romanin Jacur, "Triggering Non‑Compliance Procedures", in Treves et al. supra footnote 88, pp. 373–387.

[123] See M. Montini, "Procedural Guarantees in Non‑Compliance Mechanisms", in Treves et al., supra footnote 88, pp. 389–405.

建议而非一个直接的制裁。[124] 只有当负责程序的机构发现当事国是故意违反时，处理结果才会是处罚。最后，这些制裁通常都是内部的，在绝大多数情况下，它们只能涉及暂时取消条约所带来的利益。因此，不遵约程序的调查结果原则上并不能引发国际义务的次级规范[125]，而只能引发每个条约所具体规定的其他一系列次级规范。

在第九章中我们将详细探讨这些机制的运作。当前只是用《京都议定书》的一个案例来举例说明从援助到处罚的转变。[126]《京都议定书》的不遵约程序是由一个遵约委员会（Compliance Committee）来管理的，这一委员会包含了两个分部，即"促成"分部和"执行"分部。第一个分部试图通过提供技术和财政援助来促成遵约，[127] 而第二个分部则被授权发布制裁，例如限制灵活机制的使用，甚至施加一个处罚，减少第二承诺期（the second commitment period）内的排放总量。[128] 但是，在实践中，遵约委员会的执行权力其实是很有限的。施加压力是它们的主要办法，而这只是象征性的，例如给当事国带来的名誉伤害，或者特别情况下实质性的，例如暂时取消某些特定利益（例如援助或贸易机会）。

第六节 国际环境法中的法律环境

为了总结本章对国际环境法的概述，有必要描述这一部门法在国际法律秩序中的整体地位。从以上对国际环境法的分析和评论可以看出，国际社会为了让国际法的方法适应环境问题的特殊性，做出了各种努力。

但是，这也并不意味着国际环境法或者由多边环境协定建立的更具体

---

[124] See E. Milano, "The Outcomes of the Procedure and their Legal Effects" in Treves et al., supra footnote 88, pp. 407–418.

[125] See L. Pineschi, "Non-Compliance Procedures and the Law of State Responsibility" in Treves et al, supra footnote 88, pp. 483–497.

[126] See Art. 18 of the Kyoto Protocol, supra footnote 18 and Decision 27/CMP.1, FCCC/KP/CMP/2005/8/Add.3.

[127] See Decision 27/CMP.1, Annex, Section IV, paras.4 and 6.

[128] Ibid., Section V, para.6 and Section XV. The Committee has applied sanctions to Sections XV to Greece and Croatia. See Compliance Committee, Final Decision: Greece, 17 April 2008, CC-2007-1-8/Greece/EB; Compliance Committee, Final Decision: Croatia, 19 February 2010, CC-2009-1-8/Croatia/EB.

的条约制度就能被当作从国际秩序中割裂出来的自立的或自给自足的制度。[129] 事实情况是,我们通常称为国际环境法的一系列规范和条约其实是国际法的一部分,而且它们在发展过程中通常还必须依赖一般国际法。除了它们的特殊性,国际环境法的主要行为体和正式渊源实际上和国际法一样。另外,它的一些基本原则,例如无害、预防、合作或合理利用,都是从睦邻这一理念衍生出来的一些广义原则的不同适用。[130] 最后,不同规范(包括国际环境法的规范)的优先顺序也是由源自国际法的一般冲突规则来管理的,特别需要强调的是强行性法处于最优先的地位。

国际法与国际环境法两者之间关联的一个重要问题是,不同形式的优先排位之间的关系。有些环境规范可能会与另一个非环境领域的特别法或者通用规范发生冲突,而这些通用规范基于其实质内容因而更具权威性。为了理解环境规范与其他两类规范之间的关系,就有必要审视国际环境规范的实质性层次划分。当然,这一划分必须是基于对各个规范的逐一排查。但是,一些整体上的研究还是会有助于阐明相关术语。[131] 在国际法中,某一规范的实质位阶可以通过多种方式表现,包括将其定性为强性规范[132]或对一切义务(erga omnes obligation),[133] 或者将其表述为习惯法上必要的防卫(customary necessity defence)意义上的一种核心利益。[134] 这些概念引发了不同的位阶效果。强制性规范的核心特征是它们不得被违背,而对一切义务的特别之处则是在于它们针对所有其他国家,因此就有可能将采取行动的权利授权给任一国家。[135] 如果某个"利益"被定性为一种"核

---

[129] See generally P. -M. Dupuy, "L'unité de l'ordre juridique international: cours général de droit international public (2000) ", (2002) 297 *Recueil des Cours de L'Académie de Droit International de La Haye*, 9-489, 428 ss.

[130] See infra Chapter 3.

[131] See J. E. Viñuales, "La protección del medio ambiente y su jerarquía normativa en derecho internacional" (2008) 13 *Revista Colombiana de Derecho Internacional* 11.

[132] See A. Orakhelashvili, *Peremptory Norms in International Law* (Oxford University Press, 2006).

[133] See M. Ragazzi, *The Concept of International Obligations erga omnes* (Oxford University Press, 2000).

[134] 在国际实践中,由于特定规范的实质,因此也会通过给特定规范加上形容词来强调它的特殊重要性。See in this regard: R. Kolb, "Jus cogens, intangibilité, intransgressibilité, dérogation 'positive' et 'négative' " (2005) *Revue Générale de Droit International Public* 305.

[135] See F. Voeffray, *L'actio Popularis ou la Défense de L'intérêt Collectif Devant les Juridictions Internationals* (Paris: Presses universitaires de France, 2004).

心利益",就可以通过多种渠道将其定性为习惯法上必要的防卫,例如援引一项旨在保护这一利益的习惯法规范。[136]

在国际法的当前阶段,要想将某些环境规范当作强制性规范还是存在一定难度的。[137] 在"盖巴期科夫—拉基玛洛工程案"中,国际法院对这一问题持开放态度,因此也没有排除这一种可能性,[138] 但是另外两个要素暗示了强制性环境规范的缺失。第一个是因为多个国家的反对,国际法委员会对《1996年国家对国际不法行为的责任条款草案》(*1996 Draft Articles on the Responsibility of States for Internationally Wrongful Acts*)第19条(将故意的和大规模环境危害定性为一种犯罪)的撤回。[139] 第二个来自国际法委员会"国际法碎片化研究团队"的研究结论。[140] 这一团队分析了强行法(或者强制性规范)和对一切义务这两个概念之间的区别,得出的结论是:

> 我们认识到,强行性规范所规定的义务,正如上述第33项结论指出的那样,都具有对一切义务的特性,反之则不一定是这样。并不是所有的对一切义务都是由一般国际法的强制性规范来规定的。例如,只有那些由人类基本权利的原则和规则所规定的特定义务以及与全球公共产品相关的义务,才是由强制性规范来规定的。[141]

相反地,研究结论指出,某些环境规范由于它们自身的目的而拥有了

136　See Viñuales, supra footnote 70, 248-249.

137　On this debate, see E. Kornicker, *Ius cogens und Umweltvölkerrecht. Kriterien, Quellen und Rechtsforgen Zwingender Völkerrechtsnormen und Deren Anwendung auf das Umweltvölkerrecht* (Basel: Helbing Lichtenhahn Verlag, 1997). This author has summarised her thesis in E. Korniker, "State Community Interests, Jus Cogens and Protection of the Global Environment: Developing Criteria for Peremptory Norms" (1998-1999) 11 *Georgetown International Environmental Law Review* 101.

138　*Gabčíkovo-Nagymaros Project*, supra footnote 78, para. 112.

139　See M. Fitzmaurice, "International Protection of the Environment", (2001) 293 *Recueil des Cours de L'Académie de Droit International de la Haye*, 9-488, 141.

140　Conclusions of the work of the Study on the Fragmentation of International Law: Difficulties arising from the Diversification and Expansion of International Law, (2006) 2 (2) *Yearbook of the International Law Commission*.

141　Ibid., conclusion 38 (italics added).

一个普遍义务特性。国际法委员会针对国家责任的工作成果证实了这一结论。国际法委员会2001年条款草案第48条[142]提到了这样一种可能性,即如果被违反的义务归属于一群国家或者国际社会这一整体,则可以由受害国以外的任一国家来提起某一国的责任。这一条款是由澳大利亚诉日本(新西兰也有介入)在南极地区捕鲸这一案例引发的,虽然国际法院并未特别提到第48条,但是它还是指出,澳大利亚作为《捕鲸公约》(Whaling Convention)的一个缔约方,拥有保护鲸鱼的利益。[143] 国际法委员会条款的评注的第7段举例说明了保护环境的义务。[144]

对环境问题的重视也体现在国际法院赋予环境保护以"核心利益"的地位,第一次是在"盖巴期科夫—拉基玛洛工程案"[145]以及后续的"纸浆厂案"[146]中赋予。这重要的一步可能应当归功于一个习惯规范的出现和针对这一规范所保护利益的重视两者之间微妙的相互作用。国际法院针对"×××案"的判决明确指出了这种关联,当时国际法院承认了环境保护的核心特性。[147] 实际上,国际法院特别提到了它前一年发布的"关于威胁使用或使用核武器合法性的咨询意见"[148],强调了"尊重环境的重要意义,不仅是为了各国还是为了全人类"。[149] 对环境保护的重视还产生了其他法律效果。为了支持其结论,国际法院还指出在履行条约的过程中必须考虑

---

142 Draft Articles on the Responsibility of States for Internationally Wrongful Acts,(2001)2(2)*Yearbook of the International Law Commission*.

143 *Whaling in the Antarctic*(*Australia v. Japan*: *New Zealand intervening*),Judgment,ICJ Reports 2014,p. 226. The Court proceeded,in this regard,as in a case concerning torture brought by Belgium against Senegal: *Questions relating to the Obligation to Prosecute or Extradite*(*Belgium v. Senegal*),*Judgment*,ICJ Reports 2012,p. 422,paras. 64-70.

144 See Draft Articles on the Responsibility of States for Internationally Wrongful Acts and Commentary,(2001)2(2)*Yearbook of the International Law Commission* ad Art. 48,para. 7 of the Commentary.

145 *Gabčíkovo-Nagymaros Project*,supra footnote 78,para. 53.

146 *Pulp Mills*,supra footnote 78,para. 72.

147 See Viñuales,supra footnote 70,pp. 248-249.

148 国际法院持以下观点:环境不是一个抽象事物,而是代表了人类(包括未出生的后代)的生存空间、生活质量和人类的根本健康。各国确保其管辖和控制下的行为尊重他国或国家控制以外地区的环境这一普通义务已经成为涉及环境问题的国际法的一个有机组成部分,参见*Legality of Nuclear Weapons*,supra footnote 8,para. 29。

149 *Gabčíkovo-Nagymaros Project*,supra footnote 78,para. 53 infine.

到新的环保规范。[150] 这也是环保规范在争议地区适用的基础,无论是哪个国家对该地区拥有主权或主权权利。[151]

总之,上述研究表明,在国际法的当前状况下,有些环境规范可以被当作对一切的义务。另外,如果环境保护被理解为习惯法上必要的防卫,那么它也有资格成为一个国家的核心利益。而且,即使两国或者多国针对某一地区存在争议,这些规范仍然会适用于这一地区。

部分参考文献

[1] Andonova, L., "Public-Private Partnerships for the Earth: Politics and Patterns of Hybrid Authority in the Multilateral System" (2010) 10 *Global Environmental Politics* 25.

[2] Boisson de Chazournes, L., "Le fonds sur l'environnement mondial, recherche et conquête de son identité" (1995) 41 *Annuaire Français de Droit International* 612.

"Technical and Financial Assistance" in D. Bodansky, J. Brunnée and E. Hey (eds.), *The Oxford Handbook of International Environmental Law* (Oxford University Press, 2007), pp. 945-973.

[3] Breitmeier, H., O. R. Young and M. Zurn, *Analyzing International Environmental Regimes: From Case Study to Database* (Cambridge MA: MIT Press, 2007).

[4] Brown Weiss, E., "International Environmental Law: Contemporary Issues and the Emergence of a New World Order" (1995) 81 *Georgetown Law Journal* 675.

[5] Brown Weiss, E. and H. K. Jacobson (eds.), *Engaging Countries:*

---

[150] Ibid., para. 112 infine.

[151] *Dispute Concerning Delimitation of the Maritime Boundary between Ghana and Côte d'Ivoire in the Atlantic Ocean* (*Ghana/Côte d'Ivoire*), ITLOS Case No. 23, Order of 25 April 2015, paras. 68-73; *Request for an Advisory Opinion Submitted by the Sub-Regional Fisheries Commission* (*SRFC*), Advisory Opinion of 2 April 2015, ITLOS Case No. 21, paras. 111, 120; *In the matter of the South China Sea Arbitration before and Arbitral Tribunal constituted under Annex VII of the United Nations Convention on the Law of the Sea* (*Republic of the Philippines v. People's Republic of China*), PCA Case No. 2013-2019, Award (12 July 2016), para. 927.

Strengthening Compliance With International Environmental Accords (Cambridge MA: MIT Press, 1998).

[6] Brunnée, J., "Coping with Consent: Law – making under Multilateral Environmental Agreements" (2002) 15 *Leiden Journal of International Law* 1.

[7] Bulkeley, H., L. Andonova, M. Betsill, D. Compagnon, T. Hale, M. J. Hoffmann, P. Newell, M. Paterson, Ch. Roger and S. VanDeveer, *Transnational Climate Change Governance* (Cambridge University Press, 2014).

[8] Carlarne, C. and D. Farber, "Law Beyond Borders: Transnational Responses to Global Environmental Issuee" (2012) 1/1 *Transnational Environmental Law* 13.

[9] Churchill, R. R. and G. Ulfstein, "Autonomous Institutional Arrangements in Multilateral Environmental Agreements: A Little-Noticed Phenomenon in International Law" (2000) 94 *American Journal of International Law* 623.

[10] De Lucia, V., "Competing Narratives and Complex Genealogies: The Ecosystem Approach in International Environmental Law" (2015) 27 *Journal of Environmental Law* 91.

[11] Desai, B. H., *Multilateral Environmental Agreements. Legal Status of the Secretariats* (Cambridge University Press, 2010).

International Environmental Governance: Towards UNEPO (Leiden: Martinus Nijhoff, 2014).

[12] Dupuy, P. -M., "Soft Law and the International Law of the Environment" (1990-1991) 12 *Michigan Journal of International Law* 420.

"Où en est le droit international de l'environnement à la fin du siècle?" (1997) *Revue Générale de Droit International Public* 879.

"Formation of Customary International Law and General Principles", in D. Bodansky, J. Brunnée and E. Hey (eds.), *The Oxford Handbook of International Environmental Law* (Oxford University Press, 2007), pp. 449-466.

[13] Dupuy, P. -M. and J. E. Viñuales (eds.), *Harnessing Foreign Investment to Promote Environmental Protection: Incentives and Safeguards* (Cam-

bridge University Press, 2013).

[14] Finck, M., "Above and Below the Surface: The Status of Sub-National Authorities in EU Climate Change Regulation" (2014) 26 *Journal of Environmental Law* 443.

[15] Fisher, E., "The Rise of Transnational Environmental Law and the Expertise of Environmental Lawyers" (2012) 1/1 *Transnational Environmental Law* 43.

[16] Francioni, F. and P. -M. Dupuy, *Preliminary Feasibility Study for the Establishment of a UN Environmental Organisation or Agency* (Florence: European University Institute, 2005).

[17] Green, J. F., "Don't link carbon markets!" (2017) 543/7646 *Nature* 484.

[18] Haas, P., R. O. Keohane and M. A. Levy (eds.), *Institutions for the Earth: Sources of Effective International Environmental Protection* (Cambridge MA: MIT Press, 1993).

[19] Harrison, J., *Making the Law of the Sea. A Study in the Development of International Law* (Cambridge University Press, 2011).

[20] Heyvaert, V. and T. Etty, "Introducing Transnational Environmental Law" (2012) 1/1 *Transnational Environmental Law* 1.

[21] Iovane, M., "La participation de la société civile à l'élaboration et à l'application du droit international de l'environnement" (2008) *Revue Générale de Droit International Public* 465.

[22] Ivanova, M., "UNEP in Global Environmental Governance: Design, Leadership, Location" (2010) 10 *Global Environmental Politics* 30.

[23] Jaffe, J. M. Ranson and R. Stavins, "Linking tradable permit systems: A key element of emerging international climate policy architecture" (2010) 36 *Ecology Law Quarterly* 789.

[24] Kerbrat, Y., "La Cour internationale de justice face aux enjeux de protection de l'environnement" (2011) *Revue générale de droit international public* 39.

[25] Kiss, A., "Les traités-cadre: une technique juridique caractéristique du droit international de l'environnement" (1993) 39 *Annuaire Français de*

Droit International 792.

[26] Korniker, E., "State Community Interests, Jus Cogens and Protection of the Global Environment: Developing Criteria for Peremptory Norms" (1998–1999) 11 *Georgetown International Environmental Law* 101.

[27] Lavieille, J.M.(ed.), *Conventions de protection de L'environnement, Secrétariats, Conférences des Parties, Comités D'experts* (Limoges: PULIM, 1999).

[28] Lin, J. and J. Scott, "Looking Beyond the International: Key Themes and Approaches of Transnational Environmental Law" (2012) 1/1 *Transnational Environmental Law* 23.

[29] Martin, J.-C., "The United Nations Compensation Commission Practice with Regards to Environmental Claims", in S. Maljean-Dubois and Y. Kerbrat (eds.), *The Transformation of International Environmental Law* (Oxford: Hart Publishing, 2011), pp. 251–267.

[30] Morgera, E., *Corporate Accountability in International Environmental Law* (Oxford University Press, 2009).

[31] Pomade, A., *La Société Civile et le Droit de L'environnement. Contribution à la Réflexion sur Les Théories des Sources du Droit et de la Validité* (Paris: LGDJ, 2010).

[32] Richardson, B.J., *Socially Responsible Investment Law. Regulating the Unseen Polluters* (Oxford University Press, 2008).

[33] Romanin Jacur, F., *The Dynamics of Multilateral Environmental Agreements. Institutional Architectures and Law-Making Processes* (Naples: Editoriale Scientifica, 2013).

[34] Savadogo, L., "Le recours des juridictions internationales à des experts" (2004) 50 *Annuaire Français de Droit International* 231.

[35] Schiele, S., *Evolution of International Environmental Regimes. The Case of Climate Change* (Cambridge University Press, 2016).

[36] Speth, J.G. and P. Haas, *Global Environmental Governance* (Washington D.C.: Island Press, 2006).

[37] Stewart, R., B. Kingsbury and B. Rudyk, *Climate Finance: Regulatory and Funding Strategies for Climate Change and Global Development* (New

York: NYU University Press, 2009).

[38] Streck, C., "The Global Environmental Facility-A Role Model for International Environmental Governance?" (2001) 1 *Global Environmental Politics* 71.

[39] Treves, T., L. Pineschi, A. Tanzi, C. Pitea, C. Ragni and F. Romanin Jacur (eds.), *Non-Compliance Procedures and Mechanisms and the Effectiveness of International Environmental Agreements* (The Hague: T. M. C. Asser Press, 2009).

[40] Viñuales, J. E., "The Contribution of the International Court of Justice to the Development of International Environmental Law: A Contemporary Assessment" (2008) 32 *Fordham International Law Journal* 232.

"Legal Techniques for Dealing with Scientific Uncertainty in Environmental Law" (2010) 43 *Vanderbilt Journal of Transnational Law* 437.

"Managing Abidance by Standards for the Protection of the Environment", in A. Cassese (ed.), *Realizing Utopia* (Oxford University Press, 2012), pp. 326-339.

"La Protección Ambiental en el Derecho Internacional Consuetudinario" (2017) 69/2 *Revista Española de Derecho Internacional* 71.

第三章 国际环境法的原则

第一节 导论

在前面一章，我们没有具体讨论那些支撑国际环境法并构成其轮廓的原则和概念。因此，本章就可以被看作第二章的延续，因为它进一步对国际环境法做出定性分析。另外，对国际环境法的原则和概念的分析是研究其实质内容的重要一步，本书的后半部分将具体讨论实质内容。

为了理解国际环境法的原则和概念的重要意义以及两者间的区别，有必要首先介绍一些分析方法上的区别（本章第二节）。这些区别将会帮助我们展示那些最基本的原则和概念，正是它们才使得国际环境法的架构符合这一部门法提出的两大价值——预防（本章第三节）和平衡（本章第四节）。最后一部分（本章第五节）将会把这些原则和概念与本书第二编研究的环境制度联系起来。

第二节 不同的分析方法

针对本章主题所涉及的内容，法律评论员已经做出了比较详细的分析。但是，由于各个学者采用的标准不同，因此对内容的阐释方法也是千差万别的。为了与这些分析进行一个有益的对比，就必须首先挑明这些分析方法的区别所在（即使它们时而模糊不清），以便为一个引导性探讨打下基础。

首先，我们必须将术语"原则"的两种使用方法区分开来，一种是用于特指某一规范的表述或者阐述,[1] 另一种是用于描述某一规范的法律基础,这一规范可能是一个条约、国际习惯法或者辅助性的法律一般原则。[2] 这是两个不同的问题,因为当我们把一个规范当作一个原则来表述时(例如在软法文件中),很少会提及它的法律基础是源自国际法的一个正式渊源。评估某一原则是否具备一个特定的法律特性,应当采取具体问题具体分析的办法,逐步使其变得明朗。

其次,根据环境规范的普遍性和特殊性的程度来将其明确划分为三类(概念、原则、规则)[3] 是有益的。直观来看,这一划分意味着,当某一规范变得更加抽象时,它在某一具体案例中的实际运用就更易导致争议,反之亦然。例如,禁止向海洋中倾倒废物这样一个规范(规则)[4] 与国家有义务确保其管辖下的活动不得造成环境危害这样一个规范(原则)[5] 相比而言,前者就明确规定了一个更具体的行为。而后者则比国家管辖外的海床是一项"人类共同遗产"(common heritage of mankind)[6] 这一宣言或者生物多样性的保护是"一项人类共同关切事项"(a common concern of humankind)[7] 这一宣言(概念)更加明确。理解这种基于普遍性/特殊性程度的划分方法的另一种办法是,将概念理解为指导性规范,它通过原则

---

[1] See U. Beyerlin, "Different Types of Norms in International Environmental Law", in D. Bodansky, J. Brunnée and E. Hey (eds.), *The Oxford Handbook of International Environmental Law* (Oxford University Press, 2007), Chapter 18.

[2] G. Abi‐Saab, "Les sources du droit international: Essai de déconstruction", in *Liber Amicorum en hommage au Professeur Eduardo Jiménez de Aréchaga*, Vol. I (Montevideo: Fundación de Cultura Internacional, 1994), pp. 29–49.

[3] This distinction is taken from R. Dworkin, *Taking Rights Seriously* (Cambridge MA: Harvard University Press, 1977), p. 22, and employed in an environmental context by Beyerlin, supra footnote 1.

[4] Convention for the Prevention of Marine Pollution by Dumping of Wastes and Other Matter, 29 December 1972, as modified by the Protocol of 7 November 1996, 1046 UNTS 120, Art. 4.

[5] 这一规范(预防原则)的现代表述是由《里约宣言》第2条原则做出的。See Rio Declaration on Environment and Development, 13 June 1992, UN Doc. A/CONF. 151/26. Rev. 1 ("Rio Declaration").

[6] United Nations Convention on the Law of the Sea, 10 December 1982, 1833 UNTS 397 ("UNCLOS"), Art. 136.

[7] Convention on Biological Diversity, 5 June 1992, 1760 UNTS 79 ("CBD"), preamble, para. 3.

来实施，而原则则是通过规则来实现。

再次，在分析原则和概念的过程中，还有另一种辅助性方法，即考察原则和概念所发挥的作用。第一，它们的一个重要作用就是为某一领域的国际法提供一个特定的集体身份。正如行政法区别于劳动法和刑法是通过国内法中各个部门法的大量原则的运作来实现的，国际法的不同分支也都具有某些显著的特性。国际环境法的一个显著特性就是针对一个特定客体——环境的保护。某些非专属于环境的原则（例如无害原则），只要它们在环境语境内被再次阐述，也可以发挥这种"身份功能"。于是，无害原则的作用就不再是保护他国的"领土"，而是保护他国以及国家管辖外区域的环境本身。[8] 重要的是，这一身份功能不能被理解为构成了各部门法的合法存在。原则和概念赋予了部门法一些特性，因此它们可以被当作许多条约制度的基础，这些制度使得原则和制度更加充实和具体化。但是，只有规范、制度以及法律上相互关联的条约制度才能构成一个合法存在。[9] 第二，从国际环境法与国际法的其他分支之间的关系这一视角来看，或者更具体一点，从不同分支所精心构建的规范、条约和法律上相互关联的条约制度之间的关系这一视角看，原则和概念还可以发挥一种"协调功能"。例如，可持续发展这一概念就被当作一个概念模型来阐明国际环境法和国际经济法时而不一致的要求。[10] 正如国际法院在"×××案"中指出：

> 协调经济发展和环境保护两者关系的必要性已经在可持续发展这一概念中得以充分表述。[11]

---

[8] See J. E. Viñuales, "The Contribution of the International Court of Justice to the Development of International Environmental Law: A Contemporary Assessment" (2008) 32 *Fordham International Law Journal* 232.

[9] See J. E. Viñuales, "Cartographies imaginaires: Observations sur la portee juridique du concept de 'régime spécial' en droit international" (2013) 140 *Journal du Droit International* (*Clunet*) 405.

[10] See P. -M. Dupuy, "Où en-est le droit de l'environnement à la fin du siècle?" (1997) 101 *Revue Générale de Droit International Public* 873.

[11] *Gabčíkovo - Nagymaros Project* (*Hungary* v. *Slovakia*), Judgment, ICJ Reports 1997, p. 7 ("*Gabčíkovo–Nagymaros Project*"), para. 140.

第三，概念和原则还可以发挥一种"建筑功能"，即它们可以为某项环境制度提供基础。例如，气候变化制度主要就是依靠共同但有区别的责任这一原则而建立起来的。这一制度还同时显示出概念和原则的第四个作用，即它们的解释作用。《联合国气候变化框架公约》《京都议定书》和《巴黎协定》都用不同的方式提及《联合国气候变化框架公约》第3条所蕴含的原则并将其当作解释的指南。[12] 除了这些环境规范和手段的直接运用体现了"解释作用"，而且当其他国际法规范的运用有可能对环境造成影响时，解释作用也会发挥作用。举例来讲，国际法院就主张，在解释自卫权这一术语时就必须考虑到环境损害预防原则。[13] 第四，这些原则还拥有一个"决策功能"，换言之，发挥着"初级规范"的作用。仅举一个例证来说明，"特雷尔冶炼厂仲裁案"这样一个著名的环境争端就是根据无害原则来判决的。[14]

最后，第四种分析方法就是区分两类原则，即那些与广义预防概念相关的原则和那些与平衡考量相关的原则及概念。[15] 所谓"预防"，指的是尽可能避免那些很难修复甚至无法修复的环境危害或变化。它既包括实体性原则，例如无害原则、损害预防原则（prevention principle）和风险预防原则（precautionary principle）或方法，也包括一些程序性原则，例如合作原则（the principle of cooperation）、通知原则和协商原则（the principle of notification and/or consultation）、开展环境影响评价的要求

---

[12] United Nations Framework Convention on Climate Change, 9 May 1992, 31 ILM 849 ("UNFCCC"); Kyoto Protocol to the United Nations Framework Convention on Climate Change, 11 December 1997, 2303 UNTS 148 ("Kyoto Protocol"); Adoption of the Paris Agreement, Decision 1/CP. 21, 12 December 2015, FCCC/CP/2015/L. 9, Annex ("Paris Agreement").

[13] *Legality of the Threat or Use of Nuclear Weapons*, ICJ Reports 1996, p. 226 ("*Legality of Nuclear Weapons*"), para. 30.

[14] *Trail Smelter Arbitration*, RIAA, Vol. III, pp. 1905 – 1982 ("*Trail Smelter*"), p. 1965. A recent illustration is provided by *In the matter of the South China Sea Arbitration before and Arbitral Tribunal constituted under Annex VII of the United Nations Convention on the Law of the Sea (Republic of the Philippines v. People's Republic of China)*, PCA Case No. 2013-2019, Award (12 July 2016) ("South China Sea Arbitration"), paras. 941 and 966.

[15] 预防与平衡之间的区别不仅体现在原则和概念中，还体现在它们的实施中。See J. E. Viñuales, "Managing Abidance by Standards for the Protection of the Environment", in A. Cassese (ed.) *Realizing Utopia. The Future of International Law* (Oxford University Press, 2012), pp. 326 – 339.

(the requirement to conduct an environmental impact assessment)、事先知情同意原则（the principle of prior informed consent）。这些原则的特别之处就在于它们几乎以相同的方式适用于所有的国家。同样地，它们并不打算在各国之间或者各种人类活动领域之间进行任何正式的区分。在实践中，某一特定国家的发展程度，或者它的财政和技术状况，会在一定程度上予以考虑。但是，这些原则的目的并不是考量这些因素（或者其他涉及分配正义的因素）。国际环境法对这些其他因素的阐释是通过多个原则来实现的，例如污染者付费原则（the polluter-pays principle）、共同但有区别的责任原则（the principle of common but differentiated responsibilities）、公众参与原则（the principle of participation）、代际公平原则（the principle of inter-generational equity），还通过一些概念来实现，例如可持续发展、公地（common area）、人类共同遗产、人类共同关切事项。这些原则和概念的实际目的是管理特定资源的获取，或者是在各国间或人类活动的不同部门间分配特定环境问题的管理责任。

在我们看来，上面这一种区分方法是最有效的，它有助于我们理解后文将要研究的内容，即这些原则和概念是如何打造现代国际环境法的。它依赖于以上各种不同的分析方法，否则的话，我们就无法区分概念和原则，或者理解它们的运行和法律基础。图3-1基于上面第四种分析方法提供了国际环境法的原则和概念模型。

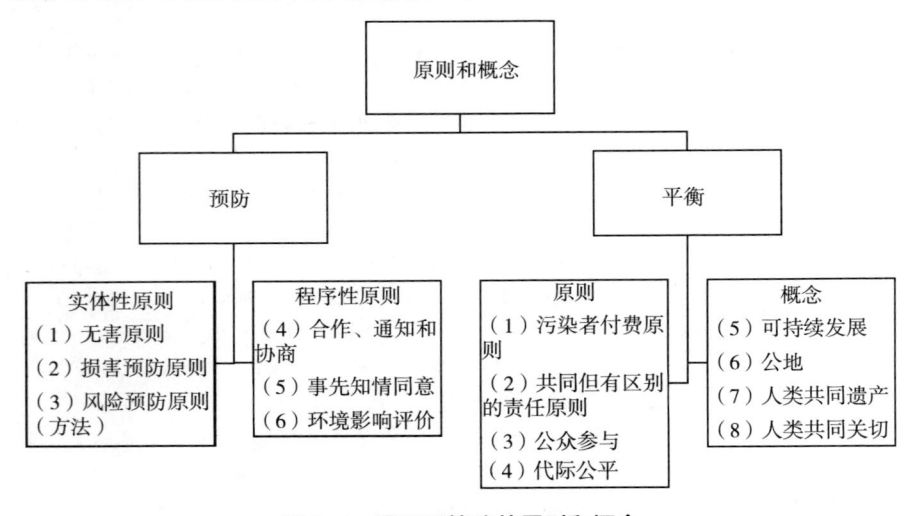

```
                          原则和概念
                ┌─────────────┴─────────────┐
              预防                          平衡
        ┌──────┴──────┐              ┌──────┴──────┐
     实体性原则      程序性原则         原则           概念
    （1）无害原则   （4）合作、通知和  （1）污染者付费   （5）可持续发展
    （2）损害预防原则    协商           原则          （6）公地
    （3）风险预防原则（5）事先知情同意  （2）共同但有区别 （7）人类共同遗产
        （方法）    （6）环境影响评价      的责任原则   （8）人类共同关切
                                   （3）公众参与
                                   （4）代际公平
```

图3-1 国际环境法的原则和概念

在后文中，我们的分析将围绕国际环境法的两个主要理念来展开，即预防环境危害的需要并在各种考量间实现令人满意的平衡。

第三节　国际环境法中的预防

一　引论

体现预防这一理念的有些原则是来自一般国际法中调整相邻国家间友好关系的古老部门法。这些古老的原则经历了多年的演化，越来越多地反映了对跨界和全球环境问题的关切。从历史的视角来看，无害原则是第一个出现的。无害原则在环境问题上的适用不仅拓展了它的适用范围，还有助于详细了解无害原则的实施方式。

如果想要把跨界危害的有限语境拓展到别国领土，就必须扩大无害原则的适用范围。重要的是，必须明确环境应当如此来加以保护，而不仅是被当作别国领土的一部分。如此一来，各国就有明确的义务去预防环境危害本身。无害原则的这一拓展将会导致一个更广泛的损害预防原则的出现。有人甚至提出了一种更宽泛的拓展，试图将损害预防原则进一步发展到风险预防原则（或方法）。但是，后文将要谈及，风险预防原则在一般国际法中的地位还存在争议。涉及履行问题时，除了在条约规定中明确表述这些原则，习惯法已经普遍承认预防环境危害这一义务的履行必须借鉴其他几个程序性义务，包括（以通知和协商的方式）合作或者开展环境影响评价。国际法院在其 2015 年 12 月针对"哥斯达黎加诉尼加拉瓜案"所做的判决中，简明陈述了国际环境法的传统模型。[16] 鉴于它的重要意义，有必要在此无删节地引用这一段文字：

> 为了履行预防重大跨界环境危害这一谨慎注意义务，在启动某项可能会对他国环境造成不利影响的活动时，一个国家必须确认是否存在重大跨界危害的风险，如果存在风险，就有必要进行一个环境影响

16　*Certain Activities Carried out by Nicaragua in the Border Area*（*Costa Rica v. Nicaragua*），*Construction of a road in Costa Rica along the river San Juan*（*Nicaragua v. Costa Rica*），*Judgment of 16 December 2015*（I. C. J.）（"Costa Rica/Nicaragua"）.

评价……如果这一环境影响评价确认存在重大跨界危害的风险，计划启动这一活动的当事国就必须遵循谨慎注意义务，通知那些有可能受到影响的国家并与它们进行善意协商，以便决定采取何种适当的方法来预防或降低这一风险。[17]

这一表述的有些内容，特别是不同义务的排序，最好将之理解为针对该项争端的具体情况，而非通用。但是，针对关于环境保护的一般国际法的现状，这一段表述还是提供了一个罕见的概括。在后文中，我们将分析国际法院提及的这些原则以及其他一些已经获得足够承认的、应当单列的真正的法律原则（而非仅仅是概念性阐述）。

二　无害原则

为了理解无害原则的起源和内容，以及它与损害预防原则的关系，就有必要回顾一下它的历史进程。无害原则在环境领域的正式形成出现于"美国诉加拿大特雷尔冶炼厂仲裁案"。仲裁庭是如此表述的：

> 如果已发生后果严重的情况，而损害又是证据确凿的话，任何国家没有权利这样地利用或允许利用它的领土，以致其烟雾在他国领土或对他国领土上的财产和生命造成损害。[18]

1949年，国际法院在"英国诉阿尔巴尼亚科孚海峡案"的判决中确认了这一原则的习惯法本质，指出：

> 存在着一些特定的一般原则和被广泛认可的原则，即各国都有义务确保不得故意允许其国土被用于开展有损他国权利的活动。[19]

17　Ibid., para. 104（emphasis added）. For study of environmental protection in customary international law see J. E. Viñuales, "La Protección Ambiental en el Derecho Internacional Consuetudinario". (2017) 69/2 *Revista Española de Derecho Internacional* 71.

18　*Trail Smelter*, supra footnote 14, p. 1965.

19　*Corfu Channel Case*（UK v. Albania）, ICJ Reports 1949, p. 4（"*Corfu Channel*"）, p. 22.

在这两个案例中,无害原则都被当作一个主要标准来确定一个国家因为对他国造成危害所应承担的责任。

对这一原则的有限认识持续了几十年。在联合国大会1803号决议[20]通过后的十年,无害原则被当作国家对其自然资源永久主权这一原则的必然结果。自然资源的自主开发因此受到了限制,即有义务不对他国造成危害。虽然1803号决议文本中并未提及这一限制,但是它在1972年通过的《斯德哥尔摩宣言》中得到了明确的承认。事实上,《斯德哥尔摩宣言》第21条原则明确地将一个国家开发其自然资源的主权与不得造成环境危害的义务联系在一起。[21] 很难抽象去界定这一义务的范围,因为涉及自然资源开发的某些措施或行为,虽然是合法的,但是还是会对他国造成影响。如果仅是出于这一原因就对这类行为进行限制,就太过于严苛了。关于这一问题,有两点需要明确。首先,无害原则不应被理解为严格责任或无过错责任的基础。它还是属于一种谨慎注意义务,或者换言之,一种行为义务。如果缘起国已经完全履行了谨慎注意义务,但是危害还是发生了,那么就不算违反了该原则。[22] 一个国家所展现出的谨慎程度,当然必须依靠基于事实的调查。其次,多大程度的危害才能构成违反无害原则,也要根据每个案例的具体情况才能确定。特雷尔冶炼厂仲裁案的法庭用了"严重后果"这一术语。国际法委员会在编撰《国际水道非航行利用法公约》时,其文本所提及的义务则是不得造成"重大危害"。[23] 与此相类似,国际法委员会在其《预防有害活动跨界危害的条款草案》中也是采用"重大危害"这一说法。[24] 近期在阿根廷诉乌拉圭"乌拉圭河纸浆厂案"

---

[20] "Permanent Sovereignty over Natural Resources", 14 December 1962, GA Res. 1803 (XVII).

[21] Commission on Sustainable Development, Report of the Expert Group Meeting on Identification of Principles of International Law for Sustainable Development, Geneva, Switzerland, 26–28 September 1995 ("Report-Principles"), paras. 51–56.

[22] See e. g. *South China Sea Arbitration*, supra footnote 14, paras. 941 and 977 (as regards the use of dynamite and cyanide as harmful fishing methods).

[23] See United Nations Convention on the Law of the Non-Navigational Uses of International Watercourses, 21 May 1997, 36 ILM 700 ("UN Convention on Watercourses"), Art. 7 (1).

[24] Draft Articles on the Prevention of Transboundary Harm from Hazardous Activities, 12 December 2001, GA Res. 56/82, UN Doc. A/RES/56/82 ("ILC Prevention Articles"), Art. 2 (a).

中,国际法院的表述是"对他国环境的重大损害"。[25]《斯德哥尔摩宣言》第 21 条原则并未对"危害"这一术语规定任何形容词。这样就意味着,后果或危害的大小判定必须具体问题具体分析,依据的标准包括对他国环境或者他国开展的活动造成重大危害的可能性,预防危害的费用与潜在损害之间的比率,对他国以类似方式利用自然资源的能力的影响,对他国人身健康的影响等。[26] 没有达到重大这一临界值的损害将不会违反无害原则,但是各国还是会受到谨慎注意义务的约束以预防危害的发生(参见损害预防原则),同时还受到其他规范的约束,例如污染者付费原则,它将可承受的损害(临界值之下)的责任分配给污染者。

需要特别强调的是,第 21 条原则不仅仅指的是跨界危害这一概念,它还涉及不得对"别国的或国家管辖范围以外区域的环境"造成危害。这一表述为预防这一概念的广义阐释打开了大门。但是,这一新的概念直到 20 世纪 90 年代才成为实证国际法的一部分,国际法院在"威胁使用或使用核武器的合法性"一案的咨询意见中承认,《斯德哥尔摩宣言》第 21 条原则编撰了国际习惯法。[27] 在 20 世纪 70 年代和 80 年代,无害原则这一有局限的概念似乎比较盛行。国际实践的两个案例可以证明这一点。第一个案例是核试验案。[28] 争议涉及法国在南太平洋进行大气核试验所造成的后果。新西兰向国际法院提出临时措施的要求,因为这些核试验可能造成的放射性尘埃不仅侵害了国际社会全体成员的权利,还侵害了新西兰的具体权利。在其命令中,国际法院仅仅批准了临时救济措施以保护新西兰的具体权利,驳回了新西兰代表国际社会进行诉求的权利。[29] 第二个案例来自国际法院针对"国际法不加禁止行为所致有害结果的国际责任"而开

---

[25] *Pulp Mills on the River Uruguay* (*Argentina v. Uruguay*), Judgment, ICJ Reports 2010, p. 14 ("*Pulp Mills*"), para. 101.

[26] Report-Principles, supra footnote 21, para. 54.

[27] *Legality of Nuclear Weapons*, supra footnote 13.

[28] *Nuclear Tests* (*New Zealand v. France*), Request for the Indication of Interim Measures of Protection, Order (22 June 1973), ICJ Reports 1973, p. 135 ("*Nuclear Tests-NZ-Order*"); *Nuclear Tests* (*Australia v. France*), Request for the Indication of Interim Measures of Protection, Order (22 June 1973), ICJ Reports 1973, p. 99.

[29] *Nuclear Tests-NZ-Order*, supra footnote 28, paras. 31-32.

展的工作。批准国际法委员会开展此项工作的联合国大会决议[30]以及那些由特别报告员在1978—2006年提交的后续报告,都明确表明这项工作的中心是跨界损害而非预防环境损害本身。我们在国际法委员会制定的最终文本中发现了这样一个狭义的概念,分别是"预防危险活动造成的跨界危害"[31]和"危险活动造成的跨界危害的损失分担"[32]。事实上,这两个文件仅仅提到了跨界危害[33],前者的重点是预防这类危害,而后者则是具体处理损害修复责任的分配。

这些案例显示了在过去几十年流行的无害原则这一有局限性的概念。后文将会谈及,无害原则在环境保护领域的运用导致了它的适用范围的重大扩展,并最终升华为一个更广泛的预防原则。

三 损害预防原则

损害预防原则在环境领域的现有表述是来自《斯德哥尔摩宣言》的第21条原则:

> 各国……拥有开发本国各种资源的主权权利……同时有责任保证在他们所管辖或控制下的各项活动不致对别国的或超出其国家管辖范围外的区域的环境造成损害。[34]

正如前文所述,第21条原则的内容不仅是一般国际法的一个反射(重新确认了无害原则),还是这一领域法演进过程中的一个尝试(规定国家有义务不得对国家管辖范围外的区域造成损害)。第21条原则想要

---

[30] Report of the International Law Commission, UN Doc. Res. 32/151 (1977), 19 December 1977, para. 7.

[31] ILC Prevention Articles, supra footnote 24.

[32] Draft Principles on the Allocation of Loss in the Case of Transboundary Harm Arising Out of Hazardous Activities, 4 December 2006, GA Res. 61/36, UN Doc. A/RES/61/36 ("ILC Principles").

[33] ILC Prevention Articles, supra footnote 24, Art. 2 (c); ILC Principles, supra footnote 32, Principle 2 (e).

[34] On this principle, see L.-A. Duvic Paoli and J. E. Viñuales, "Principle 2: Prevention", in Viñuales, J. E. (ed.), *The Rio Declaration on Environment and Development. A Commentary* (Oxford University Press, 2015), pp. 107-138.

强调的首先是保护环境本身，其次才是别国的利益。一旦这一条提示得以明确，就更容易理解无害原则和实际预防之间的区别。这一新视角的重心并非为了确认对别国造成的损害责任，而是为了明确预防环境损害这一义务。其潜在的含义是，在环境保护领域，预防显得尤其重要，因为环境损害通常都是不可逆的。用积极的预防（将风险最小化而不是修复）来保护环境本身（而非国家的利益，因此不论空间维度），正是这一新视角所设想的。在经历一些灾难之后（例如黎巴嫩油轮"托里坎荣号"在英国海岸附近沉没），对环境的关注在20世纪60年代末期就逐渐开始成形。但是，它还是应当被看作一个新视角，它要求我们重新思考各国开发本国自然资源的权利，以及各国与星球不同地区的关系。这一新视角还必须经过具体问题具体分析这样的验证，才会被允许融入一般国际法。

因此，损害预防原则在被认可为一项习惯法原则之前，首先是出现于软法文件和条约之中，也就不足为奇了。就这一点而言，就有必要提及多个重要文件，它们为损害预防原则提供了法律基础。例如，《联合国海洋法公约》第193条[35]规定"各国有依据其环境政策和按照其保护和保全海洋环境的职责开发其自然资源的主权权利"。这一条款有一个前置的一般义务，即第192条规定的保护和保全海洋环境的义务，同时还有一个更具体的后续表述（第194条第2款），它借鉴了《斯德哥尔摩宣言》第21条原则的表述。值得注意的是，这里的"海洋环境"并不仅限于各国的领海或受其控制的地区。[36] 这一点得到了近期几个案例的证实，[37] 它也可能会带来深远影响，因为这些决定指出各国必须预防重大环境危害，无论危害发生在何地，这样就把全球公地、争议地区甚至各国自有领土都包含在内。有的仲裁庭的表述就涉及这一问题。仲裁庭对《联合国海洋法公约》第12部分的环境条款以及相关习惯规范的分析都是基于以下理解：

---

[35] UNCLOS, supra footnote 6.

[36] Such as the exclusive economic zone (Part V, UNCLOS) or the continental shelf (Part VI, UNCLOS).

[37] See *Request for an Advisory Opinion Submitted by the Sub-Regional Fisheries Commission* (*SRFC*), Advisory Opinion of 2 April 2015, ITLOS Case No. 21 ("IUU Advisory Opinion"), paras. 111, 120; *Dispute Concerning Delimitation of the Maritime Boundary between Ghana and Côte d'Ivoire in the Atlantic Ocean* (*Ghana/Côte d'Ivoire*), ITLOS Case No. 23, Order of 25 April 2015 ("Ghana/Côte d'Ivoire"), paras. 68-73; *South China Sea Arbitration*, supra footnote 14, para. 940.

从一开始，仲裁庭就注意到，第 12 部分的义务适用于所有国家，涉及的是所有海域的海洋环境，包括国家管辖范围内和国家管辖范围外的区域。因此，主权问题与公约第 12 部分的适用并无关联。[38]

因此，应当采取措施来预防、减少和控制那些在"区域"（即国家管辖范围以外的公海下的海床）[39] 开展的活动对海洋环境造成的污染。同样地，深海生物资源的开发也应当遵守《联合国海洋法公约》第 116—120 条所规定的保护和管理规定。《联合国气候变化框架公约》的序言[40]和《生物多样性公约》第 3 条[41]都提及了损害预防原则的广义概念，这一概念由《斯德哥尔摩宣言》提出，后来被《里约宣言》第 2 条原则所采纳。

国际法庭的判决凸显了损害预防原则的广义表述。如前文所述，在 1996 年，国际法院在"威胁使用或使用核武器合法性的咨询意见"中指出，《斯德哥尔摩宣言》第 21 条和《里约宣言》第 2 条所体现的损害预防原则构成了一般国际法的一部分，这样就意味着损害预防原则从一项基于条约的原则转化为一项习惯法：

> 各国必须确保它们管辖和控制范围内的活动尊重别国或国家控制以外区域的环境，这是各国应当承担的一般性义务，它已经成为涉及环境的国际法的部分实体内容。[42]

国际法院后续还在三个案例中确认了损害预防原则的习惯法基础。在"盖巴斯科夫—纳基玛洛大坝案"中，国际法院指出：

> 在环境保护领域，警惕和预防是必需的，因为环境损害往往具有不可逆的特性，而且这种损害的修复机制天生具有局限性。[43]

38　*South China Sea Arbitration*, supra footnote 14, para. 940.

39　UNCLOS, supra footnote 6, Art. 145（a）. See infra footnote 45.

40　UNFCCC, supra footnote 12, preamble, para. 8.

41　CBD, supra footnote 7, Art. 3.

42　*Legality of Nuclear Weapons*, supra footnote 13, para. 29.

43　*Gabčíkovo-Nagymaros Project*, supra footnote 11, para. 140.

最近,在"纸浆厂案"和"哥斯达黎加诉尼加拉瓜案"中,国际法院进一步确认了这一原则的基础,并明确表明它是源自无害原则。[44] 在这些案件中,法院也明确指出,每个国家的"谨慎注意"义务其实来自损害预防原则。虽然法院在"纸浆厂案"中的分析借鉴了《乌拉圭河规约》(*Statute of the River Uruguay*)的条款,但是这一分析后来还是被扩展到其他语境,因此可以被认定为具有普遍应用价值。[45] 从当前的理解来看,损害预防原则具体包括:(1)不得造成重大环境损害,必须积极采取措施预防这种损害,而且必须确保这些措施得到了有效实施,这是一个一般义务;(2)派生出的第一个程序性义务就是合作义务,尤其是通知和协商;(3)派生出的第二个程序性义务就是,当计划中的活动有可能造成重大不利影响时,就必须开展环境影响评价。

包括国际海洋法法庭(International Tribunal for the Law of the Sea, ITLOS)和多个仲裁法庭在内的其他国际法庭也遵循了这一种思路。[46] 国际海洋法法庭海床分庭(ITLOS Seabed Chamber)在其"关于区域责任的咨询意见"(Advisory Opinion on the Responsibilities in the Area)中,明确提及了"纸浆厂案"判决的第 187 段,目的是将源自《联合国海洋法公约》第 139 条第 1 款的"确保"义务划定成一种"行为"义务或"谨慎注意"义务。[47] 国际海洋法法庭和其他一些法庭还将这种论证方法延伸运用于《联合国海洋法公约》第 12 部分的数个条款,包括第 123 条、第 192 条、第 193 条、第 194 条、第 197 条、第 204 条和第 206 条,并运用

---

[44] *Pulp Mills*, supra footnote 25, paras. 101 – 102, 181 – 189, 204; *Costa Rica/Nicaragua*, supra footnote 16, paras. 104, 118.

[45] *Responsibilities and Obligations of States sponsoring Persons and Entities with respect to Activities in the Area*, Case No. 17, ITLOS (Seabed Dispute Chamber), Advisory Opinion (1 February 2011) ("Responsibilities in the Area"), para. 117; *IUU Advisory Opinion*, supra footnote 37, para. 131; *In the matter of the Indus Waters Kishenganga Arbitration before the Court of Arbitration constituted in accordance with the Indus Waters Treaty 1960 between the Government of India and the Government of Pakistan signed on 19 September 1960 (Islamic Republic of Pakistan v. Republic of India)*, PCA, Partial Award (18 February 2013) ("Indus Water Kishenganga-Partial Award"), para. 451; *South China Sea Arbitration*, supra footnote 14, para. 941.

[46] See supra footnote 45.

[47] *Responsibilities in the Area*, supra footnote 45, paras. 110–120, 145.

国际法的习惯法原则来解读这些条款。[48] 除了海洋法以外，这种论证方法还被用于一个涉及共享水道的案件，[49] 也借鉴了"纸浆厂案"。

重要的是，"关于区域责任的咨询意见"又向前推进了一步，它试图将运用风险预防手段的义务，不仅视为国际海底管理局相关法规的要求，同时也视为"谨慎注意"义务的组成部分，还可能是国际习惯法的组成部分。[50] 后文将会谈及，这一结论显示了预防概念至少是在条约法中正在被拓展这一趋势，涵盖了活动对环境的影响存在着科学不确定性的情况。

四 国际法中的风险预防

风险预防作为一个法律术语是起源于德意志联邦共和国立法中 Vorsorgeprinzip 一词。[51] 其潜在的意思是，当有可能造成严重的或不可逆的后果时，对某一行为的实际或可能后果缺乏科学确定性并不能阻止国家采取适当的措施。[52] 除了这一核心内容，风险预防的法律含义是很难精确界定的。

虽然有无数尝试想要厘清这些含义，但是国际法中风险预防的性质、规范基础和内容还是存在很大的争论。这可能是因为针对风险预防的观察视角不同造成的。有些人将风险预防看作一个"原则"，[53] 而有些人（包括国际法院）则将风险预防仅仅看作一种"方法"。[54] 在这两种情况下，风险预防的规范基础都是不确定的。有论者提出，除了基于条约的风险预防义务，应当承认基于国际习惯法的风险预防原则，或者将其当作《国

48　See *IUU Advisory Opinion*, supra footnote 37, paras. 125–136; *Ghana/Côte d'Ivoire*, supra footnote 37, paras. 68–73; *South China Sea Arbitration*, supra footnote 14, paras. 940–948.

49　*Indus Water Kishenganga-Partial Award*, supra footnote 45, para. 450.

50　*Responsibilities in the Area*, supra footnote 45, paras. 125–135, particularly paras. 131 and 135.

51　See K. von Moltke, "The Vorsorgeprinzip in West German Environmental Policy", in Royal Commission on Environmental Pollution, *Twelfth Report: Best Practicable Environmental Option*, 1988, p. 57.

52　On this principle, see A. A. Cançado Trindade, "Principle 15: Precaution", in Viñuales, supra footnote 34, pp. 403–428.

53　Report-Principles, supra footnote 21, paras. 70–74.

54　*Pulp Mills*, supra footnote 25, para. 164.

际法院规约》第 38 条第 1 款所体现的一项一般法律原则。[55] 其他人，包括世界贸易组织争端解决机构（Dispute Settlement Body of the WTO），[56] 针对风险预防原则在一般国际法中的定位，则不愿意表态。风险预防所造成的困难还不仅限于此。即使我们承认习惯法上的风险预防原则的存在，它的内容还有待明确。[57] 它是否意味着，即使缺乏足够的证据证明某项活动对环境造成的危险，也有义务采取措施。或者说，它只是一个简单的授权以便采取这些措施。抑或是，当特定活动有可能损害环境时，它充当了一个程序性规则，将举证责任进行了转移（或者通过降低举证责任的标准来促成这一转移）。在风险预防无法发挥作用的情况下，是否存在一个特定的潜在损害的临界值（严重的或者不可逆转的）？所有这些问题都导致了很难在国际法中对风险预防原则进行一个准确的定位。为了进一步指明这一争论的核心要素，就有必要重新审视这一原则在条约、软法文件、司法机关或准司法机关的裁判中的特点。

首先，谈到的是条约法，越来越多的条约已经通过各种形式吸收了风险预防的内容。[58] 明确引用风险预防的第一个条约体制是 1985 年《保护臭氧层维也纳公约》[59] 以及后续的 1987 年《蒙特利尔议定书》。[60] 从 20 世纪 90 年代开始，得益于《里约宣言》第 15 条原则对风险预防原则的表

---

[55] See CFI, 26 November 2002, Case T-74/00, *Artegodan GmbH and Others* v. *Commission* ECR II-4945, para. 184 (speaking of a "general principle of Community Law"); *Pulp Mills*, supra footnote 25, Separate opinion of A. A. Cançado Trindade, paras. 67-68.

[56] *European Communities-Measures Concerning Meat and Meat Products (Hormones)*, AB Report (16 January 1998) WT/DS26/AB/R, WT/DS48/AB/R, ("*EC-Hormones*"), paras. 123-125; *European Communities-Measures Affecting the Approval and Marketing of Biotech Products*, Panel Report (29 September 2006), WT/DS291/R, WT/DS292/R, WT/DS293/R ("*EC-Biotech Products*"), paras. 7.88-7.89.

[57] Report-Principles, supra footnote 21, paras. 71-72; D. Bodansky, "Deconstructing the Precautionary Principle", in D. Caron and H. N. Scheiber (eds.), *Bringing New Law to Ocean Waters* (Leiden: Martinus Nijhoff, 2004), pp. 381-391.

[58] See, generally, A. Trouwborst, *Evolution and Status of the Precautionary Principle in International Law* (The Hague: Kluwer, 2002).

[59] Vienna Convention for the Protection of the Ozone Layer, 22 March 1985, 1513 UNTS 293 ("CPOL"), preamble, para. 5.

[60] Montreal Protocol on Substances that Deplete the Ozone Layer, 16 September 1987, 1522 UNTS 29 ("Montreal Protocol"), preamble, para. 6.

述，引用这一原则的条约的数量逐步增加。不仅《生物多样性公约》的序言进行了引用，[61]《联合国气候变化框架公约》的正文也有引用，特别是第 3 条第 3 款规定：

> 各缔约方应当采取预防措施，预测、防止或尽量减少引起气候变化的原因并缓解其不利影响。当存在造成严重或不可逆转的损害的威胁时，不应当以科学上没有完全的确定性为理由推迟采取这类措施。

后来，风险预防就被其他几项多边环境协定吸收到文本之中，例如 1995 年《跨界鱼类种群协定》（"风险预防方法"）[62]、2000 年《生物多样性公约》之《生物安全议定书》（"风险预防方法"）[63]，或者 2001 年《持久性有机污染物斯德哥尔摩公约》（"风险预防关注/风险预防方法"）。[64] 另外，在区域环境条约[65]甚至在管理其他事项的条约中，[66] 也在不同程度上体现出了风险预防原则。

其次，谈及软法文件中的风险预防的概念，在 1982 年联合国大会制

---

[61] CDB, supra footnote 7, preamble, para. 9.

[62] Agreement for the Implementation of the Provisions of the United Nations Conventions on the Law of the Sea of 10 December 1982 Relating to the Conservation and Management of Straddling Fish Stocks and Highly Migratory Fish Stocks, 4 August 1995, 2167 UNTS 88 ("Straddling Fish Stocks Agreement"), Art. 6.

[63] Cartagena Protocol on Biosafety to the Convention on Biological Diversity, 29 January 2000, 39 ILM 1027 (2000) ("Biosafety Protocol"), Arts. 1 and 10 (6).

[64] Stockholm Convention on Persistent Organic Pollutants, 22 May 2001, 40 ILM 532 (2001) ("POPs Convention"), preamble, para. 8 and Art. 1.

[65] See e. g. Bamako Convention on the ban on the Import into Africa and the Control of Transboundary Movement and Management of Hazardous Wastes within Africa, 30 January 1991, 30 ILM 773 ("Bamako Convention"), Art. 4 (3); Convention for the Protection of the Marine Environment of the North East Atlantic, 22 September 1992, 2354 UNTS 67 ("OSPAR Convention"), Annex II, Art. 3 (3) (c); Convention on the Protection and Use of Transboundary Watercourses and International Lakes, 18 March 1992, 1936 UNTS 269 ("Helsinki Convention"), Art. 2; Convention on Co-operation for the Protection and Sustainable Use of the River Danube, 29 June 1994, IER 35: 0251 ("Danube Convention"), Art. 2 (4).

[66] Treaty on the Functioning of the European Union, as amended by the Lisbon Treaty, 13 December 2007, OJ C 83, 30 March 2010 ("TFEU"), Art. 191 (2); Agreement on the Application of Sanitary and Phytosanitary Measures, 15 April 1994, 1867 UNTS 493 ("SPS Agreement"), Art. 5 (7).

定的《世界自然宪章》(*World Charter for Nature*) 已经提及了风险预防的一个变量:"如果不能完全了解可能造成的不利影响,活动即不得进行"。[67] 十年以后,这一概念被正式写入《里约宣言》第 15 条原则中,它规定了风险预防的权威表述:

> 各国根据自己的能力应广泛应用预防措施,保护环境。凡有严重威胁或不可逆转的损害,不得使用缺乏充分的科学确定性为理由推迟防止环境退化的费用低廉的措施。

这一表述后来被广泛应用于国际法针对风险预防概念的一般讨论之中。但是,它还是造成了一些难题,例如如何界定"严重威胁或不可逆转的损害""科学不确定性",或者各国"基于各自能力"而导致的义务的区别。面对这样一些尚待明确的问题,人们都期待国际法院或法庭能够进一步明确风险预防概念的轮廓。但是,有关这一问题的案例法尚有分歧。

事实上,即使调查研究有关这一问题的大量决定,还是无法提供一个更清晰的轮廓。在一般国际法中,世界贸易组织贸易争端机构似乎不太愿意承认风险预防原则的存在,[68] 而其他一些国际性法院,例如欧洲人权法院 (European Court of Human Rights, ECtHR) 或者国际海洋法法庭,对这一原则的接受程度就要高得多。国际法院的立场介于这两个极端之间。在"纸浆厂案"中,阿根廷坚持认为国际习惯法承认风险预防原则的存在,其导致的结果就是将举证责任转移到了乌拉圭。但是,国际法院并没有支持阿根廷的立场,它只是指出:

> 虽然某项风险预防措施有可能与成文法条款的解释和运用有关联,但是这并不意味着它可以导致举证责任的倒置。[69]

---

67 World Charter for Nature, GA Res. 37/7, 28 October 1982, para. 11 (b).

68 在欧共体生物技术一案中,审判委员会指出"截至目前,还没有任何国际法院或法庭做出的权威决定承认风险预防原则是一个一般原则或国际习惯法原则",*EC-Biotech*, supra footnote 56, para. 7.88. 审判委员会的这一观点实际上是采用了欧共体荷尔蒙一案中上诉机构的观点, supra footnote 56, para. 124.

69 *Pulp Mills*, supra footnote 25, para. 164.

这一观点就与欧洲人权法院的最近判决相互矛盾。为了扭转长期以来对风险预防原则的抗拒,欧洲人权法院承认了:

> 风险预防原则(在《里约宣言》中第一次有权威表述)的重要性,指出它"旨在确保在所有社区活动中能够为健康、消费者安全和环境提供一个高水平保护"。[70]

与此相类似,国际海洋法法庭在两个场合中指出,各国应"谨慎小心地开展活动",[71] 或者换言之,"谨慎和小心"要求各国必须开展合作以保护环境,[72] 在其最近的"关于区域责任的咨询意见"中,它明确接受了风险预防原则:

> 法庭注意到风险预防措施已经被越来越多的国际条约和其他文件所接受,它们大都借用了《里约宣言》第 15 条原则的表述。法庭的观点是,这已经开启了一个趋势,将风险预防措施变为国际习惯法的一部分。[73]

在欧盟层面,初审法院(Court of First Instance, CFI)和欧洲法院(European Court of Justice, ECJ)[现在的欧盟法院(Court of Justice of the European Union)]已经明确承认了风险预防原则的规范基础,并将其列为欧洲法的一个一般原则。[74]

《欧洲联盟运行条约》(*Treaty on the Functioning of the European Union*)

---

[70] *Tatar* v. *Romania*, ECtHR Application No. 67021/01, Judgment (27 January 2009, Final 6 July 2009) ("*Tatar* v. *Romania*"), para. 120.

[71] *Southern Bluefin Tuna Cases* (*New Zealand* v. *Japan*; *Australia* v. *Japan*), Provisional Measures, ITLOS Case Nos. 3 and 4, Order (27 August 1999) ("*Southern Bluefin Tuna*"), para. 77 (the French text speaks of "*Prudence et Précaution*").

[72] *MOX Plant Case* (*Ireland* v. *United Kingdom*), ITLOS Case No. 10, Order (3 December 2001) ("*MOX Plant*"), para. 84 (the French text speaks of "*Prudence et Précaution*").

[73] *Responsibilities in the Area*, supra footnote 45, para. 135.

[74] See *Pfizer Animal Health SA* v. *Council*, CFI Case T-13/99, Judgment (11 September 2002), paras. 114–15; See also *Gowan Comércio Internacional e Serviços Lda* v. *Ministero della Salute*, CJEU Case C-77/09, Judgment (22 December 2010), para. 75.

对风险预防原则的明确论述[75]和欧盟以外不同法院对案件性质的把控,以及其他一些因素,可以说明对风险预防原则的接受程度是存在差异的。事实上,欧洲人权法院和国际海洋法法庭都愿意根据自己的职权来审理那些主要涉及遵守特定环境规范的案件,它们有的与适用涉及环境的人权条款相关,或者与《联合国海洋法公约》中保护海洋环境的相关条款相关。与此相反,在国际经济法中,环境保护还是被看作针对自由贸易和投资的一种限制。这些差异就使得国际法院的立场显得尤为重要,因为国际法院是一般国际法的监护人。

五 合作、通知、协商

国际法已经明确确立了合作的一般义务。这一义务的权威表述主要是来自联合国大会"关于各国友好关系和合作国际法原则的2625号决议"[76]的第4项原则。

但是,在环境法的语境下,合作义务采用了不同的形式。[77] 联合国可持续发展委员会于1995年召集了一个专家组来确定国际环境法的基本原则,专家组把两种义务做了一个区分,第一种义务是"基于全球合作伙伴关系精神"来开展合作,[78] 第二种义务是"在跨界背景下"来开展合作。[79] 第一种义务是通过"全球公域"将各国之间关联起来,它后来具体体现为一些"原则"和"概念",例如"人类共同关切事项"[80] "人类共

---

75 See TFEU, supra footnote 66, Art. 191 (formerly EC Treaty, Art. 174).

76 "Declaration on Principles of International Law concerning Friendly Relations and Cooperation among States in accordance with the Charter of the United Nations", Res. 2625 (XXV), 26 October 1970.

77 See L. Boisson de Chazournes and K. Sangbana, "Principle 19: Notification and consultation on activities with transboundary impact", in Viñuales, supra footnote 34, pp. 492-507; P. Okowa, "Principle 18: Notification and Assistance in Case of Emergency", in Viñuales, supra footnote 34, pp. 471-492; P. H. Sand, "Principle 27: Cooperation in a Spirit of Global Partnership", in Viñuales, supra footnote 34, pp. 617-632.

78 Rio Declaration, supra footnote 5, Principle 7.

79 Report-Principles, supra footnote 21, paras. 75-122.

80 UNFCCC, supra footnote 12, preamble, para. 1; CBD, supra footnote 7, preamble, para. 3.

同遗产"[81]、各国"共同但有区别的责任"[82]，或者更笼统一点，由各国的具体情况所导致的"有差别的待遇"[83]。根据这一报告，第二种义务包含了一些在跨界背景下开展合作的最低要求，它所依据的规范标准包括共享资源的合理及公平利用原则[84]、通知和协商义务（如果导致环境后果的某项活动可能会影响到相关国家）[85]、开展环境影响评价的义务[86]、事先知情同意原则[87]，以及避免重新安置对环境有害的活动。[88]

因此，涉及环境问题的合作义务在本质上似乎是一个实体性义务而非一个程序性义务，同时它还包含了基本"原则"和"概念"。事实上，我们最好将联合国可持续发展委员会专家组给出的风险预防的定义理解为是一个致力于推动国际环境法发展的努力。如此一来，它就无须精确反映出合作义务在一般国际法中的性质和内容。合作仍然是一种行为义务，它的

81　UNCLOS, supra footnote 6, Art. 136.

82　UNFCCC, supra footnote 12, Art. 3. 1.

83　Ibid., Arts. 3（2）, 4（4）-（6）and 4（9）; UNCLOS, supra footnote 25, preamble and Art. 207. 4; United Nations Convention to Combat Desertification in those Countries Experiencing Serious Drought and/or Desertification, Particularly in Africa, 17 June 1994, 33 ILM 1328（"UNCCD"）, preamble and Arts. 5-6.

84　Helsinki Rules on the Uses of the Waters of International Rivers, adopted by the International Law Association at its 52nd Conference, Helsinki, 20 August 1966, Art IV; "Charter of Economic Rights and Duties of States", Res. 3281（XXIX）, 12 December 1974, Art. 3; UN Convention on Watercourses, supra footnote 23, Art. 5.

85　Convention on Long-Range Transboundary Air Pollution, 13 November 1979, 1302 UNTS 217（"LRTAP Convention"）, Art. 5; UNCLOS, supra footnote 6, Arts. 198 and 206; Convention on the Transboundary Effects of Industrial Accidents, 17 March 1992, 2105 UNTS 457, Arts. 10 and 17; Convention on Early Notification of a Nuclear Accident, 26 September 1986, 1439 UNTS 275; Rio Declaration, supra footnote 5, Principles 18 and 19.

86　See Convention on Environmental Impact Assessment in a Transboundary Context, 25 February 1991, 1989 UNTS 310（"Espoo Convention"）.

87　Rotterdam Convention on the Prior Informed Consent Procedure for Certain Hazardous Chemicals and Pesticides in International Trade, 10 September 1998, 2244 UNTS 337（"Rotterdam Convention" or "PIC Convention"）.

88　Basel Convention on the Control of Transboundary Movements of Hazardous Wastes and their Disposal, 22 March 1989, 1673 UNTS 57（"Basel Convention"）, Arts. 4（5）-（6）; Bamako Convention, supra footnote 65, Art. 4; Rio Declaration, supra footnote 5, Principle 14.

具体表现依赖于一个采取善意行动的国家能够做些什么。[89] 因为这一义务具有相对模糊的特性，所以要将其讲清楚，也可以采取多种不同方法。

一般来讲，各国在必要时应当寻求某一国际组织的帮助，或者缔结一项条约来具体规定开展合作所应遵循的程序。[90] 如果上述安排还无法完全避免歧义，那么就可以用善意合作义务来明确某一条约义务的内容。在实践中，一个重要的结果就是：

> 各方为了预防对某一方的重大损害而开展合作，一旦合作的程序性机制按照正常程序进行，计划开展活动的国家就有义务不得批准此项活动，更不得实施此项活动。[91]

在某些案件中，义务的具体内容可以由某一国际司法机构来明确。在环境这一语境下，这种合作义务可以被解释成是必须进行信息交换[92]、对某项活动的环境影响开展合作评估[93]，或者咨询与之相关的某一环境条约的秘书处。[94] 最基本的要求是，在所有情况下，合作义务都要求通知那些

---

[89] See *Corfu Channel*, supra footnote 19, p. 22; *North Sea Continental Shelf Case*, Judgment, ICJ Reports 1969, p. 3 ("*North Sea ContinentalShelf*"), para. 85; *Nuclear Tests* (*Australia v. France*) (*New Zealand v. France*), Judgments, I. C. J. Reports 1974, p. 268, paras. 46 and 49; *Pulp Mills*, supra footnote 25, paras. 145–146; *MOX Plant*, supra footnote 72, para. 82; *Land Reclamation in and around the Straits of Johor* (*Malaysia v. Singapore*), ITLOS Case no. 12, Order (10 September 2003), para. 92; *Ghana/Côte d'Ivoire*, supra footnote 37, para. 73; *IUU Advisory Opinion*, supra footnote 37, para. 140.

[90] UN Convention on Watercourses supra footnote 23, Art. 8; ILC Prevention Articles, supra footnote 24, Art. 4; *Lake Lanoux Arbitration* (*Spain v. France*), Award (16 November 1957), RIAA XII, p. 281 ("*Lake Lanoux Arbitration*"), pp. 22–23; *North Sea Continental Shelf*, supra footnote 89, para. 85; *Southern Bluefin Tuna*, supra, footnote 71, para. 90 (e).

[91] *Pulp Mills*, supra footnote 25, para. 144.

[92] *MOX Plant*, supra footnote 72, para. 89 (a).

[93] See *Fisheries Jurisdiction Case* (*UK v. Iceland*), Decision on Jurisdiction, ICJ Reports 1974, p. 3 ("*Fisheries Jurisdiction*"), para. 72; *Pulp Mills*, supra footnote 25, para. 281; *MOX Plant*, supra footnote 72, para. 89 (b).

[94] *Certain Activities Carried Out by Nicaragua in the Border Area* (*Costa Rica v. Nicaragua*), Provisional Measures, Order of 8 March 2011, ICJ Reports 2011, p. 6 ("*Costa Rica v. Nicaragua*"), paras. 80 and 86 (2).

六 事先知情同意

在国际法中,事先知情同意这一要求包含两层含意。首先,它指的是如果土著人有可能受到某一措施的影响,就有义务咨询土著人的意见。事先知情同意这一要求的含义其实在"平衡"这一语境下讨论更加合适,因为它寻求的是保护特定群体的利益。要避免将事先知情同意当作两个分开的部分来对待。《国际劳工组织关于独立国家土著和部落民族的第169号公约》规定,各国政府在对土著人进行特别迁移或重新安置之前,有义务与他们进行协商并获取他们的事先知情同意。[96] 与此相类似,联合国大会第61/295号决议,即《联合国土著人权利宣言》第10条规定,"土著人不可被强迫迁离其土地。若无该土著人自主的事先知情同意,不得有任何重新安置之情事"。[97] 第一层含意的一个变量出现在生物多样性制度中。《生物多样性公约》第8条第10款规定,利用土著人的传统知识的前提条件是征得他们的"同意和参与"。[98] 这一规定后来在2010年10月的《获取和惠益分享名古屋议定书》和2016年制定的后续指南中得以进一步明确。[99]

其次,事先知情同意这一要求还意味着国家有义务不得出口特定的废物、物质或产品到其他国家,除非后者已经给出事先知情同意。[100] 这一要

---

95 *Certain Questions of Mutual Assistance in Criminal Matters*(*Djibouti v. France*), I. C. J. Reports 2008, p. 231, para. 150; *Costa Rica/Nicaragua*, supra footnote 16, para. 106; *South China Sea Arbitration*, supra footnote 14, paras. 946, 984-985.

96 Convention (No. 169) concerning Indigenous and Tribal Peoples in Independent Countries, 27 June 1989, 28 ILM 1382 (1989) ("ILO Convention 169"), Arts. 16 (2) and 6.

97 See "United Nations Declaration on the Rights of Indigenous Peoples", 2 October 2007, UN Doc. A/RES/61/295 ("UNDRIP"), Annex, Arts. 10 and 19.

98 CBD, supra footnote 7, Art. 8 (j).

99 Nagoya Protocol on Access to Genetic Resources and the Fair and Equitable Sharing of the Benefits arising from their Utilization to the Convention on Biological Diversity, 29 October 2010, available at: www.cbd. int (visited on 4 January 2013), Arts. 6 (2) and 7. See also Decision XIII/18 "Article 8 (j) and related provisions: Mo'otz Kuxtal voluntary guidelines", 17 December 2016, CBD/COP/DEC/XIII/18.

100 See M. Mbengue, "Principle 14: Dangerous Substances and Activities', in Viñuales, supra footnote 34, pp. 383-402.

求的目的是确保这类废物、物质或产品只会被发往那些愿意接收并有技术能力管理它们的国家。一般而言,有两种方法可以用于实施事先知情同意这一要求,第一种是一般事先知情同意程序(单个物质一事一报),第二种是特定事先知情同意程序(批量发货,即使是同一物质)。通过借鉴 1998 年《关于在国际贸易中对某些危险化学品和农药采用事先知情同意程序的鹿特丹公约》(*1998 Rotterdam Convention on the Prior Informed Consent Procedure*)〔又称《事先知情同意公约》(*PIC Convention*)〕,可以举例说明第一种方法。[101] 自 2006 年生效以来,这一公约已经建立了一套产品鉴定[102]和信息交换制度[103]。针对每个受到事先知情同意程序规制的产品(附录三名录),一个"决定的指导性文件"都会被制定并传达给缔约国,[104] 以便各个缔约国可以自主决定是否接受这一产品进入其领土。[105] 公约秘书处会将哪些缔约方愿意接受这一产品进口的信息传达给其他缔约国。[106] 出口国必须采取措施确保在其领土上的出口商遵守进口国的决定。[107]

上述这种方法与特定事先知情同意程序形成了鲜明对比,后者的典型案例来自《控制危险废物越境转移及其处置巴塞尔公约》(《巴塞尔公约》)第 6 条。[108] 这一条款建立了一项制度,出口国的职能机关必须(遵循特定要求)将其计划运输危险废物或其他废物的方案通知到进口国(和所有中转国)的对应机关,或者要求其私人经营者这样做。[109] 如果出口国获取了进口国的书面同意,它就可以许可进行废物的越境转移。[110] 与一般事先知情同意程序相比较,第 6 条第 6—8 款还规定了特定事先知情

---

101 PIC Convention, supra footnote 87. 这一国际法律文本的渊源来自世界粮农组织和联合国环境规划署分别管理的两个文件,即"Code of Conduct on the Distribution and Use of Pesticides"(1985 年制定,后来被修订)和"London Guidelines for the Exchange of Information on Chemicals that are the Subject of International Trade"(1987 年制定,后来被修订)。

102 PIC Convention, supra footnote 87, Arts. 5, 6 and 8.

103 PIC Convention, supra footnote 87, Art. 14.

104 PIC Convention, supra footnote 87, Art. 7.

105 PIC Convention, supra footnote 87, Art. 10.

106 PIC Convention, supra footnote 87, Art. 10 (10).

107 PIC Convention, supra footnote 87, Art. 11.

108 Basel Convention, supra footnote 88.

109 Basel Convention, Art. 6 (1).

110 Basel Convention, Art. 6 (2) — (3).

同意程序的一个便利版。在便利版程序下,拥有类似物理或化学特性的废物可以依据同一个许可来定期运输,而许可的最长时限是 12 个月。[111] 除了这些与一般事先知情同意程序相类似的地方,第 6 条第 6—8 款所规定的程序依然还是一个特定事先知情同意程序,因为它适用于一个特定的出口方而且是批量进行的。

在谈及事先知情同意要求在一般国际法中的地位时,无论是一般事先知情同意还是特定事先知情同意,要想把它当作一个国际习惯法规范似乎还是言之过早。但是,我们可以这样认为,这一要求的程序性特质并不会妨碍一般国际法将其认定为风险预防原则的一种表述,正如国际法院对待其他程序性原则的法律地位的态度,这些原则包括(以通知和协商的方式)合作和开展环境影响评价的义务,这也是后文将要探讨的。

七 环境影响评价

开展环境影响评价的义务的起源最早可以追溯到某些国家的国内法,特别是美国早在 1969 年制定的《国家环境政策法》。[112] 后来,许多其他国家的国内立法[113]和多个区域[114]及全球范围的条约[115]也规定了这一义务。《里约宣言》第 17 条原则也吸收了这一义务,它规定:

---

[111] Basel Convention, Art. 6 (6) — (8).

[112] National Environmental Policy Act, 42 USC ch. 55.

[113] See N. A. Robinson, "EIA Abroad: The Comparative and Transnational Experience", in S. G. Hildebrand and J. B. Cannon (eds.), *Environmental Analysis: The NEPA Experience* (Boca Raton: Lewis, 1993), pp. 679–702; N. Craik, *The International Law of Environmental Impact Assessment* (Cambridge University Press, 2008); N. Craik, "Principle 17: Environmental Impact Assessment", in Viñuales, supra footnote 34, pp. 451–470.

[114] According to Kiss and Beurier, the first international conventions to provide for this requirement was the Kuwait Regional Convention for Cooperation on the Protection of the Marine Environment from Pollution, 24 April 1978, Art. 11 (a), and the Apia Convention on the Conservation of Nature in the South Pacific, 12 June 1976, Art. 5 (4). They were followed by the Kuala Lumpur (ASEAN) Cooperation Plan on Transboundary Haze Pollution, 9 July 1985, Art. 14. See A. Kiss and J.-P. Beurier, *Droit international de l'environnement* (Paris: Pedone, 2004), para. 324.

[115] See UNCLOS, supra footnote 6, Art. 206; Protocol on Environmental Protection to the Antarctic Treaty, 4 October 1991, 30 ILM 1455 (1991) ("Madrid Protocol"), Art. 8 and Annex I; UN Convention on Watercourses, supra footnote 86, Art. 12.

应对可能会对环境产生重大不利影响的活动和要由一个有关国家机构作决定的活动作环境影响评价,作为一项国家制度。

为了理解开展环境影响评价这一义务的范围,需要解决三个问题。第一,这一义务的正式来源(条约、习惯、法律的一般原则);第二,这一要求的空间范围(国家的、跨界的、全球的);第三,这一义务的具体内容。

谈及第一个问题,有些条约规定了开展环境影响评价这一义务。一个主要的例证是1991年制定的《关于跨界情况下环境影响评价的埃斯波公约》(*Convention on Environmental Impact Assessment in a Transboundary Context*)[《埃斯波公约》(*Espoo Convention*)],它也构成了联合国欧洲经济委员会(United Nations Economic Commission for Europe,UNECE)的部分活动。[116] 根据这一公约,缔约国在批准那些有可能造成"重大不利跨界影响"的特定活动(由附录一列出)之前,必须在其国内法中规定环评义务。[117] 除了条约法以外,在"纸浆厂案"中,国际法院也承认,环评义务具有一个习惯法上的基础。法院认为,实践已经发展到:

> 近年来,环评义务得到各国的广泛承认,以至于它可以被当作一般国际法的一项要求,也就是说,当计划中的工业活动有可能造成重大不利跨界影响时(特别是涉及共享资源时),只要这一风险存在,就必须开展环评。[118]

法院的这一表述就直接把我们带到了前文提及的第二个问题,即这一要求的空间范围。《埃斯波公约》(以及其他公约)和法院在"纸浆厂案"中的表述似乎都将开展环评的义务局限于跨界背景下。这也就引发了一个问题,当计划中的活动完全是发生在一国国内,或者发生在国家管辖以外地区时,这一习惯法义务是否也能适用。《里约宣言》第17条原

---

[116] Espoo Convention, supra footnote 86.

[117] Espoo Convention, Art. 2 (3).

[118] *Pulp Mills*, supra footnote 25, para. 204. The Court confirmed this view in *Costa Rica/Nicaragua*, supra footnote 16, para. 104. Moreover, two other tribunals (ITLOS' Seabed Chamber and an Arbitral Tribunal) have followed this view: *Responsibilities in the Area*, supra footnote 45, para. 145; *South China Sea Arbitration*, supra footnote 14, paras. 947-948.

则（将环评看作一项国家制度）的表述或者《联合国海洋法公约》第206条（它的目的是预防"对海洋环境造成重大污染或重大和有害的变化"）的表述倾向于将环评这一习惯法义务的空间范围进行拓宽。有两个裁判为环评在跨界背景以外的运用提供了支持。国际海洋法法庭海床分庭在它的"关于区域责任的咨询意见"中指出，开展环评的义务同样适用于跨界背景以外地区：

> 国际法院在跨界背景下的论证也可以适用于那些对国家管辖以外地区的环境造成影响的活动，而且法院所提到的"共享资源"也同样适用于那些属于人类共同遗产的资源。[119]

这一观点得到了某些仲裁法庭的确认，[120] 它不仅将《联合国海洋法公约》第206条比作依据国际习惯法开展环评之要求，而且它对《联合国海洋法公约》第12部分的分析是基于这样一个认识，即"就与所有海域的海洋环境，包括国家管辖范围之内和以外的海域"而言，[121] 第12部分的条款适用于"所有国家"。

谈及环评的具体内容，它依赖于这一义务的来源。整体上看，源自条约的环评义务的内容可以被非常精确地确定，[122] 而根据国际法院的观点，源自习惯法规则的环评义务的内容则是由各国的国内法所确定的。[123] 但是，关于环评的范围和内容，各国并不拥有完全的自由裁量权。这种自由裁量权受到三种方式的限制。第一，国际习惯法确定了一些最低要求，包括环评必须在活动被批准启动之前开展，[124] 而且活动的影响必须受到监

119　*Responsibilities in the Area*, supra footnote 49, para. 148.
120　*South China Sea Arbitration*, supra n. footnote 14, paras. 947–948.
121　Ibid., para 940, referring also to the *IUU Advisory Opinion*, supra footnote 37, para. 120.
122　See, e.g., Appendices II and III of the Espoo Convention, supra footnote 86.
123　在"纸浆厂案"中，法院认为"应该由各国在其国内法或针对项目的批准过程中决定各个环境影响评价所需的具体内容"，supra footnote 25, para. 205。
124　在纸浆厂一案中，法院认为"应该由各国在其国内法或针对项目的批准过程中决定各个环境影响评价所需的具体内容"，para. 205；*Costa Rica/Nicaragua*, supra footnote 16, para. 161。

督。[125] 第二，环评属于预防和谨慎注意问题，因此环评的内容应当与预期活动的具体情况相对称。[126] 第三，国际法院可以评估那些由各国依据国际标准组织开展的环评的整体效果[127]并有权认定其不合格。[128] 这样一来也就引发了一个重要的问题，即环评是否必须包含与那些可能受影响人群的协商。在《埃斯波公约》的框架中，这个问题在第2条第6款和第3条第8款得到了肯定的答复，并将其当作一个标准来判断某项活动的环境影响的重要程度。[129] 国际金融公司在其项目资金活动所遵循的涉及环境的运行政策中明确规定了协商这一义务。[130] 而在条约和行政框架之外，这一问题就显得模糊不清了。国际法委员会的预防条款在第13条指出，有义务向公众提供信息。[131] "纸浆厂案"也涉及了这一问题，但是法院的结论仅仅是，根据阿根廷所引用的文件[132]，乌拉圭没有法律义务去与可能受影响的人群进行协商，何况实际上已经进行了一个协商。[133] 这一结论没有解决这一问题，因为法院回避了一个问题，即在一般国际法中是否存在一个与公众协商的义务（即便是最少内容的协商）。

第四节 国际环境法中的平衡

一 体现平衡观念的原则

这一部分谈及的原则的目的都是将保护环境的各种义务分配给不同的利益相关方，并在环保和其他考量之间寻求一个平衡。在这些原则中，第

---

[125] *Pulp Mills*, supra footnote 25, para. 205; *Costa Rica/Nicaragua*, supra footnote 16, para. 161.

[126] *Pulp Mills*, supra footnote 25, para. 205; *Costa Rica/Nicaragua*, supra footnote 16, para. 104.

[127] *Costa Rica/Nicaragua*, supra footnote 16, paras. 157–161.

[128] *South China Sea Arbitration*, supra footnote 14, paras. 988–990.

[129] Espoo Convention, supra footnote 86, Arts. 2 (6), 3 (8), and Appendix III, para. 1 (b) *in fine*.

[130] International Finance Corporation, Operational Policy 4.01 - Environmental Assessment, October 1998, paras. 12 and 13.

[131] ILC Prevention Articles, supra footnote 24, Art. 13.

[132] *Pulp Mills*, supra footnote 25, para. 216.

[133] *Pulp Mills*, supra footnote 25, para. 219.

一个以当前形式出现的就是所谓的"污染者付费"原则，它试图将污染的成本进行"内部化"，换言之就是确保这一污染的经济负担是由污染制造者来承担的。共同但有区别的责任原则的目的是将解决某个全球环境问题的成本在不同国家间分配，依据是各国的历史责任和各自能力。在个人层面，当人们参与某项有环境后果的活动或者受到该活动的影响时，公众参与原则所发挥的作用就是权衡不同群组和个人的利益。谈及"代际公平"，它的目标是将环保的责任在当代和后代之间进行分配。

（一）污染者付费原则

可以采用不同的方式来理解污染者付费原则。[134] 第一印象是，它看起来就是一个修复对他人造成的损害的义务，只不过是在环境这一语境下。但是，这样一个存在局限性的理解就剥夺了这一原则固有的自主内容，因为这一义务在国际习惯法中已经通过无害原则和预防原则得以很好地体现。

通过进一步深究，我们会发现污染者付费原则确实拥有一个足够闪亮的内容。想要精确把握这一内容，就必须考量在环保问题出现之前工业活动的运行方式。首先我们要提及的是"外部性"（externalities）理论，即一个交易（或者更笼统地说，一个经济活动）对那些没有参与该活动的第三方造成的影响。[135] 当这一影响是负面的而且没有得到补偿时，我们就可以将其称为"负外部性"。例如，某一公司的正常经营或者意外事故造成了河流的污染，就会给整个社会带来成本。重要的是，这一活动所带来的利益是由个人所占有的，而成本则是由全社会来承担。这就带来一个问题，谁应当支付成本：公司（也就是获取利益的主体），消费者（既享受了消费其选择的产品所带来的利益，作为社会的一部分也承担了这一活动的成本），或者是全社会的所有成员（仅仅是承担责任而没有从活动中获取单独利益）？如果什么都不做，那么全社会或者那些最相关的个体（即社会的一个部门）将会承担这一成本。同理，如果国家机关介入处理污水，那么成本也是由全社会来承担的（因为它是由纳税人承担的）。但

---

[134] On this principle, see P. Schwartz, "Principle 16: The Polluter–pays Principle", in Viñuales, supra footnote 34, pp. 429-450.

[135] See A. C. Pigou, *The Economics of Welfare* (London: Mcmillan, 1920) (who suggested a tax to correct this market failure and increase welfare) and R. Coase, "The Problem of Social Cost" (1960) 3 *Journal of Law and Economics* 1 (who suggested trading as better policy response).

是，如果成本是由造成污染的公司来承担，或者转移给消费者（是他们导致了相关产品的需求）来承担，我们就可以说成本实现了"内部化"。这一观点的最早表述来自经济合作与发展组织理事会在1972年的一项建议。[136] 根据这一文件，"政府机关采取污染防治措施而产生的费用应当在那些在生产和消费过程中造成污染的商品和服务的成本中体现出来"。[137] 现在，《里约宣言》第16条原则正式收录了污染者付费原则，它规定：

> 国家当局考虑到造成污染者在原则上应承担污染的费用并适当考虑公共利益而不打乱国际贸易和投资的方针，应努力倡导环境费用内在化和使用经济手段。

环境成本的内部化也是（国内和国际）环境政策迈向市场机制这一整体趋势的一个潜在主张。遗憾的是，我们经常会忽略一个重要方面，那就是内部化只有在两个严格的条件下才能适用于外部性：第一，造成外部性的活动是社会所期望的；第二，负外部性仍然处于可容忍的环境损害（小于重大损害）这一范围之内。事实上，如果超出了"重大损害"这一临界值，那就不再是一个成本的内部化（市场机制）问题了，而是一个预防问题，它就包含了各种规制手段，包括暂停活动甚至取消活动（通过逐步停止和逐步减少的方式）。[138] 只有承认临界值造成的这一区别，并将其当作一个政策指南来高效利用，我们才能认可任何成本（包括人的生命和不可逆转的损害）都可以被内部化，换言之，为了治理污染付出任何代价都是值得的。

即使我们是在适当范围之内运用污染者付费原则，但是想要界定内部化的具体形式还是会有难度，因为有几个参数还需要明确，包括社会成本本身、概率（当发生事故时，或者某项活动的后果尚不确定）、各个污染

---

[136] OECD Council Recommendation on Guiding Principles concerning the International Economic Aspects of Environmental Policies, C (72) 128 (1972), 14 ILM 236 (1975).

[137] Ibid., Annex, para. A. 4.

[138] See Chapters 5 and 7 of this book. On the proper province of cost internalisation and prevention see J. E. Viñuales, "La distribution de la charge de protéger l'environnement: Expressions juridiques de la solidarité", in A. Supiot (ed.), *La responsabilité solidaire* (Paris: Conférences du Collège de France, 2017).

者份额的确定（当一个负外部性是由多个公司的活动造成时）、补偿的方式（事前或者事后），以及其他许多因素。在某些有关石油污染损害民事责任的公约的文本中，成本的内部化是通过如下一套制度来确定的：（1）商业经营者的严格责任制度；（2）投保足够保险的义务；（3）基于产业贡献的额外赔偿方式。[139] 在此背景下，石油运输就会被认为是一项有益的活动，但是，它还是造成了负外部性，必须通过预防和响应调节[140]来将其减少到可容忍的层次，在发生事故的情况下，就必须完全补偿。

污染者付费原则也出现于其他一些管理文件中。例如涉及河流保护的某些条约就吸收了污染者付费原则并将其当作指导性原则。[141] 另外，除了《里约宣言》之外，许多软法文件也提到了这一原则。[142] 这些文件在本质上是促进个人和企业层面的成本内部化。因此，要想将污染者付费原则用于国家导致的社会成本（即国际社会所承担的成本）的分担是非常困难的。在这方面，无害原则、预防原则或者后文谈及的"共同但有区别的责任原则"似乎更加适用。

（二）共同但有区别的责任原则

共同但有区别的责任原则的目的是：基于两个关键标准，即历史上（和当前的）责任以及各自能力（财政能力和技术能力），在各国间分配责任以便管理某一个全球性环境问题，例如臭氧层的保护[143]、应对气候变化[144]或者生物多样性的保护和利用[145]。

这一原则处于经济发展和环境保护两者间的交叉点，它的目标是调解那些可能相互冲突的要求。一方面，发展中国家将其当作承认它们的发展需求、薄弱的环境问题管理能力以及它们并非这些环境问题的主要成因的

---

[139] See infra Chapter 8.

[140] See infra Chapter 4 (specifically the discussion of MARPOL, the Intervention Convention, and the OPRC Convention).

[141] Helsinki Convention, supra footnote 65, Art. 2 (5) (b); OSPAR Convention, supra footnote 65, Art. 2 (2) (b); Danube Convention, supra footnote 65, Art. 2 (4).

[142] See e. g. "ILA New Delhi Declaration of Principles of International Law Relating to Sustainable Development", 6 April 2002 ("New Delhi Declaration"), para. 3. 1.

[143] CPOL, supra footnote 59, Art. 2 (2).

[144] UNFCCC, supra footnote 12, Art. 3 (1).

[145] CBD, supra footnote 7, Art. 20 (4).

一种方式；另一方面，发达国家将其当作一个工具，以便确保发展中国家参与到全球环境问题的管理中，并确保发展进程与特定环保要求保持同步。

这样的一些考量给《里约宣言》第7条原则提供了基础，它规定：

> 各国应本着全球伙伴关系的精神进行合作，以维持、保护和恢复地球生态系统的健康和完整。鉴于造成全球环境退化的原因不尽相同，因此各国肩负着不同程度的共同责任。发达国家承认，鉴于其社会对全球环境造成的压力和它们掌握的技术和资金，它们在国际寻求可持续发展的进程中应当承担相应的责任。

这一表述展现了共同但有区别的责任原则的两个维度，第一个是"共同的"，即有义务基于全球伙伴关系的精神来开展合作以保护环境；第二个是"有区别的"，即发达国家承认它们对环境退化负有主要责任，而且它们在应对环境退化的后果上拥有更强的能力。共同但有区别的责任原则这两个维度的起源可以在两个更早的观念中一窥端倪，一个是共同利益这一观念，涉及的是某些特定地区例如南极[146]、外空[147]或者海床；[148] 另一个则是差别待遇的观念，体现于国际贸易法[149]或海洋法中。[150]

即便共同但有区别的责任原则与这两个早期确立的观念非常相似，它还是应被当作一个新的概念；它最早体现于臭氧层制度中，后来在1992年通过的《里约宣言》《联合国气候变化框架公约》和《生物多样性公

146　The Antarctic Treaty, 1 December 1959, 402 UNTS 71, preamble, para. 2.

147　Treaty on Principles Governing the Activities of States in the Exploration and Use of Outer Space, including the Moon and Other Celestial Bodies, 27 January 1967, 610 UNTS 205 ("Outer Space Treaty"), Art. 1.

148　"Declaration of Principles Governing the Seabed and the Ocean Floor, and the Subsoil Thereof, Beyond the Limits of National Jurisdiction", Res. 2749 (XXV), 17 December 1970 ("Seabed Declaration"), preamble, para. 4, Arts. 1-3; UNCLOS, supra footnote 6, Art. 136.

149　See R. Prebisch, "Towards a New Trade Policy for Development", Report of the Secretary General to UNCTAD I, in Proceedings of the United Nations Conference on Trade and Development, UN Doc. E/CONF. 46/141, Vol. II, 1965, p. 1; "Declaration on the Establishment of a New International Economic Order", Res. 3201 (S-VI), 1 May 1974, para. 4 (n) - (p).

150　See e.g. UNCLOS, supra footnote 6, Arts. 69, 254.

约》中对这一原则都有进一步的体现。这样三个规范文本（臭氧层、气候变化和生物多样性）也可以被当作具体运用这一原则的四种方法。第一种方法是有关臭氧层的制度，1985年《维也纳公约》的前言提到了"发展中国家的情况和特殊需要"。[151] 公约的正文文本也包含了这一内容，各缔约方应当据此"在其能力范围内"[152] 来履行他们的义务，并履行合作义务，包括进行技术转让。[153] 公约的《蒙特利尔议定书》更进了一步，它在第5条为发展中国家规定了有区别的义务。[154] 在特定情况下，给予发展中国家更长的时间来完成议定书规定的义务，同时还包括其他一些优待（特别是援助和某种义务的豁免）。落实共同但有区别的责任原则的第二种方法是《联合国气候变化框架公约》及其《京都议定书》。事实上，《联合国气候变化框架公约》第3条第1款明确规定了这一原则：

> 各缔约方应当在公平的基础上，并根据它们共同但有区别的责任和各自的能力，为人类当代和后代的利益保护气候系统。因此，发达国家缔约方应当率先对付气候变化及其不利影响。

《联合国气候变化框架公约》所规定的发达国家（即附件一国家）的主要责任已经通过《京都议定书》得以实施，《京都议定书》要求这些发达国家达到附件二规定的量化的减排目标，[155] 对于发展中国家（即《联合国气候变化框架公约》附件一以外的国家）则没有要求新的义务。[156] 《巴黎协定》[157] 从根本上改变了这一方法。两种主要方法被用来落实共同但有区别的责任原则。给予发展中国家援助（财政、技术和能力建设）以换取它们为控制排放贡献自己的力量。但是，这种贡献的大小完全是由各国确定

---

[151] CPOL, supra footnote 59, preamble, para. 3.

[152] CPOL, supra footnote 59, Art. 2 (2).

[153] CPOL, supra footnote 59, Art. 4 (2).

[154] Montreal Protocol, supra footnote 60, Art. 5 (1).

[155] Kyoto Protocol to the United Nations Framework Convention on Climate Change, Kyoto, 11 December 1997, 2303 UNTS 148 ("Kyoto Protocol"), Art. 3 (1).

[156] Kyoto Protocol to the United Nations Framework Convention on Climate Change, Kyoto, 11 December 1997, 2303 UNTS 148 ("Kyoto Protocol"), Art. 10.

[157] Paris Agreement, supra footnote 12. See further Chapter 5.

的，各国可以自由确定各自的减排目标，只需要定期更新（至少五年更新一次）并且不断进步（或者更高目标）则可。如此一来，与《京都议定书》自上而下的方式不同，《巴黎协定》采用的是一种自下而上的方式来落实共同但有区别的责任原则。因此，《巴黎协定》可以被当作运用共同但有区别的责任原则的第三种方法。运用共同但有区别的责任原则的第四种方法可能是来自《生物多样性公约》，它为发展中国家履行其保护义务规定了前提条件，即发达国家应当事先履行其承担的财政和技术转让义务。[158]

即使这一原则在这些及其他条约文本中可以找到依据，它的法律地位仍然存在着争议。[159] 但是，目前看来，这种不确定性并不会导致任何严重的问题，因为这一原则已经被用于发挥两个主要作用，即影响某些特定协定的内容并帮助解释它们的条款，因此，阐明这一原则在一般国际法中的地位也就显得不那么紧迫了。

(三) 公众参与原则

前文分析的原则涉及的是国家之间的关系，而公众参与原则或者采用更精确的说法，国家为那些有可能受到项目、活动或环境政策影响的团体和个人提供各种渠道的参与方式，目的是将这些利益相关者间的利益也考虑在内，包括它们自身之间的关系（例如企业和受影响的个人之间）或者私人利益相关者和国家之间的关系。[160] 与合作原则相类似，公众参与原则的范围是宽泛的，超出了环境问题的范畴。通过举例说明，1966年《公民权利和政治权利国际公约》第25条规定了参与公共事务的一般权利。[161] 但是，这一原则在过去25年变得突出和重要还应得益于环境问题提供的广阔舞台。公众参与有些方面的问题已经在探讨土著人的事先知情同意原则时有所论及，读者可以参考那一部分。在此，我们主要关注两个重点，即这一原则的来源和内容。

---

[158] CBD, supra footnote 7, Art. 20 (4).

[159] See P. Cullet, "Principle 7: Common but Differentiated Responsibilities", in Viñuales, supra footnote 34, pp. 229-244; L. Rajamani, *Differential Treatment in International Environmental Law* (Oxford University Press, 2006).

[160] On this principle, see J. Ebbesson, "Principle 10: Public Participation", in Viñuales, supra footnote 34, pp. 287-309.

[161] International Covenant on Civil and Political Rights, 16 December 1966, 999 UNTS 171.

谈及来源问题，《里约宣言》第 10 条原则确认，在环境问题中公众参与的理念更应得到增强，它规定：

> 环境问题最好在所有公民在有关一级的参加下加以处理。在国家一级，每个人应有适当的途径获得有关公共机构掌握的环境问题的信息，其中包括关于他们的社区内有害物质和活动的信息，而且每个人应有机会参加决策过程。各国应广泛地提供信息，从而促进和鼓励公众的了解和参与。应提供采用司法和行政程序的有效途径，其中包括赔偿和补救措施。

这一表述表明，公众参与的重要性不仅体现于它是一个分配手段（权衡各种相关的利益），同时，它通过对环境问题的决策过程进行民主控制，在一定程度上充当了一个预防手段。其他一些文件，特别是一些条约，[162] 共同为公众参与原则在实证国际法中的地位提供了一个更坚实的基础，虽然它的习惯法特质还是引发了争议。特别是联合国欧洲经济委员会支持制定的《奥胡斯公约》[163] 为公众参与环境事项提供了一个强有力的推动。所有国家都可以申请加入这一公约，我们可以从三个层面来分析这一公约的影响：第一，各国有义务为公众参与环境事项采取内部措施；第二，建立了一个不遵约程序并向公众开放，并被公众广泛运用；第三，欧洲人权法院的案例法中接受了《奥胡斯公约》，它在解释相关人权问题时引用了这一公约。在联合国拉丁美洲和加勒比经济委员会（UN Economic Commission for Latin America and the Caribbean，ECLAC）的支持下，一个旨在制定一个类似条约的谈判进程已经开始。这一进程是在 2012 年里约峰会时通过发布《关于将〈里约宣言〉第 10 条原则用于环境和发展的宣言》来启动的。[164] 这一进程得到了广泛的参与，包含了各种不同的利益相

---

[162] See P. Cullet and A. Gowlland-Gualtieri, "Local Communities and Water Investments", in E. Brown Weiss, L. Boisson de Chazournes and N. Bernasconi-Osterwalder (eds.), *Fresh Water and International Economic Law* (Oxford University Press, 2005), pp. 303–330.

[163] Aarhus Convention on Access to Information, Public Participation in Decision-making and Access to Justice in Environmental Matters, 25 June 1998, 2161 UNTS 447 ("Aarhus Convention").

[164] "Declaration on the application of Principle 10 of the Rio Declaration on Environment and Development", 25 July 2012, UN Doc. A/CONF. 216/13.

关者，它所达成的一个公约草案在撰写的时候就接近于定稿。[165] 另外，在2010年，联合国环境规划署理事会（Governing Council of UNEP）制定了一个有关环境问题中的公众参与的软法文件，即《就在环境事项中获取信息、公众参与决策和诉诸司法方面制定国家立法的指南》，[166] 通常被称为《巴厘指南》（Bali Guidelines），它的目的是在世界其他国家和地区促进类似实践的开展。

谈及公众参与的内容，《里约宣言》第10条原则规定了所谓"环境民主"的三个主要组成部分，即获取环境信息的权利，在环境事项上参与决策过程的权利，以及诉诸司法的权利。前文已经提到，这些权利后来分别在《奥胡斯公约》中得以制定，其中第4—5条是关于信息获取，第6—8条是关于决策，第9条是关于诉诸司法。公约的遵约委员会还广泛论述了公约后续条款（例如诉诸司法的费用）中某些方面的内容，这是基于它们在实践中的重要意义。

公约与其他条约的交叉为这一"三件套"被用于解释相关条款［例如《欧洲人权公约》（European Convention on Human Rights）第8条］铺平了道路，它不仅适用于身为《奥胡斯公约》缔约方的当事国（罗马尼亚），也适用于身为《奥胡斯公约》非缔约方的当事国（土耳其）。[167] 虽然后面这一点似乎可以说明公众参与原则有可能具备了一个成为习惯法的基础，但是，在"纸浆厂案"中，国际法院似乎抵制了这一观点，虽然

---

[165] Preliminary Document on the Regional Agreement on Access to Information, Participation and Justice in Environmental Matters in Latin America and the Caribbean, available at http//repositorio. cepal. org（visited on 17 April 2017）.

[166] Decision SS. XI/5, Part A "Guidelines on Developing National Legislation on Access to Information, Public Participation in Decision-Making and Access to Justice in Environmental Matters", 26 February 2010, Doc GCSS. XI/11. On these guidelines and their impact see U. Etemire, "Insights on the UNEP Bali Guidelines and the Development of Environmental Democratic Rights"（2016）23 *Journal of Environmental Law* 393. See also the implementation guide relating to these guidelines: UNEP, *Putting Rio Principle 10 into Action: An Implementation Guide for the UNEP Bali Guidelines for the Development of National Legislation on Access to Information, Public Participation and Access to Justice in Environmental Matters*（October 2015）.

[167] *Taskın and Others* v. *Turkey*, ECtHR Application no. 46117/99, Decision（10 November 2004）, paras. 99-100; *Tatar* v. *Romania*, ECtHR Application no. 67021/01, Decision（27 January 2009）, para. 69.

它采用的是模糊不清的术语。事实上，法院在分析了阿根廷所引用的一些法律文书（不包括《奥胡斯公约》）后指出，这些文件并不能证明征求受影响人群的意见是一项法律义务。但是，从它的表述来看，法院的结论并没有明确肯定或否定公众参与这一习惯法原则的存在。这一问题仍然是开放的。无论如何，即使是在《奥胡斯公约》这么激进的文件中，有关公众参与的规定也没有发展到给予受影响人群否决计划中活动的权利。[168]

（四）代际公平原则

代际公平原则的目的是将自然资源的质量和可用性及其所需的保护义务在当代和后代之间进行分配。如此一来，这一原则就可以被看作自然保护这一古老理念和最近的可持续发展概念的表现形式。

在一些新旧文件中我们都可以发现这些起源的踪迹。例如，1946 年《捕鲸管理国际公约》的前言就提到了那些为了后代而保卫重大自然资源（例如鲸种群）的国家的利益。[169] 与此相类似，当 1972 年斯德哥尔摩大会凭借其通过的《斯德哥尔摩宣言》来界定环境保护的范畴时，它指出：

> 人类……负有为当代人类及其子孙后代保护和改善环境的庄严义务。[170]

后来，当《布伦特兰委员会报告》在 1987 年提出可持续发展这一概念时，焦点就变为满足当前需要而又不损害子孙后代满足其需要之能力。[171] 现代的代际公平原则在《里约宣言》第 3 条原则中的表述正是基于这一认识，它指出：

> 必须履行发展的权利，以便公正合理地满足当代和世世代代的发

---

168 See Aarhus Convention, supra footnote 163, Arts. 6 (8), 7, and 8 *in fine*; Aarhus Convention: An Implementation Guide, pp. 109–110 (available at: www.unece.org).

169 International Convention for the Regulation of Whaling with Schedule of Whaling Regulations, 2 December 1946, 161 UNTS 361, preamble, para. 1.

170 Declaration on the United Nations Conference on the Human Environment, 16 June 1972, 11 ILM 1416 (1972) ("Stockholm Declaration"), Principle 1.

171 Report of the World Commission on Environment and Development: Our Common Future, UN Doc. A/42/427, Annex, 4 August 1987, para. 1.

展与环境需要。

事实上,第 3 条原则提及后代的目的是强调发展权并不是无边界的。[172]

这一原则在国际和国内法院的判例法中都得到了一定的认可。国际法院在"威胁使用或使用核武器的合法性的咨询意见"中指出,在判定核武器的合法性时,代际公平是一个必须考量的因素。[173] 国际法院在"盖巴斯科夫—拉基玛洛工程案"中进一步指出:

> 因为新的科学认知,人类也逐步认识到对自然毫无顾虑和无休止的干预和索取对人类(当代和后代)所造成的风险,所以我们制定了新的规范和标准。[174]

但是,尽管在条约、判例法和评注中为了明确这一原则的轮廓都做出了重大的努力,[175] 但是这一原则在实证法中的基础仍然受到争议。在某些人权案件中,在解释相关条款时会参考代际公平这一因素。[176] 在国内法中,这一原则被当作一个参数来评估是否应当核发某项开发许可。[177] 重要的是,这一原则已经成为当前为后代发声的各种努力的一部分。有关这一问题,菲律宾最高法院 20 世纪 90 年代初期在"欧博萨等未成年人案"

---

[172] 这也是早些年流行的观点,参见 the *E. H. P. v Canada*, HRC Complaint no 67/1980 (27 October 1982), para. 8 (a),提及后代仅仅被当成为了表现出一种关切。

[173] *Legality of Nuclear Weapons*, supra footnote 13, para. 36.

[174] *Gabčíkovo-Nagymaros Project*, supra footnote 11, para. 140.

[175] See E. Brown Weiss, *In Fairness to Future Generations: International Law, Common Patrimony, and Intergenerational Equity* (Dobbs Ferry: Transnational Publishers, 1989); C. Molinari, "Principle 3: From a Right to Development to Intergenerational Equity", in Viñuales, supra footnote 34, pp. 139-156.

[176] See e. g. *Mayagna (Sumo) Awas Tingni Community v. Nicaragua*, ICtHR Series C No. 79, Judgment (31 August 2001), para. 149 (as discussed in Chapter 10, this is a leading case that prompted an entire jurisprudential line as regards the protection of the rights of indigenous and tribal peoples).

[177] See *State of Himachal Pradesh and others v. Ganesh Wood Products and others*, 1995 (6) SCC 363, cited in R. Ramlogan, *Sustainable Development: Towards a Judicial Interpretation* (Leiden: Martinus Nijhoff 2011), p. 226.

中迈出了有意义的一步。在此案中,一群菲律宾儿童代表他们以及后代的利益发起了这一诉讼,而代际公平原则为这一集体诉讼提供了诉讼资格的基础。[178] 更新的进展是,2011 年里约峰会鼓励联合国大会起草一份报告,探讨用何种方式将后代的代表用制度加以落实。[179] 虽然这些新制度的巩固工作比想象中更困难,甚至有些制度已经被推迟或减少,但是,在国内层面,就这一问题还是开展了大量工作。[180]

二 表述平衡观念的概念

(一) 概述

自其现代起源以来,国际环境法就不断通过各种概念或内涵来给自身定型,它们的作用并不是充当初级规范,而是为了指导这些规范(以及特定环境制度的总体框架)的制定。在这一领域,术语会经常发生变化,这就导致很难确定最相关的概念或者明确它们之间的关系。因此,当某一环境制度用到这些概念时,就有必要去了解其内涵。一般来说,设计这些概念的目的是分配环境利用所导致的利益和责任,也许是在某国的增长/发展政策这一背景下,或者更具体一点,在各国共享某一共有资源时。

在这一部分,我们将要讨论四个概念,选择它们的原因是基于它们想要表达的内涵。第一个概念"可持续发展"的目的是采用多种方式来整合增长和发展(经济和社会)的需要与环境保护的要求。然后,我们会

---

[178] See *Juan Antonio Oposa and others. v. Fulgencio S. Factoran, Jr., and others*, Supreme Court of the Philippines, Decision (30 June 1993), para. 22.

[179] See UN Secretary-General, *Intergenerational Solidarity and the Needs of Future Generations. Report of the Secretary-General*, 15 August 2013, UN Doc A/68/322.

[180] For a discussion of the experience in some countries see S. Shoham, N. Lamay, "Commission for future generations in the Knesset: Lessons learnt", in J. C. Tremmel (ed.), *Handbook of Intergenerational Justice* (Cheltenham: Edward Elgar, 2006), pp. 244 – 281; E. T. Ambrusné, "The Parliamentary Commissioner for Future Generations of Hungary and his impact" (2010) 10/1 *Intergenerational Justice Review* 18; M. Nesbit, A. Illés, *Establishing an EU "Guardian for Future Generations", Report and recommendations for the World Future Council* (London: Institute for European Environmental Policy, 2015); H. Davies, "The Well-being of Future Generations (Wales) Act 2015-A Step Change in the Legal Protection of the Interests of Future Generations?" (2017) 29 *Journal of Environmental Law* 165.

探讨其他三个概念，虽然它们的术语十分相似，但是表达的是单独的内涵。[181] 即"公地"的概念（其内涵是在承担特定义务的前提下，自由获取或禁止使用某一资源），"人类共同遗产"的概念（其内涵是合作管理某个处于国家控制以外区域的资源）以及"人类共同关切事项"的概念（其内涵是各国合作管理某个资源，这一资源的共同特质与其地理位置并无关联）。[182]

（二）可持续发展

没有任何一个国际环境法的概念能比可持续发展出现得更频繁。它最早是于1980年在一份由联合国环境规划署、世界自然基金会和世界自然保护联盟发布的联合报告中被提出。[183] 1987年布伦特兰委员会的报告《我们共同的未来》的发表，标志着可持续发展这一概念被正式承认。后来，它又出现在各种形式的文本中，特别是在1992年里约大会之后更是如此。但是，针对当前的目的，这一原则的政治意义不及它的法律意义。基于这一原因，我们在此聚焦于它的法律基础以及它在国际环境法中的作用。[184] 换言之，我们将通过与《21世纪议程》（*Agenda21*）或《2030年可持续发展议程》（*2030 Agenda for Sustainable Develeopment*）针对可持续发展所制订的行动方案进行对比，来分析可持续发展原则所传达出的法律方案的类型。

《里约宣言》第4条原则明确表述了这一概念的核心要素，它规定"为了实现可持续发展，环境保护应成为发展进程中的一个组成部分，不能同发展进程孤立开看待"。这一定义后来在十年后的约翰内斯堡可持续发展峰会上得到了进一步的明确。在这次峰会上通过了一份政治宣言，它

---

[181] On the theoretical foundations of these programmes, see P. ‑ M. Dupuy, *Droit international public* (Paris: Dalloz, 2008), pp. 775‑777.

[182] See J. Brunnée, "Common Areas, Common Heritage, and Common Concern", in Bodansky et al., supra footnote 1, pp. 552‑573.

[183] IUCN, UNEP, WWF, *World Conservation Strategy. Living Resource Conservation for Sustainable Development* (1980).

[184] See N. Schrijver, "The Evolution of Sustainable Development in International Law", (2007) 328 *Recueil des cours de l'Académie de droit international de La Haye*, 217‑412; V. Barral and P. ‑ M. Dupuy, "Principle 4: Sustainable Development through Integration", in Viñuales, supra footnote 34, pp. 157‑179.

使用的术语对明确可持续发展这一概念的要素发挥了重要的作用。根据这一文件的第 5 段,"经济发展、社会发展和环境保护"构成了"相互依存、相互增强的可持续发展支柱"。[185] 在此之前不久,国际法协会(International Law Association, ILA)已经制定了《关于可持续发展国际法原则的新德里宣言》(*New Delhi Declaration on the Principles of International Law Related to Sustainable Development*),在其前言中,它将可持续发展这一概念所传达的内涵表述为:

> 一种经济、社会和政治发展的综合性、整体性方法,其是为了地球自然资源的可持续利用,保护自然和人类生命以及社会和经济发展所依赖的环境,也是为了实现所有人类享有一个适当生活标准的权利,这是基于他们能够积极、自由、有意义地参与到发展进程及其成果的合理分配之中,同时也要照顾到后代的需要和利益。[186]

这一表述包含了法律评论员看重的可持续发展概念的主要要素,包括:(1)必须考虑到后代人的需要;(2)各国有义务用可持续的方式来开发其自然资源;(3)在开发资源时,各国有义务考虑到别国的利益;(4)各国有义务将环境保护融入它们的发展政策中。[187] 我们在分析代际公平原则、无害原则和预防原则时已经研究了前面三个要素。但是,为了理解可持续发展原则所传达的内涵,首先,就有必要更进一步,因为我们还没有开发这一内涵的某些方面(包括将环境考量融入整体发展政策之中);其次,法律实践为了表现可持续发展的内涵,也经常会涉及其他原则,这也值得我们关注。

关于整体性问题,其实在斯德哥尔摩大会期间就已经被强调了。《斯德哥尔摩宣言》第 13 条原则指出:

185　Report of the World Summit on Sustainable Development, 4 September 2002, A/CONF. 199/20, Chapter I, item 1 Political Declaration, para. 5.

186　New Delhi Declaration, supra footnote 142, preamble(italics added).

187　See P. Sands, *Principles of International Environmental Law*(Cambridge University Press, 2003), p. 253. See more generally Schrijver, supra n footnote 184, pp. 339-365.

> 为了达到更合理地管理各种资源并由此而改善环境的目的，各国应对它们的环境规划采取统一的和协调的做法，以保证为了本国人民的利益而使各种发展与保护和改善人类环境的需要相协调。[188]

《里约宣言》在第 4 条原则回应了这一观点，虽然它采用了更笼统的术语。但是，整体性问题还是引发了一个重要的实际问题：如何在争端解决中运用整体性原则？在"盖巴斯科夫—拉基玛洛工程案"中，国际法院提到了可持续发展这一概念的适用问题，但是并没有将其定性为一个主要的规范或者原则。法院指出："这种协调经济发展和环境保护的需要已经在可持续发展这一概念中得以适当表述。"[189] 但是，法院的副院长威拉曼特雷（Weeramantry）法官对这一结论提出了挑战，他的单独观点认为：

> 法院在其判决的第 140 段将可持续发展当作一个概念提出。但是，我认为它不仅是一个概念，而应是一个具有规范价值的原则，这对本案的判决也至关重要。[190]

2005 年 5 月的"比利时诉荷兰莱茵铁路仲裁案"（Iron Rhine Arbitration）的仲裁庭肯定了 Weeramantry 法官的立场，它指出：

> 当发展有可能对环境造成重大危害时，就有义务来预防（至少是减缓）这一危害。仲裁庭认为，这一义务已经成为一般国际法的一条基本原则。这一原则不仅适用于自治活动，也适用于那些为了实施各国间的特定条约而采取的活动。[191]

然而，国际法院在"纸浆厂案"中的判决还是再次肯定了"盖巴斯

---

[188] Stockholm Declaration, supra footnote 170, Principle 13.

[189] *Gabčíkovo-Nagymaros Project*, supra footnote 11, para. 140 (emphasis added).

[190] *Gabčíkovo-Nagymaros Project*, Separate Opinion of Judge Weeramantry, p. 85.

[191] Iron Rhine Arbitration ("Ijzeren Rijn") (Belgium/Netherlands), Award (24 May 2005), RIAA XXVII, pp. 35–125, para. 59.

科夫—拉基玛洛工程案"中多数人针对可持续发展的定义,将可持续发展看作一个用于指导各方间的协商的概念或者目标。[192] 也许观点冲突的来源在于可持续发展概念与那些有关发展的可持续维度(尤其是预防)的法律表述之间产生了交叉重叠。"印度河 kishenganga 水电工程案"就显示出这一点,法庭不正确地将可持续发展这一"原则"获得认可的原因归结于国际法院的多数意见(其实国际法院用的术语是可持续发展这一"概念"),但是它随后又明确表示,通过借鉴莱茵铁路仲裁案,国际环境法的原则(特别是预防原则以及开展环评的要求)应适用于各方之间的关系,也可用于解释《印度河水条约》(*Indus Water Treaty*)。[193] 如此一来,从法律的视角来看,可持续发展是一个原则还是一个概念就变得毫无实际意义了,无论如何,当把可持续发展当作一个原则来运用时,也就意味着运用了国际环境法其他具有坚实习惯法基础的原则,例如预防原则及其被承认的程序性表现方式(合作及环境影响评价)。

这样就引发了第二个更基础的问题,即运用其他原则来传达可持续发展的内涵。事实上,诸如《新德里宣言》、可持续发展委员会的专家组报告[194],或者欧洲委员会 2000 年起草的报告[195]等文件,都表明其他一些原则确实发挥了作用。这些报告提到的原则涵盖了贫困消除[196]、风险预防[197]、善治[198]、自然的伦理价值[199]、受打扰的生态系统的强制恢复[200]、小型和脆弱

---

[192] *Pulp Mills*, supra footnote 25, paras. 75–77 and 177.

[193] *Indus Water Kishenganga-Partial Award*, supra footnote 45, paras. 448–452.

[194] Report-Principles, supra footnote 21.

[195] European Commission, *The Law of Sustainable Development. General Principles*, 2000 ("*EC-General Principles*").

[196] "The Principle of Equity and the Eradication of Poverty", New Delhi Declaration, supra footnote 142, Principle 2.

[197] "The Principle of the Precautionary Approach to Human Health, Natural Resources and Ecosystems", Ibid., Principle 4.

[198] "Principle of Good Governance", Ibid., Principle 6.

[199] "Principle of the Aesthetic Value of Nature", *EC-General Principles*, supra footnote 195, p. 121.

[200] "Principle of the Obligatory Restoration of Disturbed Ecosystems", Ibid., p. 91.

生态系统的发展[201]、开展合作预防有害活动和物质的重新安置[202]、国际义务的履行[203]以及监督国际义务的遵守[204]等多个方面。显而易见的是，这些原则中的一部分仅仅是概念上的创新，在国际法中缺乏实际的基础。例如，自然的伦理价值这一原则的目的就是将特定的国内法文件移植到国际法层面。其他一些原则则是环境条约规定的某些义务的概括，或者只是那些得到确认的原则的构成部分。例如，与"开展合作以阻止或预防那些造成严重环境退化或者对人体健康有害的活动及物质的重置和转移"相关的一系列原则都属于这一类型。[205]最后，有些原则本质上的目的是推广某些进程，例如许多条约所规定的"国际义务的监督"或者"国际义务的国家履行"。我们必须承认，这些努力对推动国际环境法的发展及其概念或组件的重组都具有重要意义，同时，我们认为，围绕这些原则，国际环境法学者最紧迫的工作不再是发明更多的概念，而是更谨慎认真地将那些真正得到足够法定权威支持的原则确定下来，当它们的运行遇到模棱两可的情况时，做出进一步的概念澄清。

(三) 公地

"公地"或者"公有物"这一概念具有悠久的历史。它古代的起源是在罗马法中，16 世纪的法学家维多利亚和苏亚雷斯（Vitoria 和 Suarez）发展了这一概念，在 17 世纪，格老秀斯（Grotius）系统化地表述了这一概念，它的首次使用是为了表述公海在国际法中的地位。这一概念所传达出的内涵有两个主要内容，即获取某一公共资源的自由，以及不得据为己有。但是，这一内涵也有可能为某些国家（尤其是那些占主导地位的国家）滥用公地打开了方便之门。

解决这一问题的一种可能途径是将公共资源的获取和利用与它的保护

---

[201] "Principle of the Restrained Development of Fragile Ecosystems", Ibid., p. 101.

[202] "Cooperation to Discourage or Prevent the Relocation and Transfer of Activities and Substances that Cause Severe Environmental Degradation or are Harmful to Human Health", Report - Principles, supra footnote 21, paras. 121-122.

[203] "National Implementation of International Commitments", Report - Principles, supra footnote 21, paras. 153-154.

[204] "Monitoring of Compliance with International Commitments", Report-Principles, supra footnote 21, paras. 155-160.

[205] See supra Section 3.3.5.

义务关联起来。这是《联合国海洋法公约》采取的办法之一,[206] 它保证了对公海的自由获取和利用,同时对生物资源的利用规定了限制条件,[207] 并概括规定了一些与海洋环境保护[208]以及别国利益相关的义务。[209] 公海自由还包括了飞越公海上空的自由,这也相当于另一种"公地"的分配。[210]

"公地"的第二个例证是南极地区。签订于1959年《南极条约》的前言承认南极只能用于和平目的符合"全人类的利益"。[211] 这一概念表达的内涵与其他两个公地(公海及其上空)的内涵有相似之处,但是它还是存在一些细微区别。例如,该条约"冻结了"针对南极地区在其生命周期内的所有主权诉求,[212] 这就暗示着在将来的某个时间节点"据为己有"成为可能。南极资源(生物、矿业即其他资源[213])的利用则是受到一项具体制度的规制,这一制度是由《南极条约》体系(Antarctic Treaty System)框架下的一系列条约所建立的[214]。

"公地"的第三个例证是外空,包括月球和其他天体。这一背景下的自由获取和不得据为己有原则是联合国大会在1963年制定的《各国探索

---

[206] 《联合国海洋法公约》也制定了一种不同于"公地"概念的方法,在涉及海洋资源的开发和保护上,这种方法被认为更有效,即将原属于公海的大片地区实行"领土化"。如此一来,根据《联合国海洋法公约》第五部分,沿海国可以针对那些位于其"专属经济区"(从测算领海宽度的基线量起不超过200海里的范围)的资源行使"主权权利"(不应等同于"行使主权")。参见《联合国海洋法公约》,前文脚注6。

[207] Ibid., Arts. 116-120.

[208] Ibid., Art. 192.

[209] Ibid., Art. 87 (2).

[210] Ibid., Art. 87 (1) (b).

[211] Antarctic Treaty, supra footnote 146.

[212] Antarctic Treaty, Art. IV.

[213] 例如构成冰盖的巨量淡水资源。See J. E. Viñuales, "Iced Freshwater Resources: A Legal Exploration" (2009) 19 *Yearbook of International Environmental Law* 188.

[214] This includes, in the area of biological resources, the Convention for the Conservation of Antarctic Seals ("CCAS"), 1 June 1972, and the Convention for the Conservation of Antarctic Marine Living Resources ("CCAMLR"), 20 May 1980. In terms of mineral resources, a Convention on the Regulation of Antarctic Mineral Resource Activities ("CRAMRA") was concluded in June 1988. However, it has not been ratified, and in any event, it has been deprived of its object with the adoption, on 4 October 1991, of the Protocol to the Antarctic Treaty on the Protection of the Environment, Art. 7 providing that "[a] ny activity relating to mineral resources, other than scientific research, shall be prohibited".

与利用外层空间活动的法律原则的宣言》,[215] 它强调指出,为了和平目的探索和开发外空是"全人类的共同利益"。[216] 1967 年制定的《外空条约》对其进行了确认[217],它的第 1 条和第 2 条分别规定了自由获取和不得据为己有的原则。这就在一定程度上缓和了抢占和开发外空竞赛所带来的风险。另外,《外空条约》规定了其他一些义务,例如禁止在轨道布置大规模杀伤性武器,[218] 避免外空的污染或者地球环境的改变[219],以及一项责任制度(对另一成员国造成损害所引发)。[220] 这一法律地位后来被 1979 年完成的《月球协定》所修订,该条约将月球列为"人类共同遗产"。[221]

(四)人类共同遗产

"人类共同遗产"这一概念所传达的构想与我们前面探讨的构想不同。它将对某一资源的据为己有(公地涉及这一问题)排除在外,同时将资源的开发置于共同管理之下。其结果就是,资源获取这一权利是由负责联合管理的机构独享的。但是,联合管理是为了所有国家的利益,既包括那些拥有开发资源所需技术和财政手段的国家,也包括那些不具备这些能力的国家。当然,构想的具体内容还是要具体问题具体分析。

在谈及《月球协定》时,正如前文所提,月球被赋予了"人类共同遗产"这一地位,《月球协定》第 11 条第 5 款规定:

> 本协定缔约各国承诺一俟月球自然资源的开发即将可行时,建立指导此种开发的国际制度,其中包括适当程序在内。[222]

---

[215] "Declaration of Legal Principles Governing the Activities of States in the Exploration and Use of Outer Space", 13 December 1963, UN Doc. A/18/1962, paras. 2 and 3.

[216] "Declaration of Legal Principles Governing the Activities of States in the Exploration and Use of Outer Space", 13 December 1963, preamble.

[217] Outer Space Treaty, supra footnote 147.

[218] Outer Space Treaty, supra footnote, Art. IV.

[219] Outer Space Treaty, Art. IX.

[220] Outer Space Treaty, Art. VII. This system was completed with the adoption of the Convention on International Liability for Damage Caused by Space Objects, 29 March 1972 961 UNTS 187.

[221] Agreement Governing the Activities of States on the Moon and Other Celestial Bodies, 18 December 1979, 1363 UNTS 3 ("Moon Treaty"), Art. 11 (1).

[222] Agreement Governing the Activities of States on the Moon and Other Celestial Bodies, 18 December 1979, 1363 UNTS 3 ("Moon Treaty"), Art. 11 (5).

但是，由于那些在外空开发上最积极的国家没有批准该项协定，它的实际效果还是非常有限的。

通过与海床管理发生关联，"人类共同遗产"这一概念得到了进一步的发展。[223] 第一次进展发生在1970年，联合国大会通过了《各国管辖范围以外海床洋底及底土原则宣言》(Declaration of Principles Governing the Seabed and the Ocean Floor, and Subsoil Thereof, beyond the Limits of National Jurisdiction),[224] 将"人类共同遗产"这一地位赋予"区域"及其资源。《联合国海洋法公约》第十一部分沿用了这一定性，将"区域"置于一套国际管理制度之下，并授权国际海底管理局（International Seabed Authority）进行管理。[225] 第137条第2款特别规定：

> "区域"内资源的一切权利属于全人类，由管理局代表全人类行使。这种资源不得让渡。但从"区域"内回收的矿物，可按照本部分和管理局的规则、规章和程序予以让渡。[226]

这条规定所传达的构想引起了很大的争议，它也导致《联合国海洋法公约》十余年都没有正式生效。只是在1994年《关于执行1982年12月10日〈联合国海洋法公约〉第十一部分的纽约协定》(New York Agreement on the application of Part XI of the UNCLOS) 通过以后，《联合国海洋法公约》的生效才成为可能。[227] 在《纽约协定》中，为了回应发达国家的关切，这类"区域"的勘探和开发制度被冲淡，但是，它还是针对"人类共同遗产"这一概念所传达的构想做出了最清晰的表述。

除了以上两个例证，人类共同遗产这一概念很少在其他场合被提及，且通常会受到抵制。值得一提的是，1972年联合国教科文组织

---

[223] See R. J. Dupuy, "La notion de patrimoine commun de l'humanité appliquée aux fonds marins", in *Mélanges Colliard* (Paris: Pedone, 1984), pp. 197–205.

[224] See Seabed Declaration, supra footnote 148.

[225] UNCLOS, supra footnote 6, Part XI. On the development of this regime see J. Harrison, *Making the Law of the Sea* (Cambridge University Press), pp. 115–153.

[226] UNCLOS, supra footnote 6, Ibid., Art. 137 (2).

[227] See generally, R. R. Churchill and A. V. Lowe, *The Law of the Sea* (Manchester University Press, 3rd edn, 1999), Chapter 11.

(UNESCO)《世界文化和自然遗产保护公约》提到了这一概念,[228] 另外,在一个不同语境下,1977 年《世界人类基因组人权宣言》(Universal Declaration on the Human Genome and Human Rights) 也提到了这一概念。[229] 但是,与前面的例证不同,这两个都不涉及相关事项的联合管理。当"人类共同遗产"这一地位的授予可能引发分配和管理问题时,发达国家通常都会极力反对。一个适当的例证来自《联合国海洋法公约》框架中涉及国家管辖范围外生物多样性问题的谈判(参见第六章)。那些有能力开发公海资源(包括遗传资源)的国家坚决反对此项制度,这项制度试图从公海(公地)的自由获取向"区域"(人类共同遗产)的全球管理转向。类似的担忧已经在其他资源的利用上得以显现,这就导致了"人类共同关切事项"这一概念的出现。

(五) 人类共同关切事项

人类共同关切事项这一概念产生于 20 世纪 90 年代,虽然我们有可能找到更早的相似观点。这一概念所传达的构想与人类共同遗产的构想存在明显区别,人类共同关切事项涉及的资源可以由单个国家来开发,并不是作为一个共有资源被联合管理。在进行开发时,各国应当遵循特定要求。根据具体情况的不同,具体要求也有所不同,但是重点始终是合作以及资源的获取规制和保护。《生物多样性公约》和《联合国气候变化框架公约》为这一概念提供了两个主要案例。

谈及《生物多样性公约》,拥有地球上绝大多数陆地生物多样性的发展中国家的抵制使得人类共同遗产这一概念无法适用于生物多样性这一资源。[230] 因此,《生物多样性公约》的序言只是提出"保护生物多样性是全

---

[228] Convention Concerning the Protection of the World Cultural and Natural Heritage, 16 November 1972, 1037 UNTS 151 ("World Heritage Convention"). The preamble provides, notably, that "parts of the cultural or natural heritage are of outstanding interest and therefore need to be preserved as part of the world heritage of mankind as a whole".

[229] Resolution 29 C/17, UNESCO GC, 29th Sess. (1997), endorsed by UNGA A/RES/53/152. According to Article 1, "In a symbolic sense, [the human genome] is the heritage of humanity". See S. Maljean-Dubois, "Bioéthique et droit international" (2000) 46 Annuaire Français de Droit International 82.

[230] On the origin of the CBD, see M.-A. Hermitte, "La convention sur la diversité biologique" (1992) 38 Annuaire Français de Droit International 844.

人类共同关切的事项",紧接着又马上指出"各国对它自己的生物资源拥有主权权利",而且"各国有责任保护它自己的生物多样性"。[231] 因此,《生物多样性公约》就建立了国家保护生物多样性的义务,[232] 还建立了一套制度来规定其他国家对生物资源(特别是遗传资源)的有限获取。[233]

谈及《联合国气候变化框架公约》,它的重点在于履行合作义务以便应对气候变化对地球造成的"不利影响",这也属于"人类共同关切事项"。[234] 与《生物多样性公约》不同,《联合国气候变化框架公约》关注的焦点是公约第2条间接定义的一个全球性资源。这一资源在本质上是一个稳定的气候系统,我们应当通过控制对大气成分的人为干预来保护这一资源。虽然这一资源是全球性的(因为它横跨了所有国家的领土),但是它的保护既要求各国独自采取适当措施(国内措施),还要与别国开展合作(国际措施)。采取这些措施的责任并不是同等分配的。前文我们在讨论共同但有区别的责任时提到,当我们将气候变化当作一个人类共同关切事项来应对时,就会涉及不同的责任、时间范围和利益,这些问题将会在第五章继续讨论。

第五节　从原则到规制

前文分析的国际环境法的概念模型在实践中可以被看作履行环境条约的一套原则和概念。深刻理解这些原则和概念以及它们的运行和法律基础,有助于我们了解那些更复杂的环境制度的基石,本书的随后四章将会分析这些制度。

在一些案例中,某项条约有时会被专门用于推广某条原则。这样的例证包括《奥胡斯公约》(Aarhus Convention),它具体体现了公众参与原则,或者《埃斯波公约》,它的目的是落实环评这一要求。但是,更常见的情况是,环境制度有时会体现多个原则或制度。举例来讲,《持久性有机污染物国际公约》(POP Convention)就同时涉及风险预防方法和损害

231　CBD, supra footnote 7, preamble (italics added).
232　Ibid., Arts. 6–11.
233　Ibid., Arts. 15 and 19, especially.
234　UNFCCC, supra footnote 12, preamble.

预防原则。与此相类似，臭氧层和气候变化制度同时依赖于数个原则，包括风险预防（现已称为预防）、共同但有区别的责任和代际公平。

不同的制度可能会采用不同的方式来阐释同一个隐含的原则或概念。因此，正如后文第五章和第七章所要讨论的，共同但有区别的责任原则在几个不同的环境制度中被转化为大不相同的术语，例如，臭氧层制度的表述是，所有国家都有相似的量化的减排目标，但是发展中国家被给予了额外的援助和更长的期限；气候变化制度的表述是，部分国家有量化的减排目标，其他一些国家没有量化的减排目标，或者在《巴黎协定》之后，各国都应决定其各自的减缓程度；《持久性有机污染物国际公约》的表述是，责任的区分是由一套复杂的制度来进行管理的，这套制度为所有国家都提供了灵活性安排。

另外，可能还存在这样一些案例，即某个原则被认定是某项条约的基石，但是条约内容反而禁止有效体现这一原则。出现这种冲突的原因有可能是因为条约本身的模棱两可，例如《联合国海洋法公约》第十一部分将"区域"放置于人类共同遗产制度之下，现在被证明很难落实。

就当前来讲，最重要的是，当我们着手研究后续章节中的具体条约制度时，必须将这些问题牢记于心。

部分参考文献

[1] Agius, E. and S. Busuttil (eds.), *Future Generations and International Law* (London: Earthscan, 1998).

[2] Ambrusné, E. T., "The Parliamentary Commissioner for Future Generations of Hungary and his impact" (2010) 10/1 *Intergenerational Justice Review* 18.

[3] Barral, V., "Sustainable Development in International Law: Nature and Operation of an Evolutive Legal Norm" (2012) 23 *European Journal of International Law* 377.

Le développement durable en droit international: Essai sur les incidences juridiques d'une norme évolutive (Brussels: Bruylant, 2016).

[4] Barrios, P., "The Rotterdam Convention on Hazardous Chemicals: A Meaningful Step towards Environmental Protection?" (2004) 16 *Georgetown International Environmental Law Review* 679.

[5] Beyerlin, U., "Different Types of Norms in International Environmental Law", in D. Bodansky, J. Brunnée and E. Hey (eds.), *The Oxford Handbook of International Environmental Law* (Oxford University Press, 2007), pp. 425-448.

[6] Birnbacher, D., *La responsabilité envers les générations futures* (Paris: Presses universitaires de France, 1994).

[7] Bodansky, D., "Deconstructing the Precautionary Principle", in D. Caron and H. N. Scheiber (eds.), *Bringing New Law to Ocean Waters* (Leiden: Martinus Nijhoff, 2004), pp. 381-391.

[8] Boisson de Chazournes, L. and S. Maljean-Dubois, "Les principes du droit international de l'environnement", in *Juris-classeur environnement*, fascicule 146-215 (2011).

[9] Boyle, A., "Making the Polluter Pay? Alternatives to State Responsibility in the Allocation of Transboundary Environmental Cost", in F. Francioni and T. Scovazzi (eds.), *International Responsibility for Environmental Harm* (London: Graham & Trotman, 1991), pp. 363-379.

[10] Brown Weiss, E., *In Fairness to Future Generations: International Law, Common Patrimony, and Intergenerational Equity* (Dobbs Ferry: Transnational Publishers, 1989).

[11] Brunnée, J., "Common Areas, Common Heritage, and Common Concern", in D. Bodansky, J. Brunnée and E. Hey (eds.), *The Oxford Handbook of International Environmental Law* (Oxford University Press, 2007), pp. 552-573.

[12] Commission on Sustainable Development, Report of the Expert Group Meeting on Identification of Principles of International Law for Sustainable Development, Geneva, Switzerland, 26-28 September 1995.

[13] Craik, N., *The International Law of Environmental Impact Assessment* (Cambridge University Press, 2008).

[14] Cullet, P., "Differential Treatment in International Law: Towards a New Paradigm of Inter-State Relations" (1999) 10 *European Journal of International Law* 549.

Differential Treatment in International Environmental Law (The Hague:

Kluwer, 2003).

[15] Davies, H., "The Well-being of Future Generations (Wales) Act 2015-A Step Change in the Legal Protection of the Interests of Future Generations?" (2017) 29 *Journal of Environmental Law* 165.

[16] De Sadeleer, N., *Essai sur la genèse et la portée juridique de quelques principes en droit de l'environnement* (Bruxelles: Bruylant, 1999).

[17] Dupuy, P. -M., "Où en-est le droit de l'environnement à la fin du siècle?" (1997) *Revue générale de droit international public* 873.

"Formation of Customary International Law and General Principles", in D. Bodansky, J. Brunnée and E. Hey (eds.), *The Oxford Handbook of International Environmental Law* (Oxford University Press, 2007), pp. 449-469.

[18] Dupuy, R. -J., "La notion de patrimoine commun de l'humanité appliquée aux fonds marins", in *Mélanges Colliard* (Paris: Pedone, 1984), pp. 197-205.

[19] Duvic Paoli, L. -A., *The Prevention Principles in International Environmental Law* (Cambridge University Press, 2018).

[20] Ebbesson, J., "The Notion of Public Participation in International Environmental Law" (1997) 8 *Yearbook of International Environmental Law* 51.

[21] Epiney, A. and M. Scheyli, *Strukturprinzipien des Umweltvölkerrechts* (Baden-Baden: Nomos, 1998).

[22] Etemire, U., "Insights on the UNEP Bali Guidelines and the Development of Environmental Democratic Rights" (2016) 23 *Journal of Environmental Law* 393.

[23] European Commission, *The Law of Sustainable Development. General Principles* (2000).

[24] Francioni, F., "Sviluppo sostenibile e principi di diritto internazionale dell'ambiente", in Società Italiana di Diritto Internazionale, *Il principio dello sviluppo sostenibile nel diritto internazionale ed europeo dell'ambiente* (Naples: Editoriale Scientifica, 2007), pp. 40-61.

[25] Francioni, F. and H. Neuhold, "International Cooperation for the Protection of the Environment: The Procedural Dimension", in W. Lang,

H. Neuhold and K. Zemanek (eds.), *Environmental Protection and International Law* (Dordrecht: Martinus Nijhoff, 1991), pp. 203–226.

[26] French, D., "Developing States and International Environmental Law: The Importance of Differentiated Responsibilities" (2000) 49 *International and Comparative Law Quarterly* 35.

[27] Gaines, S., "The Polluter-Pays Principle: From Economic Equity to Environmental Ethos" (1991) 26 *Texas International Law Journal* 463.

[28] Hostiou, R., "Le lente mais irrésistible montée en puissance du principe de participation" (2003) 112 *Droit de l'environnement* 182.

[29] Kindall, M. P. A., "UNCED and the Evolution of Principles of International Environmental Law" (1992) 25 *John Marshall Law Review* 19.

[30] Kiss, A., "The Rio Declaration on Environment and Development", in L. Campiglio, L. Pineschi, D. Siniscalco and T. Treves (eds.), *The Environment after Rio: International Law and Economics* (London: Martinus Nijhoff, 1994), pp. 55–64.

[31] Kovar, J. D., "A Short Guide to the Rio Declaration" (1993) 4 *Colorado Journal of International Environmental Law and Policy* 119.

[32] Lecucq, O. and S. Maljean-Dubois (eds.), *Le rôle du Juge Dans le Développement du Droit de L'environnement* (Bruxelles: Bruylant, 2008).

[33] Lucchini, L., "Le principe de précaution en droit international de l'environnement: Ombres plus que lumières" (1999) 45 *Annuaire Français de Droit International* 710.

[34] Maljean-Dubois, S., "L'accès à l'information et la reconnaissance d'un droit à l'information environnementale", in S. Maljean-Dubois (ed.), *L'Effectivité du Droit Européen de L'environnement: Contrôle de la Mise en Oeuvre et Sanction du Non Respect* (Paris: La documentation française, 2000), p. 25.

[35] Martin-Bidou, P., "Le principe de précaution en droit international de l'environnement" (1999) *Revue générale de droit international public* 631.

[36] Mbengue, M., *Essai sur une théorie du risque en droit international public. L' anticipation du risque environnemental et sanitaire* (Paris: Pedone, 2009).

[37] McDorman, T., "The Rotterdam Convention on the Prior Informed Consent Procedure for Certain Hazardous Chemicals and Pesticides in International Trade: Some Legal Notes" (2004) 13 *Review of European Community and International Environmental Law* 187.

[38] Morgera, E. and J. Wingard, *Principles for Developing Sustainable Wildlife Management Laws*, *FAO Legal Papers* (2008).

[39] Munro, R. D. and J. G. Lammers, Environmental Protection and Sustainable Development, Expert Group on Environmental Law of the World Commission on Environment and Development (1986).

[40] Nesbit, M. and A. Illés, *Establishing an EU "Guardian for Future Generations"*, *Report and recommendations for the World Future Council* (London: Institute for European Environmental Policy, 2015).

[41] Panjabi, R. K. L., "From Stockholm to Rio: A Comparison of the Declaratory Principles of International Environmental Law" (1993) 21 *Denver Journal of International Law and Politics* 215.

[42] Paradell-Trius, L., "Principles of International Environmental Law: An Overview" (2000) 9 *Review of European Community and International Environmental Law* 93.

[43] Porras, I. M., "The Rio Declaration: A New Basis for International Co-operation" (1992) 1 *Review of European Community and International Environmental Law* 245.

[44] Rajamani, L., *Differential Treatment in International Environmental Law* (Oxford University Press, 2006).

[45] Ramlogan, R., *Sustainable Development: Towards a Judicial Interpretation* (Leiden: Martinus Nijhoff, 2010).

[46] Redgwell, C., "The International Law of Public Participation: Protected Areas, Endangered Species and Biological Diversity" in D. Zillman, A. Lucas and G. Pring (eds.), *Human Rights in Natural Resource Development-Public Participation in the Sustainable Development of Mining and Energy Resources* (Oxford University Press, 2002), pp. 187-214.

"Regulating Trade in Dangerous Substances: Prior Informed Consent under the 1998 Rotterdam Convention", in A. Kiss, D. Shelton and K. Ishibashi (eds.), *Economic Globalization and Compliance with International Environmental Agreements* (The Hague: Kluwer, 2003), pp. 75–88.

[47] Robinson, N. A., "EIA Abroad: The Comparative and Transnational Experience", in S. G. Hildebrand and J. B. Cannon (eds.), *Environmental Analysis: The NEPA Experience* (Boca Raton: Lewis, 1993), pp. 679–702.

[48] Romi, R., "Le principe pollueur–payeur, ses implications et ses applications" (1991) 8 *Droit de L'environnement* 46.

[49] Sands, P., "International Law in the Field of Sustainable Development" (1994) 65 *British Yearbook of International Law* 303.

[50] Schrijver, N., "The Evolution of Sustainable Development in International Law" (2007) 329 *Recueil des Cours de L'Académie de Droit International de La Haye 217–412*.

[51] Schwartz, P., "The Polluter–pays Principle", in J. E. Viñuales (ed.), *The Rio Declaration on Environment and Development. A Commentary* (Oxford University Press, 2015).

[52] Scotford, E., *Environmental Principles and the Evolution of Environmental Law* (Oxford: Hart, 2017).

[53] Scovazzi, T., "Sul principio precauzionale nel diritto internazionale dell'ambiente" (1992) *Rivista di diritto internazionale* 699.

[54] Shelton, D., "Stockholm Declaration (1972) and Rio Declaration (1992)", *Max Planck Encyclopedia of Public International Law*, www.mpepil.com.

[55] Shoham, S. and N. Lamay, "Commission for future generations in the Knesset: Lessons learnt", in J. C. Tremmel (ed.), *Handbook of Intergenerational Justice* (Cheltenham: Edward Elgar, 2006), pp. 244–281.

[56] Smets, H., "Le principe pollueur payeur, un principe économique érigé en principe de droit de l'environnement?" (1998) *Revue générale de droit international public* 85.

[57] Supanich, G., "The Legal Basis of Intergenerational Responsibility: An Alternative View–The Sense of Intergenerational Identity" (1992) 3 *Yearbook of International Environmental Law* 94.

[58] Trouwborst, A., *Evolution and Status of the Precautionary Principle*

in International Law (The Hague: Kluwer Law International, 2002).

[59] UN Secretary-General, *Intergenerational Solidarity and the Needs of Future Generations. Report of the Secretary-General*, 15 August 2013, UN Doc A/68/322.

[60] Viñuales, J. E., "The Contribution of the International Court of Justice to the Development of International Environmental Law: A Contemporary Assessment" (2008) 32 *Fordham International Law Journ*al 232.

"Managing Abidance by Standards for the Protection of the Environment", in A. Cassese (ed.) *Realizing Utopia. The Future of International Law* (Oxford University Press, 2012), pp. 326-339.

"Cartographies imaginaires: Observations sur la portee juridique du concept de 'régime spécial' en droit international" (2013) 140*Journal du droit international* (*Clunet*) 405.

(ed.), *The Rio Declaration on Environment and Development. A Commentary* (Oxford University Press, 2015).

"La Protección Ambiental en el Derecho Internacional Consuetudinario" (2017) 69/2*Revista Española de Derecho Internacional*71.

"La distribution de la charge de protéger l'environnement: Expressions juridiques dela solidarité", in A. Supiot (ed.), *La responsabilité solidaire* (Paris: Conférences duCollège de France, 2018).

[61] Virally, M., "Le rôle des 'principes' dans le développement du droit international", *Le droit international en devenir. Essais écrits au fil des ans* (Paris: Presses Universitaires de France, 1990), pp. 195-212.

[62] Voigt, C., *Sustainable Development as a Principle of International Law* (Leiden: Martinus Nijhoff, 2009).

[63] Wirth, D. A., "The Rio Declaration on Environment and Development: Two Steps Forward and One Back, or Vice Versa" (1995) 29 *Georgia Law Review* 599.

[64] Woods, C., *The Environment, Intergenerational Equity and Long-term Investments* (doctoral dissertation, University of Oxford, 2011).

[65] Xue Hanqin, *Transboundary Damage in International Law* (Cambridge University Press, 2003).

第二编　实体规制

第四章　大洋、海洋和淡水

第一节　引论

本章开始介绍国际环境法中的实体规制，重点是有关大洋、海洋和淡水管理的规则。

虽然从规制的视角来看，这些客体（海洋环境和淡水）是分开的，但是它们实际上是相互紧密关联的，因为海洋污染的主要源头是陆源污染物，其中一部分是由河流携带的。另外，海洋法和水道法（特别是涉及航运时）都可以在国际法的悠久历史中溯源，虽然对这些区域内环境问题的规制是近期才发生的事。另一个共同的特征是，管理这些客体的一些规则都具有习惯法的特性。一般而言，从环境法的视角来看，这些不同的规制制度都与地球的"水圈"或者水体有关。基于这些原因，所以将大洋、海洋和淡水放在同一章节讲述。

第一个实体部分包括海洋环境的规制（本章第二节）。广义来讲，海洋法主要采用两种方法来保护海洋环境。一方面，它将广阔海域的管辖权（及其环境保护的主要责任）分配给各国；另一方面，它规定了一整套义务来保护海洋环境，并通过其他文件来明确这些义务。这些文件有些是关于具体问题的（例如海洋环境的某个污染源），有些是针对某个特定的海洋地区或客体（例如区域海洋公约或者第六章中将讨论的、正在进行中的"国家管辖范围外区域生物多样性"谈判）。遵循这一框架，我们首先分析了《联合国海洋法公约》[1] 规定的管辖权的分配（本章第二节第一部

---

[1] United Nations Convention on the Law of the Sea, 10 December 1982, 1833 UNTS 397 ("UNCLOS").

分），然后分析各国保护海洋环境的义务，所采取的方法都是从概述（本章第二节第二部分）、特定污染源（本章第二节第三部分）或地理区域（本章第二节第四部分）着手。

本章的后续部分将会研究淡水的国际规制（本章第三节）。在介绍这一部门法的总体框架（本章第三节第二部分）之后，我们将讨论管理国际水道（本章第三节第三部分）、地下水（本章第三节第一部分）和淡水（冰封的形式）（本章第三节第四部分）的法律。关于水获取的人权问题以及它在环境条约中的表述，例如《水和健康议定书》（*Protocol on Water and Health*），则留给第十章来讨论。

第二节 海洋环境的国际规制

一 针对海洋地区的环境管辖权

（一）概述

这一部分的目的并不是详细介绍毗邻海岸的各个海域或者各国对其水域的控制程度，[2] 而仅仅是为了显示各国对于这些区域的管辖权对环境保护有何影响。

从历史上看，海洋区域主要是用于航运、渔业，以及最近的矿产（例如离岸石油和天然气）和其他资源（例如离岸风能和生物勘探）的开发。对这三种活动的管理需要在沿海国家和其他想要利用这些区域的国家（船旗国）的利益之间达成一个妥协。另外，自1972年《斯德哥尔摩宣言》发布以后，重心就逐渐转移到环境保护本身。为了协调这些因素，各种方案被不断提出，从一国独享海域（领海）到所有国家都可以自由

---

[2] See P. -M. Dupuy, *Droit international public* (Paris: Dalloz, 2008), paras. 639–655. For three recent contributions to the law of the sea that provide a detailed discussion of these areas see D. Attard, M. Fitzmaurice, and N. A. Martinez Gutierrez (eds.), *The IMLI Manual on International Maritime Law. Vol.* Ⅰ: *The Law of the Sea* (Oxford University Press, 2014), chapters 2, 6, 7 and 9; D. R. Rothwell et al (eds.), *The Oxford Handbook on the Law of the Sea* (Oxford University Press, 2015), chapters 5, 8, 9 and 10; R. Rayfuse (ed.), *Research Handbook on International Marine Environmental Law* (Cheltenham: Edward Elgar, 2015); A. Proelß (ed.), *TheUnited Nations Convention on the Law of the Sea. A Commentary* (Berlin/Oxford/Baden-Baden: C. H. Beck/Hart/Nomos, 2017).

利用（公海），以及介于这两者之间的多个变种。³ 在整个20世纪，沿海国家一直都在通过单边宣示的方式来加强对濒临其海岸的海域的控制，这也常常引起政治争端。⁴ 在联合国层面，主要立法工作已经逐步开展。虽然在第一次联合国海洋法大会（1958年）和第二次联合国海洋法大会（1960年）上取得了重大进展，特别是定义了大陆架和承认了沿海国对其领海和其毗连区的管辖权，但是，仍然有一些基本问题尚无定论，尤其是领海的范围以及国家针对海域的权利范畴。⁵ 只是在第三次联合国海洋法大会（1974—1982年）期间，随着《联合国海洋法公约》的制定，针对各国对不同海域（特别是领海）的管辖权的范围才达成了一项整体协议。⁶

这一部"海洋宪法"得以通过是得益于多个观点，其中一个就是必须明确各国在海洋生物资源（渔业）保护上的义务。授予沿海国在这些海域的"财产权"也就意味着，各国在享有这些资源的开发权的同时也必须尽到保护义务。财产权有望给资源的可持续管理提供必要的刺激。⁷ 如此一来，《联合国海洋法公约》规定的沿海国对不同海域的所有权就有助于引发保护义务。为了举例说明这一点，就有必要简要研究一下三个在沿海国家管辖之下的主要区域，即离海岸线12海里以内的领海、专属经济区和大陆架。图4-1提供了《联合国海洋法公约》从环境视角来定义的主要区域的一个概览。

（二）领海

适用于领海的法律制度主要体现于《联合国海洋法公约》第二部分。领海的定义是内水以外邻接的一带海域，⁸ 领海的宽度从"基线"量起到

3　See T. W. Fulton, *The Sovereignty of the Sea* (Clark NJ: The Lawbook Exchange, 1911).

4　See *Fisheries Case* (*United Kingdom* v. *Norway*), Judgment, ICJ Reports 1951, p. 116.

5　这一问题仍然是国际冲突的一个源头。See e. g. *Fisheries Jurisdiction* (*Federal Republic of Germany* v. *Iceland*), Merits, Judgment, ICJ Reports 1974, p. 175; *Fisheries Jurisdiction* (*United Kingdom* v. *Iceland*), Merits Judgment, ICJ Reports 1974, p. 3.

6　See J. Harrison, *Making the Law of the Sea* (Cambridge University Press, 2011), Chapter 2.

7　关于这一逻辑在海洋领域的运用，参见 R. Barnes, *Property Rights and Natural Resources* (Oxford: Hart, 2009), pp. 165-220。

8　UNCLOS, supra footnote 1, Art. 2 (1).

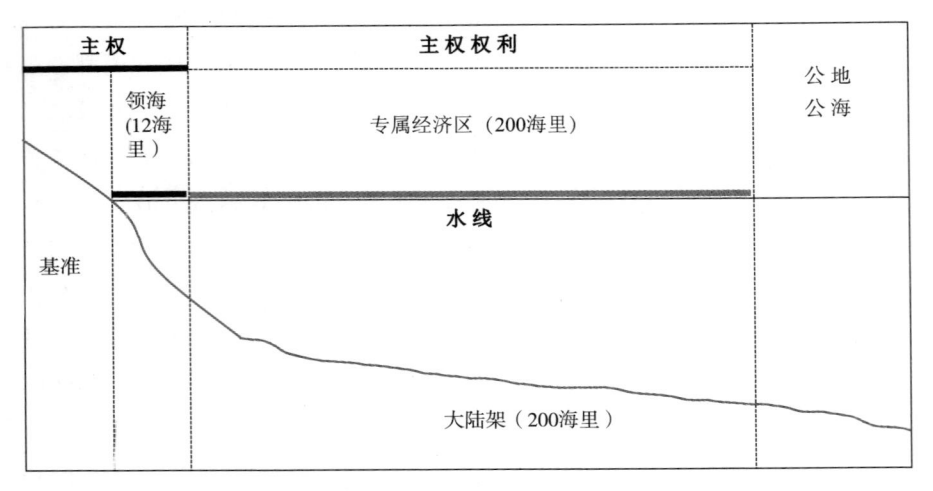

```
         主权                主权权利
        ┌──┬─────┬────────────────────┬──┐
        │  │ 领海 │                    │公地│
        │  │(12海 │  专属经济区（200海里）│公海│
        │  │ 里） │                    │  │
        │基准                水 线
        │
        │         大陆架（200海里）
```

图 4-1 《联合国海洋法公约》下管辖权的分布

不超过 12 海里[9]的界线为止（通常是沿海国官方承认的大比例尺海图所标明的沿岸低潮线[10]）。领海受到沿海国的主权管辖,[11] 但是有一个重要的限制条件，即沿海国必须保证别国船舶的"无害通过"的权利。[12]

对主权的承认也就带来了对领海的义务。根据《联合国海洋法公约》第 21 条第 1 款，沿海国有权而且应当"依本公约规定和其他国际法规则"，制定法律和规章，特别是针对"养护海洋生物资源""保全环境"和"预防污染"。[13] 但是，正如前文所述，这些权利有一个重要的限制条件，即沿海国制定的法律和规章在书面表述和实践中都不得妨碍外国船舶的无害通过。公约在一般条款[14]和涉及船舶造成的海洋环境污染的特别规定中都明确表述了这一限制条件。[15] 而且它还明确提及了一

---

[9] UNCLOS, supra footnote 1, Art. 3.

[10] UNCLOS, supra footnote 1, Art. 5.

[11] UNCLOS, supra footnote 1, Art. 2 (1).

[12] UNCLOS, supra footnote 1, Arts. 2 (3) and 17 to 32.

[13] UNCLOS, supra footnote 1, Art. 21 (1) (d) and (f). Although this Article is not formulated in terms of a duty, this is the interpretation suggested by Arts. 2 (1), 192 and 194 (1).

[14] UNCLOS, supra footnote 1, Art. 24 (1). 必须指出的是，当一艘通过领海的外国船舶进行了"任何故意或严重的污染行为"或"任何渔业捕捞行为"时，它就不被看作无害通过 [Art. 19 (2) (h) - (i)].

[15] UNCLOS, supra footnote 1, Art. 211 (4).

些反面例证，例如对任何国家有歧视[16]，或者更为严重的是那些特别针对外国船舶的设计、构造、人员配备或装备（CDEM 条款）的法律和规章。[17] 后者被认为是公约第 21 条对沿海国权利的一个具体限制，这种法律和规章只有在"能促使一般承认的国际规则或标准有效"时才能适用。

国内措施和国际规范及标准的交叉关系有可能是复杂的。举例来讲，Erika 和 Prestige 油污事故的发生导致欧盟制定了一部法规，加速双壳体船舶逐步替代单壳体船舶。[18] 这就引发了很大的争议，焦点是这条法规是否违反了 CDEM 条款。最终，通过修订《防止船舶污染国际公约》（MARPOL Convention）的附录，一个新的国际 CDEM 规范作为折中方案得以出台，它规定立即停止用单壳油船运输重油，但是仍然允许用较新的单壳船运输轻质燃料并将其淘汰的期限延长到 2015 年。[19]

（三）专属经济区

专属经济区法律制度的核心部分是在《联合国海洋法公约》第五部分。专属经济区是领海以外并邻接领海的一个区域[20]，专属经济区从测算领海宽度的基线量起，不超过 200 海里。[21] 沿海国对专属经济区并不享有主权，只是拥有旨在勘探和开发、养护和管理在专属经济区内发现的自然资源的

---

[16] UNCLOS, supra footnote 1, Art. 24 (1) (b).

[17] UNCLOS, supra footnote 1, Art. 21 (2).

[18] Regulation (EC) 1726/2003 of the European Parliament and of the Council of 22 July 2003 amending Regulation (EC) 417/2002 on the accelerated phasing-in of double-hull or equivalent design requirements for single-hull oil tankers, OJ L 249, 1-4, 1 October 2003.

[19] See M. Gavouneli, "State jurisdiction in relation to the protection and preservation of the marine environment", in Attard et al, supra footnote 2, pp. 15-16. Gavouneli 还提到了另一个例证（即 Directive 2005/35/EC）来说明欧盟法疑似没有与《联合国海洋法公约》和《防止船舶污染国际公约》保持一致。原告针对英国对此指令的实施向英国法院提起了诉讼，而英国法院则把该指令与《联合国海洋法公约》和《防止船舶污染国际公约》的一致性这一问题提交给了欧洲法院。但是，欧洲法院认为无法评估这一一致性，因为"《联合国海洋法公约》并没有制定那些旨在直接并立即适用于个人的规则，也就没有授予个人那些可以用来对抗国家的权利或自由"，*International Association of Independent Tanker Owners (Intertanko) and others v. Secretary of State for Transport*, ECJ (Grand Chamber), Case C-308/06, Judgment (3 June 2008), para. 64.

[20] UNCLOS, supra footnote 1, Art. 55.

[21] UNCLOS, supra footnote 1, Art. 57.

主权权利。[22] 在行使这些权利时，沿海国应适当顾及其他国家的权利，[23]这些权利不应仅仅局限于无害通过权，而应参考各国在公海中的自由来界定。[24] 值得一提的是，这些广义的自由包含了抗议权（包括环保激进行动），沿海国应当在一定范围内予以尊重。[25]

赋予沿海国更广泛权利这一项规定同时也伴随一个相关义务，即沿海国有义务保护专属经济区内的生物资源和海洋环境。第56条第1款授予沿海国在"海洋环境的保护和保全"方面的管辖权。[26] 第61条具体规定了沿海国在生物资源养护上的义务。[27] 当这些生物资源由于它们独有的特性，在专属经济区和公海间洄游，相关国家（沿海国和捕捞这些鱼种的船旗国）就有义务开展合作以确保养护。[28] 要想确保这种合作通常并不容易，[29] 直到1995年《跨界鱼类种群协定》[30] 制定了一项有关这些鱼种养护

---

[22] UNCLOS, supra footnote 1, Art. 56（1）（a）. 主权的行使与主权权利的行使存在着两个主要区别：（1）在行使主权权利时，专属经济区的航行制度与公海的制度相似，因此规定得更宽泛（第58条）；（2）第三方的权利，特别是"内陆国"和"区位劣势的国家"享有更广阔的权利。（第69—70条）. See Dupuy, supra footnote 2, para. 654.

[23] UNCLOS, supra footnote 1, Art. 56（2）. 沿海国这一义务的范围是由船旗国所享有的权利决定的。它可能包含程序步骤，例如在采取一个影响到他国的环保措施之前应当进行适当的协商，而如果没有实现一个令人满意的平衡，就可能会导致违约。See *In the matter of the Chagos Marine Protected Area Arbitration before an Arbitral Tribunal constituted under Annex VII of the United Nations Convention on the Law of the Sea* (*Mauritius v. UK*), Award (18 March 2015), paras. 518-519, 534-536.

[24] UNCLOS, supra footnote 1, Art. 58（1）-（2）.

[25] Arctic Sunrise Arbitration (The Netherlands v. Russia), Award on the Merits (24 August 2015), paras. 227-228 (where the tribunal interpreted the freedom of navigation in the light of human rights law).

[26] UNCLOS, supra footnote 1, Art. 56（1）（b）（iii）.

[27] UNCLOS, supra footnote 1, Art. 61.

[28] UNCLOS, supra footnote 1, Arts. 63 and 64.

[29] 所谓的"比目鱼战争"提供了一个很好的例证。在1995年3月，A good illustration is given by the so-called "turbot war". In March 1995, 一艘西班牙渔船（埃斯泰号），正在加拿大专属经济区外围附近进行捕捞时，遭到了加拿大巡逻队的登船检查，造成了加拿大和欧盟之间的一次国际事件。See *Fisheries Jurisdiction* (*Spain v. Canada*), Judgment, ICJ Reports 1998, p. 432 ("*Estai*").

[30] Agreement for the Implementation of the Provisions of the United Nations Convention on the Law of the Sea of 10 December 1982 Relating to the Conservation and Management of Straddling Fish Stocks and High Migratory Fish Stocks, 8 September 1995, 2167 UNTS 3 ("Straddling Fish Stocks Agreement").

的具体制度。[31]

除了生物资源的养护，沿海国"可以"制定法律和规章以"预防、减少和控制来自船舶的污染"[32]，同时还有权"采取为确保其依照本公约制定的法律和规章得到遵守所必要的措施，包括登临、检查、逮捕和进行司法程序"。[33]

前文"可以"这类包含有自由裁量意味的表述，不得模糊海洋环境保护义务的本质。事实上，沿海国家负有保护海洋环境的主要义务已经成为一个共识，[34] 这一义务被理解为一种谨慎注意义务，来源于《联合国海洋法公约》第十二部分和国际习惯法。[35] 事实上，来源于第十二部分的义务适用于所有国家和所有海域，包括那些有争端的地区。[36] 其导致的结果是，除了沿海国以外，船旗国也负有保护海洋环境这一谨慎注意义务，这是由第十二部分的一般义务和其他一些条款所决定的。[37] 本章后面才会具体讨论第十二部分的一般适用和含义，但是，为了理解适用于其他海洋空间的框架（例如我们马上要谈到的大陆架），我们应当将它们时刻铭记于心。

（四）大陆架

有关大陆架的法律制度是在《联合国海洋法公约》第六部分。第 76 条第 1 款规定：

---

[31] See Chapter 6.

[32] UNCLOS, supra footnote 1, Art. 73（1）.

[33] UNCLOS, supra footnote 1, Art. 73（1）.

[34] See *Request for an Advisory Opinion Submitted by the Sub-Regional Fisheries Commission (SRFC)*, Advisory Opinion of 2 April 2015, ITLOS Case No 21（"IUU Advisory Opinion"）, paras. 104-106.

[35] *In the matter of the South China Sea Arbitration before and Arbitral Tribunal constituted under Annex VII of the United Nations Convention on the Law of the Sea (Republic of the Philippines v. People's Republic of China)*, PCA Case No. 2013-2019, Award（12 July 2016）, para 941.

[36] *Dispute Concerning Delimitation of the Maritime Boundary between Ghana and Côte d'Ivoire in the Atlantic Ocean (Ghana/Côte d'Ivoire)*, ITLOS Case No. 23, Order of 25 April 2015, paras. 68-73; *IUU Advisory Opinion*, supra footnote 34, paras. 111, 120; *South China Sea Arbitration*, supra footnote 35, para 927.

[37] See *IUU Advisory Opinion*, supra footnote 34, paras. 108-109（stating that such obligations are of two sorts, those generally applicable to all States, and those applicable to flag States with regard to marine areas of a coastal State）.

沿海国的大陆架包括其领海以外依其陆地领土的全部自然延伸,扩展到大陆边外缘的海底区域的海床和底土,如果从测算领海宽度的基线量起到大陆边的外缘的距离不到 200 海里,则扩展到 200 海里的距离。[38]

与专属经济区相似,沿海国家对其大陆架行使其"主权权利"以便进行自然资源的勘探和开发。[39]

与第二部分和第五部分不同,《联合国海洋法公约》第六部分并没有具体条款专门针对生物资源的养护或者海洋环境的保护。大陆架制度的重心绝大部分是在于非生物资源(矿产)和固着种类。[40] 但是,《联合国海洋法公约》第 208 条第 1 款规定,沿海国家应当"制定法律和规章,以防止、减少和控制陆地来源,包括河流、河口湾、管道和排水口结构对海洋环境的污染,同时考虑到国际上议定的规则、标准和建议的办法及程序"。[41] 另外,第十二部分和国际习惯法所规定的涉及海洋环境保护和养护的一般义务也完全适用于大陆架。[42]

二 海洋环境保护概览

《联合国海洋法公约》的环境维度并不是仅限于分配各国的管辖权。相反,《联合国海洋法公约》第十二部分的内容全都聚焦于"海洋环境的保护和保全"。[43] 它包含了 11 节,共计 46 项条款:第一节一般规定;第二节全球性和区域性合作;第三节技术援助;第四节监测和环境评价;第五节防

---

38 UNCLOS, supra footnote 1, Art. 76 (1). 如果大陆边的外缘是位于 200 海里以外地区,那么该国可以主张拥有一个更长的大陆架,但不应超过从测算领海宽度的基线量起 350 海里。See Ibid., Arts. 76 (4) – (8) and 82.

39 Ibid., Art. 77 (1).

40 Ibid., Art. 77 (4).

41 Ibid., Art. 208 (1). See also Art. 214 on the implementation of Art. 208.

42 See *Ghana/Côte d'Ivoire*, supra footnote 36, paras. 68–72 (addressing the applicability of Arts. 192 and 193 as well as of the prevention principle in customary law to activities in the seabed); *South China Sea Arbitration*, supran. footnote 35, paras. 950–966 (addressing the applicability of Arts. 192 and 194 to the harvesting of threatened or endangered species, including corals attached to the seabed).

43 See: P. - M. Dupuy, "La préservation du milieu marin", in R. - J. Dupuy and D. Vignes (eds.), *Traité du nouveau droit de la mer* (Paris/Brussels: Economica/Bruylant, 1985), Chapter 20. On the duties arising from Part XII see also the more recent works mentioned supra footnote 2.

止、减少和控制海洋环境污染的国际规则和国内立法；第六节执行；第七节保障办法；第八节冰封区域；第九节责任；第十节主权豁免；第十一节关于保护和保全海洋环境的其他公约所规定的义务。因此，《联合国海洋法公约》的这一部分不仅提供了一个框架，还同时为海洋环境保护制定了实实在在的义务，部分义务在前文已有所提及。为了理解《联合国海洋法公约》第十二部分的运作方式，我们必须关注它的三个主要构成要件，分别是：(1) 有关环境保护的义务；(2) 与污染源相关的问题；(3) 管理与其他公约之间关系的条款。图 4-2 提供了一个公约针对海洋环境制定的框架概览。它只提及了那些在本章中讨论过的文件。[44]

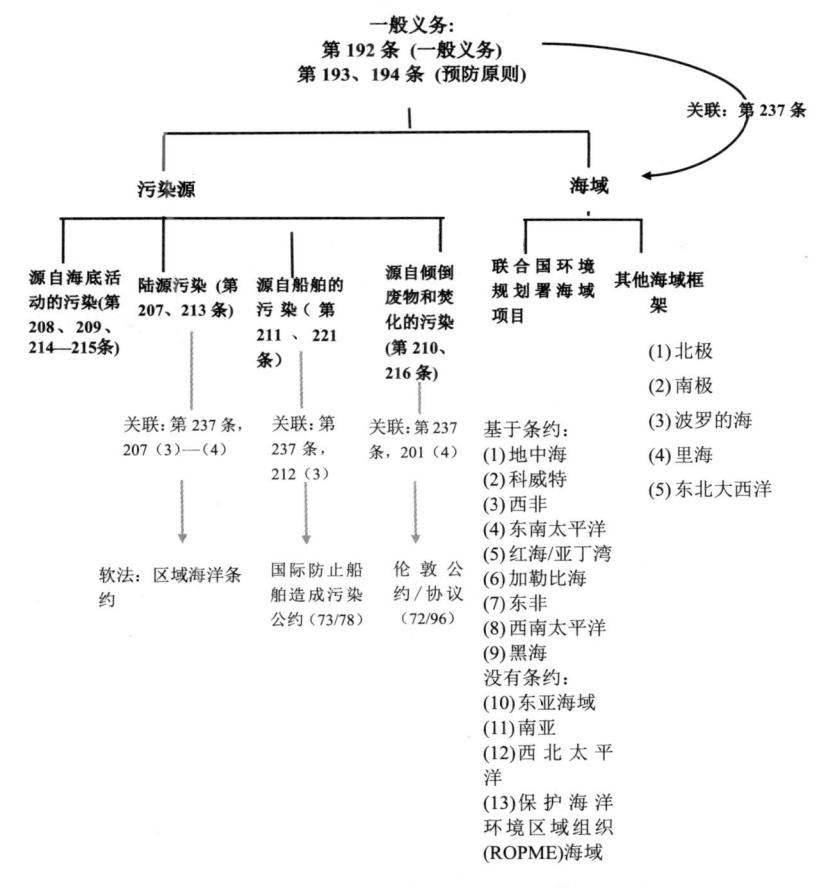

```
                        一般义务：
                     第192条（一般义务）
                   第193、194条（预防原则）
                                              关联：第237条
         ┌──────────────┴──────────────┐
       污染源                          海域
   ┌────┬────┬────┬────┐          ┌──────────┬──────────┐
  源自  陆源  源自  源自          联合国环境   其他海域
  海底  污染  船舶  倾倒          规划署海域   框架
  活动  （第  的污  废物           项目
  的污  207、 染（  和焚           
  染(第 213   第    化的           
  208、 条）  211、 污染           基于条约：  (1)北极
  209、       221   （第          (1)地中海   (2)南极
  214—       条）  210、          (2)科威特   (3)波罗的海
  215条）           216            (3)西非     (4)里海
                  条）           (4)东南太平洋(5)东北大西洋
   ↓      ↓      ↓      ↓        (5)红海/亚丁湾
 关联：  关联：  关联：  关联：    (6)加勒比海
 第237  第237  第237  第201      (7)东非
 条，   条，   条，   (4)         (8)西南太平洋
 207    212    201                (9)黑海
 (3)—   (3)    (4)               没有条约：
 (4)                               (10)东亚海域
                                   (11)南亚
   ↓      ↓      ↓      ↓        (12)西北太平洋
 软法：  国际   伦敦              (13)保护海洋
 区域   防止   公约/              环境区域组织
 海洋   船舶   协议               (ROPME)海域
 条约   造成   (72/96)
        污染
        公约
        (73/78)
```

图 4-2 《联合国海洋法公约》环境框架概览

44　For a more detailed statement, including several other instruments, see Attard et al, supra footnote 2.

关于上述第一个要件，《联合国海洋法公约》第 192 条规定国家负有一项一般义务（习惯法中的问题）去"保护和保全海洋环境"。[45] 这一条款的重要性应当引起高度重视。这是在一个国际层面的条约中首次明确表述保护和保全海洋环境这一义务。[46] 它适用于所有海域和所有国家，这一特点在实践中非常重要，因为它适用于两国或多国存在争议的地区。[47] 另外，第 192 条规定的义务内容还通过公约的其他条款得以进一步阐明，例如第十二部分和其他地方（参见本章前文）以及国际习惯法（主要指损害预防原则）。[48] 因此，它适用于所有国家，无论是公约的缔约国与否。谈及这一义务的内容，它的特点可以从三个主要方面来进行分析。第一，它是一种谨慎注意义务，要求各国采取积极的措施来保护和保全海洋环境并确保这些措施得到有效执行。[49] 即使采取了充分的措施，但是，如果这些措施没有得以执行，那么也会构成对 192 条所规定义务的违反。[50] 但是，环境危害的发生并不足以构成违法，因为这不是一个结果义务。[51] 第二，这一义务有一个广义的范畴，它涵盖了海洋环境的所有方面，它们在《联合国海洋法公约》的其他一些条款（尤其是生物资源的保护和管理以及污染的预防、减少和控制）中得到了进一步的明确。第 194 条还特别阐述了各国涉及海洋环境污染的义务。它在谈及预防海洋环境危害时重述

---

[45] UNCLOS, supra footnote 1, Art. 192.

[46] See M. H. Nordquist, S. N. Nandan and J. Kraska (eds.), *United Nations Convention on the Law of the Sea: A Commentary*, Vol. IV (Dordrecht/Boston: Martinus Nijhoff, 1991), pp. 35–43.

[47] See supra footnote 36.

[48] *South China Sea Arbitration*, supra footnote 35, para. 941.

[49] *South China Sea Arbitration*, supra footnote 35, para. 944. See also *Pulp Mills on the River Uruguay (Argentina v. Uruguay), Judgment*, I. C. J. Reports 2010, p. 14, para. 197; *Responsibilities and obligations of States sponsoring persons and entities with respect to activities in the Area*, Advisory Opinion of 1 February 2011, ITLOS Case No. 17, para. 117; *IUU Advisory Opinion*, supra footnote 34, para. 131; *In the matter of the Indus Waters Kishenganga Arbitration before the Court of Arbitration constituted in accordance with the Indus Waters Treaty 1960 between the Government of India and the Government of Pakistan signed on 19 September 1960 (Islamic Republic of Pakistan v. Republic of India)*, PCA, Partial Award (18 February 2013), para. 450-451.

[50] *South China Sea Arbitration*, supra footnote 35, para. 964.

[51] *South China Sea Arbitration*, supra footnote 35, para. 974. See further *Pulp Mills*, supra footnote 49, para. 187; *Responsibilities in the Area*, supra footnote 49, para. 110; *IUU Advisory Opinion*, supra footnote 34, para. 129.

了风险预防原则，[52] 并明确了可以采取何种类型的措施，[53] 还针对这些措施的外延做出了限制，即"不应对其他国家依照本公约行使其权利并履行其义务所进行的活动有不当的干扰"。[54] 所谓超越这一外延，指的是干扰了其他国家在公约中的实际（而非预期）权利或对它们履行义务的能力造成了不相称的侵犯。[55] 第三，第192条规定的一般义务，恰如习惯法中的损害预防原则，是由两种主要的程序性义务来进一步阐明的，即合作义务[56]以及监测和评估义务。[57] 这两种义务都有习惯法基础，[58] 它们相当于是环境保护习惯法（谨慎、预防、合作和环评）在海洋法具体内容中的重述。[59]

关于上述第二个要件，《联合国海洋法公约》对海洋污染的五种主要形式做了区分，分别是陆源（包括内陆水道）污染、[60] 来自船只的污染、[61] 倾倒或焚化造成的污染、[62] 来自大气层或通过大气层的污染、[63] 海底活动或"区域"内活动造成的污染。[64] 第207—212条规定了各国（包括

---

52 UNCLOS, supra footnote 1, Art. 194 (2).

53 UNCLOS, supra footnote 1, Art. 194 (3) and (5).

54 UNCLOS, supra footnote 1, Art. 194 (4). (emphasis added).

55 *Chagos Island Arbitration*, supra footnote 23, paras. 540 ［法庭功能地将第2条第3款、第56条第2款和第194条第4款的范围等同起来并得出结论，由于英国没有与毛里求斯进行适当协商就建立了一个海洋保护区，英国就侵占了毛里求斯的实际捕捞权（违反了第194条第4款）。但是，法庭指出，英国的环保措施并没有违反兰卡斯特承诺（英国承诺将查戈斯群岛归还给毛里求斯）所引发的权利（特别是涉及石油勘探和开发时），因为这些权利是"预期的"，毛里求斯并没有基于这些权利来有效开展任何活动］。

56 UNCLOS, supra footnote 1, Part XII, Section 2, Arts. 197-201.

57 UNCLOS, supra footnote 1, Part XII, Section 2, Part XII, Section 4, Arts. 204-206.

58 *South China Sea Arbitration*, suprafootnote 35, paras. 946-948.

59 See *Certain activities carried out by Nicaragua in the Border Area* (Costa Rica v. Nicaragua), *Construction of a road in Costa Rica along the river San Juan* (Nicaragua v. Costa Rica), Judgment of 16 December 2015 (I.C.J.), para. 104. For a detailed analysis of this set of customary norms relating to environmental protection see J. E. Viñuales, "La Protección Ambiental en el Derecho Internacional Consuetudinario (2017) 69/2 *Revista Española de Derecho Internacional* 71.

60 Ibid., Arts. 207 and 213.

61 Ibid., Arts. 211 and 217-221.

62 Ibid., Arts. 210 and 216.

63 Ibid., Arts. 212 and 222.

64 Ibid., Arts. 208, 209, 214, and 215.

沿海国和船旗国）预防、减少和控制这些污染源造成污染的相关义务。[65] 整体来看，这些条款其实是规定了两种类型的义务，即横向义务（合作义务以便制定议定的国际规则）和纵向义务（采取措施以便处理每个污染源造成的污染）。根据污染源的不同情况，纵向义务不得低于国际规则或标准的效力（针对区域内活动造成的污染、倾倒和船只污染），或者相对保守一点，应当"适当考虑"这些规则和标准（针对陆源污染和大气污染）。例如，针对倾倒造成的污染，第210条规定，各国制定的法律、规章和措施应确保非经各国主管当局准许不得进行倾倒，[66] 而且非经沿海国事前明示核准，不得在领海、专属经济区内、大陆架上进行倾倒。[67] 另外，根据第210条第6款，国内法律、规章和措施在防止、减少和控制这种污染方面的效力应不低于"全球性规则和标准"。[68] 相比之下，针对陆源污染，第207条仅仅要求各国应考虑到国际上议定的标准和实践。[69] 但是，第207条第5款则规定，所采取的措施"应尽量减少有毒、有害或有碍健康的物质，特别是持久性物质"，但是这一义务的前提是"最大可能范围内"。从一些专门应对特定类别污染（倾倒污染和船只造成的污染）的条约以及政治因素（特别针对陆源污染）中，我们都可以发现这些不同层级的要求。

关于上述第三个要件，那些参加过《联合国海洋法公约》谈判的人都知道，自1974年的第三次法律编撰大会以来，就必须要明确公约与现有（或将来的）涉及海洋环境保护的条约和协定的关系。[70] 《联合国海洋法公约》第237条负责管理公约第十二部分与其他条约和协定的关系（不同于公约整体与其他条约和协定的关系[71]）。虽然看起来似乎有点模棱

65　Ibid., Arts. 207（1）-（2），208（1）-（2），209（2），210（1）-（2），211（1），212（1）.

66　Ibid., Art. 210（3）.

67　Ibid., Art. 210（5）.

68　Ibid., Art. 210（6）. 本段可以被当成后文将要谈到的1972年《伦敦公约》的参考来解读。针对来自海底活动造成的污染和区域内的污染都规定了类似要求［但是指的是国际标准和实践（Arts. 208（3）and 209（2）］and pollution from ships（Art. 211（2））.

69　Ibid., Art. 207（1）. 针对空气和越界空气污染规定了类似要求（Art. 212（1））.

70　On the history of Art. 37, see Nordquist et al., supra footnote 46, para. 237.2-237.6.

71　Ibid., para. 237.7（a）, referring to the UNCLOS, supra footnote 1, Art. 311.

两可,但是这种关系遵循的还是特别法(lex specialis)原则。各国在现有(或将来的)特别条约和协定中承担的特殊义务应优先于第十二部分规定的义务,除非它们不符合"本公约一般原则和目标"。[72] 这种不相符应当是相当严重的,否则它就无法触发本公约"一般"原则和目标这一门槛。在国际海事组织框架下制定的大量条约和标准就更加注意它们与《联合国海洋法公约》第十二部分之间的关系。国际海事组织的立场是,公约的第 237 条(以及第 311 条)并不妨碍它的规范性行为或者限制它的管理权限。相反,《联合国海洋法公约》似乎在很多方面还依赖于国际海事组织的规范作用以实现自己的目标。[73] 后文将会谈及,有几个国际文件涉及海洋环境的保护,它们是对《联合国海洋法公约》第十二部分所构思的框架的补充。[74]

三 污染源的规制

(一)概述

在国际海事组织框架下,制定了多个文件以保护海洋环境免受污染。《联合国海洋法公约》对不同的污染源做出了区分,这也为我们组建本节的内容结构提供了一个便捷的基础。在此背景下,我们将依次分析有关船舶污染(运行或事故)、(故意的)倾倒或焚化造成的污染和陆源污染的主要国际文件。需要强调指出的是,虽然前两种海洋污染受到了国际层面的关注,但是陆源污染在所有海洋污染中的占比约是 80%。2015 年制定的《2030 年可持续发展议程》回顾了陆源污染的重要影响,并将其列为 17 项可持续发展目标之一(第 14 项可持续发展目标下 14.1 子目标)。[75] 本节将在最后分析陆源污染,因为它的国际法律规范在本质上是区域性的。

72　UNCLOS, supra footnote 1, Art. 237(2).

73　See IMO, Implications of the United Nations Convention on the Law of the Sea, 1982, for the International Maritime Organization (IMO), Doc. LEG/MISC/1 (1986 mimeo.), paras. 71-73, cited in Nordquist et al., supra footnote 46, para. 237.7 (e).

74　See Nordquist et al., supra footnote 46, para. XII. 26.

75　Resolution 70/1, "Transforming our World: The 2030 Agenda for Sustainable Development", 21 October 2015, UN doc A/RES/70/1, including the statement of 17 Sustainable Development Goals, each with several targets. Target 14.1 under SDG 14 aims to "prevent and significantly reduce marine pollution of all kinds, in particular from land-based activities, including marine debris and nutrient pollution" by 2025.

（二）源自船舶的污染

这种类型的污染来自船舶货运的正常运行以及其在运输过程中可能发生的事故。[76] 这一领域制定的国际文件的目标主要是：（1）尽量减少（包括预防）石油或者其他有害物质的泄漏；（2）在发生意外事故时促进局面的管控；（3）为造成的损害建立一套赔偿制度。我们在此将主要关注第（1）点和第（2）点，第（3）点将在第八章讨论。

早在1954年，许多国家就通过了《国际防止海上油污公约》。[77] 20世纪60年代，这个公约的缺点越发明显，特别是在一艘悬挂利比里亚国旗的油轮"托里坎荣号"在英国海滩搁浅并导致约12万吨原油泄漏到海里的事件发生之后。其导致的后果是，这一公约被1973年制定的《防止船舶污染国际公约》及其1978年议定书所取代。[78]《防止船舶污染国际公约》适用于船舶[79]所"排放"[80] 的"有害物质"[81]。这些术语都是从广义上定义的，但是存在着两个关键性的细微差别。谈及"船舶"这一术语，它可能是一艘船，或者是一艘潜水艇，还可能是一个固定或漂浮的平台，它们悬挂着某一缔约国的国旗或者由其负责运营。[82] 但是，用于政府目的的船舶，例如军事船舶，则不包含在内。[83] 谈及"排放"这一术语，第2条第3款将《伦敦公约》规定的倾倒（后文将会讨论这一问题）及其他一些排放排除在其定义之外。[84]《防止船舶污染国际公约》框架下旨在预

---

[76] See in general, A. K. -J. Tan, *Vessel-Source Marine Pollution* (Cambridge University Press, 2006).

[77] International Convention for the Prevention of Pollution of the Sea by Oil, 12 May 1954, 327 UNTS 3.

[78] International Convention for the Prevention of Pollution from Ships, 2 November 1973, amended by the Protocol of 17 February 1978, 1341 UNTS 3 ("MARPOL 73/78"). See J. Kindt, "Vessel Source Pollution and the Law of the Sea" (1984) 17 *Vanderbilt Journal of Transnational Law* 287; M. Fitzmaurice, "The International Convention for the Prevention of Pollution from Ships (MARPOL)", in Attard et al., supra footnote 2, pp. 33-77. The 1978 Protocol facilitated the entry into force of the Convention by allowing for more time for the implementation of Annex II of the Convention.

[79] Ibid., Art. 2 (4).

[80] MARPOL, supra footnote 78, Art. 2 (3).

[81] MARPOL, supra footnote 78, Art. 2 (2).

[82] MARPOL, supra footnote 78, Art. 3 (1).

[83] MARPOL, supra footnote 78, Art. 3 (3).

[84] MARPOL, supra footnote 78, Art. 3 (3) (b) (i).

防和减少排放的规章被收录于六个附录之中。[85] 前两个附录是强制性的，只有接受它们才能成为缔约国。针对不同的污染种类，《防止船舶污染国际公约》相应地采取了不同的手段。针对油污染，一方面，制定了一套各国必须达到的要求（运行排放的技术要求、油轮的建造——用双壳体船舶逐步替代单壳体船舶、建设充足的岸上装置来接收油渣和含油混合物、船上应急方案的制订、界定那些对污染预防有着更严格要求的海上"特别地区"）；另一方面，针对这些要求建立一套控制系统（认证、运行登记、船舶检查）。简言之，各国必须采取技术措施来落实那些旨在减少排放和预防事故的制度。[86] 总体而言，《防止船舶污染国际公约》对应对船舶造成的污染做出了重大的贡献，但还存在一些挑战，特别是在执行方面（例如船旗国对悬挂方便旗的船舶的执法力度偏弱）以及发展中国家对某些要求的落实方面（例如有关充足的岸上装置的规定）。[87]

在发生事故的情况下，其他一些规则就会适用于事故应对措施的管理。这些事故有可能会造成重大损害，因此非常有必要组织这套应对措施。1967年"托里坎荣"号、1978年"卡迪兹"号、1989年"埃克森·瓦尔迪兹"号、1999年"埃里卡"号、2002年"威望"号、2007年"河北精神"号油轮的搁浅，或者墨西哥湾的"深水地平线"钻井平台爆炸事故（2010年）造成的重大石油泄漏为这类风险的严重程度提供了大量实例。《联合国海洋法公约》针对这类事故的应对措施的管理作了一些基本规定，[88] 而在国

---

85 Annex I (Regulations for the Prevention of Pollution by Oil); Annex II (Regulations for the Control of Pollution by Noxious Liquid Substances in Bulk); Annex III (Regulations for the Prevention of Pollution by Harmful Substances Carried at Sea in Packaged Form); Annex IV (Regulations for the Prevention of Pollution by Sewage from Ships); Annex V (Regulations for the Control of Pollution by Garbage from Ships); Annex VI (Regulations for the Prevention of Air Pollution from Ships).

86 Other relevant texts in this regard include: the International Convention for the Control and Management of Ships Ballast Water and Sediments, 16 February 2004, available at www.ecolex.org (TRE-001412); the International Convention on the Control of Harmful Anti-fouling Systems on Ships, 5 October 2001, available at www.ecolex.org (TRE-001394) ("AFS Convention").

87 See Fitzmaurice, supra footnote 781, pp. 75-76.

88 UNCLOS, supra footnote 1, Arts. 198 (Notification of Imminent or Actual Damage), 199 (Contingency Plans against Pollution), and 211 (7) (Pollution from Vessels).

际和区域层面针对这一问题的法律文书则构成了一个更广泛的网络体系。[89] 在"托里坎荣"号事故发生后不久,在国际海事组织框架下,《国际干预公海油污事件公约》(《干预公约》)得以制定。[90] 该公约确认,沿海国为了保护自身不受海事事故后果的影响有权采取干预措施,同时,这一干预权利的行使也必须在一定范围内[只能采取必要措施,而且必须是在与相关利益方(包括船旗国)协商之后]。《防止船舶污染国际公约》通过将应急方案列为必备要求进一步强化了这一框架。后来,在1989年"埃克森·瓦尔迪兹"号沉没后不久,《国际油污防备、反应和合作公约》[91] 得以制定以便进一步巩固全球反应机制。这一公约的每个缔约国都必须落实到位一套制度以应对石油泄漏,其内容至少应当包含相关职能机构的指派和一个应对紧急情况的国家应急方案。[92] 各国还必须要求在其管辖下的船舶和平台拥有一个紧急情况应急方案以便应对任何意外事故。[93] 除了这些安排以外,还应补充一些通知程序,用于告知某一"事件"(例如石油泄漏)正在发生或可能发生,[94] 以及在预防[95]和管理此类事件时应承担的合作义务。[96] 2000 年 3 月,《国际油污防备、反应和合作

---

[89] On this body of rules see G. Gonzalez, F. Hébert, "Conventions relating to Pollution Incident Preparedness, Response and Cooperation", in Attard et al., supra footnote 2, pp. 195-256 (including a discussion of the frameworks applicable in regional seas).

[90] International Convention relating to Intervention on the High Seas in cases of Oil Pollution Casualties, 29 November 1969, available at www.ecolex.org (TRE-000111) ("Intervention Convention"). On this instrument see A. Blanco-Bazán, "Intervention in the High Seas in case of Marine Pollution Casualties", in Attard et al., supra footnote 2, pp. 261-282.

[91] International Convention on Oil Pollution Preparedness, Response and Cooperation, 30 November 1990, available at www.ecolex.org (TRE-001109) ("OPRC Convention").

[92] International Convention on Oil Pollution Preparedness, Response and Cooperation, 30 November 1990, Art. 6.

[93] International Convention on Oil Pollution Preparedness, Response and Cooperation, 30 November 1990, Art. 3.

[94] International Convention on Oil Pollution Preparedness, Response and Cooperation, 30 November 1990, Arts. 4 and 5.

[95] International Convention on Oil Pollution Preparedness, Response and Cooperation, 30 November 1990, Arts. 8-10.

[96] International Convention on Oil Pollution Preparedness, Response and Cooperation, 30 November 1990, Art. 7.

公约》的一项议定书得以制定,[97] 将公约的适用范围从石油污染拓展到有害和有毒物质。

(三) 倾倒、焚烧和海洋地质工程

废物和其他物质的倾倒在海洋污染的占比接近 10%,为此,一项全球范围的条约得以制定。[98] 这一条约的最早推动力在于,20 世纪 40 年代,向海洋倾倒被当作解决放射性废物处置问题的一种方法。1958 年联合国第二次海洋法大会决定,这类物质的倾倒必须符合相关组织 [特别是国际原子能机构 (International Atomic Energy Agency, IAEA)] 制定的安全标准。国际原子能机构在 1961 年制定了安全标准,从那时起将这一问题纳入自己的职权范围。但是,直到 1972 年《伦敦公约》(《倾废公约》) 制定之前,还没有一项全球性规制架构来管理放射性废物以及其他各种废物的倾倒。这项条约后来被修订了几次,特别是在 1996 制定的《伦敦议定书》(London Protocol)。[99]

《伦敦公约》共计 22 条和 3 个附录。它的一般方法其实很简单:缔约国应采取措施来禁止或限制特定废物的排放,附录三则按照有害程度的大小顺序列举出了这些废物。除了那些最有害物质之外,向海洋倾倒并不被禁止,而只是受到规制。第 3 条第 1 款对"倾倒"的定义是"在海洋中故意处置废物或来自船舶、航空器、平台及海洋中其他人造建筑物的其他物质";同时为了避免歧义,还包含了"在海洋中故意处置船舶、航空器、平台及海洋中其他人造建筑物"。《防止船舶污染国际公约》涵盖的正常运行排放则被排除在这一定义之外。[100] 术语"海洋"涵盖了除内陆水

---

[97] Protocol on Preparedness, Response and Cooperation to Pollution Incidents by Hazardous and Noxious Substances, 15 March 2000, available at: www.ecolex.org (TRE - 002482) ("Protocol OPRC-HNS").

[98] For a study of the global and regional regulation of dumping see H. Esmaeili, B. Grigg, "Pollution from Dumping", in Attard et al., supra footnote 2, pp. 78-94.

[99] Convention on the Prevention of Marine Pollution by Dumping of Wastes and Other Matter, 29 December 1972 ("London Convention"), subsequently modified by the Protocol of 7 November 1996 to the Convention of 1972 on the Prevention of Marine Pollution by Dumping of Wastes and Other Matter, 7 November 1996, 1046 UNTS 120 ("London Protocol").

[100] London Convention, supra footnote 99, Art. III (1) (b).

之外的所有海洋地区。[101] "废物和其他物质"是一个广义的定义，[102] 针对不同附录中列举的各种特定的废物应适用相应的具体制度。根据公约第3条的规定，附录一中的废物（例如石油、水银、放射性废物等）的倾倒是被禁止的，[103] 而附录二中的物质（砷、铅、铜、锌等）和附录三中的物质（受到数量限制或处置地限制的其他废物）的倾倒则必须符合一个特别[104]或一般的许可制度。[105]

随着《伦敦议定书》在2006年3月开始生效，这种一般方法（除非有特别禁止，倾倒就可以被批准）被修订。《伦敦议定书》是基于风险预防原则，[106] 它修改了公约这一基本方法。新的规则是，除非被明确批准，那么在海洋中倾倒和焚化就是被禁止的，[107] 例如议定书附录一列举的物质在许可颁发之前不得倾倒。[108] 对那些同为《伦敦公约》和《伦敦议定书》的缔约国而言，议定书替代了《伦敦公约》，[109] 但是《伦敦议定书》还是会对那些并非《伦敦公约》的缔约国开放。[110]

1996年的议定书是涉及气候变化的艰难谈判的多种积极尝试中的一个，它特别涉及碳捕获和隔离（如果隔离采用的是掘土储存的方式）以及海洋地质工程（涉及"海洋发酵"的提议）。[111] 关于碳捕获和隔离，公约在2006年被修订，将掘土储存的二氧化碳也纳入附录一中的安全物质。这一修订在2007年开始生效。[112] 谈及"海洋发酵"，这一问题指的是向海

---

[101] London Convention, supra footnote 99, Art. 3 (3). 《伦敦议定书》进一步阐明了这一表述，它将"海底和底土"也纳入海洋空间的范畴 [London Protocol, supra footnote 99, Art. 1 (7)] 并规定了与适用于内陆水的国内法等同的要求 [Art. 7 (2)]。

[102] London Convention, supra footnote 99, Art. III (4).

[103] London Convention, supra footnote 99, Art. IV (1) (a).

[104] London Convention, supra footnote 99, Art. IV (1) (b).

[105] London Convention, supra footnote 99, Art. IV (1) (c).

[106] London Protocol, supra footnote 99, Art. 3 (1).

[107] London Protocol, supra footnote 99, Art. 5.

[108] London Protocol, supra footnote 99, Art. 4 (1).

[109] London Protocol, supra footnote 99, Art. 23.

[110] London Protocol, supra footnote 99, Art. 24 (1).

[111] See Esmaeili, Grigg, supra footnote 98, pp. 83-85.

[112] 一个针对第6条（关于废物和其他物质的出口，它允许为了倾倒的目的而将二氧化碳出口到非缔约方）的相关修订在2009年被制定但是尚未生效。

洋中排放特定物质以促进浮游植物的生长（这样一来就相当于是一种碳捕获和隔离机制）这一事项是否应当受到议定书的规制。在议定书确实应当涵盖这一事项的初步决议达成后，相关修订案在2013年获得一致通过。这一修订案到目前为止尚未生效，它在第5条增加了一段（用于定义"海洋地质工程"）和两个附录（附录四和附录五），规定除非可以被适当证明是用于科学研究，否则禁止海洋发酵。这些进展强调了气候变化问题（第五章）的延伸范围，应对气候变化必须通过多种规制架构。

（四）陆源污染

陆源污染占到了海洋污染的80%，它有的是由城市和农业排放直接造成，或者是由水道或地下水间接造成。正如前文所述，第14项可持续发展目标下14.1子目标已经回顾了陆源污染的重大影响以及解决这一问题的紧迫性。[113] 但是，因为造成这一污染的来源和活动是各式各样的，各国和各个地理地区的情况也不尽相同，这就使得全球性的规制变得困难。[114]《联合国海洋法公约》包含了针对陆源污染的条款，包括第207条（各国防止、减少和控制此类污染的义务）和第213条（执行的义务）。[115] 另外，根据第207条第1款，各国应当考虑到"国际上议定的规则、标准和建议的办法及程序"。这一要求其实要低于那些适用于其他污染源的要求，即各国必须采取效力不低于全球标准的措施。

伴随《联合国海洋法公约》的通过，（国际社会）采取了数个步骤制定陆源污染的国际标准。最早的例证来自1985年制定的《关于保护海洋环境免受陆源污染影响的蒙特利尔导则》(*Montreal Guidelines for the Pro*

---

[113] *Transforming our World*, supra footnote 75, SDG 14, target 14.1. See also target 14.3 relating to ocean acidification which is mainly the result of land-based pollution.

[114] See M. Qing-Nan, *Land-based Marine Pollution: International Law Development* (Leiden: Martinus Nijhoff, 1987); T. Mensah, "The International Legal Regime for the Protection and Preservation of the Marine Environment from Land Based Sources", in A. Boyle and D. Freestone (eds.), *International Law and Sustainable Development: Past Achievements and Future Challenges* (Oxford University Press, 1999), pp. 297–324; Y. Tanaka, "Regulation of Land-based Marine Pollution", in Attard et al., supra footnote 2, pp. 139–168.

[115] See Qing-Nan, supra footnote 114, Chapter 4.

tection of the Marine Environment against Pollution from Land-based Sources）。[116] 《蒙特利尔导则》明确了各国为了防止、减少和控制陆源污染所能采取的数种措施，包括环境影响评价和监测、通知、协商和其他形式的合作，以及一些基于地方的管理手段（导则附录一中的"特别保护区"）和对发展中国家的援助。数年之后，在 1992 年环境与发展里约大会上，《21 世纪议程》第 17 章[117]要求联合国环境规划署召集一次政府间会议来讨论保护海洋环境不受陆源污染。这一会议于 1995 年 10—11 月在华盛顿特区召开，它的结果是通过了两项重要的软法文件，即《保护海洋环境免受陆上活动污染华盛顿宣言》（Washington Declaration on Protection of the Marine Environment from Land-Based Activities）和《保护海洋环境免受陆上活动污染全球行动方案》（Global Programme of Action for the Protection of the Marine Environment from Land-Based Activities）。[118]《全球行动方案》认可将风险预防的方法用于陆源污染，这其实是对《21 世纪议程》的遵循。对此方案的落实在不同场合得到了再次确认，包括在 2012 年 1 月通过的《马尼拉宣言》（Manila Declaratio）中。[119]

与管理船舶污染和倾废污染不同，陆源污染缺少一个全球性框架；幸运的是，国际习惯法的发展以及一些区域性法律文书的存在在一定程度上弥补了这一缺憾。正如本章前文所述，《联合国海洋法公约》第十二部分所规定的一般义务，特别是第 192 条和第 194 条，适用于所有国家（作为风险预防原则在国际习惯法中的反映）和所有海洋空间。有人担心这样的一般义务到底能发挥多大实际作用，而近些年的司法实践表明，这些义务在涉及重大法律后果的情况下可以适用。[120] 另外，1997 年《联合国国际水道非航行利用法公约》[121] 在 2014 年开始生效，它特别针对的是陆源污染抵达

---

[116] Reproduced in: H. Hohmann (ed.), *Basic Documents of International Environmental Law* (London, 1992), Vol. I, pp. 130-147. See Qing-Nan, supra footnote 114, Chapter 6.

[117] Report of the United Nations Conference on Environment and Development, A/CONF. 151/ 26/ Rev. 1 (Vol. 1), Resolution 1, Annex 2: Agenda 21 ("Agenda 21").

[118] UN Doc. UNEP (OCA) /LBA/IG. 2/7.

[119] UNEP/GPA/IGR. 3/CRP. 1/Rev. 1, 26 January 2012, available at www. unep. org (visited on 2 April 2017).

[120] See supra section 4. 2. 2.

[121] See infra footnote 147.

海洋环境的多个渠道中的一个。该公约的第 23 条要求各国"对国际水道采取一切必要措施以保护和保全海洋环境"。同时，后文将会谈及，在区域层面，包含陆源海洋污染相关规定的多个条约和制度安排也得以制定。[122]

四 区域海洋环境的保护

关于区域海洋环境的保护，已经有了超过 40 个公约、协定和议定书。其中绝大多数是根据联合国环境规划署在 1974 年建立的"区域海洋项目"（Regional Seas Programme，RSP）而制定的，而这一项目的依据则是 1972 年斯德哥尔摩会议通过的行动计划。[123]

区域海洋项目包含了 13 个行动计划，分别针对全球范围内的不同海域，包括 9 个已建立地区公约的海域（地中海地区、[124] 科威特区域行动方案、[125] 西非地区、[126] 东南太平洋地区、[127] 红海和亚丁湾地区、[128] 加勒比海地区、[129] 东非

---

[122] See Tanaka, supra footnote 114, pp. 150ff.

[123] UNEP, Report of the Governing Council on the Work of Its First Session (12-22 June 1973), New York, Decision 1 (I), Section III, para. 12 (e): Report of the Governing Council on the Work of its Second Session (11-22 March 1974), New York, Decision 8 (II), Section A I, Chapter 4. See on this subject, the Internet site of the RSP, available on: www.unep.org/regionalseas/about/default.asp (visited on 15 October 2012).

[124] Convention for the Protection of the Mediterranean Sea against Pollution, 16 February 1976, as amended and later becoming the Convention for the Protection of the Marine Environment and the Mediterranean Coastal Environment, 10 June 1995 ("Barcelona Convention"), available at: www.ecolex.org (TRE-001284).

[125] Regional Convention for Cooperation on the Protection of the Marine Environment from Pollution, 24 April 1978 ("Kuwait Convention"), available at: www.ecolex.org (TRE-000537).

[126] Convention for Co-operation in the Protection and Development of the Marine and Coastal Environment of the West and Central African Region, 23 March 1981 ("Abidjan Convention"), available at: www.ecolex.org (TRE-000547).

[127] Convention Concerning the Protection of the Marine Environment and Coastal Area of the South East Pacific, 1981 ("Lima Convention"), available at: www.ecolex.org (TRE-000741).

[128] Regional Convention for the Conservation of the Marine Environment of the Red Sea and Gulf of Aden, 14 February 1982 ("Jeddah Convention"), available at: www.ecolex.org (TRE-000743).

[129] Convention for the Protection and Development of the Marine Environment of the Wider Caribbean Region, 24 March 1983 ("Convention"), available at: www.ecolex.org (TRE-000763).

地区、[130] 西南太平洋地区、[131] 黑海地区[132]）。这些公约在绝大多数情况下都会配套有相应的议定书以补充规定具体事项，例如陆源污染、[133] 意外事故造成的石油和其他物质污染、[134] 倾倒废物造成的污染、[135] 海床勘探和开发

---

[130] Convention for the Protection, Management and Development of the Marine and Coastal Region of East Africa, 21 June 1985 ("Nairobi Convention"), available at: www.ecolex.org (TRE-000821).

[131] Convention for the Protection of Natural Resources and Environment of the South Pacific Region, 25 November 1986 ("Noumea Convention"), available at: www.ecolex.org (TRE-000892).

[132] Convention on the Protection of the Black Sea against Pollution, 21 April 1992 ("Bucharest Convention"), available at: www.ecolex.org (TRE-001149).

[133] Protocol of the Protection of the Mediterranean Sea against Pollution from Land-Based Sources, 17 May 1980, available at: www.ecolex.org (TRE-000544); Protocol for the Protection of the South-East Atlantic against Pollution from Land-based Sources, 22 July 1983, available at: www.ecolex.org (TRE-000768); Kuwait Protocol on the Protection of the Marine Environment Against Pollution from Land-based Sources, 21 February 1990, available at: www.ecolex.org (TRE-001129); Protocol on the Protection of the Marine Environment of the Black Sea Against Pollution from Land-based Sources, 21 April 1992, available at: www.ecolex.org (TRE-001392).

[134] Protocol Concerning Cooperation in Preventing Pollution from Ships and, in Cases of Emergency, Combating Pollution of the Mediterranean Sea, 25 January 2002, available at: www.ecolex.org (TRE-001402); Protocol Concerning Cooperation in Combating Pollution in Cases of Emergency, 23 March 1981, available at: www.ecolex.org (TRE-000548); Agreement on Regional Cooperation in Combating Pollution of the South-East Pacific by Hydrocarbons or Other Harmful Substances in Cases of Emergency, 12 November 1981, available at: www.ecolex.org (TRE-000742); Supplementary Protocol on the Agreement on Regional Cooperation in Combating Pollution of the South-East Pacific by Hydrocarbons or Other Harmful Substances in Cases of Emergency, 22 July 1983, available at: www.ecolex.org (TRE-000769); Protocol Concerning Regional Cooperation in Combating Pollution by Oil and Other Harmful Substances in Cases of Emergency, 14 February 1982 (Red Sea and Gulf of Aden), available at: www.ecolex.org (TRE-000745); Protocol Concerning Cooperation in Combating Oil Spills in the Wider Caribbean Region, 24 March 1983, available at: www.ecolex.org (TRE-000764); Protocol Concerning Cooperation in Combating Marine Pollution in Cases of Emergency in the Eastern African Region, 21 June 1985, available at: www.ecolex.org (TRE-000825); Protocol on Cooperation in Combating Pollution of the Black Sea Marine Environment by Oil and other Harmful Substances in Emergency Situations, 21 April 1992, available at: www.ecolex.org (TRE-001391).

[135] Protocol for the Prevention and Elimination of Pollution of the Mediterranean Sea by Dumping from Ships and Aircraft, 16 February 1976, available at: www.ecolex.org (TRE-001285); Protocol for the Prevention of Pollution of the South Pacific Region by Dumping, 25 November 1986, available at: www.ecolex.org (TRE-000893); Protocol on the Protection of the Marine Environment of the Black Sea Against Pollution by Dumping of Waste, 21 April 1992, available at: www.ecolex.org (TRE-001393).

造成的污染、[136] 该区域生物多样性的保护[137]、废物的越境转移。[138] 在区域海洋项目之外的其他一些海域也受到了特别体制的管理。现有的 5 个制度安排（北极、南极、波罗的海、里海和东北大西洋）中，除了北极之外的所有海域都有一个针对海洋环境保护的特别条约体制。[139]

在绝大多数情况下，区域体制的建立遵循了联合国环境规划署区域海洋项目实践中产生的模式。[140] 第一步是针对目标地区制订一项"行动计

---

[136] Protocol for the Protection of the Mediterranean Sea against Pollution Resulting from Exploration and Exploitation of the Continental Shelf and the Seabed and its Subsoil, 14 October 1994, available at: www.ecolex.org (TRE-001206); Protocol concerning Marine Pollution resulting from Exploration and Exploitation of the Continental Shelf (ROPME Sea Area), 29 May 1989, available at: www.ecolex.org (TRE-001128).

[137] Protocol Concerning Specially Protected Areas and Biological Diversity in the Mediterranean, 10 June 1995, available at: www.ecolex.org (TRE-001220); Protocol Concerning Cooperation in Combating Marine Pollution in Cases of Emergency in the Eastern African Region, 21 June 1985, available at: www.ecolex.org (TRE-000825); Protocol for the Conservation and Management of Protected Marine and Coastal Areas of the South East Pacific, 21 September 1989, available at: www.ecolex.org (TRE-001085); Protocol Concerning Specially Protected Area and Wildlife (SPAW), 18 January 1990, available at: www.ecolex.org (TRE-001040); Black Sea Biodiversity and Landscape Conservation Protocol, 14 June 2002, available at: www.ecolex.org (TRE-154497).

[138] Protocol on the Prevention of Pollution of the Mediterranean Sea by Transboundary Movements of Hazardous Wastes and their Disposal (Hazardous Wastes Protocol), 1 October 1996, available at: www.ecolex.org (TRE-001334); Protocol on the Control of Marine Transboundary Movements and Disposal of Hazardous Wastes and other Wastes (ROPME Sea Area), 17 March 1998, available at: www.ecolex.org (TRE-001298).

[139] For the Antarctic: Antarctic Treaty, 1 December 1959, 402 UNTS 71 ("Antarctic Treaty"); Convention for the Conservation of Antarctic Seals, signed in London, 1 June 1972, 1080 UNTS 175 ("Antarctic Seals Convention"); Convention for the Conservation of Marine Living Resources, signed in Canberra, 20 May 1980, 1329 UNTS 47 ("CCAMLR"); Protocol to the Antarctic Treaty on Environmental Protection, signed in Madrid, 4 October 1991, 30 ILM 1455 (1991) ("Madrid Protocol"). For the Baltic Sea: Convention on the Protection of the Marine Environment of the Baltic Sea Area, 9 April 1992, available on www.ecolex.org (TRE-001153). For the North-East Atlantic: Convention for the Protection of the Marine Environment of the North-East Atlantic, 22 September 1992, 2354 UNTS 67 ("OSPAR Convention"). For the Caspian Sea: Framework Convention for the Protection of the Marine Environment in the Caspian Sea, 4 November 2003 ("Tehran Convention"), available at: www.ecolex.org (TRE-001396).

[140] See generally E. M. Mrema, "Regional Seas Programme. The Role played by UNEP in its Development and Governance", in Attard et al., supra footnote 2, pp. 345-378.

划"。如果政治上可行，接下来就是制定一个框架公约。最后一步是针对具体问题为相关公约制定议定书。对这些框架内容的具体分析不在本章讨论范围之内。[141] 无论如何，还是必须强调这些已通过法规的综合性特征。总体上看，上述框架协定都包含三个主要内容。[142] 第一，它们规定了在相关海域预防、减少和控制海洋污染的义务，并根据污染源（陆源、倾废、船舶污染、海床勘探和开发造成的污染、废物转移、大气污染、意外排放）的不同做出了区分。第二，针对监测、合作和技术援助、信息交换、环评等做出了一些技术和程序要求。第三，正如在处理环境事项上的通用方式，这些协定都会有一个体制安排，以便各缔约方可以根据事先定好的规则定期会面，也规定了秘书处的支持（联合国环境规划署在六个场合中发挥了这一功能）。与全球性方法相比，区域性法规具有多方面的好处。除了可以为某些地方的陆源污染制定更为具体的规定以外，[143] 它也为促进各国间的合作提供了机会，而不论这些国家之间的关系是否长期政治紧张。[144]

第三节　淡水资源的国际规制

一　规制框架

淡水资源大约占到了地球上所有水资源的 2.5%（剩余的 97.5% 是海水）。这个 2.5% 的绝大部分被冰封于北极冰盖和其他冰体之下（69.6%）。剩余的淡水主要集中在含水层（30.1%）中，极少部分分布在湖泊和河流（0.3%）中。[145] 然而，正如后文所述，针对淡水资源的国

---

[141] See Ibid.; M. Haward and J. Vince, *Oceans Governance in the Twenty-first Century: Managing the Blue Planet* (Cheltenham: Edward Elgar, 2008), Chapter 3.

[142] See P. Sands, *Principles of International Environmental Law* (Cambridge University Press, 2003), pp. 406 ff.

[143] See D. L. Vander Zwaag and A. Powers, "The Protection of the Marine Environment from Land-Based Pollution and Activities: Gauging the Tides of Global and Regional Governance" (2008) 23 *International Journal of Marine and Coastal Law* 423.

[144] Mrema, supra footnote 140, p. 373.

[145] World Development Report 2010: Development and Climate Change (World Bank), p. 139.

际规制最大部分是集中于国际水道,以及最近引起更多关注的地下水。换言之,这一领域的国际法只管理了世界上很小部分的淡水资源(特别是河流和湖泊,以及有限的含水层)。图4-3概括了这一现状。

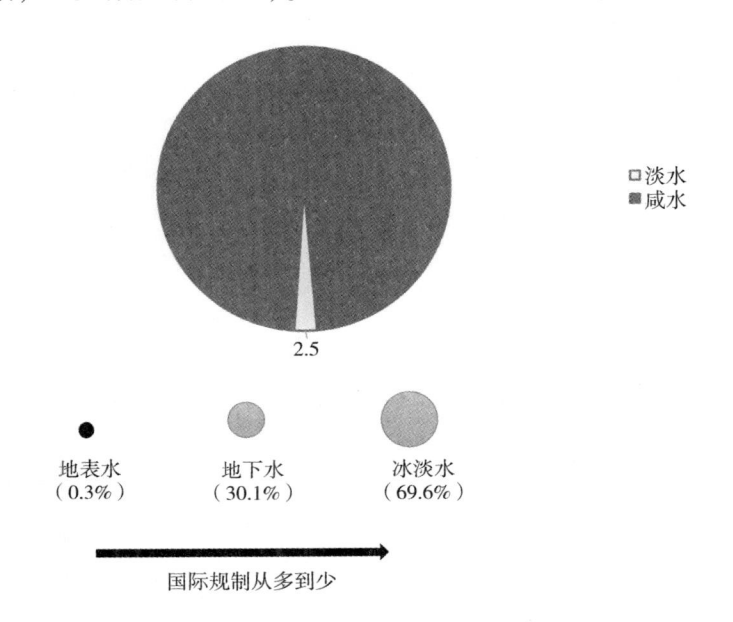

淡水
咸水

2.5

地表水（0.3%）　地下水（30.1%）　冰淡水（69.6%）

国际规制从多到少

图4-3　淡水资源及其国际规制

传统上,国际法是从两个基本视角来解决淡水的规制问题的,即(1)国际水道(包括湖泊)的航行利用;(2)淡水资源在沿岸国之间的分配。但是,从20世纪50年代开始,[146] 随着淡水资源更多地被用于农业、发电、工业利用和国内供给,连同人权的发展和环保意识的日益觉醒,针对管理水道的非航行利用的努力尝试成倍增加。[147] 这些尝试包括:(1)保全水质和受影响地区的环境;(2)将水权确定为一种人权。对淡

146　An earlier attempt was made under the aegis of the League of Nations and led to the adoption, on 9 December 1923, of a Convention relating to the Development of Hydraulic Power Affecting More than One State, 36 LNTS 77.

147　These efforts have been conducted mainly under the aegis of the *Institut de Droit International* (IDI) [particularly: "Utilization of Non-Maritime International Waters (except for Navigation)", Salzburg, 1961 ("Salzburg Resolution")], of the International Law Association (ILA) [particularly: Helsinki Rules on the Uses of the Waters of International Rivers, adopted at the 52nd conference of the ILA in August 1966 ("Helsinki Rules")]; Seoul Complementary Rules, adopted at the 62nd Conference

水资源的认知变化在《2030年可持续发展议程》中得到了显著体现。第六项可持续发展目标要求各国确保"水的提供和可持续管理"并列举了一整套涉及水的获取、水的善治以及水体和相关生态系统的保护。[148]

在后续部分，我们将不会谈及航行问题，[149] 而将关注水资源的分配和环境保护问题。将水权确定为一种人权这一问题将在第十章讨论。国际水道（本章第三节第二部分）、跨界含水层（本章第三节第三部分）、冰冻淡水（本章第三节第四部分）这几节的文本将会分析水资源的分配和环境保护这两个问题。

二　国际水道

国际水道的国际法主要包含了国际习惯法的一些原则，这些原则是从大量国家实践的立法编撰工作提炼出来的[150]，最终形成了一个全球范围的框架公约，即《联合国水道公约》（*UN Convention on Watercourses*）。这些原则随后也通过大量的双边和多边条约而适用于他特定的区域或水道。在这一部分，我们将集中讨论这些原则以及它们的相互关系。在描述"水道"这一术语后，我们将分析这一领域的管理所适用的四个主要原则，并在参考区域性和单行性水道文件的基础上得出结论。

---

of the ILA in 1986 ("Seoul Rules"); Berlin Rules on Water Resources, adopted by the ILA on 21 August 2004 ("Berlin Rules"), of the United Nations Economic Commission for Europe (UNECE) [Convention on the Protection and Use of Transboundary Watercourses and International Lakes, 18 March 1992, 1936 UNTS 269 ("Helsinki Convention")]; Protocol on Water and Health to the 1992 Convention on the Protection and Use of Transboundary Watercourses and International Lakes, 17 June 1999, 2331 UNTS 202 ("Protocol on Water and Health"), and of the United Nations International Law Commission (ILC) [United Nations Convention on the Law of the Non-Navigational Uses of International Watercourses, 21 May 1997, 36 ILM 700 ("UN Convention on Watercourses")]; "Draft Articles on the Law of Transboundary Aquifers", 11 December 2008, GA Res. 63/124, UN Doc. A/RES/63/124 ("ILC Aquifers Draft"). See S. Bogdanovic, *International Law of Water Resources: Contribution of the International Law Association (1954–2000)* (London: Kluwer Law International, 2001); E. Brown Weiss, "The Evolution of International Water Law", (2007) 331 *Recueil des cours de l'Académie de droit international de La Haye*, 161–404.

[148]　*Transforming our World*, supra footnote 75, SDG 6.

[149]　See S. McCaffrey, *The Law of International Watercourses* (Oxford University Press, 2nd edn, 2007), pp. 171–197.

[150]　See the work of the IDI, the ILA and the ILC, supra footnote 147.

正是"水道"这一概念给了这一部门法一定的整体性。作为法律规制的客体,这一概念随着时间的推移经历了重大变化。在理论上,可以从狭义上定义这一概念(例如连续或依次跨越某个国际边界的河流或湖泊),或者从广义上定义(流域及其生态系统),也可以采取一种折中的方法来定义(例如一个由连接的或非连接的地表水和地下水组成的系统,无论它是否流入一个共同的终点)。[151] 在过去十年中,国际实践中采用的概念越来越接近于流域这一概念,[152] 虽然《联合国水道公约》的概念依然将一些重要组成部分排除在外。事实上,公约将一个"国际水道"定义为"地面水和地下水的系统,由于它们之间的自然关系,构成一个整体单元,并且通常流入共同的终点",[153] 它并未包含受影响生态系统的其他要素,例如生态系统中流域的组成部分——土地(以及国家)或者与地表水无关的地下水(承压含水层)。

从一个概念化的角度来看,这些水道资源的分享可以采取以下四种不同的方法,即(1)"完全主权";(2)"完全领土完整";(3)"有限主权";(4)"利益共同体"。[154] 依据完全主权,某一国际水道的部分河段流经的国家可以针对这一段水道为所欲为,而无须顾及其行为对水道流经国家的影响和国际法的相关规定。[155] 与此相反,依据完全领土完整,水道上游国家开展的活动不得对下游国家的正常水流造成任何限制(无论大小或是否正当)。[156] 其他两个折中方法(有限主权和利益共同体)的区别在于沿岸国之间的合作及平等程度所起到的作用。有限主权指的是合作并未

---

[151] See L. Teclaff, "Evolution of the River Basin Concept in National and International Water Law" (1996) 36 *Natural Resources Journal* 359.

[152] See: Helsinki Rules, supra footnote 147, Art. 2; Helsinki Convention, supra footnote 147, Art. 1 (1) – (2); Protocol on Water and Health, supra footnote 147, Art. 5 (j); *Gabčíkovo-Nagymaros Project* (*Hungary v. Slovakia*), Judgment, ICJ Reports 1997, p. 7 ("*Gabčíkovo-Nagymaros Project*"), paras. 53 and 85.

[153] UN Convention on Watercourses, supra footnote 147, Art. 2 (a).

[154] See McCaffrey, supra footnote 147, pp. 111–170.

[155] 这一立场被称为"哈蒙主义",从1895年美国司法部长在一个与墨西哥有关格兰德河的争议中坚持这一主义之后,就受到了国际社会的抵制。Ibid., pp. 76–110.

[156] 这一立场是西班牙在与法国之间的 Lanoux 河一案中所坚持的,但是被法庭驳回,*Lake Lanoux Arbitration* (*Spain v. France*), Award of 16 November 1957, RIAA, Vol. XII, pp. 281ff ("*Lake Lanoux Arbitration*").

正式固定下来,但是水道上的每个国家都对水道的利用施加了限制,以免严重妨碍其他国家对水道的利用。利益共同体这种方法则对合作和平等程度提出了更高要求,通常的表现方式是建立一个制度框架来体现水道各国间的利益共同体。现代国际法的实践是处于有限主权和利益共同体两者之间。[157] 事实上,利益共同体这一方法最早是由国际常设法院(Permanent Court of International Justice, PCIJ)在"奥得河国际委员会管辖权案"的判决中提出的,[158] 它针对的是水道的航行利用,后来,在国际法院关于××××案的判决中被延伸到非航行利用。[159] 但是,国际法院在此案中将"利益共同体"这一概念等同于公平及合理利用原则,目的可能是强调在非航行利用的背景下沿岸国的平等并未剥夺某个(上游)国家在一定范围内使用水道的权利。在我们根据国际惯法来研究那些国际水道的非航行利用所应遵循的基本原则时,我们应当考虑到这一广义内涵。公平及合理利用、预防重大危害、合作和通知、保护和保全水道环境的义务这四个原则在《联合国水道公约》中都有体现。第一项原则是公平及合理利用以及公众参与。参照以前的文件,[160] 《联合国水道公约》第5条规定"水道国应在各自领土内公平合理地利用国际水道"。[161] 公约第6条第1款列举的标准[例如自然特征(包括地理特征)、经济和广义的社会因素、当前及可能的利用(包括替代方案、效果)等]可以用于分析某一利用是否公平合理。[162] 在国内法律体系中,水权是按照级别排序的;与这种情况

---

[157] M. Kohen, "Les principes généraux du droit international de l'eau à la lumière de la jurisprudence de la Cour internationale de Justice", in SFDI, *L'eau en droit international*, *Colloque d' Orléans* (Paris: Pedone, 2011), pp. 61-78.

[158] *Case relating to the territorial jurisdiction of the International Commission on the River Oder*, PCIJ Series A No. 23, Judgment (10 September 1929), p. 27.

[159] *Gabčíkovo-Nagymaros Project*, supra footnote 152, para. 85.

[160] See: Salzburg Resolution, supra footnote 147, Art. 3; Berlin Rules, supra footnote 147, Art. IV; J. A. Barberis and R. D. Hayton (eds.), *Droits et obligations des pays riverains desfleuves internationaux* (The Hague: Martinus Nijhoff, 1990), see the "Bilan des recherches" by J. A. Barberis.

[161] UN Convention on Watercourses, supra footnote 147, Art. 5. See also Helsinki Convention, supra footnote 147, Art. 2 (2) (b); Berlin Rules, supra footnote 147, Art. 12; *Gabčíkovo-Nagymaros Project*, supra footnote 152, para. 78.

[162] UN Convention on Watercourses, supra footnote 147, Art. 6 (1). Compare with Helsinki Rules, supra footnote 147, Art. V (2); Berlin Rules, supra footnote 147, Arts. 13 (2) and 14.

不同的是，在国际法中，水道的各种不同利用方式是没有层级排序的。唯一的一个提醒是，应当"特别关注"到"至关重要的人类需求"。[163] 当人权文件和混合型文件［例如《联合国欧洲经济委员会/世界贸易组织关于水和健康的欧洲议定书》（UNECE/WHO - Europe Protocol on Water and Health）］将水权认定为一项人权后，这一提醒就变得越来越重要。[164] 我们将在第十章中讨论这一问题。

公平及合理利用原则与预防对其他水道国造成重大危害的义务这两者之间的关系定位是一个难题。这一义务可以被理解为一个标准，用于评估某一水道利用的公平合理程度，[165] 或者被当作一个独立运行的原则，正如《联合国水道公约》第7条第1款之规定。但是，当这一义务被当作一个原则时，禁止造成危害有可能会剥夺公平或合理利用原则的内容，两者的区分就成为一个难题。反之，如果将无害义务仅仅当作一个标准，就会给上游国家的利益更多的优先权，它们比下游国家更有机会利用水道。可以在两个层面来解决这一冲突。第一个层面涉及危害的程度。只有达到一定严重程度（"重大的"）的危害才会构成对无害原则的违反，而一个较低程度的危害则只能被看成一个标准，这一标准与其他标准一起被用于评估公平合理利用原则的运用是否合理。第二个层面涉及的是预防对其他水道国造成重大危害这一义务的本质问题。国际法委员会对公约的巩固工作以及最终文本谈判委员会的工作都清楚表明，无害义务是"谨慎注意义务"的一种，换言之，只有重大危害的发生并不会触发活动缘起国的责任，这一点与严格责任的情况不同。即使活动缘起国尽到了谨慎注意义务，如果某一国际水道的利用还是造成了重大危害，该国将不被认为是违反了无害原则，但是它必须承担一个持续的义务来消除或减缓这一危害（将水道的利用纳入合理和公平利用的范畴之内），还必须商讨如何赔偿那些受伤害影响的国家。[166]

公平及合理利用原则与无害原则（要求预防环境危害）的关系同样

---

163 UN Convention on Watercourses, supra footnote 147, Art. 10.

164 Protocol on Water and Health, supra footnote 147.

165 As suggested by: Helsinki Rules, supra footnote 147, Art. IV; Berlin Rules, supra footnote 147, Art. 13; Helsinki Convention, supra footnote 147, Art. 2 (2) (b); UN Convention on Watercourses, supra footnote 147, Art. 6 (1) (d).

166 UN Convention on Watercourses, supra footnote 147, Art. 7 (2).

也提出了一些观念上的难题。我们其实在第三章中分析无害原则和预防原则之间的关系时已经讨论了这些难题。但是，需要指出的是，《联合国水道公约》通过第 20 条表明，它沿用了一种综合性方法来保护环境，它赋予各国"保护和保全国际水道生态系统"这一义务。[167] 这一义务的表述方式，以及更广义来看，《联合国水道公约》第四部分的表述其实都沿用了《联合国海洋法公约》第十二部分所采用的方法。《联合国水道公约》第 20 条与《联合国海洋法公约》第 192 条所发挥的作用相似，它规定了一项一般的、无条件的义务，即各国有义务不得危害水道的生态系统并有义务采取积极措施来保全它们。另外，第 20 条甚至在对其他水道国尚未造成任何危害（实际危害或威胁）的情况下也同样适用，[168] 这就使得它对那些水道一部分存在主权争议的案件显得尤其重要。《联合国水道公约》第 20 条把污染和生态平衡关联起来，它的这一突破进一步确认了《联合国海洋法公约》的影响。《联合国水道公约》第 21 条和第 23 条直接规定了"预防、减少和控制污染"的义务（专门针对水道），[169] 同时也间接规定了这一义务（当水道构成了海洋污染的一个来源）。[170] 第 22 条要求各国"采取一切必要措施，防止把那些可能对水道生态系统造成不利影响的外来物种或新的物种引入水道"。[171] 这类"入侵物种"所造成的有害影响的主要例证包括斑马贻贝入侵美国五大湖以及亚洲鲤鱼入侵密西西比河流域。[172] 关于这些预防义务在一般国际法中的基础，我们必须区分实体和程序这两个方面的问题。在实体方面，预防环境危害（包括在国际水道的语境下）是国际习惯法的一项要求，这一点已经确认无疑。[173] 关于程序性

---

[167] Ibid., Art. 20. Compare with the more detailed approach of the Helsinki Convention, supra footnote 147, Arts. 2 (2) and 3 and Annexes I–III.

[168] S. McCaffrey, "International Watercourses, Environmental Protection" (2011) *Max Planck Encyclopedia of Public International Law*, available at: http://opil.ouplaw.com (visited on 4 April 2017), para. 8.

[169] Ibid., Art. 21.

[170] Art. 23.

[171] UN Convention on Watercourses, supra footnote 147, Art. 22.

[172] McCaffrey, supra footnote 147, para. 15.

[173] See *Pulp Mills*, supra footnote 49, para. 101; *Indus Water Kishenganga*, supra footnote 49, paras. 448–450; *Costa Rica/Nicaragua*, supra footnote 59, para. 104. See further our analysis on the principle of prevention, supra Chapter 3.

规定，包括在《联合国水道公约》下如何开展环境合作，它们包含了习惯法和实践演进两方面的内容。[174]

最后一点就引发了国际水道中的合作义务这一问题。[175] 我们已经在第三章中讨论了这一义务的一般问题。在此，有必要再补充两点。第一，《联合国水道公约》的目的只是提供一个整体框架，各国可以根据各自需要在具体协定文本中对其进行修改。[176] 由此而论，公约对合作义务的表述[177]不如其他文件的表述精确。第二，公约第 9 条（数据和信息的定期交换）以及第 11—18 条（通知和协商）针对合作机制提供了一个精确的描述，这些合作机制被定期用于应对那些进行中的或计划开展的、有可能对其他水道国造成负面影响的活动。但是，有一个问题依然存在，即这些规定在多大程度上反映了习惯法。在实践中，答案就在于对善意原则的要求。虽然看起来各国没有权利否决其他国家的活动，[178] 但是，善意原则要求各国在启动那些有可能对他国造成重大负面影响的活动之前必须发布充分的告知，同时在开展此类活动之前还要安排一个合理的等待时间段。[179] 当存在不同意见时，习惯法施加了一项开展善意协商的义务，[180] 而且，在协商过程中，当事国无权开展此类活动，[181] 除非它们是非常紧急的而且已经被事先宣布。[182] 同样地，接到通知的国家基于善意原则不得以不答复的方式来阻止发出通知的国家开展计划中的活动。[183]

在缺乏更具体协定的情况下，这些原则提供了"共同体法"（droit

---

[174] See L. Caflisch, "La Convention du 21 mai 1997 sur l'utilisation des cours d'eaux internationaux a des fins autres que la navigation" (1997) 43 *Annuaire français de droit international* 751, 787.

[175] For a comprehensive study of this question see C. Leb, *Cooperation in the Law of Transboundary Water Resources* (Cambridge University Press, 2015).

[176] UN Convention on Watercourses, supra footnote 147, Arts. 3 and 4.

[177] UN Convention on Watercourses, Art. 8 (2). Compare with: Helsinki Convention, supra footnote 147, Arts. 9, 11 and 12.

[178] See supra footnote 162.

[179] 这一延迟不必是 6 个月（或 12 个月），这是《联合国水道公约》规定的，supra footnote 147, Art. 13. See also *Pulp Mills*, supra footnote 49, para. 120。

[180] *Lake Lanoux*, supra footnote 156, para. 22.

[181] *Pulp Mills*, supra footnote 49, para. 144.

[182] See UN Convention on Watercourses, supra footnote 147, Art. 19.

[183] See UN Convention on Watercourses, supra footnote 147, Art. 16 (1).

commun）这一概念来管理各水道国之间的关系。《联合国水道公约》第 3 条明确认可这类协定，无论它们的制定是在公约之前或之后。俄勒冈大学编撰的一个国际淡水协定合集收集了将近 300 个水道协定（针对航行和非航行利用），它们是在 1948—2002 年制定的、涉及世界上 263 个国际流域。[184] 其中大部分流域已经有了某种形式的合作机制。[185] 一个突出的例证就是 1992 年制定的联合国欧洲经济委员会《跨界水道和国际湖泊保护和利用公约》（*UNECE Convention on the Protection and Use of Transboundary Watercourses and International Lakes*）[《赫尔辛基公约》（*Helsinki Convention*）]，[186] 它成为联合国欧洲经济委员会地域内大约 200 条国际河流和湖泊的框架性文件，并逐渐适用于全球层面。《赫尔辛基公约》在后续大量的水道特别条约中得以进一步落实，例如那些与莱茵河[187]或多瑙河[188]相关的条约。针对各大洲的水道，还可以举出大量例证。例如，有两个典型案例值得一提，一个是《1975 年乌拉圭河规约》，[189] 它与国际法院受理的"纸浆厂案"密切相关，[190] 另一个是《1960 年印度河水条约》，[191] 它与 2013 年判决的"印度河基申甘加水坝仲裁案"密切相关。[192] 这两个案例清楚地阐明了习惯法原则和水道协议两者间的交叉。虽然这些协定的条款应当依据国际习惯法来解释，[193] 但是它们具体的条款有可能违背了习惯法

---

[184] UNEP/Oregon State University/FAO, *Atlas of International Freshwater Agreements* (Nairobi: UNEP, 2002), p. 3.

[185] 对有关案例的分析参见 McCaffrey, supra footnote 149, Chapter 8（探讨了适用于尼罗河、湄公河、印度河、莱茵河、约旦河或格兰德河水等河流的机制）。

[186] Helsinki Convention, supra footnote 147. On this important instrument see A. Tanzi et al (eds.), *The UNECE Convention on the Protection and Use of Transboundary Watercourses and International Lakes. Its Contribution to International Water Cooperation* (Leiden: Brill, 2015).

[187] Convention on the Protection of the Rhine, 12 April 1999, available at www.ecolex.org (TRE-001307).

[188] Convention on Cooperation for the Protection and Sustainable Use of the Danube River, 29 June 1994, available at www.ecolex.org (TRE-001207).

[189] Statute of the River Uruguay (Argentina/Uruguay), 26 February 1975, 1295 UNTS 340.

[190] *Pulp Mills*, supra footnote 49.

[191] Indus Water Treaty (India/Pakistan), 19 September 1960, 419 UNTS 126.

[192] *Indus Water Kishenganga*, supra footnote 49.

[193] *Pulp Mills*, supra footnote 49, paras. 101-102, 144-147; *Indus Water Kishenganga*, supra footnote 49, paras. 448-450.

规范,甚至对环境造成了负面影响。[194] 事实上,虽然那些管理国际水道的原则具有重要意义,但是它们在当前都没有被当成国际法的强制性规范。为了体现各水道国在政治上达成的妥协,协定条款有可能会违背这些原则。当我们在分析那些拥有丰富水资源的国家为何抵制将水权发展成一种人权时(参见第十章),这是一个值得我们关注的重要因素。

三 跨界含水层

前文提到的法律编撰尝试主要涉及的是地表水或者与地表水相连接的地下水。除了最终达成《赫尔辛基公约》的尝试之外,[195] 其他的法律编撰工作并没有充分考虑到承压地下水的问题。[196]

这一空白最终通过两种主要方法得以填补。第一种方法就是通过制定一项涉及地下水的附加文件这一特别方式来补充现有文件。因此,国际法协会在1986年制定了一项《关于跨界承压地下水的决议》(*Resolution on Confined Transboundary Groundwater*)[《首尔决议》(*Seoul Resolution*)],它包含了四个条款,第一个条款明确指出,无论跨界含水层是否与地表水有关联,都构成了某个国际流域(其含义由《赫尔辛基规则》所规定)的组

---

[194] In the matter of the Indus Waters Kishenganga Arbitration before the Court of Arbitration constituted in accordance with the Indus Waters Treaty 1960 *between the Government of India and the Government of Pakistan signed on 19 September 1960* (*Islamic Republic of Pakistan v. Republic of India*),PCA,Final Award(20 December 2014),para. 111.

[195] 作为联合国欧洲经济委员会工作的一部分,一系列的声明都早已承认有必要针对未连接的地表水采取一种综合方法:A "Declaration of Policy on Prevention and Control of Water Pollution",Decision B(XXV),Geneva – 1980;"Decision on International Cooperation on Shared Water Resources",Decision D(XXXVII),Geneva–1982;"Declaration of Policy on Rational Use of Water",Decision C(XXXIX),Geneva – 1984;"Charter on Groundwater Management",Decision E(44),Geneva–1989. The Helsinki Convention Has Remained at the Forefront of the Work on Transboundary Aquifers,Including Through the Adoption in 2012 of "Model Provisions on Transboundary Groundwaters" to the attention of States。

[196] On the international law of aquifers see McCaffrey,supra footnote 149,Chapter 14;K. Mechlem,"Groundwater Protection"(2010)*Max Planck Encyclopedia of Public International Law*,available at:http://opil. ouplaw. com(visited on 4 April 2017);Special issue of *Water International*,Vol. 36,issue 5(2011)(with contributions from Yamada,McCaffrey,Eckstein,Dellapenna,Salman,Linton/Brooks,Jarvis,among others);G. Eckstein,F. Sindico,"The Law of Transboundary Aquifers:Many ways of going forward,but only one way of standing still"(2014)23 *RECIEL* 32.

成部分。[197] 同样地，在1994年，国际法委员会制定了一项《关于跨界承压地下水的决议》(*Resolution on Confined Transboundary Groundwater*),[198] 承认有必要制定规则来管理这一问题，并指出在这些规则缺位的情况下，各国应当原则上遵循那些适用于地表水的基本原则。[199] 第二种方法是制定一套包含有地下水问题的一般规定，例如国际法协会2004年《柏林规则》(*ILA Berlin Rules of 2004*)第八章的做法，[200] 或者针对地下水制定一套具体条款，例如国际法委员会在2008年制定的《关于跨界含水层法的条款草案》(*Draft Articles on the Law of Transboundary Aquifers*)。[201]

关于这些法律编撰尝试的内容，其所确定的原则其实就是那些涉及国际水道的原则（公平及合理利用以及公众参与、[202] 无害、[203] 防止环境危害、[204] 合作[205]）。但是，与国际水道的体制相比较，还是有一些值得重视的区别。第一，含水层具有水文地质的特点，因此我们在定义含水层时就必须把水和地质容器都包含在内。[206] 这是因为容器管理着含水层的运行以及水的获取和质量，同时也是因为一个耗尽的含水层的容器可以被用于其他用途（例如二氧化碳的储存）。[207] 这一延伸同时也可以说明国际法委员会《关于跨界含水层法的条款草案》的范围不仅包含"含水层的利用"（第1条第1款），也包括"对含水层或含水层系统有影响或可能造成影响的其他活动"（第1条第2款）。2011年前，特别报告人山田中正（Chusei

---

[197] Seoul Rules, supra footnote 147, Art. 1.

[198] "Resolution on Confined Transboundary Groundwater", (1994) 2 (2) *Yearbook of the International Law Commission* 135.

[199] Ibid., para. 1.

[200] Berlin Rules, supra footnote 147, Arts. 36 and 42 (1) (b).

[201] ILC Aquifers Draft, supra footnote 147.

[202] Seoul Rules, supra footnote 147, Art. 2; Berlin Rules, supra footnote 147, Arts. 37 and 40; ILC Aquifers Draft, supra footnote 147, Arts. 4 and 5.

[203] Berlin Rules, supra footnote 147, Art. 42 (6); ILC Aquifers Draft, supra footnote 147, Art. 6.

[204] Seoul Rules, supra footnote 147, Art. 3; Berlin Rules, supra footnote 147, Arts. 38 and 41; ILC Aquifers Draft, supra footnote 147, Arts. 10–12.

[205] Seoul Rules, supra footnote 147, Art. 4; Berlin Rules, supra footnote 147, Art. 42 (2) – (5); ILC Aquifers Draft, supra n footnote 147, Arts 7–9.

[206] ILC Aquifers Draft, supra n footnote 147, Art. 2 (a).

[207] C. Yamada, "Codification of the Law of Transboundary Aquifers (Groundwaters) by the United Nations" (2011) 36 *Water International* 557, p. 562.

Yamada）用东京的城市开发来举例说明，为了确保城市地底下的含水层自我补充的能力，城市建设就受到了各种潜在的限制。当某国在其含水层开展活动而对他国造成影响时，就会导致特别的问题。[208] 第二，公平及合理利用原则在含水层的运用似乎显得不太急需。国际水道的利用期望达到的目标是可持续的利用（更具体的说法是永不枯竭的利用），而含水层则需要较长的时间才能补充，甚至部分含水层是无法补充的（承压地下水）。因此，国际法委员会条款草案在制定类似于"公平及合理"利用的条款时采用了更灵活的方法。[209] 第三，反之，适用于无害原则的"重大"危害应当根据不同含水层的具体情况来进行调整，在涉及承压地下水时，构成"重大"危害可能会比地表水容易得多。[210] 第四，地表水的管理手段一般将重点放在预防、[211] 联合管理[212]以及技术合作的具体方式。[213] 很大部分是因为含水层（特别是那些承压地下水）更容易受到污染和枯竭（因为微小或缓慢的补充水流）的伤害。最后但并非最不重要的是，在法律框架中的一个重大区别在于，国际法委员会在2008年制定的《关于跨界含水层法的条款草案》第3条指出：

> 每个含水层国家对跨界含水层或含水层系统在其领土范围内的那一部分拥有主权。

针对这一草案的注释[214]指出，许多国家是根据自然资源永久主权原则而明确支持这一条款的制定。[215] 但是，这一条款同时指出，各国应当"依据国际法和现有条款草案"来行使它们的主权。这是对不断发展的国际

208　Yamada, supra footnote 207, p. 561.

209　Ibid., pp. 562–563.

210　Ibid., p. 563.

211　ILC Aquifers Draft, supra footnote 147, Art. 6（1）–（2）.

212　Berlin Rules, supra footnote 147, Art. 2（2）; ILC Aquifers Draft, supra footnote 147, Art. 9.

213　ILC Aquifers Draft, supra footnote 147, Art. 16.

214　"Draft Articles on the Law of Transboundary Aquifers, with commentaries", (2008) 2 (2) *Yearbook of the International Law Commission*, Part 2, commentary ad Art. 3, para. 1.

215　"Permanent Sovereignty over Natural Resources", 14 December 1962, UN Doc. A/RES/1803/XVII, ("Resolution 1803").

习惯法（包括环境保护规范）的一种借鉴。

在国际法委员会通过 2008 年《关于跨界含水层法的条款草案》之后，联合国大会注意到了这一点并决定由其第六委员会来考虑如何确定这一文件的最终形式。已经讨论的多个选项包括一套指南、一项原则宣言或一项框架公约。2017 年年初，第六委员会将自己的作用限制为将这一文件当作指南"推荐"给政府，同时将这一事项纳入其立法议程留待以后讨论。[216]

四 冰冻淡水资源

（一）概述

如前文所述，世界上绝大多数的淡水资源（70%）是以冰的形式封存于极地或其他区域。虽然这些资源极具重要意义，但是它们的占有、开发和转移（从开发地转移到利用地）到目前为止尚未引起足够关注。[217] 虽然大量学术文献分析了极地地区的法律地位，[218] 但是冰冻淡水资源还是很少被特别提及，可能是因为这些资源的开发所面临的技术和经济挑战令人却步，也可能是因为此类工程所要满足的环保要求。

在这一部分，讨论将局限于环保问题。为了让冰冻淡水资源得以利用或者"开发"，首先必须有一个国家来"占有"这一资源，换言之，这一资源归属于某个国家的主权或主权权利。针对那些位于南极或北极的资源，关于占有的规则也是不一样的。

（二）南极

关于南极，《南极条约》（*Antarctic Treaty*）第 4 条[219]确定的多项基本

---

216 "The Law of Transboundary Aquifers", 4 November 2016, UN Doc. A/C. 6/71/L. 22.

217 See e. g. F. Quilleré-Majzoub, "Glaces polaires et icebergs: Quid juris gentium?" (2006) 52 *Annuaire Français de Droit International* 432; J. E. Viñuales, "Iced Freshwater Resources: A Legal Exploration" (2009) 20 *Yearbook of International Environmental Law* 188.

218 On the Antarctic treaty system, see F. Francioni and T. Scovazzi (eds.), *International Law for Antarctica* (Leiden: Martinus Nijhoff, 2nd edn, 1996). On the Arctic, see D. R. Rothwell, "International Law and the Protection of the Arctic Environment" (1995) 44 *International and Comparative Law Quarterly* 280; E. Lennon, "A Tale of Two Poles: A Comparative Look at the Legal Regimes in the Arctic and the Antarctic" (2008) 8 *Sustainable Development Law & Policy* 32.

219 See supra footnote 139.

原则之一就是所谓的"冻结"或中止多个国家[220]针对条约第6条定义的南极部分地区及其周边海洋所主张的主权要求。这一基本原则及其对南极资源能否被占有的影响应当通过一套相对复杂的程序来进行评估,还需要借鉴南极条约体系(Antarctic Treaty System, ATS)(包含其他条约[221]和大量由《南极条约》管理机构通过的决议)。[222] 这些程序所展现出的轮廓是各国在一定程度上享有海洋生物资源,这主要是由《1972年海豹公约》(*1972 Seals Convention*)和《南极海洋生物资源养护委员会公约》(*CCAMLR Convention*)特别规定的。[223] 因此,这类资源被占有的可能性是不被禁止的。而矿产资源的情况则有所不同,随着《南极矿产资源活动管理公约》[224]的失败和《环境保护议定书》的制定,涉及矿产资源的活动(科研活动除外)是被禁止的。[225]

冰冻淡水资源的情况则是位于这两种机制的中间地带,因为它们没有被认定是议定书第7条所禁止的"矿产资源"。[226] 另外,在1989年10月于巴黎召开的《南极条约》缔约方会议上,开发这些资源(意味着占有)的可能性被明确提出。这次会议通过了第15—21号建议,主要涉及"冰山的开发"。[227] 这一建议的前言特别指出:

---

[220] 在《南极条约》的12个原始签署方中,有7个国家(阿根廷、澳大利亚、智利、法国、新西兰、挪威和英国)在签署时提出了领土诉求。但是,苏联和美国维持了一个受第4条第1款保护的"诉求基础"。

[221] See supra footnote 139.

[222] 在32次会议中,《南极条约》的缔约方针对与南极相关的各种问题制定了将近200个决议。See the website of the Antarctic Treaty Secretariat, at: www.ats.aq/devAS/info_measures_list.aspx (last visited on 12 April 2017).

[223] CCAMLR, supra footnote 139.

[224] A Convention for the Regulation of Antarctic Mineral Resource Activities, 2 June 1988, 27 ILM 868 (1988) ("CRAMRA")专门针对这一问题,但是它从未生效,后来它的目标随着《马德里议定书》的制定和生效而被排除。

[225] Madrid Protocol, supra footnote 139, Art. 7.

[226] The Final Act of the Eleventh Antarctic Treaty Special Consultative Meeting, Madrid, October 1991, 在第6段指出,"会议指出冰开采不被看作一种南极矿产资源活动,因此大家同意如果冰开采在将来成为可能,那么就应当适用议定书而非第7条"。[available at: www.state.gov/documents/organization/15291.pdf (last visited on 12 April 2017)].

[227] Recommendation ATCM XV-21, available at: www.ats.aq (last visited on 12 April 2017).

"科技的发展有可能在某一天使得利用冰山(特别是在沿海地区)来获取淡水成为可能",[228] 同时指出这一可能性引发了对"南极冰山不受控制的开发活动有可能对南极独一无二的环境及其依赖和关联的生态系统造成负面影响"的关注;[229] 同时,由于获取的信息有限,可取的办法是"南极冰山的商业开发活动在任何情况下都必须事先通过《南极条约》缔约方针对这一活动的调查"。[230]

这一建议其实是要求提供此类潜在开发所造成环境影响的更多信息。[231] 2004年1月29日,在这一建议被通过大约15年之后,根据《南极条约》第9条第4款,随着最后一个缔约方(比利时)的批准,它才最终得以生效。但是,在后续会议中,并没有采取具体的跟进行动。因此,这一问题尚待解决。

(三) 北极

与南极不同,北极并非由某一单一条约或条约体系来管理,而是由一套由软法[232]和硬法[233]文件与体制组成的联合体来管理。[234] 能否对北极资源进行占有这一问题受到基本的国际规则的支配,即那些适用于各国对土地和海洋空间行使主权和主权权利的规则。[235] 我们可以用一个适当的例证来说明在冰冻淡水资源的占有中如何行使这些权利以及它可能引发的问题,加拿大纽芬兰省的法律和法规为加拿大海域内发现的冰山的开发颁发了许可

---

[228] Ibid., preamble, Recital 2.

[229] Ibid., preamble, Recital 5.

[230] Ibid., preamble, Recital 9.

[231] Ibid., operative part, paras. 1-2.

[232] See Arctic Environmental Protection Strategy (AEPS), adopted in Rovaniemi, Finland, June 1991, available at: www.arctic-council.org (last visited on 12 April 2017).

[233] Most notably the UNCLOS, supra footnote 1. See H. Corell, "Reflections on the Possibilities and Limitations of a Binding Legal Regime" (2007) 37 *Environmental Policy and Law* 321.

[234] See "Declaration on the Establishment of the Arctic Council", 19 September 1996, 35 ILM 1382 (1996); E. T. Bloom, "Establishment of the Arctic Council" (1999) 93 *American Journal of International Law* 712.

[235] See C. Joyner, "Ice-Covered Regions in International Law" (1991) 31 *Natural Resources Journal* 213.

证。[236] 但是这些权利受到了丹麦的抗议，丹麦主张加拿大无权出售这些在加拿大海域内发现的冰山，因为它们来自格陵兰冰盖。[237]

《联合国海洋法公约》除了划分主权和主权权利之外，还针对这些资源的开发制定了环境标准。在《联合国海洋法公约》的谈判过程中，加拿大提议制定一条特别针对冰山管理的条款；[238] 在1970年的加拿大《北极海域污染预防法》中采用了一种方法，[239] 而加拿大认为有必要将这一方法引入公约。而最终的条款，即《联合国海洋法公约》第234条并没有将冰直接当成一种资源而是将其看作一个风险因素，认为它增加了航海事故及其引发的北极环境污染的可能性。但是，《联合国海洋法公约》的其他条款，虽然并非特别针对海冰，但是与冰冻淡水资源潜在开发的环境要求之间拥有一个更直接的联系。我们在此借鉴了我们对环境义务（尤其是《联合国海洋法公约》第十二部分所规定的义务）的分析。[240]

针对北极地区这些活动的管理受到了其他硬法和软法文件的进一步影响，而在极地地区国际法的研究分析中，这些文件都受到了不同程度的关注。一方面，已制定的法律文书数量庞大，尤其是那些在《北极环境保护战略》（Arctic Environmental Protection Strategy，AEPS）或北极理事会（Arctic Council）框架下的文件。[241] 另一方面，针对冰冻淡水资源潜在开发的评论则是几乎没有。在这一点上，我们也许可以借鉴灵活性框架中的各种做法，例如1991年启动的《北极环境保护战略》和1996年建立的北极理事会。北极理事会由六个工作组构成，其中一个工作组［北极海洋环境保护工作组（Protection of the Arctic Marine Environment，PAME）］关注的是政策以及非紧急污染的预防和控制方法，保护北极海洋与沿海环境不受陆地和海洋活动的影响。例如，北极海洋环境保护工作组2015—

236　Incident reported by Quilleré-Majzoub, supra footnote 217, 443.

237　虽然这一起源一般来说是事实正确的，但是丹麦的诉求的法律基础尚不明确。构成一个冰盖的水是源自一国的领土这一事实还不足以禁止他国的适当挪用。

238　See D. M. McRae, "The Negotiation of Article 234", in F. Griffiths (ed.), *Politics in the Northwest Passage* (Montréal: McGill-Queens University Press, 1987), pp. 98-114.

239　See R. M. M. Gonigle, "Unilateralism and International Law: The Arctic Waters Pollution Prevention Act" (1976) 34 *University of Toronto Faculty of Law Review* 180.

240　See supra Sections 4.2.2 and 4.2.3.

241　See supra footnote 234 and the bibliography at the end of this chapter.

2017年工作计划的其中一个目标就是评估海冰减少的环境后果以及这一变化导致的自然资源（虽然没有明确指向冰冻淡水资源）开发的更多机会。[242] 这仅仅是大量案例中的一个，这些案例可以用来说明"灵活性"做法是如何用于北极环境保护的。但是，它们共同的目标在于试图影响北极国家的国家政策以及其他相关国家和组织。

部分参考文献

［1］ Arcari, M. and A. Tanzi, *The United Nations Convention on the Law of International Watercourses* (The Hague: Kluwer, 2001).

［2］ Attard, D., M. Fitzmaurice, and N. A. Martinez Gutierrez (eds.), *The IMLI Manual on International Maritime Law. Vol. I: The Law of the Sea* (Oxford University Press, 2014).

［3］ Barberis, J. A. and R. D. Hayton (eds.), *Droits et obligations des pays riverains des fleuves internationaux* (The Hague: Martinus Nijhoff, 1990).

［4］ Barnes, R., *Property Rights and Natural Resources* (Oxford: Hart, 2009).

［5］ Bederman, D., "Antarctic Environmental Liability: the Stockholm Annex and Beyond" (2005) 19 *Emory International Law Review* 1383.

［6］ Bloom, E. T., "Establishment of the Arctic Council" (1999) 93 *American Journal of International Law* 712.

［7］ Bogdanovic, S., *International Law of Water Resources, Contribution of the International Law Association (1954-2000)* (London: Kluwer Law International, 2001).

［8］ Boisson de Chazournes, L. and S. Salman (eds.), *Water Resources and International Law/Hague Academy of International Law* (Leiden: Martinus Nijhoff, 2005).

［9］ Bourne, C., *International Water Law: Selected Writings of Professor Charles B. Bourne* (Boston: Kluwer Law, 1997).

"The Primacy of the Principle of Equitable Utilization in the 1997 Water-

---

242 See Arctic Council, PAME Work Plan 2015-2017, available at: www.pame.is (last visited on 12 April 2017).

course Convention" (1998) 35 *The Canadian Yearbook of International Law* 215.

[10] Boyle, A., "The Environmental Jurisprudence of the International Tribunal for the Law of the Sea" (2007) 22 *International Journal of Marine and Coastal Law* 369.

[11] Brown Weiss, E., "The Evolution of International Water Law", (2007) 331 *Recueil des cours de l'Académie de droit international*, 161-404.

[12] Brunnée, J., "Environmental Security and Freshwater Resources: The Role of International Law", in Y. Le Bouthillier, D. M. McRae and D. Pharand (eds.), *Selected Papers in International Law: Contribution of the Canadian Council of International Law* (Toronto: Canadian Council of International Law, 1999), pp. 371-383.

[13] Bush, W., *Antarctica and International Law* (Dobbs Ferry NY: Oceana Publications, 3 vols., 1982-1988).

[14] Caflisch, L., "Règles générales du droit des cours d'eaux internationaux" (1989) 219 *Recueil des cours de l'Académie de droit international*, 9ff.

"La Convention du 21 mai 1997 sur l'utilisation des cours d'eaux internationaux à des fins autres que la navigation" (1997) 43 *Annuaire français de droit international* 751.

[15] Cohen, H. K. (ed.), *Handbook of the Antarctic Treaty System* (Washington DC: US Department of States, 9th edn, 2002).

[16] Corell, H., "Reflections on the Possibilities and Limitations of a Binding Legal Regime" (2007) 37 *Environmental Policy and Law* 321.

[17] Dejeant-Pons, M., "Les Conventions du Programme des Nations Unies pour l'Environnement relatives aux mers régionales" (1984) 33 *Annuaire français de droit international* 689.

[18] De la Fayette, L., "New Developments in the Disposal of Offshore Installations" (1999) 14 *International Journal of Marine and Coastal Law* 523.

"The Role of the United Nations in International Oceans Governance", in D. Freestone, R. Barnes and D. Ong (eds.), *The Law of the Sea: Progress and Prospects* (Oxford University Press, 2006), pp. 63-74.

"Oceans Governance in the Arctic" (2008) 23 *International Journal of Marine and Coastal Law* 531.

［19］ Dellapenna, J., "The Customary International Law of Transboundary Fresh Waters", in M. Fitzmaurice and M. Szuniewicz (eds.), *Exploitation of Natural Resources in the 21st Century* (Boston: Kluwer Law International, 2003), pp. 143–190.

［20］ Dellapenna, J. and J. Gupta (eds.), *The Evolution of the Law and Politics of Water* (Dordrecht: Springer, 2009).

［21］ Dupuy, P.-M., "La préservation du milieu marin", in Dupuy, R.-J. and Vignes, D. (eds.), *Traité du nouveau droit de la mer* (Paris/Bruxelles: Economica/Bruylant, 1985), Chapter 20.

［22］ Eckstein, G. and F. Sindico, "The Law of Transboundary Aquifers: Many ways of going forward, but only one way of standing still" (2014) 23 *Review of European, Comparative and International Environmental Law* 32.

［23］ Elferink, A. O. and E. Molenaar (eds.), *The International Legal Regime of Areas beyond National Jurisdiction: Current and Future Developments* (Leiden: Martinus Nijhoff, 2010).

［24］ Fitzmaurice, M., "General Principles Governing the Cooperation between States in Relation to Non-Navigational Uses of International Watercourses" (2004) 14 *Yearbook of International Environmental Law* 3.

［25］ Francioni, F. and T. Scovazzi (eds.), *International Law for Antarctica* (Leiden: Martinus Nijhoff, 2nd edn, 1996).

［26］ Franckx, E., "Regional Marine Environment Protection Regimes in the Context of UNCLOS" (1998) 13 *International Journal of Marine and Coastal Law* 307.

［27］ Freestone, D. and Z. Makuch, "The New International Environmental Law of Fisheries: The 1995 United Nations Straddling Stocks Agreement" (1995) 7 *Yearbook of International Environmental Law* 3.

［28］ Freestone, D. and S. Salman, "Ocean and Freshwater Resources", in D. Bodansky, J. Brunnée and E. Hey (eds.), *The Oxford Handbook of International Environmental Law* (Oxford University Press, 2007), pp. 337–361.

［29］ Fuentes, X., "Sustainable Development and the Equitable Utilization of International Watercourses" (1999) 69 *British Yearbook of International Law* 119.

"The Criteria for the Equitable Utilization of International Rivers" (1997) 67 *British Yearbook of International Law* 337.

"The Utilization of International Groundwater in General International Law", in G. S. Goodwin-Gill and S. Talmon (eds.), *The Reality of International Law: Essays in Honour of Ian Brownlie* (Oxford University Press, 1999), pp. 177-198.

[30] Fulton, T. W., *The Sovereignty of the Sea* (Clark NJ: The Lawbook Exchange, 1911).

[31] Gavouneli, M., "A Human Right to Groundwater?" (2011) 13 *International Community Law Review* 305.

[32] Gonigle, R. M. M., "Unilateralism and International Law: The Arctic Waters Pollution Prevention Act" (1976) 34 *University of Toronto Faculty of Law Review* 180.

[33] Gupta, J., R. Ahlers and L. Ahmed, "The Human Right to Water: Moving Towards Consensus in a Fragmented World" (2010) 19 *Review of European Community and International Environmental Law* 294.

[34] Haas, P., "Save the Seas: UNEP's Regional Seas Programme and the Coordination of Regional Pollution Control Efforts" (1991) 9 *Ocean Yearbook* 188.

[35] Harrison, J., *Making the Law of the Sea* (Cambridge University Press, 2011).

[36] Hassan, D., "International Conventions Relating to Land-based Sources of Marine Pollution Control: Applications and Shortcomings" (2004) 16 *Georgetown International Environmental Law Review* 657.

Protecting the Marine Environment from Land-based Sources of Pollution: Toward Effective International Co-operation (Aldershot: Ashgate, 2005).

[37] Haward, M. and J. Vince, *Oceans Governance in the Twenty-first Century: Managing the Blue Planet* (Cheltenham: Edward Elgar, 2008).

[38] Helal, M. S., "Sharing Blue Gold: The 1997 UN Convention on the Law of the Non-navigational Uses of International Watercourses Ten Years On" (2007) 18 *Colorado Journal of International Environmental Law Policy* 337.

［39］Joyner, C., "Ice-Covered Regions in International Law" (1991) 31 *Natural Resources Journal* 213.

［40］Kindt, J., "Vessel Source Pollution and the Law of the Sea" (1984) 17 *Vanderbilt* 287.

［41］Koivurova, T., "Governance of Protected Areas in the Arctic" (2009) 5 *Utrecht Law Review* 44.

［42］Koivurova, T. and D. L. Vanderzwaag, "The Arctic Council at 10 Years: Retrospect and Prospects" (2007) 10 *University of British Columbia Law Review* 121.

［43］Kramer, L., "The Contribution of the European Union to Marine Pollution Prevention", in J. Basedow and U. Magnus (eds.), *Pollution of the Sea: Prevention and Compensation* (Dordrecht: Springer, 2007), pp. 63–83.

［44］Leb, C., *Cooperation in the Law of Transboundary Water Resources* (Cambridge University Press, 2015).

［45］Lennon, L., "A Tale of Two Poles: A Comparative Look at the Legal Regimes in the Arctic and the Antarctic" (2008) 8 *Sustainable Development Law & Policy* 32.

［46］McCaffrey, S., "The 1997 United Nations Convention on International Watercourses" (1998) 92 *American Journal of International Law* 97.

The Law of International Watercourses (Oxford University Press, 2007).

"International Watercourses, Environmental Protection" (2011) *Max Planck Encyclopedia of Public International Law*, available at: http://opil.ouplaw.com (visited on 4 April 2017).

［47］McRae, D. M., "The Negotiation of Article 234", in F. Griffiths (ed.), *Politics in the Northwest Passage* (Montréal: McGill-Queens University Press, 1987), pp. 98–114.

［48］Mensah, T., "The International Legal Regime for the Protection and Preservation of the Marine Environment from Land Based Sources", in A. Boyle and D. Freestone (eds.), *International Law and Sustainable Development: Past Achievements and Future Challenges* (Oxford University Press, 1999), pp. 297–324.

［49］Nollkaemper, A., "Balancing the Protection of Marine Ecosystems with Economic Benefits from Land-Based Activities: the Quest for International Legal Barriers" (1996) 27 *Ocean Development and International Law* 154.

[50] Nordquist, M. H., S. N. Nandan and J. Kraska (eds.), *United Nations Convention on the Law of the Sea: A Commentary*, Vol. IV (Dordrecht/Boston: Martinus Nijhoff, 1991).

[51] Osborn, D., "Land-based Pollution and the Marine Environment", in R. Rayfuse (ed.), *Research Handbook on International Marine Environmental Law* (Cheltenham: Edward Elgar, 2015), pp. 81-104.

[52] Proelß, A. (ed.), *The United Nations Convention on the Law of the Sea. A Commentary* (Berlin/Oxford/Baden-Baden: C. H. Beck/Hart/Nomos, 2017).

[53] Qing-Nan, M., *Land-based Marine Pollution: International Law Development* (Leiden: Martinus Nijhoff, 1987).

[54] Quilleré-Majzoub, F., "Glaces polaires et icebergs: Quid juris gentium?" (2006) 52 *Annuaire français de droit international* 432.

[55] Rayfuse, R., "Differentiating the Common?: The Responsibilities and Obligations of States Sponsoring Deep Seabed Mining Activities in the Area" (2011) 54 *German Yearbook of International Law* 459.

Research Handbook on International Marine Environmental Law (Cheltenham: Edward Elgar, 2015).

[56] Rayfuse, R. and R. Warner, "Securing a Sustainable Future for the Oceans Beyond National Jurisdiction: the Legal Basis for an Integrated Cross-Sectoral Regime for High Seas Governance for the 21st Century" (2008) 23 *International Journal of Marine and Coastal Law* 399.

[57] Redgwell, C., "From Permission to Prohibition: The 1982 Convention on the Law of the Sea and Protection of the Marine Environment", in D. Freestone, R. Barnes and D. Ong (eds.), *The Law of the Sea: Progress and Prospects* (Oxford University Press, 2006), pp. 180-191.

[58] Rothwell, D. R., "International Law and the Protection of the Arctic Environment" (1995) 44 *International and Comparative Law Quarterly* 280.

[59] Rothwell, D. R. and T. Stephens, *The International Law of the* Sea

(Oxford: Hart Publishing, 2010).

［60］Rothwell D. R., A. G. O. Elferink, K. Scott and T. Stephens (eds.), *The Oxford Handbook on the Law of the Sea* (Oxford University Press, 2015).

［61］Salman, M. A. S., "The Helsinki Rules, the UN Watercourses Convention and the Berlin Rules: Perspectives on International Water Law" (2007) 23 *Water Resources Development* 625.

［62］Salman, S., *Regulatory Frameworks for Water Resources Management: A Comparative Study* (Washington DC: The World Bank, 2006).

"The United Nations Watercourses Convention Ten Years Later: Why Has Its Entry into Force Proven Difficult?" (2007) 22 *Water International* 1.

［63］Tan, A. K.-J., *Vessel-Source Marine Pollution* (Cambridge University Press, 2006).

［64］Tanaka, Y., "Regulation of Land-Based Marine Pollution in International Law: AComparative Analysis between Global and Regional Legal Frameworks" (2006) 66 *Zeitschrift für ausländisches öffentliches Recht und Völkerrecht* 535.

"Reflections on Reporting Systems in Treaties Concerning the Protection of the Marine Environment" (2009) 40 *Ocean Development and International Law* 146.

The International Law of the Sea (Cambridge University Press, 2012).

［65］Tanzi. A., O. McIntyre, A. Kolliopoulos, A. Rieu - Clarke and R. Kinna (eds.), *The UNECE Convention on the Protection and Use of Transboundary Watercourses and International Lakes. Its Contribution to International Water Cooperation* (Leiden: Brill, 2015).

［66］Tarlock, D., "The Changing Environment of International Water Management Law" (2001) 12 *Water Law* 351.

"National Water Law: the Foundation of Sustainable Water Use" (2004) 15 *The Journal of Water Law* 120.

"Integrated Water Resources Management: Theory and Practice", in P. Wouters, V.Dukhovny and A. Allan (eds.), *Implementing Integrated Water Resources Management in Central Asia* (Dordrecht: Springer, 2007), pp. 3-21.

"Water Security, Fear Mitigation and International Water Law" (2008) 31 *Hamline Law Review* 704.

[67] Tarlock, D. and P. Wouters, "Are Shared Benefits of International Waters an Equitable Apportionment?" (2007) 18 *Colorado Journal of International Environmental Law and Policy* 523.

"Reframing the Water Security Dialogue" (2009) 20 *The Journal of Water Law* 53.

[68] Teclaff, L., "Evolution of the River Basin Concept in National and International Water Law" (1996) 36 *Natural Resources Journal* 359.

[69] UNEP/Oregon State University/FAO, *Atlas of International Freshwater Agreements* (Nairobi: UNEP, 2002).

[70] Vander Zwaag, D. L. and A. Powers, "The Protection of the Marine Environment from Land-Based Pollution and Activities: Gauging the Tides of Global and Regional Governance" (2008) 23 *International Journal of Marine and Coastal Law* 423.

[71] Verhoeven, J., P. Sand and M. Bruce (eds.), *The Antarctic Environment and International Law* (London: Graham & Trotman, 1992).

[72] Vidas, D. (ed.), *Protecting the Polar Marine Environment: Law and Policy for Pollution Prevention* (Cambridge University Press, 2000).

[73] Viñuales, J. E., "Access to Water in Foreign Investment Disputes" (2009) 21 *Georgetown International Environmental Law Review* 733.

"Iced Freshwater Resources: A Legal Exploration" (2009) 20 *Yearbook of International Environmental Law* 188.

"La Protección Ambiental en el Derecho Internacional Consuetudinario" (2017) 69/2 *Revista Española de Derecho Internacional* 71.

[74] Vitanyi, B., *The International Regime of River Navigation* (Alphen aan den Rijn: Sijthoff & Noordhoff, 1979).

[75] Warbrick, C., D. McGoldrick and E. Kirk, "The 1996 Protocol to the London Dumping Convention and the Brent Spar" (1997) 46 *International and Comparative Law Quarterly* 957.

[76] Watts, A., *International Law and the Antarctic Treaty System* (Cambridge: Grotius Publications, 1992).

［77］Wouters, P., "National and International Water Law: Achieving Equitable and Sustainable Use of Water Resources" (2000) 25 *Water International* 499.

"The Legal Response to International Water Conflicts: The UN Watercourses Convention and Beyond" (2000) 42 *German Yearbook of International Law* 292.

"Reframing the Water Security Dialogue" (2009) 20 *The Journal of Water Law* 53.

"The International Law of Watercourses: New Dimensions", in *Collected Courses of the Xiamen Academy of International Law*, 2011, pp. 347–541.

［78］Wouters, P. and S. Hendry, "Promoting Water (Law) For All: Addressing the World's Water Problem: A Focus on International and National Water Law and the Challenges of an Integrated Approach" (2009) 20 *The Journal of Water Law* 44.

［79］Yamada, C., "Codification of the Law of Transboundary Aquifers (Groundwaters) by the United Nations" (2011) 36 *Water International* 557.

［80］Young, O. R., "Arctic in Play: Governance in a Time of Rapid Change" (2009) 24 *International Journal of Marine and Coastal Law* 423.

第五章 大气保护

第一节 导论

本章的标题似乎意味着在国际法中地球的大气是被当作一个单一客体来进行保护的。但是，规制通常是针对具体问题制定的，而不是针对大气这一客体。大气问题是各式各样的，例如造成跨界影响的烟气排放、气候变化、环境的酸化或者臭氧层耗竭。但这也并不意味着不能确定几项支配性原则，正如《联合国海洋法公约》[1] 第十二部分针对海洋环境的做法。但是，国际法委员会在将"大气法"原则录入法律文本的过程中从一开始就遭受了重要的、有争议的限制，[2] 因此这一努力的前景还不明朗。[3]

为了教学上的方便，我们通常的提法是大气保护，本章讨论的法律文书所涉及的各种问题都与大气圈的构成相关，大气圈从地球的表面延伸到

---

[1] United Nations Convention on the Law of the Sea, 10 December 1982, 1833 UNTS 397 ("UNCLOS").

[2] 国际法委员会在 2013 年第 65 次会议上决定将"空气保护"纳入其工作计划并委任 S. Murase 教授担任这一主题的特别报告人。但是，基于一个存在争议的认识（为了避免侵占气候谈判），国际法委员会对工作范围做出了一个限制，将义务、污染者付费原则、风险预防原则、共同但有区别的责任原则以及炭黑问题排除在外。See ILC, Report of the Commission to the General Assembly on the Work of its 65th Session, UN Doc. A/68/10, 2013, para. 168. On this process see P. H. Sand and J. B. Wiener, "Towards a New International Law of the Atmosphere?" (2015) 7 *Göttingen Journal of International Law* 2.

[3] On the original vision underlying this project see S. Murase, "Protection of the Atmosphere and International Law: Rationale for Codification and Progressive Development" (2012) 55 *Sophia Law Review* 1.

太空，直到地球引力内的范围，[4] 特别是与地球表面最近的两层，即对流层（12 千米高度以内）和平流层（处于 12—50 千米高度）。

应对大气保护的另一个替代和补充的方法是根据规制所适用的地理范围来区分不同的问题。从这一立场，不同的规制安排可以根据它们是否是应对本地、区域或全球问题来进行划分。值得注意的是，在国际法中即使是在处理一个"本地"问题时，我们也会碰到一种情况，由于它的跨界影响，会牵扯到两个或多个国家。从严格意义上讲，想要确定"本地""区域"和"全球"这几个种类的具体临界值，必须依据相关法规中明确规定的空间范围。这一范围通常会与该法规应对的环境问题的空间维度保持一致。但是，这两者之间并没有必然的关联。全球问题，例如气候变化的某些方面或者海洋环境的陆源污染，[5] 也有可能是在一个地方或区域层面来解决。同样地，区域或地方环境问题，例如越界空气污染或者森林火灾造成的雾霾，[6] 也有可能是在一个更大的平台上来解决。某项规制安排的空间范围在很大程度上是由各种变量决定的，例如在一个特定时间点对某一问题的科学认识，或者政治上的可行性。这些变量有时会导致某项管理制度的范围与它所应对的环境问题的范围这两者间发生变异。

将这两种方法综合在一起，我们进行分析的顺序依次是，从越界问题（本章第二节）开始，然后到区域问题（本章第三节），例如 1979 年在联合国欧洲经济委员会框架下制定的《远程越界空气污染公约》，[7] 最后到全球问题，特别是臭氧层保护的法律文书（本章第四节）和气候制度

---

[4] See the entry "Atmosphere" in M. Allaby (ed.), *Oxford Dictionary of Ecology* (Oxford University Press, 2005); I. H. Rowlands, "Atmosphere and Outer Space", in D. Bodansky, J. Brunnée and E. Hey (eds.), *The Oxford Handbook of International Environmental Law* (Oxford University Press, 2007), p. 316.

[5] See Chapter 4.

[6] ASEAN Agreement on Transboundary Haze Pollution, 10 June 2002, available at www.ecolex.org (TRE‑001344). See P. Nguitragool, *Environmental Cooperation in South‑East Asia: ASEAN's Regime for Transboundary Haze Pollution* (London: Routledge, 2011). 在印度尼西亚发生的森林大火（主要与棕榈油的开发有关），直到 2014 年印度尼西亚加入后才被纳入这一协定。但是，该协定还只是一个未获实际效果验证的框架，2015 年下半年印度尼西亚一次森林大火造成了雾霾这一重要事件就说明了这一点。

[7] Convention on Long‑Range Transboundary Air Pollution, adopted in Geneva on 13 November 1979, 1302 UNTS 217.

(本章第五节)。

第二节 "本地"越界空气污染

在第一章和第三章中,我们已经提到了越界空气污染,把它当作国际法应对的早期环境问题之一。虽然长期以来我们在国内和国际层面已经采取了广泛措施来解决这一问题,但是空气污染仍然是重要的全球性环境问题之一,这一点被 2014 年和 2015 年的联合国世界环境大会(UN World Environment Assembly)⁸[其前身是联合国环境规划署指导理事会(UNEP's Governing Council)]和世界卫生组织(World Health Organization)所承认。⁹ 遏制空气污染的必要性已经被纳入数个可持续发展目标,特别是第 3 项可持续发展目标(健康)下的第 9 个子目标以及第 11 项可持续发展目标(可持续城市)下的第 6 个子目标。¹⁰

国际法应对这一问题的传统方法是基于无害原则和风险预防原则,《斯德哥尔摩宣言》第 21 条原则和《里约宣言》第 2 条原则对此明文确认。¹¹ 这些原则的历史根源来自"特雷尔冶炼厂仲裁案",在该案中仲裁庭运用了无害原则做出了判决,即加拿大有义务修复其境内一个冶炼厂的排放对美国造成的损害。¹²

正如第三章所述,这一案例及其对后续法律进程的影响为分析这一领

---

8 UNEA Resolution 1/7 "Strengthening the Role of the United Nations Environment Programme in Promoting Air Quality", 2 September 2014, UN Doc. UNEP/EA. 1/10.

9 WHO Resolution 68.8 "Health and the Environment: Addressing the Health Impact of Air Pollution", 26 May 2015, WHA68.8.

10 Resolution 70/1, "Transforming our World: The 2030 Agenda for Sustainable Development", 21 October 2015, UN doc A/RES/70/1 (including the SDGs). On the integration of air pollution in the SDGs se B. Lode, P. Schönberger and P. Toussaint, "Clean Air for All by 2030? Air Quality in the 2030 Agenda and International Law" (2016) 25 RECIEL 27.

11 *Legality of the Threat or Use of Nuclear Weapons*, Advisory Opinion, ICJ Reports 1996, p. 226, para. 29; *Gabčíkovo-Nagymaros Project (Hungary v. Slovakia)*, Judgment, ICJ Reports 1997, p. 7, para. 53; *Pulp Mills on the River Uruguay (Argentina v. Uruguay)*, Judgment, ICJ Reports 2010, p. 14, para. 101.

12 *Trail Smelter Arbitration (United States v. Canada)*, Arbitral Award (11 March 1941), RIAA, Vol. III, pp. 1905–1982. However, the origins of the principles can be traced back much further in the history of law, even to Roman times.

域的国际习惯法提供了一个可用的切入点。它也把美国和加拿大两国之间管理越界污染的方法做出了一个说明。这一问题对这两国间的关系至关重要,因为它们都应对对方的环境酸化负责。事实上,美国和加拿大地表水的酸化主要是"酸雨"造成的,而"酸雨"则是由工业活动排放的二氧化硫和氧化氮造成的。[13] 这一现象在几十年前就广为人知,早在20世纪70年代,美国和加拿大就开始试图寻求一个双方同意的解决方案。这一进程的结果就是1991年3月13日达成的《空气质量协定》,[14] 它后来在2000年被扩展到减少越界烟雾(对流层臭氧)排放。这一协定针对空气质量规定了一般和具体目标以及评估和减少排放的义务。[15] 整体上看,该协定对这一问题的解决起到了积极作用,事实表明,1990—2012年,加拿大的二氧化硫的排放量减少了58%,美国减少了78%,而且在一个更短的周期内(2000—2012年),加拿大和美国的氧化氮的排放量都减少了近45%。[16]

越界空气污染的问题有时是通过更广泛的、涵盖不同环境问题的双边协议来进行管理的。简单列举几个例证,《1991年阿根廷和智利环境条约》(*1991 Treaty on the Environment between Argentina and Chile*)、[17]《1993年乌克兰和匈牙利协定》(*1993 Agreement between Ukraine and Hungary*)、[18]《1994年俄罗斯和白俄罗斯协定》(*1994 Agreement between Russia and Belarus*)[19] 或者《1998年乌兹别克斯坦和乌克兰协定》(*1998 Agreement between Uzbekistan and Ukraine*)[20] 都属于此类情况。

---

[13] 森林大火、海洋中的火山和细菌活动也是造成降雨酸化的原因。

[14] Agreement between the Government of Canada and the Government of the United States of America on Air Quality, 3 March 1991, available at: www.epa.og/usca/agreement.html ("Air Quality Agreement"). See J. L. Roelof, "United States-Canada Air Quality Agreement: A Framework for Addressing Transboundary Air Pollution Problems" (1993) 26 *Cornell International Law Journal* 421.

[15] Air Quality Agreement, supra footnote 14, Arts. 3 to 5 and Annex I (entitled "Annex on Acid Rain").

[16] See *Canada-United States Air Quality Agreement. Progress Report* 2014, available at: www.ec.gc.ca (last visited on 12 April 2017).

[17] See www.ecolex.org (TRE-149484).

[18] See www.ecolex.org (TRE-150828).

[19] See www.ecolex.org (TRE-150417).

[20] See www.ecolex.org (TRE-150933).

着眼于当前的研究目的，我们更应关注这些双边协议的广义特性而非它们的具体内容，也就是说，有各种不同的方法可以用于解决局部越界空气污染。后文我们将会看到，随着我们对越界空气污染的认识逐步加深，规制的方法也变得越来越复杂。

第三节 远程越界空气污染

一 制度的起源

有关远程越界空气污染国际制度的起源可以在三个发展进程的交汇中一窥端倪。

第一个进程的本质是社会经济问题，涉及欧洲20世纪50—70年代的工业发展进程及其导致的空气污染。这一时间段被称为欧洲工业发展的（更广义来讲是欧洲经济从第二次世界大战废墟中恢复的）"辉煌三十年"。但是，早在20世纪60年代，已经有研究成果开始关注德国、英国和法国排放的特定物质（尤其是二氧化硫）与斯堪的纳维亚半岛地表水酸化之间的关联。在同一时间段，美国的二氧化硫排放与加拿大湖泊的酸化这两者之间的关联也被确定。污染的"接收者"国家（特别是北欧国家和瑞士）和污染的"排放者"国家（例如美国或英国）之间的争议被提交到一些国际仲裁法庭。

第一个进程对第二个进程起到了催化的作用，后者指的是国际层面的环境意识的觉醒。这一意识最显著的表现是1972年斯德哥尔摩会议的筹备过程，本书第一章已有论述。在斯德哥尔摩会议期间，北欧国家的代表的确提出了酸雨问题，但成效不大。[21]

北欧国家的关注在第三个进程中获得了大好机遇，第三个进程指的是西方国家和苏联集团之间的和解努力，它发生于1973—1975年在赫尔辛基召开的欧洲安全和合作会议（Conference on Security and Cooperation in

---

21 See V. Sokolovsky, "Fruits of a Cold War", in J. Sliggers and W. Kakebeeke (eds.), *Clearing the Air. 25 Years of the Convention on Long-Range Transboundary Air Pollution* (New York/Geneva: United Nations, 2004), p. 8.

Europe）期间。这次会议将解决越界空气污染问题当作开展合作的出发点，[22] 它对欧洲监测和评估项目网络（European Monitoring and Evaluation Programme，EMEP）的建立起到了决定性的推动作用，而这一项目网络则为《远程越界空气污染公约》（Convention on Long-Range Transboundary Air Pollution）的制定提供了科学基础。[23]

这三个发展进程的交汇在 1979 年 11 月的日内瓦会议上达到了顶峰，这次会议是在联合国欧洲经济委员会的组织框架下召开的。在本次会议上，34 个国家的代表和欧洲共同体订立了《远程越界空气污染公约》（LRTAP Convention）。[24]

二 《远程越界空气污染公约》

《远程越界空气污染公约》是第一项在欧洲大陆并横越大西洋订立的、应对越界空气污染具有法律约束力的文件。[25] 在 1983 年生效以后，该公约对超过 50 个国家具有约束力，这些国家不仅包括位于欧洲的国家（包括东欧），还包括北美和中亚国家。

---

[22] Final Act of the Conference on Security and Cooperation in Europe, 1975, 14 ILM 1292, p. 32.

[23] See T. Schneider and J. Schneider, "EMEP–Backbone of the Convention", in Sliggers and Kakebeeke, supra footnote 21, Chapter 3.

[24] On the origins and function of this treaty see P. Okowa, "The Legal Framework for the Protection of the Environment Against Transboundary Air Pollution", in H. G. Post（ed.）, *The Protection of Ambient Air in International and European Law* (The Hague: Eleven Publishing, 2009), pp. 53–71; Sliggers and Kakebeeke, supra footnote 21; A. Byrne, "The 1979 Convention on Long-Range Transboundary Air Pollution: Assessing its Effectiveness as a Multilateral Environmental Regime after 35 Years" (2015) 4 *Transnational Environmental Law* 37.

[25] Other regional instruments on this issue have been developed over time: the Nordic Convention on the Protection of the Environment, 19 February 1974, available in English at www.ecolex.org（TRE-000491）; European guidelines in this field（see M. Montini, "EC Legislation on Air Pollution: From Guidelines to Limit Values' in Post, supra footnote 24, pp. 73–87）; ASEAN Agreement on Transboundary Haze Pollution, supra footnote 6; Framework Convention on Environmental Protection for Sustainable Development in Central Asia, 22 November 2006, available in English at www.ecolex.org（TRE-143806）; SADC Regional Policy Framework on Air Pollution, 7 March 2008, available at www.unep.org; Eastern Africa Regional Framework Agreement on Air Pollution, 23 October 2008, available at www.unep.org; West and Central Africa Regional Framework Agreement on Air Pollution, 22 July 2009, available at www.unep.org.

虽然该公约并没有包含任何具体的实际义务（虽然北欧国家试图主张这一点，但是受到了英国和联邦德国的抵制），但是它的结构在当时还是非常有意义的，因为它提出了一种重要的法律方法，这一方法后来被称为"框架公约/议定书方法"。事实上，在这个存在着相当大的不确定性和重大政治分歧（污染"接收者"和污染"排放者"之间）的背景下，该公约最终用于：(1) 定义其目标；(2) 确立基本原则；(3) 提供一个体制以便通过后续的文件（议定书）来明确各国的目标和义务。

公约第1条将"空气污染"定义为：

> 人类将有害的物质或能量直接或间接地引入空气，以致造成危害人类健康、损害生物资源和生态系统、损坏物质财产、减损或妨碍环境优美以及环境的其他正当用途等有害影响。

如此一来，污染就被理解为是人类干预（与造成排放的自然进程相反），它对人类（人类中心主义要素）或者环境（生态中心主义要素）造成了损害［包括人造环境（例如财产）］。当某国的排放源和他国的不利影响的距离达到"一般无法区分单个排放源或多个排放源的比例大小"这一标准时，该污染就会被定性为"远程"。同时应当注意的是，排放源和不利影响必须都是在某个国家的管辖范围之内，这就排除了那种仅仅影响国家管辖以外地区（例如公海）环境的污染。这也反映出当时的预防原则还是一个狭义的概念，即使《斯德哥尔摩宣言》第21条原则提出了更积极的表述，将国家管辖以外区域的环境也包含在内。

该公约在第2—6条建立了一些"基本原则"。这些原则分为两类。一方面，各国承诺采取国家措施来限制和逐步减少那些源自其管辖范围的空气污染（包括越界污染），但是一系列限定性条件又使这一承诺变得不够坚定。[26] 另一方面，各国承诺通过"信息交换、协商、科研和监测"来开展合作。[27] 这一点看起来比较适当，但是，在东—西两个世界对抗的背景下，污染接收者国家拥有一个法律依据（第5条）来提起协商这一事

---

[26] LRTAP Convention supra footnote 7, Arts. 2, 3 and 6.

[27] Ibid., Art. 3, as well as Arts. 4 and 8（exchange of information）, 5（consultations between State emitters and State receivers）, and 7（research and development）.

实、与一个旨在加深和拓宽实际义务的体制结构之间还隔着重要的一步。

公约建立的体制结构包含了一个执行机构,[28] 与我们第二章探讨的缔约方大会相似,它拥有一个闭会期工作局、一个秘书处[29]和一个科研机构,这一科研机构的职权是由欧洲监测和评估项目网络指导组(Steering Body of the EMEP)授予的,它发挥了更为统一和宽泛的功能。[30] 这一体制经过多年的发展,通过一些辅助机构的建立,例如"效果工作组""战略和评估工作组"以及"执行委员会",逐步变得成熟。数十年来,它的科研机构通过协商和公约的体制所收集的信息有力促成了不少于8个包含有具体义务的议定书的制定。

最后,我们还应指出,公约所采用的方法是限制排放而不是分配修复责任。[31] 公约不太愿意解决责任问题,部分是因为想要在排放和损害之间建立精确的因果联系还存在一定难度,同时也是政治分歧的结果,后文我们要讨论的有关臭氧层保护和气候变化的制度也是如此。

三 《远程越界空气污染公约》之议定书

20世纪80年代以来制定的议定书具有重要意义,因为它们对各缔约国有关空气质量的立法产生了实际影响(这一点有时是非常重要的),同时也是因为它们为空气污染的管理提供了一个重要的实验场地。我们不想按照时间顺序来依次介绍这些议定书,而是采用一种更具启发性的方法,通过三种分析性区分方法来形成一个交叉整合的观点。

第一种区分涉及议定书的本质。《远程越界空气污染公约》第一个议定书的目的是增强欧洲监测和评估项目网络(特别是在资金方面),[32] 而后续的七个议定书则是在空气污染领域制定具体义务。鉴于公约的文本缺少一个中心资助机制(用于那些不属于欧洲监测和评估项目网络下的活

---

[28] Ibid., Art. 10.

[29] Ibid., Art. 11.

[30] Ibid., Art. 9.

[31] In the footnote to Art. 8 (f) of the LRTAP Convention, it is expressly stated that "The present Convention does not contain a rule on State liability as to damage".

[32] Protocol to the 1979 Convention on Long-Range Transboundary Air Pollution on the long-term Financing of the Cooperative Programme for Monitoring and Evaluation of the Long-Range Transport of Air Pollutants in Europe ("EMEP"), 28 September 1984, 1491 UNTS 167.

动,即使是核心活动),因此欧洲监测和评估项目网络赖以支撑的国家强制贡献制度就值得高度关注。[33] 第二,这些文件所采取的每个方法都是针对某一特定种类的污染(二氧化硫、[34] 氧化氮、[35] 挥发性有机化合物、[36] 重金属[37]和持久性有机污染物[38])。直到1999年11月《哥德堡议定书》通过,[39] 规制手段的重心才从污染源分类转移到问题分类(酸化、富营养化、对流层臭氧),这就涵盖了更多的污染物(包括细小的微粒物质)和污染源(固定的、移动的、新的和现有的)。[40] 第三,规制手段已经变得更加复杂。这一特点也阐释了这些议定书的法律演进。

酸化问题(尤其是酸雨)起初是通过一种相对严格的方式来进行管

33　See Byrne, supra footnote 24, pp. 52–53.

34　Protocol to the 1979 Convention on Long-Range Transboundary Air Pollution on the Reduction of Sulphur Emissions or their Transboundary Fluxes by at Least 30 Per Cent, 8 July 1985, 1480 UNTS 215 ("Sulphur Protocol I"); Protocol to the 1979 Convention on Long-Range Transboundary Air Pollution on the Reduction of Sulphur Emissions, 14 June 1994, 2030 UNTS 122 ("Sulphur Protocol II").

35　Protocol to the 1979 Convention on Long-Range Transboundary Air Pollution Concerning the Control of Emissions of Nitrogen Oxides or their Transboundary Fluxes, 31 October 1988, 28 ILM 212, 216 ("NOx Protocol").

36　Protocol to the 1979 Convention on Long-Range Transboundary Air Pollution Concerning the Control of Emissions of Volatile Organic Compounds or their Transboundary Fluxes, 18 November 1991, 31 ILM 573 ("VOC Protocol").

37　Protocol to the 1979 Convention on Long-Range Transboundary Air Pollution on Heavy Metals, 24 June 1998, 2237 UNTS 4 ("Heavy Metals Protocol").

38　Protocol to the 1979 Convention on Long-Range Transboundary Air Pollution on Persistent Organic Pollutants (POPs), 24 June 1998, 2230 UNTS 79 ("POP Protocol").

39　Protocol to the 1979 Convention on Long-Range Transboundary Air Pollution on the Reduction of Acidification, Eutrophication and Ground-Level Ozone, 30 November 1999, Document of the Economic and Social Council EB. AIR/1999/1 ("Gothenburg Protocol").

40　起初,该议定书包含了二氧化硫、氧化氮、挥发性有机化合物和氨的排放。现在它也适用于细颗粒物的排放,包括炭黑这一种强大的温室气体,黑炭持续的时间较短而且它的影响是局部的。See "Parties to UNECE Air Pollution Convention approve new emission reduction commitments for main air pollutants by 2020", Press release, 4 May 2012, available at: www.unece.org/index.php?id=29858 (last visited on 12 October 2012). Note that this amendment will enter into force after ratification by two thirds of the parties, in the following presentation, we incorporate the amendments into the analysis.

理的,从取得的成果来看这种方法还是比较有效的。[41] 1984 年,在瑞典的倡议下,一项政治性的《酸雨宣言》(*Declaration on Acid Rain*)通过,并成立了一个"30%俱乐部",它是由数个同意将其二氧化硫排放量减少 30%的国家组成。虽然这种方法太过于严厉,以至于受到了数个排放国(例如波兰、西班牙、英国或美国)的抵制,但是,这一宣言还是促成了 1985 年第一项实质性议定书——《硫黄第一议定书》的制定。这项议定书为每个缔约方规定了一项无差别的义务,即必须在基准年的基础上尽早(不迟于 1993 年)将二氧化硫排放量减少 30%。[42]

不久之后,一个类似的方法被尝试用于应对氧化氮排放问题。1986 年《减少 30%氧化氮的索菲亚宣言》(*Sofia Declaration on 30% Reduction of NOx*)得以通过,但是这项与《氧化氮议定书》(*NOx Protocol*)同时制定的文件还不足以维持《硫黄第一议定书》所采用的严格的自上而下的手段。[43]《氧化氮议定书》设计了一种更复杂的减排制度,它由三个要件构成:(1)根据各国的具体情况来调整减排义务(包括可以选择一个特定的基准年份);[44] (2)根据"经济可行的最佳可得技术"(Best Available Technology which is Economically Feasible, BATEF)这一标准,针对特定污染源制定国家排放标准,包括固定污染源(例如发电厂)和移动污染源(例如小车、卡车、火车和飞机);[45] (3)根据"关键容量"(Critical Load)这一概念,制定一个综合的、节省成本的方法。所谓关键容量,指的是"一个或多个污染物暴露在数量上的估值,在这一估值之下,基于现有认识,对特定易感环境要素的重大损害后果就不会发生"。[46] 因此,每个保护区都必须为各种类型的污染物规定一个容量。这种方法后来一直

---

[41] 截至 1993 年,排放量被减少了 50% 以上。See Byrne, supra footnote 24, p. 65 (Appendix, table 1: Compliance with the Protocols' Major Objectives).

[42] Sulphur Protocol I, supra footnote 34, Art. 2.

[43] See Byrne, supra footnote 24, p. 43.

[44] NO_x Protocol, supra footnote 35, Art. 2 (1).

[45] Ibid., Art. 2 (2) and Technical Annex, paras. 6 and 41. 一个例子是把催化转换器[该设备可以将有毒气体(例如主要由汽车排放的氧化氮)转化为毒性较小的污染物(例如二氧化碳、氮和水)]的使用当作一种经济可行的最佳可得技术。这是一种"末端"解决方法而非一个结构性改变。See Byrne, supra footnote 24, pp. 48 and 66.

[46] Ibid., Art. 1 (7). See also: J. Nilsson and P. Grennfelt (eds.), *Report: Critical Loads for Sulphur and Nitrogen* (Copenhagen: Nordic Council of Ministers, 1988).

被沿用，但是它在当时就引发了大量的科学挑战，[47] 例如，如何定义保护区，如何选择指标来估量保护区的容量，或者如何理解污染物从源头到保护区的运行轨迹。[48] 需要强调指出的是，关键容量这一概念与风险预防的理念是有冲突的，[49] 因为它仅仅根据现有科学认识就确定了污染的上限——关键容量。[50] 同时，这一方法也为各国所要求的在保护层级上采取差异化方式提供了一个科学依据，它对确保那些拥有相关产业的国家的参与至关重要。为了相似的目的，关键容量这一方法后来还被用于 1994 年通过的《硫黄第二议定书》和 1999 年通过的《哥德堡议定书》（Gothenburg Protocol）（针对二氧化硫和氧化氮）。

在《氧化氮议定书》之后，1991 年通过的《挥发性有机化合物议定书》（VOC Protocol）进一步发展了那些用于增强灵活性的手段。这一议定书采用的方法包含三个要件：（1）各缔约国可以选择三种不同种类的减排义务；（2）根据经济可行的最佳可得技术这一标准来为固定和移动污染源制定排放标准；[51]（3）使用"关键程度"（critical levels）这一概念。主要的创新点体现于第一个和第三个要件中。关于第一个要件，各缔约国可以根据各自的具体情况来从三种不同的减排义务中选择一个，这三种减排义务是：（1）不晚于 1999 年将国家年度排放量减少 30%（在一个特定时间段内选择一个基准年）；[52]（2）在国家领土的核心区域（所谓的

47　NO_x Protocol, supra footnote 35, Art. 6.

48　关于旨在实现这一目标的相关模式在提升政策应对的成本效益上所发挥的作用，参见 W. Tuinstra, L. Hordijk and M. Amann, "Using Computer Models in International Negotiations: The Case of Acidification in Europe" (1999) 41 *Environment* 33。

49　See Chapter 3.

50　但是风险预防可以用于定量过程（例如使关键容量变得更保守）。See R. A. Skeffington, "Quantifying Uncertainty in Critical Loads: (a) Literature Review" (2006) 169 *Water, Air, and Soil Pollution* 3. 这一警示性说明对评估《哥德堡议定书》前言提及的风险预防方法非常重要。事实上，这一文件也包含了关键容量这一方法。

51　VOC Protocol, supra footnote 36, Art. 2 (3). 从经济可行的最佳可得技术到最佳可得技术（或者更具体一点，不会导致过度花费的最佳可得控制技术）的转变是随着 1994 年《硫黄第二议定书》的制定而发生的。概念上的区别主要在于鼓励结构性解决方法而非终端解决方法。《硫黄第二议定书》第 2 条第 4 款要求各国采用结构性措施（例如效率和涉及可再生能源时）以及采用最佳可得技术（附录四）。See Byrne, supra footnote 24, p. 49.

52　VOC Protocol, supra footnote 36, Art. 2 (2) (a).

对流层臭氧区域）减少30%排放量；[53]（3）针对排放量不大的国家规定一个不太严格的目标，保持基准年（1988年）的排放量即可。[54]

关于"关键程度"这一概念想法与"关键容量"相似，但它并不是紧盯某些地区或生态系统的污染程度，而是关注空气中的污染现状，这一污染有可能"对那些受体（例如人类、植物、生态系统或物质）造成直接的不利影响"。[55] 如此一来，这一方法与风险预防的理念之间的关系也显得模糊不清，因为容量程度是根据"现有认识状态"来预估的。

1998年制定的《重金属议定书》也设计了两项内容：（1）依据每个国家特定的基准年排放量来减少附录中确定的特定重金属（镉、铅、水银）的排放量；[56]（2）采用"最佳可得技术"这一标准和"限值"这一概念来制定固定污染源的排放标准。[57] 所谓限值，指的是在特定设施正常运行期间，某种特定重金属在每个时间段（例如每个小时）的平均排放量。该公约的附录五针对某些"主要固定污染源"规定了一般限值和特别限值。[58] 各国必须遵从最佳可得技术的要求，并按照附录四来确定特定时间段（时间段的长短由固定污染源的种类决定）的排放限值。同年制定的《持久性有机污染物议定书》（POP Protocol）[59] 则更进了一步。针对附录三中列举的物质（例如二氧芑和呋喃），公约设计了一套类似于《重金属议定书》的制度，即减少排放、采用最佳可得技术和限值。但是，它同时规定附录一指定的物质的生产和利用必须被排除，[60] 而附录二中物质的利用则是仅限于该附录规定的情形下。[61] 后面这一方法在三年后被一

---

[53] Ibid., Art. 2 (2) (b) and Annex I.

[54] Ibid., Art. 2 (2) (c).

[55] Ibid., Art. 1 (8).

[56] Heavy Metals Protocol, supra footnote 37, Art. 3 (1) and Annex I.

[57] Ibid., Art. 3 (2). 附录三（最佳可得技术）的修订案在2012年12月被制定并于2014年开始生效。其他修订案尚未开始生效。

[58] Ibid., Annexes II and V.

[59] POP Protocol, supra footnote 38. 2009年12月，该议定书被修订，列入了7种新物质并修订了涵盖物质的相关义务，但是该修订案尚未开始生效。

[60] Ibid., Art. 3 (1) (a) and Annex I. 同时参见第3条第1款规定的更多义务（关于应当如何开展清除）。

[61] Ibid., Art. 3 (1) (c) and Annex II. 例如，滴滴涕杀虫剂（蕾切尔·卡逊在1962年就报告了它的后果）的使用被特别许可用于对抗疟疾和脑炎。

个全球性的条约所复制,该条约就是 2001 年制定的《关于持久性有机污染物的斯德哥尔摩公约》。[62]

最后,关于《哥德堡议定书》,[63] 由于它的多重目标(遏制酸化、富营养化和地平面臭氧层),[64] 它整合了前文提及的多个规制手段。这就使该议定书变得非常复杂,但是也特别重要,因为它提供了《远程越界空气污染公约》框架下开展的法律实践的一个汇总。该议定书规定了:(1)量化的义务,针对特定污染物(硫黄、氧化氮、氨、挥发性有机化合物和微粒物质,例如炭黑)的减排为每个国家规定了单独的上限;[65](2)与对流层臭氧(烟雾)问题相关的"关键程度"这一概念的使用;[66](3)与酸化和富营养化(针对硫黄和氧化氮)问题相关的"关键容量"这一概念的使用;[67](4)依据最佳可得技术标准[68]和"限值"这一概念,[69]在特定时间期限内制定部分污染物(例如硫黄、氧化氮、挥发性有机化合物或燃料)的固定和移动污染源排放标准,制定具体措施以控制农业造成的氨排放。[70] 综合使用这些手段的目的是实现有害排放的稳定和减少。事实上,一般来说,针对特定污染物排放管理的规定(上限和限值)的目的就是符合关键容量和关键程度。

表 5-1 概括了《远程越界空气污染公约》之议定书所采用的这四种主要类型的规制手段(即减排目标、排放技术标准、污染限值和禁止/限制)。

---

62 Stockholm Convention on Persistent Organic Pollutants, 22 May 2001, 2256 UNTS 119, discussed in Chapter 7 of this book.

63 Gothenburg Protocol, supra footnote 39.

64 Ibid., Art. 2.

65 Ibid., Art. 3 (1) and Annex II. See supra footnote 40.

66 Ibid., Art. 2 (c) and Annex I (III).

67 Ibid., Art. 2 and Annex I.

68 Ibid., Art. 3 (6) and 3 (8) (b).

69 Ibid., Art. 3 (2) – (5) (and (7)) and Annexes IV – VI and VIII as well as X for black carbon and XI for VOC contents of products once the amendment enters into force (limit values), Annex VII (time).

70 Ibid., Art. 3 (8) and Annex IX.

表 5-1　　大气污染规制手段

减排目标		排放技术标准				污染限值		产品/利用	
严格	灵活	污染源类型 固定/移动，现有/新的	标准类型			关键容量	关键程度	清除	限制使用
			最佳可得技术	限值	特别措施				
硫黄I	氧化氮 硫黄II 挥发性有机化合物 金属 持久性有机污染物 《哥德堡议定书》	氧化氮 硫黄II 挥发性有机化合物 金属 持久性有机污染物 《哥德堡议定书》	氧化氮 硫黄II 挥发性有机化合物 金属 持久性有机污染物 《哥德堡议定书》	金属 持久性有机污染物 《哥德堡议定书》(附录四)	《哥德堡议定书》	氧化氮 硫黄II 《哥德堡议定书》	挥发性有机化合物 《哥德堡议定书》	持久性有机污染物(附录一)	挥发性有机化合物(附录二)

在《远程越界空气污染公约》框架下开展的法律实践是非常有用的，其有助于我们理解那些为了应对全球性问题（例如臭氧层消耗和气候变化）而采用的方法。

第四节　臭氧层的保护

一　制度的起源

为了应对臭氧层耗竭而制定的国际制度[71]与那些应对空气污染的前期努力存在着一些共同点，但是它还是有着不同的特征，原因在于这一问题不仅具有全球性，而且对它的初步认识还存在科学不确定性。

谈及两者的相似之处，臭氧层的保护要面对的困难与远程越界空气污染所面临的困难高度相似，即（1）科学—政策的相互作用（正如欧洲监测和评估项目网络监测空气污染，联合国环境规划署和世界气象组织以及其他一些机构定期评估臭氧层状态[72]）；（2）环境保护与经济利益之间的

---

[71] See O. Yoshida, *The International Legal Regime for the Protection of the Stratospheric Ozone Layer* (The Hague: Kluwer, 2001); R. E. Benedick, *Ozone Diplomacy: New Directions in Safeguarding the Planet* (Cambridge MA: Harvard University Press, 1998).

[72] 早在 20 世纪 80 年代，联合国环境规划署和世界气象组织就会定期发布一份关于臭氧层状态的评估报告。在此可以与政府间气候变化专门委员会的作用及其对气候变化科学的现状的定期评估进行一个类比。

冲突体现于"多伦多集团"和欧洲共同体之间的艰难谈判；一方面，包含了美国、加拿大、瑞士、北欧各国、新西兰和澳大利亚的"多伦多集团"支持国际规制；另一方面，欧洲共同体本身划分为两个派别，有些国家（例如法国和英国）不愿意接受强力规制这一观念，而有些国家（例如德国和荷兰）则支持这些规制；（3）应对这些挑战所必需的法律试验（例如"框架公约/议定书"的方法）。这些问题是史无前例的，这也更加加剧了其难度。

事实上，臭氧层保护是国际法面对的第一个真正的全球性环境问题。地球大气中大约90%的臭氧位于平流层（距离地球表面12—50千米），在25千米处臭氧的密度最大。围绕地球的这一稀薄的臭氧层吸收了很大一部分的太阳紫外线照射，否则的话就会对环境和人类健康造成严重后果。因此，这一问题就不再是一个地方、区域甚至大洲的管理问题了。臭氧层的保护必须考虑到所有国家的利益以及当代和后代的利益。想要做到这点非常困难，因为消耗臭氧层的主要物质——氟氯化碳的生产和使用会涉及重大经济利益，而氟氯化碳又被广泛使用于工业活动和产品之中（例如冰箱、溶剂、气溶胶推进剂），同时还因为存在着科学不确定性。1974年，首次明确了氟氯化碳对臭氧层的潜在威胁，[73]从那时起直到20世纪80年代末期，越来越多的科研成果进一步阐明了这一问题，虽然发展道路还是蜿蜒曲折的。即使在1985年公布的一个重大发现（即在南极上方的臭氧层中存在着一个周期性的"空洞"，尺寸相当于美国国土面积）[74]之后，氟氯化碳和臭氧层消耗之间的因果联系依然没有被完全理解。[75] 这一不确定性导致在谈判的进程中很晚才触及规制这一

---

[73] See R. S. Stolarski and R. J. Cicerone, "Stratospheric Chlorine: A Possible Sink for Ozone" (1974) 52 *Canadian Journal of Chemistry* 1610-1615; M. J. Molina and F. S. Rowland, "Stratospheric Sink for Chlorofluoromethanes: Chlorine Atomic Catalyzed Destruction of Ozone" (1974) 249 *Nature* 810-812.

[74] See B. Farman, G. Gardiner and J. D. Shanklin, Large Losses of Total Ozone in Antarctica Reveal Seasonal ClO_x/NO_x International'(1985) 315 *Nature* 207-210. A "hole" was also found in 2011 above the Arctic.

[75] On the evolution of the problem, see O. B. Toon and R. P. Turco, "Polar Stratospheric Clouds and Ozone Depletion" (1991) 264 (6) *Scientific American* 68-74.

问题。[76]

在此背景下，我们有必要来评估1985年制定的《保护臭氧层维也纳公约》[77]。虽然公约并未规定具体的实质性义务，但是它还是为最进取的国际环境法文件之一——《蒙特利尔议定书》的制定提供了一个框架。[78]

二 1985年《维也纳公约》

与《远程越界空气污染公约》相似，《维也纳公约》也是一个框架公约。虽然"多伦多集团"的部分国家试图制定一个附录来规定氟氯化碳管控的具体义务，但是这一点在1985年是无法做到的。[79] 与《远程越界空气污染公约》相似，《维也纳公约》只限于：（1）定义它的客体；（2）规定一些广义的义务；（3）规定了一个体制来明确各国的义务并制定一项有区别的履约制度（这是最重要的一点）。考虑到问题的范畴，以及当时对氟氯化碳和臭氧消耗之间因果关系的认识还存在科学不确定性，我们不应低估这一成果的价值，因为与《远程越界空气污染公约》不同，《维也纳公约》依据的是风险预防这一理念，而当时这一理念在外交圈并不被熟知，甚至受到质疑。[80]

《维也纳公约》的第一个贡献在于，在表述臭氧消耗这一问题时，强调指出它的全球性特征并把它与某个地方或区域问题（例如越界污染，特别是地平面臭氧问题）加以区分。根据第1条第1款，保护的客体实际上是"行星边界层以上的大气臭氧层"。[81] 也规定了对臭氧层保护的其他

76　See Benedick, supra footnote 71, pp. 19–20.

77　Vienna Convention on the Protection of the Ozone Layer, 22 March 1985, 1513 UNTS 293 ("Vienna Convention").

78　Montreal Protocol on Substances that Deplete the Ozone Layer, 16 September 1987, 1522 UNTS 29 ("Montreal Protocol").

79　Yoshida, supra footnote 71, pp. 49ff.

80　Benedick, supra footnote 71, p. 24.

81　Yoshida认为臭氧层的状态（公约文本对其表述不够清晰）是一个"人类共同关注"。Yoshida, supra footnote 71, p. 61.

三种方式，即明确应避免的变化种类（"不利影响"[82]），改变的成因（"人类活动"[83]），以及造成损害的物质。[84] 值得注意的是，公约的前言和第 1 条第 2 款都将公约定位为一个旨在预防臭氧层变化的手段，即使人类活动与指定物质之间，以及臭氧层的改变与它对人类健康和环境的不利影响之间的联系还没有得到科学地认证。这一点有助于我们理解预防和风险预防这两个理念之间的紧密关联，风险预防在很多方面相当于是预防的更进取（更少固化）版本。

关于各缔约国应当承担的义务，该公约只是规定，一方面，各方必须采取"适当"措施（纵向义务）[85]，另一方面，它鼓励各国相互之间并与有关的国际组织开展合作（横向义务）以便加深对臭氧消耗的研究，[86] 目的是协调各国间的内部政策[87]和制定国际制度（尤其是通过公约的议定书这一方式）。[88] 就当前目的而言，值得关注的是合作科研制度以及合作制度。

与其他多边环境协定一起，《维也纳公约》创造了一个永久的体制来明确合作义务及制度制定义务。基于公约第 6 条设立的缔约国大会发挥的主要功能是分析有关臭氧层状况的科学信息，启动科研项目，与国际科研机构（包括世界气象组织下的全球空气观察项目）保持联系，[89] 以及检查和制定公约的议定书。[90] 在此背景下，1986 年年末，缔约国大会启动了旨在制定《蒙特利尔议定书》的谈判。公约的秘书处[91]设在肯尼亚内罗毕，归属于联合国环境署。

---

[82] 《维也纳公约》第 1 条第 2 款将这一术语定义为"自然环境或生物区系内发生的，对人类健康或自然的和受管理的生态系统的组成、弹性和生产力或对人类有益的物质造成有害影响的变化，包括气候的变化"。

[83] Ibid., Art. 2（1）.

[84] 公约附录一提到了各种物质（这些物质的影响应受到监测）。这部分反映出围绕这一问题还存在较大的科学不确定性。《蒙特利尔议定书》规定了一个更精确的定义。

[85] Ibid., Arts. 2（1），2（2）（b），3（authorisation to adopt more stringent national measures）and 5（communication of information）.

[86] Ibid., Arts. 2（2）（a），3，4 and Annex II.

[87] Ibid., Arts. 2（2）（b）and 4.

[88] Ibid., Arts. 2（2）（c）– (d) and 8.

[89] Ibid., Art. 6（4）（b），(d) and (j).

[90] Ibid., Art. 6（4）（h）.

[91] Ibid., Art. 7.

三 1987 年《蒙特利尔议定书》

在国际环境法的历史进程中,《蒙特利尔议定书》无疑是一个成功标杆。[92] 我们从《蒙特利尔议定书》可以学到很多东西,包括它的积极进取以及法律上的精致和复杂,而且用回顾的视角来看,它无疑是有效的。[93] 为了采用一种清晰的方式来概括它的贡献,就有必要区分议定书结构中的两个维度,即缔约方义务的构造以及为了确保遵约而设计的制度。

缔约方的义务包含了一套复杂的内容组合,既有议定书文本规定的义务,也有各个附录规定的细则。这一制度的核心可以被划分成四个主要部分:(1)受控物质的种类(例如氟氯化碳、哈龙、氢氯氟碳化合物等[94]);(2)缔约方的类别(发展中国家的义务更具灵活性[95]);(3)管理的客体(即"消费量"和"生产量"),[96] 数量的计算方法由议定书规定[97]);(4)减排义务的构造(一个日程表首先"冻结"生产或消费,然后依据某一基准年来确定一定百分比的减排目标,并规定实现这一目标的期限[98])。议定书的文本不太容易理解,主要原因是该文本经历了各种调

---

[92] For an overview see D. S. Bryk, "The Montreal Protocol and Recent Developments to Protect the Ozone Layer" (1991) 15 *Harvard Environmental Law Review* 275.

[93] See D. Kaniaru (ed.), *The Montreal Protocol: Celebrating 20 Years of Environmental Progress* (London: Cameron May, 2007). 截至 2012 年,《蒙特利尔议定书》对世界上所有 197 个国家具有约束力,与 1987 年相比,将受管控物质的生产减少了 98%(1987 年是 180 万吨,2010 年是 45000 吨)。See the Ozone Secretariat, *Stratospheric Ozone Protection: Progress Report 1987–2012*, available at: www.ozone.unep.org (last visited on 13 August 2012).

[94] Montreal Protocol, supra footnote 78, Art. 1(4) and Annexes A, B, C, E and F(附录六关注的是氢氟碳化合物,该附录是在 2016 年 10 月由《基加利修正案》添加的,尚未生效)。该议定书采用了分门别类的方法,即义务是由围绕着义务的种类来构建的(例如聚焦于附录一组别一中的物质而不是该组别中的单个具体物质)。See Ibid., Art. 3.

[95] Ibid., Art. 5(1).

[96] Ibid., Art. 1(5)(production) and 1(6)(consumption).

[97] Ibid., Art. 1(7) and 3(calculated levels).

[98] Ibid., Arts. 2 to 2I, and Annexes A, B, C and E. 如果将本章后文论及的 2016 年 10 月制定的《基加利修正案》(see section 5.4.4)考虑在内,那么有关氢氟碳化合物的第 2 条 J 款和附录六则必须被添加在内。发展中国家(适用于第 5 条第 1 款)从该条款规定的灵活性、援助和被给予的更长期限中获益。see, in particular, Art. 5, paragraphs 1bis, 3 and 8bis to 8qua.

整（6次系列调整）[99]，还有那些通过修订（5次系列修订，最近的一次发生于2016年10月）而增加的新条款。后文这个例证有助于我们来理解这四个部分是如何相互作用的。

议定书的第2A条（附录A种类1）规定了部分氟氯化碳（氟氯化碳-11、氟氯化碳-12、氟氯化碳-113、氟氯化碳-114和氟氯化碳-115）的管控措施。随着时间的推移，人们对臭氧消耗的原因有了更深的认识，议定书也随之扩展到其他物质，包括第2C—2J条和附录B（涉及完全卤化的氟氯化碳、四氯化碳和甲基氯仿），附录C（涉及氢氯氟碳化合物、氟溴烃和溴氯甲烷），附录E（涉及溴化甲烷），以及有待生效的附录F（涉及氢氟烃）。针对每种类型的受控物质，议定书都规定了两种有区别的义务，一个是针对发达国家（那些不适用第5条第1款的国家），另一个是针对发展中国家（那些适用第5条第1款的国家）。各缔约方首先会被要求冻结并减少受控物质的消费和生产的计算数量，但是针对那些适用第5条第1款的国家所规定的要求要相对宽松一些。第1条第5款对生产量的定义是"受控物质（在一定时间段）的生产量减去特定方式销毁的数量再减去完全用作其他化学品制造原料的数量之后所得的数量"。第1条第6款对消费量的定义是"受控物质的生产量加上进口量减去出口量之后所得的数量"。后文我们将会看到，议定书具体规定了出口这些物质的可能性。根据第3条，生产量和消费量的起始控制限值是由每种受控物质（由附录A、附录B、附录C、附录E确定）的每年生产量乘以该物质的消耗臭氧潜能值（ozone depleting potential）。计算所采用的标准（或者采取一种类比的方法来说明，用某种货币来计算其他货币的价值）是氟氯化碳-11，它的潜能值被直接指定为1。部分更具危害的物质（例如哈龙）拥有一个更高的潜能值。例如，哈龙-1301的消耗臭氧潜能值是10，这样就意味着到达平流层的一吨哈龙-1301所消耗的臭氧层是氟氯化碳-11的10倍。这些潜能值会随着科学认识的不断发展而进行定期调整。

有了以上的认识基础，我们现在开始研究义务的构造。我们用氟氯化碳来举例说明。根据议定书第2A条的规定，工业化国家承诺，依据基准年（1986年），在1989年7月1日到1993年12月31日，首先冻结它们

---

[99] Ibid., Art. 2 (9).

的部分氟氯化碳（附录A种类1）的消费和生产。因此，这些国家必须按照百分比来逐步减少它们的排放量，直到最终实现这些物质的生产或消费的完全消除（淘汰）。减排采用的是一种分阶段方式，依据1986年的排放量来确定每年的排放量。据此，在1994年1月1日到1995年12月31日，氟氯化碳的每年生产量或排放量不得超过1986年排放量的25%（相当于每年的生产量或排放量减少75%）。然后，从1996年1月1日起，生产或消费就不再被允许（100%减排）。针对发展中国家，义务的构造也是类似的，但是基准排放量（在这里是1995年、1996年、1997年的平均排放量）和期限则更具灵活性。[100] 发展中国家应在1999年1月1日到2004年12月31日实现冻结，采用的是一种三步走的渐进式减排：在2005年1月1日到2006年12月31日，排放量不得超过基准排放量的50%（减排50%）；在2007年1月1日到2009年12月31日，排放量不得超过基准排放量的15%（减排85%）；从2010年1月1日起，这些物质的生产或消费就不再被允许（100%减排）。想要用文字来表述这一结构太过于困难，用图表的方式会更容易（见图5-1）。

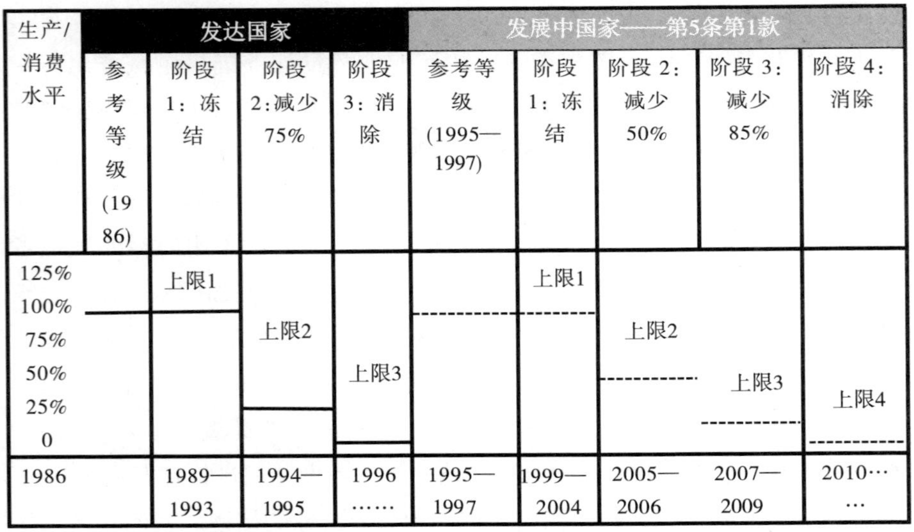

生产/消费水平	发达国家				发展中国家——第5条第1款				
	参考等级(1986)	阶段1:冻结	阶段2:减少75%	阶段3:消除	参考等级(1995—1997)	阶段1:冻结	阶段2:减少50%	阶段3:减少85%	阶段4:消除
125% 100% 75% 50% 25% 0		上限1	上限2	上限3		上限1	上限2	上限3	上限4
1986		1989—1993	1994—1995	1996……	1995—1997	1999—2004	2005—2006	2007—2009	2010……

图5-1 《蒙特利尔议定书》——承诺的结构（氟氯化碳）[101]

100 Ibid., Art. 5 paragraphs (1), (3) (a) and (c), and (8*bis*) (a).
101 来源：这一数字改编自臭氧秘书处网站显示的数据。See ozone. unep. org/new_ site/en/index. php.

这些义务的强制性本质不应被低估,特别是随着一系列针对议定书的调整和修订,它们已经变得越来越严格。

为了履行这一套雄心勃勃的义务制度,《蒙特利尔议定书》得到了一些机制的配套支持,以便采用一种同样进取的方式来鼓励公众参与、促进遵约和管理不遵约。有四个机制值得我们关注,它们是:(1)贸易规制;(2)提供给发展中国家的利益;(3)灵活机制;(4)管理不遵约的程序。

公约第 4 条负责管理与第三方开展的受控物质、包含此类物质的产品以及它们的生产技术和手段的贸易。[102] 这一条款非常重要,它可以刺激各国加入议定书,[103] 通过减少需求(这一现象被称为"泄漏")来控制那些不受议定书制度规制的此类物质的生产或消费。[104] 基于这些原因,第 4 条第 1 款和第 2 款禁止从非本议定书缔约国的任何国家进口或出口受控物质。同样地,第 4 条第 3 款(由 1991 年的附录 D 进一步补充)禁止从非本议定书缔约国的任何国家进口含有受控物质的产品。最后,第 5 款和第 6 款禁止向非本议定书缔约国的任何国家出口受控物质(或相关产品)的生产技术和手段。这些限制首先被用于附录 A 中的物质(氟氯化碳和哈龙),后来被陆续拓展到其他物质。[105] 控制这些物质的蔓延以及鼓励第三方国家加入议定书的目标在很大程度上得以实现,但是,正如我们后文所述,有必要增加其他一些刺激手段来确保中国和印度等国的参与。

在议定书生效后不久,1990 年在伦敦召开的缔约方会议上,它就被修订,目的是更好地回应某些发展中国家的诉求。事实上,适用第 5 条第

102　Ibid., Art. 4, paras. (1), (2), (3), (5) and (6). 这一条款也针对那些不含此类物质但是由此类物质生产的产品贸易(第 4 条第 4 款),但是各缔约方在 1993 年达成共识,认为不可能限制此类物质的贸易。See Decision V/17, 19 November 1993, Doc. UNEP/OzL. Pro. 5/12.

103　依据《蒙特利尔议定书》第 4 条,与议定书缔约国开展的受管控物质的贸易不被禁止,除非这一物质已经被完全淘汰。同时,受管控物质的贸易应当满足适用于"新的、使用过的、循环的和再生的受管控物质的进出口"的许可要求。当《基加利修正案》开始生效后,这一许可制度同样适用于氢氟碳化物(under the new paragraph 2*bis* of Article 4B)。

104　See R. Twum-Barima and L. B. Campbell, *Protecting the Ozone Layers through Trade Measures: Reconciling the Trade Provisions of the Montreal Protocol and the Rules of the GATT* (Geneva: UNEP, 1994), pp. 51ff.

105　Montreal Protocol, supra footnote 78, Art. 4, paragraphs 1*bis*-1*sex*, 2*bis*-*sex* and 3*bis*-3*ter*.《基加利修正案》针对第 4 条增加了几个段落(禁止向议定书非缔约国进出口氢氟碳化物)。

1 款的国家所获取的额外灵活性对某些国家（例如印度和中国）的吸引力似乎还不够大。通过一个交织了压力和让步的精巧方案，这些修订最终成功说服各个发展中国家加入这一议定书。谈及压力，议定书第 5 条被修订，确定了一个具体日期（1999 年 1 月 1 日），超出这一日期，发展中国家将不再享有那些适用第 5 条第 1 款的国家被给予的 10 年宽限期。谈及让步，通过修订议定书第 10 条（财政援助）和制定第 10A 条（技术转让），援助义务得以实质性增强。修订后的第 10 条创立了一个多边基金，它的主要作用是支付那些适用第 5 条第 1 款的国家为了执行议定书的管控措施而产生的"议定的额外费用"。[106] 这一措施在当时是极具创新性的。虽然美国作为主要出资方试图避免这一措施成为一个先例，[107] 但是这类基金还是得以建立，并在后来的多边环境协定中变得相当普遍。在伦敦会议上，援助义务的增强是一个非常重要的议题，第 5 条第 5 款也得以修订，写入了共同但有区别的责任原则这一强制性概念。这一条款文本的表述非常有技巧，掩盖了工业化国家和发展中国家之间的深刻分歧：

> 增进其履行义务的能力……（以便发展中国家实现其义务）……将有赖于第 10 条所规定财务合作及第 10A 条所规定技术转让的有效履行。

"有赖于"这一术语说明，在发展中国家的减排义务和工业化国家的援助义务之间存在着一定的不确定性。仔细阅读可以发现议定书提出的并不是一个制约性关系（只有援助到位才能要求履行义务），而是一个正当性关系（援助的缺位可以证明规制措施运用不足的正当性）。换言之，发展中国家如果觉得没有能力运用规制措施，它可以在缔约方会议上寻求援助。[108]

106　这些"议定的额外费用"填补了两种情况的差额，一种是没有环境限制的产业发展（即经济成本较低），另一种是遵守了议定书中的义务（即经济成本较高）。在当时，在激进运行的头三年议定的额外费用预估是 1.6 亿美元（随着中国和印度的加入，另外又增加了 0.8 亿美元）。基于联合国框架下的分担额度，美国在此期间的出资额是 0.4 亿—0.6 亿美元（预算的 25%）。鉴于需要如此大的总额，美国支持建立多边基金。See Benedick, supra footnote 71, pp. 187-188.

107　See Ibid., pp. 183-190.

108　关于谈判中的妥协，参见 Benedick, supra footnote 71, pp. 188-190. 如果没有寻求援助（寻求援助基本上是一个善意表示），那么不履行议定书中的义务（包括向议定书机构提供数据的义务），涉事国就会丧失获得多边基金的机会。See Yoshida, supra footnote 71, p. 222.

除了给予发展中国家这些利益，议定书也为工业化国家提供了一定的"灵活性"以便帮助它们完成义务。首先，如果某一国家特定受控物质的产量低于议定书设定的限值，那么它就有权根据第 2 条第 5 款将它未用的产能转让给另一个缔约国，前提条件是这两个国家任一种类受控物质生产的计算数量（由第 3 条规定）没有超出这类物质在特定时间段的生产限值。这种可能性在涉及消费能力时应受到一定的限制，它得以成立的条件是：(1) 只针对发达国家；(2) 受控物质的消费必须满足特定条件；(3) 与氢氯氟碳化合物相关（第 2F 条）。其次，第 2 条第 8 款允许一批国家加入某个区域性经济一体化组织以便在集体层面而非个体层面来共同完成它们的义务。这一机制，有时候被称为欧洲"泡泡"，允许某一区域组织的部分国家继续消费受控物质，前提条件是其他拥有更低消费量的成员国抵消了这一消费超额。再次，议定书允许各式各样的"豁免"。[109] 缔约方会议在不同场合批准了豁免，例如因为"核心用途""关键用途"[110] "实验和分析用途"[111] "加工剂用途"[112] "在高湿度天气用溴化甲烷烟熏消毒农场"，[113] 以及《基加利修正案》（*Kigali Amendment*）中的"高温豁免"。[114]

最后，《蒙特利尔议定书》针对"不遵约"的管理也有所创新。我们

---

[109] On this complex regime see Ozone Secretariat, *Briefing Note on Exemption Mechanisms under the Montreal Protocol* (4-8 April 2016), available at http://conf.montreal-protocol.org/meeting/oewg/oewg-37/presession/Background_documents/Briefing_note_on_exemptions.pdf (visited on 17 April 2017).

[110] "核心用途"和"关键用途"都是由缔约方会议授予给特定缔约方的，它们针对的是某一物质在其整体淘汰期后特定时间段内的特定数量。See Decision IV/25 "Essential uses", 23-25 November 1992, Doc. UNEP/OzL. Pro. 4/Prep/2 (subsequently revised several times) and for the specific regime for HCFCs see Decision XIX/6; Decision IX/6 "Critical use exemptions for methyl bromide", 15-17 September 1997, Doc. UNEP/OzL. Pro. 9/12.

[111] Decision VI/9 "Essential use nominations for controlled substances other than halons for 1996 and beyond", 6-7 October 1994, Doc. UNEP/OzL. Pro. 6/Prep/2. This exemption has been subsequently extended several times, most recently until 2021 by Decision XXVI/5 "Global laboratory and analytical-use exemption", 10 December 2014, Doc. UNEP/OzL. Pro. 26/10.

[112] Decision X/14 "Process agents", 3 December 1998, Doc. UNEP/OzL. Pro. 10/9, subsequently revised several times.

[113] Decision XV/12 "Use of methyl bromide for the treatment of high-moisture dates", 11 November 2015, Doc. UNEP/OzL. Pro. 15/9. However, since 2013-2014 alternatives to this use of methyl bromide have been deemed available by the Protocol's Technology and Economic Assessment Panel (TEAP).

[114] See infra section 5.4.4.

将在第九章用一个更综合的概念来定义"不遵约"（与"违约"相比较）这一术语。在这里，我们只需指出它是遵约（遵守被认为是一个包含不同步骤和层次的过程）的一种更灵活的方法，同时还要考虑到"不遵约"的原因（特别是当各国愿意履行他们的义务但是缺乏财政和技术手段去完成）。缔约方会议建立了一个"不遵约"程序并授权一个执行委员会来负责，该委员会包含了缔约方的十名代表。[115] 这一程序可以由某个缔约方（包括"不遵约"国家）[116] 或秘书处触发，[117] 它的目的主要不是处罚"不遵约"[118] 而是管理这一问题，包括通过技术和财政援助来提高各国的履约能力。[119] 自它启动以来，执行委员会已经处理了大量案件。[120] 例如，在 1995 年它碰到了一个涉及俄罗斯的敏感案件，俄罗斯生产并出口了受控物质，并宣称它没有能力来完成它的义务。委员会建议了各种措施，包括对受控物质出口的限制，但是缔约方会议用一种模糊的表述淡化处理了这一建议。[121] 部分原因是受到了俄罗斯的抵制，尤其是因为受控物质的出口在当时是俄罗斯经济一个重要的外汇来源。[122] 这一问题最终通过监测、信息披露和财政援助（以及压力）的组合运用而得以解决，其中的财政援助由全球环境基金负责，它干预此事并为俄罗斯提供财政援助的原因在于俄罗斯不够资格接受议定书多边基金的资助。最后，2002 年 11 月，缔约方会议宣布，它"赞赏"俄罗斯为遵守《蒙特利尔议定书》规制措施所付出的努力。[123]

---

[115] See Decision II/5, 29 June 1990, Doc. UNEP/OzL. Pro. 2/3; Decision IV/5 and Annexes IV and V, 25 November 1992, Doc. UNEP/OzL. Pro. 4/15 ("Annex IV" and "Annex V"); Decision X/10 and Annex II, 3 December 1998, Doc. UNEP/OzL. Pro. 10/9 ("Annex II").

[116] Annex II, supra footnote 115, paras. 1 and 4.

[117] Ibid., para. 3.

[118] Annex V, supra n. footnote 115, paras. B (warning) and C (suspension of rights and privileges under the Protocol).

[119] Annex V, supra n. footnote 115, para. A (technical assistance, technology transfer, financial assistance, training, etc.).

[120] See D. G. Victor, *The Early Operation and Effectiveness of the Montreal Protocol's Non-Compliance Procedure* (Laxenburg: IIASA, 1996).

[121] Decision VII/18, 27 December 1995, Doc. UNEP/Ozl. Pro. 7/12, para. 8.

[122] Victor, supra footnote 120, pp. 28–31.

[123] Decision XIV/35, 5 December 2002, Doc. UNEP/OzL. Pro. 14/9, para. 3.

以上讨论显示了《蒙特利尔议定书》的复杂性及其重要创新之处。图 5-2 概括了这一复杂的结构。

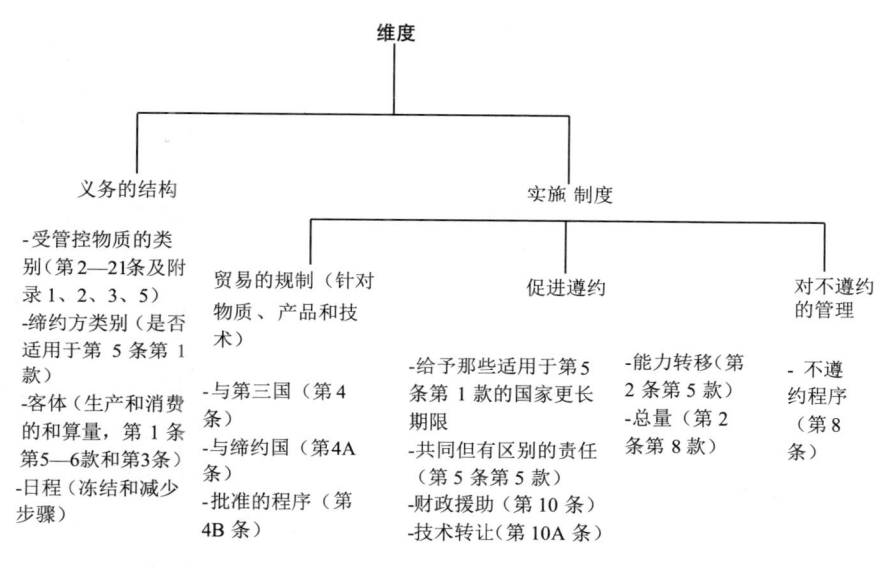

图 5-2 《蒙特利尔议定书》的维度

```
                          维度
                           │
            ┌──────────────┴──────────────┐
         义务的结构                    实施制度
            │                            │
  -受管控物质的类        ┌────────────┬─────────────┬──────────┐
   别（第2—21条及附     贸易的规制      促进遵约        对不遵
   录1、2、3、5）       （针对物质、                   约的管理
  -缔约方类别（是否      产品和技术）                    
   适用于第 5 条第 1                  -给予那些适用于第5  -不遵约
   款）                -与第三国（第4    条第1款的国家更长   程序
  -客体（生产和消费      条）            期限              （第8
   的和算量，第 1 条    -与缔约国（第4A  -共同但有区别的责任   条）
   第5—6款和第3条）     条）            （第5条第5款）
  -日程（冻结和减少     -批准的程序（第   -能力转移（第
   步骤）               4B 条）          2条第5款）
                                        -总量（第2
                                         条第8款）
                                        -财政援助（第10A 条）
                                        -技术转让（第10A 条）
```

《蒙特利尔议定书》对臭氧消耗以外的问题也造成了深远影响。因为有些受控物质（氟氯化碳、哈龙、氢氯氟碳化合物）同时也是温室气体，《蒙特利尔议定书》成为应对气候变化的一个关键手段（以有效性而论）。2016 年 10 月，当缔约方会议制定了《基加利修正案》并将氢氟碳化物这一氢氯氟碳化合物的替代品纳入议定书的管理范围之后，这一作用得到了确认。[124] 还需要特别指出一个事实，即氢氟碳化物并不是臭氧消耗物质而是一种强有力的温室气体。将它划归《蒙特利尔议定书》管理进一步证明了议定书作为一个有效政策回应的可靠性。它同时表明了气候变化问题的宽广范围，正如我们在第四章（涉及废物倾倒）和本章前文所讨论的，气候变化问题需要各种法律文件的一种协同

---

124 Decision XXVIII/1, Further amendment of the Montreal Protocol', 14 October 2016, Doc. UNEP/OzL. Pro. 28/CRP/10; Decision XXVIII/2, "Decision related to the amendment phasing down hydrofluorocarbons", 14 October 2016, Doc. UNEP/OzL. Pro. 28/CRP/10 (together the "Kigali Amendment").

回应。

四 2016年《基加利修正案》

正如前文所述,《蒙特利尔议定书》的《基加利修正案》是在2016年10月召开的第28次缔约方会议上通过的,它的独树一帜源自两个原因。第一,直到这一修正案之前,《蒙特利尔议定书》关注的仅仅是那些消耗臭氧层的物质,而氢氟碳化物则不在其中。事实上,氢氟碳化物是作为一种臭氧层友好型替代品而开发的,目的是替代其他拥有较大臭氧消耗潜力的物质(例如氢氯氟碳化合物)。但是氢氟碳化物是强有力的温室气体[125],它们逐步增加的实际利用和计划利用与氢氯氟碳化合物的淘汰之间的关系充分表明了将氢氟碳化物置于《蒙特利尔议定书》管辖下的必要性。因此,《基加利修正案》可以被看成《蒙特利尔议定书》的议定书,直接应对气候变化问题。第二,《基加利修正案》对气候变化国际法具有重要的象征意义和实际价值。所谓象征意义,指的是它说明各国更愿意根据《蒙特利尔议定书》而非《京都议定书》(在其附录A中特别涵盖了氢氟碳化物)来管理这一问题,[126] 同时也表明有必要依赖各种不同的条约来应对气候变化。所谓实际价值,指的是《基加利修正案》设计的"逐步减少"方案有助于帮助降低地球平均温度的上升(整体上降低0.5摄氏度),我们在后文将会谈到,它造就了一个巨大的区别。

最终达成《基加利修正案》的进程开始于2009年,由加拿大、墨西哥和美国倡议,也有赖于其他几个岛国的共同努力。2009—2015年,进行了修订《蒙特利尔议定书》的数次尝试。2015年,缔约方会议决定建立一个联络组来解决各国间遗留的分歧,这一过程通常被称为"氢氟碳化物迪拜路线图"(Dubai pathway on HFCs)。[127] 总体上看,有四个

---

[125] See G. J. M. Velders et al., "The large contribution of projected HFC emissions to future climate forcing" (2009) 106/27 *Proceedings of the National Academy of Sciences* 10949.

[126] Decision XXVIII/1, supra footnote 124, specifically states, in Article III, 该议定书并不是《联合国气候变化框架公约》和《京都议定书》所规定义务的例外,换言之,各国不应认为它们仅需要实施《基加利修正案》就算是完成了它们依据《联合国气候变化框架公约》和《京都议定书》所应承担的涉及氢氟碳化物的义务。

[127] Decision XXVII/1 "Dubai pathway on HFCs", 30 November 2015, UNEP/OzL. Pro. 27/13.

修改意见被纳入考虑范畴。除了"北美建议"（North American Proposal）之外，其他三个建议被欧盟、印度和一群岛国搁置。[128] 议定书的最终版本反映了各种不同的核心利益，不仅涉及环境保护，还有产业竞争力的考量，以及消费产业和国家的具体情况，特别是在那些环境温度很高的国家，制冷物质（例如氢氟碳化物）的使用是一个优先问题。

《基加利修正案》主要包含三个部分：（1）发达国家和发展中国家逐步减少氢氟碳化物的日程安排（与逐步淘汰不同），针对两类国家规定了不同时间段；（2）旨在刺激批准议定书和促进履约的某些措施（特别是财政上的灵活性、贸易措施和一些豁免）；（3）有关批准和条款适用的一些细则。第一个部分从根本上将逐步淘汰氢氟碳化物的启动时间定于2019年（针对绝大多数发达国家，给予前期经济转型国家一些额外时间），将结束时间定于21世纪40年代晚期（针对部分适用公约第5条第1款的国家）。氢氟碳化物的生产和消费的整体减排量相当于基准量的80%—85%，各类国家的基准量也是不同的。[129] 表5-2概括了这一部分的具体内容。

表5-2　　　　　　　　　《基加利修正案》[130]

	淘汰时间表（从左到右，轨迹越来越宽松）			
	不适用于第5条第1款的国家（发达国家）		适用于第5条第1款的国家（发展中国家）	
	发达国家	某些转型经济体※	第一组团	第二组团※※
基准	2011—2013年氢氟烃类平均消费水平+15%的氢氟氯化碳类基准	2011—2013年氢氟烃类平均消费水平+25%的氢氟氯化碳类基准	2020—2022年氢氟烃类平均消费水平+65%的氢氟氯化碳类基准	2024—2026年氢氟烃类平均消费水平+65%的氢氟氯化碳类基准
冻结			2024年	2028年

---

[128] See *Consolidation of the Amendment Proposals Submitted by Parties to the Montreal Protocol. Note by the Secretariat*, 7 June 2016, UNEP/OzL. Pro. ExMOP/3/INF/1.

[129] 法律上，这一部分的修订主要包括增加了一个新的条款（2J），一个新的段落（8*qua* in Article 5），一个新的附录六（针对氢氟碳化物）和一个修订后的附录三（增加了含氢氟氯化碳导致全球变暖的可能）。See Decision XXVIII/1, supra footnote 124, Art. I.

[130] Adapted from UNEP, Frequently Asked Questions relating to the Kigali Amendment to the Montreal Protocol, 3 November 2016, available at http：//ozone. unep. org（visited on 17 April 2017）.

续表

	淘汰时间表（从左到右，轨迹越来越宽松）			
	不适用于第5条第1款的国家（发达国家）		适用于第5条第1款的国家（发展中国家）	
	发达国家	某些转型经济体※	第一组团	第二组团※※
第一步	2019年（-10%）	2020年（-5%）	2029年（-10%）	2032年（-10%）
第二步	2024年（-40%）	2025年（-35%）	2035年（-30%）	2037年（-20%）
第三步	2029年（-70%）	2029年（-70%）	2040年（-50%）	2042年（-30%）
第四步	2034年（-80%）	2034年（-80%）		
稳定时期（最后等级）	2035年（-85%）	2035年（-85%）	2045年（-80%）	2047年（-85%）

注：※转型经济体包括：白俄罗斯、俄罗斯、哈萨克斯坦、塔吉克斯坦、乌兹别克斯坦。
※※第二组团包括：巴林、印度、伊朗、伊拉克、科威特、巴基斯坦、卡塔尔。

第二个部分包含了大量实施措施，包括针对那些适用公约第5条第1款的国家的灵活机制以及财政和技术援助，[131] 针对特殊情况国家的特定豁免，以及贸易措施。需要注意的是"高温豁免"，缔约方会议的决议规定它适用于一些特定范围（空调设备），针对的是那些连续十年每年平均至少两个月的最高月平均气温高于35℃的国家。[132] 这是因为，正如我们前文所述，氢氟碳化物被大量用于空调设备中，而这些国家则需要大量的空调。这一豁免是临时性的（最初定为四年，有可能延长），那些想要运用此条豁免的国家必须提交一个正式的通告。同时，它还受到其他参数的约束，包括一项技术评估（评估物质）和一个遵约程序的中止。修正案规定的贸易措施也值得关注。贸易措施包括对议定书第4条（禁止与非缔约国开展特定受控物质的贸易）的修订。[133] 虽然这一修订后的条款指的是

---

[131] Decision XXVIII/2, supra footnote 124, paras. 9-21.

[132] Ibid., paras. 26-37 and Appendix II（列举了下列这些可以从豁免中获利的国家：阿尔及利亚、巴林、贝宁、布基纳法索、中非共和国、乍得、科特迪瓦、吉布提、埃及、厄立特里亚国、冈比亚、加纳、几内亚、几内亚比绍、伊朗、伊拉克、约旦、科威特、利比亚、马里、毛里塔尼亚、尼日尔、尼日利亚、阿曼、巴基斯坦、卡塔尔、沙特阿拉伯、塞内加尔、苏丹、叙利亚、多哥、突尼斯、土库曼斯坦、阿联酋）。

[133] See Decision XXVIII/1, supra footnote 124, Art. I.

针对"本议定书的任何非缔约方"的进出口,但是,该条款应当被理解为针对的是《基加利修正案》的任何非缔约方。[134] 否则,鉴于《蒙特利尔议定书》的缔约国遍布全球,这一措施的目的就无法达到。

修订案的第三个部分具有过渡性质。它规定议定书直到2019年才可能生效,而且必须满足一个前提条件,即届时它已经获得至少20个缔约方的批准。唯一的例外是修订后的议定书第4条(禁止与非缔约方开展贸易活动),它将于2033年开始生效,前提是至少27个缔约方已经批准这一修订案。[135] 这一区分的理由在于,除了产业调整的原因之外,只有足够数量的国家加入了议定书,贸易措施才能成为一种有效的刺激手段来鼓励更多国家加入。修订案包含了一项来自北美建议的有条件适用条款,它规定,"任何缔约方可以在修正案对其生效之前的任何时间宣布它将有条件地适用第2条J款规定的任何管理措施以及第7条规定的报告义务,直到它们生效为止"。[136] 条约的有条件适用通常是由《维也纳条约法公约》第25条来管理的,[137] 国际法委员会正在对它的大量实质性影响开展研究。[138]

虽然《基加利修正案》很重要,但是它所应对的只是一个非常具体的温室气体,而且这一气体仅仅是用于少量特定活动(最大部分是制冷和空调)。后文将会谈及,温室气体的主要来源(特别是二氧化碳)的应对要困难得多,因为这些来源正是那些决定我们人类文明的活动,即电力和热能生产、交通和农业(以及土地利用)。

第五节 气候变化

一 问题概述

气候变化问题与化石燃料的使用密切相关,而化石燃料从18世纪晚

---

134 Ozone Secretariat, *Ratification of the Kigali Amendment. Briefing Note* (February 2017), p. 4.
135 Decision XXVIII/1, supra footnote 124, Annex, Art. IV (2).
136 Ibid., Art. V.
137 Vienna Convention on the Law of Treaties, 23 May 1969, 1155 UNTS 331.
138 See, in particular, *Substantive analysis of the legal effects of the provisional application of treaties. Second report of theSpecial Rapporteur, Mr. Juan Manuel Gómez-Robledo*, 9 June 2014, A/CN. 4/675, paras. 53ff (某个已宣称它将有条件适用某一条约的国家的义务渊源就是它所采取的这一单边行动)。

期的工业革命时起就成为我们人类文明的基础。为了理解这一现象，就有必要说明某些气体在全球气候系统中的作用。

大气的第一层，通常被称为对流层（距离地球表面12千米范围内），包含了某些气体的浓聚物，它们允许太阳紫外线的进入，而且当这一射线被地球表面以红外线的形式反射到太空时，这些气体保存了部分红外线。这种对能量的留存所发挥的作用是维持地球的平均温度（当前是约15摄氏度），这一温度在不同地质时代一直在发生变化（在上一个冰川期，即116000—17000年前，达到了顶点或最后一个冰河时期的峰值，全球平均气温要比今天低3—5摄氏度）。这些温室气体（包括二氧化碳、甲烷、氧化氮、氟氯化碳、含氢氟氯化碳、氢氟碳化物、炭黑、对流层臭氧和其他大量物质）的浓度升高，就会导致一个更高的能量留存，也就会造成地球气温的升高。[139] 这就是通常所说的"全球变暖"。但是，"气候变化"这一术语并不仅限于全球变暖问题。它还涉及气候更大的可变性，或者更具体地说，极端天气事件（例如热浪、暴雨、暴风、干旱和其他问题）的更频繁发生。

基于这一背景，我们就能更好地理解自工业革命以来化石燃料的广泛使用所造成的影响。源自人类活动（人为排放）的温室气体的排放增加了这些气体在对流层中的数量，因此也提升了地球的平均温度。这就非常可能会导致一系列后果，虽然当前想要精确预测这些后果还是有一定难度，但是，冰川融化、海平面上升、极端干旱和荒漠化、物种和疾病在地理上的重新分布等都是能够基本确定的。人类现在已经充分认识到解决这一问题的必要性。17个可持续发展目标中的一个目标（第13个）致力于"采取紧急措施应对气候变化及其影响"，其认知基础是，应对气候变化的主要国际框架是《联合国气候变化框架公约》。但是，因为清晰和可信赖的科学信息是政策应对的基础，所以该公约并不是气候变化体制的唯一支柱。

---

[139] 大气中温室气体浓度是通过百万体积的空气中所含污染物的体积数（通常是二氧化碳的体积数）来计算的。为了在21世纪末期把全球平均气温较工业化前水平（14摄氏度）升高控制在2摄氏度之内，就必须把二氧化碳的体积浓度控制在450以下。当前，预测表明体积浓度大约是400，考虑到许多国家日益增加的排放，要在21世纪末期将浓度控制在450似乎很难实现。

二 体制的两大支柱

现有体制的特点可以用两个关键"支柱"来归纳，即科学支柱和政策支柱。我们应当看到，这两个支柱是紧密相关的。

"科学支柱"指的是政府间气候变化专门委员会［Intergovernmental Panel on Climate Change (IPCC)］。[140] 这一组织的起源可以追溯到20世纪70年代晚期的研究项目，特别是世界气象组织下的项目。在20世纪80年代，一系列报告和科学会议关注了人类对气候系统造成影响的可能性。特别是1985年在奥地利菲拉赫召开的一次会议上，一名来自瑞典的权威专家Bert Bolin起草了一份报告，强调指出20世纪上半叶温室气体的人为排放可能已经造成了气温的升高。[141] 不久之后，联合国环境规划署、世界气象组织和国际科学理事会 (International Council for Science, ICSU)[142] 联合提出了一个倡议，促使成立政府间气候变化专门委员会以便应对20世纪80年代盛行的科学认识上的混乱，其中还包括所谓的"垃圾科学"（它是由那些担忧这一领域的潜在规制可能威胁到自身的利益团体资助的）。[143] 政府间气候变化专门委员会的使命是审查这一主题所有重要的科学问题并得出结论；换言之，在面对争议各方提出的证据和主张时，采用一种法庭判决的方式来评估各种对抗性的主张。这种审查评估采用了各式各样的"评估报告"这一方式，每个报告都有成千页的内容。这些内容分为三卷，分别是自然科学基础（卷1），影响、适应和脆弱性（卷2）以及减缓措施（卷3）。对此的一个重要补充是一份综合报告，它包含了一份"决策者摘要"，它的每一条都必须经过各缔约方派驻该委员会代表

140　On the IPCC and its legal framework, see R. Encinas de Munagorri (ed.), *Expertise et gouvernance du changement climatique* (Paris: LGDJ, 2009), Chapters 1 and 2.

141　See J. E. Viñuales, "Legal Techniques for Dealing with Scientific Uncertainty in Environmental Law" (2010) 43 *Vanderbilt Journal of Transnational Law* 437, at 486.

142　Previously known as International Council of Scientific Unions.

143　See N. Oreskes and J. Conway, *Merchants of Doubt. How a Handful of Scientists Obscured the Truth on Issues from Tobacco Smoke to Climate Change* (Bloomsbury Press, 2010)（针对美国化石燃料产业开展的故意信息误报运动进行了一个详细分析，这些运动的目的并不是挑战气候变化而只是想制造疑问以便延缓政策回应）。For the situation in France see S. Foucart, *L'avenir du climat: enquête sur les climato-sceptiques* (Paris: Folio, 2015).

的一致同意。[144] 在其成立后的近三十年内，政府间气候变化专门委员会已经提交了五份评估报告（1990 年、1995/1996 年、2001 年、2007 年和 2013/2014 年）。

虽然最近几年政府间气候变化专门委员会受到了严厉的批评，但是它还是非常认真地完成了这项复杂的工作。有必要指出的是，从评估报告发表至今，对气候变化的理解还是进展缓慢。在 1990 年的第一份报告中，委员会得出的结论是：

> 在过去十年或更长时期内，通过观察似乎尚未明确发现温室气体影响的增强。[145]

在其 1995/1996 年发布的第二份报告中，委员会还是很谨慎地指出，各种证据"表明人类对全球气候造成了一个可识别的影响"。[146] 甚至在其 2001 年发布的第三份报告中，委员会还是很谨慎地声明"有新的和更有力的证据表明，过去五十年被观测到的气候变暖是由人类活动造成的"。[147] 直到 2007 年第四份评估报告的发布，政府间气候变化专门委员会才明确证实"气候系统的变暖是毋庸置疑的"，而且"温室气体的人为聚集很有可能是 20 世纪中叶以来绝大多数观测到的全球平均气温上升的成因"。[148] 第五份评估报告用更肯定的术语再次确认了这一结论。综合报告中的决策者摘要指出：

> 气候系统变暖是毋庸置疑的。自 20 世纪 50 年代以来，许多观察到的变化在以前的几十年至几千年是前所未有的。……自从工业化前时代起，温室气体的人为排放就出现了上升，这主要是由于经济和人

144　See the Principles Governing IPCC Work, Appendix A: Procedures for the Preparation, Review, Acceptance, Adoption, Approval and Publication of IPCC Reports (including the modifications of June 2012), Section 4.6.1.

145　IPCC, *Climate Change* 1990, General Overview, Section 1.0.5., p.53.

146　IPCC, *Climate Change* 1995, Second Assessment Synthesis, para.2.4, p.5.

147　IPCC, *Climate Change* 2001, Synthesis Report, Summary for Policymakers, p.5.

148　IPCC, *Climate Change* 2007, Synthesis Report, Summary for Policymakers, p.2 (SPM 1.1.) and 5 (the term "very likely" indicates, in IPCC terminology, a probability of no less than 90 per cent).

口增长造成的,现在已达到最高水平。这造成大气二氧化碳、甲烷和一氧化二氮的浓度增加到了前所未有的水平(至少是过去 80 万年以来)。在整个气候系统中都已经探测到了这类影响以及其他人为驱动因素的影响,而且这些影响极有可能是 20 世纪中叶以来所观察到的变暖的主要成因。[149]

需要指出的是,每一份评估报告都与气候变化体制下政策支柱的每次重大进展相关联。在分析那些调整气候变化问题的国际法律文件的内容之前,有必要将它们的进展与科学支柱的进展关联起来进行概括。政府间气候变化专门委员会的成立以及它在 1990 年发布的第一份评估报告促成了《联合国气候变化框架公约》的通过和开放签署(1992 年 6 月)。[150],实际上,正是受到了政府间气候变化专门委员会的工作(特别是第三工作组有关减缓的工作)的推动,联合国大会才通过决议要求建立一个"政府间谈判委员会"(Intergovernmental Negotiating Committee)。[151] 后来,1995年,在其第一份评估报告发布前不久,政府间气候变化专门委员会与《联合国气候变化框架公约》缔约方大会分享了它的调查结果。这一信息影响了缔约方大会的第一个决议,即所谓的《柏林授权》,[152] 它为两年后《京都议定书》的制定奠定了基础。[153] 《柏林授权》还加大了发达国家(所谓的《联合国气候变化框架公约》附件一国家)与发展中国家之间的差别,这一点通过《京都议定书》建立的分隔墙得以体现。这一划分比前文谈及的《蒙特利尔议定书》的划分(它也针对适用第 5 款第 1 条的

---

[149] IPCC, *Climate Change* 2014, Synthesis Report, Summary for Policymakers, pp. 2 (SPM 1.1) and 4 (SPM 1.2) (the term "extremely likely" indicates, in IPCC terminology, a probability of no less than 95 per cent).

[150] United Nations Framework Convention on Climate Change, 9 May 1992, 1771 UNTS 107 ("UNFCCC").

[151] Protection of the Global Climate for Present and Future Generations of Mankind, Resolution 45/212, 21 December 1990, UN Doc. A/RES/45/212.

[152] The Berlin Mandate: Review of Paragraphs a) and b) of Paragraph 2 of Article 4 of the Convention to Determine if They are Adequate, Plans for a Protocol and Follow-up Decisions, Decision 1/CP.1, 2 June 1995, Doc. FCCC/CP/1995/7/Add.1.

[153] Kyoto Protocol to the United Nations Convention on Climate Change, 11 December 1997, 2302 UNTS 148 ("Kyoto Protocol").

国家规定了义务）更为明显，从 2007 年开始它就成为谈判的核心问题。于 2001 年发布的第三份评估报告极大地影响了所谓的《马拉喀什协议》（*Marrakesh Accords*），[154] 它是缔约方大会通过的一系列决议，用于细化《京都议定书》建立的制度，即使这一法律文书尚未开始生效。[155] 于 2007 年发布的第四份评估报告推动了《巴厘授权》（*Bali Mandate*），[156] 而《巴厘授权》的目的则是推动在 2009 年的哥本哈根气候大会上制定一项新的议定书。虽然哥本哈根气候大会以失败告终，但是《巴厘授权》的目标——减少或消除发达国家（《联合国气候变化框架公约》附件一国家）和发展中国家（特别是新兴经济体）两者间义务的差别依然还是谈判的优先内容。引起争议的《哥本哈根协议》[157] 以及后来的《坎昆协议》（*Cancun Agreements*）[158] 都曾试图减少这两类国家所承担义务的差别，而它们对共同但有区别的责任原则的作用都持一个模棱两可的态度。[159] 为此，2011 年 12 月在南非德班召开的缔约方大会上，一个新的工作组（不同于那个于 2007 年在巴厘岛建立的工作组）被授权"在公约框架下制定一份适用于所有缔约方的议定书、法律文书或具有法律效力的议定成果"。[160] 这一项协商授权最终促成在 2015 年 12 月召开的缔约方大会上制定了《巴黎协定》。这一协商的时间范围经过了特别设定，目的是能顺利发布第五次评估报告（2013/2014 年）。图 5-3 概括说明了科学进展与外交进展之间的关系。

154　Decisions 2/CP.7 to 14/CP.7, 21 January 2002, Doc. FCCC/CP/2001/13/Add.1.

155　在 2005 年第一次议定书缔约方会议上，这些决议被并入为议定书机构的决议。

156　Bali Plan of Action, Decision 1/CP.13, 14 March 2008, Doc. FCCC/CP/2007/6/Add.1.

157　Copenhagen Accord, Decision 2/CP.15, 30 March 2010, Doc. FCCC/CP/2009/11/Add.1.

158　《坎昆协议》包含三个协议，一个是由缔约方大会制定的，另外两个是由《京都议定书》缔约方会议制定的。See "The Cancun Agreements: Outcome of the work of the Ad Hoc Working Group on Long-term Cooperative Action under the Convention", Decision 1/CP.16, 15 March 2011, Doc. FCCC/CP/2010/7/Add.1; The Cancun Agreements: Outcome of the work of the Ad Hoc Working Group on Further Commitments for Annex I Parties under the Kyoto Protocol at its fifteenth session, Decision 1/ CMP.6, 15 March 2011, Doc. FCCC/KP/CMP/2010/12/Add.1; The Cancun Agreements: Land use, land-use change and forestry, Decision 2/CMP.6, 15 March 2011, Doc. FCCC/KP/CMP/2010/ 12/Add.1.

159　See L. Rajamani, "The Durban Platform for Enhanced Action and the Future of the Climate Regime" (2012) 61 *International and Comparative Law Quarterly* 501, 505-506.

160　Establishment of an Ad Hoc Working Group on the Durban Platform for Enhanced Action, Decision 1/CP.17, 15 March 2012, Doc. FCCC/CP/2011/9/Add.1, 2.

科学支柱　政治支柱

1988/1990年——政府间气候变化专门委员会的建立和评估报告1　⟷　1990/1992年——开始筹备《联合国气候变化框架公约》

1995年——评估报告2　⟷　1995/1997年——导致《京都议定书》的《柏林授权》

2001年——评估报告3　⟷　2001年——《马拉喀什协议》ccords

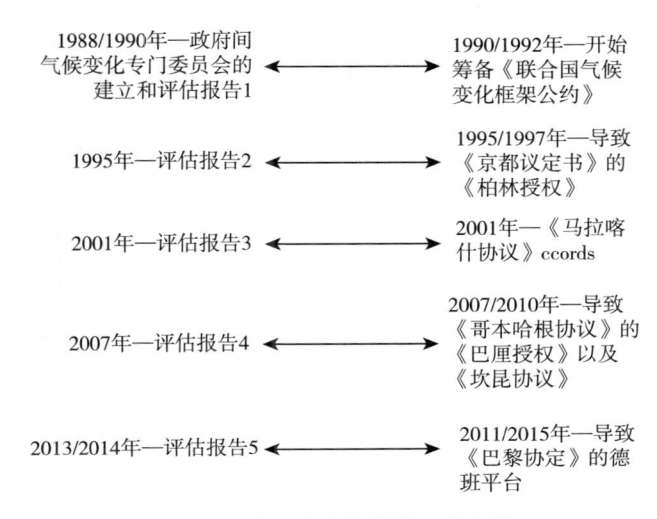

2007年——评估报告4　⟷　2007/2010年——导致《哥本哈根协议》的《巴厘授权》以及《坎昆协议》

2013/2014年——评估报告5　⟷　2011/2015年——导致《巴黎协定》的德班平台

图5-3　气候变化体制的两大支柱

其他场合也开展了气候谈判。但是，我们的研究将聚焦于《联合国气候变化框架公约》所建立的制度，同时也会留意其他文件，例如关于废物倾倒的《伦敦议定书》《哥德堡议定书》（特别是炭黑修订）或者《蒙特利尔议定书》（以及《基加利修正案》），它们都属于为了应对气候变化而采取的措施。

三　《联合国气候变化框架公约》

1990年联合国大会启动了谈判进程,[161] 目的是促进《联合国气候变化框架公约》的通过,[162] 这一进程面临着两大难题，即如何设定公约的范围

161　See, supra footnote 151.

162　有关国际气候变化的论著数不胜数。See among many others D. Bodansky, "The United Nations Framework Convention on Climate Change: A Commentary" (1993) 18 *Yale Journal of International Law* 451; F. Yamin and J. Depledge, *The International Climate Change Regime* (Cambridge University Press, 2004); J. Gupta, *The History of Global Climate Governance* (Cambridge University Press, 2014); C. Carlarne, K. Gray, R. Tarasofsky (eds.), *The Oxford Handbook of International Climate Change Law* (Oxford University Press, 2016); G. Van Calster, W. Vandenberghe, L. Reins (eds.), *Research Handbook on Climate Change Mitigation Law* (Cheltenham: Edward Elgar, 2015); D. Farber, M. Peeters (eds.), *Climate Change Law* (Cheltenham: Edward Elgar, 2016); D. Bodansky, J. Brunnee, L. Rajamani, *International Climate Change Law* (Oxford University Press, forthcoming 2017).

以及如何应对发达国家和发展中国家之间的差别。[163] 关于第一个难题，某些国家（例如美国或者一些石油输出国）主张制定一个框架公约，类似于1995年《维也纳公约》，针对排放不规定具体义务。其他一些国家（例如小岛国或者一些欧洲国家）认为关于气候变化的谈判进程已经相当深入，其成果不应仅仅是一项简单的框架公约。关于第二个难题，当前的情况与以前一样迫切。不论是过去还是现在，关键的问题一直都是如何计算不同国家在气候变化这一问题上的责任。这就意味着必须建立一个法律架构来分配各国的责任以应对气候变化。谈判者们在这两个问题上都达成了妥协。为了理解这一妥协及其对气候变化制度演进的重要影响，有必要将《联合国气候变化框架公约》的实体安排和体制安排进行区分。

关于实体安排，《联合国气候变化框架公约》设定了一个目标、一些原则、程序以及实质性义务。第2条用广义的术语对目标做了设定：

> 本公约以及任何相关法律文书的最终目标是……将大气中温室气体的浓度稳定在防止气候系统受到危险的人为干扰的水平上。

这一目标的优点是明确了那些必须受到限制的排放源——人为排放，同时对涉及这一问题的科学认识的未来进展持开放态度。事实上，直到2007年政府间气候变化专门委员会发布了第四次评估报告以后，缔约方大会才针对这一目标指定了一个具体数值，即与前工业时代（14摄氏度）相比在21世纪末期气温升高不超过2摄氏度[164]。《巴黎协定》第2条第1款的表述与这一目标存在着细微差别，[165] 它将目标表述为"把全球平均气温升幅控制在工业化前水平以上低于2摄氏度之内"。

《联合国气候变化框架公约》在第3条陈述了这一制度的一些基本原则，包括风险预防原则（第3条第3款）、代际公平原则（第3条第1款）

---

[163] See Bodansky, supra footnote 162 and D. Bodansky, "The History of the Global Climate Change Regime", in U. Luterbacher and D. F. Sprinz (eds.), *International Relations and Global Climate Change* (Cambridge MA: MIT Press, 2001), pp. 23-40.

[164] See Copenhagen Accord, supra footnote 157, para. 1; and the Cancun Agreements (Decision 1/CP. 16), supra footnote 158, Chapter V, paras. 138-140（规定了更新目标这一要求）。如前文所述，这一目标相当于把体积浓度控制在450。

[165] See infra footnote 184.

以及共同但有区别的责任原则（第3条第1款）。共同但有区别的责任原则对气候变化制度的整体架构意义重大，《联合国气候变化框架公约》文本对这一原则的承认实际上是沿袭了《蒙特利尔议定书》所采用的办法。

事实上，《联合国气候变化框架公约》第4条是按照三个层次来分配缔约方所承担的不同义务：（1）所有缔约方的义务（减排：第4条第1款；信息收集和交流的义务：第12条第1款）；（2）针对发达国家和市场经济转型中国家的义务（附件一国家）（减排：第4条第2款和第4条第6款针对转型国家的灵活机制；补充信息的交流：第12条第2款）；（3）仅由发达国家（附件二国家）承担的财政和技术援助义务（第4条第3—5款和第12条第3款）。根据《蒙特利尔议定书》第5条第5款，发达国家的援助义务与发展中国家的减排义务之间的关系被表述成一种正当性关系，其依据是共同但有区别的责任原则（第4条第7款）。

这一项差异化制度本来可以通过各种方式来实施，包括采取与《蒙特利尔议定书》相似的方式，即对发达国家和发展中国家都规定量化义务。但是，我们在后文讨论《京都议定书》时将会发现，从1995年第一次缔约方大会开始，所采取的方法就是不断扩大附件一国家（发达国家）和非附件一国家（发展中国家）之间义务的差别。

关于体制安排，与《维也纳公约》相似，《联合国气候变化框架公约》主要是一项框架文件，允许对其广义义务进行进一步的发展。《联合国气候变化框架公约》精心设计成立了缔约方大会（第7条），一个秘书处（第8条），以及两个辅助机构（第9条下的科研机构和第10条下的履行机构，多年来这一履行机构对条约机制的发展起到了非常重要的作用）。

另外，第11条为公约规定了一个财政机制。这一条款为2010年12月建立的"绿色气候基金"（Green Climate Fund）[166] 提供了重要基础，这一基金汇集了大量资源（数以十亿美元计[167]），它不仅负责支付"议定的额外成本"（也适用于大量其他环境基金，包括多边基金）还负责支付发

166　Cancun Agreements（Decision 1/CP. 16），supra footnote 158，Chapter IV, Section A.

167　哥本哈根和坎昆谈判的数字是2010—2012年为300亿美元，2020年前达到每年1000亿美元。每年1000亿美元现在被认为是谈判的地板价。但是，实际情况是，无论是否达到这一地板价，这一数额的很大部分将会来自私营部门，而且只能通过担保或其他等同金融工具由基金提供。

展中国家开展适应或减缓项目所花费的"议定的全部成本"。[168] 同样地，2010 年，缔约方大会决定建立一个"技术机制"来鼓励减缓和适应技术的发展并确保将这些技术推广到发展中国家。[169]

《联合国气候变化框架公约》的制度完善对公约而言是属于一种广义上的"回归"，特别是在《京都议定书》中建立了市场机制。2010 年缔约方大会特别建议了这一"回归"，而 2011 年缔约方大会则予以确认。[170] 这一回归有两个重要的表现，即 2013 年在波兰召开的缔约方大会建立的"损失和损害"机制[171]和通过的《在发展中国家通过减少砍伐森林和减缓森林退化而降低温室气体排放并增加碳汇的华沙框架》(Warsaw Framework for REDD-plus)[172]。《联合国气候变化框架公约》的核心作用并未因《巴黎协定》的通过而受质疑，虽然有几个国家认为《巴黎协定》并没有包含约束性减缓义务。另外，鉴于《京都议定书》的前景尚不明朗，对《联合国气候变化框架公约》的回归可以被看作对某些规制手段（例如灵活机制，议定书正是因为它才被认定是非常有用的）的一个"抢救行动"。

四 1997 年《京都议定书》

正如前文所述，《京都议定书》[173] 的前景尚不明朗。在 2011 年 12 月

---

[168] Establishment of the Green Climate Fund, Decision 3/CP.17, 15 March 2012, Doc. FCCC/CP/2011/9/Add.1, Annex: Governing instrument for the Green Climate Fund, para. 35. On the concepts of "agreed incremental costs" and "agreed full costs", see Chapter 9.

[169] Cancun Agreements (Decision 1/CP.16), supra footnote 158, Chapter IV, Section B. See also: Technology Executive Committee-Modalities and Procedures, Decision 3/CP.17, 15 March 2012, Doc. FCCC/CP/2011/9/Add.1.

[170] Cancun Agreements (Decision 1/CP.16), supra footnote 158, Chapter III, Section D and Outcome of the Work of the Ad Hoc Working Group on Long-term Cooperative Action under the Convention, Decision 2/CP.17, 15 March 2012, Doc. FCCC/CP/2011/9/Add.1, paras. 79-80.

[171] Warsaw International Mechanism for Loss and Damage Associated with Climate Change (Decision-/CP.19).

[172] 这一框架包含了在华沙制定的《联合国气候变化框架公约》下的 7 项决议，包括一个有关在发展中国家通过减少砍伐森林和减缓森林退化而降低温室气体排放的资金的重要决议。Work Programme on Results-based Finance to Progress the Full Implementation of the Activities Referred to in Decision 1/CP.16, para. 70 (Decision-/CP.19).

[173] On this instrument, see: J. Depledge, "Tracing the Origins of the Kyoto Protocol: An Article-by-Article Textual History", Technical Paper, FCCC/TP/2000/2 (2000); D. Freestone and C. Streck, *Legal Aspects of Carbon Trading* (Oxford University Press, 2009).

的德班会议上,有些国家例如加拿大、俄罗斯甚至日本都拒绝接受一个新的承诺期,因此《京都议定书》很有可能不会成为将来气候制度的一个主要构成部分。另外,此后一年制定的、旨在制定一个第二承诺期的《多哈修正案》在技术上尚未开始生效,[174] 虽然这一修正案所设计的义务其实是源自许多国家自身的国内法(或欧盟法)。尽管如此,为了本书的目的,对《京都议定书》进行分析还是很重要的,因为它提出了一种"自上而下"的方法,这一方法在适用于远程越界空气污染和臭氧消耗时取得了成功经验,但是在应对气候变化时它并不是一个适当的一般手段。[175] 正如《蒙特利尔议定书》之《基加利修正案》所述,《京都议定书》作为一个具体的应对手段还是比较重要的,但是它还不足以充当一个一般应对手段来处理温室气体如此宽泛的活动和来源。我们在此将要介绍的是这种应对气候变化的"自上而下"的方法,《京都议定书》通过其四个主要维度具体体现了这一方法。

第一个维度是我们所熟悉的。与本章讨论的其他议定书一样,《京都议定书》也是"框架公约/议定书"这一方式的一个例证。《联合国气候变化框架公约》第 17 条规定应当制定议定书以规定更具体的义务。每个议定书的生效条件由各个议定书自己确定。《京都议定书》第 25 条第 1 款要求不少于 55 个缔约国的批准,其中应包括一定数量的附件一缔约方,而且这部分缔约方合计的二氧化碳排放量至少应占到附件一缔约方 1990 年二氧化碳排放总量的 55%。当美国否决了这一议定书之后,只有俄罗斯在 2004 年 11 月之前批准这一议定书才可能满足上述要求。但是,俄罗

---

[174] Amendment to the Kyoto Protocol pursuant to its Article 3, paragraph 9 (the Doha Amendment), Decision 1/CMP-8, 28 February 2013, Doc. FCCC/KP/CMP/2012/13/Add. 1. 截至 2017 年 4 月,已经有 77 个国家批准了《多哈修正案》,它需要 144 个国家的批准(表示接受的文件)才能生效。

[175] 必须指出的是,根据一个近期研究,附录二中完全加入了《京都议定书》的所有 36 个国家(排除了从未批准议定书的美国和退出的加拿大)都完成了它们在第一承诺期(2008—2012 年)的目标。其中,只有 9 个国家的排放量超出了它们的原定目标并必须依靠灵活机制(以获取碳信用额)以便实现它们的承诺。即使将所谓的"大话"(即转型国家因为紧缩而导致的减排,从而并非是由真正的减缓行动造成的)和土地政策(土地政策可以实现碳消除而且可以被算入总体配额)也考虑在内,这一发现也是成立的。但是,如果将美国和加拿大也算在内,那么就不会实现这一目标。See I. Shishlov, R. Morel, and V. Bellassen, "Compliance of the Parties to the Kyoto Protocol in the first commitment period" (2016) Climate Policy doi:10.1080/14693062.2016.1164658.

斯的批准来得太迟了。事实上，当议定书在2005年开始生效时，显而易见的是，其附录B所设定的减排目标已经远不足以控制大气中的温室气体浓度。后续年份的排放最应受到限制的那些国家——新兴经济体国家，事实上并没有受到议定书规定的量化义务的约束。

这就把我们带入第二个维度，即议定书是采用合作方式来表述共同但有区别的责任原则。在1995年缔约方大会制定了《柏林授权》之后，显而易见的是，（旨在通过《京都议定书》的）谈判应当专注于增强公约附件一国家的义务，并关注"这一进程尤其不得针对非附件一国家规定新的承诺"。[176]《京都议定书》一丝不苟地维持了这一承诺，只是对那些仅适用于附件一国家的义务做出了规定（第3条第1款和附录B）。也正是这样一个事实导致15年后《京都议定书》大部变得过时。事实上，那些排放量大的国家（例如美国、中国、印度、巴西等）并没有受到量化义务的约束。也许我们当时应当采用另一种、类似于《蒙特利尔议定书》所采取的办法，针对所有国家都规定量化义务，同时为发展中国家提供一个宽限期或者重大的灵活性。事实上，我们在规制上面临的两项挑战——臭氧消耗和气候变化两者之间存在着关键的不同点，这也就能够解释为什么发展中国家采取了更强硬的立场。特别是，与限制《蒙特利尔议定书》涉及的物质的生产或利用相比，对能源生产的限制有可能会对经济和社会发展造成更大的整体影响。但是，随着时间的流逝，发达国家和发展中国家之间的差别只会变得越来越大。在过去十年，国际社会做出了多个努力，试图制定一项新的制度以便将新兴经济体吸收进来，这些努力实质上就是为了推翻1995年做出的选择。2015年制定的《巴黎协定》就是这么做的。但是，将这一制度推广到所有国家的代价是削弱了该制度的国际化，换言之，将该制度实质上转变成一种"自下而上"的方法。

第三个维度指的是量化义务。《京都议定书》附录B中的国家所承担的量化义务可以被分为五个组成部分：（1）规制的客体［议定书附录A确定的、源头位于某国境内的温室气体排放，不包含他国消费该国出口的产品或资源（例如石油）所造成的排放］。（2）计算排放量所依据的基准年（第3条第1款、第3款、第4款、第5款、第7款指的是1990年，

---

[176] Berlin Mandate, supra footnote 152, para. II. 2（b）.

还有两个例外，其一，针对某些特定气体的排放各国可以选择1995年作为基准年，[177] 其二，转型中国家可以选择另一个基准年[178]）。（3）减排目标（议定书附录B用数字术语表述，每个数字代表的是依据基准年所应达到的排放量的百分比。例如，针对德国的数字是92，当规定第二承诺期的修正案开始生效后，数字就是80，这就分别意味着，与1990年的排放量相比，在第一承诺期应当减排8%，在第二承诺期应当减排20%）。（4）承诺期（减排目标应当在此期间完成，一旦修正案得以生效，议定书第3条第1款将会规定两个承诺期——2008—2012年以及2013—2020年，在此期间每年的平均排放量必须等于或少于附录B中的目标值）。（5）为实现目标所应采取的措施，国内措施（第1条第1款）[179] 要优先于国际措施（即第6条、第12条、第17条规定的灵活机制的运用）。

第四个维度指的是国际措施。《京都议定书》在国际措施方面是具有开创性的。《蒙特利尔议定书》已经提出了市场机制，但是与《京都议定书》相比，它只能算是萌芽。《京都议定书》第6条、第12条、第17条规定了灵活机制（缔约方会议大量决议对其做了补充），这些机制更加复杂，并得到了一套复杂体制的支持。这三种机制是基于主要由第17条规定的排放权"转移"或"交易"理念。排放权交易意味着有可能将某国（或者获许进行排放交易的私营组织）的排放配额转移给另外一国。这种转移可能会涉及不同种类的排放单位，每类排放单位的使用（以及它们的价值）也是不尽相同的。为了说明这一问题，有必要区分以下两类排放单位。

某些排放单位（"分配排放单位"和"减排单位"）是附录B针对名录中国家设定的整体排放限额的一部分。这些排放单位之间的交换必然就意味着售出国排放配额的减少以及买入国排放配额的增加。这一交易可

177　Kyoto Protocol, supra footnote 153, Art. 3 (8).

178　Ibid., Art. 3 (5). 根据某一个国家经济的发展轨迹，选择一个不同的基准年就可以使义务变得更轻或更重。鉴于排放水平是与经济发展水平紧密相关的，选择一个更近期的年份（即排放量更高的年份）当作基准年就会留有更大余地。相反地，如果1990年的排放水平要高于后续年份（因为经济衰退的原因），该国则可以选择把1990年作为基准年，这样就可以为其在承诺期的经济发展提供更大空间。

179　Principles, Nature and Scope of the Mechanisms pursuant to Article 6, 12 and 17 of the Kyoto Protocol, Decision 2/CMP. 1, 30 March 2006, Doc. FCCC/KP/CMP/2005/8/Add. 1, para. 1.

以在一个排放市场中进行,[180] 或者采取议定书第 6 条所规定的项目的形式在附件一国家的领土上进行。[181] 这类项目的目标是向那些处于市场经济转型中的国家转让技术,并通过"绿化"终点国的高污染设施来实现比缘起国的成本更低的减排。用会计学的术语来讲,项目东道国(改进后的设施所在国)用分配排放单位来"支付"其获得的技术提升,这些排放单位是采用减排单位的形式被转移给这一项目的资助国。这些交易通常会发生于私营企业之间以便它们能够遵守相关的附件一国家赋予它们的义务。

作为议定书第 12 条规定的"清洁发展机制"的一部分,这些项目也可以在一个非附件一国家的领土上进行,例如中国、印度和巴西。[182] 逻辑还是一样的,即向发展中国家转让技术以便实现更低成本的减排。但是,第 6 款中的机制与第 12 款中的机制还是存在着一个关键区别。在第 6 款的机制下,虽然排放权进行了交换,但是核准的排放量的总量还是保持不变。与此不同的是,在第 12 款的机制下,减排量可以超出议定书设定的整体限额下可交易的排放量。这些项目新鲜出炉的排放权在一定程度上可以为那些被限额束缚的国家用于履行他们的义务。基于这一原因,同时为了避免滥用,获取这类排放权(核准减排单位)的程序就比第 12 款的条件更加严格,它包含了一系列来自独立第三方认证的要求,还需要一个执行委员会的参与以便管理这一机制。尽管有了这样一些保障,清洁发展机制还是遭到了广泛的批评,主要的问题在于它有可能诱发那种违背其初衷的行为。事实上,只要某一方(某一发展中国家或在其领土上的私营主体)在减排量越大的时候就能获取更多的利益,这一方就有可能被诱导

---

[180] See, S. Simonetti and R. de Witt Wijnen, "International Emissions Trading and Green Investment Schemes", in Freestone and Streck, supra footnote 173, pp. 157-175.

[181] Guidelines for the Implementation of Article 6 of the Kyoto Protocol, Decision 9/CMP.1, 30 March 2006, Doc. FCCC/KP/CMP/2005/8/Add.1. See A. Hobley and C. Roberts, "Joint Implementation Transactions: An Overview", in Freestone and Streck, supra footnote 173, pp. 195-212.

[182] Modalities and Procedures for a Clean Development Mechanism as defined in Article 12 of the Kyoto Protocol, Decision 3/CMP.1, 30 March 2006, Doc. FCCC/KP/CMP/2005/8/Add.1. See M. Netto and K. -U. Barani Schmidt, "The CDM Project Cycle and the Role of the UNFCCC Secretariat", in Freestone and Streck, supra footnote 173, pp. 213-230.

去从源头增加排放量以便最大化它的减排潜力,并凭此吸引更多的清洁发展机制项目(意味着更多的经费)。[183] 换言之,清洁发展机制有可能会处罚那些低排放国家和设施,因为它们没有为自己创造大幅度减排的机会。

尽管存在这些困难,正如我们下一部分所述,《巴黎协定》的条款还是规定了各种市场机制,虽然这一文件所采用的"自下而上"的方法对市场机制的运行造成了重大影响。也就是说,《巴黎协定》的重心在于别处,即一套广泛的国际协作和实施系统,而所要采取的实施措施则是完全由各国自己决定。

五 2015年《巴黎协定》

(一)达成《巴黎协定》的国际谈判

前文所述已经为分析气候变化谈判的演变提供了足够的背景资料,这一演变主要由三个过程构成,即(1)旨在增强《京都议定书》的过程,它导致的结果是2012年《多哈修正案》;(2)在巴厘岛启动并在多哈结束的过程,它的目的是缩小附件一国家与其他国家之间的差距[由公约下长期合作行动特设工作组(Ad Hoc Working Group for Long-term Cooperative Action under the Convention——AWGLCA)领导];(3)于2011年12月启动的所谓"德班平台"进程,它导致了2015年12月第21次缔约方大会上《巴黎协定》的通过。[184]

这三个谈判过程以复杂的方式相互交叉在一起。第一个和第二个过程

---

183 For practical applications (including the case of HCFC-23), see M. Wara, Measuring the Clean Development Mechanism's Performance and Potential' (2007) 55 *UCLA Law Review* 1759.

184 Adoption of the Paris Agreement, Decision 1/CP.21, 12 December 2015, FCCC/CP/2015/L.9 ("Paris Decision")。《巴黎协定》被当作一个附录添加到《巴黎决议》。《巴黎协定》技术上是国际条约法下的一个条约(虽然在某些宪法秩序下它可能不够资格成为条约),2016年4月22日有175个国家签署了该协定。See "List of representatives to High-level signature ceremony", available at: http://newsroom.unfccc.int/paris-agreement/175-states-sign-paris-agreement/ (visited on 17 April 2017). The authentic version of the Paris Agreement (hereafter "Paris Agreement") is available at: http://unfccc.int (visited on 17 April 2017). Our discussion of the Paris Agreement relies upon J. E. Viñuales, "The Paris Agreement on Climate Change: Less is More" (2016) 59 *German Yearbook of International Law* [11-45] (see also the literature devoted to the Paris Agreement cited therein). See also S. Maljean-Dubois and L. Rajamani, "L'Accord de Paris sur les changements climatiques du 12 décembre 2015" (2015) 61 *Annuaire Français de Droit International* 615.

自它们分别于 2005 年和 2007 年启动以来就被联系在一起。从一个政治视角来看，《京都议定书》附录 B 国家对第二承诺期的承认多半是对新兴经济体的一个让步，目的是换取它们接受巴厘进程所规定的具体义务。但是，新兴经济体对巴厘进程具体义务的接受并不如发达国家所愿。随着哥本哈根的外交失败，以及部分弥补这一失败的《坎昆协议》的制定（它确实考虑到了减缓措施的增强，包括针对发展中国家的措施），[185] 发达国家得出一个结论，即巴厘进程的基石还不够清晰。正如评论员指出的那样，发展中国家对巴厘进程的理解是，在适应其国情的减缓行动与那些发达国家做出的减缓承诺之间建造一道"隔离墙"，而发达国家则把《巴厘授权》当作一座旨在缩小《柏林授权》造成的差异的"桥梁"。[186]

德班平台试图在以上两种立场中找到一条中间路线。值得一提的是，启动这一谈判进程的决定并未提及共同但有区别的责任原则。另外，它还强调指出，这一谈判进程产生的所有"议定的成果"必须拥有法律效力。应当选择何种词汇来表述这一目标也引发了激烈争论，特别是在欧洲与印度的谈判之间。[187] 最后，达成共识使用如下术语："适用于所有缔约方的议定书、法律文书或具有法律效力的议定成果"。[188] 另外，德班平台的实体范围涵盖了一系列广泛的领域，包括"减缓、适应、财政、技术开发和转让、行动和支持的透明度以及能力建设"。[189] 但是，不同国家和组织针对这些领域各自的重要程度以及如何从法律视角来进行应对都持有大相径庭的观点。现在看来，考虑到谈判过程中的政治和法律变量，谈判授权的广义表述所提供的灵活性其实是最终成果的一个重要组成部分。

（二）政治基础

在一个宏观背景下理解《巴黎协定》，不仅会涉及德班平台的参数，更重要的是温室气体的主要排放国（特别是美国和中国）在进行谈判时所依据的社会经济、政治和法律边界。另外，第 21 次缔约方大会在正式谈判进程以外所激发的动力，包括城市、区域、私人企业、民间团体和其

---

185 Cancun Agreements（Decision 1/CP.16）, supra footnote 158, Chapter Ⅲ, section B.
186 Rajamani, supra footnote 159, pp. 505-506.
187 Ibid., pp. 506ff.
188 Decision 1/CP.17, supra footnote 160, para. 2.
189 Ibid., para 5.

他非缔约方利益相关者所付出的努力也值得一提。[190]

　　奥巴马政府所采取的战略也是这一宏观背景下的一个重要组成部分。鉴于共和党反对美国加入气候协议，奥巴马政府转而寻求起草一份可以约束美国政府而无须参议院批准（参议院基本不可能批准）的文件。这一方法也符合其他一些国家的利益，它们希望美国能够正式成为《巴黎协定》的一员以避免重蹈《京都议定书》的覆辙。为了达成这一点，美国的谈判立场聚焦于制定一个可以被定性为"执行协议"的文件，而非一个美国宪法管辖下的"条约"。[191] 为了实现这一可能，谈判者制定了一个法律战略，依据这一战略，美国政府在国际层面宣布的所有目标的内容本身并不具有国际约束力（虽然可能负有义务去宣布这些目标），而只是根据诸如《清洁空气法》等各种法律的授权而具有国内约束力。[192] 还有另一种选择，即所有减缓承诺的约束性来自美国已经批准的《联合国气候变化框架公约》。

　　中国作为世界上温室气体的主要排放国，它的发展战略对气候谈判具有重大影响。事实上，中国在第 21 次缔约方大会上的态度与其在前些年气候谈判（特别是在哥本哈根）中的态度不同，一个主要的原因在于中国在其第 12 个"五年计划"（2011—2015 年）中转变了经济（不仅是环境）政策。[193] 中国国家主席习近平指出，中国的经济发展的"新常态"模式包含了一个较低的增长目标（7%），注重服务和高附加值产业，扩大内需和减少不均衡。[194] 在第 21 次缔约方大会的前几年，中国的能源消费

---

[190] See *Harriet Bulkeley et al.*, Transnational Climate Change Governance (Cambridge University Press, 2014).

[191] 应当注意的是，根据国际法，条约和执行协议都被认为是"条约"，从而对美国具有约束力。但是根据美国宪法第二部分第 2 条之规定（要求参议院对"条约"的"建议和同意"），国内批准程序的进行是不同的。

[192] Clean Air Act, 42 U.S.C. § 7401 *et seq.* (1970). For a detailed analysis see D. Wirth, "Cracking the American Climate Negotiators' Hidden Code: United States Law and the Paris Agreement" (2016) 6 *Climate Law* 152.

[193] See I. Hilton and O. Kerr, "The Paris Agreement: China's 'New Normal' Role in International Climate Negotiations" (2016) 17, *Climate Policy* 48.

[194] Ibid., 51.

和排放速度已经开始下降，2015年，中国的二氧化碳排放减少了0.1%。[195]从国际气候谈判的视角来看，根据两位观察员的观点，这将把中国置于一个令人羡慕的地位，因为它可以实现"低承诺和高履行"。[196]

2016年9月3日，美国（通过执行行动）和中国都批准了《巴黎协定》，这就为协定的生效提供了极大推动力，并成功使其在2016年11月4日开始生效。这就有力地反驳了许多国家政治势力的一个借口（它们把主要排放者没有批准协定当作一个不采取行动的借口）。遗憾的是，即使从政治视角来看《巴黎协定》是非常重要的，但是该协定的广泛获批还是不可能平息所有担心，甚至是那些善意表达的担忧。这归根于《巴黎协定》的具体法律结构，因为该协定体现的是一种"自下而上"的方式。

（三）《巴黎协定》的架构

1. 概述

作为一项法律文书，《巴黎协定》有三个主要组成部分，即它的目标（如本章第五节第五部分第三点第二项内容）、行动领域（如本章第五节第五部分第三点第三项内容）和履行手段（如本章第五节第五部分第三点第四项内容）。每个组成部分不仅包含了协定文本中的一系列条款，还应包括那些技术上应被当作协定内容（根据《维也纳条约法公约》第31条的定义）的外部相关材料。[197] 图5-4概括了协定的整体架构。

在分析这些组成部分之前，值得注意的是，对《巴黎协定》的一个简明的审视还是会遗漏大量内容。从协定的序言开始，我们就可以从字斟句酌的简明表述中发现整个文本所蕴含的各种冲突，包括发达国家与发展中国家之间，易受影响的国家与其他国家之间，可能会遭受气候变化应对措施的伤害的国家与其他国家之间，气候变化行动与脱贫或劳动力的顺利过渡之间，干预与资源保护之间，科学与公平之间的关系，等等。值得特

---

[195] Ibid., 52 (referring to estimations by *Korsbakken et al.*, 2016a and the National Bureau of Statistics).

[196] F. Green and N. Stern, "China's 'new normal': structural change, better growth, and peak emissions", *Policy Brief-Grantham Research Institute on Climate Change and the Environment*, June 2015, 4 (referring to China's political commitment to peak emissions around 2030), available at: www.lse.ac.uk (accessed on 17 April 2017).

[197] VCLT, supra footnote 137, Art. 31 (2) – (3).

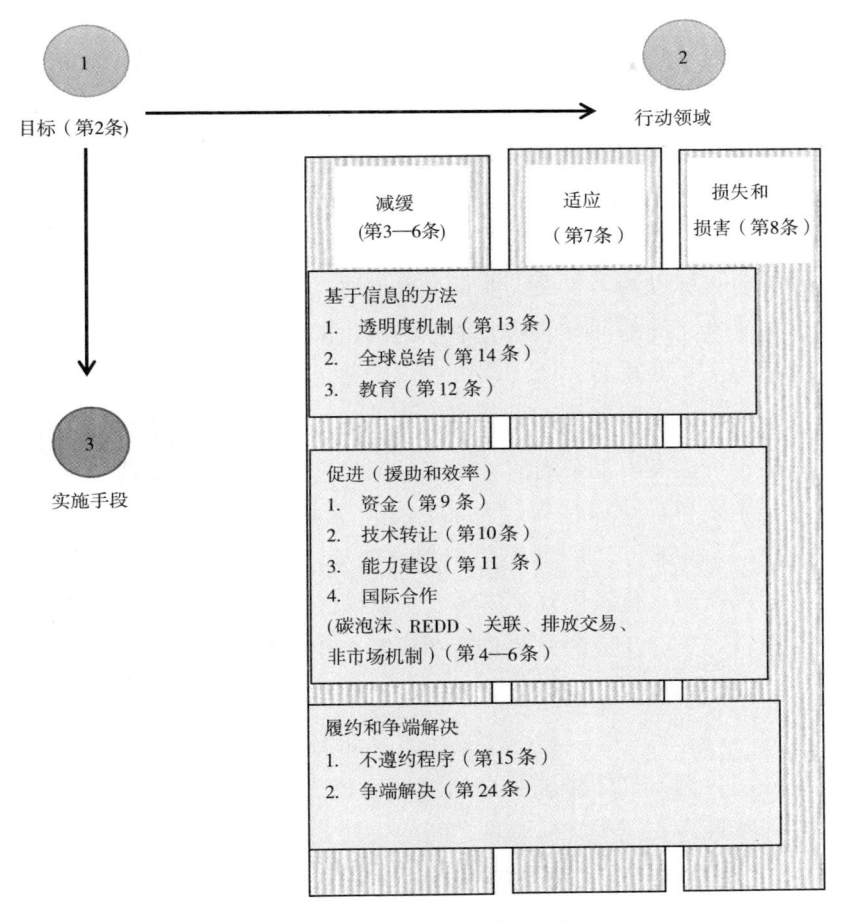

```
        1                            2
    目标(第2条)  ──────────►      行动领域

                    ┌──────────────┬──────────┬──────────┐
                    │   减缓       │  适应    │ 损失和   │
                    │ (第3—6条)    │ (第7条)  │ 损害(第8条)│
                    └──────────────┴──────────┴──────────┘

                    ┌─────────────────────────────────────┐
                    │ 基于信息的方法                       │
                    │ 1. 透明度机制(第13条)                │
        3           │ 2. 全球总结(第14条)                  │
                    │ 3. 教育(第12条)                      │
    实施手段        └─────────────────────────────────────┘

                    ┌─────────────────────────────────────┐
                    │ 促进(援助和效率)                     │
                    │ 1. 资金(第9条)                       │
                    │ 2. 技术转让(第10条)                  │
                    │ 3. 能力建设(第11条)                  │
                    │ 4. 国际合作                          │
                    │ (碳泡沫、REDD、关联、排放交易、       │
                    │ 非市场机制)(第4—6条)                 │
                    └─────────────────────────────────────┘

                    ┌─────────────────────────────────────┐
                    │ 履约和争端解决                       │
                    │ 1. 不遵约程序(第15条)                │
                    │ 2. 争端解决(第24条)                  │
                    └─────────────────────────────────────┘
```

图 5-4　《巴黎协定》的结构

别指出的是序言第 12 段，它第一次明确提出了气候变化条约中的人权问题。[198]

在后续分析中，我们会研究这些暗藏冲突的部分内容，毫无疑问的是，它们需要更多的具体研究。只有当序言提炼的可能性演变为更具体的工作流程时，其意义才可能变得清晰。这些工作可以在《巴黎协定》和公约下长期合作行动特设工作组或其他背景之下开展，例如联合国人权

---

[198] Paris Agreement, supra footnote 184, preamble, para. 12. On this question see B. Mayer, "Human Rights in the Paris Agreement" (2016) 6 *Climate Law* 109.

理事会（UN Human Rights Council）所开展的有关人权和气候变化的工作。[199]

2. 目标

在《联合国气候变化框架公约》第2条这一宏观目标之下，《巴黎协定》第2条设定了三个目标。在谈判的过程中，将全球平均气温升幅设为2摄氏度对某些国家来说是否不够充分这一问题引起了很大关注，更具体地说，将目标设为1.5摄氏度是否更加适当。这一讨论背后隐藏的是有效性和公平性之间的冲突。从公平性的视角来看，似乎1.5摄氏度这一目标更好，因为，虽然只相差了一点点（只有0.5摄氏度），但是在实际中可能因为海平面的上升和极端天气事件而导致低海拔岛国的灾难性后果。这一目标也可能发出复杂的信号效应，因为它看起来很难实现。将1.5摄氏度设为主要目标可以使得《巴黎协定》显得雄心勃勃，而不是将其仅仅定位成一个规制手段。如果协定想要给生产者和消费者一个清晰的信号，并明确指明从化石燃料经济转变为低碳经济的必要性，那么这两个目标都应顾及。最终达成的办法是第2条第1款所规定的将气温升幅控制在"低于2摄氏度之内，并努力将气温升幅限制在工业化前水平以上1.5摄氏度之内"。另外，为了稳定21世纪末全球平均气温的上升，协定第4条第1款采用"温室气体排放的全球峰值"的方式进一步规定了一个中期减缓目标并最终实现排放与清除之间的长期"平衡"。后文在谈及行动领域之一的减缓时将会继续探讨这些目标。

重要的是，《巴黎协定》第2条不仅超出了减缓这一中心点，还有争议地超出了《联合国气候变化框架公约》设定的目标范围（它仅仅提出"温室气体浓度的稳定"），它增加了"提高适应气候变化不利影响的能力"以及"使资金流动符合温室气体低排放和气候适应型发展的路径"，后者标志着投资从"棕色"向"绿色"的转移。

第2条第2款根据公平、共同但有区别的责任原则以及各自能力设定

---

[199] 联合国人权理事会针对这一问题制定了几项决议，2009年，联合国人权事务高级专员办公室发布了《联合国人权事务高级专员办公室关于气候变化与人权之间关系的报告》[UN Doc. A/HRC/10/61（2009）]。在《巴黎协定》后，人权理事会制定了一项决议将这两者联结起来，参见"Human Rights and Climate Change"，28 June 2016，Res. A/HRC/32/L. 34。参见本书第十章。

了这些目标。正如前文所述，在启动德班平台的决议中并未出现共同但有区别的责任原则，但是这一原则在气候变化谈判中已经是无法回避的。值得注意的一个事实是，《联合国气候变化框架公约》第 3 条中的其他两个重要原则（风险预防和代际公平）并未被重申。《巴黎协定》只是在前言中提到了《联合国气候变化框架公约》的原则，但是，它也只是单独提及共同但有区别的责任原则。可以很公平及科学地认为，气候变化不再仅仅是一个风险预防问题而成为一个损害预防问题，即预防一个已被确认的风险。

目标的多样性并不仅仅是为了告诫。它也出现于协定的其他两个组成部分，即每个行动领域中的义务和实施手段。

3. 行动领域

《巴黎协定》可以被认为是应对三个主要行动领域的问题。其中的两个——减缓（第 3—6 条）和适应（第 7 条）被给予了特别的重视，虽然针对减缓的措辞整体上显得更肯定一些，[200] 而第三个领域——损失和损害（第 8 条）则受限于较窄范围。

《巴黎协定》想要应对的核心行动领域是减缓。但是减缓也是该协定的"软肋"，因为整套制度是依赖于"国家自主贡献"［Nationally Determined Contributions（NDCs）][201]（第 3 条和第 4 条）这样一个柔性结构，这些自主贡献由各缔约国自由设定并被记录在一个灵活的"公共登记册"（public register）（第 4 条第 12 款）。各国可以选择它们的力度大小，前提是必须满足两个要求，即定期更新它们的国家自主贡献——每五年至少通报一次（第 4 条第 9 款），以及逐步增加其国家自主贡献（第 4 条第 3 款）。后一条款还规定了一个更有抱负的期望，即各国的国家自主贡献应

---

[200] See L. Rajamani, "The 2015 Paris Agreement: Interplay Between Hard, Soft and Non-obligations" (2016) 28 *Journal of Environmental Law* 337.

[201] 这些起初（直到《巴黎协定》的签署）被称为"预期的国家自主贡献"［Intended Nationally Determined Contributions（INDCs）］，各国是依据 2013 年在波兰华沙召开的第 19 次缔约方大会制定的决议［Decision 1/CP. 19, para. 2（b）］而提交的。它们涵盖了全球年度排放量的 90% 以上，但是许诺的减排还是无法满足将升温幅度控制在 2 摄氏度这一要求，更不论 1.5 摄氏度了，《巴黎决议》（Paris Decision, supra footnote 184, para. 17）也承认了这一点。这些预期的国家自主贡献和国家自主贡献的记录是被分别保存的。前者出现在一个"国家自主贡献平台"［http://unfccc.int/focus/indc_portal/items/8766.php（2017 年 4 月 17 日访问）］，而后者则出现于《巴黎协定》设计的一个临时的"国家自主贡献注册"，它是针对那些已经批准了协定的国家，参见 http://unfccc.int/focus/ndc_registry/items/9433.php（2017 年 4 月 17 日访问）。

反映其"尽可能大的力度"。关于国家自主贡献的具体内容,虽然在巴黎会议以前已经有了一些指南,[202] 但是它们还有待明确。在第 21 次缔约方大会之前提交的预期的国家自主贡献,在性质和内容上都是千差万别的。[203] 正是考虑到这一点,《巴黎协定》认为有必要进一步明确和加强透明度(第 4 条第 8 款),而且《通过〈巴黎协定〉的决定》已经授权特设工作组负责制定该指南并提交给缔约方会议批准。[204]

这样一个柔性结构沿袭了各国在哥本哈根会议后作出的并在《坎昆协定》中得以固定的保证,它在政治上和法律上都是非常重要的。从政治的视角来看,各国可以选择它们的力度大小,这就给区别对待留下了很大空间。[205] 想要将那些高排放发展中国家以及美国纳入这一规制系统,这也是必须付出的部分代价,而且第 9 款规定自主贡献必须逐步扩大,这也会促使各国在开始时设定适度的国家自主贡献。法律上讲,预期的国家自主贡献通常是来源于各国国内法或欧洲法设定的目标,而这些目标也给私营部门发出了更明显的信号。另外,《巴黎协定》第 4 条第 2 款进一步巩固了这些目标,根据国际法,这些目标有资格成为一项"后续协议"或"后续实践",[206] 用于解释《联合国气候变化框架公约》和《巴黎协定》,[207] 并有可能

---

[202] See "Further advancing the Durban Platform", Decision 1/CP. 19, 31 January 2014, FCCC//CP/2013/10/Add. 1, para. 2(b); "Lima Call for Climate Action", Decision 1/CP. 20, 2 February 2015, FCCC/ /CP/2014/10/Add. 1, para. 14.

[203] 但是,必须指出的是,在提交给《联合国气候变化框架公约》的 160 余个预期的国家自主贡献中,有 90 个设计了某种形式的碳定价工具(碳税、碳交易机制等)。See World Bank, *Carbon Pricing Watch* 2016, May 2016.

[204] Paris Decision, supra footnote 184, paras. 26-28. 特殊工作组还有一项工作是为各缔约方计算国家自主贡献制定指南。(see Paris Decision, para. 31; Paris Agreement, supra footnote 184, Art. 4(13)).

[205] On the question of differentiation in the Paris Agreement see C. Voigt and F. Ferreira, "Differentiation in the Paris Agreement" (2016) 6 *Climate Law* 58.

[206] VCLT, supra footnote 137, Art. 31(3)(a)-(b).

[207] See *Kasikili/Sedudu Island (Botswana/Namibia)*, Judgment, I. C. J. Reports 1999, p. 1045, para. 49. See also ILC Annual Reports, Report on the work of the sixty-fifth session (2013), A/68/10. Chapter IV "Subsequent agreements and subsequent practice in relation to the interpretation of treaties", Commentary of 4th Conclusion of Special Rapporteur, para. 17.

成为有约束力的单边行动。[208] 通过这一方法，它们的解释力就不仅会符合那些认为自主贡献具有国际约束力的国家（例如欧盟[209]）的观点，也会符合其他那些认为自主贡献只具有国内约束力的国家（例如美国）的观点。

重要的是，除了预期的国家自主贡献之外，《巴黎协定》另一个重要的补充还涉及全球排放的整体趋势以及在21世纪后半叶实现碳中和的必要性。正如前文所述，这就要求尽早实现排放峰值的到来，根据共同但有区别的责任原则给予发展中国家更长的时间，以便实现大幅减排并达到排放和消除的"平衡"（第4条第1款）。《通过〈巴黎协定〉的决定》的第36段"邀请"各缔约方在2020年之前交流"第4条第19段规定的远期温室气体低排放发展战略"，这些战略将会发布在秘书处网站。

《巴黎协定》第7条涉及第二个行动领域，其重点是"适应"。多年以来，适应的政治特性变得越来越重要，特别是在2010年《坎昆协定》建立了一个《坎昆适应框架》之后。[210]《巴黎协定》可以被看作这些特性提升努力的顶点。适应现在被看作一个可追踪的目标，第7条要求每个国家都应制订适应计划（第9段）并强调发展中国家的适应努力不仅应当被"承认"（第3段），还应当被通报（第10段），并被记录于公共登记

---

[208] 这一结论有赖于发布国家自主贡献时的具体情况。当提及美国和其他国家拒绝将国家自主贡献当作京都类目标或"应当履行的义务"时，某个评论员认为国家自主贡献永远无法等同于一个有约束力的单方行为（D. Bodanksy, "The Paris Climate Change Agreement: A New Hope?"（2016）110 *American Journal of International Law* 288, p. 304）。但是这一观点既不符合国际法中单方行为的理论（某一相关条约的准备工作材料只是在评估某一行为的法律含义时所要考虑的一个要件，它们并不会防止某国或某个组织（例如欧盟）通过单方行为来使自身受到约束），而且从根本上讲，也不符合单方行为可以造成一个有约束力的方法义务或行为义务（而不是一个"应履行义务"或"结果义务"）这一事实。关于"行为义务"与"结果义务"的区别，参见ICJ, *Pulp Mills on the River Uruguay*（Argentina v. Uruguay）, Judgment, I. C. J. Reports 2010, 14, para. 187; *Responsibilities and obligations of States sponsoring persons and entities with respect to activities in the Area*, Advisory Opinion（1 February 2011）, ITLOS Case No. 17, para. 110; *Request for an Advisory Opinion Submitted by the Sub-Regional Fisheries Commission*（SR-FC）, Advisory Opinion（2 April 2015）, ITLOS Case No. 21, para. 129。

[209] 由拉脱维亚和欧洲委员会代表欧盟及其成员国在2016年3月6日提交，参见www.unfccc.int（2017年4月17日访问）。

[210] Cancun Agreements（Decision 1/CP. 16）, supra footnote 158, paras. 13-14. On the Cancun Adaptation Framework and the development of adaptation institutions see German Watch/WWF, *Institutions for Adaptation. Towards an Effective Multilevel Interplay*（2011）, available at http://german-watch.org（visited on 17 April 2017）.

册上（第12段），甚至还应被收入协定第14条设计的全球总结之中（第14段）（参见后文本章第五节第五部分第三点第四项内容）。但是，适应行动的流程设计还是非常困难的，因为它可能比减缓行动更加多样。另外，各国给予适应的优先程度也不尽相同，发达国家更愿意促进（包括在财政上）发展中国家采取减缓行动。这两个原因就可以解释为什么有关适应的条款整体上不如有关减缓的条款那么坚定，它们被定性为"软性义务"甚至是"无义务"，因为针对它们的措辞都是建议性术语，或者满足一定前提条件才能成立，或者仅是为了获得缔约方的理解，而没有试图去创建可执行的义务。[211]

《巴黎协定》的第三个行动领域涉及"损失和损害"，这是第一次在气候变化制度中用一项专门条款（第8条）来处理这一问题。[212] 适应与损失和损害在概念上的边界很难划分。在理论上，适应是一个预防性战略，它的目的是尽可能避免气候变化的不利影响，而损失和损害则是为了应对那些已经发生的损害或无法避免的损害。换言之，适应依然还是一个预防问题，而损失和损害则是一个"回应"（有可能还是"修复"[213]）问题。但是，在实践中，除了修复问题这个被损失和损害明确排除的问题，这些概念的分类并不明显。一定程度上，这不是一个纯概念问题，因为协定规定的履约措施（包括财政措施）仅明确适用于适应（第7条）而不适用于损失和损害（所以造就了前文图5-4中的问号）。与损失和损害相关的两个重要问题是对已造成损失的赔偿和与气候变化相关的移民。这两个问题都没有在第8条中被明确提及，但是《通过〈巴黎协定〉的决定》做出了两个说明。决定的第50段明确计划了与气候变化的不利影响相关的移民问题，缔约方大会正是据此授权华沙损失与损害国际机制（Warsaw

---

211 See Rajamani, supra footnote 200, pp. 352 (characterising different types of obligations) and 356-357 (placing adaptation provisions mostly under the categories of "soft-obligations" or "non-obligations").

212 On loss and damage in the Paris Agreement see M. Burkett, "Reading Between the Red Lines: Loss and Damage and the Paris Outcome" (2016) 6 *Climate Law* 118.

213 On the distinction of the stages (internalisation, prevention, response, reparation) of environmental policy intervention, see J. E. Viñuales, "La distribution de la charge de protéger l'environnement: Expressions juridiques de la solidarité", in A. Supiot (ed.), *La responsabilité solidaire* (Paris: Conférences du Collège de France, 2017).

International Mechanism on Loss and Damage)[214] 去建立一个工作组，与其他组织一起合作制定"关于采取综合方法来防止、最小化和解决与气候变化的不利影响相关的移民问题的建议"。与直截了当地否认损失和损害与义务之间两者间的关联性（这是美国一直顽固坚持的观点）相比，[215] 这是一个受人欢迎的进展。

这三个行动领域的区别体现在它们各自拥有的履约机体中。减缓和适应的共同点较多，而损失和损害的情况则显得有些受到了局限。

4. 履约手段

《巴黎协定》的主要创新之处在于它的履约手段，特别是第13条建立的"关于行动和支持的强化透明度框架"。这一机制体现了一种方法，从2011年德班平台的启动开始，甚至更早的长期合作行动特设工作组和《哥本哈根协议》都是采用的这种方法；根据这一方法，排放目标由各国设定而它的监测、报告与核查则应当在国际层面进行。[216] 当然，它并不是唯一的方法，协定还设计了其他几种方法。但是，很明显的是，《巴黎协定》采用的"自下而上"方法的上半部分（实施）关注的焦点是协作而非国内层面的行动。为了分析的需要，有必要区分那些基于信息的方法、促进遵约的方法和针对不遵约的管理方法。

《巴黎协定》规定了三种所谓的基于信息的手段，它们不仅是依赖于信息，它们的真正目的是提供短期或长期信息的透明度。除了《联合国气候变化框架公约》对教育的特别强调之外（第12条），[217]《巴黎协定》

---

[214] On the evolution of this workstream and the Warsaw mechanism see: E. L. Roberts and S. Huq, "Coming full circle: the history of loss and damage under the UNFCCC" (2015) 8, *International Journal of Global Warming* 141; D. Stabinsky and J. P. Hoffmaister, "Establishing institutional arrangements on loss and damage under the UNFCCC: the Warsaw International Mechanism for Loss and Damage" (2015) 8, *International Journal of Global Warming* 295.

[215] See Paris Decision, supra footnote 184, para. 52 指出 "缔约方大会同意协定第8条不涉及任何责任或赔偿或为其提供一个基础"。

[216] Ibid., para. 98.

[217] 关于将环境教育当作一个政策这一更广义的问题，以及更具体的气候变化教育问题，参见 O. M. J. Langer, "Principle 21: The Role of Youth", in J. E. Viñuales (ed.), *The Rio Declaration on Environment and Development. A Commentary* (Oxford University Press, 2015), 519–539。第12条也提到了公众教育问题。On the latter question see J. Ebbesson, "Principle 10: Public Participation", in Viñuales, pp. 287–309.

也提出了两个相互关联的创新点。第一个创新点由第 13 条规定，它是一个"公开谴责"（naming and shaming）机制，目的是推动各国遵守它们的国家自主贡献和其他义务。根据第 13 条，这一透明性机制适用于所有缔约方，但是条款也强调指出了它的灵活性和非侵入性的特质，还必须考虑到各缔约方能力上的差异（第 1—3 段）。机制的这一目的与其对"行动"和"支持"的关注是一脉相承的。关于行动，这一机制的目的是追踪每个缔约方在实施和实现其国家自主贡献上的"单个"进展情况（根据第 4 条）以及各方（并未提及"单个"）在适应上的进展情况（根据第 7 条，并将第 8 条下的行动排除在外）。[218] 关于支持，这一机制的目的是清楚地表明各个缔约方所提供或者所接受的支持，这些支持被分为几类，即减缓（第 4 条）、适应（第 7 条）、财政（第 9 条）、技术转让（第 10 条）和能力建设（第 11 条）。[219] 显而易见的是，这些种类中并没有损失和损害（第 8 条）。各缔约方被要求定期（最少两年一次[220]）通报信息，这些信息包括减缓[221]以及其他一些信息（根据缔约方种类的不同），特别是援助（包括财政、技术转让和能力建设）。[222] 减缓（指所有缔约方）和支持（基本上指发达国家）的信息都应进行一个"技术专家评审"，涉及支持的事项还应接受"促进性的多方审议"这样一种同行评审过程。[223] 行动和支持的透明度是为了满足协定第 14 条设定的全球总结的需要。这一全球总结是《巴黎协定》的第二个创新点。在第 21 次缔约方大会上，谈判者（我们在这里必须假定为全世界）非常担忧这样一个事实，即目前已经提交的预期的国家自主贡献虽然涵盖了绝大部分的温室气体排放和排放源，但是与 2 摄氏度的目标还是相差太远。为了保证气候变化制度的整体有效，对"树木"（通过透明度机制对各国履行情况进行的评估）的关注不应取代对"森林"（对流层中温室气体的总量以及各国应对气候变化影响的能

---

[218] Paris Agreement, supra footnote 184, Art. 13 (5).

[219] Ibid., Art. 13 (6).

[220] Paris Decision, supra footnote 184, para. 90.

[221] Paris Agreement, supra footnote 184, Art. 13 (7)（这是一个要求，术语"应"的使用说明了这一点，而且它适用于所有缔约方）。

[222] Ibid. Art. 13 (9)（这一条款针对发达国家采用了"应"这一术语，而针对其他提供援助的国家则只采用了"应该"这一术语）。

[223] Ibid., Art. 13 (11).

力）的关注，即不能只见树木不见森林。第 14 条设定的全球总量应对的就是这一问题。这项工作将会根据特设工作组规定的形式定期（从 2023 年开始，每五年一次）开展。[224] 特设工作组还被授权去确定相关信息来源以便设定全球总量，包括来自各缔约方的单个通报信息。如此一来，第 14 条就规定了一个所谓的"信息圈"，单个通报可以为全球总量提供信息；反过来，全球总量可以为各国应在将来的国家自主贡献上展示多大的力度提供信息（第 14 条第 3 款）。

与那些基于信息的手段不同，《巴黎协定》在涉及促进遵约上并没有创新，无论是通过支持（财政[225]、技术转让[226]和能力建设[227]）还是效率手段，因为它主要（也是无可非议地）依靠的是现有机制。[228] 但是，它还是包含了多个极具潜力的市场机制，[229] 从一个相当稳固的土地利用机制（包

---

[224] Paris Decision, supra footnote 184, para. 102.

[225] 美国和其他发达国家成功地将任何具体数字排除在《巴黎协定》第 9 条之外，但是《巴黎决议》做出了两点澄清，即缔约方会议将在 2025 年之前设定一个新的集体性量化目标，而且"地板价"将会是在早前谈判中出现的数字，即每年 1000 亿美元（Paris Decision, supra footnote 184, para. 54）。关于《巴黎协定》文本中财政问题的讨论，参见 Zahar, "The Paris Agreement and the Gradual Development of a Law on Climate Finance" (2016) 6 *Climate Law* 75。

[226] 关于技术转让，第 10 条第 4 款建立了一个新的技术框架，目的是开展技术需求评估并促进技术开发和转让，包括为发展中国家的早期技术开发提供帮助。重要的是，虽然决议并未明确提及知识产权问题，但是它将"为社会和环境友好型技术的开发与转让创造有利条件并解决障碍"当作这一新框架的部分使命提了出来 [Paris Decision, supra footnote 184, para. 68 (d)]。

[227] 能力建设也被看作一个关键手段（《巴黎协定》第 11 条），因为它是准确计算和实施减缓义务的前提条件。决议建立了一个能力建设巴黎委员会，它的工作其中一项就是管理 2016—2020 年的一个旨在合理化能力建设运行的工作计划（指明差距并消除不一致和冗余）（Paris Decision, supra footnote 184, paras. 72-74）。

[228] See e. g. Art. 9 (8) of the Paris Agreement and Paris Decision, both supra footnote 184, paras. 59-60（提及了《巴黎协定》机制下的四个现有财政机制，也许还会有第五个，当前它与《京都议定书》紧密相关）。See also Article 10 (3) of the Paris Agreement and Paris Decision, para. 67 (reliance on the Technology Mechanism under the UNFCCC).

[229] 《巴黎协定》设定的市场机制引发了极大关注。See e. g. T. Jevnaker and J. Wettestad, "Linked Carbon Markets: Silver Bullets or Castle in the Air?" (2016) 6 *Climate Law* 142; A. Marcu, *Carbon Market Provisions in the Paris Agreement* (*Article* 6), Special Report, Centre for European Policy Studies (2016); M. Ranson and R. Stavins, "Linkage of greenhouse gas emissions trading systems: Learning from experience" (2015) 15 *Climate Policy* 1; J. F. Green et al, "A Balance of Bottom-Up and Top-Down in Linking Climate Policies" (2014) 4 *Nature Climate Change* 1064; C. Voigt and F. Ferreira, "The Warsaw Framework for REDD+: Implications for National Implementation and Access to Results-based Finance" (2015) 9 *Carbon and Climate Law Review* 113.

括所谓的"在发展中国家通过减少砍伐森林和减缓森林退化而降低温室气体排放并增加碳汇"（REDD-plus））,[230] 到一个将各国不同制度联结在一起的呼吁,[231] 或者一个通用的新项目机制。[232]《通过〈巴黎协定〉的决定》已经授权特设工作组来制定这些机制的运行细节，目的是达成一项类似于 2001 年《马拉喀什协议》提交给《京都议定书》的报告之类的成果。[233]

最后一个部分涉及这样一些情况，即现有信息表明，即使某个缔约方采取了多种手段来努力遵守协定规定的义务，但是它还是处于一个不遵约的状态。《巴黎协定》规定应建立一个不遵约机制，它由一个委员会管理（第 15 条第 2 款），包含了由《联合国气候变化框架公约》缔约方大会（充当《巴黎协定》缔约方会议的作用）根据一定的分配标准挑选产生的 12 名专家。[234] 重要的是，与《京都议定书》的程序不同，《巴黎协定》所设计的程序仅限于发挥促进性作用（区别于"执行"作用）。这也符合美国所坚持的约束性承诺仅适用于国内层面（以避免需要参议院的同意才能批准协定）这一立场。[235] 最后但并不是最不重要的一点是，《巴黎协定》第 24 条指出,《联合国气候变化框架公约》第 14 条中的争端解决条款经

---

[230] 所谓的"在发展中国家通过减少砍伐森林和减缓森林退化而降低温室气体排放并增加碳汇"终于在一个条约的条款中得以落地。它的运行的细节，具体来讲，非常重要的资金问题在《巴黎决议》中得以解决，supra footnote 184, para. 55。On REDD‐plus see further S. Jodoin and S. Mason‐Case, "What Difference does CBDR Make? A Socio‐Legal Analysis of the Role of Differentiation in the Transnational Legal Process for REDD+"（2016）5 *Transnational Environmental Law* 255.

[231] 一个联结的过程通常会包含一个机制承认另一个国内或国际排放交易机制下的减排单位。每个机制下的总量就会在一定程度上融合并被扩大，以确保更高效的收益。欧洲和挪威、冰岛和利希滕斯坦、加利福尼亚和魁北克之间碳排放交易机制的联结都是这样的案例。《巴黎协定》允许此种出于自愿的联结 [Paris Agreement, supra footnote 184, Art. 6（2）-（3）]。

[232] See Ibid., Art. 6（4）-（7）. 这一机制的目的是"促进温室气体排放的减缓并支持可持续发展"。这一机制在早期草案文本中被称为"可持续发展机制"（SDM），将会同时体现《京都议定书》下的联合履行（JI）和清洁发展机制（CDM）的一些特点。

[233] See supra section 5.2.2.

[234] Paris Decision, suprafootnote 184, para. 103.

[235] 参见美国国务卿克里在《巴黎协定》通过后的声明，reproduced in Wirth, supra footnote 192, p. 168（指出该协定"无须经过美国国会的批准，因为它并不包含强制性减排目标，而且它没有一个执行遵守机制"）。

过适当变通也可以适用于该协定。这一条款，为各国接受国际法院或仲裁庭的强制性司法管辖提供了可能性，但是迄今为止还从未使用过。

《巴黎协定》针对气候变化而采取的应对措施看起来似乎比较温和，但是它的作用要比绝大多数观察员实际期望的更大。另外，应当在国际层面的其他进展这一宏观背景下对其进行评估，例如前文提到的《基加利修正案》，以及 2016 年 10 月 16 日国际民航组织（International Civil Aviation Organization，ICAO）大会通过的建立一个"针对国际航空业的碳抵消和减排计划"（Carbon Offsetting and Reduction Scheme for International Aviation，CORSIA）这一重要决议。[236] 另外，甚至在《巴黎协定》之前，在国内以及区域和跨国层面也进行了很多重要的尝试。[237] 这些行动构成了《巴黎协定》真实的基础，而《巴黎协定》其实是一个协调工具，它提供了一个大框架来引导和组织各式各样的行动。事实上，与《京都议定书》和其他大量多边环境协定所采取的自上而下的方法不同，《巴黎协定》将气候政策的原动力交到各国（它们各自确定贡献力度和实现目标的政策）及其他利益相关者手中。这就为正在进行中的运动加了一把保护伞，使得这一运动目前沿着气候变化规制的真实轨迹继续前进。事实上，在制定《巴黎协定》[238] 以及当前流行的碳定价工具（碳税和排放交易机制）数年之前，就已经出现了很多法律权威意见，它们认为有必要采取行动来应对

---

[236] ICAO Assembly, Resolution 22/2 "Consolidated statement of continuing ICAO policies and practices relating to environmental protection-Global Market-Based Measure（GMBM）scheme", 6 October 2016, Doc. ICAO/A/39-WP/530, para. 5.

[237] 关于气候立法的一个数据库参见 http：//www. lse. ac. uk/GranthamInstitute/legislation/the-global-climate-legislation-database/（2017 年 4 月 17 日访问）。这一数据库源自为了起草《全球气候立法研究》年度报告而开展的早期工作，这一工作是国会议员的一个协会 GLOBE 委托的。另一个有用的数据库包含了非缔约方利益相关者（例如城市、区域、商业等）所采取的行动（虽然不是太具体），它是在秘鲁利马召开的缔约方大会上启动的，名称是针对气候行动的非国家行动者空间 [NAZCA（Non-State Actor Zone for Climate Action）]，参见 http：//climateaction. unfccc. int/（2016 年 9 月 16 日访问）。See also World Bank, *Carbon Pricing Watch* 2016（May 2016）and the previous World Bank reports on the State and Trends of Carbon Pricing.

[238] See The 2015 *Global Climate Legislation Study. Summary for Policy Makers*，它表明超过 75% 的世界排放都应受到一个经济系统的减缓目标的规制，参见 http：//www. lse. ac. uk/GranthamInstitute（2017 年 4 月 17 日访问）。

气候变化。[239] 而《巴黎协定》则是将这些分散的、各式各样的行动转变为一个全球的回应，它有利于维持和增强行动的动力。只有时间才能告诉我们，《巴黎协定》用降低国际化换来的扩张是否是一个有效的战略。

部分参考文献

[1] Aldy, J. E. and R. N. Stavins, *Post-Kyoto International Climate Policy. Implementing Architecture for Agreement* (Cambridge University Press, 2010).

[2] Bankobeza, G. M., *Ozone Protection: The International Legal Regime* (Utrecht: Eleven, 2005).

[3] Barrett, S., *Environment and Statecraft: The Strategy of Environmental Treaty-Making* (Oxford University Press, 2005).

[4] Benedick, R. E., Ozone Diplomacy: *New Directions in Safeguarding the Planet* (Cambridge MA: Harvard University Press, 1998).

[5] Bodansky, D., "The United Nations Framework Convention on Climate Change: A Commentary" (1993) 18 *Yale Journal of International Law* 451.

"The History of the Global Climate Change Regime", in U. Luterbacher and D. F. Sprinz (eds.), *International Relations and Global Climate Change* (Cambridge MA: MIT Press, 2001), pp. 23-40.

"The Paris Climate Change Agreement: A New Hope?" (2016) 110*American Journal of International Law* 288.

[6] Bodansky, D., J. Brunnee, L. Rajamani, *International Climate Change Law* (Oxford University Press, 2017).

[7] Boisson de Chazournes, L., "La gestion de l'intérêt commun à l'épreuve des enjeux économiques – Le Protocole de Kyoto sur les changements climatiques" (1997) 43 *Annuaire français de droit international* 700.

[8] Bratspies, R. and R. Miller (eds.), *Transboundary Harm in International Law. Lessons from the Trail Smelter Arbitration* (Cambridge University

---

[239] 根据世界银行的一份研究，在《巴黎协定》通过之前，已经有了约40个碳定价机制。See World Bank, *State and Trends of Carbon Pricing* 2015 (Washington, September 2015).

Press, 2006).

[9] Brunnée, J., *Acid Rain and Ozone Layer Depletion: International Law and Regulation* (Dobbs Ferry: Transnational Publishers, 1988).

[10] Bryk, D. S., "The Montreal Protocol and Recent Developments to Protect the Ozone Layer" (1991) 15 *Harvard Environmental Law Review* 275.

[11] Bulkeley, H. et al., *Transnational Climate Change Governance* (Cambridge University Press, 2014).

[12] Burkett, M., "Reading Between the Red Lines: Loss and Damage and the Paris Outcome" (2016) 6 *Climate Law* 118.

[13] Byrne, A., "The 1979 Convention on Long-Range Transboundary Air Pollution: Assessing its Effectiveness as a Multilateral Environmental Regime after 35 Years" (2015) 4 *Transnational Environmental Law* 37.

[14] Carlarne, C., K. Gray and R. Tarasofsky (eds.), *The Oxford Handbook of International Climate Change Law* (Oxford University Press, 2016).

[15] Caron, D., "La protection de la couche d'ozone stratosphérique et la structure de l'activité normative internationale en matière d'environnement" (1990) 36 *Annuaire Français de Droit International* 704.

[16] Depledge, J., "Tracing the Origins of the Kyoto Protocol: An Article-by-Article Textual History", Technical Paper, FCCC/TP/2000/2 (2000).

[17] Doumbe-Bille, S. and A. Kiss, "Conférence des Nations Unies sur l'environnement et le développement (Rio de Janeiro, June 1992)" (1992) 38 *Annuaire Français de Droit International* 823.

[18] Ellis, J., "Extraterritorial Exercise of Jurisdiction for Environmental Protection: Addressing Fairness Concerns" (2012) 25 *Leiden Journal of International Law* 397.

[19] Encinas de Munagorri, R. (ed.), *Expertise et Gouvernance du Changement Climatique* (Paris: LGDJ, 2009).

[20] Farber, D. and M. Peeters (eds.), *Climate Change Law* (Cheltenham: Edward Elgar, 2016).

[21] Flachsland, C., R. Marchinski and O. Edenhoffer, "Global

Trading versus Linking: Architectures for International Emissions Trading" (2009) 37 *Energy Policy* 1637.

[22] Freestone, D. and C. Streck, *Legal Aspects of Carbon Trading* (Oxford University Press, 2009).

[23] Gillespie, A., *Climate Change, Ozone Depletion, and Air Pollution: Legal Commentaries within the Context of Science and Policy* (Leiden: Martinus Nijhoff, 2006).

[24] Green, J. F. et al, "A Balance of Bottom-Up and Top-Down in Linking Climate Policies" (2014) 4 *Nature Climate Change* 1064.

[25] Gupta, J., *The History of Global Climate Governance* (Cambridge University Press, 2014).

[26] Haas, H., "Banning Chlorofluorocarbons: Epistemic Community Efforts to Protect Stratospheric Ozone" (1991) 46 *International Organization* 187.

[27] Hilton, I. and O. Kerr, "The Paris Agreement: China's 'New Normal' Role in International Climate Negotiations" (2016) 17, *Climate Policy* 48.

[28] Jaffe, J., M. Ranson and R. Stavins, "Linking Tradable Permit Systems: A Key Element of Emerging International Climate Policy Architecture" (2009) 36 *Ecology Law Quarterly* 789.

[29] Jevnaker, T. and J. Wettestad, "Linked Carbon Markets: Silver Bullets or Castle in the Air?" (2016) 6 *Climate Law* 142.

[30] Jodoin, S. and S. Mason-Case, "What Difference does CBDR Make? A Socio-Legal Analysis of the Role of Differentiation in the Transnational Legal Process for REDD+" (2016) 5 *Transnational Environmental Law* 255.

[31] Keohane, R. O. and D. G. Victor, "The Regime Complex for Climate Change" (2011) 9 *Perspectives on Politics* 7.

[32] Lammers, J. G. (ed.), *Transboundary Air Pollution* (Dordrecht: Martinus Nijhoff, 1986).

[33] Lang, W., "Is the Ozone Depletion Regime a Model for an Emerging Regime on Global Warming?" (1991) 9 *UCLA Journal of Environmental Law and Policy* 161.

[34] Langer, M. J., "Principle 21: The Role of Youth", in J. E.

Viñuales (ed.), *The Rio Declaration on Environment and Development. A Commentary* (Oxford University Press, 2015), pp. 519-539.

[35] Lawrence, P. M., "International Legal Regulation for Protection of the Ozone Layer: Some Problems of Implementation" (1990) 2 *Journal of Environmental Law* 17.

[36] Lode, B., P. Schönberger and P. Toussaint, "Clean Air for All by 2030? Air Quality in the 2030 Agenda and International Law" (2016) 25 *Review of European, Comparative and International Environmental Law* 27.

[37] Maljean-Dubois, S., "La mise en route du Protocole de Kyoto à la Convention-cadre des Nations Unies sur les Changements Climatiques" (2005) 51 *Annuaire français de droit international* 43.

[38] Maljean-Dubois, S. and L. Rajamani, "L' Accord de Paris sur les changements climatiques du 12 décembre 2015" (2015) 61 *Annuaire Français de Droit International* 615.

[39] Mayer, B., "Human Rights in the Paris Agreement" (2016) 6 *Climate Law* 109.

[40] Murase, S., "Protection of the Atmosphere and International Law: Rationale for Codification and Progressive Development" (2012) 55 *Sophia Law Review* 1.

[41] Nguitragool, P., *Environmental Cooperation in South-East Asia: ASEAN's Regime for Transboundary Haze Pollution* (London: Routledge, 2011).

[42] Okowa, P., *State Responsibility for Transboundary Air Pollution in International Law* (Oxford University Press, 2000).

"The Legal Framework for the Protection of the Environment Against Transboundary Air Pollution", in H. G. Post (ed.), *The Protection of Ambient Air in International and European Law* (The Hague: Eleven Publishing, 2009), pp. 53-71.

[43] Ozone Secretariat, *Handbook for the Montreal Protocol on Substances that Deplete the Ozone Layer* (UNEP, 9th edn, 2012).

Handbook for the Vienna Convention on the Protection of the Ozone Layer (UNEP, 9th edn, 2012).

Briefing Note on Exemption Mechanisms under the Montreal Protocol (4-8 April 2016).

[44] Rajamani, L., "From Berlin to Bali and Beyond: Killing Kyoto Softly?" (2008) 57 *International and Comparative Law Quarterly* 909.

"Addressing the Post-Kyoto Stress Disorder: Reflections on the Emerging Legal Architecture of the Climate Regime" (2009) 58 *International and Comparative Law Quarterly* 803.

"The Making and Unmaking of the Copenhagen Accord" (2010) 59 *International and Comparative Law Quarterly* 824.

"The Cancun Climate Change Agreements: Reading the Text, Subtext and Tealeaves" (2011) 60 *International and Comparative Law Quarterly* 499.

"The Durban Platform for Enhanced Action and the Future of the Climate Regime" (2012) 61 *International and Comparative Law Quarterly* 501.

"The 2015 Paris Agreement: Interplay between Hard, Soft and Non-Obligations" (2016) 28 *Journal of Environmental Law* 337.

[45] Roelof, J. L., "United States-Canada Air Quality Agreement: A Framework for Addressing Transboundary Air Pollution Problems" (1993) 26 *Cornell International Law Journal* 421.

[46] Rowlands, I. H., "Atmosphere and Outer Space", in D. Bodansky, J. Brunnée and E. Hey (eds.), *The Oxford Handbook of International Environmental Law* (Oxford University Press, 2007), pp. 315-336.

[47] Sand, P. H. and J. B. Wiener, "Towards a New International Law of the Atmosphere?" (2015) 7 *Göttingen Journal of International Law* 2.

[48] Skjærseth, J., "International Ozone Policies: Effective Environmental Cooperation", in E. Lerum Boasson and G. Hønneland (eds.), *International Environmental Agreements: An Introduction* (London: Routledge, 2012), pp. 38-48.

[49] Sliggers, J. and W. Kakebeeke (eds.), *Clearing the Air. 25 Years of the Convention on Long-Range Transboundary Air Pollution* (New York/Geneva: United Nations, 2004).

[50] Stabinsky, D. and J. P. Hoffmaister, "Establishing institutional arrangements on loss and damage under the UNFCCC: the Warsaw International

Mechanism for Loss and Damage" (2015) 8, *International Journal of Global Warming* 295.

[51] Tripp, J. T. B., "The UNEP Montreal Protocol: Industrialized and Developing Countries Sharing the Responsibility for Protecting the Stratospheric Ozone Layer" (1988) 20 *New York University Journal of International Law and Politics* 733.

[52] Tuinstra, W., L. Hordijk and M. Amann, "Using Computer Models in International Negotiations: The Case of Acidification in Europe" (1999) 41 *Environment* 33.

[53] Twum–Barima, R. and L. B. Campbell, *Protecting the Ozone Layers through Trade Measures: Reconciling the Trade Provisions of the Montreal Protocol and the Rules of the GATT* (Geneva: UNEP, 1994).

[54] Van Calster, G., W. Vandenberghe and L. Reins (eds.), *Research Handbook on Climate Change Mitigation Law* (Cheltenham: Edward Elgar, 2015).

[55] Victor, D. G., *The Early Operation and Effectiveness of the Montreal Protocol's Non-Compliance Procedure* (Laxenburg: IIASA, 1996).

[56] Viñuales, J. E., "El Régimen Jurídico Internacional relativo al Cambio Climático: Perspectivas y Prospectivas", in Organization of American States (OAS), *Course on International Law*, Vol. 36, 2009/2010, pp. 233–305.

"Du bon dosage du droit international: Les négociations climatiques en perspective" (2010) 56 *Annuaire français de droit international* 437.

"Legal Techniques for Dealing with Scientific Uncertainty in Environmental Law" (2010) 43 *Vanderbilt Journal of Transnational Law* 437.

"The Paris Agreement on Climate Change: Less Is More" (2016) 59 *German Yearbook of International Law* 1.

"La distribution de la charge de protéger l'environnement: Expressions juridiques de la solidarité", in A. Supiot (ed.), *La responsabilité solidaire* (Paris: Conférences du Collège de France, 2018).

[57] Voigt, C. and F. Ferreira, "The Warsaw Framework for REDD+: Implications for National Implementation and Access to Results-based Finance" (2015) 9 *Carbon and Climate Law Review* 113.

"Differentiation in the Paris Agreement" (2016) 6 *Climate Law* 58.

[58] Wara, M., "Measuring the Clean Development Mechanism's Performance and Potential" (2007) 55 *UCLA Law Review* 1759.

[59] Wirth, D., "Cracking the American Climate Negotiators' Hidden Code: United States Law and the Paris Agreement" (2016) 6 *Climate Law* 152.

[60] Yamin, F. and J. Depledge, *The International Climate Change Regime* (Cambridge University Press, 2004).

[61] Yoshida, O., *The International Legal Regime for the Protection of the Stratospheric Ozone Layer* (The Hague: Kluwer, 2001).

[62] Zahar, A., "The Paris Agreement and the Gradual Development of a Law on Climate Finance" (2016) 6 *Climate Law* 75.

第六章 物种、生态系统和生物多样性

第一节 导论

野生动物的保护是国际环境规制最早关注的问题之一。虽然随着时间的推移规制的重心已经发生了重大改变，从主要考虑经济因素转变为环境自身的保护，再逐步发展为两者的结合［通过"自然资产"（natural capital）和"生态系统服务"（ecosystem services）的方法］，这部分的规范应对的问题多种多样，例如海豹的开发、[1] 捕鲸、[2] 濒危物种贸易，[3] 对那些具有生态、文化或美学价值的物种的保护[4]，以及最近的转基因物种的越境转移、[5] 遗传资源的获取和惠益分享，[6] 这些都对国际环境法的发展造成了深刻影响。

---

[1] Convention between the United States, Great Britain, Japan and Russia Providing for the Preservation and Protection of the Fur Seals, 7 July 1911, 37 Stat. 1542, TS 564.

[2] Convention for the Regulation of Whaling, 24 September 1931, available at: www.ecolex.org (no. TRE-000073); International Convention for the Regulation of Whaling, 2 December 1946, 161 UNTS 72 ("Whaling Convention"); Convention on the Conservation of Migratory Species of Wild Animals, 23 June 1979, available at: www.ecolex.org (no. TRE-000495).

[3] Convention on International Trade in Endangered Species of Wild Fauna and Flora, 3 March 1973, United Nations, 993 UNTS 243 ("CITES").

[4] Convention on Wetlands of International Importance especially as Waterfowl Habitat, 2 February 1971, 996 UNTS 245 ("Ramsar Convention"); Convention Concerning the Protection of the World Cultural and Natural Heritage, 23 November 1972, 1037 UNTS 151 ("WHC").

[5] Cartagena Protocol on Biosafety to the Convention on Biological Diversity, 29 January 2000, 2226 UNTS 208 ("Biosafety Protocol").

[6] The Nagoya Protocol on Access to Genetic Resources and the Fair and Equitable Sharing of Benefits Arising from their Utilization to the Convention on Biological Diversity, 29 October 2012, available at: www.ecolex.org (TRE-155959) ("Nagoya Protocol").

因为针对动植物保护的国际法律文本的数量和种类繁多,[7] 所以想要尝试抓住这一规制领域的轴心是颇具挑战性的。在20世纪80年代早期,联合国大会试图以《世界自然宪章》的通过来为这一系列文件提供一个纲领。[8] 这一文件不具有法律约束力,而且它强烈的保护主义色彩对实现初衷而言被证明是一个障碍而非一个优点。在20世纪80年代,基于同一目的的其他尝试也时有发生。值得一提的是联合国环境规划署在1987年开始研究在此领域制定一个框架公约的可行性。[9] 1988年11月,这项工作被授权给一个生物多样性专家委员会,该委员会在1991年2月成为政府间谈判委员会并制定了《生物多样性公约》,提交给1992年6月的里约峰会签署。[10] 虽然《生物多样性公约》在技术层面上并不是一个框架公约,但是它还是将其他主要条约和公约的一些工作组合进了"生物多样性集群"。[11]

从特定物种保护的早期公约开始,直到《生物多样性公约》的通过及其后续进展,国际环境法的发展轨迹可以通过参考所规制客体的复杂程度来进行分析。这些客体起初是物种,或者更通俗地讲,是某个特定区域的植物和动物。[12] 随着对生态进程的认识不断深入,规制的重点转移到了

---

[7] See generally M. Bowman, P. Davies and C. Redgwell, *Lyster's International Wildlife Law* (Cambridge University Press, 2nd edn, 2010).

[8] World Charter for Nature, 28 October 1982, UN Doc. A/RES/37/7. See H. W. Wood, "The United Nations World Charter for Nature: The Developing Nations' Initiative to Establish Protections for the Environment" (1984/1985) 12 *Ecology Law Quarterly* 977.

[9] See Governing Council of UNEP, Res. 14/26 (1987).

[10] Convention on Biological Diversity, 5 June 1992, 1760 UNTS 79 ("CBD"). On the developments that led to the adoption of the CBD, see L. Glowka, F. Burhenne-Guilmin, H. Synge, J. A. McNeely and L. Gundling, *Guide de la Convention sur la Diversité Biologique* (Gland: IUCN, 1996), pp. 2ff.

[11] See G. Futhazar, "The Diffusion of the Strategic Plan for Biodiversity and its Aichi Biodiversity Targets within the Biodiversity Cluster: An Illustration of Current Trends in the Global Governance of Biodiversity and Ecosystems" (2015) 25 *Yearbook of International Environmental Law* 133.

[12] See Convention on Nature Protection and Wild Life Preservation in the Western Hemisphere, 12 October 1940, 56 Stat 1354 ("Western Hemisphere Convention"); African Convention on the Conservation of Nature and Natural Resources, 15 September 1968, amended 11 July 2003, 1001 UNTS 3 ("African Conservation Convention"), available at: www.ecolex.org (TRE-001395); Convention on the Conservation of European Wildlife and Natural Habitats, 19 September 1979, ETS No 104 ("Bern Convention"); ASEAN Agreement on the Conservation of Nature and Natural Resources, 9 July 1985, 15 EPL 64 ("Kuala Lumpur Agreement"); Convention on the Conservation of Nature in the South Pacific, 12 June 1976, available at: www.ecolex.org (TRE-000540) ("Apia Convention"); Protocol to the Antarctic Treaty on Environmental Protection, 4 October 1991, 30 ILM 1455 ("Madrid Protocol").

这些物种的环境,或者更具体地讲,它们的栖息地,[13] 或者不同物种复杂的交互作用而形成的生态系统。[14] 最终,国际规制的重点转变为物种内的、物种之间的以及生态系统之间的可变性,或者换言之,生物多样性[15]以及它蕴含的生物和遗传资源。[16]

前文所述的物种、空间和生物多样性之间的区别,虽然存在过分简单化的风险,但是还是为我们分析国际环境法在此领域的主轴提供了一个有用的基础。在本章中,在考察不同文件尝试的多种方法之后,我们分析了针对物种、空间和生物多样性的国际保护,焦点是那些为这一领域设计的日益复杂的规制手段。

第二节 规制方法

长期以来,法律客体的多样性导致规制它们的方法也是各种各样的。在各种方法中,有三种方法应当引起重视:(1)资源开发的规制;(2)空间的保护;(3)特定物种的贸易规制。[17]

这每一种方法都是基于不同考量,它们都依次表述了一个由来已久的等式,即反对资源的营利性利用(或者用当今的术语表述就是"开发"或"增长")就等于是环境保护。广义来讲,第一种和第三种方法更注重反对资源的营利性利用,而第二种方法则更注重环境保护。当然,经过进一步审视,我们可以找出更多的细微差别。举例来讲,1946年《捕鲸公约》这样一个资源开发制度起初是将经济考量置于保护之前,但是后来也变得极具保护性。这一转变源于一种具体规制手段——暂停——的运

---

13 最早采用这一方法的文件之一是《拉姆萨公约》,这一条约后来被重新解释为是体现了一种生态系统的方法。

14 第一个明确采用这一方法的文件是《南极海洋生物资源保护公约》[Convention on the Conservation of Antarctic Marine Living Resources, 20 May 1980, 1329 UNTS 47 ("CCAMLR")]. See further V. De Lucia, "Competing Narratives and Complex Genealogies: The Ecosystem Approach in International Environmental Law" (2015) 27 *Journal of Environmental Law* 91.

15 See CBD, supra footnote 10, Art. 2, para. 5.

16 Ibid., Art. 2, paras. 13–14.

17 See R. Rayfuse, "Biological Resources", in D. Bodansky, J. Brunnée and E. Hey (eds.), *The Oxford Handbook of International Environmental Law* (Oxford University Press, 2007), pp. 362–93, 374ff.

用，即中止作为商业活动的捕鲸以促进鲸鱼的保护。[18] 我们在讨论中提及"方法""考量"和"规制手段"的目的是提供一个宽泛的概念图表，在我们分析繁杂的具体规范和文件时可以参考这一宏观背景。

资源开发作为一种方法，它的特性可以从多个方面来分析：它针对的是那些由两国或多国共享的资源，或者是位于公地的资源（与此相反的是，全部都在一国管辖下的资源则归属于该国的主权和主权权利）；它涉及的是某种特定资源的分配或者某一濒危资源的保护；它通常是在资源开发已经开始时介入；它有时会呈现出一个对资源管理的肤浅认识，因为它并不一定考虑到资源与其系统的相互作用。[19] 实施这一方法的法律手段包括设定开发配额（采用物种、国家、区域、渔船数量等形式），规定何种方式和技术可用于资源开发，对这些活动可以开展的时间段和区域进行限制，[20] 针对遗传资源的获取及惠益分享达成协议，以及其他许多手段。

空间保护作为一种规制方法，它体现了对某个或多个物种与其生态系统的相互作用的一个更完整的认识。但是，这个"空间"的定义可能会面临挑战，因为"地点""栖息地"和"生态系统"这些概念之间存在重大区别。一个"地点"本身就可能受到保护，即使不考虑到它在某种或多种植物和动物上的价值。例如，这适用于受《世界遗产公约》（*World Heritage Convention*）保护的文化遗产以及一些自然遗产。[21] 从法律的视角看，"栖息地"是一个很难定义的概念。它可以指保全特定物种或保护某一物种在特定地理位置的一个特定种群所必需的条件。虽然这些条件一般是根据某一群物种、某一物种或种群来确定，但是它们也可以用更通用的方式来定性。《拉姆萨公约》之所以将那些受保护的湿地纳入"拉姆萨名录"，不仅是把它们当作水鸟的栖息地，还考虑到了它们的"生态学、植物学、动物学、湖沼学或水文学方面"。[22] 因此这些湿地是同时被当作地点和栖息地来保护。"生态系统"这一概念则更为复杂，它超出了

---

[18] See Bowman et al., supra footnote 7, pp. 165ff.

[19] Rayfuse, supra footnote 17, pp. 374ff.

[20] See K. M. Wyman, "The Property Rights Challenge in Marine Fisheries" (2008) 50 *Arizona Law Review* 511.

[21] WHC, supra footnote 4, Art. 1. 当然，也可以主张这一保护是基于这类地点对人类的价值。

[22] Ramsar Convention, supra footnote 4, Arts. 1 and 2 (2).

一个或多个特定物种的范畴而试图涵盖一个更宽泛的功能区——植物、动物和微生物群落和它们的无生命环境作为一个生态单位交互作用形成的一个动态复合体。[23] 地理的术语和功能的术语都可用于定义受保护的生态系统的轮廓,正如《南极海洋生物资源保护公约》第1条所述。[24] 用于实施这一方法的法律手段是多种多样的,但是特别重要的是建立保护区以及其他一些辅助手段,例如建立缓冲区或者开展环境影响评价和监测。[25] 公众参与或自下而上的方法也偶尔被使用,特别是涉及后文谈及的荒漠化问题时。[26]

最后,针对物种或资源的贸易规制可以被看成一个减少它们的开发的办法,也可以用于预防外来物种(或者有能力扰乱某一生态系统平衡的物种)入侵所导致的风险。[27] 这种方法与以上两种方法的不同之处在于它为了实现政策目标采取了不同的法律手段,即限制出口[28]或进口那些受规制物种标本或某些品种的有机物(即转基因生物)。[29]

正如本章后文所述,规制方法的选择在很大程度上取决于规制的客体。"资源"或"物种"通常是采用第一种和第三种方法,而第二种方法则更适用于"地点""栖息地"和"生态系统"的规制。图6-1为本章涉及的主要内容提供了一个概览。正如《生物多样性公约》以及正在进行中的国家管辖范围外区域生物多样性谈判显示的那样,各种规制办法和手段有时候会被联合用于一项单一的法律制度,以便应对客体的复杂性或者充分考虑到资源/物种保护与地点/栖息地保护之间的紧密关系。

---

[23] CBD, supra footnote 10, Art. 2, para. 6.

[24] See CCAMLR, supra footnote 14, Art. 1.

[25] See A. Gillespie, "The Management of Protected Areas of International Significance" (2006) 10 *New Zealand Journal of Environmental Law* 93.

[26] See United Nations Convention to Combat Desertification in those Countries Experiencing Serious Drought and/or Desertification, Particularly in Africa, 17 June 1994, 1954 UNTS 3 ("Convention to Combat Desertification" or "UNCCD"), Art. 10 (2) (f).

[27] Rayfuse, supra footnote 17, pp. 384ff.

[28] See WTO/CTE, Matrix on Trade Measures pursuant to Selected Multilateral Environmental Agreements, 14 March 2007, WT/CTE/W/160/Rev. 4, TN/TE/S/5/Rev. 2, Section II. More specifically, see CITES, supra footnote 3, Art. III.

[29] Cartagena Protocol, supra footnote 5.

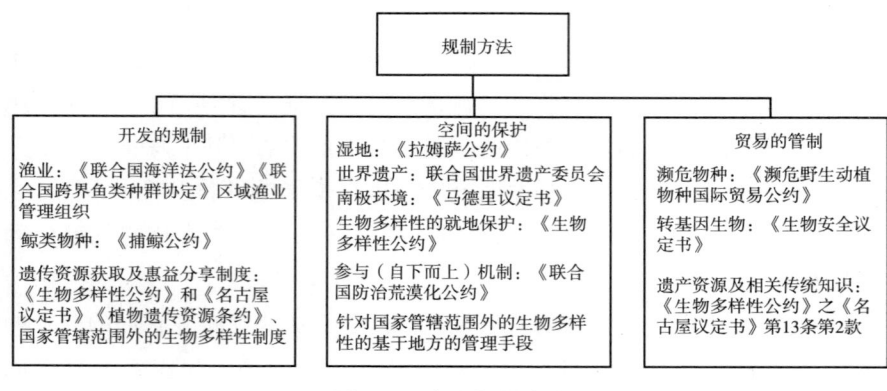

```
                           规制方法
         ┌─────────────────┼─────────────────┐
     开发的规制          空间的保护          贸易的管制
 渔业：《联合国海洋法公约》《  湿地：《拉姆萨公约》       濒危物种：《濒危野生动植
 联合国跨界鱼类种群协定》区域渔业 世界遗产：联合国世界遗产委员会  物种国际贸易公约》
 管理组织               南极环境：《马德里议定书》    转基因生物：《生物安全议
 鲸类物种：《捕鲸公约》      生物多样性的就地保护：《生物  定书》
 遗传资源获取及惠益分享制度：   多样性公约》           遗产资源及相关传统知识：
 《生物多样性公约》和《名古屋   参与（自下而上）机制：《联   《生物多样性公约》之《名
 议定书》《植物遗传资源条约》、  合国防治荒漠化公约》      古屋议定书》第13条第2款
 国家管辖范围外的生物多样性制度  针对国家管辖范围外的生物多样
                     性的基于地方的管理手段
```

图 6-1　广义规制方法

第三节　物种的保护

一　开发的规制：渔业

在实践中渔业管理是一个非常重要的问题，不仅是因为它所涉及的数量（仅水产养殖市场在 2014 年的价值就高达约一千六百亿美元[30]），还在于某些资源的耗尽甚至某些物种的灭绝这类重大风险。《2030 年可持续发展议程》在其第 14 个目标的第 4 个和第 6 个子目标中回顾了这一风险，并特别强调有必要在 2020 年之前结束过度捕捞和其他有害实践，[31] 这看起来雄心勃勃。

关于目标和规制方法的一些区别，还是有必要做出说明。关于前者，渔业管理历史上一直被当作商用资源保护的一个主要例证。但是，近期以来，受规制的客体不再仅仅被看成一种"资源"，它还被当作一种需要保护的"物种"。相关的规制方法经历了三个过程的演进：

---

[30] Food and Agriculture Organization, *The State of World Fisheries and Aquaculture* 2016, part I, 5.

[31] Resolution 70/1, "Transforming our World：The 2030 Agenda for Sustainable Development", 21 October 2015, UN doc A/RES/70/1, including the statement of 17 Sustainable Development Goals ("SDGs"), each with several targets. See specifically targets 14.4 and 14.6 under SDG 14.

(1) 所有国家在海域（除了被认定为沿海国领海的海峡以外）都可以自由捕捞；(2) 创立那些被延伸的管辖区域（领海和专属经济区），在此区域内沿海国行使开发的主权或主权权利同时负有管理义务；(3) 逐步增强在国家管辖范围以外地区的资源利用和保护上的制度化合作，特别是通过区域渔业管理组织（Regional Fisheries Management Organisations, RFMOs）。今天，渔业管理的结构依赖于多个综合性文件，特别是 1982 年《联合国海洋法公约》、[32] 1995 年《联合国跨界鱼类种群协定》、[33] 其他三个在世界粮农组织框架下制定的文件，[34] 以及大量的国际、区域和双边渔业协定。[35]

当然，演进到当前结构的发展轨迹并不是直线型的。在制定《联合国海洋法公约》之前，已经建立了多个区域渔业管理组织。但是，我们可以发现所追求目标（越来越关注环境要素）与资源开发规制通常所采取手段之间的一个特定交集，一些体制的发展可以说明这一点，例如《捕鲸公约》和西北大西洋渔业组织（Northwest Atlantic Fisheries Organization, NAFO）。[36]

在我们讨论渔业管理的一般框架时将要强调的就是这样一种发展轨

---

[32] United Nations Convention on the Law of the Sea, 10 December 1982, 1833 UNTS 397 ("UNCLOS").

[33] Agreement for the Implementation of the Provisions of the United Nations Convention on the Law of the Sea of 10 December 1982 relating to the Conservation and Management of Straddling Fish Stocks and Highly Migratory Fish Stocks, 4 August 1995, 2167 UNTS 88 ("Straddling Fish Stocks Agreement").

[34] These include the Agreement to Promote Compliance with International Conservation and Management Measures by Vessels on the High Seas, 24 November 1993, 2221 UNTS 91; the Code of Conduct for Responsible Fisheries adopted on 31 October 1995, available at: www.fao.org (visited on 2 April 2017); and the Agreement on Port State Measures to Prevent, Deter and Eliminate Illegal, Unreported and Unregulated Fishing, 22 November 2009, [2010] ATNIF 41. On the role of the FAO see J. Harrison, *Making the Law of the Sea* (Cambridge University Press, 2011), chapter 7.

[35] For an overview see D. Freestone, "Fisheries Commissions and Organizations" (2010) *Max Planck Encyclopedia of Public International Law*, available at: http://opil.ouplaw.com (visited on 4 April 2017).

[36] Convention on Future Multilateral Cooperation on Northwest Atlantic Fisheries, 24 October 1978, available at: www.nafo.int ("NAFO").

迹，这些框架包括 1995 年《联合国跨界鱼类种群协定》[37] 以及两个具体的体制化合作，即西北大西洋渔业组织和《捕鲸公约》。

（一）《联合国海洋法公约》

第四章已经介绍了调整涉及海域的国家权利和义务的一般框架。但是，为了更好地理解渔业问题以及那些适用于这些海域的生物资源的制度，就有必要介绍另外两个问题。

第一个问题是关于这些资源的位置。根据预估，90%的商业开发渔业资源是位于基准线 200 海里之内，这一片海域是被领海和专属经济区环绕。[38] 根据《联合国海洋法公约》第 61 条第 1 款，沿海国"应决定其专属经济区内生物资源的可捕量"。这一条款从而就规定了"通过正当的养护和管理措施，确保专属经济区内生物资源的维持不受过度开发的危害"这一义务。[39] 这一义务可以被分为三个组成部分：（1）限制采取单边行动［通过规定有义务与胜任的国际组织（不论是分区域、区域或全球性组织）合作，[40] 并"考虑到捕捞方式、种群的相互依存以及任何通用的国际最低标准（不论是分区域、区域或全球性的）"[41]］；（2）最低存量（措施应"使捕捞鱼种的数量维持在或恢复到能够生产最高持续产量的水平，并考虑到与所捕捞鱼种有关联或依赖该鱼种才能生存的鱼种所受的影响"[42]）；（3）有一个非对抗的争端解决机制，即通过调解而不是司法手段，除非沿海国同意采用司法手段。[43] 国际海洋法法庭在 2015 年提交的一份咨询意见中已经详细说明了这一义务的前两个组成部分。[44] 提交给法庭的其中一个问题是关于分区域渔业委员会（Sub-Regional Fisheries Commission）中沿海国涉及共享鱼种的可持续管理的权利和义务。国际海洋

---

[37] Agreement for the Implementation of the Provisions of the United Nations Convention on the Law of the Sea of 10 December 1982 relating to the Conservation and Management of Straddling Fish Stocks and Highly Migratory Fish Stocks, 4 August 1995, 2167 UNTS 88 ("Straddling Fish Stocks Agreement").

[38] Bowman et al., supra footnote 7, p. 125.

[39] UNCLOS, supra footnote 32, Art. 61 (2).

[40] Ibid., Art. 61 (2) infine and (5).

[41] Ibid., Art. 61 (3) infine (emphasis added).

[42] Ibid., Art. 61 (3) - (4) (emphasis added) and 62.

[43] Ibid., Art. 297 (3).

[44] Request for an Advisory Opinion Submitted by the Sub-Regional Fisheries Commission (SRFC), Advisory Opinion of 2 April 2015, ITLOS Case No. 21.

法法庭将"可持续管理"这一术语等同于《联合国海洋法公约》第 63 条下的"种群的养护和发展",并依据第 61 条、第 63 条第 1—2 款和第 64 条第 1 款判定沿海国有义务(本质是谨慎注意义务或行为义务)开展合作并基于最佳科学证据(在其缺位的情况下则是基于风险预防的方法)来采取保护措施。[45]

这一咨询意见对第二个问题同样重要。除了沿海国的义务,根据《联合国海洋法公约》有关渔业的规定,船旗国——不论是在他国专属经济区还是在公海捕捞——也负有特定义务。虽然专属经济区生物资源的保护和保全的主要义务应由沿海国承担,但是这并没有解除其他国家(船旗国)在这一问题上的义务。[46] 这些不仅源自船旗国在他国专属经济区进行捕捞所应承担义务的具体条款,即第 58 条第 3 款和第 62 条第 4 款,还来自那些适用于所有海域的所有国家的通用条款,即《联合国海洋法公约》第 91 条、第 92 条、第 94 条、第 192 条、第 193 条。[47] 这两套义务都应被理解为要求的是"谨慎注意义务"而非一个具体结果。[48] 在其他背景下,谨慎注意义务的履行包含了适当的规制措施的制定以及它们的恰当执行。这就是国际海洋法法庭针对那些在某国注册的船只在他国专属经济区进行非法、未受控制的、未报告的捕捞所得出的结论。一般来讲,第七部分(第 2 节)表述的在公海可以自由捕捞这一原则[49]应受到一个保护框架(与第 61 条的规定非常类似)的约束。保全义务适用于所有国家(不仅是沿海国)。[50] 各国也有义务开展合作,包括通过区域或分区域渔业组织,[51] 而且它们必须要考虑到最小存量要求(类似于第 61 条的规定)。[52] 因此,我们可以得出结论,《联合国海洋法公约》制定的框架明确规定了

45　Ibid., paras. 207-210. It must be noted that the precautionary approach was derived from the specific regional agreement applicable *in casu*. The tribunal limited its analysis to the States parties to the SRFC but it suggested that it was relevant for other States as well (paras. 214-215).

46　Ibid., para. 108.

47　Ibid., para. 111.

48　Ibid., paras. 125, 129.

49　UNCLOS, supra footnote 32, Art. 87 (1) (e).

50　Ibid., Art. 117.

51　Ibid., Art. 118.

52　Ibid., Art. 119.

合作这一要求。这种合作的形式也是多种多样的。在某些情况下，针对特定物种或者特定区域已经有了一些早先存在的文件，例如《捕鲸公约》就属于特定物种这种情况，而西北大西洋渔业组织则属于特定区域这种情况。在其他情况下，一些新的文件也被制定，例如《联合国跨界鱼类种群协定》。[53]

（二）《联合国跨界鱼类种群协定》

这一协定对举例说明前述问题特别重要，[54] 因为它在《联合国海洋法公约》制度与区域渔业管理组织有关专属经济区以外的渔业管理之间建立了一个特别联系。另外，为了与里约大会的进展保持一致，协定针对渔业管理制定了一种风险预防和生态系统方法。[55] 这一协定的核心在于它建立的合作和实施机制，首先，是通过鼓励沿海国和船旗国之间的合作，特别是通过区域渔业管理组织（首选机制）来开展合作；其次，如果这样的合作没有落实，就会制定一个辅助的合作和实施机制。为了理解它的运作，我们将简要讨论为合作和实施而建立的（首选和辅助的）合作机制和（首选和辅助的）实施机制。

关于合作，首选机制的目标是增强区域渔业管理组织。[56] 在这一问题上，第8条第3款显得尤其重要。它要求协定各缔约国必须加入相关的区域渔业管理组织（同时要求区域渔业管理组织，或者更精确一点，要求那些也是协定缔约方的缔约国接受如此安排，即只要某国有一个真实的兴趣，即使它不大可能成为一个成员，也应接受它的尝试），或者换一种方式，运用该组织制定的保护和管理措施。另外，第8条第4款规定，只有那些遵守第8条第3款所规定义务的国家才有资格获取相关渔业资源。人们也许会问，这一要求是否仅仅涉及《联合国跨界鱼类种群协定》的缔约国，抑或还包含了其他国家。第17条表明，依据排斥他人行为原则（res inter alios acta principle），只有缔约国才受到这一禁令的约束。[57] 但是，这一条款的措辞也可以被宽泛解释为它不仅指协定中的保护义务，同

53　Other instruments have also been adopted. See Bowman et al., supra footnote 7, pp. 134–135.

54　See Harrison, supra footnote 34, pp. 99–113.

55　Straddling Fish Stocks Agreement, supra footnote 33, Art. 5 (c) – (e) and 6.

56　Ibid., Art. 8 (1) – (2). The reinforcement objective is expressly provided for in Article 13 of the Agreement.

57　Ibid., Art. 17 (1).

时还包含了《联合国海洋法公约》规定的那些义务（部分义务在本质上属于习惯法）。[58] 在没有区域渔业管理组织的情况下，辅助机制就会发生作用。但是，这一机制只是一个宏观上的表达。协定的各缔约国都有义务开展合作以便创建一个组织或做出类似安排（必须具备特定基本内容）。[59]

关于履约的问题，首选机制在捕捞船舶的船旗国[60]和其他国家之间分配了权力，[61] 它必须确保各国履行相关区域渔业管理组织制定的保护和管理措施。第 21 条第 1 款还特别规定，区域渔业管理组织的任一缔约国（通常是最近的沿海国）都可以在公海上登船并检查某只悬挂他国（特指《联合国跨界鱼类种群协定》缔约国）国旗的船只，即使该缔约国并非是这一区域渔业管理组织的成员。在区域渔业管理组织没有制定登船和检查程序的情况下，第 22 条规定了"基本程序"这样一个辅助机制。我们会发现，《联合国跨界鱼类种群协定》所建立的框架高度依赖于区域渔业管理组织的存在或其他具体安排。在后文中，我们将分析这类体制的两个主要案例。

（三）西北大西洋渔业组织

第一个案例是西北大西洋渔业组织，这一区域渔业管理组织成立于 1978 年，它的萌芽早在 1949 年就开始显现。它可以充当一个有意义的案例来举例说明一个区域渔业管理组织在保护、管理和履约领域是如何运作的，而且它有助于更好地理解《联合国跨界鱼类种群协定》所设计的区域渔业管理组织与《联合国海洋法公约》之间的关系。

西北大西洋渔业组织拥有各种机构，包括一个渔业委员会，它负责制定保护和管理措施，包括特定种群的捕捞配额。[62] 委员会所制定的措施具有约束力，并对每个缔约国同时生效，除非有缔约国根据第 12 条第 1 款提出了"反对"。对这些反对的频繁运用给这一制度的正当运行造成了困难。[63] 例如，1995 年 3 月，因为欧洲反对委员会制定的某些捕捞配额，导致加拿大登上了西班牙的"埃斯泰"号船，这条船当时在加拿大专属经

58　See Chapter 4.

59　Straddling Fish Stocks Agreement, supra footnote 33, Art. 8（5）-（6）and 9.

60　Ibid., Art. 19.

61　Ibid., Arts. 20 and 21.

62　NAFO, supra footnote 36, Art. XI.

63　Bowman et al, supra n footnote 7, p. 137.

济区的外围进行捕捞作业。这一事件导致西班牙到国际法院针对加拿大提起了一个诉讼。[64] 它也为《联合国跨界鱼类种群协定》的尽早通过施加了一个紧迫感,因为协定早在两年前就已经开始谈判了。

基于风险预防理念和生态系统方法而达成的这一协定后来影响了西北大西洋渔业组织的运行。实际上,2005—2007 年,在西北大西洋渔业组织内部开展了一个改革进程,并导致其构成条约的修订。这一修正案目前尚未开始生效,[65] 在第 16 条第 5 款中针对那些已经提交了反对的国家增加了一项义务,要求它们必须提供一个解释并陈述它们为了保护和管理相关渔业资源而计划采取的替代措施。

(四)《捕鲸公约》

第二个案例是《捕鲸公约》。在经历了 1931 年和 1937 年的两次早期尝试之后,《捕鲸公约》在 1946 年得以通过。[66]

起初,公约针对鲸鱼的开发建立了一套制度,这套制度不仅可以巩固早先的规范,而且可以根据后续的发展需要来修订这些规范。实质性条款其实是出现于公约的"日程表"中而非公约正式文本中。与现代多边环境协定相似,国际捕鲸委员会(International Whaling Commission,IWC)可以凭借 3/4 多数表决通过(第 3 条第 2 款)来对这个日程表进行不定期的修订,目的是将科学及其他因素考虑在内(第 5 条第 2 款)。通过后的修正案将对所有国家都具有约束力,除了那些依据公约第 5 条第 3 款提起反对的国家。

1982 年,一项暂停令中止了商业用途的捕鲸。从技术立场来看,这个中止令采取的方式是修订公约日程表的第 10 段第 5 点,它规定:

> 从 1986 年滨海季节以及 1985/1986 年远洋季节开始,为了商业用途宰杀所有种群的鲸鱼的捕捞配额应当为零。这一条款将会依据最佳科学建议来接受评估。

64　*Fisheries Jurisdiction（Spain v. Canada）*, Judgment, ICJ Reports 1998, p. 432.

65　截至 2016 年,只有七个国家(加拿大、古巴、丹麦、欧盟、冰岛、挪威和俄罗斯)批准了这一修正案。它需要至少 3/4 的缔约方的批准才能开始生效。See: NAFO, supra footnote 36, Art. XXI.

66　Whaling Convention, supra footnote 2. For a comprehensive and up-to-date study see M. Fitzmaurice, *Whaling and International Law*（Cambridge University Press, 2015).

这一有争议的修订深刻影响了《捕鲸公约》的方法，它使得公约成为一个真正的保护性文件，而不是为了迎合一个产业的繁荣。在 Patricia Birnie 提出的极具创造性的术语中，这一制度已经从"捕鲸的保护"转变为"鲸鱼的保护"。[67] 一些国家，特别是日本，对此持保留态度。日本起初提起反对，但是后来迫于美国的压力将它撤回。[68] 但是，日本已经启动了一系列涉及鲸鱼捕捞的项目（日本鲸类研究项目1、项目2），日本认为这些项目是为了科研用途而不是商业用途，因此根据公约第8条第1款可以获得批准。

这些项目的真实目的一直以来都是争议的焦点，并导致澳大利亚在国际法院提起了一个针对日本的诉讼，起诉其违反了《捕鲸公约》。在法院2014年的判决中，法院支持了澳大利亚的主张，得出结论认为日本鲸类研究项目2并不属于公约第8条第1款规定的研究豁免范围，导致的结果是，该项目下开展的捕鲸活动违反了日程表第10段第5点。[69]

二 贸易的规制：《濒危野生动植物种国际贸易公约》

（一）《濒危野生动植物种国际贸易公约》的框架

通过人为减少资源的需求来间接规制一个或多个物种的开发，是《濒危野生动植物种国际贸易公约》（通常简称为 CITES）所采用的方法。[70]这一文件的重要性体现在几个方面。第一，野生动物物种的国际贸易数以百亿美元计。第二，CITES 已经相当成功地实现了保护濒危物种的既

---

67 See P. Birnie, *International Regulation of Whaling: From Conservation of Whaling to Conservation of Whales and Regulation of Whale Watching*, 2 vols. (Oceana Publications, 1985).

68 1984年，联合国警告日本，如果日本继续无视商业捕鲸这一禁令，那么依据所谓的 Pelly 修正案和 Packwood-Magnuson 修正案它可能会面临贸易限制。这就导致日本撤回了反对意见并承诺在1987年之前停止商业捕鲸。See "US Sanctions against Japan for Whaling" (2001) 95 *American Journal of International Law* 149.

69 *Whaling in the Antarctic (Australia v. Japan: New Zealand intervening)*, Judgment, ICJ Reports 2014, p. 226.

70 CITES, supra footnote 3. On CITES see W. Wijnstekers, *L'évolution de la CITES* (Budakeszi: CIC, 9th edn, 2011); Bowman et al., supra footnote 7, Chapter 15.

定目标。[71] 第三，同样地，CITES 制度的有效性有力促成了多个尝试，这些尝试试图将这一制度延伸至其他一些物种（例如金枪鱼），这些物种由更具体但更低效的制度进行规制。[72] 第四，CITES 是一种规制手段普遍化的生动例证，这种手段被频繁运用于国际环境法中并被称为"名录方法"。为了理解 CITES 的基本结构，有必要对这一手段进行特征描述。图 6-2 展示了它的核心内容。

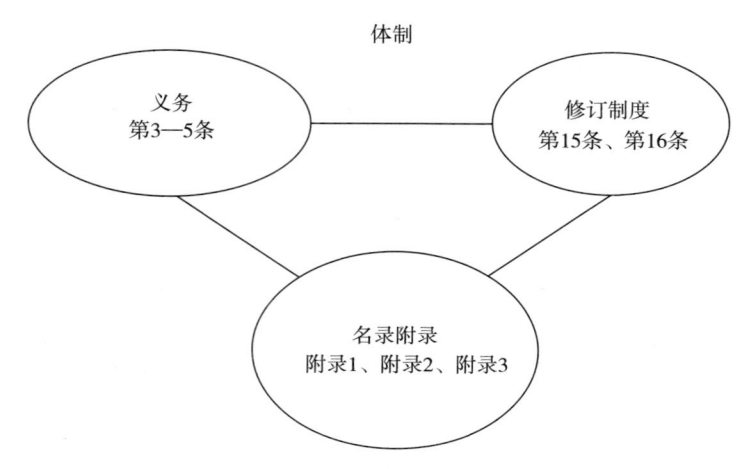

```
              体制

        义务              修订制度
       第3—5条           第15条、第16条


              名录附录
           附录1、附录2、附录3
```

图 6-2 《濒危野生动植物种国际贸易公约》以及名录方法

这一图所描述的结构其实很简单。条约规定的义务适用于特定物种和空间（或者其他一种客体，例如物质），它们通常都会在条约的一个附录中被列举出来。名录修订制度允许更新名录以便反映出某一具体问题的深化认识和实际情况。通过不同渠道，例如针对不同物种或空间制定不同的名录和义务，可以使这一基本结构变得更为复杂。另外，修订制度通常会让各国有机会去反对将某一特定物种或空间收入名录。虽然名录方法看似

---

[71] 但是有些作者认为《濒危野生动植物种国际贸易公约》从事的是一个衰退的趋势。See O. R. Young, "Effectiveness of International Environmental Regimes: Existing Knowledge, Cutting-Edge Themes, and Research Strategies" (2011) 108 *Proceedings of the National Academy of Sciences* 19853.

[72] 在 2010 年大会上，摩纳哥提议将蓝鳍金枪鱼列入《濒危野生动植物种国际贸易公约》附录一，但是没有成功，原因是遭到了多个国家的反对（主要是日本和加拿大），这些国家认为区域性渔业管理组织［例如大西洋金枪鱼保育委员会［International Commission for the Conservation of Atlantic Tunas（"ICCAT"）］已经是一个适当的安排。但是，必须指出的是，大西洋金枪鱼保育委员会在预防这一鱼种的过度捕捞上显得毫无能力。

简单，但是它的三个组成部分有助于我们去掌控多个环境条约（包括CITES）的基本架构。

到 2017 年 4 月，这一条约已经有 183 个缔约方，它分别在附录一、附录二和附录三中拥有三个名录。各个附录名录中物种标本贸易[73]的相关义务是不尽相同的。附录一列举的物种（超过 600 种动物物种和 300 种植物物种被列为"濒危"物种）除了几个例外之外基本是被禁止进行贸易的，[74] 而附录二列举的物种（约 4800 种动物物种和近 30000 种植物物种的贸易如果不受规制，它们将可能成为濒危物种）贸易则是被允许的，但是必须受到严格的管控。[75] 针对附录三列举的物种（由某个缔约方单边规制的 135 种动物物种和 12 种植物物种），CITES 建立了一个制度来促进其他国家对这一单边规制提供支持。[76] 这一名录修订制度受到了严格的管控（第 15 条和第 16 条）并包含了解除保护的可能性（第 15 条第 3 款、第 16 条第 2 款和第 23 条）。CITES 这一基本结构得到了一个体制和一套实施制度的补充，[77] 它们的一个重要内容就是规制那些与 CITES 非缔约方进行的贸易。[78] 但是，CITES 的基石是它的出口/进口许可制度。

（二）许可制度

为了理解这一制度，我们必须审视它的五个组成部分。第一个组成部分是，颁发许可所需的严格要求是由相关物种受到的威胁造成的。附录一列举的物种标本的贸易[79]只有在例外情况下才会被许可。它不仅需要进口国颁发的许可［基于管理的考量（即标本不得用于"主要为商业用途"

---

73 公约第 1 条对贸易、物种和标本这些术语做出了广义的定义。某一物种的标本可以是：（1）任何活的或死的动物或植物；（2）动物或植物的任何可辨认的部分；（3）动物或植物衍生物的任何可辨认的部分。贸易不仅包含了进口和出口，还包含了"再出口"（原先进口的任何标本的出口）以及"从海上引进"（从公海取得的标本输入某个国家）。针对每一种类所需的许可类型做出了特定调整。

74　Ibid., Art. III.

75　Ibid., Art. IV.

76　Ibid., Art. V.

77　See infra Chapter 9.

78　CITES, supra footnote 3, Art. X. See also infra Chapter 12.

79　See Wijnstekers, supra footnote 70, Chapter 10.

的用途）和生态的考量（贸易是否会对物种的生存造成影响）]，[80] 还需要出口国颁发的另一个许可（同样是基于管理的考量，例如标本的获取是否合法，以及生态的考量）。[81] 与此不同的是，附录二列举的物种标本的贸易[82]只需要一个出口许可（基于管理和生态的考量）。[83] 针对附录2列举的物种标本，[84] 一个基于管理的考量的出口许可就足够了。[85] CITES规定了"豁免"，在此情况下物种标本的越境转移不受许可制度的约束。[86] 这种情况指的是，例如，处于运输[87]或装载中的标本，或者用于个人或家用的标本，[88] 属于巡展的一部分的标本，[89] 以及用于科研的标本。[90] 表6-1概括了第一个组成部分。[91]

表 6-1　　《濒危野生动植物种国际贸易公约》许可制度

	出口许可		进口许可	
	管理的考量	生态的考量	管理的考量	生态的考量
附录一	必需	必需	必需	必需
附录二	必需	必需	必需	可选—国内法
附录三	必需	可选—国内法	可选—国内法	可选—国内法

80　Ibid., Art. III（3）. 缔约方大会的一个决议（Resolution Conf. 5.10（1985），revised in 2010）进一步明确了标本不得主要用于商业用途这一规定。根据这一决议，如果某一用途的非商业利用没有明显凸显出来，那么这一用途就会被定性为主要是商业用途，导致的结果就是不得许可附录一中物种标本的进口。因为有些进口国对此进行了不同的解读［see e. g. *Born Free USA v. Norton*, 278 F. Supp 2d 5（DDC 2003）］，后来这一决议被修订以便为某些原来相对模糊的用途（例如生物医学产业所开展的科研或用于商业用途的圈养繁殖）提供一个具体应对。

81　CITES, supra footnote 3, Art. III（2）.

82　See Wijnstekers, supra footnote 70, Chapter 11.

83　CITES, supra footnote 3, Art. IV（2）.

84　Wijnstekers, supra footnote 70, Chapter 12.

85　CITES, supra footnote 3, Art. V（2）.

86　CITES, supra footnote 3, Art. VII. See Wijnstekers, supra footnote 70, Chapter 15.

87　Ibid., Art. VII（1）and resolution Conf. 9.7（1994），revised in 2010.

88　Ibid., Art. VII（3）and resolution Conf. 13.7（2004），revised in 2007.

89　Ibid., Art. VII（7）and Resolution Conf. 12.13（2002），revised in 2007.

90　Ibid., Art. VII（6）.

91　Source：D. Hunter, J. Salzman and D. Zaelke, *International Environmental Law and Policy*（New York：Foundation Press, 4th edn, 2011），pp. 1071-1072.

表 6-1 同时也提到了第二个组成部分,即许可制度可以通过国内法得以延伸。第 14 条第 1 款明确保留了这一可能性,即各缔约国可以在其国内立法中进一步并针对许可的颁发施加附加要求(表 6-1 通过"可选—国内法"来表示)。

第三个组成部分指的是,为了与 CITES 保持一致,许可所应拥有的最基本内容。公约第 6 条列举了多个要求,它们的目的是将许可的内容进行标准化并确保这一制度的可靠性。[92]

第四个组成部分是各国应当依据公约第 8 条和第 9 条建立的组织结构,目的是实施和管理这一许可制度。各国应指定或建立一个"管理机构"来负责发放许可,一个"科学机构"以便对许可颁发涉及的环境问题提供建议,一个"救助中心"来负责照顾活着的标本(特别是涉及没收时),并保存那些颁发给公约附录一、附录二、附录三中物种的许可的记录。

第五个组成部分是一个制度,它的目的是将物种分别收录于公约各附录的名录之中。作为公约文本的补充,公约指定了一个生态和经济的标准来确定哪些物种可以被收录进附录一和附录二。[93] 但是,列入名录必须经过投票表决,从而在适用这些标准时就会引起一些政治波动。如果想要修订附录一和附录二,就必须通过"在场并投票"缔约方的 2/3 多数同意。[94] 在计算所需的 2/3 多数时,只有那些表示了同意或反对的缔约方才会被计算在内。当达到这一多数时,修订案就会对所有缔约国开始生效(包括那些投票反对的缔约国),但是,任何国家都可以在 90 天以内以书面形式提出一个保留意见,通过这种方式就可以不受修订案的约束。[95] 针对附录三,任一缔约国都可以通过向秘书处发出一个简单通告来将某一物种列入名录。[96] 修订案会在秘书处发出通告 90 天后开始对所有缔约国生效(除了那些提出了保留的国家),但是与附录一和附录二的情况不同的

---

[92] See Wijnstekers, supra footnote 70, Chapter 13.

[93] Resolution Conf. 9.24 (1994), revised in 2010. Note that this resolution urges States parties to take due account of the precautionary principle when considering proposals for the amendment of Annexes I and II. See Wijnstekers, supra footnote 70, Chapters 6-7.

[94] CITES, supra footnote 3, Art. XV (1) (b).

[95] Ibid., Art. XV (3).

[96] Ibid., Art. XVI (1).

是，这种保留意见可以在任何时间点提出，以便各国即使在修订案生效以后也能选择退出修订案。[97]

对保留意见效力的解释引发了一些争议，这也导致缔约方大会在1983 年通过了一项决议并在 2007 年进行了修订，来明确这一问题。该决议"建议""针对附录一中任一物种提交了保留意见的所有缔约方不论是出于何种用途都应将这一物种当作附录二中的物种来对待，包括文件记录和管控"。[98] 这一制度的另一个特点是它可以通过通信投票程序在两次缔约方大会（三年召开一次）的间歇期做出修订。[99]

（三）《濒危野生动植物种国际贸易公约》的实践

为了理解上述组成部分的运作，有必要更细致地分析两个案例。

第一个案例是非洲象案。这一案例不仅可以例证 CITES 的效力，还可以说明影响修订制度的考量因素和社会力量是多种多样的。在 20 世纪 80 年代，非洲一些国家［例如肯尼亚、坦桑尼亚、赞比亚、扎伊尔（现在称为刚果民主共和国）］对大象的捕杀使得非洲象的数量大幅下降。[100] 这一现象主要归因于对发达国家的象牙出口，它导致在 80 年代末期多个国家呼吁要禁止象牙贸易，这些国家包括肯尼亚、美国、英国、法国和德国。虽然其他一些国家（特别是日本以及其他一些出口国）表示了反对，缔约方大会最终还是决定将非洲象收录于 CITES 附录一中。这一收录（或者更精确地讲，从附录二转移到附录一）对大象数量的恢复起到了重要作用，以至于在 1997—2000 年，位于津巴布韦、博茨瓦纳、纳米比亚和南非的大象的数量大幅增加，非洲象降级到附录二。[101] 用于证明降级的正当性的一个主要论点是象牙贸易带来的收入可以造福当地居民，而且政府可以用它来资助保护措施。这些争论下暗藏了一种复杂的紧张关系，即

---

97 Ibid., Art. XVI (2).

98 Resolution Conf. 4. 25 (1983), revised in 2007.

99 CITES, supra footnote 3, Art. XV (2).

100 See M. Glennon, "Has International Law Failed the Elephant?" (1990) 84 *American Journal of International Law* 1, 4.

101 在 1997 年哈拉雷会议期间，缔约方大会成立了两个监测项目，即监测对大象的非法捕杀（Monitoring Illegal Killings of Elephants, MIKE）和大象贸易信息系统（Elephant Trade Information System, ETIS）以确保监测到对附录二的回归对环境造成的影响以及大象数量状况。See Resolution Conf. 10. 10 (1997), revised in 2010.

从经济视角来管理某个"资源"与保护某个"物种"之间的关系。后来，津巴布韦、博茨瓦纳、纳米比亚和南非曾试图将大象数量变回附录一，但是没有成功。2016年10月，一项建议被提交表决但是没有达到所需多数票，虽然博茨瓦纳这个拥有最大规模大象的国家（接近总数的1/3）也支持这一主张。拥有28票的欧盟反对升级到附录一，理由是这四个非洲国家的大象数量并没有急剧下降，而附录一收录标准则要求数量应是急剧下降的。

1997年，在哈拉雷会议期间，缔约方大会采取了一些措施来保护鲟鱼（鱼子酱的来源）这一物种。随着苏联的解体，因为不受控制地过度捕捞和非法鱼子酱贸易，里海地区这一物种的数量急剧下降。一些鲟形类物种已经被收录于CITES附录一和附录二中。但是直到1997年，在美国和德国的努力下，鲟形类将近20个物种才被收录于附录二。另外，缔约方大会采取了其他一系列措施，包括一个用于管控这些物种主要产品（鱼子酱标本）的贸易的标签制度，以及涉及捕捞和出口配额（国家配额、物种配额和标本配额）的具体规定。[102] 2011年，因为这一物种涉及的数个国家并没有遵守配额的规定，秘书处依据大会12.7号决议建议对这些国家实行临时零配额。[103] CITES缔约国被要求不得从那些不遵守配额规定的国家进口。[104]

在以上两个案例中，CITES都对受规制的物种数量发挥了积极作用。在非洲象案例中，在CITES总秘书处的授权和严格监督下，针对那些政府所有的，从博茨瓦纳、纳米比亚、南非和赞比亚合法收集来的象牙（排除了查封的象牙和来源不明的象牙）进行了多场一次性拍卖。在2016年约翰内斯堡缔约方大会上，探讨了在2017年以后进行更多拍卖的可能

---

[102] Resolution Conf. 12.7（2002），revised in 2004（"Resolution Conf. 12.7"）. This resolution incorporates and repeals the resolutions adopted between 1997 and 2000（in Harare and Gigiri）. For more information, see the website of CITES: www.cites.org/eng/prog/sturgeon.php（last visited on 21 April 2017）.

[103] 根据这一决议，如果相关国家没有在第4分段规定的期限之前将配额通报给秘书处，那么在这些国家将配额书面提交给秘书处并由秘书处通告给各缔约方之前，它们的配额就会是零。这些国家应将所有延误情况通知到秘书处并且由其通知各缔约方。

[104] Ibid., second recommendation, para.（a），chapeau.

性，但是被否决了。缔约方大会反而决定关停象牙市场，[105] 这一进程实际已经开始了，因为中国政府已经在 2017 年 3 月底决定在 2017 年年底之前关停其象牙市场。针对鱼子酱，苏联解体导致的管理空窗期也在一定程度上得以弥补。虽然有些国家没有遵守捕捞和出口配额，非法捕捞和贸易也没有消除，但是 CITES 所建立的日趋严格的制度还是展现了一种进步。欧盟在其野生动植物贸易规章（Wildlife Trade Regulations）[106] 中基于生态考量（"未发现有害"）规定了进口要求，这样就为出口配额的要求增加了一个管控层级。

　　另一些案例也证实了 CITES 的影响。其中一个是小羊驼案，秘书处在 2008—2009 年的年度报告中将其称为"羊毛的成功"。[107] 这一物种的羊毛需求量很大，造成它在 20 世纪 70 年代近乎灭绝。后来它被收录于附录一（在阿根廷、智利和秘鲁的物种因为数量的原因被收录于附录二），通过各国和当地居民的共同努力，这一物种的数量已经恢复。另一个案例是自 1977 年开始的针对犀牛角贸易的持续禁止以及可能的美国制裁（依据是《佩利修正案》[108]），导致了日本和韩国犀牛角市场的崩溃。目前，主要的市场位于越南等国。在 2016 年的缔约方大会上，斯威士兰提出了一项建议，希望能够允许一定数量犀牛角的出售，但是这一建议没有达到所需的多数。但是，这并不意味着 CITES 下犀牛的保护措施已经足够了。主要的挑战不是一个法律问题而是一个履行问题。在某些国家（例如越南），针对非法野生动植物交易的管控很弱，有的是因为法律没有被正确执行，或者即使执行了法律，但是与其他犯罪的处罚相比，该领域处罚的威慑力还远远不足。实际上，这一现象导致那些活跃于人、毒品或武器非法交易的跨国有组织犯罪集团将魔爪伸向了野生动植物非法交易。正是因为意识到这一问题，联合国大会在 2015 年围绕"应对野生动植物违法交易"制定了一项决议，[109] 敦促各国和其他组织"加强……执法和刑事司法

　　105　See Draft Decsions and Amendment to Resolution Conf. 10. 1（Rev. COP16）on Trade in Elephant Specimens, 24 September-5 October 2016.

　　106　Council Regulation（EC）No. 338/97of 9 December 1996on the protection of species of wild fauna and flora by regulating trade therein, OJ L 61, 3. 3. 1997, p. 1.

　　107　*Activity Report of the CITES Secretariat 2008-2009*（Geneva：Secretariat CITES, 2010），p. 6.

　　108　See supra footnote 68（the Pelly Amendment also concerns species protected under CITES）.

　　109　"Tackling illicit trafficking in wildlife", 15 July 2015, UN Doc. A/69/L. 80.

回应"并号召它们将这类犯罪更多地归于《联合国打击跨国有组织犯罪公约》之下。[110] 这一决议是在《2030年可持续发展议程》制定后不久通过的，该议程在其第15个发展目标第7个子目标指出，必须"采取紧急行动，制止偷猎和贩运受保护的动植物种群，解决非法野生动植物产品的供需问题"。[111]

这些案例不仅显示了CITES作为一个环境保护多边机制的效力，还反映了它的局限性。正如后文所述，CITES另一个局限在于，因为它关注的是贸易问题，因此它没有解决其他因素对野生动植物保护造成的严重威胁，例如栖息地的破坏或退化。

第四节 空间的保护（地点、栖息地、生态系统）

一 "自上而下"的规制和"自下而上"的规制

将空间的保护作为一种规制方法可以用两种主要方式来进行法律表述。第一种也是最常见的方式，是所谓的"自上而下的"或"垂直的"方法。各国通过制定国内法和规章来承担它们必须完成的条约义务。各个国家此类法律和规章的内容都不尽相同，但是国际法通常会施加一些特别的手段，例如通过战略计划或建立保护区。本章将通过三项主要条约来分析这一方法，这三个条约是《拉姆萨公约》《世界遗产公约》和《关于南极环境的马德里议定书》（*Madrid Protocol on the Antarctic Environment*）。

第二种方式较少被用到，它把战略设计安排在有可能受到涉事问题影响的各利益相关团体这一层面上进行。这种通常被称为"自下而上的"方法一般是通过公众参与机制来体现的，这些机制允许利益相关团体发表它们的意见甚至参与决策过程。它的目的是在利益相关者这一层面将社会和经济发展考量与环保战略整合在一起。主要的一个例证是《联合国防治荒漠化公约》（*UN Convention to Combat Desertification*）。

《2030年可持续发展议程》并未在以上两种方式中做出选择。第15

---

[110] United Nations Convention against Transnational Organized Crime, 15 November 2000, 2225 UNTS 209.

[111] *Transforming our World*, supra footnote 31, target 15.7（see more generally target 155）.

个可持续发展目标关注的是"陆地生态系统"的保护、恢复和可持续利用,它涉及的领域包含了森林管理、荒漠化、土地退化和生物多样性减少,它的提法是各国在"国际条约下的义务",从而对方法持开放态度。[112]

二 自上而下的方法:建立保护地

(一) 湿地的保护:《拉姆萨公约》

《拉姆萨公约》是在1971年年初缔结的,也就是在斯德哥尔摩人类环境会议一年多之前。因此它是最早的现代环境法律文本之一。公约起初被设计成一个针对水鸟栖息地的条约,后来它的重心逐渐转变为将湿地作为一个生态系统进行保护,最近则是转向关注湿地提供的生态服务(包括湿地与水循环的关联)。本书无法详细分析这一演变过程。[113]我们的讨论将会聚焦于公约的两个方面,即(1)它所规制的具体客体;(2)它以名录方法为特色的基本结构。

关于这一公约的规制客体,第1条第1款对"湿地"做出了一个广义的定义:

> 不问其为天然或人工、长久或暂时的沼泽地、泥炭地或水域地带,带有静止或流动的淡水、半咸水或咸水水体,包括低潮时水深不超过6米的水域。[114]

不同的标准都可以用于湿地的定义,包括从科学视角或者描述性视角(海洋的、河口的、湖泊的、河边的、沼泽的)。[115]为了当前目的,必须强调这一定义的四个主要方面。

---

112 *Transforming our World*, supra footnote 31, SDG 15, target 15.1.

113 On this treaty, see Bowman et al., supra footnote 7, Chapter 13; Ramsar Convention Secretariat, *The Ramsar Convention Manual* (Gland: Ramsar Convention Secretariat, 6th edn, 2013); Ramsar Convention Secretariat, *An Introduction to the Ramsar Convention on Wetlands* (Ramsar Handbooks: 5th edn, 2016).

114 Ramsar Convention, supra footnote 4. See also Art. 2 (1).

115 《拉姆萨公约》有一个湿地分类制度,它将湿地划分成42个种类及三个大类:海洋和沿海湿地、内陆湿地以及人造湿地。See the *Ramsar Convention Manual*, supra footnote 112, pp. 7 and 55-56.

第六章　物种、生态系统和生物多样性

第一，公约中受保护湿地的定义是非常宽泛的，它涵盖了自然湿地和人为湿地（例如被灌溉的农田、稻田甚至养殖池塘），无论淡水还是咸水。最重要的是，在这些地区，"水是控制环境及其附属植物和动物生命的重要因素"。[116]

第二，这些湿地值得保护的原因越来越多地归根于它们提供的服务。[117] 如果我们用当前的术语来理解公约的起源，我们可以这样认为，起初这些湿地的主要（虽然不是唯一的）"服务"是为特定物种（水鸟）提供一个栖息地。现在我们已经更深刻了解并记录了湿地所提供的各种生态系统服务。它们涵盖了美学价值、娱乐价值、防洪甚至温室气体的存储。近年来，重点放在湿地在水循环中的作用，更通俗地讲，是湿地带来的"利益"。[118]

第三，公约在那些具有"生态学、植物学、动物学、湖沼学或水文学方面的国际意义"[119] 的湿地与其他湿地之间做了一个区分。我们应当看到，这两种情况下的国家义务是有差异的。

第四，第2条第3款指出，将一个具有国际意义的湿地收录于由秘书处保管的名录"并不损害其所属缔约国的专有主权"。这一术语不能混同于"主权权利"这一概念（用于表述各国对其专属经济区和大陆架所拥有的权利）。[120] 它指的是国家的领土主权以及它所有的属性和局限。在这

---

[116] Ibid.

[117] 联合国前秘书长科菲·安南在2000年启动的"千年生态系统评估"这一尝试中提出了"生态系统提供的服务"这一术语，它的目的是阐明生态系统的经济价值以便促进它们的保护。See in particular the *Synthesis Report of the Millennium Ecosystem Assessment*（2005），p. 13. A reinterpretation of the older Ramsar terminology with regard to the one introduced by the Millennium Ecosystem Assessment is contained in Resolution IX.1（2005），Appendix A.

[118] 2016—2024年拉姆萨战略计划将其目标确定为"湿地受到保护及合理利用，而且它们的用处被所有人承认和欣赏"。另外，针对第3个战略目标，第11个目标指出，"湿地的功能、服务和用得到广泛展示、记载和传播"。参见2016—2024年第四版拉姆萨战略计划（Ramsar Handbooks：5th edn，2016）。这一计划（Resolution XII.2 of COP12）2015年在乌拉圭埃斯特角城召开的缔约方大会上被制订。它将公约的工作纳入了《2030年可持续发展议程》及其可持续发展目标这一更大框架下（参见本书第一章）。

[119] Ramsar Convention, supra footnote 4, Art. 2（2）. The COP developed a set of criteria for the identification of wetlands having an international importance. See *Ramsar Convention Manual*, supra n. 93, pp. 52–54.

[120] See Chapter 4.

一点上，湿地的跨界属性无关紧要。如果涉及跨界问题，公约第 5 条敦促各国开展合作，包括通过建立双边或区域安排的方式。[121] 各国已经创立了多个此类安排并通报给了公约秘书处。[122] 但是，这些地点的领土地位还是归属于相关国家的主权管辖，同时主权国应承担多项义务，这些义务主要源自有关国际水道和跨界含水层的法律。[123]

上述受规制客体的保护是通过前文 CITES 中的名录方法来组织进行的。为了理解《拉姆萨公约》的基本结构，就有必要审视这一手段的三个组成部分：名录、相应的义务以及名录修订所应遵循的制度。

公约在第 2 条第 1 款规定，[124] 应建立一个由秘书处保管的《国际重要湿地名录》(List of Wetlands of International Importance)（第 8 条第 2 款）。截至 2017 年，这一名录收录了 2263 个世界各地的湿地。名录提及了地名、指定日期、国内地理位置、表面面积以及每个地点中心点的坐标（纬度和经度）。名录是由各国组织编写的，但是也可以通过指定的时间顺序来查询每个地点。另外，一个《拉姆萨名录评注》(Annotated Ramsar List) 针对每个地点提供了一个简短说明（200 字），它可以在秘书处获取。此外，秘书处保管的第二个名录，即《蒙特勒档案》(Montreux Record)，[125] 包含了拉姆萨名录中那些"在生态特性上已经发生、正在发生或可能发生一个负面变化，因此需要优先保护"的地点。[126] 将某个地点收录进《蒙特勒档案》（截至 2007 年，它收录了 47 个地点）具有一定的法律含义，它不仅会触发援助而且会提高保护等级。

关于公约设定的义务，可以分为三个层面来理解。第一个层面适用于公约缔约国领土上的所有湿地，不论其是否被列入名录。在第 3 条第 1 款

---

[121] See Resolution VII. 19 (1999) "Guidelines for International Cooperation under the Ramsar Convention" Annex.

[122] *Ramsar Convention Manual*, supra footnote 113, pp. 60–64.

[123] See Chapter 4.

[124] See also Resolution VII. 11 (1999).

[125] 这一名录是在 1990 年于瑞士蒙特勒召开的缔约方大会上制定的。参见 1990 年《拉姆萨地点生态属性的改变》第 4 条建议第 8 款 [Recommendation 4.8 (1990) "Changes in the Ecological Character of Ramsar Sites"]。

[126] See Resolution VI. 1 (1996), Annex 3, "Operating Principles of the Montreux Record", para. 3.1. The guidance on the operation of the Montreux Record was updated in 2015, by Resolution XII. 6 (2015).

中，各国承诺"制订和执行规划，以促进对列入名录的湿地的保护，并尽可能地合理使用其领土内的湿地"。因此"合理"利用这一义务是适用于所有湿地的，无论是否被列入名录。第4条第1款消除了在这一问题上的任何可能模糊之处，它规定各国有义务"在湿地（不论是否已列入名录）建立自然保护区，以促进对湿地和水禽的保护"。如此一来，没有被列入名录的湿地就并未被排除在公约范围之外。但是，针对那些具有国际意义并被列入名录的湿地，相应的要求会更加严格。一方面，"合理利用"义务指的是一个宽泛的范围，它不仅涉及湿地所在国还涉及其他缔约国；[127] 另一方面，被列入名录就意味着更多的监测和报告义务（第3条第2款和第8条第2款），[128] 而这些义务也可能引发另一个义务，即采取措施来应对这一地点受到的威胁或损害。[129] 最终，在《蒙特勒档案》中的地点在实践中就会得益于一个优先制度，即各国有义务汇报这一地点的演变情况，还能根据具体情况来更好地获取技术和财政援助。[130]

有关地点的指定和名录的修订，是由各国独自负责的。这是《拉姆萨公约》一个很特别的特点，它几乎没有给第三方国家和条约机构发表意见的机会。这一制度的两个主轴是列入名录和从名录中删除。第2·条是它的主要法律基础。根据这一条款，每个国家在加入公约时都应指定至少一个湿地（第2条第4款）并随之：

> 有权将其领土内的其他湿地增列入名录，扩大已列入名录的湿地的边界，或者出于紧急的国家利益的考虑，取消列入名录的湿地或缩小其边界（第2条第5款）。

在各个情况下都是由各国做出单边决定，但是，如果这一决定蕴含了保护的减少（从名录中删除或减少表面面积），它就会受到更多的限制，

---

[127] See Bowman et al., supra footnote 7, pp. 424–426.

[128] See also Resolution IX.1 (2005), Annex A, paras. 15–21.

[129] 参见1990年《拉姆萨地点生态属性的改变》第4条建议第8款。根据这一建议，各缔约国在威胁或损害发生时应采取迅速有效的行动来防止改变或做出救济。

[130] Bowman et al., supra footnote 7, pp. 443–448.

该国就会被要求去证明它的决策是为了它的"紧急国家利益",[131] 并通知秘书处(秘书处会通知其他缔约方并安排在下次大会上讨论这些问题,第8条第2款),以及采取适当的补偿措施(第4条第2款)。在实践中,只发生了极少数的边界调整,从拉姆萨名录中删除地点也只发生了三次,而且都没有调用"紧急国家利益"这一原因。[132] 另外,管理局还可以建议将某一地点列入《蒙特勒档案》,虽然这种列入必须事先征得湿地所在国的批准。[133] 当某一地点的领土主权存在争议或者它处于国家管辖范围以外地区时,就会造成困难。第一种情况由公约第5条规定的合作义务来处理。这一合作义务主要适用于跨界地点,不论其是否在名录中,而且它还应适用于那些位于争议地区的湿地。如果默许领土争端中的一方将一个存在争议的地点列入名录,就可能导致法律后果,[134] 因此在这种情况下最好的办法应当是各国开展合作并达成一项共同的保护制度,即使该地并没有被列入名录。针对那些位于国家管辖范围以外的湿地,例如那些位于南极的湿地,瑞士向2005年在坎帕拉(乌干达首都)召开的缔约方大会提交了一个建议,邀请《南极条约》提交一份符合拉姆萨名录列入标准的地点的名录。[135] 但是,这份建议引发了很大争议,最终被撤回。图6-3概括了这一制度的基本结构。

这一制度唤起了对湿地重要性的意识,并对它们在国内和国际层面的保护力度产生了积极影响。名录上庞大数量的地点(其面积超过2.15亿公顷)只是这一影响的其中一个表现。更为重要的可能还是国家层面保护政策的有效实施。[136] 正如后文所述,世界遗产的保护遵循了一个类似的

---

[131] This point has been clarified by Resolution VIII. 20 (2002) "General Guidance for Interpreting 'Urgent National Interests' under Article 2. 5 of the Convention and Considering Compensation under Article 4. 2".

[132] See *An Introduction to the Ramsar Convention*, supra footnote 113, p. 42 (noting that these deletions took place before the listing criteria were adopted, and they were justified on the grounds that the sites in question did not meet these criteria).

[133] "Operating Principles", supra footnote 126, para. 3. 2. 1.

[134] 如后文所述,世界卫生组织在第11条第3款对这一问题做出了明确规定,指出"某一财产位于一个不止一个国家主张拥有主权或管辖权的领土上,并不会妨碍争端各方的权利"。

[135] See Ramsar COP9 DR 23, Rev. 1, 7 November 2005, para. 8.

[136] See M. Bowman, "The Ramsar Convention on Wetlands: Has it Made a Difference" (2002) *Yearbook of International Co-operation on Environment and Development* 61, 63-65.

体 制

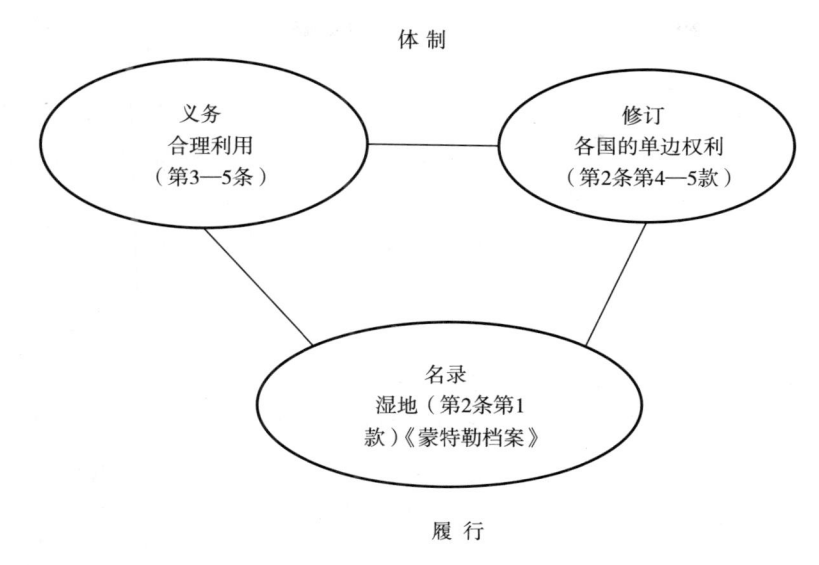

```
     义务                           修订
   合理利用                     各国的单边权利
  （第3—5条）                  （第2条第4—5款）


              名录
         湿地（第2条第1
         款）《蒙特勒档案》
```

履 行

图 6-3 《拉姆萨公约》的基本结构

模式，只是它的方法更加制度化。

（二）世界遗产的保护：《世界遗产公约》

《世界遗产公约》[137] 从很多方面来看是一项混合性文件。它既保护文化遗迹也保护自然环境的特定部分。它还体现了全人类想要保护这些地点的愿望（通过"世界遗产"这一概念显示）与它们位于一国或多国领土之内这一事实之间的冲突。另外，与其他那些在 20 世纪 70 年代制定的环境条约不同，它还明确考虑到了后代可以从世界遗产获取的利益。最后，世界遗产的保护也是和平努力的一个重要组成部分。摧毁敌方标志性的文化地点已经成为一个特殊的战争策略，例如阿富汗塔利班破坏了巴米扬大佛，叙利亚伊斯兰国武装破坏了巴尔米拉庙。2017 年 3 月，联合国安理会在一项一致通过的决议中承认了世界遗产在维护国际和平与安全中的重要作用。[138] 这四个维度凸显了《世界遗产公约》多年来所面临的多个挑战。对公约演变过程的具体介绍不在本书范围之内。[139] 与《拉姆萨公约》

137　WHC, supra footnote 4.

138　Resolution 2347（2017）, 24 March 2017, UN Doc. S/RES/2347/2017.

139　See F. Francioni and F. Lenzerini（eds.）, *The 1972 World Heritage Convention：A Commentary*（Oxford University Press, 2008）；Bowman et al., supra footnote 7, Chapter 14.

的情况相似，我们将只会分析《世界遗产公约》的具体规制客体和它的基本结构。

《世界遗产公约》所保护的客体是世界自然和文化遗产。这一复杂表述有三个组成部分：文化遗产、自然遗产以及将这一遗产的部分构成提升至世界遗产层次的"突出的普遍价值"。

《世界遗产公约》的环境维度涉及的是它的客体的自然遗产部分。第2条中对"自然遗产"的定性是相当严格的。事实上，通过借用第1条中文化遗产的概念（遗迹、建筑群、地点），第2条将自然遗产基本看作自然遗迹（自然特征、地理和地文学构造、地点）。空间维度占据了主导地位。[140] 举例来讲，根据公约，像蓝鲸这样的标志性物种就不能被认定为自然遗产，因为它是可移动的。[141] 这一特性也凸显了公约所采用的聚焦于空间的规制方法，并把它从前文探讨的其他用于物种和资源保护的方法区分开来。

针对"突出的普遍价值"的判定，世界遗产委员会（World Heritage Committee）在其制定并定期更新的《操作指南》（Operational Guidelines）中提供了一些澄清说明：

> 突出的普遍价值指的是文化/自然上的重要意义是如此特别，以至于超出了国家边界而对全人类当代和后代都具有重要意义。[142]

这一定义后来在世界遗产委员会制定的标准中得到了进一步明确，并在操作指南中得以解释。必须满足三种标准：地点的利益［自然遗产[143]应具备特别的美感，象征性地代表一个地质过程或生态进程，或者对生物多样性或特定物种的就地保护（in situ conservation）具有特殊意义］；完整

---

[140] Bowman et al., supra footnote 7, p. 457. See also the *Operational Guidelines for the Implementation of the World Heritage Convention*, 26 October 2016, WHC. 16/01（"Operational Guidelines"）, para. 48（"Nominations of immovable heritage which are likely to become movable will not be considered"）.

[141] Ibid.

[142] Operational Guidelines supra footnote 140, para. 49.

[143] Ibid., para. 77 (vii) - (x).

性或原真性[144]（针对自然遗产而言，整体性可以被理解为"自然/文化遗产及其附属物的完全和完整无缺"[145]）；有一套针对地点的保护制度，用于表达国家保护这一地点的价值的承诺[146]（包括现有适当立法、地点的描绘以及一套管理制度）。

将"突出的普遍价值"赋予某一地点会带来许多法律难题。例如，人们可能会问，承认这一价值以及"世界遗产"这一地位会给地点所在国行使主权带来何种后果。在第三章中，我们发现"人类共同遗产"这一概念体现了一种方法，它排除了某个国家对相关资源的所有权并安排了联合管理。但是，《世界遗产公约》则采取了一个不同的立场。第6条第1款明确尊重"文化和自然遗产的所在国的主权"，同时强调各国有义务开展合作以确保遗传的保护，还有义务不得故意采取"任何可能直接或间接损害本公约其他缔约国领土内的……文化和自然遗产的措施"（第6条第3款）。然而，在有些情况下，世界遗产委员会的干预遭到了国家机关的强烈反对，特别是当委员会试图将某一地点列入《濒危世界遗产名录》（*List of World Heritage in Danger*）以应对来自经济开发项目的威胁时。[147] 人们也许还会问，"突出的普遍价值"这一定性是否仅限用于列入名录的地点，或者这一定位也可以授予那些不在名录中的地点，甚至是一个已经被拒绝登记的地点。《世界遗产公约》明显选择了后一种方法。实际上，第12条规定：

> 未被列入第11条第2段和第4段提及的两个目录的属于文化或自然遗产的财产，决非意味着在列入这些目录的目的之外的其他领域不具有突出的普遍价值。

这就引发了另一个问题，即列入名录的性质是构成性还是宣告性。但是，在解决这一问题之前，有必要解释公约的基本结构。

144　Ibid., paras. 78–95.

145　Ibid., para. 88.

146　Ibid., paras. 78 and 96–118.

147　See N. Affolder, "Mining and the World Heritage Convention: Democratic Legitimacy and Treaty Compliance" (2007) 24 *Pace Environmental Law Review* 35.

与 CITES 和《拉姆萨公约》高度相似,《世界遗产公约》也采用了名录方法,它包含三个组成部分:目录、公约下的义务以及名录修订制度。

关于名录,公约第 11 条创立了两种不同的名录。第 11 条第 2 款规定的《世界遗产名录》包含了 1000 多个地点,其中 1/5 是自然遗产。它们中的一部分可能会被列入第二个名录中,即《濒危世界遗产名录》,前提条件是该地点正在:

> 受到下述严重的特殊危险威胁,这些危险是,蜕变加剧、大规模公共或私人工程、城市或旅游业迅速发展计划造成的消失威胁;土地的使用变动或易主造成的破坏;未知原因造成的重大变化;随意摈弃;武装冲突的爆发或威胁;灾害和灾变;严重火灾、地震、山崩;火山爆发;水位变动、洪水和海啸等(第 11 条第 4 款)。[148]

截至 2017 年年初,这一名录包含了 55 个地点,其中 18 个是自然遗产。值得注意的是,将某一地点转入第二个名录是属于世界遗产委员会的职权范围,这一特点有时会造成地点所在国与委员会的紧张关系。

谈及各国所承担的保护义务,我们必须区分两种不同的义务,一种义务是适用于符合公约的文化或自然遗产定义的所有地点,不论其是否在名录中,而另一种义务则是仅适用于名录中的地点。第一种义务包含了一项"垂直"义务,即有义务在国内层面采取措施以确保"第 1 条和第 2 条中提及的、该国领土内的文化和自然遗产的确定、保护、保存、展出和遗传后代(第 4 条)"。[149] 这一义务的范围及其效果还需要一些说明。两位著名的评论员在参考了第 6 条第 1 款和第 2 款以及第 12 条之后,对第 4 条、第 5 条的内容进行了一个语境解读,认为保护义务并不仅限于名录中的地点。[150]

---

[148] Operational Guidelines, supra footnote 140, para. 177.

[149] See also WHC, supra footnote 4, Art. 5 (listing specific measures that States are urged to adopt).

[150] Bowman et al., supra footnote 7, p. 454 (and cited references). See also F. Francioni and F. Lenzerini, "The Destruction of the Buddhas of Bamiyan and International Law" (2003) 14 *European Journal of International Law* 619, 631.

如此看来，列入目录并不只有一个宣告性效果。[151] 关于义务的效果，第4条和第5条已经被国内法院解释为授予了地点所在国一个自由裁量权。[152] 这一观点并不必然事关条约的其他内容，因为其他国家的法院赋予了条约条款一种直接的效力，这种效力与《世界遗产公约》第4条和第5条一样宽泛甚至更宽泛。[153] 同时在第一种义务中，公约还规定了"水平"义务，特别是合作义务，包括一般义务（通过建立一些机构，例如世界遗产委员会[154]）和更具体的义务（例如通过财政和技术援助机制[155]），以及前文提到的义务：

> 不得故意采取任何可能直接或间接损害本公约其他缔约国领土内的第1条和第2条中提及的文化和自然遗产的措施（第6条第3款）。

这是风险预防原则的早期构想。关于第二种义务，第6条第2款规定了一项仅适用于名录中地点的援助义务。这一义务的范围明确仅限于"第11条第2段和第4段所指的文化和自然遗产"（因此排除了第1条和第2条所指的遗产）。列表还可以拓展各国获取援助的可能性，特别是当涉事地点是在《濒危世界遗产名录》之中。

关于名录制度，与《拉姆萨公约》不同，《世界遗产公约》没有授予各国一个单边权利去将某一地点列入名录。它建立了一套提名制度，世界

---

[151] See, however, *Southern Pacific Properties (Middle East) Limited (SPP) v. Arab Republic of Egypt*, ICSID Case No. ARB/84/3, Award (20 May 1992), para. 154.

[152] See Bowman et al., supra footnote 7, pp. 455–456 (referring to Australian jurisprudence in particular: *Richardson v. Forestry Commission* [1988] HCA 10, (1988) 164 CLR 261). See also B. Boer and G. Wiffen, *Heritage Law in Australia* (Oxford University Press, 2006), Chapter 3.

[153] See *Netherlands Crown Decision (in Dutch) in the case lodged by the Competent Authority for the Island of Bonaire on the annulment of two of its decisions on the Lac wetland by the Governor of the Netherlands Antilles*, 11 September 2007, Staatsblad 2007, 347 ("*Bonaire*"). J. Verschuuren, "Ramsar soft law is not soft at all" (2008) 35 *Milieu en Recht* 28 (English translation of a text in Dutch, available on www.ssrn.com, discussing the case of *Bonaire*, in which an administrative authority in the Netherlands granted direct effect to Art. 3 of the Ramsar Convention).

[154] See WHC supra footnote 4, Arts. 6 (1) and 8–14.

[155] See Ibid., Parts IV (Fund for the Protection of the World Heritage) and V (terms and conditions of international assistance).

遗产委员会有权接受（从而将地点列入名录）或者拒绝（第 11 条第 6 款）。[156] 这套制度是基于公约第 11 条以及操作指南的多个部分（特别是第三部分，第 120—168 段）。必须对《世界遗产名录》和《濒危世界遗产名录》做一个区分。前者中某个地点的动议必须是来自地点所在国（第 11 条第 1 款和第 3 款）。第 11 条第 3 款指出，列入本名录需要征得当事国的同意。如此一来，当某一地点的主权存在争议时就会造成问题。柏威夏寺一案就说明了这一点。1962 年，柬埔寨和泰国之间的一个领土定界争议问题被提交给国际法院，国际法院得出的结论是支持柬埔寨。[157] 自 2001 年以来，柬埔寨就申请将该寺庙列入《世界遗产名录》，这就激起了泰国的抗议，主要原因在于柬埔寨试图列入的具体面积。2008 年，柬埔寨提出了一个新的建议，并获得了泰国的同意，这一建议对这一地点的边界做出了更窄的划定。这一建议导致该寺庙被列入名录，虽然泰国在最后一分钟又改变了主意。国际法院后来确认了柬埔寨将寺庙周边涵盖在内的诉求。[158] 将某一地点列入名录并不是一成不变的。在特定情况下，名录可以被修订[159]甚至从名录中除名（例如如果这一地点恶化到不再具有突出的普世价值）。[160]

适用于《濒危世界遗产名录》的制度与我们刚刚探讨的制度存在着一个重大区别，即它的收录是掌握在世界遗产委员会手中，而当事国并没有否决权（第 11 条第 4 款）。但是，委员会应当尽可能地与地点所在国开展协商与合作，[161] 第 11 条第 3 款（列入名录需征得当事国的同意）则

---

[156] *Operational Guidelines*, supra footnote 140, para. 158. 该委员会包含了由世界卫生组织大会选出的 21 个缔约方代表。以出席并参加表决的缔约方的 2/3 多数票通过决定。参见委员会程序规则第 29 条第 2 款。在实践中，该委员会拒绝了数次列入目录的申请，也从名录中除名了数个地点（在德国和阿曼），虽然这种情况比较少见。

[157] *Preah Vihear Case* (*Cambodia v. Thailand*), Judgment, ICJ Reports 1962, p. 6.

[158] *Request for Interpretation of the Judgment of* 15 *June* 1962 *in the Case concerning the Temple of Preah Vihear* (*Cambodia v. Thailand*) (*Cambodia v. Thailand*), Judgment, ICJ Reports 2013, p. 281.

[159] Operational Guidelines supra footnote 140, paras. 163-167.

[160] Ibid., paras. 192-198 (the withdrawal is made by a decision of the World Heritage Committee adopted by a majority of two thirds of the members present and voting, in accordance with Art. 13 (8) of the Convention).

[161] Operational Guidelines supra footnote 140, para. 183-184.

不适用于这种情况。在实践中,正是考虑到这一程序可能导致的危机,[162] 委员会一般都会试图在当事国同意的情况下来操作。图 6-4 展示了这一制度的基本结构。

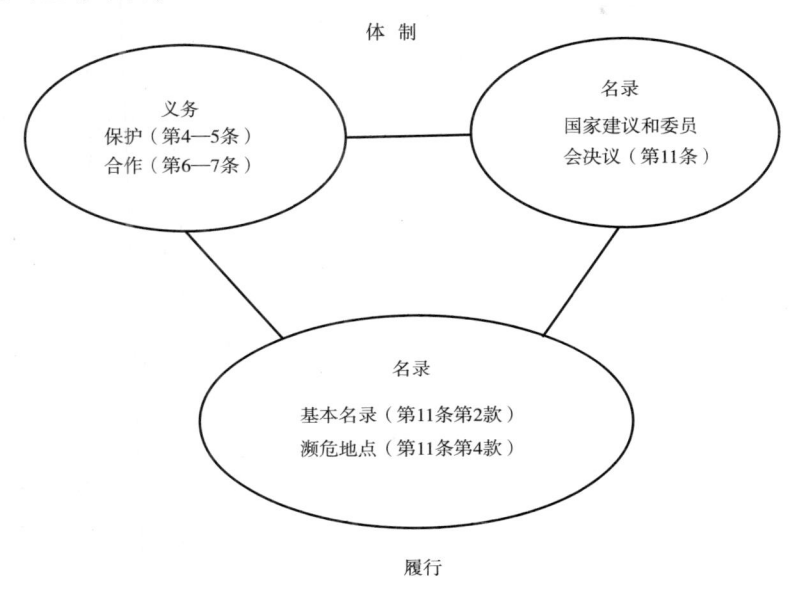

体 制

```
        义务                          名录
    保护（第4—5条）              国家建议和委员
    合作（第6—7条）              会决议（第11条）

                    名录
            基本名录（第11条第2款）
            濒危地点（第11条第4款）

                    履行
```

图 6-4　《世界遗产公约》的基本结构

《世界遗产公约》为一项环境条约中的名录方法提供了又一个实证。但是,《世界遗产公约》关注的重点其实是文化遗迹,自然环境的保护只是排在次要位置。也就是说,将空间保护当作一个规制方法,《世界遗产公约》可能是最具代表性的国际文件。

（三）南极环境的保护:《马德里议定书》

南极作为一个公地,早在 20 世纪 50 年代就受到了南极条约体系（Antarctic Treaty System, ATS）的调整。[163] 在这一体系下,1991 年《马德里议定书》是环境保护战略的核心。[164] 虽然长期以来也制定了其他一些法

162　See Affolder, supra footnote 147.

163　Antarctic Treaty, 1 December 1959, 402 UNTS 71.

164　Madrid Protocol, supra footnote 12. See J. ‐ P. Puissochet, " Le Protocole au Traité sur l'Antarctique relatif à la protection de l'environnement‐Madrid" (1991) 37 *Annuaire français de droit international* 755; Committee on Environmental Protection, *25 Years of the Protocol on Environmental Protection to the Antarctic Treaty* (Buenos Aires: Secretariat of the Antarctic Treaty, 2016).

律文本，包括保护海豹[165]以及海洋动植物的条约，[166] 而《马德里议定书》则是涵盖了整个南极环境并将其看作一个生态系统，并使其成为一个"自然保护地"（第 2 条）。[167] 事实上，它是最先进的环境制度之一，也第一次创立了一个真正国际性的保护区。

《马德里议定书》的结构与框架公约的结构相似，但同时存在两个重大差异。第一，那些用于细化相关框架协定的文件一般是议定书的附录，而议定书本身也是一个更宽泛框架协定（即《南极条约》）的进一步细化。《马德里议定书》目前拥有 6 个附录：附录一（环境影响评价）、附录二（南极动植物的保护）、附录三（废物处置和废物管理）、附录四（防止海洋污染）、附录五（保护区管理）、附录六（环境紧急事件的责任）。第二，从实质视角来看，议定书的文本比我们所述的那些框架协定更具体。一些更多的评论将有助于阐明这一点。

议定书的文本针对涉及矿产资源的活动（根据第 7 条应当被禁止）与其他可以获批的活动进行了一个区分，可以获批的活动应受到一定的约束，主要是必须经过环境影响评价（第 3 条第 2 款和第 3 款，第 8 条和附录一）。关于采矿，《马德里议定书》推翻了 1988 年制定的一项有关矿产资源开发的制度，并规定在 50 年内中止一切采矿活动（第 7 条和第 25 条）。[168] 而其他的一些活动（科研、旅游、其他政府或非政府活动），[169] 则可以在履行了环评这一义务的前提条件下开展，环评的范围有赖于涉事活

---

[165] Convention on the Protection of Antarctic Seals, 1 June 1972, 1080 UNTS 175.

[166] Convention on the Conservation of Antarctic Marine Living Resources, 20 May 1980, 1329 UNTS 47.

[167] 《南极条约》的规定应适用于南纬60°以南的地区，包括一切冰架（《南极条约》第 6 条，《马德里议定书》第 2 条第 1 款所指）。值得注意的是，《马德里议定书》第 2 条和第 8 条第 1 款将保护延伸至南极环境的"赖以生存的和相关的生态系统"。

[168] 谈判过程中针对修订制度的讨论，参见 Puissochet supra footnote 164, pp. 764ff。针对矿产资源活动的禁令从议定书在 1998 年生效时开始，直到 2048 年（第 25 条第 2 款）。在此期间，只有经过南极条约体系的所有协商方的一致同意才能修订议定书（第 25 条第 1 款）。另外，第 7 条针对矿产资源活动的禁止在 2048 年以后还会继续有效，除非针对南极矿产资源活动制定了一个有约束力并具有特定内容的法律制度（第 25 条第 5 款）。

[169] Madrid Protocol, supra footnote 12. Arts. 3 (4) and 8 (2). Note that the Final Act excludes certain activities from the obligation to conduct an EIA, namely fishing, whaling, and sealing, Puissochet, supra footnote 164, p. 766.

动所造成的风险。针对这一问题，第 8 条第 1 款和附录一将活动分为了三个层次，依据是该活动是否造成了"不到一个较小或短暂影响"（不需要环评），[170] "等于一个较小或短暂影响"（有义务针对环境影响开展一个初步评估），[171] "大于一个较小或短暂影响"（有义务针对环境影响开展一个综合评估）。[172] 在门槛以下的活动无须满足更多的要求就可以开展，而那些被认定为有较小或短暂影响的活动则必须是在一个初步环评确认了影响之后才能开展，而且它们还有赖于适当监测程序的建立。[173] 针对那些可能造成大于一个较小或短暂影响的活动，它们在通过了一个综合环评后才可能获得批准，而综合环评则是一个复杂得多的程序。从实践的视角来看，人们也许会问，何种机构有能力做出：（1）决定某项活动是否符合这三个层次中的一个；（2）在需要的时候开展相应的环评；（3）批准这项活动。议定书把这些决定权交到了活动缘起国手中。[174] 但是，当涉及那些需要开展综合环评的活动时，当事国应与议定书环境保护委员会（Protocol's Committee on Environmental Protection）、南极条约咨询会议（Antarctic Treaty Consultative Meeting，ATCM）以及公众开展协商。[175]

除了这项一般制度，针对特定地区还有一些特别限制，这是根据《马德里议定书》附录五来规定的。这一附录借用了南极条约体系下制定的一项旧的体系，它指定了"南极特别保护区"（Antarctic Specially Protected Areas，ASPA）和"南极特别管理区"（Antarctic Specially Managed Areas，ASMA）。这些地区受到"管理计划"的约束，这些管理计划明确了可适用的制度。"南极特别保护区"的设立是为了保护某一种客体（环境的、科学上的、历史的或美学的），[176] 而"南极特别管理区"则主要是为了促进缔约方之间的协作，包括对不同活动造成的累积影响进行管控，

---

[170] Madrid Protocol, supra footnote 12. Annex I, Art. 1 (2).

[171] Ibid., Annex I, Art. 2.

[172] Ibid., Annex I, Art. 3.

[173] Ibid., Annex I, Art. 2 (2).

[174] Ibid., Art. 8 (2) and Annex I, Art. 2 (1).

[175] Ibid., Annex I, Art. 3 and "Revised Guidelines for Environmental Impact Assessment in Antarctica", Resolution 1 (2016) -ATCM XXXIX-CEP XIX, 1 June 2016, Santiago.

[176] Madrid Protocol, supra footnote 12, Annex V, Art. 3.

以便"将环境影响最小化"。[177] 附录五的第 6 条规定了这些地区的认定程序。决定是由南极条约咨询会议做出。[178] 但是，进入这些地区或开展活动的授权则是由各国主管机关根据适用的管理计划所设定的条件来发布的。[179]

以上对《马德里议定书》所建立制度的综述，充分显示了针对空间保护的自上而下的方法。现在我们将转向不太常见的自下而上的方法，用《防治荒漠化公约》来举例说明。

三　自下而上的方法：《联合国防治荒漠化公约》

与有关湿地保护的《拉姆萨公约》相对照，1994 年《联合国防治荒漠化公约》[180] 的目的是保护干旱地区不会进一步"荒漠化"，第 1 条第 1 款对荒漠化的定义是：

> 包括气候变异和人类活动在内的种种因素造成的干旱、半干旱和亚湿润干旱地区的土地退化。[181]

这一公约的起源可以追溯到 20 世纪 70 年代，它得以通过受到 1992 年里约峰会的推动。它在 1996 年开始生效并在 2012 年实现了全球的参与。在此部分，我们将聚焦于公约是如何试图保护那些具有高度经济和社会价值的大片地区。[182]

为了理解《联合国防治荒漠化公约》的核心，就有必要将它所应对的问题种类熟记于心。干旱地区的面积占到了世界陆地面积的约 40%，有约 20 亿人居住于此。[183] 这些人的绝大部分生活在发展中国家，他们的

---

[177] Ibid., Annex V, Art. 4.

[178] Ibid., Annex V, Art. 6 (1).

[179] Ibid., Annex V, Art. 7.

[180] UNCCD, supra footnote 26.

[181] See also World Resources Institute, *Ecosystèmes et bien-être humain: Synthèse sur la désertification* (Washington: Island Press, 2005) ("Synthesis on Desertification").

[182] See A. Tal and J. A. Cohen, "Bringing 'Top-Down' to 'Bottom-Up': A New Role for Environmental Legislation in Combating Desertification" (2007) 31 *Harvard Environmental Law Review* 163.

[183] Synthesis on Desertification, supra footnote 181, p. 1.

生存依赖于他们耕作的土地的产量。荒漠化导致的产量损失造成了这些人的贫困。防治荒漠化的潜在动力不是土地退化本身,而主要是它的社会经济后果。在此背景下,为了解决荒漠化造成的问题,设立保护区看起来就不是一个适当的手段。但是,公约并未将这一手段排除在外(第5条规定了一个自上而下的战略,虽然它并未明确提及建立保护区),但是它强调了一种公众参与的方法,它的核心要件是制定区域、次区域,特别是国家级行动计划(第9条和第10条)。这些计划可以被看作这一问题的本地化管理的手段,它们必须整合各种各样的利益相关团体,包括那些开展的活动对干旱地区造成了重大压力的团体(第10条第2款)。

与许多框架协定相似,这一公约下的义务也是采用一种宽泛的模式来进行表述的。但是,公约的附录对这些义务进行了细化,它们相当于发挥了议定书的作用,类似于《马德里议定书》。《联合国防治荒漠化公约》目前有五个附录(附录一:非洲;附录二:亚洲;附录三:拉丁美洲和加勒比海地区;附录四:北地中海地区;附录五:中欧和东欧),它们采取了同一种逻辑,即明确规定国家的、次区域的以及区域的行动计划必须采用的方式,并规定了一个特定基本内容。针对非洲的附录一的内容是最详细的。这是基于历史原因(非洲国家引领了制定条约的倡议)和实证原因(非洲大陆遭受的荒漠化影响是最大的)两个方面。在实践中,制订这些行动计划所花费的时间超出了预期,虽然现在已经有了大约一百个国家计划及一些区域和次区域计划。另外,这些计划的实际影响,或者通俗地讲,这种自下而上方法的实际效果还有待证实。[184] 这一论点源自《联合国防治荒漠化公约》的"十年战略",它是在2007年第八次缔约方大会上通过的,[185] 目的是加强公约的实施。

遗憾的是,《联合国防治荒漠化公约》并不是唯一一个面临严重实施困难的法律文本。正如后文所述,《生物多样性公约》也面临着相似的困境,即使它在规范制定中发挥了重要作用。

---

[184] See Tal and Cohen, supra footnote 182, pp. 178–180. These authors thus propose a return to a top-down approach.

[185] See Decision 3/COP. 8, "The 10-year strategic plan and framework to enhance the implementation of the Convention", 23 October 2007, ICCD/COP(8)/16/Add. 1.

第五节 生物多样性的保护

一 一个复杂的规制客体

除了物种和空间（地点、栖息地、生态系统）的保护，这些生物资源本身的多样性并未受到明确的保护，直到1992年生物多样性大会制定了《生物多样性公约》。[186] 这一复杂客体的保护在20世纪80年代的一些软法文件中就有所构思，包括世界自然保护联盟在1980年制定并于1991年修订的《世界自然保护战略》，[187] 以及布伦特兰委员会所做的工作。[188] 但是直到《生物多样性公约》通过后，生物资源本身的多样性才被确定应当受到保护。[189]

《生物多样性公约》第2条将多样性定义为：

> 所有来源的活的生物体中的变异性，这些来源除其他外包括陆地、海洋和其他水生生态系统及其所构成的生态综合体；这包括物种内、物种之间和生态系统的多样性。

这一定义明确了生物多样性必须在三个层次进行保护，即（1）物种内的基因多样性；（2）物种多样性；（3）生态系统的多样性。这三个层次生物多样性的保护和管理就要求必须对这些多样性赖以存在的物种和栖

---

[186] CBD, supra footnote 10.

[187] See IUCN, UNEP, WWF, *World Conservation Strategy. Living Resource Conservation for Sustainable Development* (Gland: IUCN, 1980), Section 6 ("Priority Requirements: Genetic Diversity"); IUCN, *Caring for the Earth: A Strategy for Sustainable Living* (Gland: IUCN, 1991), Chapter 4.

[188] See R. D. Munro and J. G. Lammers, *Environmental Protection and Sustainable Development: Legal Principles and Recommendations adopted by the Experts Group on Environmental Law of the World Commission on Environment and Development* (London: Graham & Trotman, 1987).

[189] See M. -A. Hermitte, S. Maljean - Dubois and E. Truilhé - Marengo, "Actualités de la convention sur la diversité biologiques: science et politique, équité, biosécurité" (2011) 57 *Annuaire français de droit international* 399; Bowman et al., supra footnote 7, Chapter 17; E. Morgera andE. Tsioumani, "Yesterday, Today, and Tomorrow: Looking Afresh at the Convention on Biological Diversity" (2010) 21 *Yearbook of International Environmental Law* 3.

息地进行保护。正是基于这个原因,《生物多样性公约》才会被看作一个中心轴,它为物种和空间保护的大量(全球性、区域性、双边性)法律文本提供了一个共同基础。[190]

为了应对这一复杂客体,《生物多样性公约》将保护与经济考量联合在一起。生物多样性这两个维度的区别体现在《生物多样性公约》所做的区分,一方面,"生物多样性的保护"是一个"人类共同关注事项",[191]另一方面,资源所在国主权下的"生物资源"的"可持续利用"应当符合一套获取和惠益分享制度。[192]

二 生物多样性的规制

前文所述的一般框架也显示了《生物多样性公约》规范性行为的两个主要领域,即生物多样性的保护和生物资源的可持续利用,特别是遗传资源的管理。这些领域在实践中相互间的交叉是如此密切,以至于单独展示它们可能会使条约的运行变得模糊不清。从一个分析的立场来看,最好对三个轴心做一个区分,我们可以沿着这三个主轴来研究公约及其演进过程。

第一个主轴指的是前文提到的生物多样性的保护和生物与遗传资源的可持续利用之间的区分。可持续发展目标(SDGs)在一定程度上维持了这一观点,[193]它有助于理解《生物多样性公约》文本的基本结构以及在公约框架下制定的其他文件。表6-2展示了这一基本结构,强调了公约中的一些重要条款。

---

190 关于《生物多样性公约》战略计划和目标与"生物多样性集群"其他公约的整合,参见 Futhazar, supra footnote 11。

191 CBD, supra footnote 10, Preamble, paras. 3 and 5, and Art. 1.

192 Ibid., Preamble, paras. 4 and 5, and Art. 1, 3 and 15. 获取和惠益分享通常被当作一个单独的目标。但是,从规制的视角来看,它可能是《生物多样性公约》所建立的资源管理制度的核心要件。

193 *Transforming our World*, supra footnote 31, 第2个可持续发展目标(聚焦于食品安全,参见目标第4个和第5个子目标)和第15个可持续发展目标(聚焦于生态系统和生物多样性的保护、恢复和可持续管理)。

表 6-2　　　　　　　　　《生物多样性公约》的基本结构

生物多样保护	生物资源的可持续利用	
	总体	遗传资源的管理
—国家计划（第6条） —查明及监测（第7条） —就地保护（第8条）和移地保护（第9条） —外来物种（第8条及指导原则，decision CP. VI/23） —将生物多样性的保护和持续利用订入有关的部门或跨部门计划、方案和政策内（第6条第2款和坎昆指南，decision CP. XIII/3）	—国家计划（第6条） —可持续利用（第10条和指导原则） —鼓励措施（第11条） —环境影响评价（第14条）	—获取和惠益分享（第15条、第16条、第19条、第8条第9款） —《生命之根自愿准则》，Decision XIII/18 —《名古屋议定书》（2010）	—生物安全风险管理《卡塔赫纳生物安全议定书》（2000）和《卡塔赫纳生物安全议定书关于赔偿责任和补救的名古屋—吉隆坡补充协议》（2010）

不论是从规范视角还是从实践来看，都很难判断公约这两个目标中的哪一个更早出现。正如前文所述，这两个目标是紧密关联在一起的。例如，遗传资源的某些利用所涉及的风险（例如生物技术）被纳入了《卡塔赫纳生物安全议定书》（Cartagena Protocol on Biosafety），但是这一文件其实是处于保护和可持续利用的交叉点。它的逻辑起点是，遗传资源确实可以被加以利用，同时还试图减少转基因生物带来的风险。类似的分析也可用于《名古屋议定书》或者缔约方大会多年来通过的数个指导原则。

为了理解这两个目标之间的关系以及《生物多样性公约》的规范性工作，我们必须采取比保护和可持续利用这种宏观目标更具体的分析类别。

第二个主轴聚焦于数次缔约方大会多年以来所应对的"主题"问题，以及那些横跨这些主题的"多部门"问题。正是在这一层面我们才能理解《生物多样性公约》的规范性实践。针对这些问题所采用的工作方法具有高度相似性。缔约方大会可以决定从事某项工作计划，工作计划根据情况的不同，可以有一定程度的组织建设（常设工作组、特别专家组、非正式团体）并通常会与科研辅助机构相关联，这一科研机构有的是在公约之下，有的是在缔约方大会决定成立的履行评估工作组之下。为了在这样一个浓密的行政"森林"中找到一个出路，就必须将主题工作计划与交叉性或多部门计划进行区分。一方面，每个主题工作计划都是聚焦于某种生物群系（海洋和沿海生物多样性、森林、干旱地、内陆水域、岛屿或山脉）[194]或农业的关键问题；另一方面，交叉性或多部门计划有的被授权给了常设工作组（例如针对第8条或保护区的工作组）。这些计划的表现形式各式各样，涵盖了整体的问题，例如生物多样性的可持续利用和生态系统方法，还有一些更具体的问题，例如外来物种入侵、技术转让或影响评价。《生物多样性公约》正是通过这些项目来开展它重要的规范性行为。事实上，如果不是顾忌过于简单，我们完全可以将《生物多样性公约》建立的制度称为一个"规范的动力室"，因为公约及其框架下建立的机构所关注的重点都是制定大量的标准、指南和其他措施以便指导国内措施的制定。[195]一个重要的例证是，为了落实《生物多样性公约》第6条第2款和2011—2020年战略计划的第一个目标，2016年缔约方大会制定了一些指南，用于将生物多样性整合进其他部门并使之主流化。[196]国际社会普遍认为这些指南是缔约方大会的主要成就之一，因为它们应对的是生物多样性减少的潜在（社会—经济）成因，并将战略计划放置于《2030年可持续发展议程》整体框架之中。

　　履行的需要也是第三个主轴的起点。主轴从《生物多样性公约》作为一个规范的动力室这一概念延伸为一个模式；在此模式下，公约及其议定书下的义务通过一个管控体系得以有效履行。2002年，战略计划的制订以及履行评估工作组（Working Group on the Review of Implementation）的成立是制定一套实施监督制度的第一次尝试。[197]但是，这些举措还远不够充分，没有实现"2010年目标"（减少生物多样性丧失的比率）就说明了这一点。在名古屋举办的第十次缔约方大会启动了第二次尝试。工作

---

[194] Some of these biomes have been specifically targeted for protection, restoration and/or sustainable use under SDG 15, see *Transforming our World*, suprafootnote 31.

[195] See the section of the CBD website on guidelines and tools: http://www.cbd.int/guidelines/ (last visited on 10 December 2013).

[196] Decision XIII/3 "Strategic actions to enhance the implementation of the Strategic Plan for Biodiversity 2011-2020 and the achievement of the Aichi Biodiversity Targets, including with respect to mainstreaming and the integration of biodiversity within and across sectors", 16 December 2016, CBD/COP/XIII/3. See also *Transforming our World*, suprafootnote 31, SDG 15, target 15.9.

[197] See Decision CP VII/30 "Strategic Plan: Future Evaluation of Progress", 13 April 2004, UNEP/CBD/COP/DEC/VII/30.

的一个重要部分是建立机制来监督公约中义务的履行并固化义务，例如一个不遵约程序，[198] 用于评估进展［朝向战略目标和本次会议通过的"生物多样性爱知目标"（Aichi Targets on Biological Diversity）］的具体指标，[199] 为生物多样性管理制定战略的区域讲习班，[200] 或者一套责任追究制度。[201] 自2010年以来已经取得了一些进展。最近于2016年年底在墨西哥坎昆举办的缔约方大会上，通过了一项名为"履行附属机构的特定做法"（Modus operandi）的决定，它的目的是评估《生物多样性公约》（特别是《2011—2020年战略计划》）的履行进展。[202]

三 转基因生物的规制

在缔结《生物多样性公约》时，转基因生物造成的潜在风险就已经被确定。实际上第8条和第19条第3款规定应当通过一个议定书：

> 建立适当程序，特别包括事先知情同意，适用于可能对生物多样性的保护和可持续利用造成不利影响的、由生物技术改变的任何活生物体的安全转让、处理和使用。

在第二次缔约方大会上，针对这一问题成立了一个特别工作组。[203] 这一工作组的工作花费了几年时间，原因在于转基因生物出口国（所谓的"迈阿密集团"）和进口国（包括大部分发展中国家和欧盟）之间的紧张关系。最终，2000年1月，在缔约方大会的一次特别会议上，《卡塔赫纳

---

[198] CP decision X/2 "Strategic Plan 2011-2020 and the Aichi Targets on Biological Diversity", 27 October 2010, UNEP/CBD/COP/DEC/X/2, subsections 14 and 15.

[199] Decision CP XI/3 "Monitoring Progress in Implementation of the Strategic Plan for Biodiversity 2011-2020 and the Aichi Biodiversity Targets" (advanced version), Annex.

[200] Morgera and Tsioumani, supra footnote 189, p. 10.

[201] See Section 6.5.3.

[202] See CP decision XIII/25 "Modus operandi of the Subsidiary Body on Implementation and mechanisms to support review of implementation", 9 December 2016, CBD/COP/XIII/25.

[203] CP. II/5, "Consideration of the Need for and Modalities of a Protocol for the Safe Transfer, Handling and Use of Living Modified Organisms", UNEP/CBD/COP/2/19.

生物安全议定书》得以签署。[204] 虽然议定书已经拥有了大量缔约国（截至2017年4月有170个缔约国），但是转基因生物的一些主要出口国（例如阿根廷、澳大利亚、加拿大或美国）并不受约束。必须要强调这一点，因为它对议定书的运行造成了重大影响。

议定书所建立的制度是相对简单的：两类转基因生物的越境转移受到两个管控程序的约束。[205] 为了理解这一制度，就有必要阐明两个问题。关于转基因生物的分类，在议定书的谈判过程中这一问题就引发了很大争论。存在着两种观点，一种是限制性的（受到出口国的支持），另一种是扩张性的（受到进口国的支持）。最终的解决办法是这两个立场的妥协。议定书不是仅限于规制改性活生物体（LMOs，[206] 包括种子），这些生物体是被有意引入环境中，继而对生物多样性造成了风险。它还涵盖了那些用于食物或饲料（未加工的农产品）的改性活生物体或者在进口国进行的加工过程（面粉、石油等）。相反地，议定书并不规制出口国用改性活生物体生产出的产品（例如番茄酱、面粉、石油）、药物、[207] 过境运输中的改性活生物体[208]或者那些用于"封闭"使用的改性活生物体。[209]

关于第二个问题，议定书规制的两类改性活生物体受到了两个单独程序的约束。进口国为了将改性活生物体有意引入环境中而进行的越境转移应当受到"提前知情同意"（advance informed agreement）这一具体程序的约束（第7—10条，第12条）。[210] 这一制度可以拿来与《巴塞尔公约》建立的制度作一个比较，[211] 虽然与《卡塔赫纳生物安全议定书》不同，《巴塞尔公约》是在一个国际层面起草的名录中确定受规制的废物。这一程序的主要特点可以被概括为以下七点：（1）应在越境转移之前获得同

204　Biosafety Protocol, supra footnote 5. See M. - C. Cordonier - Segger, F. Perron - Welch, C. Frison (eds.), *Legal Aspects of Implementing the Cartagena Protocol on Biosafety* (Cambridge University Press, 2013).

205　Biosafety Protocol, supra footnote 5, Art. 3 (k).

206　Ibid., Art. 3 (g).

207　Ibid., Art. 5.

208　Ibid., Art. 6 (1).

209　Ibid., Art. 6 (2) and 3 (b).

210　See Chapter 3.

211　See Chapter 7.

意（规制的客体是"越境转移"而不是一种转基因生物，获得了同意就意味着该生物被批准）；(2) 通知应由计划出口该性活生物体的经营者发起（这些生物体还应受到出口国依据议定书所进行的规制）；[212] (3) 进口国应在一定时限内确认已收到通知，并表明何种制度（议定书制度或者国内法建立的制度）将会用于管理越境转移；[213] (4) 进口国应在上述规定的时限内把它对越境转移的决定[214]以书面方式告知出口国，[215] 它可能会导致核准（在满足特定条件的情况下）或禁止故意转移；[216] (5) 即使对改性活生物体的影响还缺乏科学定论，还是可以根据风险预防原则来做出决定，而且可以随时重新审议决定；[217] (6) 决定必须通告出口方以及议定书的缔约国［通过生物安全资料交换所（Biosafety Clearing House, BCH）］；(7) 最后，议定书指出，进口国的沉默并不意味着其对越境转移表示同意。[218] 这一程序看起来似乎很烦琐，特别是当它无差别地适用于所有改性活生物体（包括主要出口国的农产品）时。谈判达成的妥协的一个核心内容是将那些用于人类或动物消费的改性活生物体（包括农产品）适用议定书第 11 条规定的一个简易程序。这一程序与《鹿特丹公约》创立的一般事先知情同意相类似。[219] 这一程序的焦点不是越境转移而是涉事的改性活生物体，各国应当把授予进口方的许可告知生物安全资料交换所，包括进口应满足的条件（例如许可的有效期或有关产品标签的规定）。在实践中，这一程序显得不是那么烦琐，因为一个许可可以被用于同一产品的多次进口。值得注意的是，议定书为其他改性活生物体采用简易程序提供了机会，各进口国通过向生物安全资料交换所发出一个通告，指明何种改性活生物体是它不打算采用提前知情同意的，或者指明在

---

[212] Biosafety Protocol, supra footnote 5, Art. 8 and Annex I.

[213] Ibid., Art. 9 (2) (c).

[214] Ibid., Art. 10 (2) (b).

[215] Ibid., Art. 10 (2) (a).

[216] Ibid., Art. 10 (3).

[217] Ibid., Art. 10 (6) and 12 (1). 议定书第 15 条和附录三为风险评估提供了一个框架，并将其当作依据第 10 条所做出决定的基础。应当注意的是，风险评估可能会对出口方和通知方造成较大负担。

[218] Ibid., Art. 9 (4) and 10 (5).

[219] See Chapter 7.

何种情况下越境转移可以基于一个简易通知来进行。[220]

人们对这些涉及转基因生物风险预防的措施是否充分还存有疑虑，特别是想知道当这些转基因生物的引入对生物多样性和人类健康造成了伤害时会发生什么。议定书第 19 条敦促各缔约国考虑责任问题并制定国际规则和程序。这一进程花费的时间比预想的要长，而且只产生了一个相当保守的文件，对国内法的影响微乎其微。事实上，不论是有意还是无意，签订于 2010 年 10 月的《吉隆坡补充议定书》[221] 并没有如有些人期望的那样建立一个国际制度来规定改性活生物体的越境转移所造成损害的责任。正是因为受到了这些生物体的生产公司以及主要出口国的重大影响，议定书才将绝大多数的干预措施交付给一个补偿性制度，而这项制度由各国的国内法负责制定（第 12 条）。[222]

四　遗传资源的获取和惠益分享

（一）"种子战争"

遗传资源的获取问题是非常重要的，其一，它是利润极高的经济活动的基础；其二，它是一个主要的规制挑战。《2030 年可持续发展议程》从几个方面来应对这一问题，特别是它们的收获及其关联的重新分配范围。[223] 另外，这一问题为《生物多样性公约》在当前热议的粮食安全中的关键作用提供了一个例证。[224]

数个世纪以来，拥有更高产量的各类种子是通过从最佳标本中进行挑

---

[220] Biosafety Protocol, supra footnote 5, Art. 13 (1).

[221] Nagoya-Kuala Lumpur Supplementary Protocol to the Cartagena Protocol on Biosafety, 15 October 2010, UNEP/CBD/BS/COP-MOP/5/17. 截至 2017 年 4 月，该议定书只差几个国家的批准就可以达到生效所要求的数量（40 个）。

[222] See Hermitte et al., supra footnote 189, pp. 426ff; S. Jungcurt and N. Schabus, "Liability and Redress in the Context of the Cartagena Protocol on Biosafety" (2010) 19 *Review of European Community and International Environmental Law* 197.

[223] *Transforming our World*, suprafootnote 31, SDGs 2 (targets 2.5 and 2.a) and 15 (target 15.6).

[224] See J. Kloppenburg, *First the Seed: The Political Economy of Plant Biotechnology*, 1492-2000 (Cambridge University Press, 1988); J. Kloppenburg, "Impeding Dispossession, Enabling Repossession: Biological Open Source and the Recovery of Seed Sovereignty" (2010) 10 *Journal of Agrarian Change* 367.

选这样一个缓慢的进程而得以确定的，这些最佳标本被当成"人类共同遗产"[225] 的一部分，因为这些不同品种标本的获取及其后续利用都是免费的。这一方法并不是共享愿景导致的必然结果，而是限制获取各类品种种子所引发的挑战导致了这一结果。种子真的就是生命的源头。它们会转变为植物并生产出可以出售（为了终端利用，例如消费或加工）或者重新栽种的新种子。农民只需要单次获取一个更优良品种的种子。其后，他们只用从收成中保存部分种子并再次栽种它们，因为这些种子可以无限期地再生产。但是，在20世纪，受两个主要因素的影响，这一情况经历了深刻变化。

第一个因素是那些限制种子的再生产能力以及再种植能力的技术的发展。无论是通过杂交（改良种子以限制再生产）、灭菌法（对某一种子进行基因改良使其在首次使用后变得不育，或者对那些更易被产业掌握的一些化学成分的使用设定再生产前提条件）或者标识（依据交易的不同种子来辨别植物），重新种植的可能性都受到了严重制约。另外，基于各种原因，包括改良种子对抵抗力较弱的种子的影响、这一领域公共研究的削弱以及产业所采取的过激的市场营销策略，改良种子的利用最终导致了单一栽培的发展；换言之，造成的结果是仅有一小部分种子可以被随处利用。种子数量的减少导致植物更容易受到害虫的伤害，因为害虫会更容易适应新种子的特性并能在数年后大幅降低产量。造成的结果就是，种子的新品种只能在一个有限的期限（数年）内提供高产量，在此之后市场又会需要一个新的品种。

第二个因素具有法律属性。因为当前在技术上已经可以限制重新种植的可能，下一步就是用法律术语来表述这一限制。用于这一目的的工具是针对商业化种子授予国内层面[226]和国际层面[227]的知识产权。这些权利（育种者权利）就与农民的权利产生了直接的冲突。因此种子的重新种植就

---

[225] 值得一提的是，"人类共同遗产"这一概念所引发的项目并不是千篇一律的。在涉及国家管辖范围以外的海底时，针对获取和开发的规制是大不相同的。参见第三章。

[226] See TRIPS Council, Review of the Provisions of Article 27.3 b: Illustrative List of Questions Prepared by the Secretariat-Revision, Document IP/C/W/273/Rev.1, 18 February 2003.

[227] International Convention for the Protection of New Varieties of Plants of December 2, 1961, as revised at Geneva on 10 November 1972, 23 October 1978 and 19 March 1991 ("UPOV Convention"), available at: www.ecolex.org (TRE-001119), Agreement on Trade-Related Aspects of Intellectual Property Trade, 15 April 1994, 1869 UNTS 299 ("TRIPS"), Art. 27 (3) (b).

侵犯了商业化种子品种的知识产权。当然，这些发展引起了极大的争议。发展中国家根据共同遗产这一方式已经批准在其领土上收集遗传资源，它们现在面临的问题是必须尊重那些位于发达国家的跨国公司对这些种子品种的知识产权。

正是在这样一个对抗的背景下，（国际社会）围绕多个国际文件进行了谈判工作，包括《生物多样性公约》和《名古屋议定书》。值得一提的是，这样争论不仅涉及遗传资源的地位（"人类共同遗产"对"主权和所有权"）及其法律后果（"获取""可专利性""重新种植的权利"），还涉及某一特定地位的不同表述方式。事实上，在20世纪80年代早期，世界粮农组织曾尝试将"共同遗产"这一地位延伸到遗传资源利用所生产的产品，包括跨国公司开发的植物品种。[228] 在另一个极端，第二个选择是将植物品种和遗传资源都纳入一个占有制度中。这是《生物多样性公约》（及其《名古屋议定书》[229]）所采用的方法，更具体来讲，后文所述的《植物遗传资源国际条约》[230] 也采用了这一方法。

（二）国际法的作用

在"种子战争"中，国际法的作用是什么？通常情况是，法律的定型往往是主要战场之一。[231] 在20世纪80年代末期，一个日益清晰的事实是，所有权这种模式更容易推广，战场的前线转移到遗传资源获取和惠益分享管理的具体安排。在此背景下，必须审视两个重要的问题，即（1）规制所涉及的客体；（2）资源获取管理的具体安排。

《生物多样性公约》第15条体现的这一制度的直接客体是"遗传资源"，第2条将其定义为：

---

[228] See J. R. Kloppenburg and D. L. Kleinman, "Seeds of Controversy: National Property vs Common Heritage", in J. R. Kloppenburg (ed.), *Seeds and Sovereignty: The Use and Control of Plant Genetic Resources* (Durham, NC: Duke University Press, 1988), p. 174.

[229] On this instrument see E. Morgera, E. Tsiumani, M. Buck, *Unravelling the Nagoya Protocol. A commentary on the Nagoya Protocol on Access and Benefit-sharing to the Convention on Biological Diversity* (The Hague: Brill, 2014).

[230] International Treaty on Plant Genetic Resources for Food and Agriculture, 3 November 2001, 2400 UNTS 379 ("ITPGR").

[231] See M.-A. Hermitte, "La construction du droit des ressources génétiques-Exclusivismes et échanges au fil du temps", in M.-A. Hermitte and P. Kahn (eds.), *Les ressources génétiques et le droit dans les rapports Nord-Sud* (Brussels: Bruylant, 2004).

具有实际或潜在价值的……来自植物、动物、微生物或其他来源的任何含有遗传功能单位的材料。

这一客体是一个广义的类别,在它之下还有一个具体类别,即"用于食物和农业的植物遗传资源",[232] 受到了特别的规制［《植物遗传资源国际条约》（ITPGR）］。将"遗产资源"定性为保护的客体还应考虑到《生物多样性公约》另一个相关客体,即"土著和地方社区体现传统生活方式而与生物多样性的保护和持续利用相关的知识、创新和实践"（第 8 条第 10 款）。《名古屋议定书》第 3 条解释了"遗传资源"和"传统知识"之间的联系,第 3 条涵盖了"与遗传资源相关的传统知识"。在实践中,这一关联涉及传统医学知识、农业实践以及更通用的防虫或个人护理。[233] 因此,正如前文所述,谈判超出了种子的范畴而延伸到了其他有争议的领域。[234] 在当前涉及客体拓展的讨论中,两个问题值得特别关注。一个问题是与遗传资源并没有具体关联的传统知识的利用。[235] 另一个问题是,遗传物质的数字信息（而非实际的遗传物质）的交换在多大范围可以被当作遗传资源的利用。《生物多样性公约》（及其《名古屋议定书》）和《植物遗传资源国际条约》都是针对遗传物质本身而设计的。合成生物学科研中数字信息的利用可以使得它们无须接触现实。在 2016 年的缔约方会议上,这一问题尚无定论,但是已经启动了一个进程来探索它的整合,[236] 正如《植物遗传资源国际条约》文本规定的一样。[237]

---

[232] ITPGR, supra footnote 230, Art. 1. 必须指出的是《植物遗传资源国际条约》并未涵盖那些用于医疗用途的动植物遗传资源。

[233] Hermitte et al., supra footnote 169, p. 415.

[234] See S. Safrin, "Hyperownership in a Time of Biotechnological Promise: The International Conflict to Control the Building Blocks of Life" (2004) 98 *American Journal of International Law* 641.

[235] 针对这一问题,2016 年缔约方大会制定了一套有关原住民和当地社区的传统知识（即使这些知识与遗传资源没有关联）的利用的自愿性指南。See Decision XIII/18 "Article 8 (j) and related provisions: Mo'otz Kuxtal voluntary guidelines", 17 December 2016, CBD/COP/DEC/XIII/18.

[236] Decision 2/14 "Digital sequence information on genetic resources", 16 December 2016, CBD/NP/MOP/DEC/2/14.

[237] 与植物遗传资源相关的信息已经被整合进《植物遗传资源国际条约》第 17 条所设立的全球信息系统及其工作计划之中。See Resolution 3/2015 "The Vision and the Programme of Work on the Global Information System", IT/GB-6/15/Res3.

第二个问题涉及管理受规制客体的具体安排。《生物多样性公约》在第 15 条规定的一般制度通过《名古屋议定书》和《植物遗传资源国际条约》得到了进一步细化。这一制度的基石是资源所在国有权规制资源的获取，可以选择批准或者拒绝。[238] 更具体来讲，获取是有条件的，它有赖于遗传资源原产国的同意，[239] 有时还需要相关"土著人和当地社区"的同意。[240] 而这种同意则是有赖于资源利用带来的惠益分享的具体安排（与资源原产国分享，有时还会涉及土著人和当地社区）。[241] 在实践中，惠益分享这一条款有可能包括资金返还、知识产权的使用许可甚至共同所有权，它是由协议在个案基础上决定的，它应包含法律普遍规定的最基本内容。用于粮食和农业的植物遗传资源则是受到一个特别制度的约束，这一制度是参照一个"获取和分享的多边制度"（《植物遗传资源国际条约》第 10 条）而构建的。这一制度适用于《植物遗传资源国际条约》的一个附录所指定的一个名录（代表了人类消费的近 80%），它的目的是通过限制协商过程的交易成本来促进这些资源的交易，并根据具体情况来促成获取和惠益分享协议。

这些就是在资源占有模式这一整体框架下达成的妥协。想要具体评估已建立制度的表现是比较困难的。一些研究暗示了形形色色或不令人满意的结果，[242] 但是在某些案例中还是实现了真实的协同增效。[243] 为了当前的目的，首先必须强调的是《生物多样性公约》在食品安全上发挥的作用

---

[238] See CBD, supra footnote 10, Art. 15（1）; Nagoya Protocol, supra footnote 6, Art. 6（1）, ITPGR, supra footnote 230, Art. 10（1）.

[239] CBD, supra footnote 10, Art. 15（5）; Nagoya Protocol, supra footnote 6, Art. 6（1）.

[240] Nagoya Protocol, supra footnote 6, Arts. 6（2）and 7. See also the "Mo'otz Kuxtal voluntary guidelines", supra footnote 235.

[241] CBD, supra footnote 10, Arts. 15（7）, 16 and 19; Nagoya Protocol, supra footnote 6, Art. 5. Article 13（2）of the Protocol introduced a written certification of the legality of access to regulated resources. On the complexities of benefit sharing see E. Morgera, "The Need for an International Concept of Fair and Equitable Benefit Sharing"（2016）27 European Journal of International Law 353.

[242] See *When Nature Goes Public*: *The Making and Unmaking of Bioprospecting in Mexico*（Princeton University Press, 2003）; S. Greene, "Indigenous People Incorporated? Culture as Politics, Culture as Property in Biopharmaceutical Bioprospecting"（2004）45 *Current Anthropology* 211.

[243] See M. D. Coughlin, "Using the Merck-INBio agreement to clarify the Convention on Biological Diversity"（1993）31 *Columbia Journal of Transnational Law* 337. See also R. Lewis-Lettington and S. Mwanyiki, *Case Studies on Access and Benefit Sharing*（Rome: International Plant Genetic Resources Institute, 2006）.

以及生物多样性保护和资源开发之间的紧密联系。正如后文所述,关于遗传资源获取的争论,以及更整体的关于生物多样性保护的争论已经延伸到国家管辖范围以外区域。

五 国家管辖范围外的生物多样性

在过去几十年,技术的发展为勘探和开发海洋环境遥远地区的各种生物及遗传资源提供了越来越多的机会。多个拥有相关技术手段的国家也因此能够对这些资源攫取不成比例的份额,而这些资源的法律地位也各不相同。根据一些估计,超过70%的海洋种源基因序列专利集中于三个国家,而且十个国家就占到了2000—2010年在国家管辖范围以外地区所获捕捞总量的70%。[244] 除了这些基于公平的考量,国家管辖范围外生物多样性的保护问题也是非常重要的。事实上,各种各样的活动,从海底采矿到生物质移除(包括渔业),从塑料降解到海洋酸化,都对国家管辖范围外生物多样性造成了重大威胁。[245]

在这一整体背景下,2004年,海洋生物多样性的保护和可持续利用问题被提上了联合国海洋和海洋法大会(UN General Assembly on Oceans and the Law of the Sea)的工作日程。在这一场合,(联合国)决定建立一个不限成员名额特设非正式工作组(Ad Hoc Open-ended Informal Working Group)来"研究与国家管辖范围外的生物多样性的保护和可持续利用相关的问题"。[246] 国家管辖范围外生物多样性工作组(BBNJ Working Group)花了十年讨论这些问题。这些讨论中两个重大里程碑是工作组在2011年提出的建议(后来受到了联合国大会的认可),即在《联合国海洋法公约》下制定一项协定,[247] 并为2012年里约峰会成果文件的出台提供更多

---

[244] R. Blasiak, J. Pittman, N. Yagi, H. Sugino, "Negotiating the Use of Biodiversity in Marine Areas beyond National Jurisdiction" (2016) 3 *Frontiers in Marine Science* 1, p. 2.

[245] See A. Eassom et al., *Horizon scan of pressures on Biodiversity Beyond National Jurisdiction*, UNEP-WCMC (2017), Cambridge, UK.

[246] Resolution 59/24 "Oceans and the law of the sea", 4 February 2005, UN Doc. A/Res/59/24 (4 February 2005) para 73.

[247] See Letter dated 30 June 2011 from the Co-Chairs of the Ad Hoc Open-ended Informal Working Group to the President of the General Assembly, UN Doc. A/66/119, Annex (Recommendations), and Resolution 66/231 "Oceans and the law of the sea", 5 April 2012, UN Doc. A/Res/66/231, para. 166 (endorsing the recommendation).

的推动力。[248] 最后，工作组终于就一份成果文件达成了共识并将其提交到2015年1月的联合国大会。[249] 在此基础上，联合国大会建立了一个筹备委员会以便确定《联合国海洋法公约》下协议草案的要素，并在2017年年底之前向联合国大会重提建议。[250] 预计联合国大会将召集一个政府间会议来制定该项条约。

这是一个复杂的行政过程，从一个工作组的非正式讨论、到同一工作组的有组织讨论、到筹备委员会制定一份草案、到可能由一个政府间会议来制定一项条约，这都表明在当前这一问题上达成协议的难度。在本书即将出版之际谈判仍然在继续，后文讨论的主要目的在于：（1）描述一个可能制定的协议的实质框架；（2）针对某些问题提供一些观点。

联合国大会决议所定义的实质框架已经相对完善了，虽然还是有点模糊不清。这一协议将会是《联合国海洋法公约》下的一项有约束力的文件，[251] 聚焦于"国家管辖范围外海洋生物多样性"的"保护"和"可持续利用"（以回应《生物多样性公约》的支柱），[252] 并更具体地应对一系列问题（所有问题都应被涵盖，包括其他那些潜在问题）：

> 特别是，作为一个整体，海洋遗传资源，包括惠益分享和各种措施，例如基于区域的管理手段，包括海洋保护区、环境影响评价和能力建设以及海洋技术转让。[253]

重要的是，该决议明确指出：

---

[248] "The Future We Want", 11 September 2012, UN Doc. A/Res/66/288, para. 162.

[249] Letter dated 13 February 2015 from the Co-Chairs of the Ad Hoc Open-ended Informal Working Group to the President of the General Assembly, 13 February 2015, UN Doc. A/69/780, Annex (outcome document).

[250] Resolution 69/292 "Development of an international legally-binding instrument under the United Nations Convention on the Law of the Sea on the conservation and sustainable use of marine biological diversity of areas beyond national jurisdiction", 19 June 2015, UN Doc. A/RES/69/292 ("BBNJ Resolution").

[251] Ibid., para. 1.

[252] Ibid., paras. 1 and 2.

[253] Ibid., para. 2.

协定"不得损害现有的相关法律文件和框架以及相关的全球、区域和部门机构"。[254]

鉴于涉及这一问题的法律文件是多种多样的（例如区域性渔业管理组织、第四章讨论的海洋法文件及其他大量文件[255]），以及"不得损害"这一术语的模棱两可，这一"保留条款"有可能会造成实施上的困难。这就引发了下一个要讨论的问题。

事实上，"不得损害"这一术语可以被解释成确保一个针对国家管辖范围外生物多样性的最低级别的保护（新协议将因此提供公平的条件）；或者，相反地，也可以被理解为一个提醒，即现有的法律文件（包括功能紊乱的区域性渔业管理组织和那些收获国家管辖范围外的生物多样性的国家当前享有的自由）将会优先于任何潜在的协议。这些含意凸显了谈判中的深刻分歧。谈判的目标被确定为达成一个在《联合国海洋法公约》下的实施协议，这一事实表明《生物多样性公约》不被当作一个合适的场合来解决这一问题。[256] 即使在《联合国海洋法公约》框架下，国家管辖范围外生物多样性的地位也是模糊不清的，因为它可以被简单当成生物资源的一部分，从而作为"公地"交由公海自由来管理；或者，相反地，它可以被授予"人类共同遗产"这一地位，这样就在获取、占有和惠益分享方面拥有了深刻含意（参见第三章），特别是涉及遗传资源时。[257] 另外，运用这一揽子交易确定的手段（特别是区划管理工具和环境影响评价）也对治理结构（需要一定程度的制度化建设并与现有体系开展协作）

---

[254] Ibid., para 3.

[255] For two attempts at scanning the instruments that are potentially relevant see E. Barritt, J. E. Viñuales, "Legal Scan: A Conservation Agenda for Biodiversity Beyond National Jurisdiction" (2016) C-EENRG Report (draft version); T. Scovazzi, "Negotiating Conservation and Sustainable use of Marine Biological Diversity in Areas Beyond National Jurisdiction: Prospects and Challenges" (2014) 24 Italian Yearbook of International Law 63.

[256] 虽然，如许多评论者所述，与国家管辖范围外的生物多样性相关的活动没有被《生物多样性公约》的范围或其规范性实践排除在外。See Bowman et al, supra footnote 7, pp. 595–596（与其他著作共同指出《生物多样性公约》的近海范围已经在诉讼中被成功确认）。

[257] On this question see D. Tladi, "The Common Heritage of Mankind and the Proposed Treaty on Biodiversity in Areas beyond National Jurisdiction: The Choice between Pragmatism and Sustainability" (2015) 25 Yearbook of International Environmental Law 113.

和财政具有重大影响。[258] 关于种子战争，围绕国家管辖范围外的生物多样性的谈判提供了一个反面教材，即法律可以在多大程度上被当作一个反射潜在力量和利益的战场，而仅有其中一部分是真正旨在保护生物多样性。

部分参考文献

［1］Affolder, N., "Mining and the World Heritage Convention: Democratic Legitimacy and Treaty Compliance" (2007) 24 *Pace Environmental Law Review* 35.

［2］Anvar, S. L., Semences et droit, Doctoral dissertation (University of Paris I, 2008).

［3］Bail, C., R. Falkner and H. Marquard (eds.), *The Cartagena Protocol on Biosafety-Reconciling Trade in Biotechnology with Environment and Development*? (London: Earthscan, 2002).

［4］Batisse, M. and G. Bolla, *L' invention du patrimoine mondial. Cahiers du Club d' Histoire No.* 2 (Paris: AAFU, 2003).

［5］Bekhechi, M., "Une nouvelle étape dans le développement du droit international de l'environnement: la Convention sur la desertification" (1997) 101 *Revue générale de droit international public* 5.

［6］Birnie, P., *International Regulation of Whaling: From Conservation of Whaling to Conservation of Whales and Regulation of Whale Watching*, 2 vols. (Oceana Publications, 1985).

［7］Boer, B. and G. Wiffen, *Heritage Law in Australia* (Oxford University Press, 2006).

［8］Bourrinet, J. and S. Maljean-Dubois (eds.), *La régulation du commerce international des OGM* (Paris: La Documentation française, 2002).

［9］Bowman, M., "The Ramsar Convention on Wetlands: Has it Made a Difference" (2002) *Yearbook of International Co-operation on Environment and Development* 61.

" 'Normalizing' the International Convention for the Regulation of Whal-

---

[258] See R. Fletcher et al., *Biodiversity Beyond National Jurisdiction: Legal Options for a New International Agreement*, UNEP-WCMC (2017), Cambridge, UK.

ing" (2008) 29 *Michigan Journal of International Law* 293.

[10] Bowman, M., P. Davies and C. Redgwell, *Lyster's International Wildlife Law* (Cambridge University Press, 2nd edn, 2010).

[11] Chandler, M., "The Biodiversity Convention: Selected Issues of Interest to the International Lawyer" (1993) 4 *Colorado Journal of International Law and Policy* 141.

[12] Cordonier‐Segger, M.‐C., F. Perron‐Welch and C. Frison (eds.), *Legal Aspects of Implementing the Cartagena Protocol on Biosafety* (Cambridge University Press, 2013).

[13] Coughlin, M. D., "Using the Merck–INBio Agreement to Clarify the Convention on Biological Diversity" (1993) 31 *Columbia Journal of Transnational Law* 337.

[14] Davis, P. G. G. and C. Redgwell, "The International Legal Regulation of Straddling Fish Stocks" (1996) 67 *British Yearbook of International Law* 199.

[15] . De Lucia, V., "Competing Narratives and Complex Genealogies: The Ecosystem Approach in International Environmental Law" (2015) 27 *Journal of Environmental Law* 91.

[16] Farrier, D. and L. Tucker, "Wise Use of Wetlands under the Ramsar Convention: A Challenge for Meaningful Implementation of International Law" (2000) 12 *Journal of Environmental Law* 21.

[17] Francioni, F., "The Madrid Protocol on the Protection of the Antarctic Environment" (1993) 28 *Texas International Law Journal* 47.

[18] Francioni, F. and F. Lenzerini (eds.), The 1972 World Heritage Convention: A Commentary (Oxford University Press, 2008).

"The Destruction of the Buddhas of Bamiyan and International Law" (2003) 14 European Journal of International Law 619.

[19] Fitzmaurice, M., *Whaling and International Law* (Cambridge University Press, 2015).

[20] Fletcher, R. et al., *Biodiversity beyond National Jurisdiction: Legal Options for a NewInternational Agreement* (Cambridge: UNEP–WCMC, 2017).

[21] Futhazar, G., "The Diffusion of the Strategic Plan for Biodiversity and its Aichi Biodiversity Targets within the Biodiversity Cluster: An Illustration of Current Trends in the Global Governance of Biodiversity and Ecosystems" (2015) 25 *Yearbook of International Environmental Law* 133.

[22] Gillespie, A., "The Management of Protected Areas of International Significance" 10 *New Zealand Journal of Environmental Law* 93.

[23] Glennon, M., "Has International Law Failed the Elephant?" (1990) 84 *American Journal of International Law* 1.

[24] Glowka, L., F. Burhenne-Guilmin, H. Synge and J. A. McNeely, *A Guide to the Convention on Biological Diversity* (Gland: IUCN, 1996).

[25] Goodwin, E. J., "The World Heritage Convention, the Environment and Compliance" (2009) 20 *Colorado Journal of International Law and Policy* 157.

[26] Hagen, P. E. and J. Wiener, "The Cartagena Protocol on Biosafety: New Rules for International Trade in Living Modified Organisms" (2000) 12 *Georgetown International Environmental Law Review* 697.

[27] Harrison, J., *Making the Law of the Sea* (Cambridge University Press, 2011).

[28] Hermitte, M.-A., "La convention sur la diversité biologique" (1992) 38 *Annuaire Françaisde Droit International* 844.

"La construction du droit des ressources génétiques – Exclusivismes et échanges au fildu temps", in M.-A. Hermitte and P. Kahn (eds.), *Les Ressources Génétiques et Ledroit Dans les Rapports Nord-Sud* (Brussels: Bruylant, 2004).

[29] Hermitte, M.-A., I. Doussan, S. Mabile, S. Maljean-Dubois, C. Noiville and F. Bellivier, "La convention sur la diversité biologique a quinze ans" (2006) 52 *Annuaire Français de Droit International* 351.

[30] Hermitte, M.-A., S. Maljean-Dubois and E. Truilhé-Marengo, "Actualités de la convention sur la diversité biologiques: science et politique, équité, biosécurité" (2011) 57 *Annuaire Français de Droit International* 399.

[31] Iles, A., "The Desertification Convention: A Deeper Focus on Social Aspects of Environmental Degradation?" (1995) 36 *Harvard International*

Law Journal 205.

[32] Jungcurt, S. and N. Schabus, "Liability and Redress in the Context of the Cartagena Protocol on Biosafety" (2010) 19 Review of European Community and International Environmental Law 197.

[33] Kimball, L., "Institutional Linkages between the Convention on Biological Diversity and Other International Agreements" (1997) 6 Review of European Community and International Environmental Law 239.

[34] Kloppenburg, J., First the Seed: The Political Economy of Plant Biotechnology, 1492-2000 (Cambridge University Press, 1988).

"Impeding Dispossession, Enabling Repossession: Biological Open Source and the Recovery of Seed Sovereignty" (2010) 10 Journal of Agrarian Change 367.

[35] Kloppenburg, J. and D. L. Kleinman, "Seeds of Controversy: National Property vs Common Heritage", in J. R. Kloppenburg (ed.), Seeds and Sovereignty: The Use and Control of Plant Genetic Resources (Durham: Duke University Press, 1988), pp. 172-203.

[36] Konate, A., "L' Afrique et la Convention des Nations Unies sur la lutte contre la desertification" (2000) 12 African Journal of International and Comparative Law 718.

[37] Lewis-Lettington, R. and S. Mwanyiki, Case Studies on Access and Benefit Sharing (Rome: International Plant Genetic Resources Institute, 2006).

[38] Matthews, V. T., The Ramsar Convention on Wetlands: Its History and Development (Gland: Ramsar Convention Secretariat, 1993).

[39] McConnel, F., The Biodiversity Convention. A Negotiating History (The Hague: Kluwer, 1996).

[40] McGraw, D., "The CBD: Key Characteristics and Implications for Development" (2002) 11 Review of European Community and International Environmental Law 17.

[41] Momtaz, D., "L' Accord relatif à la conservation et la gestion des stocks de poissons chevauchants et grands migrateurs" (1995) 41 Annuaire Français de Droit International 676.

[42] Morgera, E., "The Need for an International Concept of Fair and Equitable Benefit Sharing" (2016) 27 *European Journal of International Law* 353.

[43] Morgera, E. and E. Tsioumani, "Yesterday, Today, and Tomorrow: Looking Afresh at the Convention on Biological Diversity" (2010) 21 *Yearbook of International Environmental Law* 3.

[44] Morgera, E., E. Tsiumani and M. Buck, *Unravelling the Nagoya Protocol. A commentary on the Nagoya Protocol on Access and Benefit-sharing to the Convention on Biological Diversity* (The Hague: Brill, 2014).

[45] Orrego Vicuña, F., *The Changing International Law of High Seas Fisheries* (Cambridge University Press, 2005).

[46] Peyroux, E., "La chasse à la baleine dans le droit international public actuel" (1975) 79 *Revue Générale de Droit International Public* 92.

[47] Puissochet, J.-P., "Le Protocole au Traité sur l'Antarctique relatif à la protection de l'environnement-Madrid" (1991) 37 *Annuaire français de droit international* 755.

[48] Ramsar Convention Secretariat, *The Ramsar Convention Manual* (Gland: Ramsar Convention Secretariat, 6th edn, 2013).

[49] Ramsar Convention Secretariat, *An Introduction to the Ramsar Convention on Wetlands* (Ramsar Handbooks: 5th edn, 2016).

[50] Rayfuse, R., "Biological Resources", in D. Bodansky, J. Brunnée and E. Hey (eds.), *The Oxford Handbook of International Environmental Law* (Oxford University Press, 2007), pp. 362-393.

[51] Redgwell, C., "Environmental Protection in Antarctica: The 1991 Protocol" (1994) 43 *International and Comparative Law Quarterly* 599.

[52] Safrin, S., "Hyperownership in a Time of Biotechnological Promise: The International Conflict to Control the Building Blocks of Life" (2004) 98 *American Journal of International Law* 641.

[53] Sand, P. H., "Wither CITES? The Evolution of a Treaty Regime in the Borderline between Trade and the Environment" (1997) 8 *European Journal of International Law* 29.

[54] Scovazzi, T., "Negotiating Conservation and Sustainable use of

Marine Biological Diversity in Areas Beyond National Jurisdiction: Prospects and Challenges" (2014) 24 *Italian Yearbook of International Law* 63.

[55] Tal, A. and J. A. Cohen, "Bringing 'Top-Down' to 'Bottom-Up': A New Role for Environmental Legislation in Combating Desertification" (2007) 31 *Harvard Environmental Law Review* 163.

[56] Tladi, D., "The Common Heritage of Mankind and the Proposed Treaty on Biodiversity in Areas beyond National Jurisdiction: The Choice between Pragmatism and Sustainability" (2015) 25 *Yearbook of International Environmental Law* 113.

[57] Verschuuren, J., "The Case of Transboundary Wetlands Under the Ramsar Convention: Keep the Lawyers Out!" (2008) 19 *Colorado Journal of International Environmental Law and Policy* 49.

[58] Wijnstekers, W., *L' évolution de la CITES* (Budakeszi CIC, 9th edn, 2011).

[59] Wood, H. W., "The United Nations World Charter for Nature: The Developing Nations' Initiative to Establish Protections for the Environment" (1984/1985) 12 *Ecology Law Quarterly* 977.

[60] Wyman, K. M., "The Property Rights Challenge in Marine Fisheries" (2008) 50 *Arizona Law Review* 511.

[61] Young, O. R., "Effectiveness of International Environmental Regimes: Existing Knowledge, Cutting-Edge Themes, and Research Strategies" (2011) 108 *Proceedings of the National Academy of Sciences* 19853.

第七章 危险物质和活动

第一节 导论

正如前面章节所述，从习惯法和条约法的视角来看，对大气、水和土壤污染的源头规制已经成为国际环境法的主要关注问题之一。[1] 这些"第一代"环境问题实际上导致了大量国内法和国际法律文本的制定。整体上看，我们可以从两个不同角度来看待这一部门法，即对某一特定客体的保护[2]以及对某一特定污染源的规制。将这两个角度联结在一起也是可能的（例如，保护一个特定客体不受某一特定污染源的损害）。数个例证将用于说明这一问题。

我们在前面章节中研究的法律文本的一个重要方面在于，它们被用于保护某一特定客体对抗各种威胁，包括污染（造成栖息地退化的一个因素）。这主要适用于那些保护物种、空间和生物多样性的公约。相反地，其他一些法律文本的构造方式则是为了规制特定污染源（例如运行排放、石油泄漏、废物倾倒或焚化、污染大气的特定物质的排放、消耗臭氧层特定物质的生产和消费，或者对气候造成不利影响的特定物质的排放）。这些法律文本所追求的目标通常是保护某一特定客体（例如海洋环境、臭氧层、气候系统）。但是，它们的重心在于这些客体所面临的部分（而非

---

[1] See P.-M. Dupuy, "Overview of the Existing Customary Legal Regime Regarding International Pollution", in D. B. Magraw (ed.), International Law and Pollution (Philadelphia: University of Pennsylvania Press, 1991), pp. 61–89. See also Chapters 1 and 3.

[2] See K. Kummer, International Management of Hazardous Wastes (Oxford University Press, 1995), pp. 25–26 and Chapter 5.

全部）威胁，³ 而这些客体不断被增补，增补的节奏取决于它们对环境造成影响的认识以及政治可行性。另一种选择是，对这些污染物的规制可以着眼于同时保护多种客体，不论它们是否被明确认定。⁴

  本章聚焦于那些具有特定危险或风险的特定物质和活动的规制，它们不是被当作一个具体客体来受规制，而是被当作更宏观的环境和公共健康来受规制。有大量的法律文本与这一问题存在潜在关联，但是我们关注的重点只是这些物质和活动的预防和控制。有一些法律文本针对这些物质的利用或这些活动所导致损害的赔偿做出了规定，我们将在第八章讨论这一问题。我们将讨论危险物质和活动的国际规制所应对的问题种类以及这一规制的整体结构（本章第二节）。当前，还没有全球性的规范，虽然在过去20年进行了多个尝试想要在国际层面实现某种协作和协调（本章第三节）。尽管现有生效的国际规范是碎片化的，它针对的目标是各种物质（例如化学品、⁵ 重金属⁶和特定种类的废物⁷）或具体风险（工业事故⁸

---

  3 See, e. g., the Montreal Protocol on Substances that Deplete the Ozone Layer, 16 September 1987, 1522 UNTS 28 (which provides for specific substances in Annexes A, B, C, and E in order to protect the environment) or the Kyoto Protocol to the UN Convention on Climate Change, 11 December 1997, 2302 UNTS 148 (which provides for specific substances in Annex A with a view to protecting the climate).

  4 The Protocols to the Convention on Long-Distance Transboundary Air Pollution, 13 November 1979, 1302 UNTS 217 ("LRTAP Convention")《远程越界空气污染公约》的多个议定书针对的是特定物质，但是保护的客体不一定会被明确指定。即使是《哥德堡议定书》[30 November 1999, available at www. ecolex. org (TRE-001328)] 被某些人认定为《远程越界空气污染公约》的最精致的议定书，它采用的结构也是将特定物质的规制与应对那些影响到不同特定客体的数个问题（酸化、富营养化、对流层臭氧）关联在一起。参见第五章。

  5 See, in particular, the Rotterdam Convention on the Prior Informed Consent Procedure for Certain Hazardous Chemicals and Pesticides in International Trade, 10 September 1998, 2244 UNTS 337 ("Rotterdam Convention" or "PIC Convention"); Stockholm Convention on Persistent Organic Pollutants, 22 May 2001, 2256 UNTS 119 ("Stockholm Convention" or "POP Convention").

  6 Protocol to the 1979 Convention on Long-Range Transboundary Air Pollution on Heavy Metals, 24 June 1998, 2237 UNTS 4; Minamata Convention on Mercury, 10 October 2013, available at: www. mercuryconvention. org (last visited on 15 January 2014).

  7 Basel Convention on the Control of Transboundary Movements of Hazardous Wastes and their Disposal, 22 March 1989, 1673 UNTS 57 ("Basel Convention"); Bamako Convention on the Ban on the Import into Africa and the Control of Transboundary Movement and Management of Hazardous Wastes within Africa, 30 January 1991, 30 ILM 773 ("Bamako Convention").

  8 Convention of the United Nations Commission for Europe on the Transboundary Effects of Industrial Accidents, 17 March 1992, 2105 UNTS 457 ("Convention on Industrial Accidents").

及核能⁹），现有的法律文本还是涵盖了受规制物质的整个生命周期（生产、使用、消费、储存、运输、处置）（本章第四节）。

第二节　国际规制框架的客体和结构

化学品的生产和大规模使用是我们这一时代的标志性事件。在20世纪后半叶，这种生产以指数级方式飞速增长。在1970年它的产值接近1710亿美元，到了2010年它的产值达近4.12万亿美元。[10] 换言之，经过40年的时间，这一产品的产值就增长了24倍。另外，化学产品已经渗透到当前经济的方方面面。这些产品不仅越来越多地出现于工业生产和消费品中，而且它们作为经济发展的一个要件的作用也变得至关重要。[11] 在此背景下，人们会问是否存在一个恰当的制度框架来确保化学品日益增长的生产、利用所造成的风险可以被最小化并受到管控。对这一问题的解答应当考虑到多种因素，除了其他一些因素，下列三个问题值得关注。

第一个问题涉及我们用何种方式来评估这些风险。在此背景下，必须在"风险评估"和"风险管理"之间做一个区分。风险评估是对某一物质对人体健康或环境造成的潜在危害进行评估。长期以来，在评估风险等级时所考虑的影响范围已经变得越来越宽泛。早在20世纪40—50年代，规制主要应对的是某一物质的毒性问题（即暴露于某一物质而在短期造成的负面影响）。在60—70年代，风险评估开始将长期暴露

9　Convention on Early Notification of a Nuclear Accident, 26 September 1986, 1439 UNTS 275 ("Convention on Early Notification"); Convention on Assistance in Case of a Nuclear Accident or Radiological Emergency, 26 September 1986, 1457 UNTS 133 ("Convention on Assistance"); Convention on Nuclear Safety, 17 June 1994, 1963 UNTS 293; Joint Convention on the Safety of Spent Fuel Management and on the Safety of Radioactive Waste Management, 5 September 1997, available at: www.ecolex.org (TRE-001273) ("Joint Convention").

10　UNEP, Global Chemicals Outlook I: Synthesis Report (2012) ("GCO Report"), p. 9. The Global Chemicals Outlook II is still at the consultations stage and is expected to be concluded before 2020.

11　Ibid., p. 13.

导致的物质致癌性考虑在内。[12] 到了近期，对风险的理解已经进化到将暴露于数个物质的联合效应（即使单一物质的影响程度被认为是可以接受的）以及某些物质的内分泌干扰（它们可以像激素那样发挥作用——激素仿制——从而影响诸如性别、繁殖、生长或行为的各种进程）也考虑在内。[13] 这一趋势表明了两个结论。一方面，当前我们对风险的认识比20世纪中期更有经验了，这是毋庸置疑的；另一方面，我们不能低估化学品在经济中的泛滥带来的现实挑战（还没有被认识到的风险）。我们不能排除将来还会出现其他不利影响，它可能是某一化学品被释放而造成的没有预料到的影响。但是，在当前，针对化学品泛滥对环境和人体健康的影响，我们只拥有有限的证据，而我们的认识还必须依靠这一点。[14] 一个重要的问题是，是否有一个充分的条件可以停止这些物质的生产？答案在某些情况下无疑是肯定的，正如我们看到的，有条约（例如《持久性有机污染物公约》）就明文禁止特定物质的生产和消费。即使当前流通中的大量物质（超过248000种）[15] 造成了风险，但是还不足以禁止它们的生产。评估这些风险时必须考虑到其他因素，包括这些物质可能提供的服务。这种评估被称为"风险管理"。在这一问题上要考虑的要素具有一个社会经济属性。例如，《持久性有机污染物公约》附录五[16] 就明确指出了在规制进程的这一步应当权衡的数个要素（例如某一限制的实际可行性、社会和经济成本等）。

12　直到20世纪90年代，致癌性一直被看作某一化学品毒性的主导性要件。See T. Colborn, D. Dumanoski and J. Peterson Myers, Our Stolen Future（New York：Dutton, 1996）, p. 19.

13　D. Hunter, J. Salzman and D. Zaelke, International Environmental Law and Policy（New York：Foundation Press, 2011）, p. 911; GCO Report, supra footnote 10, pp. 19ff 指明了这三个步骤。内分泌干扰的完整性仍然存在争议。2012年，联合国环境规划署和世界卫生组织发布的一个联合出版物［UNEP/WHO, State of Science in Endocrine Disrupting Chemicals 2012（Geneva：WHO/UNEP, 2013）］提供了内分泌干扰化学品的一个科学表述。在此基础上，国际化学品管理大会（参见后文第七章第三节第二点）通过了一个决议，将内分泌干扰化学品认定为一个正在发生的政策问题。See Decision III/2 "Emerging policy issues", 29 October 2012, SAICM/ICCM. 3/24, Section F（endocrine-disrupting chemicals）.

14　UNEP, Global Environmental Outlook 5. Environment for the Future We Want（UNEP, 2005）, pp. 168 and 172ff.

15　Ibid., p. 170.

16　POP Convention, supra footnote 5.

第二个问题是化学品影响的不确定性以及化学品规制的社会经济规模带来的挑战,这些物质的生产和消费(通过贸易)向发展中国家的扩散以及适用的法律框架的潜在差异进一步放大了这种挑战,这些国家包括巴西、俄罗斯、印度、印度尼西亚、中国和南非〔所谓的金砖(BRIICS)国家〕[17]。

关于第三个也是最后一个问题,应当强调的是,化学品的规制是基于具体问题具体分析而发展起来的,当一个新的风险被确认或者不期出现的时候,一般采用反应模式。为了理解这一难题,有必要把流通中的化学品的数量(超过248000种)与受到国际规制的产品数量(约60种物质被列入《持久性有机污染物公约》和《事先知情同意公约》的名录,另外《巴塞尔公约》附录八还指定了60种危险废物)进行一个对比。当然,我们不应忽略这样一个事实,即大量物质是在国内或区域级别受到规制的。然而,上述数字之间的差距凸显了一个日益紧迫的需求,即必须在这些物质的规制中实现一定程度的统一协调。

正如本章所述,(国际社会)在这一方面采取了两个主要战略,一个是针对化学品进行普遍规制(不同于基于单一物质的规制),另一个则是试图在那些针对特定物质但是涵盖了化学品的整个生命周期的各种条约之间实现协同增效。这两个战略之间也存在着重要的相互作用,特别是它们可以互相加强。图7-1用示意图的方式展示了国际规制框架的结构。

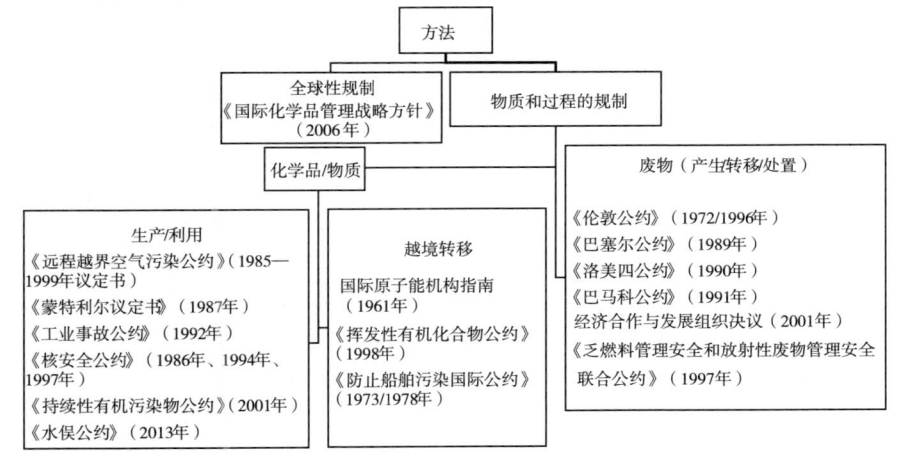

图7-1 危险物质/行为的国际规制框架

---

[17] Ibid., p. 174; GCO Report, supra footnote 10, pp. 13-14.

如图 7-1 所示，这一领域的绝大多数条约涉及的是具体的物质或加工流程。在第四章和第五章中我们已经探讨了这些法律文本中的一部分。本章关注的重点是余下的一些。为了看清这一规范"树"更完整的全貌，有必要再加上几个指南和标准，[18] 以及国内和区域的[19]法律文本，因为它们在实践中的关联性甚至高过某些条约的关联性。

第三节　制定一个全球规制框架的努力

一　政治原动力

化学品的规制是 1992 年里约峰会所讨论的一个重要内容。里约峰会制订的行动计划——《21 世纪议程》[20] 在第 19 章提到了六个优先领域以实现化学品的"环境友好型管理"，它们是：

  （1）扩大和加速对化学品风险的国际评估；（2）化学品分类和标签的一致化；（3）交换有关有毒化学品和化学品风险的资料；（4）拟订减少风险方案；（5）加强管理化学品的国家功能和能力；

 18　See e. g. below the discussion of the origins of the PIC and Basel Conventions as well as, among others: FAO, Guidelines for Legislation on the Control of Pesticides (1989); FAO, Guidelines for the Registration and Control of Pesticides (1985); ILO, Code of Practice on Prevention of Major Industrial Accidents (1991); ILO, Code of Practice concerning the Use of Chemicals at Work (1993); OECD, Council Decision on the Mutual Acceptance of Data in the Assessment of Chemicals (1981) (including Guidelines for the Testing of Chemicals and GLP, Guidelines on Accidents (1992), and others); UNEP, Code of Ethics on the International Trade of Chemicals (1994).

 19　See e. g. Regulation (EC) No 1907/2006 of the European Parliament and of the Council of 18 December 2006 concerning the Registration, Evaluation, Authorisation and Restriction of Chemicals (REACH), establishing a European Chemicals Agency, amending Directive 1999/45/EC and repealing Council Regulation (EEC) No. 793/93 and Commission Regulation (EC) No 1488/94 as well as Council Directive 76/769/EEC and Commission Directives 91/155/EEC, 93/105/EC and 2000/21/EC, OJ L 136/3 (29 May 2007) ("REACH' Regulation). On this instrument see J. Scott, "REACH: Combining Harmonization and Dynamism in the Regulation of Chemicals", in J. Scott (ed.), Environmental Protection: European Law and Governance (Oxford University Press, 2009), pp. 56-91.

 20　Report of the United Nations Conference on Environment and Development, A/CONF. 151/26/Rev. 1 (Vol. 1), 13 June 1992, Resolution 1, Annex 2: Agenda 21 ("Agenda 21").

第七章 危险物质和活动

(6) 防止有毒和危险产品的非法国际贩运。[21]

虽然这一章节并不具备法律约束力，但是在一些合作项目"国际化学品安全性论坛"（International Forum on Chemical Safety, IFCS）[22] 或"化学品无害管理组织间方案"[23] （Inter-Organization Programme for the Sound Management of Chemicals, IOMC）的协作下，它还是对国际组织的工作产生了重大影响。

国际化学品安全性论坛通过的《巴伊亚化学品安全宣言》[24] 以及2002年约翰内斯堡可持续发展峰会通过的一个实施计划提供了更多的原动力，该实施计划重申：

> 如《21世纪议程》提出的承诺，为了可持续发展以及保护人体健康和环境，尤其是为了在2020年之前使得化学品的使用和生产方式能够将其对人体健康和环境的重大不利影响最小化，应开展化学品整个生命周期的无害管理以及有害废物的无害管理。[25]

正如后文所述，这些文本提供的原动力导致了多个化学品全球规制柔性结构的制定。

---

21 Ibid., para. 19.4.

22 联合了各种国际组织、各国政府以及民间团体和私营部门。

23 包含了九个国际组织，即联合国粮农组织、国际劳工组织、联合国开发规划署、联合国环境规划署、联合国工业发展组织、联合国训练研究所、世界卫生组织、世界银行、经济合作与发展组织 [the United Nations Food and Agriculture Organization ("FAO"), the International Labour Organization ("ILO"), the United Nations Development Programme ("UNDP"), the United Nations Environment Programme ("UNEP", now UN Environment), the United Nations Industrial Development Organization ("UNIDO"), the United Nations Institute for Training and Research ("UNITAR"), the World Health Organization ("WHO"), the World Bank, and the Organisation for Economic Cooperation and Development ("OECD")].

24 Bahia Declaration on Chemical Safety, 20 October 2000, IFCS/FORUM III/23w.

25 Report of the World Summit on Sustainable Development, Johannesburg, South Africa, 26 August-4 September 2002, Resolution 2, Plan of Implementation of the World Summit on Sustainable Development, Annex, UN Doc. A/CONF. 199/20, para. 23.

二 主要成果:《联合国化学品全球统一分类和标签制度》和《国际化学品管理战略方针》

《21 世纪议程》《巴伊亚化学品安全宣言》和约翰内斯堡计划有助于各种尝试的发展,其中有两个应在这里进行回顾。

首先,从里约峰会直到约翰内斯堡峰会结束的这十年内,一个《联合国化学品全球统一分类和标签制度》[26] 被逐步制定。这一重要尝试的基础可以从《21 世纪议程》第十九章中找到,它明确呼吁"如果可行,应于 2000 年前建立全球统一和配套的危害分类和标签制度,包括物质的安全数据单和易懂的符号在内"[27]。这项工作是由化学品无害管理组织间方案(IOMC)负责协调,虽然文本是在约翰内斯堡峰会后才被正式批准的,但是其实在 2001 年就已经准备妥当。在此基础上,《约翰内斯堡履行计划》(Johannesburg Plan of Implementation)明确"鼓励各国尽快实施新的全球统一分类和标签制度,力争在 2008 年以前实现该制度的全面运行"。[28]《联合国化学品全球统一分类和标签制度》的实际影响对现有的规制手段和那些新开发手段都是非常重要的。例如,欧洲委员会改革了欧洲分类制度,[29] 加上其他因素,最终导致了《工业事故塞维索指令 II》(现在是 III)的修订,[30] 以及国际层面的《工业事故跨界影响公约》(Convention on Industrial Accidents)的修订。

其次,《约翰内斯堡履行计划》呼吁制定一个《国际化学品管理战

---

[26] United Nations Globally Harmonized System of Classification and Labelling of Chemicals, 2003, ST/SG/AC. 10/30 (GHS). See S. Smith, "GHS: A Short Acronym for a Big Idea" (2007) 69 *Occupational Hazards* 6.

[27] Agenda 21, supra footnote 20, Chapter 19, para. 27.

[28] Plan of Implementation, supra footnote 25, para. 23 (c).

[29] See Regulation (EC) No. 1272/2008 of the European Parliament and of the Council of 16 December 2008 on the classification, labelling and packaging of substances and mixtures, amending and repealing Directives 67/548/EEC and 1999/45/EC, and amending Regulation (EC) No. 1907/2006, OJ L 353/2, 31 November 2008. This regulation complements the REACH Directive, supra footnote 19.

[30] Directive 2012/18/EU of the European Parliament and Council of 4 July 2012 on the control of major-accident hazards involving dangerous substances, amending and subsequently repealing Council Directive 96/82/EC, OJ L 197/1, 24 July 2012.

略方针》(*Strategic Approach to International Chemicals Management*, SAICM)。[31] 它导致多个国际组织通过化学品无害管理组织间方案和国际化学品安全性论坛来开展工作,以制定一个柔性的、不具约束力的化学品全球性规章制度。这一法律文本的重要性在于它与框架公约的相似性。事实上,围绕《国际化学品管理战略方针》[32]的谈判是通过一个构成复杂的委员会进行的,成员包括民间团体和私营部门的代表,还有国家和国际组织的代表,这与框架公约的模式非常相似。另外,这些谈判的成果后来在2006年1月被迪拜(阿拉伯联合酋长国)举办的一个国际化学品管理大会(International Conference on Chemical Management, ICCM)所采纳。其中包括《国际化学品管理迪拜宣言》(*Dubai Declaration on International Chemicals Management*)、一个《支配性政策战略》(*Overarching Policy Strategy*)和一个《全球行动计划》(*Global Plan of Action*)。[33]

《国际化学品管理战略方针》的目标是:

> 实现化学品整个生命周期的无害管理以便在2020年之前使得化学品的使用和生产方式能够将其对人体健康和环境的重大不利影响最小化。[34]

后来,一系列更具体的目标和行动被确定下来,而且,国际化学品管理大会被授权去定期监督它们的实施。[35] 在这一点上,我们可以把国际化学品管理大会与环境条约的缔约方大会做一个类比。[36] 迄今为止,国际化学品管理大会召开了四次,最近的一次是在2015年。2015年第四次大会通过了一个《实现化学品无害管理2020年目标的总体取向和指南》(*O-*

31　Plan of Implementation, supra footnote 25, para. 23 (b)。

32　UNEP, *Strategic Approach to International Chemicals Management. SAICM Texts and Resolutions of the International Conference on Chemicals Management*, 2007, available at: www.unece.org (last visited 31 January 2013)。

33　后者尚未正式制定。

34　SAICM, supra footnote 32, para. 13。

35　Ibid., para. 24 (a) — (b)。

36　Hunter et al., supra footnote 13, p. 937。

verall Orientation and Guidance for Achieving the 2020 Goal of Sound Management of Chemicals)[37] 以便依据《2030 年可持续发展议程》及其可持续发展目标来规划它将来的工作。[38] 这一指导性文件明确指出了六个核心行动领域：（1）加强利用相关者的责任（即健康、农业、劳工、工业和公共利益团体的更多参与）；（2）建立和增强有关化学品与废物的国内立法和规章制度（绝大部分是在发展中国家，通过适当的合作和能力建设）；（3）使得化学品和废物的无害管理成为《2030 年可持续发展议程》的主流；（4）针对出现的政策问题，加强降低风险和信息共享的努力（这些问题包括内分泌干扰物、电力及电子产品的生命周期、纳米技术和人造纳米材料）；（5）提升信息获取（例如在《联合国化学品全球统一分类和标签制度》尚未实施的场合实施这一制度）；（6）对朝向 2020 年目标的进展进行评估。

评估这项工作是非常重要的，因为《国际化学品管理战略方针》是被当作单一化学品规制或"零碎规制"的替代方案（但是也可能及时提供了一个伞状框架）来启动的。作为一个不具约束力的框架，它为解决那些在其他平台可能引发更大争议的问题（内分泌干扰物或电力及电子废物）提供了一个平台。但是，有一个问题依旧存在，那就是在一个化学品全球性文件的通过无法达成政治共识的情况下，《国际化学品管理战略方针》所采用的路线是否可以为实现相似结果做出一个积极贡献。这一问题的答案必须是基于实证。在 2012 年 9 月的国际化学品管理大会第三次会议上，提交了第一份《国际化学品管理战略方针》的实施进展报告。[39] 这一报告主要总结了在这一问题上的可见进展。[40] 但是，正如《国际化学品管理战略方针》秘书处在一个总结报告中指出的那样，大量有

---

[37] Decision IV/1 "Implementation towards the achievement of the 2020 goal", 25 October 2015, SAICM/ICCM. 4/15, endorsing at para. 1 the "Orientation and guidance" document.

[38] See Resolution 70/1, "Transforming our World : The 2030 Agenda for Sustainable Development", 21 October 2015, UN doc A/RES/70/1, including the statement of 17 Sustainable Development Goals, each with several targets. Chemicals and waste generation are addressed under a number of SDGs, particularly SDGs 3 (target 3.9), 6 (target 6.3), 11 (target 11.6) and 12 (targets 12.4 and 12.5).

[39] Progress in Implementation of SAICM Reported for 2009–2010, 18 August 2012, SAICM/ICCM. 3/INF/6.

[40] Ibid., p. 3.

关风险减少、治理、技术合作或国际非法交易的这些活动似乎是受到了一些措施（这些措施是为了实施《持久性有机污染物公约》而采取的措施）的影响，还受到了《关于汞的水俣公约》（*Minamata Convention*）谈判进程的影响。[41] 在 2015 年第四次会议上，国际化学品管理大会通过了一项决议，呼吁对 2006—2015 年的《国际化学品管理战略方针》进行一个独立评估，以便为一个中期工作组提供信息，这一工作组被授权针对《国际化学品管理战略方针》从现在到 2020 年的作用提出建议。[42] 这一工作仍在进行中，但是趋势是日益趋向一个协同进程，而《国际化学品管理战略方针》则是在多个更具体条约（特别是前文提及的四个条约）的运行中充当了多方利益相关者的一个伞状框架。[43]

第四节　特定物质和活动的规制

一　受规制的客体和技术

虽然针对有害物质和活动的国际规制是碎片化的，但是它还是涵盖了化学品的整个生命周期。从法律的视角来看，我们可以把这一周期分为三个阶段。

第一个阶段涉及的是化学品的"生产"和"使用"。这些术语应当在广义上来解读。例如，"生产"这一术语也包含了废物的产生，而废物的构成成分导致其必须被当作化学品一样来小心处置。类似地，"使用"这一术语也适用于化学品的消费，正如《蒙特利尔议定书》第 1 条第 6 款之规定。总体上，"生产"和"使用"这些术语也涵盖了制造某个化学品（用于多种用途）的各种工业生产过程或者将某一产品用于另一目的（例如利用核聚变来发电，或者在生产过程中利用某一物质）。

第二个阶段关注的是这些物质的转移。这类转移可能发生在一国的领

41　Secretariat Summary Report on Progress in Implementation of the Strategic Approach, 7 June 2012, SAICM/ICCM. 3/4, paras. 13, 16-22.

42　Decision IV/4 "The Strategic Approach and sound management of chemicals and waste beyond 2020", 28 October 2015, SAICM/ICCM. 4/15, paras 1 and 2.

43　For a study of this combined approach see D. Ditz, B. Tuncak, "Bridging the divide between toxic risks and global chemical governance" (2014) 23 RECIEL 181.

土内，还可能越境或者发生在国家管辖范围以外（例如海运）。内部转移是由国内法来规制的，而国内法通常也会遵守国际指南和标准。环境条约通常都会涉及越境转移和海洋运输。"越境转移"这一术语也应从广义上来解读，它涵盖了受到管控的各种行为，例如受控物质的出口、储存、运输、中转和进口。对"转移"进行如此解读是为了抓住国际法律文本所使用的规制角度。

第三个阶段关注的是化学品或那些被当成"废物"的含化学品产品的处置。从一个分析的视角来看，这一阶段除了这些物质的实际消除之外，还包含了多种行为。事实上，从严格意义上讲，废物的"管理"这一提法可能更恰当，因为废物的产生和越境转移也属于规制的目标。但是处置这一术语还是有意义的，它可以凸显涉及"废物"的各种行为的具体目标。

正如后面章节所述，化学品生命周期的这三个阶段为针对危险物质和活动的国际规制的讨论提供了一个有用的基础。它们也可以与前面章节讨论的规制方法进行一个对比。特别是我们可以发现名录方法及其三个组成部分（名录、义务、修订制度）[44] 被广泛用于物质和危险行为的规制，《持久性有机污染物公约》所采用的复杂而精致的结构就说明了这一点。但是，在本书的文本中，我们无法针对所有相关文件提供一个详细的分析。[45] 因此后文将会聚焦于四个最重要的条约，即《持久性有机污染物公约》（对持久性有机污染物的生产或使用的规制）、《鹿特丹公约》（关于信息交换的制度）、《巴塞尔公约》（危险废物无害管理的各种方法）和《水俣公约》（覆盖汞的整个生命周期）。另外，我们也会展示两套制度是如何被建立以确保特定工业生产过程的安全，这两套制度是《工业事故跨界影响公约》（*Convention on the Transboundary Effects of Industrial Accidents*）和核能管理的综合方法。

44　See Chapter 6.

45　See Kummer, supra footnote 2; M. Pallemaerts, *Toxics and Transnational Law: International and European Regulation of Toxic Substances as Legal Symbolism* (Oxford: Hart Publishing, 2003); S. Tromans, *Nuclear Law: The Law Applying to Nuclear Installations and Radioactive Substances in its Historic Context* (Oxford: Hart Publishing, 2010); M. Montjoie, *Droit international et gestion des déchets radioactifs* (Paris: LGDJ, 2011).

二 生产和使用的规制

(一) 物质的规制:《持久性有机污染物公约》

《关于持久性有机污染物的斯德哥尔摩公约》或《持久性有机污染物公约》[46]的产生必须结合20世纪90年代进行的一些尝试来分析,这些尝试是:(1) 1992年里约峰会在化学品规制领域的成果,特别是《21世纪议程》第十九章;[47](2) 更深刻地认识《持久性有机污染物公约》的特点(持续性、能够长距离移动、生物积累性的本性,这就使得它们上升到营养链的顶端——人类),它们的动态性〔所谓的"草斗"效应,即它们在温带地区挥发,它们通过大气风力的大范围流通,它们以下雨的方式在寒冷地区(特别是极地)的凝结和沉淀〕以及它们所造成的内分泌干扰风险;[48](3) 制定了一个《关于可持续有机污染物的议定书》(《远程越界空气污染公约》在区域背景下的应用)。[49]

在此背景下,联合国环境规划署启动了一个谈判进程,第一步是要求国际化学品安全性论坛[50]来应对这一问题并提出建议,并在1997年通过了一个正式授权以制定一个有关可持续有机污染物的条约。正如其他许多环境条约所采用的模式,这一授权是由一个政府间谈判委员会领导,最终在2001年制定了《持久性有机污染物公约》。[51]谈判进程遇到了多个挑战,例如条约目标的定性(消除抑或管理),是否有必要将12种最危险持久性有机污染物(所谓的"肮脏的一打")以外的化学品陆续列入条约,条约与国际贸易中的国家义务之间的相互作用,或者提供给发展中国家的资助及援助。[52]我们在后续讨论中有必要将这些问题牢记在心,因为它们有助于我们理解那些潜在的妥协,而这些妥协有时会被公约的最终文

---

46 See P. Lallas, "The Stockholm Convention on Persistent Organic Pollutants" (2001) 95 *American Journal of International Law* 692; M. A. Olsen, *Analysis of the Stockholm Convention on Persistent Organic Pollutants* (Dobbs Ferry NY: Oceana, 2003).

47 See supra Section 7.3.1.

48 See supra Section 7.1.

49 See Chapter 6.

50 See supra Section 7.3.1.

51 POP Convention, supra footnote 5.

52 These issues are addressed by Lallas, supra footnote 46, 696.

本模糊处理。

正如前文所述，《持久性有机污染物公约》采用了名录方法，本书第六章对这一方法进行了介绍。实际上，将名录方法用于有害物质和活动的规制，《持久性有机污染物公约》是最精致的例证之一。这种精致不仅体现于名录的结构或国家所承担的义务的范围，还体现于一套分权制衡的复杂制度，让人联想到一个真正的宪法架构。图7-2概括了这一公约的基本结构。

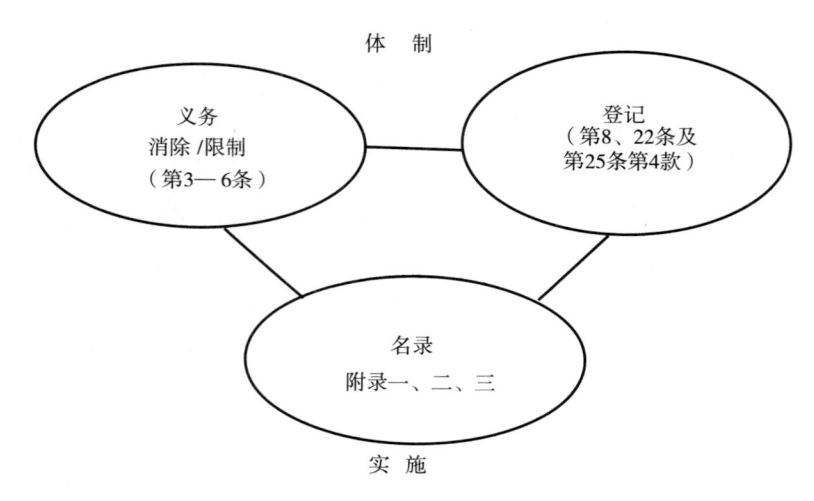

图7-2 《持久性有机污染物公约》的基本结构

这一公约包含了三个名录，即附录一、附录二和附录三。附录一（消除）及其后来在2009年、2011年、2013年和2015年的四次修订目前包含了22种物质（农药和工业化学品）。[53] 附录二（限制）只包含了两种物质，[54] 包括滴滴涕杀虫剂，美国作家蕾切尔·卡逊（Rachel Carson）于

---

[53] 如果将过去这些年的修订都考虑在内（包括那些有待生效的或必须被更多缔约方接受的），附录一就包含了下列这些物质：艾氏剂、六氯化苯、氯丹、十氯酮、狄氏剂、工艺硫丹及其同分异构体（2011年修订）；异狄氏剂、七氯、六溴联苯、六溴环十二烷（2013年修订）；六溴联苯醚和七溴联苯醚、六氯苯、六氯丁二烯（2015年修订）；林丹、灭蚁灵、五氯苯、多氯环烷及其盐分和脂类（2015年修订）；多氯联苯、多氯环烷（它们中的几个已经列入2015年修订）；四溴联苯醚、五溴联苯醚、毒杀芬。

[54] Annex B contains：DDT［1，1，1-trichloro-2，2-bis（4-chlorophenyl）ethane］；Perfluorooctane sulfonic acid, its salts and perfluorooctane sulfonyl fluoride.

1962年创作的著名著作《寂静的春天》特意提到了这一杀虫剂。[55] 附录三（非故意的生产）关注的是人类行为非故意生产或释放的持久性有机污染物，它包含6种物质，[56] 其中4种（例如多氯联苯）也被列入了附录一（涉及这些物质的故意生产或使用）。

每个附录所列举的这些物质都受制于具体义务。为了理解这些义务的结构，要弄清楚两个问题。首先，与《远程越界空气污染公约》的《关于可持续有机污染物的议定书》（在北大西洋为主的背景下制定）不同，[57]《持久性有机污染物公约》还想将许多发展中国家整合进来。因此，在大相径庭的社会经济背景下就有必要针对这些物质的消除或渐进限制采取一定程度的区别对待。针对每一个名录中的物质，"特殊豁免"被加到附录文本中，而不是在公约文本中规定不同的义务。那些想要利用任一特殊豁免的国家必须在秘书处登记。特殊豁免只能用于一个有限的时间段（一般是五年，除非被允许延长）。[58] 如此一来，附录一和附录二中这些物质的义务就受制于各种灵活性，包括这些特殊豁免。其次，如果认为《持久性有机污染物公约》仅仅是要求消除或限制附录中物质的生产或消除，那么这一定性就是不准确的。该公约还包含了针对这些物质的贸易规制（第3条第1款和第3条第2款），而且它还试图管控特定副产品（第5条和附录三）甚至进行废物管理（第6条）。从这一立场来看，该公约的制度涵盖了受规制物质的整个生命周期，虽然它的重点是关于这些物质的消除或限制。

第3条包含了缔约方的核心义务。可以把有关生产或利用的义务与有关贸易的义务做一个区分。针对前者，每个缔约国都有义务采取必须措施以消除附录一中物质的生产和使用（第3条第1款）并限制附录二中物质的生产和使用（第3条第1款）。针对贸易义务，第3条第2款规定的

55　R. Carson, *Silent Spring* (Boston: Houghton Mifflin, 1962).

56　Annex C contains (incorporating the amendment of 2015): hexachlorobenzene; pentachlorobenzene; polychlorinated biphenyls; polychlorinated dibenzo-p-dioxins and dibenzofurans; polychlorinated naphtalenes (several of them introduced by the 2015 amendment).

57　Protocol to the 1979 Convention on Long-Range Transboundary Air Pollution on Persistent Organic Pollutants (POPs), 24 June 1998, 2230 UNTS 79 ("POP Protocol").

58　See Lallas, supra footnote 46, 700. 这一区别化的手段可以与技术和财政援助联合在一起实施, 参见 POP Convention, supra footnote 5, Art. 11 (2) (c) and 12 to 14 as well as Chapter 9.

义务则是基于物质的地位以及贸易的目的。只有拟议用途被一个例外所批准，或者基于公约规定的"环境无害化处置"这一用途（第3条第2款），这一物质的进口才能被批准。同样地，某一物质的出口只有基于一个特定用途才能被批准。这就取决于某一特定物质是否被附加了一个例外，因此这一目标多少还是有限制性的。不适用例外的那些物质只有凭借"环境无害化型处置"这一用途才能被出口，而适用例外的其他物质的出口则可以凭借这些例外所设定的各种用途。这些限制同样也适用于管理那些针对公约非缔约国的出口。这些出口另外还要求进口国提供特定的保证。[59]

前文的讨论清楚表明，例外这一制度对于我们更好地理解公约所设立的义务具有重要意义。事实上，附录一和附录二中物质所涉及的两种义务的主要区别在于每个具体情况所适用的例外的种类。例外主要分为两类：特殊例外（被称为特殊豁免）和一般例外，它们各有几个变种。特殊豁免适用于附录一和附录二中的物质。这些特殊豁免针对每个物质的生产和使用规定了一些具体"种类"的豁免。如前文所述，各国如果想要某种特定物质适用于一个或多个特殊豁免（必须是基于该物质已被确定的豁免，因为各国不能基于一个未被提及的豁免），就必须做出声明。这一灵活性安排的时间期限原则上被限定为五年（第4条第7款）。秘书处针对各国已利用的特殊豁免进行"登记"。这一登记的优点在于，它无须经历公约或其附录修订的烦琐程序就可以被修订。当某一种特殊豁免没有（或者不再）被利用，它就会被去除而且任何缔约方在将来都不得利用它（第4条第9款）。[60] 有一个案例可以帮助我们理解这一方法并将特殊豁免与其他例外做一个区分。附录一包含了一条脚注（脚注1），它表明一种针对六氯苯（被当作一个封闭系统中有限场地的媒介）的特殊豁免从2009年5月17日开始不再适用，因为没有缔约方登记这一豁免。但是，如另一条脚注（脚注2）所示，这一特殊豁免的到期并不影响某一缔约国去利用一个程序上受限的一般例外（由附录一和附录二的脚注3规定），而且无须登记。换言之，一个高度相似的行为同时会涉及一个特殊豁免和

59　POP Convention, supra footnote 5, Art. 3 (2) (b) (iii).
60　举例来讲，附录一中针对艾氏剂、氯丹、狄氏剂、七氯、六氯苯、灭蚁灵的特殊豁免已经过期。同样地，附录二中针对滴滴涕的特殊豁免也已经过期。

一个一般例外。第一个过期作废了（时间限制是所有特殊豁免的一部分），而一般例外则依然有效。例如，第3条第5款规定，"除非本公约另有规定，第1款和第2款不应适用于拟用于实验室规模的研究或用作参照标准的化学品"。[61] 一个特别种类的一般例外，它也是附录一和附录二的根本区别所在，这些例外被认定为构成了附录二中物质的生产或使用的"可接受的用途"。作为一个例证，滴滴涕杀虫剂可以被生产或用于"疾病媒介物的控制……根据附录二第二部分"，它指的是世界卫生组织在抗击疟疾的战斗中建议使用农药。一般例外，不论是用"可接受的用途"这样的术语来表述或采用其他表述，并不要求特别的登记，因此任何缔约国都可以利用它。另外，与特殊豁免不同，一般例外作为一个规则是不受时间限制的。

在名录方法中，每个名录都与一套义务和例外相关联，这一方法也被用于后来出现的一系列条约中。公约第1条将这一制度放置于风险预防这一方法（由《里约宣言》第15条原则所确立）的逻辑之下。[62] 另外，公约还号召缔约方大会建立一个"可持续有机污染物审查委员会"（Persistent Organic Pollutants Review Committee），它包含了政府指定的代表并以出席并参加表决的成员的2/3多数票通过它的决定（第19条第6款）。这一委员会在公约第8条规定名录的更新过程中发挥了重要作用。如果某一缔约方想要在公约的数个名录的其中一个登记一种新物质，它就必须提交一份提议，这一提议经过秘书处的初步审核后，将交由委员会来讨论。该委员会必须首先评估附录四指定的一些挑选标准是否被遵守，而且它可以在这一阶段就拒绝这一提议。但是，如果委员会认定这些标准得到了遵守，它就会认真起草一个"风险预测"并提交给各缔约国讨论。在各缔约国提交的意见的基础上，委员会将会依据附录五起草一个最终版的风险预测。到了这一步，基于这一个风险预测，委员会可以再次决定是否继续进行或终止这一提议。如果继续进行，下一步就会包括开展一个"风险管理评估"，并将所有规制措施和社会经济影响考虑在内（附录六）。在此基础上，委员会针对是否将某种物质列入某一附录向缔约方大

---

[61] See also the notes in Roman numerals in Annexes A and B.

[62] Rio Declaration on Environment and Development, 13 June 1992, UN Doc. A/CONF.151/26 ("Rio Declaration"), Principle 15.

会提出一个建议（第8条第9款）。缔约方大会以出席并参加表决的缔约方的3/4多数票通过它的决定（第22条第4款）。登记一个新物质这一过程必须满足几个条件。应当指出的是，根据风险预防这一方法，委员会在缺乏科学确定性的情况下也可以做出决定。如果委员会决定不再继续某一份提议（在附录四或附录五这一阶段），该决定可以被上诉到缔约方大会，缔约方大会有权做出不同的决定。一个重要的问题在于，缔约方大会通过的附录一、附录二或附录三的修正案具备何种效力。鉴于这一修正案是通过有效多数投票来通过的，因而持反对意见的国家是否也应受到修正案的约束还存在疑问。公约在这个方面所采用的方法是有细微差别的。原则上，为了不受修正案的约束，某国必须在该修正案发出通知之日起一年内通知各方它不接受修正案（第22条第3款）。如果没有这类通知，修正案将会对该国生效。但是这样一种"退出"制度可以被转换为一种"加入"制度（沉默并不意味着接受），如果在批准该公约时，某国明确表示除非它明文批准涉事修正案，否则它将不受其约束（第25条第4款）。

《持久性有机污染物公约》这一复杂制度是由一个法律实验导致的，这一实验不仅允许采用那些旨在应对科学问题的规制手段（风险预防方法和建立委员会），还将社会经济因素（风险管理评估、特殊豁免和一般例外）也考虑在内。有证据表明，这一方法对管控持久性有机污染物做出了积极贡献。[63]虽然《持久性有机污染物公约》的构造比较精致，但是它仅适用于有限数量的物质，即使近年来这一数量有所增加。另外，公约也没有抓住工业生产过程造成的另一个重大风险，即工业事故的发生。如后文所述，在区域层面已经开始应对工业事故的预防和管理问题。

（二）活动的规制：《工业事故跨界影响公约》

联合国欧洲经济委员会《工业事故跨界影响公约》可以在20世纪70年代以来的一系列事件中找到源头，这些事件凸显了某些特定工业生产过

63　On the performance of the POP Convention see the special issue of Environmental Pollution, Vol. 2017（2016）and, particularly, the opening article by H. Hung, A. A. Katsoyiannis, and R. Guardans, "Ten years of global monitoring under the Stockholm Convention on Persistent Organic Pollutants: Trend, sources and transport modelling"（2016）217 Environmental Pollution 1.

程（与大量高危险或较危险的物质有关）所造成的风险。一个典型的案例就是1976年7月发生意大利北部的依米沙化学品工厂（属于瑞士吉沃丹集团）的一次事故。一大片含有高危险毒素的云状物被一个反应堆释放出并飘散到伦巴底（位于塞韦索市区），它影响了成百上千的人。随后，欧共体针对工业事故制定了一项指令，即所谓的《塞韦索指令》，后来还被修订了两次（《塞韦索指令Ⅱ》和《塞韦索指令Ⅲ》）。[64] 过去这些年来，其他一些工业事故也引起了公众的高度关注。除了重大石油泄漏和核灾难这些关注的焦点之外，在发展中国家和发达国家都发生了数次工业事故，例如1984年发生的博帕尔悲剧（印度），1991年在Anaversa（墨西哥）发生的农药厂爆炸，以及1986年在巴塞尔（瑞士）发生的山度士厂火灾和1988年在内华达（美国）发生的PEPCON厂爆炸。

在所有这些（以及其他大量）事故中，主要问题在于工业生产过程，这些过程与特定危险物质的利用和生产有关。因为这类事故有可能对相邻国家的人身健康和环境造成重大影响，所以在此背景下，国际法可以发挥重要作用。在一些情况下，特别是当事故造成了河流污染时，在距离事故发生地很远的地方都可以感受到跨界影响。最适合预防此类事故以及在事故发生后将损害最小化的规制手段与《持久性有机污染物公约》规定的手段存在很大不同。后者禁止或限制特定物质的生产和使用，而工业事故的规制目的并不是禁止受规制的活动，而是针对工业事故的预防和管理设定特定要求。这是那些有用但危险的活动所采取的方法，例如石油运输[65]或核能的生产。[66]

这也是《工业事故跨界影响公约》所采用的方法，截至2017年该公约对泛欧洲区域的41个国家具有约束力。[67] 为了了解它的运行，我们应当审视：（1）它的客体；（2）《公约》建立的标识、预防和信息管理

64　See supra footnote 30.

65　See Chapter 4.

66　See infra Section 7.3.5.2.

67　Convention on Industrial Accidents, supra footnote 8. Commentary on this instrument can be found in the manuals prepared by the United Nations Economic Commission for Europe: UNECE Industrial Accident Notification System (Geneva: ECE, 2005); Safety Guidelines and Good Practices for Pipelines (Geneva: ECE, 2008). See also, ECE, The Convention on the Transboundary Effects of Industrial Accidents: Twenty Years of Prevention, Preparedness and Response (Geneva: ECE, 2012).

制度。

关于客体，公约指的是"可能造成跨界影响的工业事故"（第2条第1款）。这一术语可以从几个方面进行定性。首先，这一术语被第1条第1款定义为"与危险物质有关的所有活动过程中由无法控制的发展导致的事件"。这一初步的定性还需要更深入的澄清。事故必须是发生于一个设施里面（也有可能包含工业场地内的交通运输）[68]，而且这些活动必须与"有害物质"有关。因此工业事故的定义有赖于物质的类别。而这些物质则是由它们的本质和数量来定性的（附录一）。定义这些物质的"有害"本质会涉及对应的"类别"，正如前文所讨论的《联合国化学品全球统一分类和标签制度》（例如"可燃"或"易燃"，"有毒"或"非常有毒"等），或者涉及物质本身（例如硝酸铵或钾、氯、石油等）。在这两种情况下，附录一都设定了一定的数量要求，只有数量够大才能让该物质危险到应由公约来规制。另外，工业事故的"影响"（广义定义[69]）必须是"越境的""严重的"，[70] 还应是其他一个国家的事故造成的。任何活动如果"可能会"造成跨界影响，那么就足以把它认定为是危险的（第1条第2款）。最后，第2条第2款将一些受到特定管理制度规制的事故（核事故、石油泄漏、转基因生物释放）排除在公约范围以外，或者，对于公约的框架而言被认为是不合适的（指军事设施）。

这一复杂客体（空间、活动、物质、事故、影响）受到了一个规制框架的规制，这一框架包括四个主要成分：（1）有害活动的认定；（2）事故的预防；（3）事故发生后的管理；（4）信息交换和公众参与。[71] 每个成分都会被公约文本一般提及，并由附录或缔约方大会的决定进一步细化。相关工业活动的认定是由第4条来管理的。公约建立了指南以便帮助各缔约方开展这一进程。[72] 每个缔约方都必须建立一个发生在其领土上的有害活动名录，通知潜在的受影响方并与之展开协商。当某一缔约国认为在别国领土上开展的某项活动是危险的并应受到公约制度的规制时，它

68　Convention on Industrial Accidents, supra footnote 8, Art. 1（a）and 2（2）（d）（ii）.

69　Ibid., Art. 1（c）.

70　Ibid., Art. 1（d）.

71　Ibid., Art. 3.

72　See "Decision 2000/3 Guidelines to facilitate the identification of hazardous activities for the purposes of the convention", 22 February 2001, ECE/CP. TEIA/2.

也可以引发认定进程。[73] 依据附录二，当各方无法达成一致意见时，任何一方都可以将其提交给一个调查委员会。另外，各缔约方可以同意将那些公约附录一以外的活动也交由公约的规章制度来进行规制。[74] 工业事故的预防是公约的主要目标。第6条规定了一个"垂直的"义务：各缔约方必须采取适当措施（附录四建议了一些措施，例如设立具体安全目标、制定安全标准、进行检查等）以预防工业事故。这些措施还包括鼓励运营方采取行动以减少事故风险，[75] 要求运营方针对如何在它们的场地确保工业生产过程的安全提供准确信息，[76] 或者对工业场地的选址进行规制以减少事故发生造成的影响。[77] 换言之，公约要求制定一个国家层面的规章制度以及在工业场地这一层面的一个具体预防制度。当然，预防制度也无法保证事故在任何情况下都不会发生。在这个方面，工业针对这些事故的管理设定了一些参数，或者说得更具体一点，为了确保一个适当的回应以便将损害最小化。除了信息披露的义务，公约还要求建立一个紧急响应制度（在当地、[78] 国家[79]和区域[80]层面）以及协作义务[81]和相互援助。[82] 信息披露的义务适用于多个阶段，包括事故认定阶段（特别是涉及与其他国家[83]和潜在被影响人群的协商[84]）、活动的开展阶段[85]或事故发生以后（通知和信息交换）。针对事故已经发生这种情况，公约规定应建立信息交换

73　Convention on Industrial Accidents, supra footnote 8, Art. 4 (2).

74　Ibid., Art. 5.

75　Ibid., Art. 4 (4). This provision refers to the Convention on Environmental Impact Assessment in a Transboundary Context, 25 February 1991, 1989 UNTS 309 ("Espoo Convention").

76　Convention on Industrial Accidents, supra footnote 8, Art. 6 (2).

77　Ibid., Art. 7 and Annexes V (1) – (8) and VI.

78　Ibid., Art. 8 (1) – (2) and Annex 7 (4).

79　Ibid., Art. 8 (3) and Annex 7 (5).

80　Ibid., Art. 8 (3) in fine.

81　Ibid., Art. 11.

82　Ibid., Art. 12 and Annex X. See also Art. 18 (4) and Annex XII.

83　Ibid., Art. 4 and Annex III.

84　Ibid., Art. 9 and Annex VIII. These requirements are now strengthened by the adoption of the Convention on Access to Information, Public Participation in Decision-Making and Access to Justice in Environmental Matters, 25 June 1998, 2161 UNTS 447 ("Aarhus Convention").

85　Convention on Industrial Accidents, supra footnote 8, Art. 15 and Annex XI.

制度，包括相关机构的认定，[86] 并要求当事国向其他缔约国提供所需的最基本信息。[87]

公约为多个有关工业事故预防和管理国内法的制定提供了指导，并为数个越界事故演习提供了框架（例如2002年在波兰和俄罗斯进行的行动，2009年保加利亚、罗马尼亚和塞尔维亚在多瑙河进行的行动，2015年摩尔多瓦、罗马尼亚和乌克兰针对多瑙河三角洲进行的行动）。但是，公约的实际影响应该在一个更宏观的背景下进行评估。事实上，这一公约是联合国欧洲经济委员会制定的一整套环境公约（共计有五项）的组成部分。[88] 这五项条约作为一个整体提供了一个精巧和平衡的框架。[89] 另外，公约当前正在依据《2030年可持续发展议程》及其可持续发展目标以及2015年在日本仙台市制定的一个有关减灾的全球框架来重新规划其工作。[90] 作为公约更新工作的一部分，出现了一个修订建议，其目的是把公约向欧洲经济委员会区域以外的国家开放加入。[91] 如果这一修订案得以制定，那么《工业事故跨界影响公约》就有可能像其他欧洲经济委员会环境公约一样成为一个全球性条约。

三　贸易的规制：《事先知情同意公约》

如前文所述，《持久性有机污染物公约》不仅涵盖了附录所认定的持久性有机污染物的生产和使用，它还负责规制它们的出口和进口。但是，

---

[86] Ibid., Art. 17 (2).

[87] Ibid., Art. 10 (2) and Annex IX.

[88] See W. Schrage, K. Bull and A. Karadjova, "Environmental Legal Instruments in the UNECE Region" (2007) 18 *Yearbook of International Environmental Law* 3.

[89] Ibid., 3.

[90] 《2015—2030年仙台减灾框架》(*The Sendai Framework for Disaster Risk Reduction 2015-2030*) 是在2015年3月的第三届世界减灾大会上通过的。它是其前身文件——《2005—2015兵库行动框架》(*the Hyogo Framework for Action 2005-2015*) 的继承者。See Fostering the implementation of the 2030 Agenda for Sustainable Development and the Sendai Framework for Disaster Risk Reduction 2015-2030. Note by the Secretariat, 7 September 2016, ECE/CP. TEIA/2/016/1.

[91] See Report of the Conference of the Parties at its ninth meeting, 10 March 2017, ECE/CP. TEIA/32, paras. 29-33. 针对修订决定草案，俄罗斯和德国持有不同意见。德国认为开放的修订（针对第29条）应当联合第9条（关于公众参与和诉诸司法）的修订，而俄罗斯则表示反对。

这一背景下贸易规制的目的是增强那些与生产和使用相关的义务。《鹿特丹公约》（也可被称为《事先知情同意公约》）[92]则采用了不同的视角。它的主要目的是规制化学品贸易。更具体地讲，它试图确保足够丰富的信息，以便让各国（尤其是发展中国家）有能力了解特定化学品造成的风险并针对它们的进口做出有根据的决定。为了了解这一制度的目标和结构，就有必要回顾一下它出现的历史原因。

20世纪70—80年代，将在发达国家被禁止的特定农药出口到发展中国家的做法，受到了强烈的批评。这一争议包含了两个主要问题。[93] 一方面，所谓的"环境正义"运动起初关注的是美国污染源的地理分布与人种议题之间的关联，后来它被扩展到危险物质的越境转移。对进口国的环境和人身健康造成的损害甚至会更加严重，因为农药出口国的法律制度已经禁止使用这些农药。至少有必要向进口国提供有关农药风险的足够信息，以便它们可以做出一个有根据的决定。另一方面，进口国的国内法规（或者它们的不足实施）往往无法充分应对这些风险。一旦获知发展中国家在物质进口问题上的立场，更优的选择是利用出口国（发达国家）的国内法律制度来管控出口方的行为。这不仅是为了保护发展中国家，也是为了避免所谓的"毒害循环"，即在北半球被禁用的农药通过那些从发展中国家进口的食品又回到北半球。这两个问题导致了两个不具约束力的法律文本的通过，它们是在世界粮农组织和联合国环境规划署的框架下制定的，分别是1985年《关于农药分配和使用行为规范的国际法典》（*International Code of Conduct on the Distribution and Use of Pesticides*）和1987年《关于国际贸易中化学品的信息交换的伦敦指南》（*London Guidelines for the Exchange of Information on Chemicals in International Trade*）。这些文件后来在1989年进行了修订以便为事先知情同意制定一个通用程序，它为《事先知情同意公约》的制定提供了基础。[94]

92　PIC Convention, supra footnote 5. See R. W. Emory, "Probing the Protections in the Rotterdam Convention on Prior Informed Consent" (2001) 12 Colorado Journal of International Environmental Law and Policy 47; P. Barrios, "The Rotterdam Convention on Hazardous Chemicals: A Meaningful Step towards Environmental Protection?" (2004) 16 Georgetown International Environmental Law Review 679.

93　See Barrios, supra footnote 92, 709ff.

94　See A. M. Mekouar, "Pesticides and Chemicals-The Requirement of Prior Informed Consent", in D. Shelton (ed.), Commitment and Compliance (Oxford University Press, 2000), pp. 146-163.

《事先知情同意公约》沿用了名录方法及其三个组成部分（名录、义务、修订制度）。图7-3概括了它的基本结构。《公约》的附录三[95]列举了多个"被禁的或严格限制的化学品"[96]和"极为危险的农药制剂"。[97]《公约》自制定以来经历了五次修订（2004年、2008年、2011年、2013年和2015年）。在当前版本，这一目录包含了43种物质，其中绝大部分是农药。

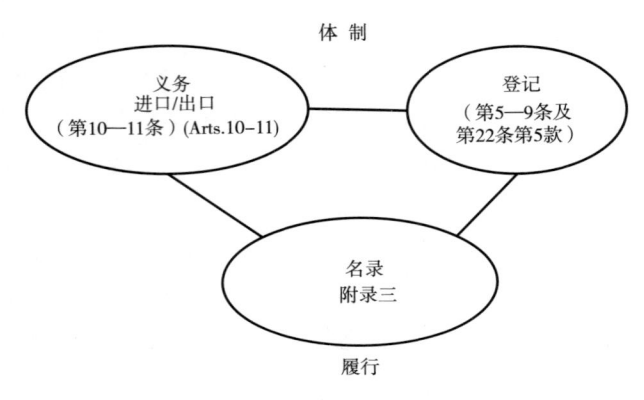

体　制

义务
进口/出口
（第10—11条）(Arts.10—11)

登记
（第5—9条及第22条第5款）

名录
附录三

履　行

图7-3　《事先知情同意公约》的基本结构

在这些物质当中，我们可以发现《斯德哥尔摩公约》附录所列举的持久性有机污染物的大部分都名列其中。针对附录三中的每种物质，《公约》建立的化学品审查委员会（Chemical Review Committee）都起草了一份"决定指南文件"，[98]并将其转发给所有缔约国。[99]这一文件为公约建立的一个信息交换制度提供了基础。

名录中物质的相应义务涉及这些物质的进口和出口。关于进口问题，各缔约国承诺，采取必要措施以便在一定期限内（通常是它们收到决定指南文件的九个月以内）针对某一特定产品的进口做出决定，并通过公

---

[95] 公约还针对受禁物质或被严格限制的物质设立了一个通知制度（特殊事先知情同意程序）（第12条）。这一制度并不适用于附录三中的物质（因为一旦被列入附录三，则应适用一般事先知情同意程序），要理解这一制度，应当参考上述问题，即把受禁或被限制的产品出口到发展中国家带来的问题。

[96] PIC Convention, supra footnote 5, Art. 2（b）-（c）.

[97] Ibid., Art. 2（d）.

[98] 这一文件必须包含《事先知情同意公约》附录一和附录四指定的特定信息。

[99] Ibid., Art. 7.

约秘书处将这一决定通报给其他缔约国。[100] 这一决定，不论是最终的还是临时的，都可能导致：（1）批准进口；（2）禁止进口；（3）在特定条件下批准进口。[101] 进口国也可以要求出口方提供更多的信息或者为评估化学品提供更多帮助。[102] 当某国决定禁止或限制某一特定化学品的进口时，它同时有义务将这一禁止或限制应用于来自其他国家的进口，并有义务禁止或限制它的国内生产。[103] 这是因为，在"最惠国待遇"和"国民待遇"条款缺位的情况下，某个国家可能会以一个歧视或保护主义的方式来决定禁止或限制进口，而这则是《事先知情同意公约》想要避免的。第 11 条要求出口国采取必要措施以确保那些试图出口名录中产品的所有私营主体能够遵守进口国的决定，从而增强了这一制度的有效性。值得注意的是，在一些例外情况下，[104] 进口国没有回应并不会妨碍出口国批准某一物质的出口。这种情况指的是，有证据表明该物质没有被进口国所禁止，即使进口国没有回应（因此进口国就必须给出一个临时的回复，说明它的决定还有待做出）。总体上，这一制度可以被看作自由贸易与严格的（风险预防的）环境保护和健康之间的一个妥协。决定是由进口国自由裁量来做出的，但是，如果进口国决定限制贸易，那么它也必须限制其国内生产以及来自其他国家的进口。这一"贸易纪律"并不适用于名录以外的物质，而这也是登记的意义所在。

正是基于登记的重要意义，各缔约方才以一种详细的方式构建了一个登记程序，用于管理如何将新物质列入《事先知情同意公约》附录三。第 5 条（化学品）和第 6 条（极为危险的农药制剂）规定了在何种条件下可以提交一个登记提名。这些条件包括：（1）一个包含地理维度的建议；[105]（2）秘书处以及化学品审查委员会进行的特定标准（附录一、附录

---

[100] Ibid., Art. 10.

[101] Ibid., Art. 10 (4) (a) and (b) (i).

[102] Ibid., Art. 10 (4) (b) (iii) – (iv).

[103] Ibid., Art. 10 (9).

[104] Ibid., Art. 11 (2).

[105] 针对化学品，必须至少有来自不同区域（非洲、北美洲、拉丁美洲和加勒比地区、亚洲、欧洲、西南太平洋地区、中东）的两个国家已经采取（并沟通了）一个涉及涉事物质的规制措施。与之相比，针对极度有害杀虫剂，一个发展中国家或经济转型中国家的建议就足以引发这一程序。See Ibid., Arts. 5 (5) and 6 (1).

二或附录四）的评估，委员会提出一个建议[106]。并提交给缔约方大会参会代表投票表决。[107] 缔约方大会就会在这一建议的基础上做出决定（第7条）。大会是以一致同意的方式来通过决定（第22条第5款）。这一条款比《持久性有机污染物公约》规定的3/4多数还要苛刻，这也解释了为什么将存在政治争议的强杀虫剂硫丹列入《事先知情同意公约》附录三的初次尝试会以失败告终。直到《持久性有机污染物公约》附录一收录了硫丹，一个新的尝试才再次被启动。

此外，《事先知情同意公约》还有多个特性比不上《持久性有机污染物公约》所展示的精致法律制度。针对《事先知情同意公约》的批评意见主要是它缺少针对发展中国家的足够援助和能力建设（以便发展中国家能够真正理解并掌握事先知情同意制度下的信息交换），[108] 它也没有限制面向第三国的出口。[109] 正如本章后文所述，[110] 通过《事先知情同意公约》与其他法律文本（例如《持久性有机污染物公约》或《巴塞尔公约》）的协同，这些不足至少可以得到部分弥补。

四　废物的规制：《巴塞尔公约》

与《事先知情同意公约》一样，《巴塞尔公约》[111] 也是起源于环境正义运动，而且它的前身也是一项不具约束力的法律文本。[112] 这一条约的根源是一个引发争议的事实，即发达国家（或者它们最富有的地区）制造了大量废物并将废物转移到发展中国家（或者贫困地区）以便进行消除或仅仅是为了排放。这一现象主要是由在废物制造国进行废物处置的高成本所引发；它受到了许多批评，主要是因为它对接收国和地区的环境与健

---

[106] Ibid., Arts. 5（6）and 6（5）.

[107] Ibid., Art. 18（6）（c）.

[108] Barrios, supra footnote 92, 743ff. 依据公约第16条，秘书处已经提供了一些技术和财政援助，绝大部分用于会议和论坛的组织。但是它只是进行中的与《斯德哥尔摩公约》和《巴塞尔公约》开展协同这一进程的部分内容，这一进程被指定为战略优先，包括在特定问题上向特定国家提供技术援助。

[109] Emory, supra footnote 92, 54ff.

[110] See infra Section 7.4.5.

[111] Basel Convention, supra n. 7. See Kummer, supra footnote 2.

[112] UNEP, Environmental Law Guidelines and Principles no. 8: Environmentally Sound Management of Hazardous Wastes (Nairobi: UNEP, 1987). See Kummer, supra footnote 2, p. 39.

康造成的不利影响。虽然这一问题还远未解决,近年来,对废物的重新认知还是影响了这一争论,废物日益被看作一种"资源"(例如发电或者循环利用为其他物质)或者至少是一种可盈利的商业"机会"(在许多发展中国家出现了垃圾产业)。[113] 这些认识有助于我们理解《巴塞尔公约》的文本以及它想要规制的问题。

《巴塞尔公约》的前执行秘书库默尔(K. Kummer)[114] 将公约的一般方法概括为:(1)将产生的危险废物减至最低限度("废物最小化原则",第4条第2款);(2)采用环境友好型方式在尽可能靠近废物产生地的设施来处置废物("就近处置原则",第4条第2款);(3)在某些情况下完全禁止危险废物的出口(出口到该公约非缔约国、[115] 出口到南极、[116] 出口到那些已经禁止进口或者没有能力采用环境友好型方式来处置废物的国家,[117] 或者由经济合作与发展组织成员国出口到非成员国[118]);(4)在所有情况下,危险废物的出口都必须遵守公约所建立的制度,即处置必须是在进口国以一种环境友好型方式进行,越界转移必须满足特定要求,主要是一个具体的事先知情同意程序(第6条);(5)被非法出口的危险废物或者无法做到环境上无害化处置的危险废物必须被运回出口国(第8条)。这一制度涵盖了危险废物管理的全部阶段,从它们的产生到越境转

---

[113] On this approach see K. Kummer Peiry, A. R. Ziegler and J. Baumgartner (eds.), Waste Management and the Green Economy. Law and Policy (Cheltenham: Edward Elgar, 2016).

[114] Kummer, supra footnote 2, pp. 47–48.

[115] Basel Convention, supra footnote 7, Art. 4 (5).

[116] Ibid., Art. 4 (6).

[117] Ibid., Art. 4 (2) (e) and (g).

[118] See Decision III/1, "Amendment to the Convention", 28 November 1995, UNEP/CHW. 3/35. 这一修正案尚未开始生效,虽然在实践中它已经通过瑞士和印度尼西亚所倡导的"国家引领的努力"而得到了广泛实施。这一修正案由出席并参加表决的缔约方的3/4多数票通过,但是它还是无法生效,除非那些已经通过或接受的国家的3/4(实质上就是上一个3/4的3/4)以上的国家再批准它(第17条第3—5款)。这一修订案引发了针对第17条第5款的争论,更具体来说,就是对3/4多数的理解。后来,缔约方大会依据《维也纳条约法公约》第31条第3款的权威解释在2011年通过了一项决定,指出"各缔约方同意《巴塞尔公约》第17条第5款应被解释为在通过议定书时的3/4缔约方中的3/4以上的接受是议定书生效的必要条件"。Decision BC-10/3 "Indonesian-Swiss country-led initiative to improve the effectiveness of the Basel Convention", 1 November 2011, UNEP/CHW. 10/28, section A, para. 2. 这一步可以推动这一禁止修订案早日生效。

移,直到处置。在这一部分,我们将关注《巴塞尔公约》的三个主要构成,即"废物"作为一个受规制客体的定性、管控制度(具体的事先知情同意程序)以及公约与涉及类似客体的其他法律文本的关系。

公约所建立的制度针对受规制废物的交易规定了重要的限制。因此,判断废物会用于何种用途是非常重要的。起初,公约采用了一种不太实际的方法,仅仅将受规制的废物定性为具备特定特征(附录三)的废物"种类"(附录一)。[119] 这一定性导致了公约所针对的客体变得不够确定。公约同样适用于被单方(不论是进口方、出口方或中转方)认定为危险废物的废物,[120] 这一特点就要求必须建立一个针对这些废物的认定制度,并把信息散发到其他缔约方。另外,在公约文本谈判过程中达成了一个妥协,即公约在"危险废物"与"其他废物"(附录二)两者间做了一个区分,虽然从规制的视角来看,应对这两种类别的方式是相似的。对受规制废物的定性模棱两可这一问题,在 1998 年的第四次缔约方大会上得以解决,本次大会制定了公约的附录八和附录九。附录八包含了一个废物名录,里面有近 60 个被公约第 1 款第 1 条认定为危险废物的条目。相反地,附录九规定了一个被假定为无害废物的名录,因此就不在公约范围以内,除非它们所包含的附录一中的物质的数量和浓度足以构成附录 3 所规定的其中一个危险特性。与附录二一起,附录八和附录九针对受规制废物的定性提供了更多的澄清。在它们被制定以后,又经历了多次修订,修订的过程使公约的名录得以不断更新。另外,公约秘书处与两个私营部门开展了合作伙伴关系,针对两类在实践中非常重要的废物(即不再使用的手机和电脑组件)共同制定具体指南。[121] 值得一提的是,"技术指南"的制定已经成为公约活动的一个非常重要的部分,自 1994 年的一个框架文件以来,已经制定了数十个这样的不具约束力的指南,尽管公约的规制内容依然还是越境转移的管控程序。

对越境转移的管控其实就是《巴塞尔公约》所建立制度的核心。与本领域的其他条约相似,名录方法为我们理解这一制度提供给了一个有用的分析

119　Basel Convention, supra footnote 7, Art. 1 (1) (a).

120　Ibid., Art. 1 (1) (b).

121　Mobile Phone Partnership Initiative (2003-2008) and Partnership for Action on Computing Equipment (2008).

框架。图7-4概括了这一制度的主要构成（名录、义务、更新制度）。

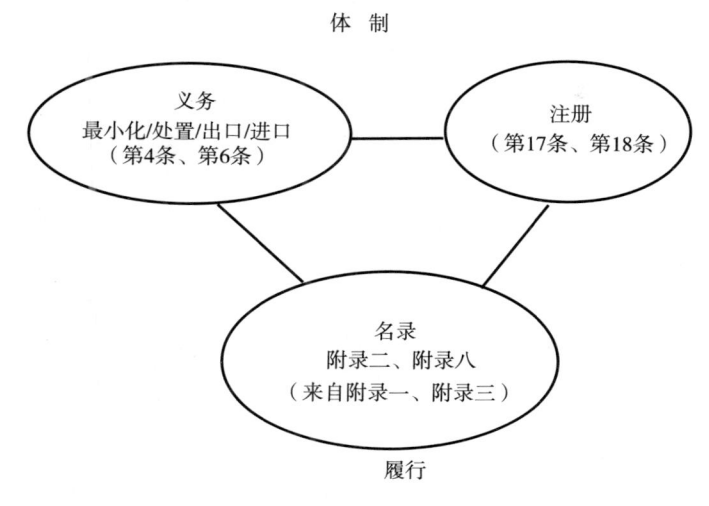

体　制

```
        义务                          注册
    最小化/处置/出口/进口         （第17条、第18条）
     （第4条、第6条）

                  名录
              附录二、附录八
            （来自附录一、附录三）

                  履行
```

图7-4　《巴塞尔公约》的基本结构

　　前文已经探讨过《巴塞尔公约》所建立的这一复杂结构。它包含了五个附录（附录一、附录二、附录三、附录八和附录九）针对受规制废物的认定所发生的相互作用，虽然所涉及的物质更多的是由附录二（"其他废物"）和附录三（"假定为危险的废物"）直接列举的。第18条第3款（它依次提及了第17条和第18条的制度）规定，附录的修正案应以出席并参加表决的缔约国的3/4多数票通过（第17条第3款）。与公约本身的修正案不同，附录的修正案会自动对每个缔约方生效，除非该缔约方在一个特定期限内提交了一份书面通知（反对声明）给秘书处（第18条第2款）。正如前文所述，适用于受规制废物的义务的重点是废物产生的最小化、在靠近废物源头的地方采用无害化方式处置，以及在越境转移被批准的情况下采用一个具体的事先知情同意程序。这一程序的规定主要在公约第6条。该条款规定，出口国应将受规制废物的越境转移（按照特定要求）通知进口国（以及中转国）的主管机关，或要求相关私营业主做出这一通知。[122] 出口国只有在得到进口国的书面同意以及其他一些保证之后（尤其是有关废物的环境无害管理）才能批准废物的越境转移。[123] 那

---

[122]　Basel Convention, supra footnote 7, Art. 6（1）.
[123]　Ibid., Art. 6（2）-（3）.

些具有相同物理化学特性的受规制废物，如果它们在 12 个月之内通过同一线路被定期装运，就可以适用于一个由第 6 条第 6—8 款规定的简易程序。

《巴塞尔公约》的另一个维度是它与其他法律文本（包括那些与废物的越境转移管理相关的区域性文件）的关系。虽然已经有文献对此维度进行了具体分析，[124] 但是它的核心内容还是值得一提，因为它们可以帮助我们了解公约在危险废物的国际规制这一问题上的总体目标。在谈判过程中，起初提出了一个想法是以达成一个框架协定（类似于《远程越界空气污染公约》[125] 或《保护臭氧层维也纳公约》[126]）为目标，但是不仅之后这一想法就被放弃，各方更倾向一个包含具体义务的条约。[127] 起初的这一尝试还是达成了少量成果，主要体现在第 11 条，它负责管理公约与其他"协定"或"安排"之间的关系，它们针对的主要目标与公约一样，即危险废物的越境转移。这些协定或安排可能是基于一个双边、区域的甚至全球的基础与公约的其他缔约国或者第三方国家在公约前后达成的。这些协定或安排可以被看作关于公约的特别法，前提条件是它们针对废物无害化处置制度的严格程度不得低于公约的规定（第 11 条第 2 款）。当前已经有了几个这类的协定和安排，[128] 例如《巴马科公约》[129] 或经济合作与发展组织针对这一问题通过的决定。[130] 为了理解这一规则的运用，我们必须澄

---

[124] See Kummer, supra footnote 2, Chapters 3 (The Basel Convention as an Umbrella for Regional Hazardous Waste Treaties), 4 (The Relationship Between the Basel Convention and the Waste Management Systems of the EU and the OECD) and 5 (The Basel Regime and Sectoral Pollution Control Treaties).

[125] LRTAP Convention, supra footnote 4.

[126] Vienna Convention on the Protection of the Ozone Layer, 22 March 1985, 1513 UNTS 293.

[127] Kummer, supra footnote 2, p. 87.

[128] A list of agreements and arrangements is available at: www.basel.int (last visited 10 December 2013).

[129] Bamako Convention, supra footnote 7. See W. F. Jones, "The Evolution of the Bamako Convention: An African Perspective" (1993) 4 Colorado Journal of International Environmental Law and Policy 324.

[130] Decision of the Council concerning the revision of Decision (92) 39/FINAL on the control of transboundary movements of wastes destined for recovery operations, 21 May 2002, C (2001) 107/FINAL. On the OECD regime see Kummer, supra footnote 2, Chapter 4; OECD, Manuel d'application pour la mise en œuvre de la Décision de l'OCDE C (2001) 107/Final modifiée concernant le contrôle des mouvements transfrontières de déchets destinés à des opérations de valorisation (Paris: OECD, 2009).

清三个方面的问题。第一，应该弄清谁来评估某项协定或安排是否具备与公约类似的环境标准。这不仅是个学术问题，因为答案也会对某一国际争端的结果造成重大反响。[131] 第一次缔约方大会建立的一个工作组讨论了这一问题。工作组倾向于把评估交由各国负责，只提供一些标准来指导各国的决策。[132] 第二，公约作为一项"普通法"仅仅适用于受规制废物在两个同是该协定（或安排）的缔约国之间的越境转移。发生于公约两个缔约国之间的转移，如果只有一方是某一协定（或特定安排）的缔约方，仍应受到公约的规制。第三，必须弄清第 11 条具体针对的是何种类型的协定或安排。事实上，有几个条约，例如有关特定物质在海洋（或在区域海洋）的运输或倾倒的条约，[133] 它们也与废物的越境转移相关。[134] 第 11 条仅适用于那些针对《巴塞尔公约》的核心要件（即危险废物在两国间的越境转移）建立了一个规范的协定或安排。如果某协定针对的是废物生命周期的其他方面，或者该协定虽然关注的是废物的越境转移但是并不满足第 11 条的条件，那么公约与该协定的关系就应受到条约法（特别是《维也纳条约法公约》第 30 条）的规制。[135]

也就是说，不同条约之间的关系并不一定是冲突的。如后文所述，《巴塞尔公约》《事先知情同意公约》和《持久性有机污染物公约》之间的协同取得了一些进展。这三个文件的合作运用就涵盖了部分化学品的整个生命周期。其他综合方法也是可能的，正如针对核能的国际规制以及 2013 年的《水俣公约》。

五　综合方法

（一）《巴塞尔公约》《事先知情同意公约》和《持久性有机污染物公约》之间的协同

如前文所述，《巴塞尔公约》《事先知情同意公约》和《持久性有机污染物公约》组合在一起，就涵盖了化学品的整个生命周期（生

---

[131] See e. g. the case S. D. Myers Inc. v. Canada, NAFTA Arbitration (UNCITRAL Rules), Award (13 November 2000).

[132] Kummer, supra footnote 2, p. 89.

[133] See Chapter 4.

[134] See Kummer, supra footnote 2, Chapter 5.

[135] Vienna Convention on the Law of Treaties, 23 May 1969, 1155 UNTS 331.

产/利用、越境转移和处置)。另外,这些文件所引发的义务通常适用于相似的活动和物质。因此,通过协同(尤其是组织上的协同)来协调那些在这三个文件框架下开展的工作就会有利于发挥每个条约的特长。[136]

2005 年,这三项公约的缔约方大会创立了一个联合工作组[137]以便分析可能的协同并提出建议。这一工作组的成果[138]在这三项公约的 2008 年缔约方大会上被讨论并得以批准。[139] 这一仍在进行中的协同进程的目标主要是研究如何提升组织上的效率。三个秘书处围绕协同所开展工作的第一步包含了提名一个共同的执行秘书以及同步组织三个缔约方大会(包括一些问题上的相同会期和存档)。这一进程的其他一些重要步骤是协同或合并这些公约在国际、区域和国内层面的管理机构(或由公约导致的机构),并采用一个综合方法来资助这些机构,或者提升公众对这些公约的认识。[140] 这一协同进程的目标是实现更高的效率(减少成本)和效力(增加影响力并提升那些提供给各国的服务)。

---

[136] On this process see K. Kummer Peiry, "The Chemicals and Waste Regime as a Basis for a Comprehensive International Framework on Sustainable Management of Potentially Hazardous Materials?" (2014) 23 RECIEL 172.

[137] Decision SC-2/15 "Synergies", 15 May 2006, UNEP/POPS/COP. 2/30; Decision RC-3/8, "Cooperation and Coordination between the Basel, Rotterdam and Stockholm Conventions", 5 January 2007, UNEP/CHW. 8/16.

[138] Report of the Ad hoc Joint Working Group on Enhancing Cooperation and Coordination among the Basel, Rotterdam and Stockholm Conventions on the Work of its Third Meeting, 29 March 2008, UNEP/FAO/CHW/RC/POPS/JWG. 3/3.

[139] Decision SC-4/34, "Enhancing Cooperation and Coordination among the Basel, Rotterdam and Stockholm Conventions", 8 May 2009, UNEP/POPS/COP. 4/38; Decision RC-4/11, "Enhancing Cooperation and Coordination among the Basel, Rotterdam and Stockholm Conventions", 31 October 2008, UNEP/FAO/RC/COP. 4/24; Decision BC-IX/10, "Cooperation and Coordination between the Basel, Rotterdam and Stockholm Conventions", 27 June 2008, UNEP/CHW. 9/39.

[140] 一个接受委托的机构提交了一份有关协同进程的评估报告,供 2017 年的联合缔约方大会讨论。这一报告针对业已取得的进展提供了一个较好的综述。See Report on the overall review of the synergies arrangements. Note by the Secretariat, 24 November 2016, UNEP/CHW. 13/INF/43, UNEP/FAO/RC/COP. 8/INF/29, UNEP/POPS/COP. 8/INF/43, Annex. On the financial integration process see Implementation of the integrated approach to financing. Note by the Secretariat, 28 March 2017, UNEP/CHW. 13/INF/40, UNEP/FAO/RC/COP. 8/INF/44, UNEP/POPS/COP. 8/INF/35.

在这一背景下开展的组织上的实验理所当然地吸引了环境治理领域的关注。事实上，全球环境治理面临着一个主要问题，即各种不同环境体制的激增，每个体制都是基于某一条约有关成立永久性体系的规定。多个不同的法律和行政部门都来处理同一个问题，就会造成矛盾以及高得多的成本。当然，针对这一协同的探索造成的挑战不只限于组织或法律方面。有时候，在多边环境协定下成立的这些组织针对某些问题可能会产生相互竞争的利益，虽然这一现象并不显著。[141] 有一些替代方案有助于应对这些挑战，例如柔性包罗框架的制定（例如国际化学品管理战略方针或更宏观的可持续发展目标），某个多边协定针对其他组织的工作制订的一个战略计划（例如《生物多样性公约》制订的 2011—2020 年战略计划[142]），或者更模糊一点，为了全面应对某一问题而建立的一个综合框架。如后文所述，综合框架这一方法被用于与核能和汞相关的领域。

（二）综合规制：核能

有关核能的国际法提供了一个很好的例证来说明涉及危险物质和活动规制的一种更集中和综合的方法。这一形式的能源及其相关活动受到了一个体制的约束，该体制包含了条约（双边和多边条约）以及各种标准和指南。但是，这一方法的主要构成是一个多边机构的建立，这一机构应是全球范围的并拥有一些规范性权力（通常是通过制定技术标准或建议），这一机构就是国际原子能机构。多年以来，在 1956 年建立的国际原子能机构这一初始体制得到了一些条约的补充，它们包括 1968 年《不扩散核武器条约》[143] 以及其他一些条约，它们分别是在 1980 年、[144] 1986 年（在

---

[141] See, e.g., K. Rosendal and S. Andresen, UNEP's Role in Enhancing Problem - Solving Capacity in Multilateral Environmental Agreements: Co-ordination and Assistance in the Biodiversity Conservation Cluster (Lysaker: Fridtjof Nansen Institute, 2004), p. 29.

[142] On this "clustering" phenomenon see G. Futhazar, "The Diffusion of the Strategic Plan for Biodiversity and its Aichi Biodiversity Targets within the Biodiversity Cluster: An Illustration of Current Trends in the Global Governance of Biodiversity and Ecosystems" (2015) 25 Yearbook of International Environmental Law 133. For the cluster on chemicals and waste see Ditz, Tuncak, supra footnote 43.

[143] Treaty on the Non-Proliferation of Nuclear Weapons, 1 July 1968, 729 UNTS 161.

[144] Convention on the Physical Protection of Nuclear Material, 3 March 1980, 1458 UNTS 125.

切尔诺贝利事故之后）、[145] 1994 年和 1997 年制定的。[146] 在 2011 年日本福岛事故发生以后，国际社会曾经试图修订 1994 年《核安全公约》，但是没有达成一致意见。[147]

为了理解这一复杂制度的环境维度，[148] 我们必须区分三个不同的"层级"：（1）国际原子能机构发布的一种包含了标准和技术规范的"普通法"或者"一般法"；（2）一套适用于这些活动的主要阶段（原料的保护、设施的建造和运行，包括事故的预防和管理、放射性原料的转移和废物管理）的多边条约制度；[149]（3）有关核合作的大批双边协定，用于应对技术转让、通知和援助，以及更宏观的核设施的风险预防等问题。[150] 这些规制的层级是互相联系的，而且它们经常会与国内或欧洲层面建立的制度发生相互作用。这样一个复杂的结构引发了两种问题。一方面，人们会问这一多层级规制的精华（除了法律文本的多样化之外）是什么；另一方面，有必要澄清主要包含了软法（不具约束力的）文件的"普通法"与相关有约束力的文件（多边/双边条约和国内法或欧洲法）之间的关系。

谈及这一体制的精华，它涵盖了民事核活动的所有阶段，从核原料的保护到核设施的建造及其运行的监测，再到放射性物质越境转移的规制，直到废物的管理。因此它是一种针对核能的综合方法。这一方法起初是基于国际原子能机构发布的一些不具约束力的标准，后来通过 1980 年针对

---

[145] Convention on Early Notification, supra footnote 9; Convention on Assistance, supra footnote 9.

[146] Convention on Nuclear Safety, supra footnote 9; Joint Convention, supra footnote 9.

[147] See infra footnote 156. On the domestic legal aspects of the Fukushima accident and subsequent reforms see J. Yokoyama, "Dysfunction of the regulation of nuclear power in Japan-Legal analysis of the Fukushima disaster and 2012 reform" (2013) 9 International Journal of Public Policy 245.

[148] See IAEA, Safeguards Legal Framework, available at: www.iaea.org (last visited 3 April 2017). See P. Birnie, A. Boyle and C. Redgwell, International Law and the Environment (Oxford University Press, 2009), Chapter 9; O. Jankowitsch-Prévor, "La compétence normative de l'AIEA, Bases juridiques et sources du droit", in OECD, Le droit nucléaire international: Histoire, évolution et perspectives (Paris: OECD, 2010), pp. 15-34; Tromans, supra footnote 45; Montjoie, supra footnote 45.

[149] 在发生核事故的情况下（如第八章所述），还应增加一个责任制度。

[150] See the agreements identified by Birnie et al., supra footnote 148, pp. 511-515 (notes 149, 150, 164, 175).

核原料的物理保护、1986 年关于事故发生后的合作及援助、[151] 1994 年关于设施的建造及合作、[152] 1997 年关于已用燃料和废物的管理[153]等数项条约的制定而得以增强。但是，多边条约这一层级在很大程度上是基于国际原子能机构所发布标准的实质内容。另外，这些文件虽然表述了一般原则，但是它们把具体程序交由各国负责，各国的国内框架也是基于国际原子能机构的标准。因此，明确说明这些国际标准的法律地位是非常重要的。

国际原子能机构的规范性权力的法律渊源来自它的规约的第 3 条第 1 款，依据这一条款，国际原子能机构可以：

> 与联合国主管机关及有关专门机构协商，在适当领域与之合作，以制定或采取旨在保护健康及尽量减少对生命与财产的危险的安全标准（包括劳动条件的标准），并使此项标准适用于机构本身的工作及利用由机构本身或经其请求或在其规制和监督下供应的材料、服务、设备、设施和情报所进行的工作；并使此项标准，于当事国请求时，适用于依任何双边或多边协议所开展的工作，或于一国请求时，适用于该国在原子能方面的任何活动。[154]

因此，国际原子能机构可以制订各种类型的技术规划和标准，但是它们是否对各缔约国具有约束力尚不明确。虽然超出本章节的有限范围，这一问题还是值得进行详尽分析。[155] 目前只需要指出这些技术规范不仅在实践中得到了广泛认可（例如《核安全公约》在"同行评审"机制这一背

---

[151] See Convention on Early Notification and Convention on Assistance, supra footnote 9 and G. Handl, "Après Tchernobyl: Quelques réflexions sur le programme législatif multilatéral à l'ordre du jour" (1988) 92 Revue générale de droit international public 5.

[152] See Convention on Nuclear Safetysupra footnote 9; G. Handl, "The IAEA Nuclear Safety Conventions: an Example of Successful 'Treaty Management'?" (2003) 72 Nuclear Law Bulletin 7.

[153] See Joint Convention, supra footnote 9; Montjoie, supra footnote 45.

[154] Statute of the International Atomic Energy Agency, 26 October 1956, as amended on 28 December 1989, available at http://www.iaea.org (last visited 5 March 2013), Article III. A. 6.

[155] See Jankowitsch-Prévor, supra footnote 148; Birnie et al., supra footnote 148, pp. 495ff; Montjoie, supra footnote 45, pp. 45ff.

景下建立的标准[156]），而且它们还可以通过并入某些协议[157]以及各国与国际原子能机构达成的安保协议来获取约束力。事实上，那些没有核武器的《不扩散核武器条约》缔约国被要求与国际原子能机构达成一个具体的安保协议，这一协议也可以包含一些标准。但是，这些协议优先考虑的是各国有义务不将国际原子能机构提供的援助用于军事用途，[158] 而遵守国际原子能机构的技术标准只是附带义务。[159]

（三）综合规制：汞

探索对化学品规制的综合方法还取得了另一个重要进展，即在2013年10月达成的《水俣公约》[160]。该公约于2017年8月生效并于次月召开了第一次会议。这一条约对目前用途具有重大意义，因为：（1）它涵盖了全球的范围；（2）它试图涵盖汞的整个生命周期；（3）它借用了《持

156　举例来讲，在2011年日本福岛核电站发生事故以后，国际原子能机构制订了一项聚焦于12种主要行动的行动计划，包括国际原子能机构安全标准的更新。2013年，瑞士提议修订《核安全公约》第18条以便进一步严格要求那些新的或现有核设施。2015年，召集了一个外交会议来讨论这一提议，但是没有达成一致意见（因为有些国家反对将修订适用于现有设施）。作为一种替代方案，该次会议通过了《关于核安全的维也纳宣言》（9 February 2015, CNS/DC/2015/2/Rev.1）。该宣言在第三段明确指出，那些旨在确保核电站整个生命周期的安全的国内要求和法规，应当把相关的国际原子能机构安全标准考虑在内。它还呼吁把适当的技术标准和规格融入《核安全公约》下的同行评审过程中。

157　Jankowitsch-Prévor, supra footnote148, pp. 32ff [referring e. g. to the Convention on Early Notification (containing the "Guidelines on Reportable Events, Integrated Planning and Information Exchange in a Transboundary Release of Radioactive Materials", INFCIRC/ 321) and the Convention on Assistance (containing the "Guidelines for Mutual Emergency Assistance Arrangements in connection with a Nuclear Accident or a Radiological Emergency", INFCIRC/310)]. See also Birnie et al., supra footnote148, p. 497 [referring e. g., to the Convention on Nuclear Safety and the Joint Convention, which includes the following standards: "The Safety of Nuclear Installations", IAEA Safety series No. 110, 1993; "The Principles of Radioactive Waste Management", IAEA Safety series No. 111-F, 1995; "Radiation Protection and the Safety of Radiation Sources", IAEA Safety series No. 120, 1996; "Code of Practice on the Transboundary Movement of Radioactive Waste", IAEA GC (XXXIV) /939 (1990)].

158　虽然在实践中国际原子能机构的作用通常是通过供应方和接收方的协议来促进那些拥有核技术和原料的国家提供帮助。

159　如果某国不是《不扩散核武器条约》的缔约国，安保协议仍然必须遵守国际原子能机构的规约，该规约特别规定，如果有某国违反了依据第11条（不得将援助用于军事用途）所做出的承诺，国际原子能机构有可能会通知联合国安理会和联合国大会。

160　See supra footnote6.

久性有机污染物公约》《事先知情同意公约》和《巴塞尔公约》(以及《远程越界空气污染公约》的多个议定书)所开发的手段来应对这一生命周期的不同阶段。让我们依次来讨论这三个问题。

关于第一个问题,值得一提的是,已经有一个区域层面(联合国欧洲经济委员会)开展了针对重金属(例如汞)的规制。如第五章所述,《远程越界空气污染公约》的一项议定书就是专门针对重金属,并将其看作越界空气污染的一个污染源。[161] 汞对人身健康和环境造成的不利影响已经得到充分证实,而且在当地以及距离污染源很远的地方(远程越界沉积)都可以感受到这些影响。联合国环境规划署从 2001 年开始就在其《全球汞评估》(*Global Mercury Assessments*,GMA)的文本中监测汞的生命周期。[162]《全球汞评估》和联合国环境规划署的其他尝试,与国内法(尤其是在美国)的规制进展一起,为建立一个政府间谈判委员会提供了动力。[163] 这一政府间谈判委员会在 2013 年年初的日内瓦会议上完成了工作,批准了汞公约的文本,后来这一文本于 2013 年 10 月在日本水俣获得正式通过,用以纪念几十年前发生在这里的一个汞毒悲剧。与《重金属议定书》不同,《水俣公约》是全球性的,它向所有国家或区域经济一体化组织开放签署,即使这些组织的成员国本身并非《水俣公约》的缔约方。[164]

《水俣公约》另一个重要特点是它涵盖了汞的整个生命周期,从汞矿开采,到它的利用和释放,再到贸易、储存以及最后的处置。这也符合公约的广义目标,正如它第 1 条的规定,即"保护人体健康和环境免受汞和汞化合物人为排放和释放的危害"。公约针对的只是汞和汞化合物的"人为"排放而不包括自然发生的汞,这一点与气候变化协定聚焦于温室气体的人为(而非自然发生的)排放很相似。汞的人为释放主要源自手工的和小规模的金矿开采(占比 37%)、燃料燃烧(占比 25%)、有色金

---

[161] See supra footnote 6.

[162] See e. g. UNEP, Global Mercury Assessment (2013) (hereafter "GMA 2013").

[163] See H. Selin, "Global Environmental Law and Treaty-Making on Hazardous Substances: The Minamata Convention and Mercury Abatement" (2014) 14 Global Environmental Politics 1, 4-7. On the negotiation of this convention see also See H. H. Eriksen and F. Perrez, "The Minamata Convention: A Comprehensive Response to a Global Problem" (2014) 23 RECIEL 195.

[164] Minamata Convention, supra footnote 6, Art. 30. The term "regional economic integration organisation" is specifically defined in Art. 2 (j) of the Convention.

属生产（占比 10%）、水泥生产（占比 9%）以及其他几个生产过程。[165] 公约通过借用其他条约的各种规制手段（如本章和第五章所述）来管理这些源头。

事实上，公约是把《持久性有机污染物公约》《事先知情同意公约》和《巴塞尔公约》以及其他条约的手段整合在一起，并将它们运用于汞、汞化合物、添汞产品和涉及汞的生产过程的规制。这一手段是如此复杂，以至于本章的文本只能做一个简要概括。[166] 有鉴于此，就有必要区分规制干预的五个阶段，即提取（开采）、利用和释放、贸易、储存及处置。《水俣公约》为每一个阶段都规定了不同的框架。

汞矿开采是由第 3 条来规制的。根据这一条款，禁止缔约国进行（本公约对其生效之际未在其领土范围内进行的）原生汞矿开采活动（即新的汞矿开采），业已进行的原生汞矿开采活动自本公约获批后继续进行最多 15 年。[167] 关于汞提取的其他重要源头（与主要开采相比，被称为次要开采），它们应当被认定，而且在某些情况下，获取的汞必须依照环境无害化管理指南来予以消除。[168]

汞的利用和释放的规制模式沿用了《持久性有机污染物公约》的模式。第 4—9 条针对产品和生产过程规定了一个具体的框架［包括金矿开采和其他过程（例如燃煤）所导致的汞向环境的排放或释放］。"名录"（附录一）所认定的一些产品和过程附带有一个逐步淘汰的义务，[169] 同时也存在一些例外情况（等同于《持久性有机污染物公约》的"一般例外"）[170] 和单个国家的时限延长（等同于《持久性有机污染物公约》的"特殊豁免"）。[171] 其他一些产品和过程则只会被限制（例如将汞用于银

165　GMA 2013, supra footnote152, p. 9. The Convention adopts a source-specific approach rather than introducing an overall national cap on mercury. On this question see You Mingqing, "Interpretation of the source-specific substantive control measures of the Minamata Convention on Mercury" (2015) 75 Environment International 1.

166　For a more detailed discussion see Selin, supra footnote163.

167　Minamata Convention, supra footnote6, Art. 3 (3) - (4).

168　Ibid., Art. 3 (5).

169　Ibid., Art. 4 (1) [in addition, Arts. 4 (2) provides a more flexible obligation which is only available under strict conditions] and 5 (2).

170　Ibid., Annex A.

171　Ibid., Art. 6.

汞合金或者用于氯乙烯单体的生产），[172] 而一些产品则会得到特批（例如根据世界卫生组织的建议将汞用于延长一些疫苗的保质期）。[173] 其他三种类型的生产过程也受到了相应的处置。第一种指的是用汞来进行手工和小规模金矿开采，它应当通过基于公约附录三的"国家计划"来处理。[174] 第二种指的是附录四认定的那种向大气排放汞的"点源"，它应受制于一些管控措施。新的点源必须符合"最佳可得技术"[175] 和"最佳环境实践"[176] 这些标准以"在实际情况允许时尽快、但最迟应自本公约被批准之日起5年内控制并于可行时减少排放"，[177] 而现有的点源则只是通过"国家计划"（包括第8条第5款提及的一些措施）来解决。最后，一个默认条款针对的是其他一些生产过程（"点源"），它们的运行将汞释放到环境中。有义务去认定这些源头并采取措施以减少这类释放。[178]

关于贸易，第3条第6—7款允许将汞出口到缔约方和非缔约方，前提条件是必须遵循一个事先知情同意程序（参照《事先知情同意公约》的模式），目的是确保接收者有能力正确管理汞。[179] 如果是从公约的非缔约方出口到缔约方，进口国只有在收到汞来自公约批准来源这样的保证之后，才能允许交易继续进行。[180]

---

[172] Ibid., Annex A, part II, and Annex B, part II. On the dental amalgam issue, which was highly debated, see T. K. Mackey, J. T. Contreras, B. A. Liang, " The Minamata Convention: Attempting to address the global controversy of dental amalgam use and mercury waste disposal" （2014） 472 Science of the Total Environment 125.

[173] Minamata Convention, supra footnote 6, Annex A.

[174] Ibid., Art. 7. On this question see S. Spiegel et al., "The Minamata Convention on Mercury: Time to seek solutions with artisanal mining communities" （2014） 122 Environmental Health Perspectives 122; S. Spiegel et al., "Implications of the Minamata Convention on Mercury for informal gold mining in Sub-Saharan Africa: From global policy debates to grassroots implementation?" （2015） 17 Environment, Development and Sustinability 765; A. Buccella, "Can the Minamata Convention on Mercury solve Peru's illegal artisanal gold mining problem?" （2014） 24 Yearbook of International Environmental Law 166.

[175] Minamata Convention, supra footnote 6, Art. 2 （b）.

[176] Ibid., Art. 2 （c）.

[177] Ibid., Art. 8 （4）.

[178] Ibid., Art. 9 （3）-（5）.

[179] Ibid., Art. 3 （6） （requiring written consent and some assurances, more demanding in the case of exports to non-parties） and 3 （7） （setting out a facilitated system based on a general notification）.

[180] Ibid., Art. 3 （8） and 3 （9） （setting out a facilitated system based on a general notification）.

第 10 条针对的是那些用于公约所允许的用途（而非汞废物）的汞或汞化合物的临时储存。各缔约国应采取措施以确保这样的储存采用了一种"环境无害化方式"。这一标准将会通过参考缔约方大会发布的指南来规定，而这一指南则必须是基于在《巴塞尔公约》框架下制定的相关指南。[181]

最后，《巴塞尔公约》还为《水俣公约》第 11 条针对汞废物处置所采用的方法提供了基础。第 11 条第 1 段和第 2 段通过直接借鉴《巴塞尔公约》来定性汞废物。关于汞废物这一客体，各国应承担三种义务，即（1）采取措施以确保汞废物的处置采用的是环境无害化的方式，并将《巴塞尔公约》的相关指南考虑在内；[182]（2）不得允许汞废物的回收、再循环、再生或直接再使用，除非它是用于公约批准的某种用途或者为了进行环境无害化处置；[183]（3）将《事先知情同意公约》的事先知情同意制度运用于汞废物的越境转移。[184] 如果某国不是《巴塞尔公约》的缔约方，第 11 条则要求该国应充分考虑这一文件及其相关标准以构建本国的法律体制。[185]

与其他多边环境协定相似，《水俣公约》也拥有一个重要的体制安排和履行安排，包括一个在谈判过程中引发激烈讨论的财政机制。[186] 本书的第二章和第九章用一种交叉的方式分析了这些安排。[187] 但是，基于当前目的，应该强调的是公约关注到了某一种物质（例如汞）的完整生命周期，以及公约从其前任那里沿用了逐步淘汰、事先知情同意程序、最佳可得技术/最佳环境实践的联合应用这一模式。

部分参考文献

[1] Andrews, A., "Beyond the Ban-Can the Basel Convention Adequately

---

[181] Ibid., Art. 10 (3).
[182] Ibid., Art. 11 (3) (a).
[183] Ibid., Art. 11 (3) (b).
[184] Ibid., Art. 11 (3) (c).
[185] Ibid., Art. 11 (1) and (3) (c).
[186] Selin, supra footnote 163, pp. 14-15.
[187] On this question see J. Templeton, P. Kohler, "Implementation and Compliance under the Minamata Convention" (2014) 23 RECIEL 211.

Safeguard the Interests of the World's Poor in the International Trade of Hazardous Waste?" (2009) 5 *Law, Environment and Development Journal* 167.

[2] Barrios, P., "The Rotterdam Convention on Hazardous Chemicals: A Meaningful Step towards Environmental Protection?" (2004) 16 *Georgetown International Environmental Law Review* 679.

[3] Bitar, F., *Les Mouvements Transfrontières de Déchets Dangereux Selon la Convention de Bâle. Etude des Régimes de Responsabilité* (Paris: Pedone, 1997).

[4] Bombier, N., "The Basel Convention's Complete Ban on Hazardous Waste Exports: Negotiating the Compatibility of Trade and the Environment" (1997) 7 *Journal of Environmental Law and Practice* 325.

[5] Brown Weiss, E., "International Environmental Law: Contemporary Issues and the Emergence of a New World Order" (1995) 81 *Georgetown Law Journal* 675.

[6] Buccella, A., "Can the Minamata Convention on Mercury solve Peru's illegal artisanal gold mining problem?" (2014) 24 *Yearbook of International Environmental Law* 166.

[7] Caron, D. and C. Leben (eds.), *Les aspects internationaux des catastrophes naturelles et industrielles–The International Aspects of Natural and Industrial Catastrophes* (The Hague/Leiden: Académie de droit international/Martinus Nijhoff, 2001).

[8] Clapps, J., *Toxic Exports: The Transfer of Hazardous Wastes from Rich to Poor Countries* (Ithaca NY: Cornell University Press, 2001).

[9] Cox, J., "The Trafigura Case and the System of Prior Informed Consent Under the Basel Convention–A Broken System?" (2010) 6 *Law, Environment and Development Journal* 263.

[10] Ditz, D. and B. Tuncak, "Bridging the divide between toxic risks and global chemical governance" (2014) 23 *Review of European, Comparative and International Environmental Law* 181.

[11] Dupuy, P.-M., "Overview of the Existing Customary Legal Regime Regarding International Pollution", in D. B. Magraw (ed.), *International Law and Pollution* (Philadelphia: University of Pennsylvania Press,

1991), pp. 61-89.

[12] Edvokia, M., "La Convention de Bâle sur les mouvements transfrontières de déchets dangereux (22 March 1989)" (1989) 93 *Revue Générale de Droit International Public* 899.

[13] Emory, R. W., "Probing the Protections in the Rotterdam Convention on Prior Informed Consent" (2001) 12 *Colorado Journal of International Environmental Law and Policy* 47.

[14] Eriksen H. H. and F. Perrez, "The Minamata Convention: A Comprehensive Response to a Global Problem" (2014) 23 *Review of European, Comparative and International Environmental Law* 195.

[15] Grosz, M., *Sustainable Waste Trade under WTO Law* (Leiden: Martinus Nijhoff, 2011).

[16] Handl, G., "Après Tchernobyl: Quelques réflexions sur le programme législatif multilatéral à l'ordre du jour" (1988) 92 *Revue générale de droit international public* 5.

"The IAEA Nuclear Safety Conventions: an Example of Successful 'Treaty Management'?" (2003) 72 *Nuclear Law Bulletin* 7.

[17] Hung, H., A. A. Katsoyiannis, and R. Guardans, "Ten years of global monitoring under the Stockholm Convention on Persistent Organic Pollutants: Trend, sources and transport modelling" (2016) 217 *Environmental Pollution* 1.

[18] Jankowitsch-Prévor, O., "La compétence normative de l'AIEA, Bases juridiques et sources du droit", in OECD, *Le droit nucléaire international: Histoire, évolution et perspectives* (Paris: OECD, 2010), pp. 15-34.

[19] Jones, W. F., "The Evolution of the Bamako Convention: An African Perspective" (1993) 4 *Colorado Journal of International Environmental Law and Policy* 324.

[20] Kummer, K., *International Management of Hazardous Wastes* (Oxford University Press, 1995).

[21] Kummer Peiry, K., "The Chemicals and Waste Regime as a Basis for a Comprehensive International Framework on Sustainable Management of Potentially Hazardous Materials?" (2014) 23 *Review of European, Comparative*

and International Environmental Law 172.

[22] Kummer Peiry, K., A. R. Ziegler and J. Baumgartner (eds.), *Waste Management and the Green Economy. Law and Policy* (Cheltenham: Edward Elgar, 2016).

[23] Lallas, P., "The Stockholm Convention on Persistent Organic Pollutants" (2001) 95 *American Journal of International Law* 692.

"The Role of Process and Participation in the Development of Effective International Environmental Agreements: A Study of the Global Treaty on Persistent Organic Pollutants" (2002) 19 *UCLA Journal of Environmental Law and Policy* 83.

[24] Lonngren, R., *International Approaches to Chemicals Control: A Historical Overview* (Stockholm: Kemi, 1992).

[25] Mackey, T. K., J. T. Contreras and B. A. Liang, "The Minamata Convention: Attempting to address the global controversy of dental amalgam use and mercury waste disposal" (2014) 472 *Science of the Total Environment* 125.

[26] McDorman, T., "The Rotterdam Convention on the Prior Informed Consent Procedure for Certain Hazardous Chemicals and Pesticides in International Trade: Some Legal Notes" (2004) 13 *Review of European Community and International Environmental Law* 187.

[27] Mekouar, A. M., "Pesticides and Chemicals-The Requirement of Prior Informed Consent", in D. Shelton (ed.), *Commitment and Compliance. The Role of Non-Binding Norms in the International Legal System* (Oxford University Press, 2000), pp. 146-163.

[28] Mintz, J., "Two Cheers for Global POP's: A Summary and Assessment of the Stockholm Convention on Persistent Organic Pollutants" (2001) 14 *Georgetown International Environmental Law Review* 319.

[29] Montjoie, M., *Droit International et Gestion des Déchets Radioactifs* (Paris: LGDJ, 2011).

[30] Olsen, M. A., *Analysis of the Stockholm Convention on Persistent Organic Pollutants* (Dobbs Ferry NY: Oceana, 2003).

[31] Ouguergouz, F. "La Convention de Bamako sur l'interdiction d'importer en Afrique des déchets dangereux et sur le contrôle des mouvements

transfrontières et la gestion des déchets dangereux produits en Afrique" (1992) 38 *Annuaire français de droit international* 871.

[32] Pallemaerts, M., *Toxics and Transnational Law: International and European Regulation of Toxic Substances as Legal Symbolism* (Oxford: Hart Publishing, 2003).

[33] Redgwell, C., "Regulating Trade in Dangerous Substances: Prior Informed Consent under the 1998 Rotterdam Convention", in A. Kiss, D. Shelton and K. Ishibashi (eds.), *Economic Globalization and Compliance with International Environmental Agreements* (The Hague: Kluwer, 2003), pp. 75-88.

[34] . Riley, P., *Nuclear Waste: Law, Policy and Pragmatism* (Aldershot: Ashgate, 2004).

[35] Rosendal, K. and S. Andresen, *UNEP's Role in Enhancing Problem-Solving Capacity in Multilateral Environmental Agreements: Co-ordination and Assistance in the Biodiversity Conservation Cluster* (Lysaker: Fridtjof Nansen Institute, 2004).

[36] Scott, J., "REACH: Combining Harmonization and Dynamism in the Regulation of Chemicals", in J. Scott (ed.), *Environmental Protection: European Law and Governance* (Oxford University Press, 2009), pp. 56-91.

[37] Selin, H., "Global Environmental Law and Treaty-Making on Hazardous Substances: The Minamata Convention and Mercury Abatement" (2014) 14 *Global Environmental Politics* 1.

[38] Smith, S., "GHS: A Short Acronym for a Big Idea" (2007) 69 *Occupational Hazards* 6.

[39] Söderholm, P., "The Political Economy of a Global Ban on Mercury-Added Products: Positive versus Negative List Approaches" (2013) 53 *Journal of Cleaner Production* 287.

[40] Szasz, P., *The Law and Practice of the International Atomic Energy Agency* (Vienna: IAEA, 1970) and Supplement (1970-1980).

[41] Tromans, S., *Nuclear Law: The Law Applying to Nuclear Installations and Radioactive Substances in its Historic Context* (Oxford: Hart Publishing, 2010).

[42] Winder, C., R. Azzi and D. Wagner, "The Development of the

Globally Harmonized System (GHS) of Classification and Labelling of Hazardous Chemicals" (2005) 125 *Journal of Hazardous Materials* 29.

[43] Winter, G., "Dangerous Chemicals: A Global Problem on its Way to Global Governance", in M. Fuhr, K. Bizer and P. H. Feindt (eds.), *Umweltrecht und Umweltwissenschaft: Festschrift für Eckard Rehbinder* (Erich Schmidt Verlag: 2007), pp. 819-833.

[44] Wirth, D. A., "Trade implications of the Basel Convention Amendment banning North-South Trade in Hazardous Waste" (1998) 7 *Review of European Community and International Environmental Law* 237.

"Hazardous Substances and Activities", in D. Bodansky, J. Brunnée and E. Hey (eds.), *The Oxford Handbook of International Environmental Law* (Oxford University Press, 2007), pp. 394-422.

[45] Yokoyama, J., "Dysfunction of the regulation of nuclear power in Japan-Legal analysis of the Fukushima disaster and 2012 reform" (2013) 9 *International Journal of Public Policy* 245.

[46] You Mingqing, "Interpretation of the source-specific substantive control measures of the Minamata Convention on Mercury" (2015) 75 *Environment International* 1.

[47] Young, G., J. Garman and S. Tupper, "A Long Way from Basel Clarity: Implications of the Basel Convention for the Consumer Electronics Sector" (2000) 9 *European Environmental Law Review* 71.

第三编 履 行

第八章　履行：传统方法

第一节　导论

在前几章中，我们已经讨论了在国际层面对环境问题的实质性规制。我们具体分析了各国在水圈、大气层、生物圈的保护以及危险物质和活动等方面所承担的义务。我们现在谈谈履行这些义务的过程。

在这方面的传统做法认为，国际义务的遵守只是取决于一个国家是否愿意遵守。从实体法的角度看，鼓励遵约的主要机制是使国家为任何违反行为付出代价，特别是通过适合国家责任的次级规范（secondary norms of State responsibility）。[1] 从程序的观点来看，违反一项规范可能会导致若干后果，从最初对不遵守国际义务的指控，随后往往是有关国家之间的谈判和协商，到解决争端的司法机制，以及在适当情况下的替代性争端解决机制，例如调解、和解或调查。[2]

然而，我们最好将遵守规范的要求到不遵守规范的要求这一转变理解为一个发展过程，这一过程存在着不同的程度。这些程度为本章的讨论提供了有益的基础，因为它们有助于在它们最可能介入的阶段确定不同的履

---

[1] 各国也可以采取反制措施，虽然这种情况并不常见。See Responsibility of States for Internationally Wrongful Acts, GA Res. 56/83, UN Doc. A/RES/56/83, 12 December 2001 (ILC Articles), Art. 22 and Arts. 49–54.

[2] Article 33 of the UN Charter, 24 October 1945, 1 UNTS 16, shows the range of traditional methods for the peaceful settlement of disputes between States. See J. Merrills, *International Dispute Settlement* (Cambridge University Press, 2011).

行机制。根据遵约的范围可以区分为四个"阶段"。[3] 图8-1生动地总结了这种理解。

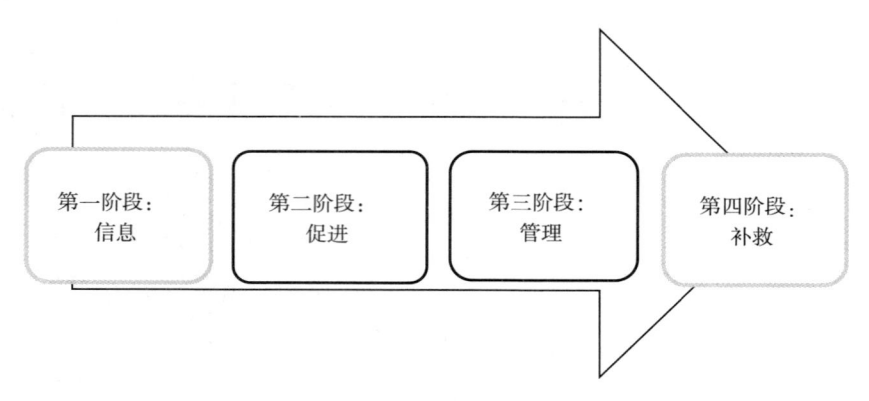

```
第一阶段：    第二阶段：    第三阶段：    第四阶段：
信息          促进          管理          补救
```

图 8-1　遵约程序的各阶段

有些机制只在不遵约指控出现之前发挥"上游"的作用（第一阶段）。在这一阶段的主要机制是监测和报告信息，这些信息是与其国际义务相关联的国家行为（本章第二节）。相比之下，在"下游"（第四阶段），我们发现，更正式的机制通过第三方（裁决或准裁决机制）来定性违约行为，以及凭借国家责任法（本章第三节）或其他次级规范来确定后续后果。在这两个极端之间存在一个灰色地带，在那里遵约的程度是不明确的。这一领域历来是所谓和平解决争端的外交或政治机制的范围。然而，我们将在第九章中看到，在国际环境法中，这一领域涌现了多个通过环境标准来促进遵约（第二阶段）和管理不遵约（第三阶段）的新方法。

第二节　监测和报告

一　义务类型

有一系列机制可以用来促进对环境义务的遵守。在本节中，我们分析

---

[3] See P. – M. Dupuy, "Oùenest le droit international de l'environnement à la fin du siècle?" (1997) *Revue générale de droit international public* 873, in particular pp. 893–895; J. E. Viñuales, "Managing Abidance by Standards for the Protection of the Environment", in A. Cassese (ed.), *Realizing Utopia* (Oxford University Press, 2012), pp. 326–339.

一种在违反义务中发挥上游作用的技术,即收集有关履行义务的信息(监测)和提交涉及义务履行的报告(即报告)。要理解这种机制是如何发挥作用的,首先看一下要履行的义务类型。

第一个区别,我们将在本章后面更深入地探讨,可以在"初级规范"和"次级规范"之间进行区分。初级规范规定了各国应采取的具体行为(例如,减少特定物质的排放、建立保护区、交流报告等)或者对某些前提条件做出定义,一旦满足这些条件就会引发特定法律后果。另外,次级规范说明了违约(或更具体地说是满足了初级规范所规定的前提条件)所导致的后果(广义上的"补救")。在本章第三节中我们将发现这种区别比它看起来要复杂得多。

在初级规范中,可以进一步区分"实体性义务"和"程序性义务"。第一类包括各种类型的义务。例如,防止环境破坏的责任被纳入习惯法[4]和条约法[5]中。其他例证包括减少特定物质的消费、生产或排放[6]或者控制其越境转移[7]的条约义务。这些实体性义务反映了一种直觉观念,即存在一种国家间义务或"横向"义务。但是,第一类还包括在国际环境法中很重要的另一种义务,即一国承担的执行条约规定而采取国内措施的"纵向"义务。纵向义务是为了落实条约的要求(例如制订保护生物多样性的国家计划[8])或为了履行横向义务(例如为履行物种或物质国际贸易

---

[4] See *Legality of the Threat or Use of Nuclear Weapons*, Advisory Opinion, ICJ Reports 1996, p. 226(Legality of Nuclear Weapons), para. 29.

[5] See United Nations Convention on the Law of the Sea, 10 December 1982, 1833 UNTS 3 (UNCLOS), Art. 194.

[6] See, e. g. the Montreal Protocol on Substances that Deplete the Ozone Layer, 16 September 1987, 1522 UNTS 29 (Montreal Protocol), Arts. 2 to 2I and Annexes A, B, C and E; Kyoto Protocol to the United Nations Framework Convention on Climate Change, 11 December 1997, 2302 UNTS 148 (Kyoto Protocol), Art. 3 and Annex B; Stockholm Convention on Persistent Organic Pollutants, 22 May 2001, 2256 UNTS 119 (Stockholm Convention or POP Convention), Art. 3 (1).

[7] See Convention on International Trade in Endangered Species of Wild Fauna and Flora, 3 March 1973, 993 UNTS 243 (CITES), Arts. III–IV; Basel Convention on the Control of Transboundary Movements of Hazardous Wastes and their Disposal, 22 March 1989, 1673 UNTS 57 (Basel Convention), Arts. 4 and 6; Rotterdam Convention on the Prior Informed Consent Procedure for Certain Hazardous Chemicals and Pesticides in International Trade, 10 September 1998, 2244 UNTS 337 (PIC Convention), Arts. 10 and 11; POP Convention, supra 66, Art. 3 (2).

[8] See Convention on Biological Diversity, 5 June 1992, 1760 UNTS 79 (CBD), Art. 6.

规制而采取国内措施的义务)。

就程序义务的类别而论,它们反过来有助于执行纵向的实体性义务。事实上,它们的主要目标是鼓励各国不仅采取国家措施和交流这些措施,还要建立机构收集必要的信息[9],从而为创建充足的数据库奠定基础,数据库的目的是监测该规定旨在控制的环境问题的变化。因此,这些程序要求是信息监测和报告机制的起点。

二 机制的类型

一般来说,环境条约规定了信息收集和义务履行情况报告的机制。[10] 在本书文本中,不会对大量的条约进行个别分析,我们将集中识别实践中使用的机制类型。在这方面,根据有关条约所赋予的权力范围,我们可以区分两种主要类型。

第一种机制相对来说没什么雄心。各国有义务向条约机构[缔约方大会(COP)、秘书处或其他机构]提交报告,说明它们为履行条约义务所采取的措施。在这些措施中,往往需要各国应要求建立一个制度来监测某些环境变量(例如某些物质的排放)。监测系统为适当履行报告义务提供了基础。这一机制可参照《远程越界空气污染公约》(*LRTAP Convention*)的《硫减排议定书》(*Protocol on the Reduction of Sulphur Emissions*)第4条和第6条来说明。[11] 第6条规定,缔约国应"制订国家政策、方案和战略,作为减少硫排放或其越界流出的一种手段,尽早最迟在1993年至少减少30%"。他们还必须"向执行机构报告实现这一目标的进展情况"。减少30%是源于该议定书第2条的实质性义务。关于这些措施和进展的报告的义务得到了第4条的确认,该条规定"各缔约方每年应

---

[9] See CITES, supra footnote 7, Art. VIII (1).

[10] R. Wolfrum, "Means of Ensuring Compliance with and Enforcement of International Environmental Law" (1998) 272 *Recueil Des Cours de L'Académie de Droit International de La Haye*, 9–154, in particular 36–55.

[11] Protocol to the Convention on Long-Range Transboundary Air Pollution 1979 on the Reduction of Sulphur Emissions or their Transboundary Fluxes by at Least 30 per cent, 8 July 1985, 1480 UNTS 215 (Sulphur Protocol I). See also Protocol to the Convention on Long-Range Transboundary Air Pollution 1979 on Further Reduction of Sulphur Emissions, 14 June 1994, 2030 UNTS 122 (Sulphur Protocol II), Art. 5.

向执行机构提供其国家年度硫排放量的水平及其计算依据"。这些安排也有助于识别实体性义务与监测和交流这些程序性义务的区别。

第二种机制与第一种机制非常相似，但有两个显著区别。一方面，程序义务更加精确。它们为信息的交流规定了具体的最后期限和格式。另一方面，收到来文的条约机构有更大的权力，根据条约，这些权力可包括：(1) 有机会核查所提交资料；(2) 可以要求提交更多信息；(3) 可以自行（proprio motu）收集信息或者将其他方式获取的信息也纳入考量。

第一个例证，《拉姆萨公约》（Ramsar Convention）[12] 缔约方大会在1990年建立了一个涉及保护区的信息交流和核查机制。[13] 这一机制履行了公约第3条第1款（纵向实体性义务）和第2款（监测和交流的程序性义务）。设立这一机制的决议附录二要求采用一种特定的信息交流格式，即《拉姆萨湿地信息表》（Information Sheet on Ramsar Sites）和"湿地类型分类系统"（Classification System for Wetland Type）。[14] 附录一规定了一个程序，各国必须向公约主席团（Bureau of the Convention）通报名单上某一地点的生态特征因人为干预而正发生的变化（或可能发生变化）的情况。[15] 该主席团可要求提供更多信息以评估有关情况，如该主席团认为有关地点的特征正在改变（或可能改变），则可与当事国合作，找出一种可接受的解决方案。该程序随后成为解决争端的政治手段，包括将案件提交给常设委员会（常设委员会也将试图寻求解决的方案）或提交给缔约方会议。我们将在第九章谈及这些程序。

第二个例证则是《濒危野生动植物种国际贸易公约》（CITES）所建立的体系。[16] 主要体现于第2—4条中的横向实体性义务，将通过纵向实体性义务（第8条第1款）来得以履行。第8条第7款规定各缔约国有程

---

[12] Convention on Wetlands of International Importance especially as Waterfowl Habitat, 2 February 1971, 996 UNTS 245 (Ramsar Convention).

[13] Recommendation 4.7. (1990) "Mechanisms for Improved Application of the Ramsar Convention" (Recommendation 4.7). This mechanism had been established earlier by the Standing Committee of the Convention, but it was not until 1990 that the COP endorsed this measure (see Recommendation 4.7, first paragraph of the operative part).

[14] 随着时间的推移，这种格式已经进行了修改。

[15] Recommendation 4.7, supra footnote 13, Annex I, para. 1.

[16] CITES, supra footnote 7.

序上的义务编制关于公约执行情况的报告并将其送交给秘书处。这些报告必须在规定的时间内（视情况而定，每年或每两年）以特定的格式提交。在这方面，秘书处向缔约国转递了两份"通知"，介绍了年度报告[17]和两年报告[18]的撰写标准格式。负责审查这些报告的秘书处也可以"要求缔约方提供它认为为确保本公约的履行所必需的有关资料"（第7条第2款d项）。

第三个例证是《联合国气候变化框架公约》（UNFCCC）建立的更复杂的体系。[19]《联合国气候变化框架公约》第12条规定的程序义务（对排放和吸收的监测，以及国家措施的制定）以第五章所研究的实体性义务（所有国家的义务，附录一国家的义务，附录二国家的义务）为基础。取决于一国的国情，报告的频率、内容和条约机构的核查程度将有所不同。我们无法在此详细解释适用于每一类国家的规则。[20] 想要了解这样一个体系所涵盖的范围和复杂性，简要回顾适用于附录一国家的制度便足够了，这些国家也是《京都议定书》（Kyoto Protocol）的缔约国。[21] 这些国家必须按照特定的格式［"共同报告格式"（Common Reporting Format，CRF）和"国家清单报告"（National Inventory Report，NIR）][22] 提交温室气体排放的年度报告，对于《京都议定书》缔约方，还必须包括《京都议定书》要求的更多信息。[23] 并且，它们还必须定期提交为减少排放而采取的

17　Notification to the Parties 2011/019, 17 February 2011. This notification refers to the guidelines for the submission of annual reports, which were adopted in 2000 and revised to introduce adjustments adopted at subsequent COPs.

18　Notification to the Parties 2005/035, 6 July 2005.

19　United Nations Framework Convention on Climate Change, 9 May 1992, 1771 UNTS 107 (UNFCCC).

20　See unfccc.int/national_reports/items/1408.php (visited on 28 January 2013).

21　Kyoto Protocol, supra footnote 6.

22　Decision 3/CP.5, "Guidelines for the Preparation of National Communications by Parties included in Annex I to the Convention, Part I: UNFCCC Reporting Guidelines on Annual Inventories", 16 February 2000, Doc. FCCC/CP/1999/7, revised several times.

23　UNFCCC Secretariat, *Kyoto Protocol Reference Manual on Accounting of Emissions and Assigned Amount* (2008).

措施的"国家信息通报"(national communications)。[24] 这些报告可能要由秘书处协调的专家小组进行"深入审查"。[25] 第一次缔约方会议审议了这些专家小组访问国家的可能性,并且随后予以确认。[26] 此外,这项审查包括专家小组与当事国之间的交流,还会要求当事国提供更多的信息。[27] 请注意,虽然数据主要是由各国提供的,但缔约方会议承认也有可能考虑到其他来源的数据。[28]

各种不同的监测机制生动形象地展示了这些体系的演变,其特点是更高层次的制度化和更详细的核查。在第九章我们将会看到,这些机制通常与其他旨在促进遵约或管理"不遵约"的程序一起运行。

第三节 争端解决及法律后果

一 前言

在20世纪下半叶,在国际法的履行上,一个日益普遍的方式是通过裁决或者准裁决(如一个委员会)对违约进行定性以及决定违约所导致的法律后果(国际不法行为所应承担的责任或其他后果)。这种方法在国

---

[24] Decision 4/CP.5, "Guidelines for the Preparation of National Communications by Parties included in Annex I to the Convention, Part II: UNFCCC Reporting Guidelines for National Communications", 16 February 2000, Doc. FCCC/CP/1999/7, revised several times.

[25] See, in particular, Decision 2/CP.1, "Review of First Communications from the Parties referred to in Annex I of the Convention", 2 June 1995, Doc. FCCC/CP/1995/7/Add.1; Decision 6/CP.3, "Communications from Parties included in Annex I of the Convention", 6 March 1998, Doc. FCCC/CP/1997/7/Add.1; Decision 11/CP.4, "National Communications from Parties included in Annex I to the Convention", 25 January 1999, Coc. FCCC/CP/1998/16/Add.1; Decision 6/ CP.5, "Guidelines for the Technical Review of Greenhouse Gas Inventories from Parties included in Annex I to the Convention", 2 February 2000, Doc. FCCC/CP/1999/6/Add.1, adopting the document FCCC/CP/1999/7 * (Examination Guidelines).

[26] See Decision 2/CP.1, supra footnote 25, para.2 (c); Decision 6/CP.3, supra footnote 25, para.3 (a); Examination Guidelines, supra footnote 25, para.20.

[27] Examination Guidelines, supra footnote 25, para.19.

[28] See Decision 6/CP.3, supra footnote 25, para.2 (b), allowing the release of inventory data "[with] relevant data from authoritative sources".

际环境法中存在许多困难。[29] 我们将会在适当时机讨论这些困难,但在当前阶段,通过介绍来确定其中一些困难似乎是有用的。

第一,补救的逻辑并不适合环境损害的特殊性质,因为环境损害的修复要困难得多和(或)昂贵得多,有时甚至是不可逆转的。如何定义可修复的环境破坏(特别是纯生态破坏),建立行为和环境影响(例如气候变化相关的损害)之间的因果关系并确定适当的补救(支付补偿金、实物补偿、恢复原状等),都是国际法仍难以解决的问题。此外,在国际环境法中,想要明确区分预防和补救是特别具有挑战性的,因为一些经济上可取的活动(例如能源生产或工业生产)必然对环境产生影响。通常,要消除这些影响而不停止活动本身是不可能的。在此情况下,国际法寻求将损失最小化,并根据具体情况提供某种形式的补救。

第二,即使在可能进行补救的情况下,制定可以确定其具体方式的规则也特别具有挑战性。例如,可以在国际层面通过有关违反横向或纵向义务的国家责任的规则来组织补救。然而,也可能是在国家或跨国层面组织补救,同时国际法会要求遵守特定的参量,例如给予受害方在损害缘起国诉诸司法的权利,或禁止歧视,或者制订一个基于严格责任规则和保险相结合的补偿方案。

第三,有些违反行为并不是因为国家缺乏遵守国际法的意愿(这是国际责任的一般理论所假定的),而是因为缺乏遵守国际法的技术或财政能力。在此背景下,正如第九章所述,对违反和后续法律后果的定性可能不是一个适当的补救办法。

在接下来的段落中,我们将讨论这些困难如何在国际法中得到解决。在简要讨论了裁决在国际环境法中的作用(第二部分)之后,我们分析了如何根据国际法管理环境损害的后果(第三部分)。

二 国际环境裁判

(一) 国际环境法的裁判机构

尽管国际环境法在过去 40 年中有了重要的规范化发展,但它并没有

---

[29] See P.-M. Dupuy, "A propos des mésaventures de la responsabilité internationale des Etats dans ses rapports avec la protection internationale de l'environnement", in M. Prieur (ed.), *Etudes en hommage à Alexandre Kiss* (Paris: Frisson-Roche, 1998), pp. 269-282, para. 2.

经历其他领域中日益增长的司法化。专门化的国际裁判（adjudication）确实在人权、国际刑法、国际贸易法、外国投资法以及海洋法等领域取得了显著进展，但在环境问题上没有做到。[30] 为了了解与环境有关的争端在多大程度上被提交到国际司法机构，就有必要要将环境法专门法院与那些所谓的"借壳法庭"（即国际法其他领域的专门法院，但解决涉及环境要素的争端）区分开来。图8-2介绍了这两种分类。

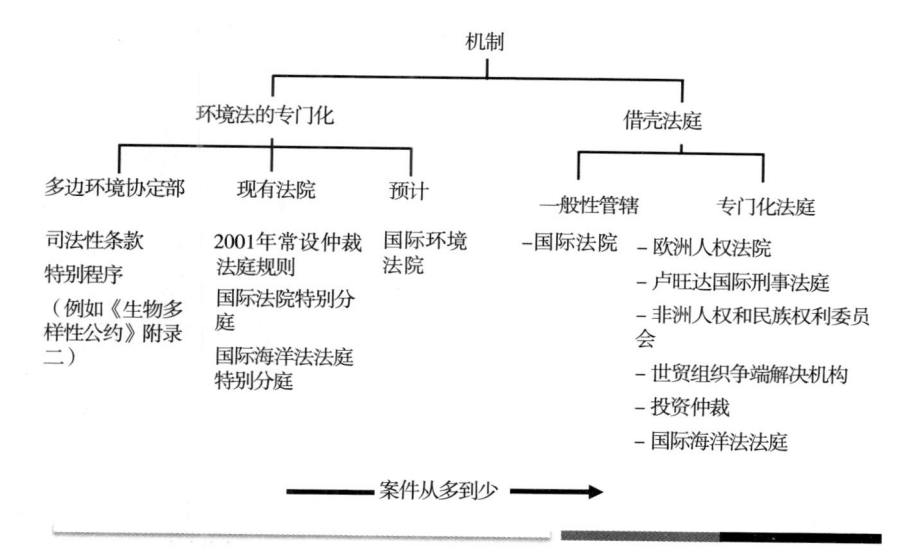

```
                           机制
              ┌─────────────┴──────────────┐
        环境法的专门化                  借壳法庭
    ┌────────┼────────┐            ┌──────┴──────┐
多边环境协定部  现有法院    预计      一般性管辖      专门化法庭
                                  －国际法院
司法性条款   2001年常设仲裁  国际环境              －欧洲人权法院
特别程序    法庭规则        法院                  －卢旺达国际刑事法庭
（例如《生物   国际法院特别分                       －非洲人权和民族权利委员
多样性公约》  庭                                  会
附录        国际海洋法法庭                         －世贸组织争端解决机构
二）        特别分庭                              －投资仲裁
                                                －国际海洋法法庭

            ◄──────── 案件从多到少 ────────►
```

图8-2　国际环境法法庭

以下各节将分析这两个大类。在这一阶段应该指出一般特征是，大多数国际环境争端都发生在那些为了专门应对环境问题而设立的管辖权和程序之外。造成这种现象的原因尚不清楚。这可能是由于各国不情愿将一项争端描述为"环境性的"，或不愿意使用新的框架，甚至不愿意将它们的

---

[30] On international environmental adjudication seeC. Romano, *The Peaceful Settlement of International Environmental Disputes: A Pragmatic Approach* (The Hague: Kluwer, 2000); O. Lecucq and S. Maljean-Dubois (eds.), *Le Rôle du Juge Dans le Développement du Droit de L'environnement* (Brussels: Bruylant, 2008); J. E. Viñuales, "The Contribution of the International Court of Justice to the Development of International Environmental Law" (2008) 32 *Fordham International Law Journal* 232; T. Stephens, *International Courts and Environmental Protection* (Cambridge University Press, 2009); A. Boyle and J. Harrison, "Judicial Settlement of International Environmental Disputes: Current Problems" (2013) 4 *Journal of International Dispute Settlement* 245.

争端置于一套相对较新和了解甚少的规则之下。人们还可以提到这样一个事实,即索赔往往是由个人(而不是国家)向他们可以诉诸的国际法院提出的。尽管如此,如本章第三节第二部分第三点所述,这种现象对国际环境法的发展具有潜在的影响。

(二) 环境问题的专门法庭

建立环境法程序和专门法庭的努力遵循了三种主要方法。第一种方法是在环境条约文本中制定一个争端解决程序。有些条约包含争端解决条款,[31] 虽然在大多数情况下这些条款缺乏司法解决争端的意向。[32]《生物多样性公约》(Convention on Biological Diversity, CBD)则更进一步,向缔约国提供了具体的仲裁程序。根据第 27 条第 3 款,各国可表示明确同意将争端提交到国际法院(ICJ)或由附录二组织的仲裁程序。但是,只有很少有国家(奥地利、古巴、格鲁吉亚和拉脱维亚)同意这种可能性,不管怎样,这一程序尚未使用过。

第二种可能性是在既有机构内制定特别程序。这种方法主要有两种形式。一方面,常设仲裁法院(Permanent Court of Arbitration, PCA)于 2001 年制定了《关于自然资源和/或环境争端仲裁的选择性规则》(Optional Rules for Arbitration of Disputes Relating to Natural Resources and/or the Environment)。[33] 这一工具只在少数情况下使用,它明确规定了一些程序性权力,例如法庭可以要求科学事项的非技术性摘要(第 24 条第 4 款),授权保护环境的临时措施(第 26 条第 1 款)或任命专家以协助法庭(第 27 条第 1 款)。另一方面,在国际法院(ICJ)和国际海洋法法庭(International Tribunal for the Law of the Sea, ITLOS)内设立了特别分庭来

---

[31] 一些条约规定了所谓的"选择加入"选项,即争端解决机制仅在国家成为条约缔约国时明确表示同意时才适用。See, e.g., Vienna Convention for the Protection of the Ozone Layer, 22 March 1985, 1513 UNTS 293, Art. 11 (3); UNFCCC, supra footnote 19, Art. 14 (2); CBD, supra footnote 8, Art. 27 (3). 其他条约提供了"选择退出"的选项,即除非国家在加入条约时另行通知,否则适用争端解决机制。See, e.g., Convention on the Physical Protection of Nuclear Material, 26 October 1979, 1456 UNTS 124, Art. 17 (3). Fora more detailed typology see Stephens, supra footnote 30, p. 25.

[32] See UNCLOS, supra footnote 5, Art. 287, Convention for the Protection of the Marine Environment of the North-East Atlantic, 22 September 1992, 2354 UNTS 67 (OSPAR Convention), Art. 32.

[33] The PCA Rules are available at: www.pca-cpa.org (visited on 4 April 2017).

处理环境问题。环境分庭（Chamber for Environmental Matters）[34] 成立于1993年，是为了回应国际法院特定的未决案件，即×××××大毛罗斯工程案[35]、关于核武器合法性的咨询意见[36]以及瑙鲁特定含磷化合物土地案。[37] 宏观来看，1992年里约热内卢首脑会议之后，正是国内、国际层面大量规范得以制定的时期，并给解决环境争端带来了很大希望。然而，尽管涉及环境要素的国际争端变得日益频繁，但它们并没有被提交到这些专门机制来化解。事实上，国际法院分庭从未被使用过，最终国际法院决定不再重新组织分庭。国际海洋法法庭于1997年成立的"海洋环境争端特别分庭"（Chamber for Marine Environment Disputes），至少到目前为止，其命运与国际法院分庭相似。本分庭的管辖权有赖于各国就某些法律问题达成一致意见，不仅包括"旨在保护和保全海洋环境"的《联合国海洋法公约》的"任一条款"的解释和运用所引发的争议，[38] 还涉及《联合国海洋法公约》第237条提及的那些有关海洋环境保护的条约或授予国际海洋法庭（ITLOS）的管辖权。[39] 这可能是一个重要的管辖范围，但是，分庭的实际意义仍然有待证明。

　　第三种方法是建立一个国际环境法庭。这方面的一个项目是在20世纪80年代后期拟订的，特别是由Amedeo Postiglione推动的，[40] 他是意大

---

[34] See R. Ranjeva, "l'environnement, la Cour internationale de justice et sa chambre spéciale pour les questions d'environnement" (1994) 40 *Annuaire français de droit international* 433.

[35] *Case Concerning the Gabčíkovo-Nagymaros Project* (*Hungary v. Slovakia*), Judgment, ICJ Reports 1997, p. 7 (*Gabčíkovo-Nagymaros Project*).

[36] *Legality of the Use by a State of Nuclear Weapons in Armed Conflict*, Advisory Opinion, ICJ Reports 1996, p. 66 (*Legality of Nuclear Weapons - WHO*); *Legality of Nuclear Weapons*, supra footnote 4.

[37] *Certain Phosphate Lands in Nauru* (*Nauru v. Australia*), Preliminary Objections, Judgment, ICJ Reports 1992, p. 240.

[38] UNCLOS, supra footnote 5.

[39] Resolution on the Chamber for the Settlement of Disputes relating to the Marine Environment, 6 October 2011, ITLOS/2011/RES. 2, para. 3.

[40] See A. Postiglione, "A More Efficient International Law on the Environment and Setting up an International Court for the Environment within the United Nations" (1990) 20 *Environmental Law* 321. For a critique by the former president of the ICJ, 参见 R. Jennings, "Need for an Environmental Court" (1992) 20 *Environmental Policy and Law* 312. On this debate, see: Stephens, supra footnote 30, pp. 56–61.

利最高法院（Corte di Cassazione）的法官，也是环境基金会国际法院（International Court of the Environment Foundation，ICEF）的创始人。[41] 除了此类项目启动的可能性极低之外，成立一个专门的环境法庭还带来了两个主要问题。第一个问题涉及这一倡议需要克服的技术困难，特别是其管辖范围（哪些条约或条款？环境习惯法？）的界定以及与人权、贸易、投资或其他事项有关的争端涉及的重大环境问题而可能与其他国际法院产生紧张关系。此外，条约中环境规范的构成通常是广泛的甚至是模糊的（"软性的"），这一特征给环境法庭带来了额外的挑战。[42] 然而，这一论点可能会被推翻：由于环境规范的相对模糊［环境规范并不比其他法庭常规运用的宽泛标准（例如投资法中的公平与公正对待标准）更模糊］，这将使专门的环境裁决变得有用。第二个问题涉及这样一个机构应该履行的职能。在这方面，程序和专门环境法庭的有限使用表明，目前没有建立一个新的机构的迫切需要。一般法庭（如国际法院和仲裁法庭）以及专门法庭和仲裁法庭（如人权、贸易、投资）似乎足以满足对环境裁判的需求。反之，也可以主张专门的环境裁判将有助于缓解"借壳法庭"的压力，并给环境法更多的空间。事实上，正如下面所讨论的，对环境保护的重视程度在不同的司法管辖下存在很大差异。

(三) 借壳法庭

1. 概述

大多数环境裁判都是在借壳法庭上审理的。当然也可以主张这些法庭不是"借来的"，因为并不存在"环境争端"，而只有"带有环境要素的争端"，这些争端由相关的专门法庭审理。这个论点在技术上是正确的。然而，"借壳法庭"一词似乎有助于强调这样一个事实，即环境裁判基本上是在国际法其他专门领域的法庭上进行的，或者提交到国际法院（尽管数量较少但有所增加）。这对了解国际环境裁判的动态和前景也很重要。实际上，专门法庭倾向于在适合其专业性的情况下来审理这些争端，有时会损害国际环境法。另一个后果是需要采用国际法其他分支的特定术语来"审理"一个环境本质的诉求，以便各法庭能够受理这些诉求。通

41　See www.icef-court.org（visited on 31 January 2013）.

42　Dupuy, supra footnote 3, 892.

常所说的环境保护的"人权方法"就是一个恰当的例证。[43] 由于管辖和可受理性方面的限制,如果环境退化与人权受到损害之间没有直接联系,这种方法就无法保护环境。[44] 此外,将环境内容融入那些旨在实现其他目标的国际义务之中的意图,并不会总能实现。同外国的移民一样,环境保护有时也受到国际法其他领域的严格规制,例如国际贸易法和外国投资法。[45]

在这一节中,我们简要分析国际环境法在"借壳法庭"中的发展。文献常常一个接一个地讨论这些法庭,或者根据它们的管辖范围来组织讨论(见图8-2)。在这方面,我们将采取一种不同的方法,试图抓住国际法院和法庭对环境考量的不同开放程度。这种方法将突出案例法中不同的断层线,可以从概念上确定一个机构是否对整合环境考量持欢迎、中立或者不愿意的态度。[46] 在进行讨论之前,有两点需要注意。第一,我们的区分是一种初步的尝试,目的是更接近实际情况,结合通常使用的方法,可能是有用的。第二,对开放程度的评估将基于两个标准或指标,其中一个是非常激进的,即对风险预防原则的态度,另一个则是不那么激进但也是重要的,即《维也纳条约法公约》第31条第3款规定的解释规则的使用,[47] 它将外部规范也考虑在内以便促进系统性整合。尽管这些指标很简单,但它们是有用的,因为它们已在大多数国际法院和法庭上被主张。对于国际法院和法庭的环境要件的更详细讨论,包括对其他环境维度的参考,参见第十章和第十二章。

2. 受欢迎的管辖

谈及最受欢迎的司法管辖,人权法院提供了最清楚的样例。随着时间

---

43 See A. Boyle and M. R. Anderson (eds.), *Human Rights Approaches to Environmental Protection* (Oxford: Clarendon, 1998).

44 See F. Francioni, "International Human Rights in an Environmental Horizon" (2010) 21 *European Journal of International Law* 41. See also Chapter 10.

45 See J. E. Viñuales, "The Environmental Regulation of Foreign Investment Schemes under International Law", in P. -M. Dupuy and J. E. Viñuales (eds.), *Harnessing Foreign Investment to Promote Environmental Protection: Incentives and Safeguards* (Cambridge University Press, 2013), pp. 273-320, at 278-285.

46 The letters (w), (n) and (r) are used to emphasise this distinction in Figure 8.2 supra.

47 Vienna Convention on the Law of Treaties, 23 May 1969, 1155 UNTS 331 (VCLT).

的推移，这些机构的开放性有了很大的变化，这表明推动变化的不是它们职权的正式要求，而是它们对环境考量的态度推动力变化。因此，欧洲人权法院（European Court of Human Rights，ECtHR）曾很长一段时间都不愿在其判例法中提及风险预防原则，但现在它承认了风险预防原则（这一原则在《里约宣言》中首次提出）的重要性，这一原则"将用于确保在所有社会活动中健康、消费者安全和环境都能得到高水平的保护"。[48]

同样，国际海洋法法庭在其关于临时措施的判例中指出，各国必须"谨慎行事"，[49] 这要求各国开展合作以保护环境。[50] 随后，在其"关于国家资助的自然人和实体在区域活动中的责任和义务的咨询意见"中，它确认了对风险预防方法的承认。[51]

环境开放性的很大部分是通过系统整合技术的使用显现出来的。因此，欧洲人权法院（ECtHR）在解释《欧洲人权公约》（*European Convention on Human Rights*）第8条时参考了《奥胡斯公约》（*Aarhus Convention*），[52] 它涉及《欧洲人权公约》缔约国（如罗马尼亚、乌克兰或意大利[53]）和非缔约国（如土耳其[54]）的争端，同样，国际海洋法法庭认为，

48　*Tatar v. Romania*，ECtHR Application No. 67021/01（27 January 2009），para. 120.

49　Southern Bluefin Tuna Cases（New Zealand v. Japan，Australia v. Japan），ITLOS Case Nos. 3 and 4，Order of 27 August 1999（*Bluefin Tuna*），para. 77. 另参见 the dissenting opinion of Judge T. Treves，who points out that the precautionary approach is the basis of paragraph 77 of the Order（Dissenting Opinion，para. 8）。

50　MOX Plant Case（Ireland v. United Kingdom），ITLOS Case No. 10，Order of 3 December 2001（MOX Plant Case），para. 84.

51　Responsibilities and Obligations of States Sponsoring Persons and Entities with Respect toActivities in the Area，ITLOS（Seabed Disputes Chamber），Case No. 17 Advisory Opinion，1 February 2011（Responsibilities in the Area），paras. 125–135.

52　1998年6月25日《在环境问题上获得信息、参与决策和诉诸司法的公约》，2161 UNTS 447（《奥胡斯公约》）。这不是法院用来解释《欧洲人权法》各项规定的唯一国际文书。See，e. g.，*Brincat and others v. Malta*，ECtHR Applications Nos. 60908/11，62110/11，62129/11，62312/11 and 62338/11，Judgment（24 July 2014），paras. 105–106（提到《石棉公约》以及其他事实可得出结论，即马耳他已经知道或应该知道石棉对工人的危险）。

53　*Tatar v. Romania*，supra footnote 48，paras. 118，120；Grimkovskaya v. Ukraine，ECtHR Application No. 38182/03，Judgment（21 July 2011），paras. 39，69 and 72；*Di Sarno and others v. Italy*，ECtHR Application No. 30765/08，Judgment（10 January 2012），para. 107.

54　*Taskin and others v. Turkey*，ECtHR Application No. 46117/99，Judgment（10 November 2004，Final 30 March 2005），paras. 99–100.

通过其他文书（条约或"软法"文书）和习惯法来解释《联合国海洋法公约》和国际海底管理局（International Seabed Authority）颁布的法规没有任何障碍。[55] 我们还可以对美洲人权法院（Inter-American Court of Human Rights）和非洲人权和民族权利委员会（African Commission on Human and Peoples' Rights）的判例进行类似的分析。我们将在第十章讨论这一问题。

3. 中立的国际法院

这些法庭对国际环境法的慷慨接受可以与国际法院更为中立（尽管在演变）的立场做一个比较。作为一般国际法的监护者，国际法院必须特别小心，因为它的立法职能（词源学意义上的"法学"）与其争端解决的职能同样重要，甚至更重要。因此，在20世纪90年代取得重大进展之后，国际法院又回到了保守的做法，这不足为奇，而这种做法现在正处于巩固的过程中。第三章围绕国际环境法的原则特别是那些具有习惯法基础的原则，对这一做法作了一些详细的讨论。在这里回顾两点就足够了。

首先，国际法院对风险预防原则给予了温和的回应。在"纸浆厂案"中，阿根廷引用这一原则，要求撤销举证责任。法院只是答复说，"尽管在解释和适用成文法的规定中可能采取风险预防方法，但并不能因此认为它是举证责任的倒置"。[56] 因此，国际法院接受风险预防的想法，但只是作为一种可能对解释有用的"方法"，而没有澄清其内容。

其次，法院坚决采用第31条第3款c项所规定的系统整合技术，包括在环境事项方面。[57] 在"盖巴斯科夫—拉基玛洛工程案"中，法院认为，可适用的条约必须根据其生效后产生的环境标准来进行解释。[58] 该案

---

[55] *Responsibilities in the Area*, supra footnote 51, paras. 135 and 148; *Dispute Concerning Delimitation of the Maritime Boundary between Ghana and Côte d'Ivoire in the Atlantic Ocean* (*Ghana/Côte d'Ivoire*), ITLOS Case No. 23, Order of 25 April 2015 ("*Ghana/Côte d'Ivoire*"), paras. 68-73; *Request for an Advisory Opinion Submitted by the Sub-Regional Fisheries Commission* (*SRFC*), Advisory Opinion of 2 April 2015, ITLOS Case No. 21 (*IUU Advisory Opinion*), paras. 130-140.

[56] Pulp Mills on the River Uruguay (*Argentina v. Uruguay*), Judgment, ICJ Reports 2010, p. 14 (*Pulp Mills*), para. 164. The reluctance of the Court has been criticised by Judge Cançado Trindade in his separate opinion, paras. 62-92 and 103-113.

[57] Oil Platforms (*Islamic Republic of Iran v. United States of America*), Judgment, ICJ Reports 2003, p. 161, para. 41.

[58] Gabčíkovo-Nagymaros Project, supra footnote 35, para. 112.

中，条约为此目的包括了一项具体规定，但这不是必要条件。事实上，在"纸浆厂案"中，法院指出：有必要考虑到阿根廷援引的一些外部文书，作为"适用于当事各方之间关系的有关国际法规则"。[59] 在"哥斯达黎加/尼加拉瓜案"中也采取了类似的立场，法院认为即使存在一条约要求较低程度的合作，但并不会因此取代来自条约或习惯法的其他环境义务。[60] 因此，我们看到，在两个评价开放性程度的指标中，国际法院只接受了一个。

4. 不情愿的法庭

国际经济法的专门法庭显示出不太接受国际环境法的意愿。但是，这一一般性结论的成立是有前提条件的。这是因为，第一，投资的判例法是复杂的；第二，如果采用不同于上述所选的指标，可能导致不同的结论。换言之，世贸组织争端解决机构（DSB）和一些投资法庭采取了一种相当限制的方法。

世贸组织争端解决机构（DSB）对两项指标的立场可以从"欧洲共同体生物技术案"（EC-Biotech）一案中一窥端倪。专家组指出："迄今为止，没有一个法院或法庭作出权威性的决定，承认风险预防原则为国际法的一般原则或习惯法原则。"[61] 这一观点可被视为上诉机构在关于《适用卫生与植物检疫措施协定》（Agreement on the Application of Sanitary and Phytosanitary Measures, SPS Agreement）[62] 的第一个案例，即"欧共体荷尔蒙案"（EC-Hormones）一案中所采取的立场的延续。[63] "欧洲共同体生物

---

[59] Pulp Mills, supra footnote 56, para. 65 (paraphrasing Article 31 (3) (c) of the VCLT). 另参见 para. 66, 阐明了可以考虑的标准类型。

[60] Certain activities carried out by Nicaragua in the Border Area (Costa Rica v. Nicaragua), Construction of a road in Costa Rica along the river San Juan (Nicaragua v. Costa Rica), Judgment of 16 December 2015 (I. C. J), paras. 108, 118. 但是，法院认为没有必要讨论条约条款（特别是1958年条约）与环境习惯法之间的相互作用。

[61] European Communities-Measures Affecting the Approval and Marketing of Biotech Products, Panel Report, 29 September 2006, WT/DS291/R, WT/DS292/R, WT/DS293/R (EC - Biotech) para. 7. 88.

[62] Agreement on the Application of Sanitary and Phytosanitary Measures, 15 April 1994, 1867UNTS 493 (SPS Agreement).

[63] EC-Measures Concerning Meat and Meat Products (Hormones), AB Report (16 January 1998), WT/DS26/ABR, WT/DS48/AB/R (EC-Hormones), para. 124.

技术案"也说明了世贸组织争端解决机构（DSB）对系统整合所采取的限制性方法。如果想在解释贸易法时将外部条约规范考虑在内，专家组展示的解释方法表现出的狭义理解会要求所有 WTO 缔约方（而不只是争端各方）都必须是该外部条约的缔约方。[64] 实际上，能够满足这一要求的环境条约并不多见。然而，必须强调的是，专家组提到了上诉机构在"海虾—海龟案"[65] 中的裁决，以支持其结论，即可以根据《维也纳条约法公约》（VCLT）第 31 条第 3 款 c 项将习惯性规范甚至一般的法律原则考虑在内。[66] 但是，这种开放的价值取决于世贸组织争端解决机构（DSB）对某些环境原则的法律地位（习惯或一般法律原则）的立场。重要的是，为了解释的目的，争端解决机构必须适用第三章所确定的国际习惯法三项核心原则，即预防、合作和环境影响评估。事实上，它在"中国原材料案"[67] 中已承认预防原则要素的适用。这并不是说可以从这一参考中获得太多益处，因为主要的障碍不是法律方面的，而是文化方面的，即目前在上诉机构中普遍存在的以贸易为中心的狭隘观念。[68] 这种不情愿是可以理解的，因为在环境问题上的差别化对待有可能严重损害贸易自由化。事实上，一条河流正在叩响 WTO 的大门，即便是一个小小的开端，也有可能把大门打开。

关于投资法庭，判例法的不稳定性导致对风险预防原则或系统整合的使用接受程度进行横向分析，变得相当困难。在一个裁判高度依赖事实和法庭的法律背景下，欢迎或拒绝适用某一环境原则的裁判的价值不具有代

64　*EC-Biotech Products*, supra footnote 61, paras. 7.68-7.70.

65　United States-Import Prohibition of Certain Shrimp and Certain Products Containing Shrimp, Appellate Body, 12 October 1998, WT/DS58/AB/R（Shrimp-Turtle）, para. 158 and note 157.

66　*EC-Biotech Products*, supra footnote 61, para. 7.67.

67　China-Measures Related to the Exportation of Various Raw Materials-Reports of the Panel, WT/DS394/R；WT/DS395/R；WT/DS398/R（5 July 2011）, para.7.381 指出 "对自然资源的主权原则使会员有机会利用其自然资源促进自身发展，同时规范这些资源的使用以确保可持续发展"。

68　最近的一个例证是关于印度-太阳能电池的决定，根据该决定，公约和《里约宣言》所载的原则不能视为《关贸总协定》第 20（d）条规定的"法律和法规"，因为它们需要行政部门执行。当然，这在一定程度上是有问题的，因为这样的测试会得出这样的结论：就第 20（d）条而言，国内法规（也需要通过法规进行具体实施）不会构成"法律和法规"。See India-Certain Measures relating to Solar Cells and Solar Modules-Report of the Appellate Body, WT/DS456/AB/R（16 September 2016）, paras. 5.91-5.151, 6.6.

表性。但是，通过参考在实践中所遵循的三种可能的方法，可以发现投资法庭对环境要素的接受程度。[69] 第一种方法将国内环境措施视为单方面和保护主义政策的表现。[70] 它忽略了一个事实，即可以根据环境条约采取国家措施。相反，要证明国际环境法受到欢迎，就必须考虑国家措施与国际环境义务之间的关系。这种方法目前看来过于激进。因此，国际环境法对投资争端的影响限于一种中间方法，即投资法的解释在不同程度上受到环境因素的影响。例如，《持续性有机污染物公约奥胡斯议定书》(*Aarhus POP Protocol*)[71] 和《持续性有机污染物公约》(*POP Convention*) 等环境条约的要求被用于解释《北美自由贸易协定》(*North American Free Trade Agreement*, NAFTA)[72] 的投资章节。同样，法庭出于解释目的，也考虑了投资计划对世界遗产[73]或用水人权[74]的影响。更常见的是，投资法庭引用国内环境法来解释传统的投资法概念，[75] 或越来越依赖于投资条约中的环

69　See Viñuales, supra footnote 45; infra Chapter 12.

70　See, e.g., *Compañia del Desarrollo de Santa Elena SA v. Republic of Costa Rica*, ICSID Case No. ARB/96/1, Award (17 February 2000), para. 71; *Metalclad Corp. v. United Mexican States*, ICSID Case No. ARB (AF) /97/1, Award (25 August 2000), paras. 109–111; *Técnicas Medioambientales Tecmed S. A. v. United Mexican States*, ICSID Case No. ARB (AF) /00/2, Award (29 May 2003), para. 128.

71　Protocol to the 1979 Convention on Long-Range Transboundary Air Pollution on Persistent Organic Pollutants (POPs), 24 June 1998, 2230 UNTS 79.

72　North American Free Trade Agreement, 17 December 1992, 32 ILM 296. See *Chemtura Corporation (formerly Crompton Corporation) v. Government of Canada*, UNCITRAL, Award (2 August 2010) (*Chemtura v. Canada*), para. 138.

73　*Parkerings-Compagniet AS v. Republic of Lithuania*, ICSID Case No. ARB/05/8, Award (11 September 2007) (*Parkerings v. Lithuania*), para. 392.

74　See *Suez, Sociedad General de Aguas de Barcelona S. A. and InterAguas Servicios Integrales del Agua S. A. v. The Argentine Republic*, ICSID Case No. ARB/03/17, Decision on liability (30 July 2010), para. 238; *Suez, Sociedad General de Aguas de Barcelona, S. A. and Vivendi Universal, S. A. v. The Argentine Republic*, ICSID Case No. ARB/03/19, Decision on liability (30 July 2010), para. 260. 然而，在这两起案件中，法庭的结论都是存在违反。

75　See e.g. *Plama Consortium Ltd v. Republic of Bulgaria*, ICSID Case No. ARB/03/24, Award (27 August 2008), paras. 219–221; e.g. *Marion Unglaube v. Republic of Costa Rica*, ICSID Case No. ARB/08/1 and *Reinhard Unglaube v. Republic of Costa Rica*, ICSID Case No. ARB/09/20, Award (16 May 2012), paras. 258, 309 (在评估被征收财产的"最高和最佳使用"时，分别考虑了投资者表现出的勤勉水平和环境保护)。

境条款来解释投资保护标准。[76]

我们将在第十章至第十二章中讨论国际环境法与国际法其他领域之间的相互作用。但是，上述意见有助于理解在欢迎、中立和不情愿的法庭背景下的演变为何能对国际环境法的发展造成重大影响，特别是在涉及对习惯性规范的缓慢承认和进一步阐明实践中需要哪些广义表述的环境规范的情况下。

三 环境损害的后果

（一）后果的类型

对于"过失""损害"或两者兼有的情况，国际法规定了某些法律后果。环境损害的责任（responsibility）/赔偿责任（liability）分析以"过失"为核心概念，区分了责任（responsibility）（因过失引发的补救）和赔偿责任（liability）（无过失但损害发生后的补救）。这个是有问题的，主要有两个原因。

首先，一项"初级"（primary）或"引发性"（triggering）规范可以用不同方式来定义一种应当承担法律后果的情况。通常情况下，它将指出在从事某种行为时应当保持相当的谨慎（例如国家应当或者不得做某事）。如果没有遵循该要求，则被视为"违反"规范，将会引发被称为"次级"（secondary）或"补救性"规范（例如，如果发生违反，以下结果将适用）所界定的后果。但是，在某些情况下，初级规范会规定某些与过失无关的后果（例如，如果某事件发生，则需要补救）。这通常被称为严格责任。有一些补救性规范将后果纳入初级规范所界定的情况中（例如，某事件的发生所导致的补救将根据下列原则来组织）。然而，这一假设在技术上并不是对一个初级规范的"违反"，只是由于这种情况满足了该规范引发补救所需的全部条件。这就是第二个问题的由来。将"过失"这一主观概念应用于国家或国际组织等抽象主体是令人困惑的。

---

[76] See e. g. *William Ralph Clayton*, *William Richard Clayton*, *Douglas Clayton*, *Daniel Clayton*, *and Bilcon of Delaware*, *Inc. v. Government of Canada*, NAFTA (UNCITRAL), Award (17 March 2015), paras. 595-601 (referring to the preamble of the North American FreeTrade Agreement); Adel A Hamadi Al Tamimi v. Sultanate of Oman, ICSID Case No. ARB/ 11/33, Award (3 November 2015), para. 389（在投资条约的全文中，特别是在第 10.10 条和第 17 章中提到"强有力地捍卫环境规制和保护"）。

"过失"在这里的意思是"非法"。这一概念很容易适用于"违反"责任的语境，但很难适用于无过错或非法行为的后果（赔偿责任）。事实上，如果一个用于定义引发法律后果的假设行为的规范不需要违法性，那么"违反"一词就用错了地方。更恰当的说法是，"发生"了引发法律后果的假设行为或达到了补救的条件。由于这种引发性规范的内容可能会在一定程度上与负责补救的次级规范的内容发生重叠，这一术语上的困境就变得更加复杂。初级（引发性）和次级（补救性）规范之间概念上的关联既适用于违约责任，也适用于某些事件的发生所导致的责任。

这是在分析环境损害的法律后果时必须依赖的概念上的背景。就像"过失"（违法性）一样，"损害"是由初级规范设定的条件。根据不同的情况，法律后果必须要由"过失""损害"和/或其他条件来引发。要引发国家因违反（国际不法行为）所应承担的责任，则必须存在过失（非法）。初级规范可能也会将损害的发生当作引发法律后果的条件（例如对损害预防原则的绝大多数违反如果没有造成损害，就无须承担法律后果），但情况并非总是如此（例如对报告或进行环境影响评价等程序义务的违反）。当这种情况涉及（私人或公共）经济运营商的行为时，损害的发生是触发某些具体条约（以核能或石油污染损害为重点）或某些一般文书所规定的责任制度的必要条件。[77] 反之，它不要求存在过失，虽然可能引起额外的后果（即运营商所承担的金额将不设上限）。至于涉及国际组织行为的案件，国际法仍处于起步阶段。在这方面，我们只指出，国际组织必须遵守可能引发国际责任制度的初级规范。此外，如世界银行或区域开发银行等组织，在其活动中必须遵守内部标准（包括环境标准）。它们必须确保它们资助的项目符合这些标准，并已设立一些向民间社会开放的程序（例如提交到世界银行审查委员会）来审查这些标准的遵守情况。这种合规审查必须与传统的"责任"（responsibility）和"赔偿责任"（li-

---

[77] 下文脚注 83 的国际法委员会原则评论指出，它与"初级规范"有关（对第 1 条第 2 款的评论）。为了避免造成误解，必须澄清此引用。也就是说国际法委员会原则为民事责任的组织设定了某些参数（在国内层面：第 4 条和第 6 条；在国际层面：第 7 条），这些参数可以被解释为要求各国采取某些国内措施的"主要"规范或义务（纵向），或针对某些条约进行谈判（横向），这些义务的内容实质上就是组织赔偿制度。因此，最好将国际法委员会原则的核心条款（限定经济运营商的严格责任参数）理解为一组"赔偿"或"次级"规范。该结论的一个例外是原则 5（在事故中有义务合作），它与预防和谨慎密切相关。

ability）区分开来。在这方面使用的术语是"可追责"（accountability），很像为审查人权或环境条约或企业社会责任标准的遵守情况而建立的程序。上述区别见表 8-1。

表 8-1　　　　　　　　　　　法律后果的类型

	国家	经济运营商	国际组织
初级规范（"引发性"）	—（损害） —未尽谨慎注意义务（国际法委员会预防条款，2001 年）	—损害 —（未尽谨慎注意义务）	—（损害） —未尽谨慎注意义务
次级规范（"补救性"）	—对国际不法行为造成的国家责任的习惯法规则（国际法委员会关于国家责任条款，2001 年） —问责机制，例如不遵约程序	—关于民事责任条约规则（例如核能和石油污染） ——般参量（国际法委员会损失分摊原则，2006 年） —问责机制，例如企业社会责任管控	—国际组织国际责任规则（国际法委员会国际组织责任的条款，2011 年） —问责机制，例如审查委员会

表 8-1 显示，与环境保护相关的初级（引发性）和次级（补救性）规范的性质根据义务承担人的不同而发生变化。这个表显现的一个重要要件是，在现代国际法中没有对国家实行严格（"无过失"）责任制度。[78] 但是，对于私营和公共经济运营商，已经确定了这种责任（赔偿 liability）。我们使用赔偿责任（liability）一词来指代它，尽管这个词在国内法中有更广泛的含义。请注意，当一个国家主体作为一个经济运营商时，它也可能会受制于严格责任的相关条约。许多活动已经制订了这类方案，这些活动的特点都是蕴含了利益与风险之间的冲突。我们将在本章第三节第三部分第三点中探讨其中一些方案。但是，在讨论这种具体形式的赔偿责任之前，有必要分析在环境背景下的相关规则（针对国家因国际不法行为所应担负责任）的运行情况。

（二）国家的国际责任

1. 制度概述

自 20 世纪 60 年代以来，阐明各国预防和修复环境损害的义务，就引

---

[78] The onlyexceptionis Art. 2 of the Conventionon International Liability for Damage Caused by Space Objects, 29 March 1972, 961 UNTS 187（发射国应当为其空间物体对地球表面或飞行中的飞机所造成的损害承担绝对赔偿责任）。

发了重大的法律挑战。[79] 主要问题是如何考量某些活动（例如核电或某些工业生产）所造成的个别或"特别"风险，这些活动对开展活动的国家有用但可能对其他国家或者国家管辖范围以外区域的环境造成不利影响，这种不利影响是由于其正常运行（影响）或事故（风险）而造成的。

关于这些活动的影响，在第三章中已经就无害和损害预防原则阐述了国际法研究院采取的方法。国家有行为义务（"谨慎注意义务"），以确保其领土不被用于对其他国家或国家管辖范围以外的环境造成重大损害。撇开这一原则范围内的一些灰色地带（见第三章），如果满足下列三个条件，就违反了国家被赋予的基本义务：（1）损害的发生（仅仅风险通常是不够的）；（2）损害的程度（低于所需门槛的损害不足以引发责任）和它的空间范围（原则上，它必须超越缘起国的领土，尽管在第四章讨论的最近的判例表明，损害预防的适用不受领土的限制）；（3）最重要的是谨慎注意义务（这意味着即使损害满足了规模和范围的条件，如果国家在行事时尽到了谨慎注意义务，它将不负责任）。值得注意的是，这种谨慎注意义务的行使并不会排除不法性或免除责任，而是初级规范或引发规范这一定义的部分内容。换言之，为了证明当事国违反了损害预防原则，受害国必须确定损害、损害的规模和范围、缘起国没有尽到谨慎注意义务以及过失与损害之间的因果关系。因此，缘起国可以选择援引那些排除不法性的习惯法条件，包括国际法委员会针对国家责任的条款第 25 条所规定的紧急避险。

针对那些可能造成重大风险的活动的规制，有两种主要方法可供选择。一方面，一些作者建议建立严格责任制度。在这一制度下，某项高风险活动所造成的任何损害将由缘起国承担，不论其在多大程度上尽到了谨慎注意义务。另一方面，一些作者认为这种方法是不切实际的，认为掌握

79　For early manifestations, see W. Jenks, "Liability for Hazardous Activities" (1966) 117 *Recueil des cours de l'Académie de droit international de La Haye*, 102-200; L. F. E. Goldie, "Liability for Damage and the Progressive Development of International Law" (1965) 14 *International and Comparative Law Quarterly* 1189; P. -M. Dupuy, *La Responsabilite Internationale des Etats Pour les Dommages D'origine Technologique et Industrielle* (Paris: Pedone, 1976). See also T. Scovazzi, " State Responsibility for Environmental Harm" (2001) 12 *Yearbook of International Environmental Law* 43; C. Négre, "Responsibility and International Environmental Law", in J. Crawford, A. Pellet and S. Olleson (eds.), *The Law of International Responsibility* (Oxford University Press, 2010), pp. 803-813.

高风险活动特点的更好方法是延伸使用基本方法（不法行为导致的责任），对谨慎注意义务提出更高要求，特别是通过国际标准，[80] 据此，仅仅造成"严重损害的风险"就足以构成违反（在极端有害活动的背景下，如果不尽到防范严重风险的谨慎注意义务，就会等同于实际损害）。就国家的责任而言，后一种方法的影响要大得多。事实上，自20世纪70年代初以来，损害预防原则在条约和习惯法中得到了越来越多的承认，[81] 它也在"软法"标准中得到了体现，该标准规定了谨慎注意义务的内容。国际法委员会最初的工作是设法制定一个适用于各国的严格责任制度，但它不得不承认，如果不重新拟订这一主题（特别是通过区分两个组成部分），就无不可能向前推进。第一种方法导致在2001年制定了《预防危险活动造成跨界损害的条款草案》（*Draft Articles on the Prevention of Transboundary Harm from Hazardous Activities*）[82]，它应当被视为在跨界背景下阐明损害预防原则（一个引发性规范）的内容的一次尝试。第二种方法继续围绕一个国际严格责任制度开展工作并做出了两个重要的修订，即机制针对的是经济运行商（而非国家）和2006年最终制定的文本，该文本仅以《危险活动造成的跨界损害案件中损失分配的原则草案》（《国际法委员会原则》）[83] 的形式提出一套指南。《国际法委员会原则》将在下一节讨论。在这里，我们只需注意，严格来讲，这两个组成部分并不是原始成果的"一半"，而是可以从初始方法中实际保留下来的东西。事实上，最初项目的核心，即适用于各国的严格责任制度，在这个过程中已经遗失。

通过以上说明，我们现在可以更好地了解有关国际不法行为所导致的国家责任的一般制度是如何将损害的责任和风险的责任都涵盖在内的。在这两种情况下，国家都有义务进行预防。它必须在任何情况下都尽到"谨慎注意义务"。为了详细说明这一点，两条附加的评论看起来很贴切。

80　See Scovazzi, supra footnote 79, p. 49. See also R. Pisillo Mazzeschi, "The Due Diligence Rule and the Nature of the International Responsibility of States" (1992) 35 *German Yearbook of International Law* 9.

81　See Chapter 3.

82　Draft Articles on the Prevention of Transboundary Harm from Hazardous Activities, GA Res. 56/82, UN Doc. A/RES/56/82 (ILC Prevention Articles).

83　Draft Principles on the Allocation of Loss in case of Transboundary Harm from HazardousActivities, GA Res. 61/36, UN Doc. A/RES/61/36 (ILC Principles).

2. 初级规范：损害预防和谨慎注意义务

第一点评论涉及可能引发责任制度的义务。到目前为止，我们只提到了损害预防的习惯法原则。但是，活动所在国的作为/不作为可能违反其他习惯法义务（例如通知、协商或进行环境影响评价的义务）或基于条约的义务（例如报告义务）。这些义务规定了遵约或违约的条款，[84] 这些条款可能不同于上述条款（即一定规模和范围的损害、过失）。这就是说，许多由条约引发的义务必须在谨慎注意义务所提供的宏观背景下加以解释。

在过去20年中，这一义务在文献中得到了越来越多的关注，[85] 也成为判例法和编纂工作的主题。除了国际法院、[86] 国际海洋法法庭[87]和其他法庭[88]承认损害预防原则的习惯法基础外，还可提及国际法研究院（Institut de Droit International，IDI）[89] 和国际法委员会（ILC）[90] 的贡献。这些贡献非常详细地说明了谨慎注意义务在实证国际法中意味着什么。这些内容可以概括为五点：(1) 谨慎注意义务是一种行为义务 [损害的发

---

[84] Pulp Mills, supra footnote 56, para. 79.

[85] For two book-length studies, see R. Pisillo Mazzeschi, *Due diligence e responsabilità interna-zionale degli Stati* (Milan: Giuffrè, 1989); A. Ouedraogo, *La diligence en droit international. Contribution à l'étude d'une notion aux contours imprécis* (PhD dissertation, The Graduate Institute, Geneva, 2011).

[86] Legality of Nuclear Weapons, supra footnote 4, para. 29; Gabčíkovo-Nagymaros Project, suprafootnote 35, para. 140; Pulp Mills, supra footnote 57, para. 110; Costa Rica/Nicaragua, suprafootnote 60, para. 104.

[87] See *Responsibilities in the Area*, supra footnote 51, in particular paras. 99-120, 123, 131-132 and 136; *IUU Advisory Opinion*, supra footnote 55, para. 131.

[88] See In the matter of the Indus Waters Kishenganga Arbitration before the Court of Arbitrationconstituted in accordance with the Indus Waters Treaty 1960 between the Government of Indiaand the Government of Pakistan signed on 19 September 1960 (Islamic Republic of Pakistanv. Republic of India), PCA, Partial Award (18 February 2013) (Indus Water Kishenganga-Partial Award); para. 451; In the matter of the South China Sea Arbitration before an Arbitral Tribunal constituted under Annex VII of the United Nations Convention on the Law of the Sea (Republic of the Philippines v. People's Republic of China), PCA Case No. 2013-2019, Award (12 July 2016) (South China Sea Arbitration), para. 941.

[89] See Institut de Droit International, Resolution on "Environment" (Rapporteur L. Ferrari Bravo) (IDI - Environment); Resolution on "Responsibility and Liability under International Law for Environmental Damage" (Rapporteur F. Orrego Vicuña) (IDI - Responsibility); Resolution on Procedures for the Adoption and Implementation of Rules in the Field of Environment) (Rapporteur F. Paolillo) (IDI-Procedures), all adopted at the Strasbourg Session (1997).

[90] ILC Prevention Articles, supra footnote 82, in particular Art. 3 and its commentary.

生（或造成严重损害的风险）并不意味着违反了这一义务]，[91]（2）谨慎注意的标准是由国家在国际法赋予它们的自由裁量权内制定的（在"合理"的界限内行使并且不是绝对的），[92]（3）根据不同的标准，谨慎注意义务可能会有所不同，尤其是在有关国家的时间，[93] 活动类型[94]以及当事国能力方面，[95]（4）谨慎注意同时关乎措施的制定以及履行这些措施的合理努力，[96] 以及（5）谨慎注意的履行不仅涉及跨界影响（或严重损害的风险）的最小化，也涉及对国家管辖范围外地区[97]甚至是活动所在国的影响（和风险）的最小化。[98]

3. 次级规范：应对复杂场景

第二点评论涉及在环境损害（损害和造成严重损害的风险）责任的背景下次级规范的运行。事实上，环境问题带来了相当独特的挑战，特别是在确定责任国和受害国方面。[99] 除了某个国家因为过失对他国造成损害这一基本场景外，还必须考虑另一个更困难的情况，即众多国家的行为以渐进和累积的方式对环境造成的损害，多数或所有国家都遭受了这种环境

---

[91] Pulp Mills, supra footnote 56, para. 187; Responsibilities in the Area, supra footnote 51, para. 110; ILC Prevention Articles, supra footnote 82, commentary to Art. 3, para. 7.

[92] See IDI-Responsibility, supra footnote 89, Art. 3, para. 2; ILC Prevention Articles, supra footnote 82, comment to Art. 3, paras. 9, 11 and 12, referring to the *Alabama* case where the court rejected the proposition of the UK that "due diligence" was a national standard. But see *Pulp Mills*, supra footnote 56, para. 205（国际法院建议，谨慎注意义务的组成部分的内容，即进行环境影响评价的习惯性义务，应留给各国）。

[93]《国家担保自然人和实体在该区域内活动的责任与义务》, supra footnote 51, para. 117。

[94] There is no doubt that "the degree of care required is proportional to the degree of risk involved in the business", ILC Prevention Articles, supra footnote 82, comment to Art. 3, para. 18; *Responsibilities in the Area*, supra footnote 51, para. 117.

[95] ILC Prevention Articles, supra footnote 82, commentary to Art. 3, para. 18; *Responsibilities in the Area*, supra footnote 51, paras. 158-159.

[96] *Pulp Mills*, supra footnote 56, para. 197; *Responsibilities in the Area*, supra footnote 51, paras. 115 and 239; ILC Prevention Articles, supra footnote 82, commentary to Art. 3, para. 10.

[97] *Responsibilities in the Area*, supra footnote 51, paras. 142-148.

[98] See IUU Advisory Opinion, supra footnote 55, paras. 111, 120; *Dispute Concerning Delimitation of the Maritime Boundary between Ghana and Côte d'Ivoire in the Atlantic Ocean (Ghana/Côte d'Ivoire)*, ITLOS Case No. 23, Order of 25 April 2015 (*Ghana/Côte d'Ivoire*), paras. 68-73; *South China Sea Arbitration*, supra footnote 88, para. 940.

[99] Scovazzi, supra footnote 79, 61-63.

损害。这样的例证不胜枚举：气候变化、海洋污染（包括陆源污染）或生物多样性的减少。这些困难由于环境损害的潜在不可逆转性和无法确定损害与特定国家的单个行为之间的因果关系，而变得更加复杂。《国际法委员会国家责任条款草案》可以适用其中一些情况，但并不总是令人满意。

关于责任国，国际法委员会条款草案包括这样一种可能性，即国际不法行为包括被整体定义为不法行为的（第 15 条第 1 款）一系列行动或疏忽，它可能是由多个责任国（第 47 条第 1 款）实施的，因此都会涉及这些国家的单独责任。但是，这些规定意味着，人们可以在那些可归因于数个国家的一系列行为和损害的发生（初级规范目前是这样要求的）之间建立因果联系。这不是一个简单的步骤。例如，如果一个海域有五个沿海国，它们在不同的时间和不同的程度上向海洋排放污染物，第五国可以认为它的四个共同沿海国应对该项综合性的国际不法行为负责。但每一个沿海国都可以辩称，其具体行为与损害之间的因果关系尚未成立。在刚才所描述的相当简单的场景内，如果因果关系都很难予以证明，那么可以想象与气候变化有关的该有多困难。[100] 结果就是经济运营商在所在国的批准下长达两个世纪的温室气体排放。在这方面，可以在国际法研究院的决议中找到一种可能的办法，正如 T. Scovazzi 所指出的，该决议建议对某些活动[101]采用因果推定，采用连带责任制度[102]以及集体赔偿制度。[103]

关于有权对他国责任提起诉求的国家，国际法委员会条款草案做了一个区分，依据是所违反的义务是否应由某个国家、多个国家抑或整个国际社会来提起诉求。后两个类别可以适应违反环境义务（习惯或基于条约）

---

[100] For an overview, see R. Lord, S. Goldberg, L. Rajamani and J. Brunnée（eds.），Climate ChangeLiability: Transboundary Law and Practice（Cambridge University Press，2011）. 这个问题是在国际气候谈判的背景下提出的，但使用的术语（"损失与损害"）避免了赔偿的想法，而是强调了援助的想法。See Adoption of the Paris Agreement, Decision 1/CP. 21, 12 December 2015, FCCC/CP/2015/ L. 9（Paris Decision）. The Paris Agreement is appended as an Annex to the Paris Decision（Paris Agreement），Art. 8（read in the light of para. 52 of the Paris Decision, which specifically excludes the use of this provision for liability purposes）.

[101] IDI-Responsibility, supra footnote 89, Art. 7.

[102] Ibid., Art. 11.

[103] Ibid., Art. 12.

的情况，这些违约行为超出了两国之间的双边（象征性）关系，通常应由条约的所有缔约国（对一切义务）或作为一个整体的国家共同体（对一切）来提起诉求。违反这些义务而导致的责任可由"受害国"（包括受到"个别"影响或"特别"影响的国家，如果违约根本改变了其他国家的地位，那么这些国家也有资格成为受害国）[104] 或由"其他"国家（采取行动的权利只是源自该国在集体利益条约中的地位或作为国际社会成员的地位）来提起诉求。[105] 关于后一类（第48条），针对国际法委员会条款草案是否反映了现行的习惯法，尚未达成明确共识，尽管国际法院已经给出了两点暗示。[106] 然而，即使该制度适用于气候变化或陆源海洋污染等假设场景，包括对国家管辖范围以外区域的环境损害，也不清楚这种损害应如何修复。正如 Scovazzi 所指出的，在不可能恢复环境的情况下，责任国支付的任何赔偿仅对受害国而不对"其他"国家有意义。然而，也有可能出现并不存在受害国的环境损害情况。目前还不清楚这种损害是否应该赔偿，以及如何赔偿。国际法研究院决议第28条在这方面提出了一项有益的建议，要求各国明确或建立在此情况下有权提出索赔和获得赔偿的主体。[107] 这项建议是在某些民事责任制度文本中规定的解决办法的概念延伸。

（三）经济运营商的赔偿责任

1. 条约体系概述

调整经济运营商（公共或私人）赔偿责任的条约在某种程度上可以

---

[104] ILC Articles, supra footnote 1, Art. 42 (b).

[105] Ibid., Art. 48. For two examples see Questions relating to the Obligation to Prosecute or Extradite (*Belgium v. Senegal*), Judgment, ICJ Reports 2012, p. 422 (where the mere fact that Belgium was a party to the Convention against Torture was enough for the Court to consider that it had an interest in the prosecution of Hissëne Habrë, the former dictator of Chad exiled in Senegal); Whalinginthe Antarctic (*Australia v. Japan*: *New Zealand intervening*), Judgment, ICJ Reports 2014, p. 226 (where the mere fact of being party to the Whaling Convention was sufficient for Australia to have an interest in requiring Japan to stop whaling in violation of the treaty).

[106] On the existence of an actio popularis in international law, seeF. Voeffray, *L'actio Popularis ou la Dëfense de L'intërët Collectif Devant les Juridictions Internationales* (Paris: Presses Universitaires de France, 2004). Although the ICJ did not refer explicitly to the rule in Article 48 of the ILC Articles, the Belgium/Senegal case and the *Whaling* case could be viewed as implicit recognitions of the rule. See supra footnote 105.

[107] IDI-Responsibility, supra footnote 89, Art. 28, noted by Scovazzi, supra footnote 79, 63.

理解为国际私法中所谓的"统一法"(droit uniforme),即数个国家共同通过条约确立的实体法。[108] 事实上,在这一领域适用国际法的主要目的是确立一些要素,以实现相关法律的协调运行(至少是对等运行),这些法律涉及的是受规制行为造成的特定损害所引发的赔偿。

针对核能生产和石油污染造成的损害,国际社会制定了第一批条约或条约体系。关于核能,已经发展了两个独立但相关联的体系,一个是经济合作与发展组织国家(OECD States)之间的体系,[109] 另一个是在国际原子能机构(IAEA)支持下的体系。[110] 这两个体系是经由1988年通过的一个共同议定书发生关联的,该议定书旨在协调受核事故影响的人的状况,这一核事故受到这两个体系其中一个的管辖。[111]

关于石油污染损害,国际海事组织(IMO)针对1967年3月利比里亚油轮"托里坎荣号"在英国海岸附近的搁浅制定了一个体系。这一事件促进了该体系两大支柱的制定,即1969年的《民事责任公约》[Convention on Civil Liability' of 1969(CLC)]和1971年的《基金公约》(FUND of 1971)。目前的体系是通过两项议定书对这两大支柱进行彻底改

---

[108] On strict liability for environmental damage, see L. Bergkamp, Liability and Environment: Private and Public Law Aspects of Civil Liability for Environmental Harm in an International Context (The Hague: Kluwer, 2001).

[109] Convention on Third Party Liability in the Field of Nuclear Energy, 29 July 1960, 956 UNTS251 (Paris Convention). Theregimeestablishedbythe Paris Conventionwassupplementedbyanother treaty, the Convention Supplementary to the Paris Convention of 29 July 1960 on Third Party Liability in the Fieldof Nuclear Energy, 31January1963, 1041UNTS358 (Brussels Supplementary Convention). 1964年、1982年和2004年对"巴黎/布鲁塞尔"体系进行了修订。后一项修正是切尔诺贝利事故后启动的一个程序的结果,是对原始体系的重大修改,但尚未生效。See M. Montjoie, "NuclearEnergy" in Crawford et al., supra footnote 79, pp. 915-928.

[110] Convention on Civil Liability for Nuclear Damage, 21 May 1963, 1063 UNTS 265 (Vienna Convention). This treaty was amended by a Protocol to amend the Vienna Convention on Civil Liability for Nuclear Damage, 12 September 1997, 2241 UNTS 302, which leaves in placethe two systems (initial system and amended system). The 1997 revision also resulted in theadoption of a Convention on Supplementary Compensation for Nuclear Damage, 12 September 1997, IAEA INFCIRC/567 (Complementary Vienna Convention, not yet inforce).

[111] Joint Protocol Relating to the Application of the Vienna Convention and the Paris Convention, 27 September 1988, 1672 UNTS 293.

革的结果，从而产生了 1992 年《民事责任公约》（CLC/92）[112] 和 1992 年《基金公约》（Convention FUND/92）。[113] 该体制得到两项文书的补充，这两项文书处理的是不在原来体制范围内的情况，[114] 并增加了额外的赔偿。[115]

最近关于工业事故导致的损害[116]或某些物质的转移，例如危险废物[117]或转基因生物，[118] 也制定了民事（赔偿）责任制度。此外，国际法委员会和欧洲理事会的努力建立了一个更通用的制度，从而产生了两个案文，即早些时候提到的国际法委员会原则和《卢加诺公约》（*Lugano Convention*）。[119] 尽管这些文书的实际影响有限（没有一项具有约束力），但它们综合了环境损害民事责任领域的其他文书所遵循的一般结构。

2. 赔偿责任制度的主要要素

前一节所介绍的责任制度有四个主要要素：（1）经济运营商的严格

---

[112] Protocol amending the International Convention on Civil Liability for Oil Pollution Damage, 27 November 1992, available at: www. ecolex. org （TRE - 001 177） （CLC/92）. SeeJ. L. Gabaldón García, Curso de Derecho Marítimo Internacional（Madrid: Marcial Pons, 2012）, pp. 783-806.

[113] Protocol to Amend the International Convention on the Establishment of an International Fund for Compensation for Oil Pollution Damage, 27 November 1992, available at: www. ecolex. org （TRE-001 176） （FUND/92）.

[114] International Convention on Civil Liability for Oil Pollution Damage, 23 March 2001, available at: www. ecolex. org （TRE-001 377） （BUNKERS 2001, not yet in force）.

[115] Protocol to the International Convention on the Establishment of an International Fund for Compensation for Oil Pollution, 16 May 2003, available at: www. ecolex. org （TRE-001 401）（FUND/2003）.

[116] Protocol on Civil Liability and Compensation for Damage Caused by the Transboundary Effects of Industrial Accidents on Transboundary Waters, 21 May 2003, Doc. ECE/MP. WAT/11-ECE/CP. TEIA/9（Kiev Protocol, not yet in force）.

[117] Convention Relating to Third Party Liability in the Field of Maritime Carriage of Nuclear Material, 17 December 1971, 944 UNTS 255; International Convention on Liability and Compensation for Damage in Connection with the Carriage of Hazardous and Noxious Substances, 3 May 1996 （amended by the Protocol of 30 April 2010）, available at: www. ecolex. org （TRE-001 245）（HNS Convention 2010, not yet in force）; Basel Protocol onLiability and Compensation for Damage Resulting from Transboundary Movements of Hazardous Wastes and their Disposal, 10 December 1999, available on: www. ecolex. org （TRE-001341） （Basel Protocol, not yet in force）.

[118] Nagoya-Kuala Lumpur Supplementary Protocol on Liability and Redress to the Cartagena Protocol on Biosafety, 15 October 2010, UNEP/CBD/BS/COP-MOP/5/17 （not yet in force）

[119] Convention on Civil Liability for Damage Resulting from Activities Dangerous to the Environment, 21 June 1993, available at: www. ecolex. org （TRE-001 166）（LuganoConvention, not yet in force）.

责任（无过失）的建立；[120]（2）对经济运营商投保的要求；（3）增设赔偿层次；（4）禁止在获得赔偿程序方面的歧视。在下面的段落中，我们将以这种一般结构为基础，介绍这种方法的主要组成部分。我们通过参考管控核能和石油污染损害的制度来说明这些组成部分。

第一个决定因素是最复杂的一个，它体现了在严格责任背景下初级规范和次级规范的表达。它涉及明确四个要素，即责任主体、责任性质、豁免理由和责任范围的所有适用限制。责任主体的确定必须考虑到几个方面。要求受益于某项活动的主体去赔偿由此可能造成的损害似乎是自然的。同样，对危险行为拥有实际权力的主体也可能成为目标，因为它处于确保该行为合理进行的最佳地位。困难在于，这些考量和其他考量[121]未必会指向相同的解决方案。例如，在核能制度中，负有责任的主体是"运营商"[122]（既是受益人又是对该行为拥有事实上权力的主体），而在石油污染制度中，责任则是主要转嫁给船舶所有人[123]（对行为的实际权力），而不是石油行业（受益人）。当损害是由若干肇事主体的联合行为造成时，就会出现另一个困难。我们稍早已经指出，在国际不法行为所致国家责任规则的背景下，存在着这样的问题。在民事责任制度的背景下，这个问题是通过建立连带责任来解决的：[124]每个经济运营商可能必须对所有的损害作出反应，但它有权对其他负有责任的主体采取行动。在所有这些情况下，责任在性质上是严格的或客观的，即没有必要确立过失（疏忽或故意不当行为）。但是，根据免责事由的范围不同，这种责任也存在不同的程度（有时在"严格责任"和"绝对责任"之间可能有概念上的区别，后者不允许有免责事由）。当给予受害方的唯一好处是举证责任倒置时，

---

[120] See ILC Principles, supra footnote 83, Arts. 4, 6 and 7. See also Survey of Liability Regimes relevant to the Topic of International Liability for Injurious Consequences arising out of Acts not prohibited by International Law (International Liability in case of Loss from Transboundary Harm arising out of Hazardous Activities) 24 June 2004, UN Doc. A/CN. 4/ 543 (Study of the Secretariat).

[121] See G. Doeker and T. Gehring, "Private or International Liability for Transnational Environmental Damage-The Precedent of Conventional Liability Regimes" (1990) 2 *Journal of Environmental Law* 7.

[122] Paris Convention, supra footnote 109, Arts. 1 (a) (vi) and 3; Vienna Convention, supra footnote 110, Arts. I (a) (c) and IV (1).

[123] CLC/92, supra footnote 112, Arts. I (3), III (1) and (4).

[124] Ibid., Art. IV; Vienna Convention, supra footnote 110, Art. II (3) (a); Paris Convention, supra footnote 109, Art. 5 (b).

经济主体可以通过建立谨慎行事（diligence）制度来免除责任。这种情况可以更恰当地描述为便利的责任（基于过失的）机制。如果不允许将谨慎行事作为免责事由，责任制度的客观（严格或绝对）性质将取决于现有的免责事由。经济运营商如果证明损害是由武装冲突、不可抗力或受害人或第三人的非法行为等情况造成的，可以免除责任。[125] 严格责任制度通常会规定最高限额，即向负有责任的主体索偿的数额会有一定的限制。[126] 这样的上限试图实现两个相互竞争的目标。一方面，为了实现受规制活动的追求，最高限额是必要的。没有这些最高限额，就很难衡量诉讼风险，从而导致经济运营商不愿从事这种活动。另一方面，最高限额不得过低，否则经济运营商将没有足够的动力来保持必要的谨慎注意。处理这种权衡的一种方法是，当经济运营商陷入严重的过错时消除这些上限。[127] 这种方法表明严格责任制度的建立并不排除在必要时恢复基于过失的责任。

可能出现的实际困难是经济运营商可能资不抵债。一般而言，严格责任制度包括经济运营商投保的义务。[128] 不管事故的影响是在缘起国还是在国外发生，保险范围通常会延伸至责任主体可承担的最高限额。保险人和责任主体之间的关系是合同性质的，根据具体情况的不同可能会发生变化，但它们仍会受到适用条约和国内法的管辖。通常情况下，受害方有权直接对保险公司提起诉讼，保险公司可以利用与责任主体相同的抗辩理由（特别是免责事由）。[129] 与最高限额一样，保险是严格责任制度的一个重要

---

[125] CLC/92, supra footnote 112, Art. III (2) – (3); Vienna Convention, supra footnote 110, Art. IV (2) – (3); Paris Convention, supra footnote 109, Art. 9.

[126] On the amounts that may be required in respect of a nuclear accident or pollution byhydrocarbons seeILC Principles, supra footnote 83, Art. 4 comments, para. 23 and notes. CLC/ 92 conditions this limitation of liability by the responsible entity having to file with the court an action for damages for an amount equal to its limit of liability. See CLC/92, supra footnote 112, Art. V (3).

[127] See CLC/92, supra footnote 112, Art. V (2); Kiev Protocol, supra footnote 116, Art. 5; Basel Protocol, supra footnote 117, Art. 5. See more generally the ILC Principles, supra footnote 83, Art. 4, commentary, para. 24.

[128] See CLC/92, supra footnote 112, Art. VII (1); Vienna Convention, supra footnote 110, Art. VII; Paris Convention, supra footnote 109, Art. 10.

[129] CLC/92, supra footnote 112, Art. VII (8); Kiev Protocol, supra footnote 116, Art. 11 (3); Basel Protocol, supra footnote 117, Art. 14 (4). See more generally the ILC Principles, supra footnote 83, Art. 4, commentary, para. 34.

组成部分,因为它允许活动的商业开发,尽管这些活动有风险,但从社会的角度来看是有益的。

即使在强制保险和可能对保险公司采取直接诉讼的情况下,追回封顶数额也可能不足以弥补所有损失。核事故和石油泄漏确实可能造成数亿欧元甚至数十亿欧元的大规模环境破坏。这就是为什么严格责任制度规定了由受益行业(在石油污染损害制度中)或国家(核能事故)承担的不同层次的赔偿。诸如《布鲁塞尔补充公约》(*Brussels Supplementary Convention*)[130]、《维也纳公约补充公约》(*Supplementary Convention to the Vienna Convention*)[131]、1971年《基金公约》(现为1992年《基金公约》)[132]和2003年《基金公约》[133]等文书增加了这些层次。当经济运营商和/或保险公司破产,或当损害超过最高保险金额和/或损害无法转给经济运营商时,它们就会发挥作用。[134] 考虑到这些补充层次的目的是确保适当的赔偿,受害方可以直接向有关基金提出索赔,因为该基金无法利用经济运营商所能利用的所有抗辩。[135] 这些资金的情况可以被理解为一种绝对责任(由损害引发),虽然严格地说,它们不能被视为对所造成的损害负责的主体。

最后,严格责任制度力求协调受损害影响者的境况。为此,一种可能性是设立一个国际救济机制,例如在海湾战争后成立的联合国赔偿委员会(United Nations Compensation Commission)或在1979年伊朗革命后设立的伊美索赔法庭(Iran-United States Claims Tribunal)。[136] 救济程序通常是在国内层面进行,重要的是避免损害缘起国(或其法院)对当地和外国受害者的任何区别对待。[137] 不得歧视是跨国赔偿的一个关键要素,这说明了这一机制的"两栖"特性,它严重依赖国内法和各国法院,各国法院是

130　Brussels Supplementary Convention, supra footnote 109.

131　Complementary Vienna Convention, supra footnote 110.

132　FUND/92, supra footnote 113.

133　FUND/2003, supra footnote 115.

134　FUND/92, supra footnote 113, Art. 4.

135　Ibid., Art. 4 (2).

136　ILC Principles, supra footnote 83, Art. 6 (4), commentary, para. 11.

137　Paris Convention, supra footnote 109, Art. 14 (a); Vienna Convention, supra footnote 110, Art. XIII.

依照条约规定的某些广义要素来运作的。[138] 还应注意,该要求包含了一项义务,即应当向那些可能受影响的人(包括外国人)提供机会去获取有关风险的信息(或者有关损害的信息,视情况而定),这凸显了第三章所讨论的公众参与原则与工业活动开展之间的关联。[139]

前述观察总结了适用于经济运营商的民事责任制度的一般方法。但是,还有一个重要的问题需要解决,这将使我们回到分析的起点,即评估和修复环境损害所采用的方法。

(四) 环境损害的评估与补救

前面各节分析的责任和赔偿责任制度组织了环境损害的补救。[140] 我们现在必须弄清楚"环境损害"这一术语的涵盖范围,以及在补救时可以采取什么具体方式。这两个问题是相关的,因为某些类型的损害"必须"被修复到它们"能够"被修复的程度。

为了便于介绍,我们首先介绍应对这一问题的基本原则。毫无疑问,对人的损害(生命或身体的损失)或财产的损害(损失或损害)和持续性利润的损失(某项活动因为环境损害的影响而导致收入的损失)必须加以修复。[141] 然而,这些假设并不包括对环境本身的损害,而是包括环境损害所造成的身体和经济损害。环境本身的损害的修复可以参照采取某些措施所涉及(或者合理推算涉及)的花费。正是在明确何种损害必须得到修复时,修复方式的选择才变得尤其重要。在这方面,可以初步区分在事件发生之前采取的措施和在事件发生后采取的措施。第一类是预防义务的一部分,有关费用并不属于损害赔偿金的一部分。相比之下,响应措施通常是可补偿的。[142] 在这一类别中,可以进一步区分清理和预防(减轻)措施。恢复、复原或清理环境的措施一般会得到补偿[143],但必须符合某些

---

138 See CLC/92, supra footnote 112, Art. X (2).

139 ILC Principles, supra footnote 83, Art. 6 (5), commentary, paras. 13–15.

140 See M. Bowman and A. Boyle (eds.), *Environmental Damage in International and Comparative Law: Problems of Definition and Evaluation* (Oxford University Press, 2002); SFDI, *Le dom-mage écologique en droit interne, communautaire et comparé* (Paris: Economica, 1992)

141 See, e.g., Paris Convention, supra footnote 109, Art. 3; Vienna Convention, supra footnote 110, Art. I (k); CLC/92, supra footnote 112, Art. I (6); Basel Protocol, supra footnote 117, Art. 2.

142 See CLC/92, supra footnote 112, Art. I (6); Basel Protocol, supra footnote 117, Art. 2.

143 See CLC/92, supra footnote 112, Art. I (6); Basel Protocol, supra footnote 117, Art. 2.

合理条件，并须证明确实采取了这些措施。[144] 关于预防性（减轻）措施，补偿取决于条约的内容。当这些措施试图减轻已经发生的损害程度时，它们依据与恢复措施相同的逻辑得到补偿。然而，当损害尚未发生时，只有在"污染损害的严重威胁迫在眉睫"的情况下才能收回这些措施的花费。[145]

一个更大的难题在于，超出现有考虑范围的环境损害（即纯生态损害）是否必须得到修复。主要的困难是这种损害往往是不可逆转的，而且即使可以确定环境质量方面的损失，这种损失也不能轻易地分配给一个可识别的权利持有人（而非环境本身）。几个例证将有助于理解这一概念。臭氧层的损耗、气候系统的变化、物种灭绝或在国家管辖范围以外区域的生态系统是否应该得到修复？解决这一问题的一个方法是参照可以采取的措施来量化这一损失。这一方法可以为（尽可能地）恢复原状或复原措施提供支撑。[146] 在气候谈判中也探讨过这一方法，尽管迄今为止没有成功。[147] 这一方法的一个变体包括在受损地区以外的地区恢复或保护一个类似的生态系统。这一方法支持各种污染配额交易计划（例如，温室气体排放交易或消耗臭氧层或酸化物质的生产/消费能力的交易，或湿地破坏的补偿配额）。[148] 另一种方法是（尽可能地）量化当前和未来物种或生态系统的损失所代表的价值，并将有关款项拨给那些为了代表这一特别利

---

[144] On the increasing role of restoration see A. Telesetsky, A. Cliquet and A. Akhtar-Khavari, *Restoration in International Environmental Law* (London: Routledge, 2017).

[145] CLC/92, supra footnote 112, Art. I (6) – (7); FUND/92, supra footnote 113, Art. 3 (b) and 4 (1) (c); IMO, Claims Manual (London, 2008), para. 1.4.5., 1.4.6., 1.4.11.

[146] See "Erika", Cour de Cassation, Chambre criminelle, Arre't No. 3439 (25 September 2012) (recognizing the existence of an "objective prejudice" to the environment as such).

[147] See supra footnote 100.

[148] See Chapter 5. See also the techniques of compensation for the loss of wetlands in the context of the Clean Water Act of the United States (Compensatory Mitigation for Losses of Aquatic Resources, 40 CFR Part 230 Subpart J and 33 CFR 332) or, more generally, the techniques of compensation under Directive 2004/35/CE of the European Parliament and Council of 21 April 2004 on environmental liability with regard to the prevention and remedying of environmental damage, OJ L143/56, 30 April 2004, para. 1.1.3: "Compensatory remediation shall be undertaken to compensate for the interim loss of natural resources and services pending recovery. This compensation consists of additional improvements to protected natural habitats and species or water at either the damaged site or at an alternative site. It does not consist of financial compensation to members of the public." see generally M. Lucas, *étude juridique de la compensation écologique* (Paris: LGDJ, 2015).

益而建立的机构（例如非政府机构、[149] 地方当局、[150] 环境专员）。这是国际法研究院推荐的解决方案。[151] 总的来说，人们可以得出这样的结论：目前，国际法主要是通过恢复或复原来处理对纯生态损害的补偿。[152]

部分参考文献

［1］ Anton, D. K. and D. Shelton, *Environmental Protection and Human Rights* (Cambridge University Press, 2011).

［2］ Barboza, J. A., "International Liability for the Injurious Consequences of Acts Not Prohibited by International Law and Protection of the Environment" (1994) 247 *Recueil Des Cours de l'Académie de Droit International* 293-405.

The Environment, Risk and Liability in International Law (Leiden: Martinus Nijhoff, 2011).

［3］ Bergkamp, L., *Liability and Environment: Private and Public Law Aspects of Civil Liability for Environmental Harm in an International Context* (The Hague: Kluwer, 2001).

［4］ Betlem, G. and E. Brans (eds.), *Environmental Liability in the EU: The 2004 Directive Compared with US and Member State Law* (London: Cameron May, 2006).

［5］ Bianchi, A., "Harmonisation of Laws on Liability for Environmental Damage in Europe" (1994) 6 *Journal of Environmental Law* 21.

［6］ Bowman, M. and A. Boyle (eds.), *Environmental Damage in International and Comparative Law: Problems of Definition and Evaluation* (Oxford University Press, 2002).

---

[149] See L. Neyret, *Atteintes au Vivant et Responsabilité Civile* (Paris: LGDJ, 2006), pp. 577ff.

[150] See Tribunal correctionnel de Paris, 11th ch., 16 January 2008, No. 9934895010, cited in Y. Kerbrat, "Le Droit International Face au défi de la réparation des dommages à L'environnement", in SFDI, *Le Droit International Face aux Enjeux Environnementaux* (Paris: Pedone, 2010), pp. 125-144, at 141.

[151] See IDI-Responsibility, supra footnote 89, Art. 28.

[152] See Manual, supra footnote 145, paras. 3.6.1. to 3.6.4; Lugano Convention, supra footnote 119, Art. 2 (9) - (11).

[7] Boyle, A., "State Responsibility and International Liability for Injurious Consequences of Acts Not Prohibited by International Law: A Necessary Distinction?" (1990) 39 *International and Comparative Law Quarterly* 1.

[8] Boyle, A. and M. R. Anderson (eds.), *Human Rights Approaches to Environmental Protection* (Oxford: Clarendon Press, 1998).

[9] Boyle, A. and J. Harrison, "Judicial Settlement of International Environmental Disputes: Current Problems" (2013) 4 *Journal of International Dispute Settlement* 245.

[10] Brans, E. H. P., *Liability for Damage to Public Natural Resources: Standing, Damage and Damage Assessment* (The Hague: Kluwer, 2001).

[11] Brunnée, J., "Of Sense and Sensibility: Reflections on International Liability Regimes as Tools for Environmental Protection" (2004) 53 *International and Comparative Law Quarterly* 351.

[12] Burns, W. C. G. and H. Osofsky (eds.), *Adjudicating Climate Change. State, National and International Approaches* (Cambridge University Press, 2009).

[13] Churchill, R. R., "Facilitating (Transnational) Civil Liability Litigation for Environmental Damage by Means of Treaties: Progress, Problems, and Prospects" (2001) 12 *Yearbook of International Environmental Law* 3.

[14] Doeker, G. and T. Gehring, "Private or International Liability for Transnational Environmental Damage – The Precedent of Conventional Liability Regimes" (1990) 2 *Journal of Environmental Law* 7.

[15] Dupuy, P. -M., *La Responsabilité Internationale des Etats Pour les Dommages D'origine Technologique et Industrielle* (Paris: Pédone, 1976).

"La diligence due dans le droit international de la responsabilité", *Aspects Juridiques de la Pollution Transfrontière* (Paris: OCDE, 1977), pp. 396-407.

"Oùen est le droit international de l'environnement àlafin du siècle?" (1997) *Revue Générale de Droit International Public* 873.

"A propos des mésaventures de la responsabilité internationale des Etats dans ses rapports avec la protection internationale de l'environnement", in M. Prieur (ed.), *Les Hommes Etl'environnement: Quels Droits Pour le Vingt-et-unième Siècle? Etudes en Hommage à Alexandre Kiss* (Paris: Frisson-

Roche, 1998), pp. 269–282.

[16] Francioni, F., "International Human Rights in an Environmental Horizon" (2010) 21 *European Journal of International Law* 41.

[17] Francioni, F. and T. Scovazzi (eds.), *International Responsibility for Environmental Harm* (London: Graham & Trotman, 1991).

[18] French, D., "Environmental Dispute Settlement: The First (Hesistant) Signs of Spring?" (2007) 19 *Hague Yearbook of International Law* 3.

[19] Gabaldòn Garcìa, J. L., *Curso de Derecho Marítimo Internacional* (Madrid: Marcial Pons, 2012).

[20] Goldie, L. F. E., "Liability for Damage and the Progressive Development of International Law" (1965) 14 *International and Comparative Law Quarterly* 1189.

"Concepts of Strict and Absolute Liability and the Ranking of Liability in Terms of Relative Exposure to Risk" (1985) 16 *Netherlands Yearbook of International Law* 175.

[21] Handl, G., "Liability as an Obligation Established by a Primary Rule of International Law" (1985) 16 *Netherlands Yearbook of International Law* 49.

[22] Jenks, W., "Liability for Hazardous Activities" (1966) 117 *Recueil des Cours de l'Académie de Doit International* 102–200.

[23] Jennings, R., "Need for an Environmental Court" (1992) 20 *Environmental Policy and Law* 312

"The Role of the International Court of Justice in the Development of International Environment Protection Law" (1992) 1 *Review of European Community and International Environmental Law* 240.

[24] Kerbrat, Y., "Le droit international face au défi de la réparation des dommages à L'environnement", in *SFDI, Le Droit International Face Aux Enjeux Environnementaux* (Paris: Pedone, 2010), pp. 125–144.

[25] Larsson, M.-L., *The Law of Environmental Damage: Liability and Reparation* (The Hague: Kluwer, 1999).

[26] Lecucq, O. and S. Maljean-Dubois (eds.), *Le Rôle du Juge Dans le Développement du Droit de L'environnement* (Brussels: Bruylant, 2008).

［27］ Lefeber, R., *Transboundary Environmental Interference and the Origin of State Liability* (The Hague: Kluwer, 1996).

［28］ Lord, R., S. Goldberg, L. Rajamani and J. Brunnée (eds.), *Climate Change Liability: Transnational Law and Practice* (Cambridge University Press, 2011).

［29］ Lozano Contreras, J. F., *La Noción de Debida Diligencia en Derecho Internacional Público* (Barcelona: Atelier Libros Jurídicos, 2007).

［30］ Lucas, M., *étude Juridique de la Compensation écologique* (Paris: Librairie générale de droit et de jurisprudence, 2015).

［31］ Magraw, D. B., "Transboundary Harm: The International Law Commission's Study of International Liability" (1986) 80 *American Journal of International Law* 305.

［32］ Maljean-Dubois, S., *La Mise en œuvre du Droit International de L'environnement* (Paris: Iddri, 2003).

［33］ Nègre, C., "Responsibility and International Environmental Law", in J. Crawford, A. Pellet, S. Olleson and K. Parlett (eds.), *The Law of International Responsibility* (Oxford University Press, 2010), pp. 803–813.

［34］ Neyret, L., *Atteintes au Vivant et Responsabilité Civile* (Paris: LGDJ, 2006).

［35］ Ouedraogo, A., *La Diligence en Droit International. Contribution à L'étude D'une Notion aux Contours Imprécis* (Thesis of the Graduate Institute of International and Development Studies, Geneva, 2011).

［36］ Pisillo Mazzeschi, R., *Due Diligence e Responsabilità Internazionale degli Stati* (Milan: Giuffrè, 1989).

"The Due Diligence Rule and the Nature of the International Responsibility of States" (1992) 35 *German Yearbook of International Law* 9.

［37］ Postiglione, A., "A More Efficient International Law on the Environment and Setting up an International Court for the Environment within the United Nations" (1990) 20 *Environmental Law* 321.

［38］ Ranjeva, R., "L'environnement, la Cour internationale de justice et sa chambre spéciale pour les questions d'environnement" (1994) 40 *Annuaire Français de Droit International* 433.

[39] Ratliff, D. P., "The PCA Optional Rules for Arbitration of Disputes Relating to Natural Resources and/or the Environment" (2001) 14 *Leiden Journal of International Law* 887.

[40] Romano, C., *The Peaceful Settlement of International Environmental Disputes: A Pragmatic Approach* (The Hague: Kluwer, 2000).

[41] Sachariew, K., "Promoting Compliance with International Environmental Legal Standards: Reflections on Monitoring and Reporting Mechanisms" (1991) 2 *Yearbook of International Environmental Law* 31.

[42] Sands, P., "Existing Arrangements for the Settlement of International Environmental Disputes: A Background Paper", in *Towards the World Governing of the Environment: IV International Conference International Court of the Environment Foundation (ICEF), 2–5 June 1994* (Pavia: Iuculano, 1996), pp. 628–647.

[43] Scovazzi, T., "State Responsibility for Environmental Harm" (2001) 12 *Yearbook of International Environmental Law* 43.

[44] Société française pour le droit international, *Le dommage écologique en droit interne, communautaire et comparé* (Paris: Economica, 1992).

[45] Stephens, T., *International Courts and Environmental Protection* (Cambridge University Press, 2009).

[46] Telesetsky, A., A. Cliquet and A. Akhtar-Khavari, *Restoration in International Environmental Law* (London: Routledge, 2017).

[47] Viñuales, J. E., "The Contribution of the International Court of Justice to the Development of International Environmental Law" (2008) 32 *Fordham International Law Journal* 232.

"Managing Abidance by Standards for the Protection of the Environment", in A. Cassese (ed.), *Realizing Utopia* (Oxford University Press, 2012), pp. 326–339.

"The Environmental Regulation of Foreign Investment Schemes under International Law", in P.-M. Dupuy and J. E. Viñuales (eds.), *Harnessing Foreign Investment to Promote Environmental Protection: Incentives and Safeguards* (Cambridge University Press, 2013), pp. 273–320.

[48] Wetterstein, P. (ed.), *Harm to the Environment: The Right to*

Compensation and Assessment of Damage (Oxford: Clarendon Press, 1997).

[49] Wolfrum, R., "Means of Ensuring Compliance with and Enforcement of International Environmental Law" (1998) 272 *Recueil Des Cours de L'Académie de Droit International* 9–154.

第九章 履行：新方法

第一节 导论

在上一章中，我们确定了一个遵守初级环境规范过程的四个阶段。我们发现，国际法用于履行国际义务的传统方法侧重于第一阶段（信息）和第四阶段（修复）。用于处理信息收集/报告、对违约行为进行定性（以裁判方式）以及确定后续法律后果（责任/赔偿责任 responsibility/liability）的这些手段在环境保护中发挥着重要作用，但它们也带来了巨大的挑战。我们在从遵约到不遵约的过程中确定了一个灰色区域，该区域的特征是遵约程度的不确定性（信息尚不构成违约本质）。这一领域可能被称为遵约过程的"软肋"，对我们的讨论很重要，因为它是许多环境条约履行体系的主要目标。

这一战略选择基于两个主要考量。一方面，在环境保护背景下，环境损害的预防比修复要重要得多，而修复往往是非常困难的；[1] 另一方面，第一阶段和第四阶段相关手段假定不遵守义务是一个意愿问题，而非财务或技术能力问题。[2] 这种假设不一定对所有国家都准确。遵守环境条约所涉及的费用和专业知识有时会使那些缺乏足够资源的国家难以遵约。此外，即使一个国家拥有资源，尽量减少与执行措施有关的费用，对于提高

---

[1] See section 8.3.3.4 of Chapter 8.

[2] See A. Chayes and A. Handler Chayes, *The New Sovereignty*, *Compliance with International Regulatory Agreements* (Cambridge, MA: Harvard University Press, 1998).

遵约效率仍然很重要。这两个因素导致形成了新的履行方法。图 9-1 [3] 确定了这些方法介入的阶段。

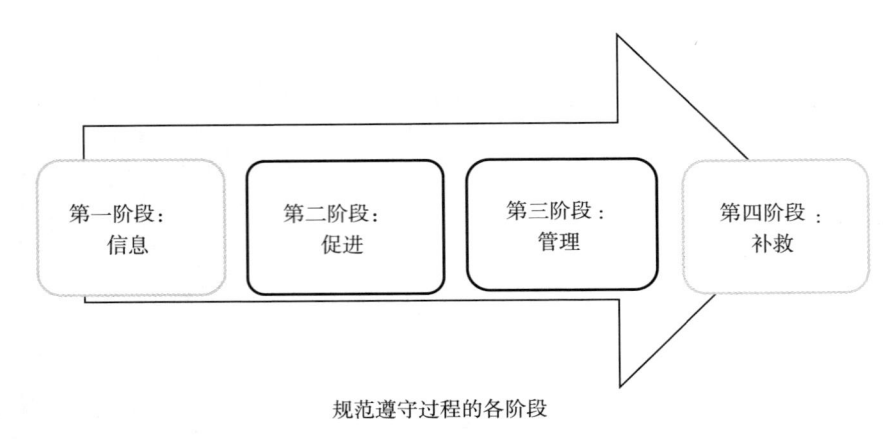

```
第一阶段：    第二阶段：    第三阶段：    第四阶段：
  信息          促进          管理          补救
```

规范遵守过程的各阶段

图 9-1　遵约流程的"软肋"

促进遵守环境义务的主要手段（第二阶段）试图提供"帮助"和"效率"收益（本章第二节）。技术和财政援助旨在为发展中国家提供途径以建立必要的基础设施来履行其环境义务。其他手段旨在提高效率，以减少履行环境义务的成本。后者与发达国家和发展中国家都有关，它们通常被构造为市场机制。就管理不遵约情况的手段（第三阶段）而言，其目的是通过新的援助、外交压力和制裁相结合，将机制的有效性保持在合理的范围内（本章第三节）。

第二节　促进遵约的手段

一　手段类型

对遵守环境标准的促进手段进行分析存在一些困难。手段的多样性以及每种机制的特殊性使它们难以被理解。此外，手段的运行既涉及政治和

---

[3] See P.‑M. Dupuy, "Où en est le droit international de l'environnement à la fin du siècle?" (1997) *Revue generale de droit international public* 873, in particular 893‑895; J. E. Viñuales, "Managing Abidance by Standards for the Protection of the Environment", in A. Cassese (ed.), *Realizing Utopia* (Oxford University Press, 2012), pp. 326‑339.

经济因素，也涉及法律。因此，必须明确应当从何种角度来讨论这些手段。

国际环境法教科书通常会描述各种机制，例如发展援助、环境资金、技术转让、能力建设等；简要介绍了几种手段的构成规则，而没有详细介绍它们的运行。如前所述，这种方法是可以被理解的，因为手段各不相同，并且每种机制都有其特征，教科书的有限文本甚至在一本巨著中都无法分析。我们的讨论采用了一种不同但互补的方法。我们没有笼统地简要介绍每种机制，而是着重于以下三个方面。

第一，在本书中，主要考虑因素是阐明环境条约采用的创新履行方法的性质。这就是为什么我们要强调各种促进手段所追求的两个目标，即提供援助和提高效率。第二，鉴于潜在的相关文件数量众多，因此不可能简单地涵盖每个示例。为了克服这一困难，我们将根据各种手段的代表性特征和实践意义来选择一些主要例证。我们必须考虑的第三个方面是分析中采用的特定角度。在介绍了每种机制的基本特征之后，我们将特别注意其运行中出现的法律问题。

二 面向援助的手段

（一）财政援助

1. 概述

履行环境协定的一个重要手段是提供财政援助。"财政援助"一词包括各种公共、私人甚至混合机制。建立这些机制的目的通常是弥合发达国家和发展中国家在条约谈判中的立场。例如，1987 年《蒙特利尔议定书》（*Montreal Protocol*）多边基金就是这种情况。[4] 实际上，1990 年通过对议定书的修订引入了该基金，目的是使某些发展中国家（特别是中国和印度）加入该体系。该机制以及《蒙特利尔议定书》提出的其他多项创新，深刻影响了发达国家与发展中国家之间在随后的环境谈判中处理分歧的方式。稍后我们将更详细地讨论该机制，但首先将其置于更广泛的财政援助手段这一背景中进行分析是很有用的。图 9-2 简要概述了这些手段。

---

[4] 1987 年 9 月 16 日《关于消耗臭氧层物质的蒙特利尔议定书》，1522 UNTS 3（Montreal Protocol）. See also the Terms of Reference for the Multilateral Fund, 25 November 1992, UNEP/OzL. Pro. 4/15, Annex IX（Terms of Reference for the Multilateral Fund）.

```
                            财政
         ┌───────────────────┼───────────────────┐
        公共                  混合                 私人
    ┌────┴────┐          ┌────┴────┐         ┌────┴────┐
  一般性      环境      混合机制    杠杆金融   直接投资   社会责任投资
```

官方开发援助
（ODA）

世界银行
区域银行

　　　　　┌────┴────┐
         一般性   具体性

全球环境基   世界遗产基金
金（GEF）
            多边基金（臭
            氧）

            绿色气候基金
            （GCF）

原型碳汇基金   绿色
（PCF）   气候
                  基金

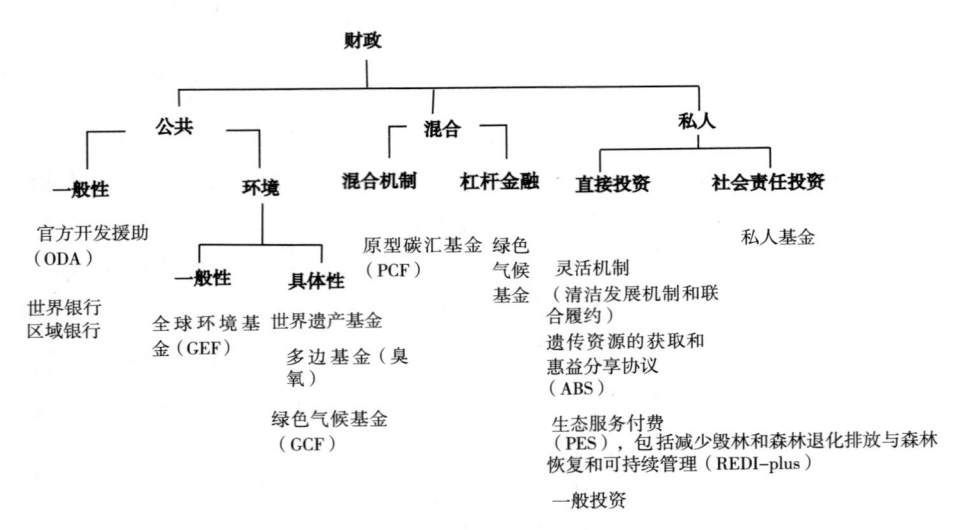

灵活机制
（清洁发展机制和联
合履约）

遗传资源的获取和
惠益分享协议
（ABS）

生态服务付费
（PES），包括减少毁林和森林退化排放与森林
恢复和可持续管理（REDI-plus）

一般投资

私人基金

图 9-2　财政援助手段

　　一般而言，在国际谈判中，资金来源发挥着重要作用。发展中国家通常更倾向于选择公共财政（Public finance），因为从理论上讲，公共财政是更可预测的，[5] 尽管发达国家在这一领域的承诺并不总是得到尊重，而且往往附带条件。

　　相比之下，发达国家通常倾向于让私人资金（private finance）发挥更大的作用，并通过资本流动的自由化和外国直接投资的更容易获取来得以实现。在公共财政（public finance）中，根据财政资源是一般性地分配给发展或更具体地分配给环境保护，可以明确两个明显不同的标准。我们无法在这里谈论宏观的官方发展援助（Official Development Aid，ODA）[6] 问题。只需指出，强调"新的和额外的"资源供给[7]是为了确保财政援助能够超越官方发展援助在环境项目中的重新分配。关于那些聚焦于环境保护的机制，可以在一般环境基金（例如全球环境基金，GEF）和条约特定基

---

[5]　Report of the United Nations Conference on Environment and Development，A/CONF. 151/26/Rev. 1（Vol. 1），Resolution 1，Annex 2：Action 21（Action 21），para. 33.11（b）.

[6]　See P. Kohona，"UNCED - The Transfer of Financial Resources to Developing Countries"（1992）1 *Review of European Community and International Environmental Law* 307.

[7]　Action 21，supra footnote 5，chapter 33，particularly para. 33.1.

金（例如世界遗产基金、多边基金或绿色气候基金）之间做一个进一步区分。关于私人资金，无论是外国直接投资、组合投资[8]还是单纯的商业贷款，自1992年地球峰会（Earth Summit）以来，其重要性都得到了越来越多的认可。这种资金来源所引发的法律问题将在第十二章中讨论。另一个日益重要的手段是混合融资（mixed financing），通常是在开发银行或全球环境基金（GEF）的主持下进行的，全球环境基金（GEF）已动员了大量的私人资本作为杠杆融资的一部分。世界银行设立的原型碳汇基金（Prototype Carbon Fund，PCF）是一个合适的例证，它为在国内建立其他混合型基金（hybrid funds）提供了模板。

这些对融资类型的一般性观察为进一步详细分析三个例证（即条约型环境基金、全球环境基金和原型碳汇基金）奠定了基础。对这些机制的分析将聚焦于其功能以及部分法律问题。

2. 条约型环境基金

根据《世界遗产公约》（*World Heritage Convention*）第15条，[9] 1972年成立了第一个条约型环境基金。尽管世界遗产基金管理的资金数额不大（每年约400万美元），但该机制仍代表着一种类型的基金，我们也能在其他环境条约中找到，包括《拉姆萨公约》（*Ramsar Convention*）[10] 和《巴塞尔公约》（*Basel Convention*）。[11] 世界遗产基金主要来自国家的捐赠，部分是强制性的，部分是自愿性的，也有来自其他主体的捐赠，例如国际

---

[8] See B. J. Richardson, *Socially Responsible Investment Law*: *Regulating the Unseen Polluters* (Oxford University Press, 2008).

[9] Convention Concerning the Protection of the World Cultural and Natural Heritage, 16 November 1972, 1037 UNTS 151 (WHC).

[10] Ramsar Convention on Wetlands of International Importance, especially as Waterfowl Habitat, 2 February 1971, 996 UNTS 245 (Ramsar Convention). The fund was established by the "Resolution on a Wetland Conservation Fund", Resolution 4.3 (1990). 实际上，该机制被称为"拉姆萨小额赠款基金"。

[11] Basel Convention on the Control of Transboundary Movements of Hazardous Wastes and their Disposal, 22 March 1989, 1673 UNTS 57 (Basel Convention), Art. 14. The COP established a "General Trust Fund" and a "Trust Fund for Technical Cooperation". see "Financial Rules of the Conference of the Parties, its subsidiary bodies and the Secretariat of the Basel Convention on the Control of Transboundary Movements of Hazardous Wastes and their Disposal", Decision BC-10/28 (2011).

组织和私人团体。[12] 基金的金额会被分配给公约设立的世界遗产委员会所规定的活动,并且数额不得超出实际可用的数额。[13] 这些活动主要涉及缔约国能力建设(提供专家和培训)和其他形式的技术援助(研究和设备供应)。基金中的某些款项被分配用于维持储备金(公约第21条第2款提到),其目的是在自然灾害等紧急情况下提供迅速援助。委员会根据其在资金分配方面的优先次序将目标活动分为三类:[14] 紧急援助(特别是《濒危世界遗产名录》中的遗址[15]);在保护和管理方面的支持;预备援助。基金当前的策略与环境基金通过共同资助项目来利用额外资本的大趋势相一致。[16] 尽管具有标志性,但世界遗产基金仅仅代表第一代(但规模不大)的条约特定环境基金。[17] 随着《蒙特利尔议定书》(Montreal Protocol)内多边基金(Multilateral Fund)的建立,第二代条约型环境基金能够动员更多的资源。

该多边基金具有两个方面的象征意义。[18] 一方面,它是第二代条约型环境基金的第一笔资金,即足够资助发展中国家因遵守环境条约而改变基础设施所产生的"议定的增量成本"的资金(每期超过4亿美元[19]);另一方面,管理机构,即由七个发展中国家和七个发达国家组成(尽管只

---

12 Financial Regulations of the World Heritage Fund, available at: www.whc.unesco.org (visited on 15 April 2017) ("Financial Regulations"), Art. 3. 1.

13 Ibid., Art. 4.

14 Operational Guidelines for the Implementation of the World Heritage Convention, 26 October 2016, WHC. 16/01 (Operational Guidelines), para. 235.

15 Ibid., para. 236.

16 Ibid., para. 225. See M. Bowman, P. Davies and C. Redgwell, *Lyster's International Wildlife Law* (Cambridge University Press, 2nd edn, 2010), pp. 475-477 for concrete examples.

17 On "generations" of financial mechanisms, see L. Boisson de Chazournes, "Technical and Financial Assistance", in D. Bodansky, J. Brunnée and E. Hey (eds.), *The Oxford Handbook of International Environmental Law* (Oxford University Press, 2007), pp. 948-972.

18 On this mechanism, see P. Lawrence, "Technology Transfer Funds and the Law: Recent Amendments to the Montreal Protocol on Substances that Deplete the Ozone Layer" (1992) 4 *Journal of Environmental Law* 15.

19 The periods were as follows: 1991-1993, 1994-1996, 1997-1999, 2000-2002, 2003-2005, 2006-2008, 2009-2011, 2012-2014.

第九章 履行：新方法   389

有发达国家出资[20]）的执行委员会，体现了共同但有区别的责任这一原则。[21] 该基金是根据1990年6月对《蒙特利尔议定书》的一项修正案设立的，成立于1991年，并于1992年成为常设基金，以支付"议定的增量成本"（根据议定书第10条第1款指定）。[22] 其中包括生产受管控物质设施的转型或提前退役，建立生产替代品的新设施，进口此类替代品或使用相关专利和外观设计等所产生的成本，这是列举的几个类别。[23] 提供资金的相关决议是由委员会以协商一致的方式做出的，否则由出席并参加表决的成员的2/3作出，但必须尊重发展中国家和发达国家的双重多数。[24] 实际上，委员会以协商一致方式行事。该财政援助体系的履行由"履行机构"管理，特别是联合国环境规划署（现为联合国环境署）、联合国开发计划署、世界银行[25]和联合国工业发展组织（United Nations Industrial Development Organization，UNIDO）。有个例证可能有助于我们了解这种机制的运作方式。2011年，执行委员会根据《蒙特利尔议定书》第2条E款核准了2.65亿美元，以减少氢氯氟烃的使用。[26] 这些物质也是潜在的温室气体。目前已经为使用氢氯氟烃（HCFCs）的数百条装配线的改造提供了财政援助。作为该项目的一部分，应该首先冻结，然后减少氢氯氟烃的消费，中国将会得到联合国开发规划署、联合国环境规划署、联合国工业发展组织、世界银行以及德国和日本政府的协助。[27] 总而言之，多边基金的特点可以归纳为所提到的三个主要特征：涵盖发展中国家为遵守条约而产生的"议定的增量成本"；由发达国家和发展中国家组成平等的委员

---

[20] Montreal Protocol, supra footnote 4, Art. 10（5）-（6）; Terms of Reference of the Executive Committee as Modified by the Ninth Meeting of the Parties in its Decision IX/16, 25 September 1997, UNEP/OzL. Pro. 9/12, Annex V（Terms of Reference of the Executive Committee）, para. 2. The Terms of Reference have been revised several times.

[21] See Chapter 3.

[22] Montreal Protocol, supra footnote 4, Art. 10（1）.

[23] Indicative List of Agreed Incremental Costs, 25 November 1992, UNEP/OzL. Pro. 4/15, Annex.

[24] Montreal Protocol, supra footnote 4, Art. 10（9）.

[25] Terms of Reference for the Multilateral Fund, supra footnote 4, paras. 2-7.

[26] Montreal Protocol, supra footnote 4, Art. 2F and Annex C（Group I）.

[27] See "China Commits to Landmark Agreement on Dual Ozone and Climate Benefits", 29 July 2011, available at: www. multilateralfund. org（visited on 15 April 2017）.

会进行决策;"履行机构"对援助的履行。如下所述,有关气候融资的谈判在某些重要方面偏离了该模板。

条约型环境基金的第三个例证是绿色气候基金(GCF)的创立。[28] 该基金是根据 2011 年 12 月《联合国气候变化框架公约》(UNFCCC)[29] 缔约方大会的一项决议设立的,但这是 2006 年已经开始的进程的结果,并且在 2009 年 12 月哥本哈根会议上得到加强。颇具争议的《哥本哈根协定》(*Copenhagen Accord*)的重点是创建一个筹集可观资源(到 2020 年达到每年 1000 亿美元)的基金,这一想法在 2010 年 12 月的"坎昆协议"中得到了采纳,并在 2011 年"德班会议"上正式确立。[30]《巴黎协定》的通过,其中包括有待审查的财务义务,为绿色气候基金(GCF)的运作提供了更多动力。[31] 尽管在撰写本书时,绿色气候基金才刚刚开始其融资业务(2015 年做出了第一笔融资决定,2016 年年末做出第一笔支出),但其机构架构值得关注,因为它很大程度上反映了过去数十年在开发环境基金方面积累的经验教训。从这个角度出发,必须突出五个主要特征。

第一,关于资金分配的决策权,由拥有平等席位的"委员会"掌握(12 名代表发达国家,12 名代表发展中国家)。[32] 决策由协商一致作出,委员会必须通过法规来处理无法达成协商一致的案件。[33] 委员会在此基础上设计了一种流程,在该流程中,通过联席主席和异议成员的交流以及同行压力的双重作用,可以保留共识规则,但更难以维持异议。[34]

28　Implementation of the Green Climate Fund, Decision 3/CP.17, 15 March 2012, FCCC/CP/2011/9/Add.1, Annex: Governing Instrument for the Green Climate Fund (GCF Instrument). On this instrument, see L. Schalatek and S. Nakhooda, "The Green Climate Fund" (November 2012) 11 Climate Finance Fundamentals.

29　UN Framework Convention on Climate Change, 9 May 1992, 1771 UNTS 107 (UNFCCC).

30　On climate negotiations, see supra Chapter 5.

31　See Adoption of the Paris Agreement, Decision 1/CP.21, 12 December 2015, FCCC/CP/2015/L.9 (Paris Decision). The Paris Agreement is appended as an Annex to the Paris Decision (Paris Agreement), Arts. 9 (on finance) and 13 (9) (on the review of financial obligations). Para. 54 of the Paris Decision introduces two clarifications, namely that a new collective quantified goal will be set by the COP acting as the meeting of the parties of the Paris Agreement (CMA) prior to 2025 and that the "floor" will be the figure, already present in previous negotiations, of US $ 100 billion per year.

32　GCF Instrument, supra footnote 28, para. 9.

33　Ibid., para. 14.

34　"Rules of Procedure of the Board", Decision B.01-13/01, 13-15 March 2013, Section 7.1.

第二点涉及委员会一方面与缔约方大会（COP）的关系，另一方面与基金"受托人"（暂定为世界银行）之间的关系。绿色气候基金是一个独立实体，但根据公约第 11 条，它是《联合国气候变化框架公约》（UN-FCCC）的资金机制。[35] 这使绿色气候基金相对于缔约方大会（COP）处于从属地位。建立绿色气候基金的文书仅声明为此达成"安排"，并设定了一些一般指导方针，包括需要遵守缔约方大会的一般准则并向缔约方大会提交年度报告。[36] 在实践中，该模式掩盖了发展中国家（资金接受国）与发达国家之间的分歧，前者希望缔约方大会能够对绿色气候基金进行更多管控，而后者则主张更大自由。虽然管理人是根据委员会的决议进行管理的，但在接受和持有基金的管理人（受托人）的选举中，各方意见也有分歧。应缔约方大会的要求（在捐助国的倡议下），世界银行担任临时受托人。[37] 任命常任受托人的程序预计将于 2017 年年底完成。

第三个要素是资金来源。就筹集的资金而言，预计绿色气候基金将成为最重要的机制。目标是到 2020 年每年调动 1000 亿美元，尽管这个目标可能过于雄心勃勃，正如绿色气候基金目前管理的大约 100 亿美元所暗示的那样。达成《巴黎协定》的谈判，将达到 1000 亿美元的"底线"的最后期限延长到 2025 年。[38] 接近这一目标的一种方法是利用可得的公共资金，并将其当作筹集更多私人资金的基础。绿色气候基金的工作明确地预见了这一点，绿色气候基金已经建立了一个私营部门基金，其具体目标是通过各种手段（特别是降低私营部门投资风险的那些手段）来利用私营部门的资金。

绿色气候基金架构的第四个重要方面是如何组织资金分配。这可能包括向那些负责资助特定项目的履行实体或组织提供资金，或者相反，绿色气候基金可以直接开展此类资金活动，这将需要更复杂的行政结构。[39] 该工具选择了第一种模式，绿色气候基金会通过委员会认可的国际、区域乃

---

35 《巴黎协定》提到了《联合国气候变化框架公约》的资金机制，see Paris Agreement, supra footnote 31, Art. 9（8）。

36 GCF Instrument, supra footnote 28, para. 6.

37 Ibid., para. 26.

38 See supra footnote 31.

39 Schalatek and Nakhooda, supra footnote 28, p. 2.

至国家实体、公共或私人实体（通过认证的实体）来分发其资源。[40] 应特别强调国内当局的作用，以确保在特定国家提交的资助提案之间的协调，以及与国家减缓和适应计划的一致性。

绿色气候基金的第五个特征是，与其他基金不同，它可以覆盖发展中国家产生的"议定的增量成本"，还可以支付与适应、减缓、技术转让和能力建设相关项目的"议定的所有成本"。[41] 这些是绿色气候基金架构的基本特征。它们很大程度上要归功于我们接下来将要研究的金融机制，即全球环境基金。

3. 一般环境基金：全球环境基金

全球环境基金是一个非条约型一般环境基金的主要例证。[42] 全球环境基金最初是作为一个原型（1991—1994年）设立的，1994年作为一个独立实体设立。[43] 与绿色气候基金一样，我们将重点关注全球环境基金的五个主要架构特征，即（1）决策权；（2）与相关缔约方大会的关系；（3）资金来源；（4）援助的履行；（5）涵盖的费用类型。但是，与其他资金机制相比，全球环境基金的主要特点是其普遍用途，换言之，它涉及若干领域（生物多样性、气候变化、荒漠化、臭氧层耗竭、持久性有机污染物和国际水域）。[44] 全球环境基金是若干环境条约的资金机制，但它的范围更广。正如本节所讨论的，这常常会引发与相应的缔约方大会的摩擦。

首先，关于决策权力，它归属于由32个成员组成的"理事会"（16个来自发展中国家，14个来自发达国家，2个来自转型国家），[45] 通常采取协商一致行动，但当无法达成共识时，通过"双重加权多数"（同意票

---

[40] GCF Instrument, supra footnote 28, para. 45. At the time of writing, there were forty-eight Accredited Entities, more than half of which are international entities (e. g. regional development banks). The list is available at: www.greenclimate.fund/partners/accredited-entities/ae-directory (visited on 15 April 2017).

[41] GCF Instrument, supra footnote 28, para. 35.

[42] See A. S. Miller, "The Global Environmental Facility and the Search for Financial Strategies to Foster Sustainable Development" (1999-2000) 24 Vermont Law Review 1229.

[43] 建立全球环境基金的法律文书此后修订了几次。当前的版本参见"Instrument for the Establishment of the Restructured Global Environment Facility" (October 2011) (GEF Instrument)。

[44] Ibid., para. 2.

[45] Ibid., para. 16.

代表了参加者60%的多数和捐款总数的60%）做决定。[46] 这一制度是捐助国（它们赞成世界银行的加权制度）和发展中国家（它们支持一种平等的方法）利益之间的妥协。

全球环境基金和缔约方大会之间的关系引发了许多难题。这些问题的根源在于发展中国家和发达国家之间的紧张关系，发展中国家（通过缔约方大会）寻求对资金分配更大的控制权，而发达国家尤其是捐助国，则倾向于一种更自主的模式。全球环境基金已与相关条约的秘书处签订了协议（谅解备忘录），随后得到缔约方大会的批准，并作为一项决议的附件。但是，一般而言，各种关系的组织方式相当广泛，缔约方大会有权制定分配资金的一般政策，全球环境基金理事会负责就具体项目作出决定。[47]

其次，关于资金的来源，它们采取参与国向受托人（即世界银行）提供捐助的形式，在四年的"资金补充"期间，首先由参与国承诺捐助一定数额。[48] 从这个角度看，全球环境基金是公共资金的一种形式。迄今为止，全球环境基金已经经历了6个增资期，第7个增资期已于2016年10月启动（第6个增资期将于2018年结束）。全球环境基金自成立至2013年，已向大约3200个与其涉猎领域相关的项目投资约115亿美元。更重要的是来自其他来源，包括私人来源的资金，这些资金是通过全球环境基金活动以杠杆化方式获取的（570亿美元）。这些"混合"活动无疑是调动所需资金以应对大规模环境挑战的最现实的方式之一。正如已经指出的，全球环境基金并不是通过求助于私人基金来发挥其影响力的唯一机制。发展中国家不愿面对私人融资日益增长的作用和推动其运作的市场逻辑，它们认为这种融资来源缺乏足够的可预见性，而且更难管理。这是实用主义与公平之间的普遍紧张关系的又一表现，全球环境治理的许多领域都暗含这种紧张关系。

全球环境基金提供的财政援助是通过"履行机构"执行的。它们主

46　Ibid., para. 25（b）and（c）(i).

47　Ibid., para. 6（a）. See "Strengthening Relations with the Conventions in the GEF Network", 21 April 2011, GEF/C. 40/15.

48　GEF Instrument, supra footnote 43, para. 10.

要包括联合国开发规划署、联合国环境规划署和世界银行,[49] 虽然全球环境基金目前是通过 10 个执行和履行机构来运作的,包括区域发展和合作银行(非洲、亚洲、欧洲和美洲国家间)。

最后,关于全球环境基金的支出类型,它原则上只涵盖在其涉猎领域所采取措施的"议定的增量成本"。[50] 我们在对《蒙特利尔议定书》多边基金的分析中阐述了这一概念,这一概念在该基金中首次出现。这一原则的一个例外涉及"议定的所有成本",事关履行《联合国气候变化框架公约》第 12 条第 1 款规定的程序义务,该义务也可由全球环境基金承担。[51]

正如前面的讨论所指出的,全球环境基金与最近的绿色气候基金之间有许多共同特征。后者的结构的确是基于前者的经验。然而,在资源调动、与私营部门的互动以及所涵盖成本的性质方面,绿色气候基金有望超越全球环境基金。相反,绿色气候基金的权力仅限于气候变化,尽管绿色气候基金文书对这一领域的定义广泛地涵盖了它与其他领域的相互作用,如生物多样性保护,特别是涉及减少森林砍伐的项目(所谓的 REDD-plus)。[52] 更重要的是,绿色气候基金是一个全新的工具,它还有大把机会得到证明,而全球环境基金已经有了 25 年的经验,并且已经为环境保护项目输送了数百亿美元的资金。

4. 混合机制:原型碳汇基金

1999 年在世界银行支持下建立的原型碳汇基金(PCF)是一种值得关注的资金机制。[53] 尽管原型碳汇基金筹集的资金相对较少(不到 2 亿美元),但这一机制作为一项制度实验还是很有意义的。其目的是促进将公共和私人资金(例如由 Electrabel 公司或三菱商事株式会社提供)用于清洁发展机制(CDM)和联合履约机制(JI)(这两个机制是由《京都议定

---

49 Ibid., para. 22.

50 Ibid., para. 2.

51 Ibid., para. 6 (a) *in fine*.

52 GCF Instrument, supra footnote 28, para. 35.

53 IBRD, " Amended and Restated Instrument Establishing the Prototype Carbon Fund ", Resolution No. 99-101 (PCF Instrument). See D. Freestone, " The World Bank's Prototype Carbon Fund: Mobilising new Resources for Sustainable Development ", in S. Schemmer-Schulte and K. Y. Tung (eds.) *Liber Amicorum Ibrahim S. I. Shihata* (The Hague: Kluwer, 2001), pp. 265-341.

书》设立的）的规则所构建的减排项目。[54]

尽管自《京都议定书》第一承诺期（包括"真正行动"）结束以来，清洁发展机制和联合履约机制失去了吸引力，但原型碳汇基金的经验不仅是有用的环境资金来源，而且是进一步发展这类机制的试验场。除了原型碳汇基金积累的项目管理专业知识外，无论是公共还是私人投资者都可以获得减排单位，这些单位可以用来履行其在该领域的义务或在排放权市场上出售。

尽管近年来碳交易遇到了严重的困难，特别是由于全球经济危机（随之而来的排放权供应过剩）和《京都议定书》的前途未卜（尽管制定了仍未批准的第二承诺期，到2020年可能将不再履行可量化的排放目标），但是绝对不能低估原型碳汇基金的贡献。除此之外，它还促进了国内层面类似机制的发展，[55] 并可以充当其他国际混合融资倡议的榜样。

（二）技术援助

技术援助与财政援助密切相关。通常，财政援助的目的是资助技术援助，而技术援助的形式则包括能力建设（人员培训、提供专家或设备、发展基础设施和管理能力）[56] 或向发展中国家转让技术（向接受国公共或私人部门转让知识产权或技术）。[57] 这两类技术援助的定义存在一些重叠。举例说明，《21世纪议程》第37章说，"技术合作，包括与技术转让和专门知识有关的技术合作，涉及旨在发展或增强个人和集体能量与能力的各种各样的活动。"[58] 同样，《21世纪议程》关于"环境友好型技术"转让的第34章一再提到必须加强发展中国家的技术和体制能力。[59]

但是，在实践中，这两种形式的技术援助有其独特的特点，这些特点

54　Kyoto Protocol to the UN Framework Convention on Climate Change, 11 December 1997, 2302 UNTS 148 (Kyoto Protocol). See Chapter 5.

55　World Bank, *Annual Report. Carbon Finance for Sustainable Development* (2010), pp. 23–77.

56　See Action 21, supra footnote 5, Chapter 37. More generally, see D. Ponce-Nava, "Capacity-Building in Environmental Law and Sustainable Development", in W. Lang (ed.), *Sustainable Development and International Law* (London: Springer, 1995), pp. 131–136.

57　See Action 21, supra footnote 5, Chapter 34. See also L. Gündling, "Compliance Assistance in International Environmental Law: Capacity-Building, Transfer of Finance and Technology" (1996) 56 *Zeitschrift für ausländisches öffentliches Recht und Völkerrecht* 796.

58　Action 21, supra footnote 5, para. 37.2.

59　Ibid., paras. 34.8, 34.14 (d), 34.20, 34.22 and 34.26 (b).

对于了解技术援助在环境条约结构中的地位是很重要的。能力建设是环境条约最初设想的技术援助类型。世界遗产基金就是一个很好的例证。[60] 我们发现，设立这一基金是为了帮助缔约国确定有突出价值的遗迹，准备申请把它们列入世界遗产名录，并采取措施保护它们，特别是当它们受到自然灾害或武装冲突等情况的威胁时。这类技术援助可与《蒙特利尔议定书》所设想的并由其多边基金资助的某些形式的援助加以区别。如前所述，[61] 1990 年修订了《蒙特利尔议定书》以吸引一些发展中国家。《伦敦修正案》创立了多边基金，但也引入了一项关于"技术转让"的规定（第 10 条 A 款）。为了了解修正案的范围，不仅是关于臭氧制度，而且更广泛地说，关于国际环境法中的技术转让问题，回顾《蒙特利尔议定书》谈判的一些方面是有益的。

《伦敦修正案》促使某些国家（如中国和印度）加入了《蒙特利尔议定书》的体系。这些国家（根据第 5 条第 1 款）承担了消除受规制物质的生产和消费的义务，这些义务与发达国家的义务大致相同（主要区别是适用于每一组的时间期限）。作为对这一承诺的交换，发达国家同意支付发展中国家为履行其义务而产生的"议定的增量成本"。[62] 但这笔交易不仅仅是资金问题。我们在第五章中研究了《蒙特利尔议定书》的谈判背景，特别是研究了寻求受规制物质的替代品所引发的对国际竞争力的考量。在这样一个背景下，承诺不再生产/消费某些物质，从工业的角度看这是重要的，对没有替代品的国家则是个不现实的选择，除非：（1）给予它们足够的时间以逐步转换工业基础设施；（2）为它们提供财政援助；（3）在合理条件下转让知识产权（IPRs）和有关替代品的专门知识。这三方面的考量非常有助于理解《伦敦修正案》所规定的技术转让条款（第 10 条第 1 款）的内容：

> 各缔约方应采取一切切实可行的步骤，并与资金机制所支持的方案保持一致，以确保：
> （1）迅速向适用于第 5 条第 1 款的缔约方转让最佳可得的、环

---

60 See supra section 9.1.2.2.
61 See supra section 9.1.2.2.
62 Lndicative list of Agreed Incremental Costs, supra footnote 23.

境安全的替代品和有关技术；

(2)(1)款所提及的转让是在公平和最有利的条件下进行的。

换言之，与能力建设不同，技术转让在实践中涉及知识产权和专门知识保护等重要问题，从而影响国际竞争力。这些问题不仅涉及转让的资金筹措，更基本的是，还涉及技术的提供。知识产权持有者可以限制某些技术的使用（拒绝授予许可），以防止其他（实际或潜在的）公司开发竞争产品。这个问题实际上产生于印度和韩国的工业，它们无法获取许可证（即使付费也不行）来生产《蒙特利尔议定书》规制物质的替代品。[63] 这种拒绝意味着必须从专利持有者手中购买替代产品。多边基金可以支付进口替代品的费用，但这不是一个令人满意的解决问题的办法，因为这种援助取决于是否有足够的资金。此外，还有一个循环性的问题，即资金"援助"正被用于支付设在捐赠国的公司的产品。这个案例阐释了技术转让所引发的一些具体问题。

知识产权和国际环境法之间的相互作用将在第十二章中进行更详细的讨论。就目前而言，就技术援助得出一些一般性结论就足够了。可以对能力建设和技术转让（如本节所述）作出区分。第二类援助提出了竞争力和知识产权保护的具体问题。我们在《蒙特利尔议定书》的背景下阐述了这种差异，但在其他背景下也出现了类似的问题，如应对气候变化[64]和持久性有机污染物的管控。[65] 印度和中国的情况也凸显了发达国家（通常支持知识产权持有者）和发展中国家（技术接受者）之间的紧张关系。这种紧张关系在法律术语中反映为技术转让所设想的"形式"。[66] 发达国

---

[63] See UNDP, *Rapport Sur le Développement Humain* 2001（Brussels: DeBoeck Université, 2001）, p. 109.

[64] See K. E. Maskus, "Differentiated Intellectual Property Regimes for Environmental and Climate Technologies"（2010）No. 17 *OECD Environment Working Papers*.

[65] See "Endosulfan ban call inspired by European interests", 29 April 2011, available at: www.news.agropages.com（visited on 4 April 2017）.

[66] The three "forms" traditionally identified in economics, namely trade, licensing and foreign direct investment, have very different political and legal implications. On the economic approach, see W. Keller, "International Technology Diffusion"（2004）42 *Journal of Economic Literature* 752.

家倾向于对这类环保产品征收较低的关税[67]（即产品替代品的进口），而发展中国家则强调需要以优惠的条件进行真正的技术转让，包括相关的专有技术。在这两个极端之间，法律学者必须找到中间的解决方案来满足双方的正当要求。这是一项严格法律上的研究，对国际环境法的有效性具有相当重要的意义。

有人可能会问，在这种情况下有哪些手段可以用来应对这种权衡？有几种可能，从知识产权强制许可证的发放[68]、发展具体机制的实施[69]到技术共享[70]，特别是通过创造知识产权的"市场"。[71] 2010 年，在坎昆举行的《联合国气候变化框架公约》缔约方大会试图建立一个创新性的工具。在这次会议上，"技术机制"（Technology Mechanism）的产生建立在两个机构支柱的基础之上，即一个"技术执行委员会"（Technology Executive Committee）和一个"气候技术中心和网络"（Climate Technology Centre and Network）。[72] 委员会的职能主要是为技术转让政策提供指导，而中心的重点则是执行。该中心目前由政府间组织（包括联合国环境规划署和联合国工业发展组织）、非政府组织和私营组织组成的财团管理。该中心的主要目的是分享信息和专门知识，但目前避免具体提及知识产权的管理。值得注意的是，它强调鼓励企业家精神，"北方"和"南方"组织之间的伙伴关系以及外国直接投资。这种形式的投资可能是保护知识产权

---

67 See OECD, *Policy Brief*: *Opening Markets for Environmental Goods and Services* (Paris: OECD, 2005); R. Steenblink and J. A. Kim, "Facilitating Trade in Selected Climate Change Mitigation Technologies in the Energy Supply, Buildings, and Industry Sectors", *OECD Trade and Environment Working Paper*, No. 2009-02 (4 May 2009).

68 See C. Correa, "Innovation and Technology Transfer of Environmentally Sound Technologies: The Need to Engage in a Substantive Debate" (2013) 22 *Review of European, Comparative and International Environmental Law* 54, at 60.

69 See L. Diaz Anadon, "Missions-oriented RD&D Institutions in Energy between 2000 and 2010: A Comparative Analysis of China, the United Kingdom, and the United States" (2012) 41 *Research Policy* 1742.

70 See Correa, supra footnote 68.

71 A. H. B. Monk, "The Emerging Market for Intellectual Property: Drivers, Restrainers, and Implications" (2009) 9 *Journal of Economic Geography* 469.

72 "The Cancun Agreements: Outcome of the Work of the Ad Hoc Working Group on Long-term Cooperative Action under the Convention", Decision 1/CP.16, 15 March 2011, Doc. FCCC/CP/2010/7/Add.1, paras. 117-127.

（仍然掌握在投资者手中）和发展中国家寻求的国家基础设施发展之间的一种很好的妥协，但它确实存在一些问题，这些问题将在第十二章中讨论。《巴黎协定》依托《联合国气候变化框架公约》建立的这一机制，进一步增加了"技术框架"，旨在为技术机制的运行提供指导。[73]

三 以效率为导向的手段

技术寻求效率收益，例如《京都议定书》所引入的市场机制，其已在第五章中进行了研究。在此，只要回顾一下为什么它们减少了遵守国际环境义务的成本就够了。

我们在第五章中看到，《京都议定书》以排放交易（第17条）和基于项目的机制［联合履行机制（第6条）和清洁发展机制第（12条）］的形式建立许多"灵活机制"。这些机制有几个优点。从援助的角度看，它们有助于将资金用于环境项目，与"按部就班"（Business As Usua，BAU）模式相比，它们在特定情况下还有助于转让某些减排技术。重要的是，它们还可以在发达国家产生效率收益。像在瑞士和德国等国的生产过程已经采用了现代技术，其实现更多减排的成本可能远远高于那些仍在广泛采用"更脏"技术的国家。因此，从成本/效益的角度来看，在瑞士或德国等国寻求减少排放的效率可能不如在中国或墨西哥等提升幅度更大的国家。这一点很重要，因为无论二氧化碳的排放是来自瑞士还是中国，它们对全球气候系统的影响都是一样的。在这种情况下，那些允许瑞士等国家通过在成本较低的国家（如中国）（直接或间接）实现减排来履行其义务的机制，显然会产生效率收益。这是通过市场机制寻求效率的合理性所在。[74]

然而，这种方法也有其缺点。主要问题与错误的信息有关，它可传达给发达的经济运营商，即在自己的生产过程（例如，通过改变其技术甚至调整他们的活动）不需要产生额外的减排，因为他们可以以更低的成本抵消在发展中国家的排放。正因为如此，根据《京都议定书》，这种"国际措施"的使用被限制不得超出量化承诺所要求的减排的一定百分

73　Paris Agreement, supra footnote 31, Art. 10 (3) - (4).

74　关于市场机制在环境法中的使用，see J. Freeman and C. Kolstad (eds.), *Moving to Markets in Environmental Regulation. Lessons from Thirty Years of Experience* (Oxford University Press, 2006).

比。在欧盟和国内层面（例如在瑞士这样的非成员国），也采取了一种类似但更为慷慨的做法。因此，必须在合理的范围内使用效率手段，以避免损害大多数环境保护文书的核心信息：降低污染水平的必要性。

第三节 管理不遵约的手段

一 不遵约程序

不遵约程序（NCPs）在环境条约的履行上发挥着非常重要的作用。[75] 通过提供资金或技术援助或采取一系列制裁，它们的主要目标是确保条约义务遵守的程度能够令人满意。下面几节将分析不遵约程序的主要组成部分。在这里，我们提供了一些关于其历史起源的背景、方法及其主要法律特征。

关于第一个元素，就像许多其他的法律创新，不遵约程序的起源可以在《蒙特利尔议定书》中找到，具体体现于第 8 条，它规定"缔约国应在其第一次会议上审议并通过据以裁定不遵守本议定书规定的情事和处理被查明不遵守规定的缔约国的程序及体制机构"。这一规定是建立第一个现代不遵约程序的基础，这一模式对《蒙特利尔议定书》之后制定的条约以及后来建立不遵约程序的一些较老的文书产生了重大影响。

正是这一模型定义了不遵约程序所蕴藏的一般遵约方法。我们已经在第二章中提到了这种方法。它的两个主要特点是程序的非对抗性和对环境损害预防的重视。这两个特征是密切相关的。某个国家不遵守一项国际义务可能不是因为缺乏遵约的意愿，而是因为某些技术或财政困难。在这种情形之下，不遵约程序的目的是帮助有关国家恢复遵约的状态，或至少将不遵约的状态保持在合理的范围内。不遵约程序这样做的目的是防止或减

---

[75] On these procedures, see T. Treves et al. (eds.), *Non-Compliance Procedures and Mechanisms and the Effectiveness of International Environmental Agreements* (The Hague: TMC Asser Press, 2009); S. Urbinati, *Les mécanismes de contrôle et de suivi des conventions internationales de protection de l'environnement* (Milan: Giuffrè, 2009).

轻不遵守规定所造成的环境损害，同时又不使有关国家蒙羞。[76] 如果由于国家不愿意遵约而造成违约，不遵约程序就可以转变成类似司法程序的程序，导致一个不遵约的调查结果甚至制裁。但是，总的来说，不遵约程序所蕴藏的遵约方法显然侧重于预防和援助。

就不遵约程序的主要法律特征而言，它们可以分为四个标题：（1）其法律依据；（2）获授权启动不遵约程序的各缔约方；（3）遵约委员会的组成；（4）可采取的措施。[77]

图9-3对这些特征提供了一个概述，并引用了来自具体不遵约程序（《蒙特利尔议定书》[78]《京都议定书》[79]《卡塔赫纳议定书》[80]《奥胡斯公约》[81]《拉姆萨公约》[82]《巴塞尔公约》[83]《濒危野生动植物种国际贸易公约》[84]《阿尔卑斯公约》[85]《水与健康议定书》[86]）的一些案例。下面我们依次分析这些特征。

---

[76] See M. Koskenniemi, "Breach of Treaty or Non-Compliance? Reflections on the Enforcement of the Montreal Protocol" (1992) 3 *Yearbook of International Environmental Law* 123.

[77] See Viñuales, supra footnote 3, pp. 335-338.

[78] "Non-compliance Procedure", Decision IV/5, 25 November 1992, UNEP/OzL. Pro4/15, Annex IV (Report of the Parties) as subsequently amended (Montreal NCP).

[79] "Procedure and Mechanisms relating to Compliance under the Kyoto Protocol", Decision 27/CMP.I, 30 March 2006, FCCC/KP/CMP/2005/8/Add. 3, Annex (Kyoto NCP).

[80] "Establishment of Procedures and Mechanisms on Compliance under the Cartagena Protocol on Biosafety", Decision BS-I/7, 27 February 2004, UNEP/CBD/BS/COP-MOP/1/15, Annex I (Cartagena NCP).

[81] "Review of Compliance", Decision I/7, 2 April 2004, ECE/MP. PP/2/Add. 8, Annex, (Aarhus NCP).

[82] "Mechanisms for Improved Application of the Ramsar Convention", Recommendation REC. C. 4. 7 (Rev) (Ramsar NCP) Annex I.

[83] "Establishment of a Mechanism for Promoting Implementation and Compliance", Decision VI/12, 10 February 2003, UNEP/CHW. 6/40 (2003), Annex, as amended by COP. 10 (Basel NCP).

[84] "CITES Compliance Procedures", Resolution Conf. 14. 3, June 2007, Annex (CITES NCP).

[85] "Mechanism for the Verification of the Compliance with the Alpine Convention and its Implementation Protocols (Compliance Procedure)", Decision XII/I, 7 September 2012, ACXII/A1/1, Annex (Alpine NCP).

[86] "Review of Compliance", Decision I/2, 3 July 2007, ECE/MP. WH/2/Add. 3, EUR/06/5069385/1/ Add. 3 (PWH NCP).

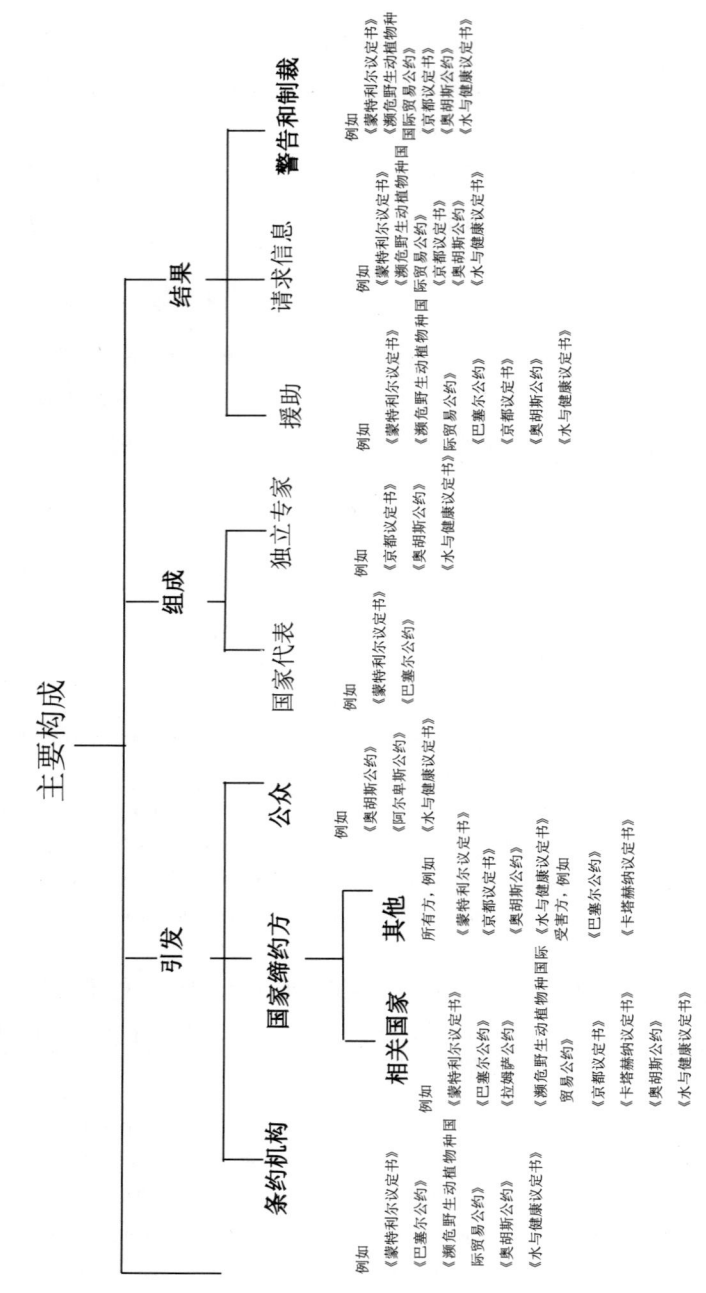

图 9-3 部分不遵约程序（NCPs）概述

二 不遵约程序的法律依据及其影响

一般来说，不遵约程序是基于一项具体的条约条款。《蒙特利尔议定书》通过后所缔结的许多条约都是如此。举例来讲，除该议定书第 8 条外，还包括《京都议定书》第 18 条、《生物安全议定书》(*Biosafety Protocol*) 第 34 条、[87]《奥胡斯公约》第 15 条、[88]《水与健康议定书》(*Protocol on Water and Health*) 第 15 条[89]等。这些条款随后由条约机构［最常见的是缔约方大会（COPs）或适用于议定书的缔约方会议（MOPs）］通过的一系列决议加以明确细化。其他一些条约在没有明确法律基础的情况下，也建立了不遵约程序。这些例证包括《拉姆萨公约》《濒危野生动植物种国际贸易公约》[90]和《巴塞尔公约》建立的程序。这种差异主要是由每个条约制定时间的不同造成的。《蒙特利尔议定书》之后制定的条约（虽然不总是这样，例如《巴塞尔公约》）一般都会包含一个关于建立不遵约程序的具体规定，而以前的文书则是通过缔约方大会的决议来进行更新。

这一差别并非没有法律意义，因为条约中法律基础的存在可能对确定程序的性质很重要，特别是用于判断不遵约程序所形成的决议是否具有约束力。这是一个复杂的问题，尽管具有现实意义，但尚未得到解决。要解决这个问题，必须区分三个层次。

首先，必须根据条约的具体内容来分析其约束力。在这个层次上，条约中某项条款的存在是特别重要的。例如，《京都议定书》第 18 条规定，涉及遵守的决定可能具有约束力，但只有通过修订案建立了不遵约程序（即有关国家已经批准）的情况下才有约束力。相反，如果没有这样的修正案，这些决定在技术上是没有约束力的。相反，基础条约也可明文规定

---

[87] Cartagena Protocol on Biosafety to the Convention on Biological Diversity, 29 January 2000, 2226 UNTS 208（Biosafety Protocol）.

[88] Convention on Access to Information, Public Participation in Decision-making and Access to Justice in Environmental Matters, 25 June 1998, 2161 UNTS 447（Aarhus Convention）.

[89] Protocol on Water and Health to the 1992 Convention on the Protection and Use of Transboundary Watercourses and International Lakes, 17 June 1999, 2331 UNTS 202（Protocol on Water and Health）.

[90] Washington Convention on International Trade in Endangered Species of Wild Fauna and Flora, 3 March 1973, United Nations, 993 UNTS 243（CITES）.

不遵约程序的可选性和协商性，从而规定不遵约程序所通过的决议的可选性和协商性。这就是《奥胡斯公约》第 15 条的情况。在其他情况下，如《蒙特利尔议定书》第 8 条或《生物安全议定书》第 34 条，条约对涉及遵约的决议是否具有约束力不置可否，这就导致了第二个层次。

在这种情况下，必须根据条约机构的一般权力，特别是缔约方大会（缔约方会议）的权力，来分析这些决议的法律性质。一些条约授权缔约方会议制定有约束力的决议。《蒙特利尔议定书》第 2 条第 9 款或《生物安全议定书》第 7 条第 4 款就是此种情况。[91] 这些条款的存在表明，事实上，缔约方会议在某些情况下有权作出有约束力的决议（因此它可以将这项权力下放）。但是，这些条款通常是为了将这种权力限制于特定类型的决议中，不一定涵盖那些涉及不遵约的决议。无论如何，如果条约不允许缔约方大会或缔约方会议制定有约束力的决议，那么不遵约程序就更没有资格来这样做了。然而，这一结论并不意味着这些决议在实践中不具有规范性作用。

在第三个层次上，重要的是要确定不遵约程序形成的决定是否受到尊重，或者它们至少是否具有某种权威性。[92] 这一问题因《京都议定书》项下希腊等国家的情势有关。[93] 遵约委员会认为希腊没有履行《京都议定书》第 5 条第 1 款和第 7 款规定的义务，并且认为希腊（将）处于不遵约的状态。在此基础上，它要求希腊"根据第 15 节第 1 款制订计划并在三个月内提交"；重要的是，同时还决定在履行问题解决方案确定期间，希腊没有资格参与议定书第 6 条、第 12 条和第 17 条规定的机制。[94] 后来，在完全没有明确委员会决议的约束性质的情况下，对希腊的中止被取消了。[95] 这个案例经常被引用来强调不遵约程序决议在实践中的权威性。在

---

[91] J. Brunnée, " COPing with Consent: Law – making under Multilateral Environmental Agreements" (2002) 15 *Leiden Journal of International Law* 1, 21-23.

[92] Ibid., 23ff.

[93] Compliance Committee, Final Decision: Greece, 17 April 2008, CC-2007-1-8/Greece/EB (Decision-Greece). See also Compliance Committee, *Final Decision: Croatia*, 19 February 2010, CC-2009-1-8/Croatia/EB.

[94] Ibid., Annex, para. 18.

[95] Compliance Committee, Final Decision: Greece, 13 November 2008, CC-2007-1-13/Greece/EB.

可以用来说明这一点的众多例证中，[96] 由《奥胡斯公约》遵约委员会通过的决议是特别恰当的。虽然公约第 15 条明确规定，涉及遵守的决议没有约束力，但它们在实践中所显示的规范性力量几乎是不容置疑的。缔约方会议根据委员会的决议向各缔约国提出的建议，实际上在很大程度上得到了遵守。[97]

三 不遵约程序的启动

不遵约程序的一个特点可以凸显它的非对抗性本质，这一特点就是不遵约程序的启动方式。与司法程序不同的是，不遵约程序可以由不遵守条约的国家启动。[98] 正如后文所述，自我启动与申请财政和/或技术援助的可能性有关。除不遵约国家启动外，不遵约程序还可根据情况由其他缔约国、某些条约机构、公众或委员会主动启动。

某些不遵约程序可以由其他缔约国启动，而不需要它们证明自身受到了特别的影响。[99] 在这里，我们采用了"所有当事方间的集体诉讼"（actio popularis inter omnes partes）这一概念（对应的是一般国际法尚未明确承认的集体诉讼[100]）。这种可能性是基于条约所保护对象的性质（例如臭氧层、气候系统、濒危物种、环境事项的某种程度的透明度、水体的质

---

96 See M. Fitzmaurice, "Non-Compliance Procedures and the Law of Treaties", in Treves et al., supra footnote 75, pp. 453–481.

97 See A. Andrusevych, T. Alge and C. Konrad (eds.), *Case Law of the Aarhus Convention Compliance Committee (2004–2011)* (Lviv: RACSE, 2nd edn, 2011), in particular Part III synthesising the "outcomes" of the actions taken by States to respond to the recommendations of the COP (made on the basis of those of the Committee). 遗憾的是，该书的第三版不再提及这些结果，参见 A. Andrusevych and S. Kern (eds.), *Case Law of the Aarhus Convention Compliance Committee (2004–2014)* (Lviv: RACSE, 3rd edn, 2016).

98 See, e.g., Montreal NCP, supra footnote 79, para. 44; Basel NCP, supra footnote 83, para. 9 (a); Ramsar NCP, supra footnote 82, para. 1; CITES NCP, supra footnote 83, para. 19; Kyoto NCP, supra footnote 79, para. VI. 1 (a); Cartagena NCP, supra footnote 80, para. IV. 1 (a); Aarhus NCP, supra footnote 81, para. 16.

99 See, e.g., Montreal NCP, supra footnote 78, para. 1; NCP Kyoto, supra footnote 79, para. VI. 1 (b); CITES NCP, supra footnote 84, para. 18; Aarhus NCP, supra footnote 81, para. 15; PWH NCP, supra footnote 86, para. 14.

100 See F. Voeffray, *L'actio popularis ou la défense de l'intérêt collectif devant les juridictions internationales* (Paris: Presse Universitaires de France, 2004).

量)。缔约国的不遵约很可能影响条约所保护的共同利益,从而影响所有其他缔约国的利益。当条约的目的不是保护一种共有资源(例如跨界环境保护)时,不遵约程序通常只向具体受影响的国家提供启动程序的权利。[101]

某些条约机构(例如秘书处)在下列情况下会被给予启动程序的机会,包括当不遵守具体义务(例如程序义务[102])发生时,或是涉及更广义的、不加区别的所有条约义务时。[103] 这种启动方式有几个优点。首先,各条约机构将关于条约执行情况的资料集中起来,因此处于发现不遵约情况的理想地位。其次,条约机构的启动避免了缔约国之间的对抗,同时在管理不遵约方面又可以实现类似的结果。最后,条约机构可以非正式地转达民间社会团体的关切,这些团体通常不被允许发起不遵约程序。然而,实际上,这种权力很少被使用,因为中立的秘书处宁愿避免对缔约国采取行动。

后一点将我们引向了启动机制的第三种形式,即公众提起。这种可能性只在区域性质的环境条约中有规定,如《阿尔卑斯公约》(*Alpine Convention*)[104]、《奥胡斯公约》[105] 或《水与健康议定书》。[106] 正是由于这种启动机制,《奥胡斯公约》遵约委员会才得以发展出关于"环境民主"这一重要的"法理学"体系。事实上,委员会收到的大多数通报是来自民间社会团体。请注意,没有必要对使用这种方式表现出特别的兴趣。有关诉讼资格(locus standi)和可受理性的规则为非政府公益组织提出通报创造了条件,它们有助于遵守公约所订定的环境透明度标准。[107] 这同样适用于《水与健康议定书》,尽管诉诸遵约委员会的通报实践才刚刚开始。

最后,在该议定书的范围内,遵约委员会基于对其授权地位的解释

---

[101] See, e.g., Basel NCP, supra footnote 83, para. 9 (b); Cartagena NCP, supra footnote 80, para. IV. 1 (b).

[102] See, e.g., Basel NCP, supra footnote 83, para. 9 (c).

[103] See, e.g., Montreal NCP, supra footnote 78, para. 3; PWH NCP, supra footnote 86, para. 15.

[104] Alpine NCP, supra footnote 85, para. 2.

[105] Aarhus NCP, supra footnote 81, para. 18.

[106] PWH NCP, supra footnote 86, para. 16.

[107] See Andrusevych et al. (2011), supra footnote 97, pp. 102ff.

（这一解释后来得到了缔约方会议的认可），有可能在某些特定条件下自行采取行动。[108] 这是一种特殊情况，发生的原因可能是各国一方面关注连通水体的共同保护，另一方面它们又不愿通过提交针对其他缔约方的意见书来追求议定书的履行。它使得《水与健康议定书》的不遵约程序成为遵约委员会在权限内处理不遵约状况的最先进的工具。

四　不遵约程序机构的组成

不遵约程序机构的组成具有一定的现实意义。可以从几个角度来考虑这个问题，这取决于是否对成员的地域分配（如环境基金）、提名程序或成员的行动能力感兴趣。一般来说，我们会区分由国家代表组成的机构和由独立专家组成的机构。然而，提名程序可能在某种程度上模糊了这两个类别，因为各国可以选择独立的专家。此外，国家代表有时可以表现出一定的独立性。但为了理解实践中的不遵约程序，对其进行区分仍然是非常有益处的，因为国家对独立专家（他们一旦获得任命就会在规定的任期内继续任职）的影响比国家对国家代表（这些代表被要求时刻代表国家行事）的影响要小得多。

《蒙特利尔议定书》不遵约程序由一个机构（遵约委员会）负责管理，该机构由缔约方会议选出的 10 名国家代表组成，任期两年，按照公平地域原则进行分配。[109] 这同样适用于其他遵约委员会，例如根据《远程越界空气污染公约》(LRTAP Convention)[110] 和《埃斯波公约》(Espoo Convention)[111] 建立的遵约委员会。在另一个极端，《京都议定书》的不遵约程序是由一个复杂的机构（也是一个遵约委员会）管理的，该机构的 20

---

[108]　PWH NCP, supra footnote 86, paras. 11 and 12, read in the light of the Report to the Compliance Committee to the Meeting of the Parties, 5 September 2016, ECE/MP.WH/ 2016/5 - EUPCR/1611921/2.1/2016/MOP-4/11, paras. 27-35, and the Decision on the Competence of the Committee to address cases of non-compliance by specific Parties, Report of the Meeting of the Parties on its fourth session, 14-16 November 2016, ECE/MP.WH/13-EUPCR/1611921/2.1/2016/MOP-4/06.

[109]　Montreal NCP, supra footnote 78, para. 5.

[110]　Convention on Long-range Transboundary Air Pollution, 13 November 1979, 1302 UNTS 217 (LRTAP Convention).

[111]　Convention on Environmental Impact Assessment in a Transboundary Context, 25 February 1991, 1989 UNTS 309 (Espoo Convention).

名专家由缔约方大会选举,并以独立身份行事。[112] 委员会举行全体会议(20 名成员),但也有两个分支(每个分支有 10 名成员),称为"促进分支"(其目的是提供援助)和"执行分支"(定性不遵约的状态并实施制裁)。成员的选择还必须虑到地域代表性以及技术专长。[113]《奥胡斯公约》遵约委员会由独立专家组成。它有 8 名以个人身份和提供无偿服务(pro bono)的成员,他们是公认的专家,包括法律事务方面的专家。[114] 同样,《水与健康议定书》的遵约委员会由 9 名独立专家组成,由缔约方会议根据某个国家的建议任命,并在特定期间内提供公益服务。[115] 在这两个极端之间,可发现其他机构,例如根据《巴塞尔公约》设立的遵约委员会,其成员实际上是各国代表,虽然在设立不遵约程序的文书中可能没有明确说明这一点。[116]

负责管理不遵约程序的机构的成员构成可以解释这些程序是如何运作的。除了独立问题(它可能由个人考量和机构的体制所推动),成员构成还有助于了解各机构倾向的(技术上或政治上的)不同方法。评论员观察到,采用更具政治性的方法则冒着使遵约变得"可协商"的风险。[117] 然而,不遵约程序的政治维度也可被视为其运作的一个必要特征,因为它们的主要目的是管理不遵约,而不是确定定性违约和决定后续法律后果。

五 不遵约程序采取的措施

我们早些时候看到,不遵约程序所通过决定的法律性质仍然没有得到解决。然而,我们也注意到它们在实践中具有重要的规范性影响。我们现在必须通过对遵约委员会可以采取的各种措施的调查来完成分析。

不遵约程序的主要目标是确定不遵约的理由,并提供资金和技术援助。这反映在它们有权采取的措施中。例如,根据《京都议定书》设立的委员会"促进分支"可以归纳为"提供建议和促进援助"或"促进资

112　Kyoto NCP, supra footnote 79, para. II (3) and (6).
113　Ibid., paras. II (6), IV (1) and V (1).
114　Aarhus NCP, supra footnote 81, para. I (1) – (2).
115　PWH NCP, supra footnote 86, paras. 4-7.
116　See Urbinati, supra footnote 75, pp. 58-59.
117　See G. Handl, "Compliance Control Mechanisms and International Environmental Obligations" (1997) 9 *Tulane Journal of International and Comparative Law* 29, 37.

金和技术援助，包括技术转让和能力建设"。[118] 这同样适用于管理不遵约程序的所有其他委员会。但是，具体到某一不遵约案件的成因分析，也可能导致采取更强硬的立场，包括采取制裁措施。这些措施可以是简单地要求提供更多的信息，[119] 也可以是发出警告[120]或发布不遵约的调查结果，[121] 甚至是采取真正的制裁，例如根据有关条约暂停某些好处或实施惩罚。[122] 重要的是，《水与健康议定书》的遵约委员会可以采取具体的补救措施以及其他具体措施来处理不遵约的情况。[123]

从非对抗性方法过渡到一个更接近国际环境法履行的传统方法（如第八章所述）的逻辑，体现了从促进性措施向更强有力措施的转变。

部分参考文献

[1] Andrusevych, A. and S. and C. Kern (eds.), *Case Law of the Aarhus Convention Compliance Committee (2004-2014)* (Lviv: RACSE, 3rd edn, 2016).

[2] Andrusevych, A., T. Alge and C. Konrad (eds.), *Case Law of the Aarhus Convention Compliance Committee (2004-2011)* (Lviv: RACSE, 2nd edn, 2011).

---

118 Kyoto NCP, supra footnote 79, para. XIV.

119 See, e.g., Montreal NCP, supra footnote 78, paras. 3 and 5 (c); Basel NCP, supra footnote 83, para. 22 (a); CITES NCP, supra footnote 84, para. 29 (b); Cartagena NCP, supra footnote 80, para. VI.1 (d); Kyoto NCP, supra footnote 79, para. IX (3); PWH NCP, supra footnote 86, para. 34 (b) - (c).

120 See, e.g., Basel NCP, supra footnote 83, para. 20 (b); CITES NCP, supra footnote 84, para. 29 (c) and (g); Cartagena NCP, supra footnote 80, para. VI.2 (b); Aarhus NCP, supra footnote 81, para. XII.37 (f); PWH NCP, supra footnote 86, para. 34 (d).

121 See, e.g., Montreal NCP, supra footnote 78, para. 9; Kyoto NCP, supra footnote 79, paras. IX (4) (a) and (7) and XV (1) (a); CITES NCP, supra footnote 84, para. 29 (g); Aarhus NCP, supra footnote 81, para. XII.37 (e).

122 See, e.g., Aarhus NCP, supra footnote 81, para. XII.37 (g) (measure adopted by the MOP on the recommendation of the CC); CITES NCP, supra footnote 84, paras. 30 and 34 (the measure is adopted by the Standing Committee which is an inter-State body); Kyoto NCP, supra footnote 79, para. XV (5) (measure adopted by the enforcement branch of the Compliance Committee); PWH NCP, supra footnote 86, para. 35 (f) (measure adopted by the MOP on the recommendation of the CC).

123 PWH NCP, supra footnote 86, para. 34 (e).

［3］Biermann, F., "Financing Environmental Policies in the South: Experiences from the Multilateral Ozone Fund" (1997) 9 *International Environmental Affairs* 179.

［4］Boisson de Chazournes, L., "La mise en œuvre du droit international dans le domaine de la protection de l'environnement: Enjeux et défis" (1995) 99 *Revue Générale de Droit International Public* 37.

"Le Fonds pour l'environnement mondial: Recherche et conquête de son identité" (1995) 41 *Annuaire Français de Droit International* 612.

"Technical and Financial Assistance", in D. Bodansky, J. Brunnée and E. Hey (eds.), *The Oxford Handbook of International Environmental Law* (Oxford University Press, 2007), pp. 948-972.

［5］Brown Weiss, E. and H. K. Jacobson (eds.), *Engaging Countries: Strengthening Compliance with International Environmental Accords* (Cambridge, MA: MIT Press, 1998).

［6］Brunnée, J., "COPing with Consent: Law-making under Multilateral Environmental Agreements" (2002) 15 *Leiden Journal of International Law* 1.

［7］Chayes, A. and A. Handler Chayes, *The New Sovereignty, Compliance with International Regulatory Agreements* (Cambridge, MA: Harvard University Press, 1998).

［8］Correa, C., "Innovation and Technology Transfer of Environmentally Sound Technologies: The Need to Engage in a Substantive Debate" (2013) 22 *Review of European, Comparative and International Law* 54.

［9］Diaz Anadon, L., "Missions-oriented RD&D Institutions in Energy between 2000 and 2010: A Comparative Analysis of China, the United Kingdom, and the United States" (2012) 41 *Research Policy* 1742.

［10］Fitzmaurice, M. and C. Redgwell, "Environmental Non-Compliance Procedures and International Law" (2000) 31 *Netherlands Yearbook of International Law* 35.

［11］Freeman, J. and C. Kolstad (eds.), *Moving to Markets in Environmental Regulation. Lessons from Thirty Years of Experience* (Oxford University Press, 2006).

[12] Freestone, D., "The World Bank's Prototype Carbon Fund: Mobilising New Resources for Sustainable Development", in S. Schemmer-Schulte and K. -Y. Tung (eds.), *Liber Amicorum Ibrahim S. I. Shihata* (The Hague: Kluwer, 2001), pp. 265-341.

"The World Bank and Sustainable Development", in M. Fitzmaurice, D. Ong and P. Merkouris (eds.), *Research Handbook on International Environmental Law* (Cheltenham: Edward Elgar, 2010), pp. 138-160.

[13] Gündling, L., "Compliance Assistance in International Environmental Law: Capacity - Building, Transfer of Finance and Technology" (1996) 56 *Zeitschrift für ausländisches öffentliches Recht und Völkerrecht* 796.

[14] Handl, G., "Compliance Control Mechanisms and International Environmental Obligations" (1997) 9 *Tulane Journal of International and Comparative Law* 29.

[15] Impériali, C. (ed.), *L'effectivité du Droit International de L'environnement. Contrôle de la Mise en œuvre Des Conventions Internationales* (Paris: Economica, 1998).

[16] Keller, W., "International Technology Diffusion" (2004) 42 *Journal of Economic Literature* 752.

[17] Kiss, A., D. Shelton and K. Ishibashi (eds.), *Economic Globalization and Compliance with International Environmental Agreements* (The Hague: Kluwer, 2003).

[18] Kohona, P., "UNCED-The Transfer of Financial Resources to Developing Countries" (1992) 1 *Review of European Community and International Environmental Law* 307.

[19] Koskenniemi, M., "Breach of Treaty or Non-Compliance? Reflections on the Enforcement of the Montreal Protocol" (1992) 3 *Yearbook of International Environmental Law* 123.

[20] Langer, M. -J., "Key Instruments of Private Environmental Finance: Funds, Project Finance and Market Mechanisms", in P. -M. Dupuy and J. E. Viñuales (eds.), *Harnessing Foreign Investment to Promote Environmental Protection: Incentives and Safeguards* (Cambridge University Press, 2013), pp. 131-175.

[21] Lawrence, P., "Technology Transfer Funds and the Law: Recent Amendments to the Montreal Protocol on Substances that Deplete the Ozone Layer" (1992) 4 *Journal of Environmental Law* 15.

[22] Maljean-Dubois, S., "Mécanismes internationaux de suivi et mise en œuvre des conventions internationales de protection de l'environnement" (2004) 9 Analyses 1.

[23] Maskus, K. E., "Differentiated Intellectual Property Regimes for Environmental and Climate Technologies", *OECD Environment Working Papers*, No. 17 (2010).

[24] Miller, A. S., "The Global Environmental Facility and the Search for Financial Strategies to Foster Sustainable Development" (1999–2000) 24 *Vermont Law Review* 1229.

[25] Monk, A. H. B., "The Emerging Market for Intellectual Property: Drivers, Restrainers, and Implications" (2009) 9 *Journal of Economic Geography* 469.

[26] Nanda, N., "Diffusion of Climate Friendly Technologies: Can Compulsory Licensing Help?" (2009) 14 *Journal of Intellectual Property Rights* 241.

[27] Nollkaemper, A., "Compliance Control in International Environmental Law: Traversing the Limits of the National Legal Order" (2002) 13 *Yearbook of International Environmental Law* 165.

[28] Ponce-Nava, D., "Capacity-Building in Environmental Law and Sustainable Development", in W. Lang (ed.), *Sustainable Development and International Law* (London: Springer, 1995), pp. 131–136.

[29] Richardson, B. J., *Socially Responsible Investment Law: Regulating the Unseen Polluters* (Oxford University Press, 2008).

[30] Romanin Jacur, F., *The Dynamics of Multilateral Environmental Agreements. Institutional Architectures and Law-Making Processes* (Naples: Editoriale Scientifica, 2013).

[31] Schalatek, L. and S. Nakhooda, "The Green Climate Fund", in *Climate Finance Fundamentals*, No. 11, November 2012.

[32] Steenblink, R. and J. A. Kim, "Facilitating Trade in Selected Cli-

mate Change Mitigation Technologies in the Energy Supply, Buildings, and Industry Sectors", *OECD Trade and Environment Working Paper*, No. 2009-02 (4 May 2009).

[33] Streck, C., "The Global Environmental Facility-A Role Model for International Environmental Governance?" (2001) 1 *Global Environmental Politics* 71.

[34] Treves, T., L. Pineschi, A. Tanzi, C. Pitea, C. Ragni and F. Romanin Jacur (eds.), *Non-Compliance Procedures and Mechanisms and the Effectiveness of International Environmental Agreements* (The Hague: TMC Asser Press, 2009).

[35] Ulfstein, G. and T. Marauhn (eds.), *Making Treaties Work: Human Rights, Environment and Arms Control* (Cambridge University Press, 2007).

[36] United Nations Environment Programme, *Manual on Compliance with and Enforcement of Multilateral Environmental Agreements* (Nairobi: UNEP, 2006).

[37] Urbinati, S., *Les Mécanismes de Contrôle et de Suivi Des Conventions Internationales de Protection de L'environnement* (Milan: Giuffrè, 2009).

[38] Viñuales, J. E., "Managing Abidance by Standards for the Protection of the Environment", in A. Cassese (ed.), *Realizing Utopia* (Oxford University Press, 2012), pp. 326-339.

[39] Wolfrum, R., P. T. Stoll and U. Beyerlin (eds.), *Ensuring Compliance with Multilateral Environmental Agreements. A Dialogue between Practitioners and Academia* (The Hague: Martinus Nijhoff, 2006).

第四编 作为一种视角的国际环境法

第十章　人权和环境

第一节　导论

环境保护与人权法在许多方面相互影响，二者关系较为复杂，我们在研究二者关系时主要依据的是"协同效应"。尊重人权的一个基本要求是为人们提供一个对身心健康无损害的高质量环境，然而，当今世界许多地区人们的身心健康都受到诸如水污染、空气污染等环境问题的影响。[1] 从法律层面看，这一系列环境问题推动了人权的发展，从而使（由条约和国家宪法规定的）人权及其相关机构（区域性法院、委员会、国内司法机关）开始应对环境法律问题。

本章主要分析两个主要问题：（1）哪些人权可以用于保护环境；（2）保护的范围是什么。这些问题的答案让评论员、倡导团体、决策者、裁判者忙碌了几十年，它还引发了其他许多涉及"环境保护的人权途径"的问题，例如，享有特定质量的环境权利的表述、人权与气候变化之间的联系等。然而，在20多年的研究里，很少有学者注意到本章所要讨论的第三个问题：（3）人权与环境保护之间的潜在冲突。这一遗漏的一个显而易见的例证是，经联合国人权理事会（UN Human Rights Council）提议，人权事务高级专员办事处（Office of the High Commissioner for Human Rights）委托撰写的《关于人权与环境之间关系的分析研究》并未明确提

---

[1] See Yuyu Chen, A. Ebenstein, M. Greenstone and Hongbin Li, "Evidence on the Impact of Sustained Exposure to Air Pollution on Life Expectancy from China's Huai River Policy" (2009) 110 *Proceedings of the National Academy of Sciences* 12936.

及这一冲突。² 这也许只是单纯的疏漏或基于政治立场，但必须强调的是，这种冲突确实存在，³ 且可能随着环境政策的变化而进一步发展。⁴

本章第一节对人权与环境保护在概念上的关系进行了探讨（本章第二节），这一部分的探讨为随后分析二者间的协同效应（本章第三节）以及二者在价值和规范（保护人权的规范和保护环境的规范）上的冲突（本章第四节）提供了一些分析。

第二节 人权与环境保护之间的关系

目前，我们对人权与环境保护之间协同效应的理解可追溯到1972年的斯德哥尔摩人类环境会议。⁵《斯德哥尔摩宣言》（*Stockholm Declaration*）强调了国际法这两个部门之间深刻的协同效应。事实上，第一条原则规定：

> 人类享有自由、平等、舒适的生活条件，有在尊严和舒适的环境中生活的基本权利。⁶

2　Office of the High Commissioner for Human Rights（OHCHR）, Analytical Study on the Relationship between Human Rights and the Environment, 16 December 2011, UN Doc. A/HRC/19/34.

3　这种冲突在其他学科领域受到广泛关注。See R. P. Neumann, *Imposing Wilderness: Struggles over Livelihood and Nature Preservation in Africa*（Berkeley: University of California Press, 1998）; M. Dowie, *Conservation Refugees: The Hundred Years Conflict between Global Conservation and Native Peoples*（Cambridge, MA: MIT Press, 2009）; A. Agrawal and K. Redford, "Conservation and Displacement: An Overview"（2009）7 *Conservation & Society* 1. In international law, growing attention is being paid to such conflicts. See, e.g., M. -C. Petersmann, "Environmental Protection and Human Rights: When Friends Become Foes – Conflict Management of the CJEU", in C. Voigt and L. J. Kotzé（eds.）, *The Environment in International Courts and Tribunals: Questions of Legitimacy*（Cambridge University Press, 2017）; M. -C. Petersmann, "Narcissus Reflected in the Lake: Anthropocentric Environmental Law and Untold Narratives"（2018）30 *Journal of Environmental Law* 1.

4　投资原则（大部分都包含类似于人权的内容，例如不歧视、程序正当、保护私有财产）与环境保护之间的冲突日益加剧。See J. E. Viñuales, *Foreign Investment and the Environment in International Law*（Cambridge University Press, 2012）.

5　See supra Chapter 1.

6　"Declaration of the United Nations Conference on the Human Environment", Stockholm, 16 June 1972, UN Doc. A/CONF 48/14/Rev. 1, pp. 2ff（Stockholm Declaration）. On this prin‑ciple, see L. Sohn, "The Stockholm Declaration on the Human Environment"（1972）14 *Harvard International Law Journal* 423, 451–455.

此后，协同效应的概念深刻影响新出台的国际文书以及司法与准司法机构的裁判文书。可以理解的是，这些国际法部门所保护的价值相互之间紧密相连。但是，这并不是忽视冲突可能性的理由；特别是考虑到，在斯德哥尔摩人类环境会议之前，"保护自然"时常与利用空间和资源以满足人类需求的理念相冲突，建立自然保护区与生活在保护地的土著或部落人民权利的冲突问题，恰好说明了这一点。[7] 我们将在本章第三节中展开讨论。在此只需要指出，自斯德哥尔摩人类环境会议以来，外交用语逐步排除提及冲突，而是重新调整术语的使用，从"自然"转变为"环境"，以强调人类与他们环境[8]之间的协同效应。

当下，协同观深深根植于国际惯例中。人权事务高级专员办事处于2011年发布的《分析研究》[9] 在确定人权与环境保护之间关系的三种"主要方法"（均是协同的）时，就体现了这一理论。

首先，在《斯德哥尔摩宣言》后，人们普遍认为，享有人权的必要条件是拥有舒适的环境。[10] 从人权的视角来看，这一观点意味着，环境保护只是在促使人们尊重人权方面体现出一种工具价值。反之，环境本身的保护（无论是否有助于保护人权）就可能是开放性的。

这种模糊性对《分析研究》确定的第二种方法具有重要意义，即人权作为一种保护环境的法律手段的工具性价值[11]。这种方法主要基于三重考量。第一，人权的权利主体广泛，且可以被具体确定（个人），而环境的保护并无明确的"权利主体"。[12] 第二，如此众多且可以明确的人权权利主体可以向越来越多的司法或准司法机构（区域性法院、委员会等）

7　See supra footnote 3.

8　See P.-M. Dupuy, "International Environmental Law: Looking at the Past to Shape the Future", in P.-M. Dupuy and J. E. Viñuales (eds.), *Harnessing Foreign Investment to Promote Environmental Protection: Incentives and Safeguards* (Cambridge University Press, 2013), p. 9.

9　OHCHR Analytical Study, supra footnote 2.

10　Ibid., para. 7.

11　Ibid., para. 8.

12　这就是国际法研究院提议设立在责任和赔偿责任方面代表国际社会的"环境事务高级专员"的原因。See "Responsibility and Liability under International Law for Environmental Damage" (1997) *Annuaire de l'IDI* (Session of Strasbourg), Art. 28.

提起诉求,而这些机构比国际环境法中的机构更为复杂。[13] 第三,人权被认为具有更高的价值,因此,它们拥有比单纯的环境考量更为强大的社会和政治吸引力。[14] 然而,因为这些驱动力的性质,通过人权来实现的环境保护的程度具有很大的局限性。[15] 具体来讲,只有环境退化与某项受保护人权的重大损害之间的直接因果关系得以建立,环境退化才构成对人权的侵犯。在没有直接因果关系的情况下,人权条款基本上不适用于环境保护。

《分析报告》所确认的第三种方法可能是三种方法中最模糊的一种。[16] 它主张必须将人权视为可持续发展概念的有机组成部分。我们可以将这一表述转换为国际环境法所使用的术语,将其称为可持续发展的"社会支柱"(另外两个支柱是"环境保护"和"经济发展")。[17] 这当然是毫无疑义的。真正的难题不限于可持续发展的三个支柱和谐共处所依据的善意条款,而是指向了许多情况,例如矿产资源开采或者水电项目的开发,这种情况下的经济、社会和环境因素并不一定是相匹配的。如此被重构之后,第三种方法不再是纯粹的协同效应(较为模糊),它为理解人权与环境保护之间的微妙关系铺平了道路,即二者确实存在发生冲突的可能性。[18]

---

[13] See A. Boyle and M. Anderson (eds.), *Human Rights Approaches to Environmental Protection* (Oxford University Press, 1996). 随着时间的推移,保护环境已经成为人权的重要组成部分。联合国特别报告员在其关于《享有安全、清洁、健康和可持续有关环境的人权义务问题》的执行情况报告(A/HRC/31/53,2015年12月28日)中提到这一点。Other reports offer some measure of the scope of the problem: Global Witness, *Deadly Environment: The Dramatic Rise in Killings of Environmental and Land Defenders* 1 January 2002–2031 December 2013 (April 2014); UNDP, *Environmental Justice: Comparative Experiences in Legal Empowerment* (June 2014). For two examples of precautionary measures recommended by the Inter-American Commission on Human Rights, see *Kevin Donaldo Ramirez and Family*, ICommHR, Precautionary Measure No. 460/15 (28 September 2015); *Ana Miran Romero and others*, ICommHR Precautionary Measure No. 589/15 (24 November 2015).

[14] See D. Shelton, "Substantive Rights", in M. Fitzmaurice, D. Ong and P. Merkouris (eds.), *Research Handbook on International Environmental Law* (Cheltenham: Edward Elgar, 2010), pp. 265–283, particularly pp. 265–266.

[15] See F. Francioni, "International Human Rights in the Environmental Horizon" (2010) 21 *European Journal of International Law* 41.

[16] OHCHR Analytical Study, supra footnote 2, para. 9.

[17] See supra Chapter 1.

[18] See J. E. Viñuales, "The Rise and Fall of Sustainable Development" (2013) 22 *Review of European Comparative and International Environmental Law* 3.

这三种方法都有助于我们理解在选定某种概念性观点时最重要的依据是什么。在此方面，"导论"所提及的问题更容易被阐释。一方面，我们将评估人权条款中环境要素的影响范围以及通过人权司法机构和准司法机构来保护环境的后续影响。在此情况下，我们应着重理解"范围"一词，因为它很大程度上概括了协同效应的核心问题。另一方面，我们也必须考虑到冲突的可能性，因为冲突经常会隐藏在诸如可持续发展等概念之下，而它明显排除了任何摩擦或冲突。表 10-1 总结了人权与环境保护之间的关系所产生的概念性问题。

表 10-1　　　　　　　　人权与环境保护之间的关系

协同效应			冲突		
问题 1	问题 2	问题 3	问题 4	问题 5	问题 6
利用人权保护环境	利用环境法保护人权	可持续发展"支柱"（环境、经济、社会）的相互支撑原则	可持续发展"支柱"之间的紧张关系	环境保护与土著和部落人民权利之间的冲突	环境干预主义与人权的紧张关系

在理论上和政策上，这六个问题打开的领域是广阔而复杂的。法律专家和国际文书通常只关注问题 1，而很少提及其他问题。[19] 在此背景下，本章将在第三节集中讨论"导论"中所提出的两个主要问题（哪些人权可以用于保护环境、保护的范围），讨论的同时会涉及表 10-1 所列的问题 2 和问题 3。其余问题将在本章第四节中简要讨论。

19　On these other issues, see e. g. S. Chuffart and J. E. Viñuales, "From the Other Shore: Economic, Social and Cultural Right from an International Environmental Law Perspective", in E. Reidel, G. Giacca and C. Golay (eds.), *Economic, Social and Cultural Rights: Current Issues and Challenges* (Oxford University Press, 2014), pp. 286-307 (focusing on issue 2 and reviewing the relevant literature); K. Murphy, "The Social Pillar of Sustainable Development: A Literature Review and Framework for Policy Analysis" (2012) 8 *Sustainability: Science, Practice, & Policy* 5 (analysing the body of literature on issues 3 and 4, within which specifically legal contributions are rare); the studies mentioned supra footnote 3 (focusing on issue 5, although most of them come from disciplines other than law); T. Hayward, *Political Theory and Ecological Values* (London: Polity Press, 1998) (analysing issue 6 from the perspective of political theory) and Viñuales, supra footnote 4 (analysing issue 6 from the perspective of how to structure environmental policies to minimise conflicts with investment disciplines).

第三节 协同效应

一 两个关键问题

自医学诞生以来,人们就意识到了环境要素对人类生命健康的重要性。公元前 5 世纪,医学之父希波克拉底(Hippocrates)曾说:

> 任何希望恰当研究医学的人,都应采取如下方法:……人们应当对居民用水的水质和水源进行考察,区分它是软水还是硬水,咸水还是淡水,若是咸水,则不宜用来烹调;发源地是高山岩石、狭窄凹地还是寒冷的高地;流域地面是干旱贫瘠的,还是树木繁茂、灌溉良好的。[20]

后来出现了在罗马时代采取的第一项公共卫生和卫生措施,18 世纪 Avicena 和 Maimonides 的发现,以及 Lavoisier 的发现,以及杰里米·边沁(Jeremy Bentham)对英格兰议会通过卫生法的努力。直到工业革命留下了疤痕、烟囱、悲惨的房屋、污染的空气和河流,以及最近人类活动各个领域的化学物质泛滥,西方世界才开始认真对待考虑到环境退化对人类生活条件的影响。在亚洲和非洲地区,工业革命远不如自然灾害、流行病所带来的影响明显,这些地区直到 20 世纪才开始慢慢出现环境污染问题。然而,对进步的信念和对利润的追求,将措施的采用推迟到 20 世纪下半叶,当时环境恶化被认为是全球关注的主要问题。即使到了今天,尽管人们对环境与人类生存之间的关系有了更好的了解,但相关的监管框架仍然是空洞的,而且常常是不力的。有些发展中国家提供了一个例子,燃煤发电厂正在污染空气和水,以至于政府现在将环境保护视为一项值得付出的优先事项。

如果人们的生命健康取决于适当的环境条件,那么明确环境损害与人

---

[20] Hippocrates, "On Airs, Waters and Places", in *The Genuine Works of Hippocrates*, translated by Francis Adams (Whitefish, MT: Kissinger Legacy Reprints, 2010), part I. See P. -M. Dupuy, " Le droit à la santé et la protection de l'environnement", in R. -J. Dupuy (ed.), *Le Droit à la Santé en Tant Que Droit de L'homme* (The Hague: Sijthoff, 1978), pp. 340-427.

权之间的关系就显得尤为重要,20世纪90年代早期以来,国际社会多次承认了环境损害与人权之间的关系。[21] 联合国人权事务高级专员办公室的《分析研究》调查了大量威胁到人权的环境问题,主要包括大气污染(空气污染、臭氧损耗、气候变化)、土地退化(森林砍伐和荒漠化)、水体污染、化学品和危险废物排放造成的污染、生物多样性减少、人为自然灾害增加(人为导致的气候变化)[22] 等问题。尽管这些清单只是描述性质的,人们可以从中得出一个重要的分析结论:环境对人权实现的影响主要(虽然不完全)是对人类健康现实或潜在的威胁。此外,环境损害还会侵害到人类的其他价值观,尤其是文化和审美价值观。因此,从人权的角度来说,对特定环境质量的保护就是对广义的人类健康的保护。

后一点还有两方面的分析后果。一方面,保护环境的人权条款主要包含那些涉及人类健康和整体尊严的权利(例如健康权、生命权、个人和家庭生活的权利、水权、食物权、享有优良生活水平权),同时也包括与文化因素相关的权利(文化权、财产权、环境信息权和参与权);另一方面,基于被保护价值(健康、文化)的不同以及这一价值能够承受的损害程度,就必须在不同程度上确定环境退化与人权保障之间的因果关系。这一因果关系就会决定人权条款作为一个法律工具可以在多大范围为环境因素提供保护。这些分析结果下面的讨论提供了概念上的基础。

二 确定含有环境内容的人权条款

(一)分析类型

一直以来,对人权条款的演化解释("目的论")都会承认在某些权利内的环境内容。如前所述,尽管其他因素(文化因素)在环境保护方面发挥了重要作用,但真正将环境损害和人权保障联系在一起的是人类健康。为了进一步研究多如牛毛的与环境相关的人权条款,人们对人权进行了很多分类。我们将在下文逐一介绍。

第一种分类涉及支持所有人权的基本结构,无论是"公民权利和政治

---

[21] See, in particular, Human Rights and the Environment. Final report presented by Mrs Fatma Zohra Ksentini, Special Rapporteur, 6 July 1994, UN Doc. E/CN. 4/Sub. 2/1994/9 (Ksentini Report), paras. 161-234 (讨论环境退化对十项具体人权的影响)。

[22] OHCHR Analytical Study, supra footnote 2, paras. 15-22.

权利"还是"经济、社会和文化权利",每一项人权都对其责任人或义务人(通常是国家)施加三项相互关联的义务:[23] (1)尊重人权内容的义务;(2)保护这一权利不受第三方(其他个人或非国家主体——包括跨国公司,甚至是自然灾害等)侵害的义务;(3)为权利主体充分享受该权利逐步提供必要条件的义务。上述义务都体现了人权的环境保护内容,因此,对这一分类的表面理解就可以说明人权的环境内容并不是仅限于第三种义务类型。

第二种分类将人权分为实体性权利和程序性权利。[24] 这两种权利往往存在某些重叠,因为许多实体性权利往往会附带一些程序性义务,但是,这一分类还是有用的,它可以被当作一个工具来检查相关文献和实践。这一分类有助于掌握20年来程序性环境权利的重大发展及其区域性爆发点《奥胡斯公约》(*Aarhus Convention*),《奥胡斯公约》是在联合国欧洲经济委员会(UNECE)[25]的主持下缔结的,目前正通过软法的形式向其他区域[26]及全球推广。[27]

---

[23] On this influential conceptualisation, see H. Shue, *Basic Rights: Subsistence, Affluence and U. S. Foreign Policy* (Princeton, NJ: Princeton University Press, 1980); *Report on the Right to Adequate Food as a Human Right. Final Report presented by the Special Rapporteur Asbjørn Eide*, 7 July 1987, UN Doc. E/CN. 4/Sub. 2/1987/23 (1987), paras. 66-69; Committee on Economic, Social and Cultural Rights, *General Comment No. 12: The Right to Adequate Food* (*Art.* 11), 12 May 1999, UN Doc. E/C. 12/1999/5 (1999), para. 15; Human Rights Committee, *General Comment No. 6: Article 6* (*Right to Life*), 30 April 1982, UN Doc. HRI/GEN/1/Rev. 9 (Vol. I), paras. 3-5; I. E. Koch, "Dichotomies, Trichotomies or Waves of Duties?" (2005) 5 *Human Rights Law Review* 81.

[24] See, e. g., the distinction made in Fitzmaurice et al., supra footnote 14, Chapters 13 and 14.

[25] Aarhus Convention on Access to Information, Public Participation in Decision-making and Access to Justice in Environmental Matters, 25 June 1998, 2161 UNTS 447 (Aarhus Convention). See also the policy basis of this instrument, namely principle 10 of the Rio Declaration on Environment and Development, 13 June 1992, UN Doc. A/CONF. 151/26. Rev. 1 (Rio Declaration).

[26] Preliminary Document on the Regional Agreement on Access to Information, Participation and Justice in Environmental Matters in Latin America and the Caribbean (ECLAC Draft), available at: http//repositorio. cepal. org (visited on 17 April 2017).

[27] Decision SS. XI /5, Part A "Guidelines on Developing National Legislation on Access to Information, Public Participation in Decision-Making and Access to Justice in Environmental Matters", 26 February 2010, Doc. GCSS. XI/11 (Bali Guidelines). On these guide-lines and their impact see U. Etemire, "Insights on the UNEP Bali Guidelines and the Development of Environmental Democratic Rights" (2016) 28 *Journal of Environmental Law* 393. See also the implementation guide relating to these guidelines: UNEP, *Putting Rio Principle 10 into Action: An Implementation Guide for the UNEP Bali Guidelines for the Development of National Legislation on Access to Information, Public Participation and Access to Justice in Environmental Matters* (October 2015) (Bali Implementation Guidelines).

第三种分类涉及环境保护在人权领域的重要性问题。从这一视角出发，可将人权分为"一般性"权利（仅与环境保护有间接联系的人权）和"具体的环境"权利（如获得优良环境的权利、水权，或环境信息权、参与权、诉诸司法权等）。

在下文中，我们将重点讨论最后一种分类，前两种分类将有助于我们进一步梳理"一般性"权利和"具体的环境"权利的相关概念。

（二）一般性权利

1. 背景

一般性权利的主要特点是，它们在被设定时并非专为环境保护目的。实际上，它们大多数规范表述在现代国际环境法诞生前的1—20年就出现了。它们的环境影响是在很晚以后引入的，特别是在20世纪90年代，是由区域人权法院或委员会或有权审理个人投诉的准司法委员会经由演化解释的方式实现的。由此，与环境有关的"一般"权利清单，例如文化权利或健康权、私人和家庭生活权、生命权、财产权、食物权或适足生活水准权，处在不断发展的过程中，因为它可能在上述权利之一或甚至以前与环境不相关的其他权利中纳入新的环境要件。[28]

许多法律学者对其中大部分进行了研究。[29] 我们的目的不是总结这方面的文献，而是重点关注多个司法和准司法机构是在何种情况下才会去明

---

[28] 举例说明，在两个涉及拥挤监狱中的被动吸烟的案件中，《欧洲人权公约》第3条（后文脚注31）所禁止的酷刑已被赋予了环境内容。See *Florea v. Romania*, ECtHR Application No. 37186/03, Judgment (14 September 2010), paras. 50-51, 60-65; *Elefteriadis v. Romania*, ECtHR Application No. 38427/05, Judgment (25 January 2011), paras. 47-55.

[29] See, e.g., D. K. Anton and D. Shelton, *Environmental Protection and Human Rights* (Cambridge University Press, 2011); Francioni, supra footnote 15; D. Shelton, "Human Rights and the Environment: Jurisprudence of Human Rights Bodies" (2002) 32 *Environmental Policy and Law* 158; F. Francioni and M. Scheinin (eds.), *Cultural Human Rights* (Leiden: Martinus Nijhoff, 2008); S. Joseph, J. Schultz and M. Castan, *The International Covenant on Civil and Political Rights. Cases, Materials and Commentary* (Oxford University Press, 2nd edn, 2004); D. J. Harris, M. O'Boyle, E. P. Bates and C. M. Buckley, *Law of the European Convention on Human Rights* (Oxford University Press, 2nd edn, 2009); L. Burgorgue-Larsen and A. Ubeda de Torres, *The Inter-American Court of Human Rights. Case Law and Commentary* (Oxford University Press, 2011); M. Evans and R. Murray (eds.), *The African Charter on Human and Peoples' Rights. The System in Practice, 1986-2006* (Cambridge University Press, 2nd edn, 2008); D. Shelton (ed.), *The Oxford Handbook of International Human Rights Law* (Oxford University Press, 2013); O. de Schutter, *International Human Rights Law. Cases, Materials, Commentary* (Cambridge University Press, 2014); R. Smith, *Textbook*

确特定权利的环境维度及其轮廓。在这一问题上,把人权条款常用的解释方法及这些解释发生的机构背景作为研究的出发点是有用的。这些解释方法是条约解释一般规则的具体运用,强调对人权规范进行演化性和目的性解读,以便适应社会变化。[30] 这种方法的影响应结合人权保护的高度组织化这一特点来评价。这个领域的主要机构包括欧洲人权法院(European Court of Human Rights, ECtHR)、美洲人权委员会(Inter-American Commission, ICommHR)和美洲人权法院(Inter-American Court of HumanRights, ICtHR)、非洲人权和人民权利委员会(African Commission onHuman and Peoples' Rights, African Commission)(以下简称非洲委员会)和非洲人权和民族权法院(African CourtonHuman and Peoples' Rights, African Court)以及联合国的内设机构,如联合国人权委员会(HumanRights Committee, HRC)和经济、社会和文化权利委员会(Committee on Economic, Social andCultural Rights, ESCR Committee)等。

如前所述,许多人权条约,诸如 1950 年《欧洲人权公约》(*European Human Rights Convention*)[31]、1966 年《公民权利及政治权利国际公约》(*International Covenants on Civil and Political Rights*)[32]、1966 年《经济、社

---

on International Human Rights Law (Oxford University Press, 2015); B. Saul, *Indigenous Peoples and Human Rights. International and Regional Jurisprudence* (Oxford: Hart, 2016); F. Sudre, *Droit européen et international des droits de l'homme* (Paris: Presses universitaires de France, 2016); L. Hennebel and H. Tigroudja, *Traité de droit international des droits de l'homme* (Paris: Pedone, 2016); I. Bantekas and L. Oette, *International Human Rights Law and Practice* (Cambridge University Press, 2nd edn 2016); D. Forsythe, *Human Rights in International Relations* (Cambridge University Press, 4th edn 2017).

[30] See *Loizidou v. Turkey* (Preliminary objections), Judgment of 23 May 1995, ECtHR Application No. 15318/89, para. 72; *The Right to Information on Consular Assistance in the Framework of the Guarantees of the Due Process of Law*, ICtHR Advisory Opinion OC-16/99, 1 October 1, 1999, Ser. A, No. 16 (1999), paras. 114–115; Human Rights Committee, *General Comment 24: General Comment on Issues Relating to Reservations made upon Ratification or Accession to the Covenant or the Optional Protocols thereto, or in Relation to Declarations under Article 41 of the Covenant*, UN Doc. CCPR/C/21/Rev. 1/Add. 6 (1994) (General Comment No. 24).

[31] Convention for the Protection of Human Rights and Fundamental Freedoms, 4 November 1950, 213 UNTS 221 (ECHR).

[32] International Covenant on Civil and Political Rights, 16 December 1966, 999 UNTS 171 (ICCPR).

会及文化权利国际公约》(*International Covenants on Economic, Social and Cultural Rights*)³³ 和 1969 年《美洲人权公约》(*American Convention on Human Rights*)³⁴，都是在 1972 年斯德哥尔摩人类环境会议之前缔结的。因此，除《非洲人权和人民权利宪章》(*African Charter*)（以下简称《非洲宪章》)³⁵ 和 1988 年《美洲人权公约圣萨尔瓦多议定书》(*San Salvador Protocol to the American Convention*)³⁶ 明确规定了环境保护外，上述其他条约可以通过演化解释的方式将环境保护的相关内容纳入其中。联合国人权和环境问题特别报告员对相关判例法进行了大量研究，完成了 14 份关于各种司法和准司法机构实践工作的单独报告。³⁷ 后文的讨论将会参考这一杰出工作成果和一些最新的决议，我们采取一种分析上的框架来

---

33 International Covenant on Economic, Social and Cultural Rights, 16 December 1966, 993 UNTS 3 (ICESCR).

34 American Convention on Human Rights, 22 November 1969, 1144 UNTS 123 (ACHR or American Convention).

35 African Charter on Human and Peoples' Rights, 27 June 1981, 21 ILM 58 (1982) (African Charter), Art. 24.

36 Additional Protocol to the American Convention on Human Rights in the Area of Economic, Social and Cultural Rights, 16 November 1988, OAS Treaty Series No. 69, Art. 11.

37 See *Individual Report on the International Covenant on Economic, Social and Cultural Rights*, Report No. 1 (December 2013) (Report on the ICESCRs); *Individual Report on the International Covenant on Civil and Political Rights*, Report No. 2 (December 2013) (Report on the ICCPRs); *Individual Report on the International Convention on the Elimination of All Forms of Racial Discrimination*, Report No. 3 (December 2013) (Report on the CERD); *Individual Report on the United Nations Convention on the Elimination of All Forms of Discrimination against Women*, Report No. 4 (December 2013) (Report on the CEDAW); *Individual Report on the United Nations Convention on the Rights of the Child*, Report No. 5 (December 2013) (Report on the CRC); *Individual Report on the UN General Assembly and the Human Rights Council, including the Universal Periodic Review Process*, Report No. 6 (December 2013) (Report on the UPR); *Individual Report on the Special Procedures of the United Nations Human Rights Council*, Report No. 7 (December 2013) (Report on Special Procedures); *Individual Report on the Rights of Indigenous Peoples*, Report No. 8 (December 2013) (Report on Indigenous Peoples); *Individual Report on Global and Regional Environmental Agreements*, Report No. 9 (December 2013) (Report on MEAs); *Individual Report on Non-Binding International Environmental Instruments*, Report No. 10 (December 2013) (Report on environmental soft law); *Individual Report on the Convention on Access to Information, Public Participation in Decision-Making and Access to Justice in Environmental Matters (Aarhus Convention)*, Report No. 11 (December 2013) (Report on Aarhus); *Individual Report on the Asia-Pacific, Arab and African Regions as well as the European Social Charter*, Report No. 12 (December

组合这些材料，以便确定人权与环境保护之间关系发展的潜在趋势。

2. 一个新起点：人权委员会

关于人权与环境的解释首次出现在 20 世纪 80 年代，特别是人权委员会的判例中。[38]《公民权利及政治权利国际公约》的环境维度第一次被检视，涉及的是生命权以及核试验和核废料造成的风险。[39] 但是，在案件受理阶段，人权委员会驳回了这些诉求。

直到 20 世纪 90 年代初，人权的环境维度才在《公民权利及政治权利国际公约》中得以表述。出人意料的是，切入点主要是公约的第 27 条，即享受个人文化的权利。人权委员会认为文化联结是一种可保护的对象，因为它将特定人群与其故土、资源和活动（他们的自然环境）关联起来。[40] 尽管在大多数情况下这一诉求是不被受理的，或在实体审理中被驳回。[41] 虽然人权委员会的判例有其局限性，但它有助于确定其他公共机构已尝试的两个环境考量切入点，即环境退化对广义的人类健康的影响以及文化权利视角上的这一影响。

2013) (Report on regional instruments); *Individual Report on the American Declaration of the Rights and Duties of Man, the American Convention on Human Rights, and the Additional Protocol to the American Convention on Human Rights in the Area of Economic, Social and Cultural Rights*, Report No. 13 (December 2013) (Report on the Inter-American system); *Individual Report on the European Convention on Human Rights and the European Union*, Report No. 14 (December 2013) (Report on the ECHR).

[38] See Report on the ICCPRs, supra footnote 37.

[39] See *E. H. P. v. Canada*, HRC Communication No. 67/1980 (27 October 1982); *Bordes et Temeharo v. France*, HRC Communication No. 645/1995 (22 July 1996). See also *Brun v. France*, HRC Communication No. 1453/2006 (18 October 2006) (relating to GMOs).

[40] See HRC, *General Comment No. 23: Protection of Minorities* (Art. 27), 4 August 1994, CCPR/C/ 21/Rev. 1/Add. 5, para. 3. 2. By way of illustration, see *Kitok v. Sweden*, HRC Communication 197/1985 (27 July 1988); *Bernard Ominayak and the Lubicon Lake Band v. Canada*, HRC Communication No. 167/1984 (26 March 1990); *Ilmari Länsman and others v. Finland*, HRC Communication No. 511/1992 (8 November 1995); *Jouni E. Länsman and others v. Finland*, HRC Communication No. 671/1995 (30 October 1996); *Apirana Mahuika and others v. New Zealand*, HRC Communication No. 547/93 (27 October 2000); *Diergaardt v. Namibia*, HRC Communication No. 760/1997 (6 September 2000); *Poma Poma v. Peru*, HRC Communication No. 1457/2006 (27 March 2009) (concluding to a violation of Art. 27).

[41] See D. Shelton, "The Human Rights Committee's Decisions", *Carnegie Council for Ethics in International Affairs*, 22 April 2005, available at: www.carnegiecouncil.org (last visited on 15 January 2014).

正如后文所述，欧洲人权法院的判例主要（并非唯一[42]）采用了第一个切入点，而美洲人权委员会和美洲人权法院的判例主要强调了第二个切入点。非洲委员会的判例则采取了两个切入点，可能是因为它将个人权利和民族权都当作重点问题。得出这些一般性结论当然必须是很慎重的，因为没有裁判机构是仅仅关注单个问题。在作出裁判时要对全案进行充分考虑，不能仅侧重案件的个别问题。但是，明确每个裁判机构在司法实践中所强调的问题还是会有助于我们理解整体发展趋势。图10-1用图形的方式展示了这一趋势。

```
                        ┌─────────┐
                        │ 人权委员会 │
                        └────┬────┘
              ┌──────────────┴──────────────┐
        ┌──────────┐                   ┌──────────┐
        │ 健康考量  │                   │ 文化考量  │
        └────┬─────┘                   └────┬─────┘
        ┌──────────┐              ┌──────────────────────┐
        │ 欧洲人权法院│              │美洲人权委员会和美洲人权法院│
        └────┬─────┘              └──────────┬───────────┘
        ┌──────────┐                   ┌──────────┐
        │ 健康考量  │                   │ 文化考量  │
        └────┬─────┘                   └────┬─────┘
              └──────────────┬──────────────┘
                        ┌─────────┐
                        │ 非洲委员会 │
                        └────┬────┘
                     ┌──────────────┐
                     │ 个人/集体权利 │
                     └──────────────┘
```

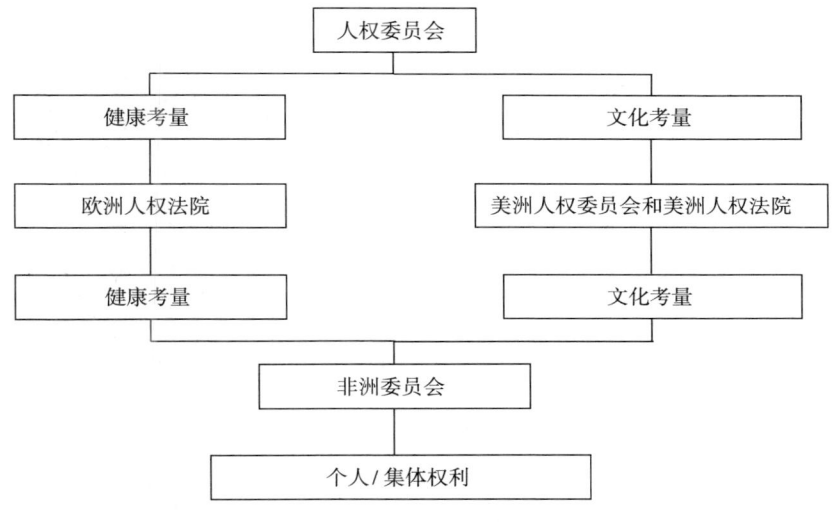

图10-1 "一般性"权利的环境维度

3. 欧洲人权法院

欧洲人权法院的环境判例[43]主要涉及的是与广义的人类健康和整体尊

---

42 See, e.g., T. Koivurova, "Jurisprudence of the European Court of Human Rights Regarding Indigenous Peoples: Retrospect and Prospects" (2011) 18 *International Journal on Minority and Group Rights* 1; G. Pentassuglia, "Towards a Jurisprudential Articulation of Indigenous Land Rights" (2011) 22 *European Journal of International Law* 165; G. Pentassuglia, "The Strasbourg Court and Minority Groups: Shooting in the Dark or a New Interpretive Ethos" (2012) 19 *International Journal on Minority and Group Rights* 1; Saul, supra footnote 29.

43 See Report on the ECHR, supra footnote 37.

严各方面相关的人权,特别是《欧洲人权公约》第 8 条规定的私人和家庭生活权利。

一个著名的案例,即"Lopez Ostra 诉西班牙案"[44] 的判决是在 20 世纪 90 年代初里约热内卢会议不久之后做出的,这不仅仅是巧合。欧洲人权法院已经在早期的案例中考虑过了某种性质的环境侵害问题(例如,机场对周边环境所造成的干扰),但当时的裁判结果是,该损害行为的社会利益优先于起诉人的个人利益。[45] Lopez Ostra 案是思维的标志性转变。法院认为,当地皮革废物处理设施的确对 Lopez Ostra 的家庭造成了损害,尽管该设施有一定的社会效益,但侵犯了私人和家庭生活的权利(第 8 条)。法院特别指出:

> 自然地,严重的环境污染会通过对私人和家庭生活造成负面影响(但是尚未严重威胁到他们的健康)而影响到个人的幸福并使得他们无法享受居家生活。[46]

因此,法院就把狭义的健康权与那些对广义的人性完整性(如私人和家庭生活的权利)的其他损害进行了区分。另外,法院为如何理解这一背景下的国家义务打下了基础:

> 无论是在国家的积极义务(即国家有义务采取合理和适当措施以保护申请人依据第 8 条第 1 段所应享有的权利)这一背景下分析这一问题(申请人希望在本案中采取这种模式),还是在某一公共机构的干预(干预的必要性由第 8 条第 2 段来确定)这一背景下分析这一问题,适用的原则在广义上都是相似的。在这两种背景下,都必须注重在相互竞争的个人利益和社会整体利益之间实现相对的平衡,在所有情况下,国家都享有一定的权衡权限。另外,当涉及第 8 条第 1

---

[44] *Lopez Ostra v. Spain*, ECtHR Application No. 16798/90, Judgment (9 December 1994).

[45] See e. g. *Powell and Rayner v. United Kingdom*, ECtHR Application No. 9310/81, Judgment (21 February 1990). Later, in *Hatton and others v. United Kingdom*, ECtHR Application No. 36022/97, Judgment (8 July 2003), the Court had rejected the claim for breach of Article 8.

[46] *Lopez Ostra*, supra footnote 44, para. 51.

段所规定的国家积极义务（实现所需的利益平衡）时，第 8 条第 2 段提及的目标也具有一定的关联度。[47]

法院接着从三个主要方面进一步明确了这一方法。第一，拓展了"一般性"权利的环境内容，尤其是：（1）承认与实体性权利相关的补充性程序性义务；[48]（2）把程序公平（第 6 条）[49]、生命权（第 2 条）[50]、言论自由权（第 10 条）[51]、集会和结社自由权（第 12 条）[52] 和禁止酷刑权（第 3 条）[53] 当作环境考量的切入点；（3）明确规定国家负有积极义务去

---

[47] Ibid., para. 51.

[48] See *Guerra and others v. Italy*, ECtHR Application No. 116/1996/735/932, Judgment（19 February 1998），para. 60；*Oneryildiz v. Turkey*, ECtHR Application No. 48939/99, Judgment（30 November 2004），paras. 91–96；*L'Erablière A. S. B. L. v. Belgium*, ECtHR Application No. 49230/07, Judgment（24 February 2009），paras. 24–30；*Taskin and others v. Turkey*, ECtHR Application No. 46117/99, Judgment（30 March 2005），paras. 118–125；*Tatar v. Romania*, ECtHR Application No. 67021/01, Judgment（6 July 2009），paras. 96–97 and 116–125；*Ivan Atanasov v. Bulgaria*, ECtHR Application No. 12853/03, Judgment（11 April 2011），para. 78；*Vilnes and others v. Norway*, ECtHR Application No. 52806/09, Judgment（5 December 2013），paras. 235–244；*Brincat and others v. Malta*, ECtHR Application Nos. 60908/11, 62110/11, 62129/11, 62312/11, and 62338/11, Judgment（24 July 2014），para. 102；*Özel and others v. Turkey*, ECtHR Application Nos. 14350/05, 15245/05, and 16051/05, Judgment（17 November 2015），paras. 170–172, 187–190；*Smaltini v. Italy*, ECtHR Application No. 43961/09, Decision（admissibility）（24 March 2015），paras. 51–54.

[49] *Okyay and others v. Turkey*, ECtHR Application No. 36220/97, Judgment（12 October 2005），paras. 61–69（on the applicability in casu of Art. 6.1）；*L'Erablière*, supra footnote 48, paras. 24–30；*Apanasewicz v. Poland*, ECtHR Application No. 6854/07, Judgment（3 May 2011），paras. 72–83.

[50] *Oneryildiz*, supra footnote 48, paras. 89–90；*Kolyadenko and others v. Russia*, ECtHR Applications Nos. 17423/05, 20534/05, 20678/05, 23263/05, 24283/05 and 35673/05, Judgment（28 February 2012），paras. 157–161；*Vilnes*, supra footnote 48, paras. 219–220；*Brincat*, supra footnote 48, paras. 59, 79–85, 101；*Özel*, supra footnote 48, paras. 170–172；*Smaltini*, supra footnote 48, paras. 49–54.

[51] *Vides Aizsardzibas Klubs v. Latvia*, ECtHR Application No. 57829/00, Judgment（27 May 2004），paras. 40–49.

[52] *Costel Popa v. Romania*, ECtHR Application Nos. 47558/10, Judgment（26 April 2016），paras. 30–47.

[53] *Florea*, supra footnote 28, paras. 50–51, 60–65；*Elefteriadis*, supra footnote 28, paras. 47–55.

保护个人人权不受第三方[54]或自然灾害[55]的侵害。第二，法院进一步拓展了环境保护，认为为了实现环保这一目标，甚至有正当理由去限制某些人权（特别是财产权）。[56] 第三，《欧洲人权公约》中的环境保护范围以环境损害与个人权利受到严重侵害之间存在直接因果关系为条件，对具体案件具体分析。[57]

总而言之，《欧洲人权公约》为环境判例的发展提供了一定基础，其不仅关注国家义务，而且（间接）关注第三方（非国家）的行为。然而，对广义的人类健康和人性完整性的强调，对公约所能提供的环境保护范畴造成了重大限制。事实上，公约仍是一个以人身损害为基础的法律制度。因此，至少就目前而言，那些仅与严重的人身伤害或损害间接相关的环境退化案件，还不在保护范畴内。

4. 美洲人权法院

美洲人权法院的环境判例以及美洲人权委员会所通过的部分报告[58]采取了截然不同的处理方式，这主要是由美洲大陆特定情况所决定的。这些决定的重点是文化方面的考虑，而用于保护它们的法律手段是《美洲人权公约》第 21 条规定的财产权或者《美洲人权宣言》所规定的财产权（第 23 条）和文化权（第 13 条）[59]。从概念上讲，环境退化与这些权利的关联之处主要在于土著居民和部落传统上居住的祖传土地的完整性，因

54　*Tatar v. Romania*, supra footnote 48, paras. 85-88; *Apanasewicz*, supra footnote 49, paras. 93-104; *Chis v. Romania*, ECtHR Application No. 55396/07, Decision (admissibility) (9 September 2014), paras. 30, 35-37.

55　*Budayeva and others v. Russia*, ECtHR Applications No. 15339/02, 21166/02, 20058/02, 11673/02 and 15343/02, Judgment (29 September 2008), paras. 128-37; *Özel*, supra footnote 48, paras. 170-175.

56　*Turgut v. Turkey*, ECtHR Application No. 1411/03, Judgment (merits) (8 July 2008), para. 90; *Depalle v. France*, ECtHR Application No. 34044/02, Judgment (29 March 2010), paras. 77-93; *Brosset-Triboulet and others v. France*, ECtHR Application No. 34078/02, Judgment (29 March 2010), paras. 80-96 (在这两起案件中，赔偿的缺位并没有改变大陪审团的结论，即不构成对财产权的侵权)。

57　*Fadeyeva v. Russia*, ECtHR Application No. 55723/00, Judgment (30 November 2005), paras. 68-70; *Apanasewicz*, supra footnote 49, para. 94; *Chis*, supra footnote 54, paras. 29, 31-34.

58　See Report on the Inter-American system, supra footnote 37.

59　American Declaration on the Rights and Duties of Man, adopted by the Ninth International Conference of American States, Bogotá, Colombia, 1948 (American Declaration).

此，土地已经成为他们生活方式不可或缺的一部分。

这方面的经典案例是 2001 年美洲人权法院审理的"Awas Tingni 诉尼加拉瓜案"，[60] 尽管在美洲人权委员会[61]先前的裁判中有过类似案件。本案中，尼加拉瓜政府向一名韩国投资者发放了伐木特许权，允许其在位于 Awas Tingni 社区传统土地内的森林里伐木。法院通过对《美洲人权公约》第 21 条进行了演化解释的方式，推理认为：

> 土著居民和土地的紧密联系必须这样来认可和理解，即土地是他们的文化、精神生活、完整性和经济生存的根本基础。对土著社区而言，与土地的关系不仅是一个占有和生产的问题，还是一个他们应当完全享有的物质和精神要件，甚至还涉及保护他们的文化遗产并移交到后代。[62]

基于以上认识，法院认为，尼加拉瓜违反了公约第 21 条。[63] 美洲人权法院在"Awas Tingni 案"中的立场随后得到了确认和进一步发展，并得到了国际社会的充分认可。这一立场的整个思路在后来的"Sarayaku 诉厄瓜多尔案"[64]

60　*Mayagna (Sumo) Awas Tingni Community v. Nicaragua*, ICtHR Series C No. 79, Judgment (31 August 2001) (*Awas Tingni v. Nicaragua*), paras. 145–155.

61　See *Yanomani Indians v. Brazil*, ICommHR case 7615 (decision of 5 March 1985), subsequently confirmed most notably in *Maya Indigenous Community of the Toledo District v. Belize*, ICommHR case 12.053 (report of 12 October 2004). 美洲委员会经常被要求解决类似的问题，包括当土著人民的权利受到商业发展或采掘工业的威胁时采取风险预防措施等。Some emblematic examples include *Community of San Mateo de Huanchor and its Members v. Peru*, ICommHR Petition 504/03, Report No. 69/04 (15 October 2004); *Community of La Oroya v. Peru*, ICommHR Petition 1473/06, Report on Admissibility 76/09 (5 August 2009) and the more recent Precautionary Measure 271-05 (3 May 2016); *U'wa People v. Colombia*, ICommHR Case 11.754, Report on Admissibility 33/15 (22 July 2015).

62　*Awas Tingni v. Nicaragua*, supra footnote 60, para. 149.

63　Ibid., para. 155.

64　See *Indigenous People Kichwa of Sarayaku v. Ecuador*, ICtHR Series C No. 245, Judgment (merits and compensation) (27 June 2012), paras. 145–147 (right to property) and 159–168 (participatory rights).

"Kuna 诉巴拿马案"[65] 和 "Kaliña、Lokono 诉苏里南案"[66] 等案例中都被概括提及。

综上,我们的讨论将仅限于下面四个结论,它们有助于我们来评估美洲人权法院判例法所认可的环境保护范围。第一,法院将公约第 21 条规定的保护对象拓展到"部落"族群(即使他们不能被当作"土著居民")[67]。第二,法院明确指出,这一背景下的保护也涵盖了这些土地上的自然资源,因为土著居民和部落族群自古以来就一直利用这些资源。[68]第三,法院还明确指出,财产权(即使是土著居民被认可的财产权)并不是绝对的,在下列情况下可以对其加以限制:(1)当事社区参与的充足程度;(2)所涉活动的利益与相关社区的分享情况;(3)事先进行的环境和社会评估。[69] 第四,当一个土著居民或部落族群的财产保护与一个私人所有者的财产保护发生冲突时,法院(默示地)建议[70]土著居民财产优先,至少可以要求国家征用这块土地(补偿所有者)以便将土地交给

---

[65] See *Case of the Kuna Indigenous People of Madungandí and the Emberá Indigenous People of Bayano and their members v. Panama*, ICtHR Series C No. 284 (Preliminary Objections, Merits, Reparations and Costs), Judgment (14 October 2014), paras. 111-113.

[66] See *Kaliña and Lokono Peoples v. Suriname*, ICtHR Case No. 12.639 (Merits, Reparations and Costs), Judgment (25 November 2015), paras. 129-132.

[67] See *Saramaka People v. Suriname*, ICtHR Series C No. 172, Judgment (28 November 2007), paras. 80-86 [(regarding black communities descending from the slave trade of the seventeenth century); *Afro-Descendant Communities Displaced from the Cacarica River Basin (Operation Genesis) v. Colombia*, ICtHR Ser. C No. 270, Preliminary Objections, Merits, Reparations, and Costs, Judgment (20 November 2013), paras. 345-347; *Kaliña and Lokono v. Suriname*, supra footnote 66, paras. 122-125 (该案涉及土著居民,但法院从其保护的角度将这两种类别的推理同化)]。

[68] See *Indigenous Community Yakye Axa v. Paraguay*, ICtHR Series C No. 125 (17 June 2005), para. 137; *Sawhoyamaxa Indigenous Community v. Paraguay*, ICtHR Series C No. 146 (29 March 2006), para. 118; *Kaliña and Lokono v. Suriname*, supra footnote 66, para. 122.

[69] See *Saramaka v. Suriname*, supra footnote 67, paras. 125-130; *Yakye Axa v. Paraguay*, supra footnote 68, para. 145; *Kaliña and Lokono v. Suriname*, supra footnote 66, para. 155.

[70] See *Sawhoyamaxa v. Paraguay*, supra footnote 68, para. 136 (法院指出,它不打算解决这两种保护财产之间的等级问题,尽管它后来就如何处理这个问题提出了一些指导); *Kaliña and Lokono v. Suriname*, supra footnote 66, para. 155 (法院认为,国家所采取的平衡措施不得对"土著居民社区的生存"造成影响)。

相关人群,[71] 或者在条件允许的情况下为土著居民和部落族群提供其他的土地。[72]

5. 非洲委员会

非洲委员会和非洲法院的判例[73]往往会重视公民的健康和文化考量。虽然《非洲宪章》文本存在一些被诟病的表述问题,[74] 但是这一文件所表达出的方法将一个个体维度（在本章的背景下，涉及的是广义的健康考量）和一个基于文化考量的团体维度（民族权）关联在一起。一般来说，这两个维度可以通过两个主要案例来展示，后续的实践都遵循了这两个案例。

第一个是"SERAC 诉尼日利亚案"[75]，尼日利亚国家石油公司和外国投资者在进行石油勘探开采的过程中严重损害了环境、影响了 Ogoni 地区人民。Ogoni 地区人民努力反抗石油开采活动，但遭到了尼日利亚政府当局的镇压，这进一步侵害了 Ogoni 地区人民的权利。该案由西班牙非政府组织 SERAC 以尼日利亚政府违反了《非洲宪章》数项条款为由诉至非洲委员会。非洲委员会考虑了石油公司开采行为所造成的环境退化对个人的健康权（第 16 条）和对集体的一般舒适环境权（第 24 条）的影响以及其他一些因素，认定尼日利亚没有尊重 Ogoni 地区人民的人权，也没有保护他们不受第三方行为的侵害。[76] 此外，委员会还明确了源自这些权利的程序性义务，特别涉及环境影响评价和公众参与的义务。[77]

Ogoni 案也存在一个文化维度，而"Endorois 案"则是更好地体现了

---

71 Ibid., para. 210; *Yakye Axa v. Paraguay*, supra footnote 68, para. 148.

72 *Kaliña and Lokono v. Suriname*, supra footnote 66, paras. 149–160.

73 See Report on regional instruments, supra footnote 37.

74 African Charter, supra footnote 35. See F. Ouguergouz, *La Charte africaine des droits de l'homme et des peuples* (Paris: Presses Universitaire de France, 1995); Evans and Murray, supra footnote 29.

75 *Social and Economic Rights Action Center (SERAC) and others v. Nigeria*, African Commission Application No. 155/96 (2001–2002) (*Ogoni*).

76 Ibid., para. 52. The ECOWAS Court took a similar stance years later in a related situation, see *SERAP v. Federal Republic of Nigeria*, ECOWAS Court of Justice, Judgment No. ECW/CCJ/JUD/18/12 (14 December 2012), paras. 91–121 [关于尼日尔三角洲漏油事件对人权的影响，并详细讨论了《非洲宪章》第 24 条（即有权享有整体上令人满意的环境）的实施情况]。

77 *Ogoni*, supra footnote 75, para. 53.

这一点。在"Endorois 案"中，肯尼亚政府采取了损害少数民族利益的措施。[78] 肯尼亚当局为了建立一块保护地，强行将 Endorois 地区的少数民族从祖传土地上驱逐出去。"Endorois 案"之所以引人关注，其中一个原因是它援引了美洲人权法院关于土著和部落财产的判例[79]，目的是确定此类少数民族与其自然环境之间存在着文化上的关联（这一关联受到了第 14 条——个人财产权和第 21 条——自由处分财产和自然资源的集体性权利的保护），[80] 而且还可以派生出协商、影响评价和补救等具体义务[81]。此外，非洲委员会还援引了人权委员会对《公民权利及政治权利国际公约》第 27 条的《一般评论意见》，认为肯尼亚侵犯了 Endorois 地区人民的文化权（第 17 条）。[82] 非洲法院审理了与"Endorois 案"相类似的案件（以环境保护为借口来驱逐少数民族），即肯尼亚政府针对 Ogiek 地区人民的案件。[83] 肯尼亚政府认为，驱逐 Ogiek 地区人民是对他们权利的一种合法和适度的限制，限制的正当性源自公共用途，即保护 Mau 森林的生态环境系统。然而，法院并未接受这一解释，认为政府的这一行为违反了《非洲宪章》的数条规定，包括第 14 条的财产权（被解释为个人权利和集体性权利），第 17 条第 2 款和第 3 款的文化权（也被看作个人权利和集体性权利），以及第 21 条人民对其自然资源的权利。

非洲委员会和非洲法院的判例不仅将健康考量和文化考量这两种途径联结在一起（区域人权法院正是通过这两种途径来给环境保护寻求一定的操作空间），它还示范了具体环境权的运作，这是后文将要讨论的。

（三）具体环境权

除前文所述的包含环境要素的一般性人权外，具体环境权中的实体性

---

[78] *Centre for Minority Rights Development (Kenya) and Minority Rights Group International on behalf of Endorois Welfare Council v. Kenya*, African Commission Application No. 276/2003 (*Endorois*).

[79] Ibid., paras. 190–198, 205–208, 257–266.

[80] Ibid., para. 209. 在一个关于肯尼亚努比亚人的案件中，少数民族与他们所占领土地之间的长期持久的事实关系得到了认可。See *The Nubian Community in Kenya v. The Republic of Kenya*, African Commission Application No. 317/06 (30 May 2016), para. 160.

[81] *Endorois*, supra footnote 78, paras. 225–238, 266–268.

[82] Ibid., paras. 250–251.

[83] See *African Commission on Human and Peoples' Rights v. Kenya*, Judgment (26 May 2017), African Court Application No. 006/2012. Such tensions have also arisen in the Inter-American system. See *Kaliña and Lokono v. Suriname*, supra footnote 66, paras. 163–198).

权利和程序性权利也逐渐得到国际社会的认可。图10-2提供了一个主要法律渊源的概览。

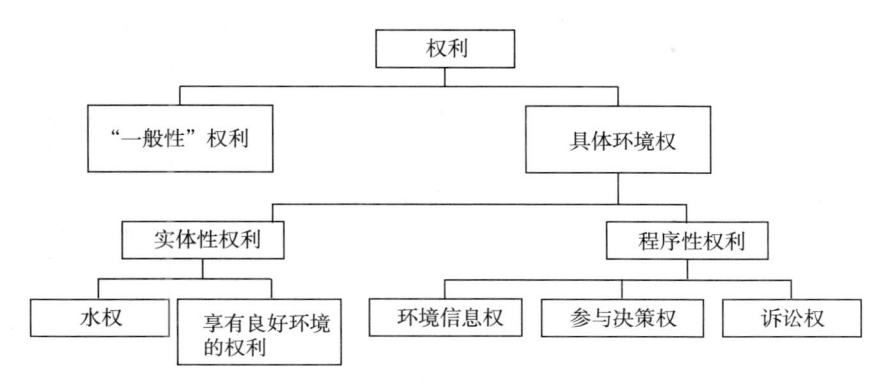

```
                        权利
                  ┌──────┴──────┐
            "一般性"权利        具体环境权
                          ┌────────┴────────┐
                      实体性权利          程序性权利
                      ┌───┴───┐      ┌──────┼──────┐
                     水权  享有良好环境  环境信息权  参与决策权  诉讼权
                            的权利
```

图10-2 具体环境权概览

1. 享有特定质量环境的权利

从实体性权利的视角来看，主要进展体现在对享有特定质量环境的权利的逐步承认。[84] 然而用来描述这种质量的形容词（"清洁的""健康的""令人满意的"）却经常被人忽视。正如我们从下文第三部分第四点可得知，这样的描述从战略视角来看有可能是非常重要的。在此，我们将仅限于讨论在国家和国际层面承认这项权利的里程碑事件。

在国家层面，1972年斯德哥尔摩人类环境会议和1992年里约热内卢会议对享有特定质量环境的权利的承认，一定程度上对成员国的国家宪法产生了影响。据联合国人权事务高级专员办公室的《分析研究》：

> 2010年，140多个国家的宪法都明确规定了环境权利及其责任，

---

[84] See P. Kromarek, *Le Droit à un Environnement équilibré et Sain, Considéré Comme un Droit de L'homme: sa Mise en Oeuvre Nationale, Européenne et Internationale*, Introductory report, European Conference on the Environment and Human Rights, Strasbourg, 19 – 20 January 1979; P. Cullet, "Definition of an Environmental Right in a Human Rights Context" (1995) 13 *Netherlands Quarterly of Human Rights* 25; M. Paellemarts, "The Human Right to a Healthy Environment as a Substantive Right", in M. Dejeant-Pons and M. Paellemarts (eds.), *Human Rights and the Environment* (Strasbourg: Council of Europe, 2002), pp. 11ff.

这意味着世界上超过 70% 的国家都在宪法层面确立了环境权。[85]

根据另一个估计,1992 年后的国家宪法绝大多数都承认健康环境权。[86] 这一研究还参考了大量国内司法判决(这些判决认为这个权利是可诉的)。[87] 在国际层面,《斯德哥尔摩宣言》第 1 条原则已经承认了享有人权与享有特定质量环境的权利两者之间的联系。

随后,许多国际性法律文件纷纷对这一联系予以肯定。如《非洲宪章》第 24 条规定"一切民族均有权享有一个有利于其发展的总体令人满意的环境"。这一条款在前文"Ogoni 案"中被讨论和应用,非洲委员会指出这一权利:

> 为政府施加了清晰的义务。它要求国家采取合理措施以防止环境污染和生态损害,促进保护并确保自然资源的生态可持续发展和利用。[88]

此外,非洲委员会强调了这一集体性权利与《经济、社会及文化权利国际公约》(International Covenant on Economic, Social and Cultural Rights, ICESCR)承认的一些个人权利(特别是健康权——公约第 12 条和《非洲宪章》第 16 条)的紧密联系。[89] 值得注意的是,委员会从这一权利中派生出了程序性义务,即针对工业项目进行环境和社会影响评价的义务,监测这一影响,提供环境信息获取,并在相关决策过程中提供有意义的公众参与机会。[90] 西非国家经济共同体法院(ECOWAS Court of Justice)在"SERAP 诉尼日利亚案"中对《非洲宪章》第 24 条作出了进

85　OHCHR Analytical Study, supra footnote 2, para. 30.

86　Shelton, supra footnote 14, p. 267. See more generally J. R. May and E. Daly, *Global Environmental Constitutionalism* (Cambridge University Press, 2104); R. Boyd, *The Environmental Rights Revolution. A Global Study of Constitutions, Human Rights and Environment* (Vancouver: UBC Press, 2012).

87　Shelton, supra footnote 14, pp. 267-268.

88　Ogoni, supra footnote 75, para. 52.

89　Ibid., para. 52.

90　Ibid., para. 53.

一步解释，该案主要涉及尼日尔三角洲的石油泄漏问题。[91] 法院在雄心勃勃地阐述这项权利时指出，它既涉及"态度义务也涉及结果义务"[92]，尽管后来澄清说，这是"警惕"和"谨慎注意"的问题，不仅包括采用全面的环境保护框架，也要有效实施。[93] 值得注意的是，法院建议只要存在石油泄漏的事实，且国家未能履行防止损害的义务，就无须证明具体的人身伤害[94]。此外，适用于第 24 条的环境损害行为不能仅通过私人间的赔偿方式解决：

> 与尼日利亚联邦共和国试图将环境损害责任归咎于拥有石油开采许可的持有者不同……石油工业对全人类至关重要的资源（例如环境）造成的损害，不能只是由石油公司自行决定，或者仅仅是它们可能与受到这一污染产业毁灭性影响的人们达成的赔偿协议。[95]

这与国际海洋法法庭（ITLOS）特别分庭在处理国家之间的"科特迪瓦与加纳海洋划界案"所采取的临时措施这一方法相类似，该案在讨论加纳许可的石油开采活动时，同时考量了《联合国海洋法公约》（UNCLOS）第 192 条和习惯法的预防原则的环境考量，认为它们不能仅仅通过赔偿来补救。[96]

在美洲，《美洲人权公约圣萨尔瓦多议定书》第 11 条第 1 款规定："公民有权生活在一个健康的环境并获取基本公共服务"。[97] 议定书第 19 条第 6 款似乎不允许因上述权利受到侵害而提出个人诉求。[98] 1989 年《儿

---

[91] *SERAP v. Nigeria*, supra footnote 76.

[92] Ibid., para. 100.

[93] Ibid., paras. 105, 108 and 111.

[94] Ibid., paras. 94, 96, 101.

[95] Ibid., para. 109.

[96] See *Dispute Concerning Delimitation of the Maritime Boundary between Ghana and Côte d'Ivoire in the Atlantic Ocean (Ghana/Côte d'Ivoire)*, ITLOS Case No. 23, Order of 25 April 2015 (Ghana/Côte d'Ivoire), paras. 89–91 and 99–101（莫名其妙地得出这样的结论，即某些钻井作业必须继续进行，因为它们一旦暂停就可能对海洋环境造成严重影响）。

[97] Protocol of San Salvador, supra footnote 37, Art. 11 (1).

[98] See *Kawas-Fernandez v. Honduras*, ICtHR Series C No. 196, Judgment (merits, reparation and costs) (3 April 2009), para. 148.

童权利公约》(*Convention on the Rights of the Child*)第 24 条第 2 款提供了另一个注解,即明确提到"环境污染的危险和风险"。[99] 最后,2012 年《东盟人权宣言》(*ASEAN Human Rights Declaration*)第 28 条第 6 款规定"每个人都有权拥有适当标准的生活……包括……一个安全、清洁和可持续的环境"。[100]

各种联合国机构(特别是联合国人权理事会及其前身人权委员会)所进行的大量法律编撰工作,为国际人权法承认这一权利提供了支持。人权委员会早在 1989 年 8 月就开始组织针对环境退化与人权之间关系的研究。这项研究成果通常被称为"Ksentini 报告"(以特别报告员 Fatma Zohra Ksentini 夫人的名字命名),于 1994 年提交。[101] 该报告在附件中附加了一个有关人权与环境间关系的原则的宏伟项目,其将环境保护明示为一系列个人的和集体的权利(义务)。遗憾的是,这个项目在当时的实际影响有限。在人权理事会的支持下,开展了一个类似的工作,目的是由一名"独立专家"来审查"与享有安全、清洁、健康和可持续的环境相关的人权义务问题"。[102] 授权给专家(John H. Knox 教授后来成为这个项目的特别报告员)的任务足够务实,可以避免得出不切实际的结论。任务的重点是对现有人权的环境维度进行评估,而不是分析享有特定质量环境这一人权的轮廓。自 2012 年被任命以来,特别报告员针对人权文件的文本和实践对环境考量的认可以及环境文件的人权维度进行了广泛的调查。在提交一份范围界定报告后[103],特别报告员对该领域做出了一个广义界定,[104] 并

---

[99] Convention on the Rights of the Child, 20 November 1989, 1577 UNTS 3 ("CRC").

[100] ASEAN Human Rights Declaration, 19 November 2012, available at: www.asean.org (last visited on 3 February 2014).

[101] Ksentini Report, supra footnote 21.

[102] Human Rights Council, Resolution 19/10: "Human Rights and the Environment", 19 April 2012, A/HRC/RES/19/10, para. 2.

[103] Report of the Independent Expert on the issue of human rights obligations relating to the enjoyment of a safe, clean, healthy and sustainable environment, John H. Knox. Preliminary Report, 24 December 2012, A/HRC/22/43.

[104] Report of the Independent Expert on the issue of human rights obligations relating to the enjoyment of a safe, clean, healthy and sustainable environment, John H. Knox. Mapping Report, 30 December 2013, A/HRC/25/53. See also the individual reports referred to supra footnote 37.

针对承认和实施人权的环境维度的"良好实践"[105] 提出了多项建议。[106]

2. 用水和环境卫生权

另一项具有特定环境性质的权利是用水和环境卫生权。[107] 国内和国际文件在不同程度地承认了这一权利。[108]

许多文件对用水权的承认是模糊的，隐现于那些规定其他权利的条款中。如《经济、社会及文化权利国际公约》（ICESCR）第 11 条（享有良好的生活水平、充足的食物以及住房的权利）和第 12 条（享有最高可获得健康标准的权利），它们被认为是经济、社会、文化权利委员会（Committee on Economic, Social and Cultural Rights）在它的《第 15 号一般评论意见》（*General Comment 15*, GC 15）中承认用水权的基础。在《第 15 号一般评论意见》中，[109] 委员会对用水权的定义如下：

> 用水人权使得人们有权获得充足的、安全的、可接受的、可实际获取和负担的个人和家庭用水。[110]

这一定性后来被进一步阐释，它体现了五个主要要件：可用性（个人和家庭用水的供应必须是充足的和持续的）、质量（水必须是安全的，即无污染物、病菌和辐射危险）、可获取性（水必须是在所有人群的安全

105　Report of the Independent Expert on the issue of human rights obligations relating to the enjoyment of a safe, clean, healthy and sustainable environment, John H. Knox. Compilation of good practices, 3 February 2015, A/HRC/28/61.

106　Report of the Special Rapporteur on the issue of human rights obligations relating to the enjoyment of a safe, clean, healthy and sustainable environment. Implementation Report, 28 December 2015, A/HRC/31/53.

107　See I. T. Winkler, *The Human Right to Water* (Oxford: Hart, 2012); M.-C. Petersmann, *Les Sources du droit à l'eau en droit international* (Paris: Johanet, 2013); P. Thielboerger, *The Human Right (s) to Water. The Multi-Level Governance of a Unique Human Right* (Berlin: Springer, 2014); M. Langford and A. F. S. Russell (eds.), *The Right to Water. Theory, Practice and Prospects* (Cambridge University Press, 2017).

108　On the extent of this recognition, see Petersmann, supra footnote 107.

109　Committee on Economic, Social and Cultural Rights, *General Comment No. 15* (2002), *The Right to Water* (*Arts. 11 and 12 of the International Covenant on Economic, Social and Cultural Rights*), 26 November 2002, UN ESCOR Doc. E/C. 12/2002/11 ("GC 15").

110　Ibid., para. 2.

使用范围内)、可负担性(所有人都负担得起用水和水设施的费用)和可接受性(必须具有符合标准的颜色、气味和味道,以供所有个人和家庭使用)。公民在享有用水权的同时,必须履行相应的义务。用水权包含多个从不同视角来定性的关联义务。一种视角是关注用水权派生出的具体权利的各种类别,主要分为两大类,"自由"(例如不受歧视、干涉)和"权利"(例如获得供水和水信息的权利)。另一种视角则是关注用水权引发的国家义务,采用关联义务的常用三部曲来表述就是"尊重"(不直接干预)、"保护"(不受第三方干预)和"实现"(为公民行使水权提供便利并提升所需服务)。需要强调指出的是,与其他人权一样,用水权的保障需要各国的谨慎注意。如此一来,用水权就蕴含了可诉的持续性的国家义务。[111] 这一点有时会被误解,原因是一个狭隘和僵化的固化思维影响了对经济、社会和文化权利的正确理解。

在其他一些文件中,用水权也得到了明确的承认,但是权利主体仅限于儿童、[112] 妇女、[113] 以及武装冲突中的战俘或平民等。[114] 如《消除对妇女一切形式歧视公约》(Convention on the Elimination of All Forms of Discrimination against Women)第14条第2款规定:

> 缔约各国应采取一切适当措施以消除对农村妇女的歧视,保证她们在男女平等的基础上参与农村发展并受其益惠,尤其是保证她们有

---

[111] See, e.g., *Children and Adolescents of the Communities of Uribia, Manaure, Riohacha and Maicao of the Wayuu People, in the Department of the Guajira, Colombia*, ICommHR Precautionary Measure No. 51/15 (11 December 2015) [美洲人权委员会要求哥伦比亚"立即采取措施,使受益社区能够尽快获得安全的饮用水,以满足女童、男童和青少年的生存需要"(翻译自西班牙语原文)]。

[112] CRC, supra footnote 99.

[113] Convention on the Elimination of All Forms of Discriminationa against Women, 18 December 1979, 1249 UNTS 13 (CEDAW).

[114] See, e.g., Convention (III) relative to the Treatment of Prisoners of War, 12 August 1949, 75 UNTS 31, Arts. 20, 26, 29 and 46; Convention (IV) relative to the Protection of Civilian Persons in Time of War, 12 August 1949, 75 UNTS 287, Arts. 85, 89 and 127; Protocol Additional to the Geneva Conventions of 12 August 1949, and relating to the Protection of Victims of International Armed Conflicts (Additional Protocol I), 8 June 1977, 1125 UNTS 3, Arts. 54 and 55; Protocol Additional to the Geneva Conventions of 12 August 1949, and relating to the Protection of Victims of Non-International Armed Conflicts (Protocol II), 8 June 1977, 1125 UNTS 609, Arts. 5 and 14.

权享受适当的生活条件,特别是在住房、卫生、水电供应、交通和通信等方面。[115]

类似地,《儿童权利公约》第 24 条第 2 款要求各国采取措施以便:

> 消除疾病和营养不良(包括在基本医疗体系内),特别是通过采取即刻可得技术和提供充足的营养食品和清洁饮水。[116]

2010 年以来,联合国大会和人权理事会通过了一系列决议,明确承认用水和环境卫生权属于人权。[117] 人权理事会针对这一权利任命的第一位特别报告员 Catarina de Albuquerque 阐释了环境卫生的维度,环境卫生现在被看作用水权和人权的一个共同要件。[118] 联合国大会明确承认:

> 享有安全饮用水的人权是指每个人都能不受歧视地享有充足、安全、可接受、现实可获取、可负担的个人和家庭用水的权利,环境卫生人权是指每个人都能不受歧视地在生活的各方面享有获得现实的、可负担的环境卫生的权利,该权利应该是安全的、卫生的、可靠的、社会和文化可接受的,并提供因素且确保尊严,同时重申这两项权利都是享有优良生活水平权的组成部分。[119]

"人人享有用水和环境卫生权"是计划于 2030 年实现的《2030 年可持续发展议程》中 17 项可持续发展目标之一。[120]

---

[115] CEDAW, supra footnote 113, Art. 14 (2) (h).

[116] CRC, supra footnote 99, Art. 24 (2) (c).

[117] Resolution A/64/292, "The Human Right to Water and Sanitation", 28 July 2010, UN Doc. A/64/L. 63/Rev. 1; Resolution 15/9: "Human Rights and Access to Safe Drinking Water and Sanitation", 24 September 2010, A/HRC/15/L. 14.

[118] See "Human Rights Obligations related to Access to Sanitation", 1 July 2009, UN Doc. A/HRC/ 12/24.

[119] Resolution 70/169, "The Human Rights to Safe Drinking Water and Sanitation", 17 December 2015, UN Doc. A/RES/70/169, para. 2.

[120] Resolution 70/1, "Transforming our World: The 2030 Agenda for Sustainable Development", 21 October 2015, UN Doc. A/RES/70/1.

准确理解的话,用水和环境卫生权介于人权法和环境法之间,特别是从《赫尔辛基公约关于水与健康的议定书》(*Protocol on Water and Health to the Helsinki Convention*)[121] 等文件的视角来看,这些权利履行的前提是国家负有"确保人人享有用水和环境卫生权"的义务。[122] 从这个角度看,议定书必须被理解为是介于人权和国家间环境与健康义务之间的混合型文件。重要的是,议定书是唯一一个详细规定各国在用水和环境卫生权上所负核心义务的"硬性法律"。国家在这方面的义务主要有四类:水质[123]、应急处理[124]、信息提供[125]和国家间合作。[126] 议定书的核心是要求在广泛的领域设定有关水质的目标,并监测和报告进展情况。这一规定明确了国家的结果义务(设定目标,监测目标,并定期报告工作)和谨慎注意的一般性义务,以实现议定书第 6 条第 1 款所规定的目标,该条规定"各缔约国'应努力实现'水的获取和环境卫生的提供这一目标,或者更具体地讲,应努力这样做"。

理解议定书的结构,有助于强调那些涉及"个人权利"(无论是积极的还是消极的)的条款和那些主要涉及"国家义务"的条款在概念上的联系。[127] 如前所述,每一项个人权利都附有三项相互关联的国家义务,即尊重权利、保护权利不受第三方剥夺以及为完全享用权利提供便利的义务。对这些义务内容的明确不能仅仅依据人权条款的要件(《第 15 号一般评论意见》采取了这种做法),还应参考那些明确规定了国家义务(但是并未具体规定个人权利)的文件(例如议定书以及其他绝大多数环境条约)。换言之,为了理解调整用水和环境卫生的法律框架,必须充分结合人权条款以及涉及国家义务和职责的规范。[128]

3. 程序性权利

谈及程序性权利,我们会发现一些国际裁判机构在一般实体性权利中

---

[121] Protocol on Water and Health to the 1992 Convention on the Protection and Use of Transboundary Watercourses and International Lakes, 17 June 1999, 2331 UNTS 202 (Protocol on Water and Health).

[122] Ibid., Art. 6 (1).

[123] Ibid., Arts. 6 and 7.

[124] Ibid., Arts. 8.

[125] Ibid., Arts. 9 and 10.

[126] Ibid., Arts. 11 to 14.

[127] See, e.g., the international humanitarian law instruments mentioned supra footnote 114.

[128] See Chuffart and Viñuales, supra footnote 19.

明确了程序性要件（评估、监督、参与等）。但也有一些程序性权利被明确指定为环境程序性权利。最初对环境程序性权利进行概述的是《里约宣言》（*Rio Declaration*）第 10 条原则[129]，此后，《奥胡斯公约》[130]《巴厘指南》（*Bali Guidelines*）[131] 以及联合国拉丁美洲和加勒比经济委员会（UN Economic Commission for Latin-America and the Caribbean）的相关文件[132]等相继做出了具体规定。《奥胡斯公约》是一个区域性法律文件（在欧洲经委会主持下通过），然而它的适用范围可以进一步扩大，因为它对其他国家也开放加入。[133] 下面我们将重点讨论这一文件，因为它不仅是第一项此种类型的文件，还是唯一一项进行了足够实践的文件。[134]

《奥胡斯公约》的主要目的是"为促进保护今世后代人人得在适合其健康和福祉的环境中生活的权利"。[135] 为此目的，公约要求各缔约国在国内法律体系中落实三类环境程序性权利。[136]

第一类是获取环境信息权（第 4 条和第 5 条）。术语"环境信息"在第 2 条第 3 款中被广泛界定，主要包括以下三类："环境要素的状况"（第 2 条第 3 款 a 项）[137]、"物质、能源、噪声和辐射等因素"[138]（第 2 条第

---

[129] See supra Chapter 3.

[130] Aarhus Convention, supra footnote 25. The following presentation draws upon Chuffart and Viñuales, supra footnote 19.

[131] See *Bali Guidelines and Bali Implementation Guidelines*, supra footnote 27.

[132] See ECLAC Draft, supra footnote 26.

[133] Aarhus Convention, supra footnote 25, Art. 19 (2) – (3).

[134] See A. Andrusevych and S. Kern (eds.), *Case Law of the Aarhus Convention Compliance Committee* (2004-2014) (Lviv: RACSE, 3nd edn, 2016) (references made in this section to the case-law of the Committee are derived from Andrusevych/Kern). On the relevance of this instrument from the perspective of human rights and the environment see Report on Aarhus, supra footnote 37.

[135] Aarhus Convention, supra footnote 25, Art. 1.

[136] 《奥胡斯公约》的条款也可能对国内法律体系造成直接影响。See *Kazakhstan* ACCC/C/2004/2, ECE/MP. PP/C. 1/2005/2/Add. 2（14 March 2005），para. 28.

[137] See *United Kingdom* ACCC/C/2010/53, ECE/MP. PP/C. 1/2013/3（11 January 2013）（UK January 2013），paras. 73-74（这些信息可能包括过程，但也包括原始数据）。

[138] See *Moldova* ACCC/C/2008/30, ECE/MP. PP/C. 1/2009/6/Add. 3（8 February 2011），para. 29（活动或措施是一个宽泛的术语，有可能包括国有林地的租赁合同）；*European Community* ACCC/C/2007/21, ECE/MP. PP/C. 1/2009/2/ Add. 1（11 December 2009），para. 30（还包括与环境相关的活动或措施的融资协议）。

3款b项）和：

> 正在或可能受环境要素或通过这些要素影响，或者上述（第2条第3款b项）所指因素、活动或措施影响的人类健康和安全状况、人类生活条件、文化遗址和建筑结构（第2条第3款c项）。

这一条款建立了"人类健康安全"或"人类生活条件"与"环境"之间的联系，凸显了扩大人权的范围以便将环境要素包含在内的意义。人权范围扩大的同时，使得这一联系越来越明确，进而将这一权利从获取环境信息权延伸到涉及各种人权的措施与政策（涉及水质标准、第三方使用公共土地、卫生系统区域规划要求的措施政策）。《奥胡斯公约实施指南》（Implementation Guide of the Aarhus Convention）进一步阐明了这种联系，它指出了如下事实：

> 人类健康包括一系列直接或间接归因于后者受环境条件变化影响的疾病和健康状况。[139]

就目前而言，环境信息与人权条件之间的联系涉及表10-1中的"问题2"，即如何通过利用环境法律文件来实现人权。扩大"环境信息"的范围有其局限性。虽然《奥胡斯公约实施指南》指出，上述三种"环境信息"的分类还不够完整，[140] 但是也无法认定其中包含了与环境无明显联系的措施。"环境信息"不包括涉及受教育权或劳动权的措施的信息，除非该信息与"环境要素的状态"或"物质、能源、噪声和辐射"等因素有充分联系。

第二类包括公众参与特定活动决策（第6条）、涉及环境的计划、方案和政策（第7条），以及参与行政规章和其他普遍适用具有法律约束力的文书的起草（第8条）。这些权利可以被看作更宽泛的公共事务参与权

---

[139] The Aarhus Convention: An Implementation Guide, available at: www.unece.org/env/pp/implementation%20guide/english/part2.pdf（last visited 24 January 2014）("Implementation Guide"), p. 38.

[140] Ibid., p. 35.

具体应用，该项参与权主要由《公民权利及政治权利国际公约》第 25 条第 1 款规定，[141] 适用于经济、社会和文化权利。[142] 这一类权利引发了多个问题，[143] 其中一个最相关的问题是确认根据《奥胡斯公约》哪些种类的行为必须经过公众参与。不同种类的行为必须符合不同的公众参与要求[144]，因此，某一特定行为与环境的关系是一个核心问题。两个基本标准被用于判断这一问题。

第 6 条第 1 款和第 8 条（序言）指的是那些"可能会对环境产生重大影响的""活动"或"行政规章和其他普遍适用的具有法律约束力的规则"。公约附件一所列的活动应符合第 6 条的规定，因此应被假定是足够重大的（第 6 条第 1 款第 1 项），针对未列入附件 1 的活动（第 6 条第 1 款第 2 项），公约并未规定满足重大所需的门槛，因此，由缔约国自主决定某一项目的决策是否适用于第 6 条。[145] 而这一"筛选性"决策应当遵守第 6 条的规定。在实质性方面，《奥胡斯公约实施指南》[146] 援引了《关于跨界背景下环境影响评价的埃斯波公约》（*Espoo Convention on Environmental Impact Assessment in a Transboundary Context*）[147] 附件三第 1 段用以阐明重

---

[141] ICCPR, supra footnote 32, Art. 25 (a).

[142] On the scope of Article 25 of the ICCPR, see HRC, *General Comment No. 25: The Right to Participate in Public Affairs, Voting Rights and the Right of Equal Access to Public Service* (Art. 25), 12 July 1996, CCPR/C/21/Rev. 1/Add. 7, paras. 5-8 (referring to applications of the Art. 25 (a)).

[143] One important question concerns the scope of public participation. This is discussed in detail in the Implementation Guide (Implementation Guide, supra footnote 139, pp. 85-122). 就我们的目的而言，只需指出公众参与这一规定并不意味着公众对活动、措施或计划具有否决权。See Aarhus Convention, supra footnote 25, Arts. 6 (8), 7, and 8 *in fine*; Implementation Guide, supra footnote 139, pp. 109 - 10; *Spain* ACCC/C/2008/24, ECE/MP. PP/C. 1/2009/8/Add. 1 (30 September 2010), para. 98; *Czech Republic* ACCC/C/2012/70, ECE/MP. PP/C. 1/2014/9 (4 June 2014) (*Czech Republic June* 2014), para. 61.

[144] On the formulation of this stratification see UK (January 2013), supra footnote 137, para. 82.

[145] See *Czech Republic* ACCC/C/2010/50, ECE/MP. PP/C. 1/2012/11 (2 October 2012), para. 82; *United Kingdom* ACCC/C/2010/45 and ACCC/C/2011/60, ECE/MP. PP/C. 1/2013/12 (23 October 2013), para. 75. 举例来说，欧盟排放交易指令在特定国家的实施策略实际上是一个"计划"，因此受公众参与要求的制约。See *Czech Republic June* 2014, supra footnote 143, para. 53.

[146] Implementation Guide, supra footnote 139, p. 94.

[147] Convention on Environmental Impact Assessment in a Transboundary Context, 25 February 1991, 1989 UNTS 309 (Espoo Convention).

大活动的界定标准。《埃斯波公约》提到了在界定"重大"活动时所应考虑的几个标准。一般来讲，这些标准包括规模、位置和影响。公约更进一步明确提及了那些位于特定地点的项目（在这些地点，计划的开发活动有可能会对居民造成重大影响）[148] 或者那些对人类造成严重影响的活动。[149] 针对规范性行为，那些涉及程序性环境权利和义务的行为被认为满足了重大这一门槛。[150]

第 7 条在提及与环境相关的"计划和项目"和"政策起草"时采用了相对较低的标准。某一行为是"活动"（就第 6 条而言）还是"计划"，是"项目"还是"政策"，并不取决于该行为的名称，而是取决于该行为的实际特点和影响。[151] 根据《奥胡斯公约实施指南》，这一相关性应当参考"环境信息"定义中蕴含的"环境"的定义（第 2 条第 3 款）来决定。[152] 如此一来，在这种情况下，那些影响人类状态及其人权的活动、措施和法规就有可能被归属为必须经过公众参与的行为。实际上，所针对的活动和措施大多是那些可能对环境造成严重后果的活动和措施，这类活动和措施在很大程度上与那些影响广义的人类健康和文化的活动和措施（例如通过水的安全和质量、食品生产、工作环境的安全等）产生了重叠。因此，《奥胡斯公约》所规定的公众参与要求可以充当一个额外的保护层次，基于这一保护层次，公众就可以进一步审视那些涉及人权保障的措施。

第三类主要包括公民在获得环境信息和参与环境决策过程中诉诸司法的权利（第 9 条）。重要的是，公约第 9 条第 3 款拓展规定，公众的成员享有"对违反涉及环境的国家法律规定的个人和当局的作为和不作为提

---

[148] Ibid., Appendix Ⅲ, para. 1（b）*in fine*.

[149] Ibid., Appendix Ⅲ, para. 1（c）.

[150] See *Belarus* ACCC/C/2009/44, ECE/MP.PP/C. 1/2011/6/Add. 1（19 September 2011）, para. 61.

[151] See *Croatia* ACCC/C/2012/66, ECE/MP.PP/C. 1/2014/4（13 January 2014）, para. 35.

[152] Implementation Guide, supra footnote 139, p. 115. 根据《奥胡斯公约实施指南》，这将包括"各级政府的土地利用和区域发展战略，以及交通、旅游、能源、重工业和轻工业、水资源、健康与卫生等方面的部门规划"。

出质疑"的权利，[153] 换言之，所涉及的法律必须是"涉及环境的"，这与狭义的"环境法"相比更具包容性。[154] 此外，赋予的救济途径必须切实有效，且成本不宜过高。[155] 在人权的语境内，这一扩展可以被视为国家有义务保护公民的环境权利不受第三方剥夺，或者在谈及与用水权的关联时，有义务在确立和履行环境保护的适当框架时谨慎注意。[156]

对于上述三类权利，有关公众主要包括符合国家法律规定的"受到或可能受到环境决策影响或与环境决策程序存在利害关系以及满足国内法其他规定的"的公众。[157] 此外，公约第9条第2款明确规定：

> 凡达到第2条第5款所指要求的任何非政府组织的利益，应视为具备上述（a）项所指充分利益（具有充分利益的所涉公众）。这种组织也应被视为具有以上（b）所指可受到损害的权利（确定某项权利受到损害）。[158]

《奥胡斯公约》框架的广泛适用使其成为实施国家义务的有力工具。此外，正如第九章讨论的，当缔约国未在国内法律体系内履行公约规定的义务时，可以按照公约关于不遵约程序的相关规定提交通报。因此，总的来说，与《关于水与健康的议定书》相似，《奥胡斯公约》是一个混合型文件，兼容了人权与环境义务。

153　On the scope of this obligation see *Denmark* ACCC/C/2006/18, ECE/MP. PP/2008/5/Add. 4（29 April 2008），para. 28. See also *European Union* ACCC/C/2008/32（Part I），ECE/MP. PP/ C. 1/2011/4/Add. 1（May 2011），para. 77（指各方在履行这一义务时所享有的"灵活性"，即这不要求颁布一项普遍措施，但也不允许一方通过严格的常设标准有效地限制诉诸司法的机会）。

154　See *Austria* ACCC/C/2011/63，ECE/MP. PP/C. 1/2014/3（13 January 2014），para. 52.

155　See *United Kingdom* ACCC/C/2008/27，ECE/MP. PP/C. 1/2010/6/Add. 2（November 2010），para. 44.

156　*Kazakhstan* ACCC/C/2004/6，ECE/MP. PP/C. 1/2006/4/Add. 1（28 July 2006），paras. 30ff.

157　Aarhus Convention, supra footnote 25, Art. 2（5）.

158　See *Belgium* ACCC/2005/11，ECE/MP. PP/C. 1/2006/4/Add. 2（28 July 2006），para. 27（指出："尽管充分利益和侵权的成立应由国内法来确定，但是，必须依据公约来体现其目标是使公众有更多机会诉诸司法"）。

三 人权文件中环境保护的范围

(一) 概述

如前所述,人权文件对环境的保护取决于环境损害与所保护的人类价值(特别是广义上的健康和完整性或文化考量)受损之间的联系。这是因为人权法与侵权法一样,提供法律保护的基础是人身受到损害。依据这一方法,就几乎不可能提供纯粹的"以生态为中心的"[159]环境保护或者整合未出生的后代的权利。[160]如此一来,人权保护规范与环境保护规范的范围就并不是完全重叠的。

利用人权保护环境虽然有效,但有一定的局限性。有一个著名学者就曾指出这一难点:

> 我们在寻求这一领域(环境正义)的过程中,应该明确以下问题:是否需要创造一些新权利——我将避免对"世代权利"进行迂腐的、徒劳的图示化——这些权利必然会涉及环境和新技术导致的风险,或者是否需要"调整"国际人权的概念性和规范性框架以顺应时代的变化,将保护的范围拓展到新的风险和环境退化对人权的影响。[161]

后文将聚焦上段提出的第二种方法,即"调整"现有的概念性和规范性框架以便适应(而非歪曲)人权的逻辑基础。我们将会讨论这一方法的局限性和可能的解决措施及其对两个问题(即集体诉请和人权与气候变化的联系)的影响。

(二) 对"联系"的要求

在现有各种人权中,根据它们对应的裁判机构的解释,其环境保护的范围取决于环境退化与某一受保护权利受损之间的"联系"。在各种不同

---

[159] On the distinction between "anthropocentric" and "ecocentric" approaches, see C. Stone, "Ethics and International Environmental Law", in D. Bodansky, J. Brunnée and E. Hey (eds.), *The Oxford Handbook of International Environmental Law* (Oxford University Press, 2007), pp. 291-312.

[160] See *E. H. P. v. Canada*, supra footnote 39, para. 8 (a),在这里,对后代的提及仅仅被视为一种"关切的表达"。

[161] Francioni, supra footnote 15, p. 42.

的法律语境中,对这一联系进行了广义或狭义解读。虽然"法律语境"这一表述在此通常指的是相关的条约(例如欧洲、美洲、非洲的人权公约),但是我们还应做一个更详细的梳理以便掌握"联系"这一要求的局限性。事实上,每个"条约语境"的裁判机构都采取了不同的立场,这不仅取决于所涉及的特定"人权"(如《欧洲人权公约》第6条或第8条),而且取决于案件的具体情况。想要设定一个合适的尺度是非常困难的,这一尺度既足够具体以便把握个案的细微差别,同时又足够宽泛以便得出一般性结论。在后文,我们设立了一个相对宽泛的尺度,以便强调对这一"联系"的普遍性需求。更具体的研究可以在专业著作中找到。[162]

最新的区域人权裁判机制已经承认,必须要有一个或多或少的"联系",联系的紧密程度则需要具体情况具体分析。欧洲人权法院在"Kyrtatos 诉希腊案"(在《欧洲人权公约》第8条背景下)中指出:

> 《欧洲人权公约》无论是第8条还是其他任意一条条款都不是专门为环境提供一般保护而制定的;针对环境保护问题,其他的国际文件或国内立法更加适用。[163]

在"Athanassoglou 诉瑞士案"中,法院依据《欧洲人权公约》第6条指出:

> 原告们在诉状中……并没有充分论证核电厂普遍存在的危险对他们个人而言形成了一个具体的和迫在眉睫的危险;他们起诉的依据大多是核能利用天生具备的安全、环境和技术特点。[164]

---

[162] See Francioni, supra footnote 15; C. Schall, "Public Interest Litigation Concerning Environmental Matters before the Human Rights Courts: A Promising Future Concept?" (2008) 20 *Journal of Environmental Law* 417; ICommHR, *Indigenous and Tribal Peoples' Rights over their Ancestral Lands and Natural Resources: Norms and Jurisprudence of the InterAmerican Human Rights System*, 30 December 2009, Doc OEA/Ser. L/V/II, Doc. 56/09; R. Pavoni, *Interesse pubblico e diritti individuali nella giurisprudenza ambientale della Corte europea dei diritti umani* (Naples: Editoriale Scientifica, 2013).

[163] *Kyrtatos v. Greece*, ECtHR Application No. 41666/98, Judgment (22 May 2003), para. 52.

[164] *Athanassoglou and others v. Switzerland*, ECtHR Application No. 27644/95, Judgment (6 April 2000), para. 52.

在美洲，美洲人权委员会针对土著居民反对修建穿越巴拿马自然保护区公路的请愿书提出了一个类似的观点：

> 委员会……认为这一诉请不应被受理，因为它涉及集团诉讼中被代表的抽象受害者问题，而不是具体确定和限定的个体。委员会认为，鉴于诉请的性质，诉状很难精确指定特定受害群体，因为巴拿马的所有公民都被看作大都市自然保护区的财产所有者。这一诉请不应被受理，还因为《美洲人权公约》认为环境、公民和科学团体（它们被认为受到了最大伤害）是法律实体，而非自然人。因此，根据在之前案例中所适用的、对公约第44条解释标准所确定的判例，委员会裁定它不具备所需的属人管辖（ratione personae）权来裁判当前事项。[165]

即使是美洲人权法院在涉及土著居民权利时所运用的较宽松标准的判例，也要求必须存在某种"联系"，没有"联系"就失去了保护环境的依据。在"Saramaka人民诉苏里南案"中，法院阐明了为什么应根据公约第21条（财产权）保护环境：

> 代表土著居民和部落所采取特别措施的目的是保证他们能够继续过传统的生活，他们独特的文化特征、社会结构、经济制度、习惯信仰等能够得到国家的尊重、确认和保护。[166]

至于非洲委员会，尽管《非洲宪章》第24条明确规定了各国人民享有舒适环境的权利，但单纯的环境退化（迄今为止）似乎并不构成对个人或民族权利的损害。事实上，在"Ogoni案"中，[167] 非洲委员会根据《非洲宪章》第16条（健康权）对第24条进行了解释，提及了"健康环

---

[165] *Metropolitan Nature Reserve v. Panama*, Case 11.533, Report No. 88/03, ICommHR, OEA/Ser. L/V/II. 118 Doc. 70 rev. 2 at 524（2003），para. 34.

[166] *Saramaka v. Suriname*, supra footnote 67, para. 121.

[167] *Ogoni*, supra footnote 75.

境权"。虽然它是用概括性的方式来定性第 24 条所引发的义务，[168] 但是它得出"违反了宪章"这一结论的基础在于所涉活动对 Ogoni 地区及其居民的影响：

> 无可置疑和必须承认的是，尼日利亚政府（通过国家石油公司）有权开采石油，并将其收入用于满足尼日利亚人民的经济和社会权利。但是，政府没有注意到前段所提及的关切，而该关切将保护所指控侵权行为的受害者的权利。更恶劣的是，政府的保安部队还参与了对当地居民权利的侵害活动，袭击、焚烧和摧毁了数个 Ogoni 地区的村庄和住宅。[169]

由于法律背景的不同，对"联系"的要求也存在不同的定性方式。欧洲人权法院采用的是《欧洲人权公约》第 8 条中环境退化与对人权的"最低严重程度的"侵害之间的"直接"联系。[170] 侵害程度应当根据多个因素来进行评估：

> 对"最低严重程度"的评估是相对的，它取决于案件的具体情况，如妨害行为的强度和持续的时间以及它造成的身体和心理影响。环境的宏观背景也应考虑在内。如果与所有现代城市生活天生就有的环境危害相比，所起诉的损害后果是可以忽略不计的，那么就不能依据《欧洲人权公约》第 8 条提出无可争辩的诉求。[171]

在"Fagerskiold 诉瑞典案"中，原告认为位于其住所附近的风力涡轮机产生的噪声和光反射这一妨害行为的严重程度，构成了对《欧洲人权公约》第 8 条的违反，但被法院驳回。法院指出，这一妨害行为的严重

---

168 According to the Commission, this right requires the State "to take reasonable and other measures to prevent pollution and ecological degradation, to promote conservation, and to secure an ecologically sustainable development and use of natural resources", Ibid., para. 52.

169 Ibid., para. 54.

170 *Fadeyeva v. Russia*, supra footnote 57, paras. 68-70.

171 Ibid., para. 69.

程度还没有达到处理环境问题的案件所确立的高门槛。[172] 关于联系的"直接性",欧洲人权法院采取了一个事实敏感测试,它在"Kyrtatos 诉希腊案"中的推理是一个很好的例证:

> 即使假设该地区的城市发展严重破坏了环境,原告还是没有提供令人信服的证据来证明,对生活在沼泽地的鸟类和其他受保护物种的损害直接影响到了他们自身的权利(即依据《公约》第 8 条第 1 款所享有的权利)。如果换一种情况,结果可能就会不同,例如,所指控的环境退化涉及对原告住所附近森林地区的破坏,这样就直接影响到了原告的切身利益。[173]

还是在欧洲这一背景下,当涉及依据《欧洲人权公约》第 6 条所提起的诉求时,对"联系"的要求似乎更加严格。在"Balmer-Schafroth 诉瑞士案"中,欧洲人权法院将对"联系"的要求定性为既要求存在着一个针对国内认可的某项"民事权利"的"争议",也要求假定有瑕疵的程序所导致的结果对所涉权利产生了直接决定性影响。[174] 该案中,原告反对延长核电厂的运行许可证,认为这一运行会威胁到他们的生命和健康。国内机关(瑞士联邦理事会)驳回了原告的诉求,原告随后上诉到欧洲人权法院。法院宣布这一诉求是不可受理的。法院指出,"只有细微的联系或遥远的因果关系还不足以启用第 6 条第 1 款",[175] 法院认为原告没有:

> 表明 Mühleberg 发电站使他们自身暴露于严重的、具体的和迫在眉睫的危险。在证明这一点之前,联邦理事会在此情况下可能批准的措施对公民的影响都只是一种假设。[176]

---

172 *Fägerskiöld v. Sweden*, ECtHR Application No. 37664/04, Decision as to admissibility (26 February 2008).

173 *Kyrtatos v. Greece*, supra footnote 163, para. 53.

174 *Balmer-Schafroth and others v. Switzerland*, ECtHR Application No. 22110/93, Judgment (26 August 1997), para. 32.

175 Ibid.

176 Ibid., para. 40.

在美洲和非洲，对"联系"的要求则更为宽松。主要是因为美洲人权法院在处理土著和部落居民案件时采取了较为激进的方式，以及《非洲宪章》对民族权利进行了明确规定。然而，当这种集体性权利没有受到威胁时，对"联系"的要求仍然较为严苛。美洲人权委员会在上述"大都市自然保护区案"中对此做出了一个区分，指出：

> 为保护共同利益而提起的诉请被认为是不应受理的，但是这并不意味着原告必须能够明确指定它所代表的每一个受害者……委员会认为某些代表受害者群体提交的诉请是可以受理的，前提是这一群体本身被明确定义，而且可辨识的成员的各自权利受到了诉请所针对情况的直接伤害。这就是所谓的"特定社区的成员"。[177]

委员会提到了两个"特定社区"的案例。一个是土著群体，他们逐渐被视为集体人权的一个主体，[178] 对于他们而言，对"联系"的要求较为宽松。另一个是哥伦比亚准军事组织的受害者们，他们不具备土著或部落属性。然而，从案件的实际情况来看（尤其是大多数受害者的尸体被扔进河里并已失踪），有正当理由把他们当作一群原告，尽管缺乏个体成员的确认。因此很难（尽管不是不可能）将这一群体（非土著或部落）与一个受到某种环境退化的影响的群体做一个类比。

如此一来就引发了一个问题，也就是文献中所提及的、向人权机构提起的"集体诉讼"[179] 以及它们在环境保护方面的潜在作用。

（三）人权集体诉讼：谁在为环境说话

有一个重大进展为人权中的环境保护拓展了更多空间，即在两个主要方面放宽了对"联系"的要求，一个是受害主体的确定，另一个是原告主体的确定。这两个问题直接关系到提起集体诉讼的可能性大小，因为集体或集团诉讼需要确定一个团体（不同于特定个人）及代表这一团体的主体（不同于个人诉讼的集合）。

反过来，集体或集团诉讼有可能成为环境保护的重要手段，因为：

177　*Metropolitan Nature Reserve*, supra footnote 165, para. 32.

178　See *Sarayaku v. Ecuador*, supra footnote 64, para. 231.

179　Pavoni, supra footnote 162, pp. 37-47.

(1) 环境退化往往会影响到许多人；(2) 团体内每个人对提起诉讼的态度（是否考虑到位置、脆弱性或影响）和能力（包括依据现有的资源）都有所不同；(3) 提供个体救济（即使针对的是大量不同人群）对解决广泛的环境危害而言是远远不够的。因此，放宽对"联系"的要求以推动集体诉讼的发展将会有助于为环境保护在人权中拓展更多空间。

在这一方面，欧洲与美洲和非洲存在着明显差异。欧洲对集体诉讼作了重大限制，然而在美洲和非洲，由于存在明确的法律基础（《非洲宪章》）或由于判例法的发展（美洲），集体诉讼被认为是可受理的。但是，这一宏观判断还应进行精细分析，因为欧洲的集体诉讼也有一定的发展空间；相反地，如果不涉及土著和部落居民，在美洲多大程度上可以提起集体诉讼还是不确定的。我们将进一步讨论这一问题。

欧洲人权法院对涉及环境的集体诉讼的态度是相当谨慎的。欧洲人权法院对"Atanasov 诉保加利亚案"的裁判可以当作我们分析这一问题的切入点。[180] 该案的意义在于，它不仅为欧洲人权法院提供了很好的环境判例，[181] 还因为本案中有欠缺的环境恢复方案对原告和一个团体（生活在矿址周围的当地社区）都构成了威胁。事实上，保加利亚法院已经意识到原告和该地区的其他居民有足够的利害关系来依据国内法提起诉讼。然而，法院却偏离了这一意识，而只是简单运用了公约第 8 条的基本标准，即要求环境退化与对个体人权的严重侵权之间必须存在直接联系。[182] 基于这一点，法院驳回了认定违反公约第 8 条的诉讼请求。另一个可能更清晰的例证是法院在"Aydin 诉土耳其案"中的判决，[183] 在该案中，许多土地主对一个影响自然公园环境的大坝和水电开发项目提出质疑。他们依据《欧洲人权公约》第 6 条和第 8 条向法院提起诉讼，要求享有健康环境的权利。法院对这两条理由都予以驳回并指出，关于第 8 条，实际上原告是试图保护环境而非他们的权利：

原告认为该开发项目会对 Munzur valley 的生态系统造成影响；然

---

[180] *Atanasov v. Bulgaria*, supra footnote 48.

[181] Ibid., paras. 66-75.

[182] Ibid., paras. 76-79.

[183] *Aydin and others v. Turkey*, ECtHR Application No. 40806/07), Decision (15 May 2012).

而却没有证明该项目的修建会对他们的生活方式或财产造成影响，也没有证明他们的一员面临着一个具体和直接的威胁。[184]

在后来的"Di Sarno 诉意大利案"中，[185] 法院稍微软化了它的立场。原告认为意大利政府未能建立一个完善的废物收集和管理制度，从而侵犯了坎帕尼亚大区（Campania）全体居民的权利。法院并未采纳这一主张，但是法院通过承认特定城区（Soma Vesuviana 地区）的居民（包括原告）受到了"垃圾危机"的威胁来含蓄地降低了证明存在着直接和严重的影响的要求。[186] 但是，总的来说，欧洲人权法院至今仍不受理集体环境诉讼，只有当这些诉讼转化为符合对"联系"要求的个人诉讼时才会被受理。换言之，受到环境退化影响的个人可以提起诉讼并寻求具体救济，但是在这一法律背景下，环境本身还是无法发声。

美洲人权法院则采取了不同的方法，虽然到目前为止只涉及土著和部落居民。如本章前文所述，美洲人权法院扩大了《美洲人权公约》第 21 条（财产权）的范围，以保护这类居民或社区与其传统土地的关系。这不仅意味着这类主体被当作人权的主体，还意味着将环境保护的范围扩大到可能对这类居民造成影响的整个区域，这一范围必然大大超出了原有范围（只影响某一特定个人）。此外，这样所提供的保护重心就不是广义上的人类健康和完整性，而是环境的一般状态，环境的保护程度至少应当能够确保土著和部落居民的传统生活方式。如此一来，涉及环境的集体诉讼就有可能出现，因为有标准来确定某一团体（界定土著和部落居民的文化标准），而且这一团体有一个集体代表（土著和部落居民当局）。受到保护的权利不再仅仅是特定个人的权利，而是一个集体主体的权利。美洲人权法院在"Kichwa de Sarayaku 诉厄瓜多尔案"中指出：

> 在以往涉及土著和部落社区或居民的案件中，法院曾认定土著或部落社区和居民的成员的权利受到侵害。但是，有关土著或部落社区和居民的国际立法将他们的权利看作国际法上集体主体的权利，而不

---

[184] Ibid., para. 28（our translation from the French text）.

[185] *Di Sarno and others v. Italy*, ECtHR Application No. 30765/08, Judgment（10 January 2012）.

[186] Ibid., para. 81.

仅看作个人的权利（参见《联合国土著人民权利宣言》《国际劳工组织第 169 号公约》和《非洲宪章》）。鉴于土著或部落社区和居民是由特殊的生活方式和身份团结在一起、以集体的方式来行使公约承认的特定权利，法院指出，应当从集体的视角来理解这一判决所表达或传递的法律考量。[187]

与任何个人相比，这些集体主体都处于一个优势地位来为环境发声并主张一般的环境救济，因为他们与环境状态的关联比居住于某一地点的任何特定个人或家庭都要广泛得多。《联合国土著人民权利宣言》指出："土著人民有权养护和保护其土地或领土和资源的环境和生产能力。"[188] 此外，《美洲人权公约》第 44 条的一项程序性规定进一步增加了提起涉及环境的集体诉讼的可能性。它规定：

> 任何团体或被美洲国家组织（OAS）一个或多个成员国法律上认可的任何非政府组织，可以就任一缔约国违反公约的行为向美洲人权委员会提起诉请（包括申诉或请求）。

如此一来，在美洲，环境在实体和程序两个层面都得益于集体性发声。

在非洲，由于《非洲宪章》明确规定了集体性权利和代表性，对集体诉讼的判例阐释就显得不是那么迫切。这一点可以在"Ogoni 案"[189] 中得以体现，该案由两个欧洲非政府组织向非洲委员会提起诉讼，案中涉及了个人权利（第 16 条）和集体权利（第 21 条、第 24 条）。

尽管集体诉讼是一种很好的环保途径，但是对集体权利及起诉资格的承认仍然受制于这类权利对"联系"的要求。想要将环境退化纳入人权文件中，必须在某国的作为或不作为、环境退化和对集体权利的侵害之间

---

[187] *Kichwa de Sarayaku v. Ecuador*, supra footnote 64, para. 231.

[188] United Nations Declaration on the Rights of Indigenous Peoples, 13 September 2007, UN Doc. A/RES/61/295, para. 29（1）. See also American Declaration on the Rights of Indigenous Peoples, 16 June 2016, OAS AG/RES. 2888（XLVI-0/16）, p. 167, Art. XIX（专注于"一项保护健康环境的权利"）.

[189] *Ogoni*, supra footnote 75.

第十章　人权和环境　　459

建立起一个联系。在有些情况下这是非常困难的，例如气候变化，想要证明这一联系就面临着无法逾越的障碍。

（四）人权与气候变化[190]

如前文所述，我们已经看到，环境保护的人权方法会要求在环境退化与对人权的侵害之间建立一种联系。这种联系可以从不同层面来理解。一种是涉及健康或文化的各种考量，这些考量已经被用于证明环境退化侵犯了人权。另一种是这一联系的法律特征（严重性和直接性）。这两个层面都会基于法律背景（条约、具体条款、具体情况）的不同而发生改变。但是，总体而言，欧洲人权法院比较重视广义上的健康考量，美洲人权法院则比较关注文化考量。由于《非洲宪章》的特别内容，非洲委员会对健康和文化考量都比较重视。

以上这一整体判断有助于我们理解现在所讨论的问题，即采用什么"形容词"来定性享有特定质量的环境这一权利。专家和裁判机构似乎很少关注"形容词"，他们可能会理所当然地认为"形容词"的使用并不会对权利的内容和运作造成改变。然而，措辞通常都会对法律上的突破发挥重大作用。我们所说的享有一个"健康的"（healthy）环境的权利，可能会超出健康这一范围并涵盖广义上的人类完整性的问题，但很少会涉及某一传统产业活动（例如烟草生产、渔业或畜牧业[191]）的保护或审美上的考量。类型的局限性可能也适用于享有一个"安全的"（safe）[或者合理的（sound）]环境的权利，虽然这一定性可能更容易适用于"集体"主体，因为"健康"是一个个人利益，只有在类比的情况下才能用于集体。相反地，享有一个"体面的"（decent）或"整体令人满意的"（generally satisfactory）环境权利的重心并不在于健康和完整性上的考量，而会更多涉及文化和审美上的考量。同样地，这样的权利更适用于集体主体。

190　This section draws partly upon J. E. Viñuales, "A Human Rights Approach to Extraterritorial Environmental Protection? An Assessment", in N. Bhuta (ed.), *The Frontiers of Human Rights. Extraterritoriality and its Challenges* (Oxford University Press, 2016), pp. 177–221.

191　根据土著居民权利的某些文书来解释《北美自由贸易协定》第 11 章，烟草生产被认定是受保护的投资。See *Grand River Enterprises Six Nations, Ltd, and others v. United States of America*, NAFTA Arbitration (UNCITRAL Rules), Award (12 January 2011), paras. 66–67, 190. 一般来讲，因为文化上的原因，渔业或畜牧业等活动被当作某些少数民族传统生计的一部分而受到保护。See *Ominayak v. Canada*, supra footnote 40; *Ilmari Länsman v. Finland*, supra footnote 40.

针对措辞的研究第一眼看起来像是纯学术的，实际上并非如此。当前，人们正在探索用人权方法来解决环境问题，包括非常难以捕捉的气候变化及其影响［例如通过所谓的"缓发事件"（slow onset events）］。[192] 值得注意的是，作为一项专门针对气候变化的条约，《巴黎协定》（Paris Agreement）首次提到了人权问题：

> 认识到气候变化是人类共同关切事项，缔约方在采取应对气候变化的行动时，应尊重、促进和考虑他们对人权、健康权、土著居民、当地社区、移民、儿童、残障人士、弱势群体的权利和发展权，以及性别平等、赋予妇女权利、代际公平等所附的各自义务。[193]

这一重要提法从两个视角强调了人权义务的相关性，第一是从协同效应的视角（各国有义务针对气候变化采取行动并尊重、促进和完成它们的人权义务），第二是从冲突的视角（应对气候变化的行动不能侵犯人权），在此我们重点讨论第一个视角。在本章末尾我们将讨论冲突问题。

为了将基于人身伤害的法律制度（例如人权法）用于促进各国采取减缓和适应措施，就必须很谨慎地选择一个措辞来对享有特定质量的环境的潜在权利进行定性。想要气候变化符合前文所述的对"联系"的要求是非常困难的，因为原告必须证明国家的作为或者不作为对气候系统造成了影响，而这一影响引发了一个影响了原告权利的具体极端（或者缓发

---

[192] 一些倡议试图从人权的角度来将气候变化问题概念化。See, e. g., OHCHR, *Report of the Office of the United Nations High Commissioner for Human Rights on the Relationship between Climate Change and Human Rights*, 15 January 2009, UN Doc. A/HRC/10/61; UNEP, *Climate Change and Human Rights* (December 2015); Human Rights Council, "Human rights and climate change", 28 June 2016, A/HRC/32/L. 34; OHCHR, *Analytical study on the relationship between climate change and the human right of everyone to the enjoyment of the highest attainable standard of physical and mental health*, 6 May 2016, A/ HRC/32/23; Report of the Special Rapporteur on the issue of human rights obligations relating to the enjoyment of a safe, clean, healthy and sustainable environment, 1 February 2016, A/ HRC/31/52.

[193] See Adoption of the Paris Agreement, Decision 1/CP. 21, 12 December 2015, FCCC/CP/2015/ L. 9 (Paris Decision). The Paris Agreement is appended as an Annex (Paris Agreement).

的）天气事件。[194] 这一复杂的逻辑结构通常发生在全球范围，人权法只有通过认定域外人权义务才能处理这一问题。[195] 概念上，在这种情况下要证明因果联系需要有三个步骤：（1）国家行为（通过作为或不作为）影响了气候系统；（2）该影响导致了极端天气事件（例如干旱、热浪、飓风等）或缓发事件（例如极地冰川融化或海平面上升）的发生；（3）这一极端或缓发事件对人权造成了一个具体的、足够严重的侵害。

人权法院的实践只涉及这一逻辑结构的部分内容。法院实践迄今为止关注的重点是地方性的环境威胁或退化，而非极端或缓发环境现象。在此背景下，需要进行两个因果关系求证，第一，国家的作为或不作为与这种环境威胁或退化之间的因果关系；第二，这种环境威胁或退化与个人人权受损之间的因果关系。图10-3 概括了这一点。

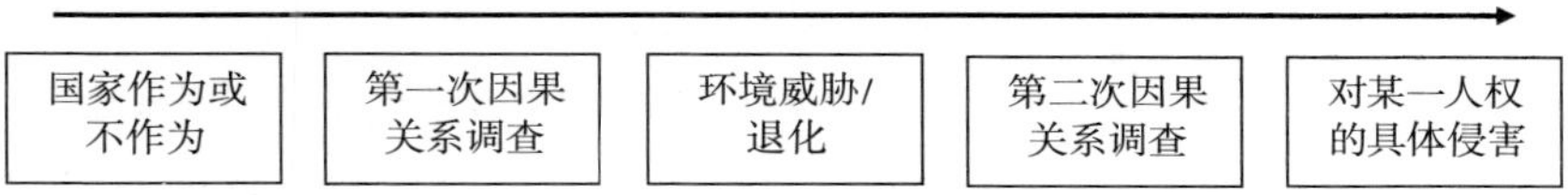

| 国家作为或不作为 | 第一次因果关系调查 | 环境威胁/退化 | 第二次因果关系调查 | 对某一人权的具体侵害 |

图 10-3　基本的因果关系求证

虽然想要证明上述因果关系可能会比较困难，但是在环境案件发生的通常情况下也并非不可能，因为正如许多判决所述，人权法院都会在环境案件认定违反相关条约的情况。在气候变化领域，这两个因果关系求证要复杂得多。虽然当下已经确定了20世纪气候变化的主要原因是温室气体

194　For two on-going attempts in this regard see：Petition to the Commission on Human Rights of the Philippines requesting for Investigation of the Responsibility of the Carbon Majors for Human Rights Violations or Threats of Violations Resulting from the Impacts of Climate Change, submitted by Greenpeace Southeast Asia et al. （22 September 2015）；Kelsey Cascadia Rose Juliana et al. v. United States of America et al., US District Court of Oregon（Eugene Division）, Case No. 6：15-cv-01517-TC, Opinion and Order（10 November 2016）［美国俄勒冈州联邦地区法院否决了政府的两项动议，第一项动议是驳回侵权（侵害了生命、自由和财产）诉讼，第二项动议是否认政府有义务受人民和后代的委托来管理自然资源，原因是政府未能遏制二氧化碳排放］。Urgenda案中政府采取了另一种做法，强调政府有义务根据国内法在其谨慎注意义务下采取减缓行动：*Urgenda Foundation v. State of Netherlands*, Hague District Court, C/09/456689/HA ZA 13-1396 Judgment（24 June 2015）.

195　See A. Boyle, "Human Rights and the Environment：Where Next?"（2012）23 *European Journal of International Law* 613, 636-641.

排放（第一次因果调查），[196] 但想要将某一具体天气事件归因于气候变化还是太过困难（第二次因果调查）。这一难题打断了这一因果关系链条。众所周知的是，气候变化导致了极端天气的频繁发生，并触发了许多缓发事件。甚至还有可能明确气候变化能够引发何种类型的事件（例如热浪、干旱、飓风、冰川融化、海平面上升、某些疾病的扩散等）。缺失的是与一个具体事件（这一事件在一个特定时间影响了特定地区）的联系。这正是第二个因果关系求证想要建立的联系。

因纽特人向美洲人权委员会提起的诉请可以证明这一困难。[197] 因纽特极地会议（Inuit Circumpolar Conference）代表 63 个有名有姓的个人和因纽特人民起诉美国政府违反了《美洲人权宣言》（American Declaration on Human Rights）。根据这一诉请，美国作为（当时）世界上主要的温室气体排放国因其作为和不作为而导致了气候变化，从而对因纽特人居住的北极地区环境造成了重大改变，进而侵犯了因纽特人的人权。这一诉求在两个因果关系求证中都面临着重大障碍。在第一个因果关系求证中，起诉书指出，估算的美国历史排放量（缺乏规制行为的结果），和据观察气温上升的 30%（约为 0.6℃）发生在 1850—2000 年[198]存在关联。但是，原告也承认"日积月累的排放量与气温上升之间的实际关联性仍然存在着一定的不确定性"。[199] 即使并非如此，一般国际法所采用的因果关系理论并不太适于把关联性替换成因果关系。关于第二个因果关系求证，起诉书在第四（C）部分明确指出了气候变化对北极地区环境造成的数个影响，包括冰川的变化、永冻层融化、物种的迁徙、日益频发的极端天气等。但是，

---

[196] See Intergovernmental Panel for Climate Change (IPCC), *Climate Change* 2013: *The Physical Science Basis*, *Summary for Policymakers*, section B, p. 2, and section D. 3, p. 15. 声明气候系统变暖是毋庸置疑的，自 20 世纪 50 年代以来，许多观测到的变化在以往的几十年甚至是几千年都是前所未有的，人类活动极有可能是气候变暖的主要原因（IPCC 使用的"极有可能"一词表示这种可能性不低于 95%）。

[197] See Inuit Circumpolar Conference, *Petition to the Inter American Commission on Human Rights Seeking Relief from Violations Resulting from Global Warming Caused by Acts and Omissions of the United States* (2005), available at: www.inuitscircopolar.com/files/uploads/iccfiles/finalpetionicc.pdf (last visited in January 2014). On this case see D. Shelton, "Human Rights Violations and Climate Change: The Last Days of the Inuit People" (2010) 37 *Rutgers Law Record* 182.

[198] Inuit petition, supra footnote 197, pp. 68–69.

[199] Ibid., p. 69.

还是无法在气候变化、某一具体天气事件和对人权的某一具体侵害之间（或者在规制上的实际缺失与这些后果之间）建立具体的联系。美洲人权委员会没有接受因纽特人诉请中的观点。[200] 因此，如果要向某个国际人权机构提起诉讼，当前可用的科学证据（指气候变化影响了北极环境的相关证据）还不一定足够充分。这一诉请为了表达诉求而采取的方法，很好地说明了涉及气候变化的国际人权诉讼所面临的各种挑战。值得注意的是，第一个因果关系求证可以从科学上加以解决（尽管是通过"关联性"），而第二个因果关系求证想要明确建立联系就要困难得多。

有不同的方法可以用于克服这一重要障碍。第一种方法具有科学的性质。我们可以一直等下去，直到将某一具体天气事件归因于气候变化在科学上成为可能，而不是去改变法律上的要求。近年来，政府间气候变化专门委员会（IPCC）一直在收集科学证据，以便开展这种具体的归因工作；[201] 尽管针对某些备受瞩目的天气事件最终可以较好地建立起这种联系，但是对可以提起诉讼的所有极端天气事件并非都能如此。

第二种方法是以排放大量温室气体的国家和企业的捐款为基础，建立补偿基金制度。这一方法实际上是通过一个法律手段来克服前述障碍，即建立一项将温室气体排放当作其他一些有害但可容忍的活动（如核能生产和石油运输等）来同等对待的制度。[202] 尽管发达国家强烈反对以"补偿"为基础来构架谈判进程，但这一方法还是有可能被纳入《联合国气候变化框架公约》和《巴黎协定》中"损失和损害"的谈判范围。[203]

第三种可能的方法是通过在法律上承认公民有权享有一个"生态平

---

[200] A. C. Revkin, "Inuit Climate Change Petition Rejected", *New York Times*, 16 December 2006, www.nytimes.com/2006/12/16/world/americas/16briefs-inuitcomplaint.html（visited in January 2014）. But see HRC Res. 10/4, UN Doc. A/HRC/RES/10/4（31 March 2009）（adopting a position on the issue）; HRC Res. 7/23, UN Doc. A/HRC/RES/7/23（28 March 2008）（deciding to study the issue）.

[201] IPCC, *Managing the Risks of Extreme Weather Events and Disasters to Advance Climate Change Adaptation*（2011）（so-called SREX）.

[202] See Chapter 8.

[203] See Warsaw international mechanism for loss and damage associated with climate change（Decision-/CP. 19）, which carefully avoids framing this issue from a compensation perspective. See also Paris Decision, supra footnote 193, para. 52 ［明确排除使用《巴黎协定》第 8 条（专门涉及损失与损害）作为赔偿责任的依据］.

衡的"或"整体上令人满意的"环境以便克服这一障碍,其逻辑性在于,对气候系统的重大干扰(第一个因果关系求证)有可能构成对这一权利的侵害,因为它破坏了环境平衡或者使环境整体上变差。目前这种可能的方法尚未被适用,而且有可能一直都不会适用,直到我们能够充分认识到挑选合适的"形容词"来定性享有特定质量的环境这一权利的重要意义。但是,这种方法还是会造成几个难题(例如,如何才能构成对气候的"重大"干扰?"生态平衡的""整体上令人满意的"这些定语的具体含义是什么?当受害人处于他国的实际管控下,排放温室气体的国家的司法管辖权能否延伸到域外?)。这些难题有可能出现于第一个事实关系(排放对气候系统的影响)这一阶段,目前比第二个因果关系求证更易于掌控。此外,将这一权利赋予集体性人权主体(例如某个土著或部落民族、某个少数民族甚至是某个完整族群),将有助于证明环境对某一人群[他们祖居的地区正在融化(例如因纽特人[204]),或者即将消失(指随着海平面上升而将沉没的低海拔岛屿)而言不再是"生态平衡的"或"整体上令人满意的"。[205] 在本书中提出这一问题,目的是希望它能启发人们进一步思考如何调整这种权利。

第四节 冲突

如本章导论所言,法学专家和国际场合的争辩在很大程度上忽视了人权法和环境法之间的冲突维度。对协同效应的关注和我们在研究环境法与其他部门法(如贸易法或投资法)的相互作用时所采用的方法不尽相同,它同时关注了协同效应和冲突这两个问题。[206] 人权与环境保护间的协同效

---

[204] Inuit petition, supra footnote 197, p. 70.

[205] See, e. g., Kalinga Seneviratne, *Tuvalu Steps up Threat to Sue Australia*, US, 8 September 2002, available at: www.tuvaluislands.com/news/archived/2002/2002-09-10.htm(描述了图瓦卢针对美国和澳大利亚提起诉讼的努力。在该案中,诉讼的性质是国与国之间的,在人权背景下图瓦卢居民可被视为一个集体主体)。马尔代夫也在很努力地试图建立气候变化与人权之间的关联。See J. Knox, "Linking Human Rights and Climate Change at the United Nations"(2009)33 *Harvard Environmental Law Review* 477.

[206] See, e. g., J. Pauwelyn, *Conflict of Norms in Public International Law* (Cambridge University Press, 2003); Viñuales, supra footnote 4.

应比其他部门法之间的协同效应更大,但并不是说这种协同效应是理所当然的。在此,我们研究的目的是寻找出人权与环境保护之间潜在的冲突类型,并应在哪一层面加以解决以实现各种利益间的平衡。

在本书的第一章和第三章,我们研究了国际环境法的产生和发展以及可持续发展的部分法律内容。可持续发展由环境保护、经济发展和社会发展这三个相互支持的支柱构成。然而,有充足证据表明,这些支柱的相互作用并不必然是和谐的。一方面是(迄今主要是以化石燃料为基础的)经济增长和发展,另一方面是环境保护,二者的冲突是许多环境谈判的首要焦点。例如,气候变化谈判中的冲突主要就是由"环境—发展等式"造成的。然而,发展并不仅仅意味着经济上的考量。2012年里约峰会的成果文件切实强调了"消除贫困是当今世界所面临的最大挑战,是可持续发展的必然要求"[207]。消除贫困也被列为第一项可持续发展目标,虽然这一排序并未明显意味着优先次序。毫无疑问,消除贫困是一个关键的优先事项。但是,环境保护也是一个必需品,因为保护环境对促进社会的包容性和消除贫困具有重大意义。但是,有一个问题似乎无法避免,当一项消除贫困的政策(如增加对贫困地区的能源供应)对环境产生不利影响(如温室气体的排放)时,我们该如何应对?我们的观点是,这样的问题不能够抽象地回答(即在可持续发展概念层面上回答),而应针对某一具体政策或具体案例采用具体问题具体分析的方法。我们在后文提供了几个例证。

通常情况下,环境政策和社会发展考量的冲突是由特定和可操作的条款来具体解决的。本书第七章探讨的《关于持久性有机污染物的斯德哥尔摩公约》(*Stockholm Convention on Persistent Organic Pollutants*)[208] 附件B,就是一个例证。该公约禁止了数种物质的生产和使用,包括所谓的"肮脏的一打",其中包括滴滴涕农药,蕾切尔·卡逊(Rachel Carson)在其1962年出版的《寂静的春天》(*Silent Spring*)[209] 一书中曾提到滴滴涕农药

---

[207] See "The Future We Want", 11 September 2012, UN Doc. A/Res/66/288, para. 2. 消除贫穷被单列为2015年后议程的第一个可持续发展目标(SDG)。

[208] Stockholm Convention on Persistent Organic Pollutants, 22 May 2001, 2256 UNTS 119 (Stockholm Convention or POP Convention).

[209] R. Carson, *Silent Spring* (Boston: Houghton Mifflin, 1962).

对环境的影响。然而滴滴涕农药并没有被完全禁止。它只是受到了限制，即为了某一特定用途，它可以被生产和使用，而根据世界卫生组织的建议，它可以用于防治疟疾。事实上，附录二第一部分将生产和使用滴滴涕农药的"目的"确定为"根据本附录第二部分进行疾病防控"。附录二第二部分指出：

> 当相关缔约方在当地缺乏安全、有效、可负担的替代品时，生产和使用滴滴涕农药的所有缔约方应当根据世界卫生组织有关滴滴涕农药的使用的建议和指南来限制这类用于疟疾防治的农药生产和使用。[210]

世界卫生组织建议仅将滴滴涕农药用于"室内残留喷洒"，其前提是当地没有可长期替代滴滴涕农药的合适的、符合成本效益的替代品。[211] 在特定条件下，由于人类健康的实际情况，滴滴涕农药对环境造成的负面影响在某些地方还是可以接受的。在《水俣公约》(*Minamata Convention on Mercury*)[212] 中，对硫柳汞的使用也采取了类似的限制措施；硫柳汞是一种含汞物质，可以使疫苗无须冷藏就能延长保质期，这样就促进了疫苗在偏远地区的使用。在《水俣公约》的谈判过程中，世界卫生组织根据它有关硫柳汞的使用建议，支持硫柳汞的这一例外用途，而无汞药物联盟 (Coalition for Mercury-Free Drugs) 则主张逐步淘汰硫柳汞。[213] 最终，代表们支持了世界卫生组织。公约附录一明确将"含硫柳汞疫苗"排除在管控措施以外。[214] 多边银行在环境筹资活动中采取了一种更为宽松的方法，

---

[210] POP Convention, supra footnote 208, Annex B, Part II, para. 2.

[211] World Health Organization, *The Use of DDT in Malaria Vector Control. WHO Position Statement* (Geneva: WHO, 2011).

[212] Minamata Convention on Mercury, 10 October 2013, available at: www.mercuryconvention.org (last visited on 10 March 2014).

[213] See H. Selin, "Global Environmental Law and Treaty-Making on Hazardous Substances: The Minamata Convention and Mercury Abatement" (2014) 14 *Global Environmental Politics* 1, 10.

[214] Minamata Convention, supra footnote 212, Annex A, chapeau, letter (e).

这些活动数次与人权的保护发生了冲突。[215] 为了解决环境项目侵犯人权的情况，金融机构通过了可持续性发展指南，设立了有权评审个案并提出建议的特别专家组。例如，绿色气候基金在出台自身的具体标准之前，临时采用了国际金融公司（International Finance Corporation，IFC）的指南（"绩效标准"）。"绩效标准"第 7 条主要侧重于土著人民，要求除非得到了严格同意并做出了惠益分享的安排，否则不得在土著居民的传统土地上开发项目。[216]

在其他一些情况下，条约文本或具体指南并未涉及潜在的冲突，裁判机构必须通过其他领域的国际法来平衡各种因素并采取具体问题具体分析的方法。可以用几个案例来说明这一方法。在非洲人权和人民权利法院审理的一个案例中，法院批准了临时措施以对抗肯尼亚政府颁布的驱逐令（以保护 Mau 森林为由强制 Ogiek 地区土著居民离开）。[217] 法院在其判决书中说道，肯尼亚的驱逐行为侵犯了 Ogiek 地区居民的多项个人权利和集体权利，虽然其主张驱逐的目的是保护环境，但没有证据证实这一点。[218] 非洲委员会也处理过类似的案件，该案中，肯尼亚政府为建立自然保护区而驱逐 Endorois 地区的人民。委员会认为，肯尼亚政府这一行为违反了《非洲宪章》。[219] 在早期一个起诉瑞典的案件中，一名来自萨米社区的萨米人认为瑞典侵犯了他享受文化方面的权利（《公民权利及政治权利国际公约》第 27 条），因为一项法令剥夺了他饲养驯鹿的权利。[220] 瑞典政府辩称，对饲养驯鹿的规制主要是基于生态原因。[221] 人权理事会支持了瑞典的观点，认为规制饲养驯鹿的法令总体上是合理的，符合公约第 27 条的规

215　On this question, see T. Gutner, *Banking on the Environment. Multilateral Development Banks and their Environmental Performance in Central and Eastern Europe* (Cambridge, MA: MIT Press 2002); B. F. Perez et al., "Rethinking the Role of Development Banks in Climate Finance: Panama's Barro Blanco CDM Project and Human Rights" (2016) 12 *Law, Environment and Development Journal* 1.

216　See generally Green Climate Fund, *Environmental and Social Safeguards at the Green Climate Fund* (December 2015).

217　*African Commission on Human and Peoples' Rights v. Kenya*, Order on Provisional Measures (15 March 2013), African Court Application No. 006/2012.

218　*African Commission v. Kenya*, supra footnote 83.

219　*Endorois*, supra footnote 78.

220　*Kitok v. Sweden*, supra footnote 40.

221　Ibid., para. 9.5.

定。在实践中,保护措施与土著和部落居民利益的冲突屡见不鲜,尽管这些冲突很少被诉至国际法院和法庭。[222]

其他一些法院也会处理人权与环境政策间的冲突。事实上,我们对协同效应的研究也涉及各种冲突,特别是涉及各国拥有多大的自由裁量空间为了环境政策而限制人权;或者相比其他权利(所有者的私人财产权)而言,更偏向于某一权利(土著或部落居民拥有其传统土地的权利)的特定维度,并进行适当的救济(征用私人所有者的土地以恢复土著居民的土地)。例如,在"Turgut 诉土耳其案"中,欧洲人权法院认为:"经济上的必要性,甚至一些基本人权(例如财产权)不应优先于环境保护的考量。"[223] 法院认为,如果发生这种情况,必须做出合理赔偿,虽然在实践中赔偿通常会低于财产的全部价值。[224] 同样地,美洲人权法院在"Sawhoyamaxa 诉巴拉圭案"中认为:"传统土地的恢复……是最符合恢复原状(restitutio in integrum)原则的补救措施。"[225] 此外,常设的人权法院在环境保护与人权间冲突中所采取的立场对与日俱增的投资案件也非常重要,因为在这些案件中环境政策与投资原则时常产生摩擦。[226] 事实上,人权与投资原则拥有一个共同的渊源,部分内容还存在重叠。[227] 因此,环境保护与外商投资保护之间的冲突也可以被看作人权与环境法之间冲突的一

---

[222] For some examples see e. g. *Kuna v. Panama*, supra footnote 65, paras. 63ff, 111ff(人权与水力发电项目之间的冲突,以及森林保护与定居者入侵之间的协同效应); *Kaliña and Lokono Peoples v. Suriname*, supra footnote 66, paras. 163–198(人权与自然保护之间的冲突); *Specific Instance regarding the World Wide Fund for Nature International (WWF) submitted by Survival International Charitable Trust*, OECD Guidelines-National Contact Point of Switzerland, Initial Assessment (20 December 2016)(人权与自然保护之间的冲突)。

[223] *Turgut v. Turkey*, supra footnote 56, para. 90 (unofficial translation of the French text)。

[224] Ibid., Judgment-Just Satisfaction (13 October 2009), para. 14. On the wider implications of this case, see Viñuales, supra footnote 4, p. 297. In some cases, no compensation may be due. See *Depalle v. France*, supra footnote 56, paras. 77–93; *Brosset-Triboulet and others v. France*, supra footnote 56, paras. 80–96.

[225] *Sawhoyamaxa v. Paraguay*, supra footnote 68, para. 210; *Yakye Axa v. Paraguay*, supra footnote 68, para. 148; *Kuna v. Panama*, supra footnote 65, paras. 143–145.

[226] See infra Chapter 12.

[227] See P.-M. Dupuy and J. E. Viñuales, "Human Rights and Investment Disciplines: Integration in Progress", in M. Bungenberg, J. Griebel, S. Hobe and A. Reinisch (eds.), *International Investment Law* (Munich/London: C. H. Beck/Hart/Nomos, forthcoming 2015), Chapter 77.

个具体表现。

这些案例说明,有大量的素材归属于我们在本章第三节提到的第4—6个问题,它们都涉及人权和环境保护之间的冲突。这一主题还需要持续地分析研究,不仅是为了评估其整体意义,也是为了了解应当如何解决这些冲突。在本书中,我们仅是提出这一需求,希望它能推动更深的研究。

部分参考文献

［1］ Agrawal, A. and K. Redford, "Conservation and Displacement: An Overview" (2009) 7 *Conservation & Society* 1.

［2］ Anaya, J., "Environmentalism, Human Rights and Indigenous Peoples: A Tale of Converging and Diverging Interests" (1999/2000) 7 *Buffalo Environmental Law Journal* 1.

［3］ Andrusevych, A. and S. Kern (eds.), *Case Law of the Aarhus Convention Compliance Committee (2004–2014)* (Lviv: RACSE, 3rd edn, 2016)

［4］ Andrusevych, A., T. Alge and C. Konrad (eds.), *Case Law of the Aarhus Convention Compliance Committee (2004-2011)* (Lviv: RACSE, 2nd edn, 2011).

［5］ Anton, D. K. and D. Shelton, *Environmental Protection and Human Rights* (Cambridge University Press, 2011).

［6］ Bantekas, I. and L. Oette, *International Human Rights Law and Practice* (Cambridge University Press, 2nd edn, 2016).

［7］ Boisson de Chazournes, L., "Le droit à l'eau et la satisfaction des besoins humains: Notions de justice", in D. Alland, V. Chetail, O. de Frouville and J. E. Viñuales (eds.), *Unity and Diversity of International Law: Essays in Honour of Professor Pierre-Marie Dupuy/Unité et Diversité du Droit International: Ecrits en L'honneur du Professeur Pierre-Marie Dupuy* (Leiden: Martinus Nijhoff, 2014), pp. 967-981.

［8］ Boyd, R., *The Environmental Rights Revolution. A Global Study of Constitutions, Human Rights and Environment* (Vancouver: UBC Press, 2012).

［9］ Boyle, A., "Human Rights and the Environment: Where Next?"

(2012) 23 *European Journal of International Law* 613.

[10] Boyle, A. and M. Anderson (eds.), *Human Rights Approaches to Environmental Protection* (Oxford University Press, 1996).

[11] Cancoado Trindade, A. A. (ed.), *Human Rights, Sustainable Development and the Environment* (San José: Instituto Interamericano de Derechos Humanos, 1992).

[12] Chuffart, S. L. and J. E. Viñuales, "From the Other Shore: Economic, Social and Cultural Rights from an International Environmental Law Perspective", in E. Reidel, G. Giacca and C. Golay (eds.), *Economic, Social and Cultural Rights: Current Issues and Challenges* (Oxford University Press, 2014), pp. 286–307.

[13] Cullet, P., "Definition of an Environmental Right in a Human Rights Context" (1995) 13 *Netherlands Quarterly of Human Rights* 25.

[14] De Schutter, O., *International Human Rights Law. Cases, Materials, Commentary* (Cambridge University Press, 2014).

[15] Dejeant-Pons, M. and M. Pallemaerts, *Droits de L'homme et environnement* (Strasbourg: Conseil de l'Europe, 2002).

[16] Desgagne, R., "Integrating Environmental Values into the European Convention on Human Rights" (1995) 89 *American Journal of International Law* 263.

[17] Dowie, M., *Conservation Refugees: The Hundred Years Conflict between Global Conservation and Native Peoples* (Cambridge, MA: MIT Press, 2009).

[18] Dupuy, P. - M., "Le droit à la santé et la protection de l'environnement", in R. -J. Dupuy (ed.), *Le droit à la santé en tant que droit de l'homme* (The Hague: Sijthoff, 1978), pp. 340–427.

"Le droit à l'eau: droit de l'homme ou droit des Etats?", in M. G. Kohen (ed.), *Promoting Justice, Human Rights and Conflict Resolution through International Law/La Promotion de la Justice, des Droits de L'homme et du Règlement des Conflits par le Droit International: Liber Amicorum Lucius Caflisch* (The Hague: Martinus Nijhoff, 2007), pp. 701–715.

[19] Dupuy, P. -M. and J. E. Viñuales, "Human Rights and Investment

Disciplines: Integration in Progress", in M. Bungenberg, J. Griebel, S. Hobe and A. Reinisch (eds.), *International Investment Law* (Munich/London: C. H. Beck/Hart/Nomos, forthcoming 2015), Chapter 77.

[20] Ebeku, K. S. A., "The Right to a Satisfactory Environment and the African Commission" (2003) 3 *African Human Rights Journal* 149.

[21] Etemire, U., "Insights on the UNEP Bali Guidelines and the Development of Environmental Democratic Rights" (2016) 23 *Journal of Environmental Law* 393.

[22] Fitzmaurice, M., "The Human Right to Water" (2007) 18 *Fordham Environmental Law Review* 537.

[23] Fitzmaurice, M. and J. Marshall, "The Human Right to a Clean Environment-Phantom or Reality? The European Court of Human Rights and English Courts' Perspective on Balancing Rights in Environmental Cases" (2007) 76 *Nordic Journal of International Law* 103.

[24] Forsythe, D., *Human Rights in International Relations* (Cambridge University Press, 4th edn, 2017).

[25] Francioni, F., "International Human Rights in the Environmental Horizon" (2010) 21 *European Journal of International Law* 41.

[26] Francioni, F. and M. Scheinin (eds.), *Cultural Human Rights* (Leiden: Martinus Nijhoff, 2008).

[27] Gattini, A., "Mass Claims at the European Court of Human Rights", in S. Breitenmoser, B. Ehrenzeller and M. Sassoli (eds.), *Human Rights, Democracy and the Rule of Law. Liber amicorum Luzius Wildhaber* (Zurich: Dike, 2007), pp. 271-294.

[28] Global Witness, *Deadly Environment: The Dramatic Rise in Killings of Environmental and Land Defenders* 1 *January* 2002-31 *December* 2013 (April 2014).

[29] Golay, C., *Droit à L'alimentation et Accès à la Justice* (Brussels: Bruylant, 2011).

[30] Gutner, T., *Banking on the Environment. Multilateral Development Banks and their Environmental Performance in Central and Eastern Europe* (Cambridge MA: MIT Press 2002).

[31] Hayward, T., *Political Theory and Ecological Values* (London: Polity Press, 1998).

[32] Hennebel, L. and H. Tigroudja, *Traité de droit international des droits de l'homme* (Paris: Pedone, 2016).

[33] Hodkova, I., "Is There a Right to a Healthy Environment in the International Legal Order?" (1991) 7 *Connecticut Journal of International Law* 65.

[34] Humphreys, S. (ed.), *Human Rights and Climate Change* (Cambridge University Press, 2009).

[35] *Individual Report on the International Covenant on Economic, Social and Cultural Rights*, Report No. 1 (December 2013).

[36] *Individual Report on the International Covenant on Civil and Political Rights*, Report No. 2 (December 2013).

[37] *Individual Report on the International Convention on the Elimination of All Forms of Racial Discrimination*, Report No. 3 (December 2013).

[38] *Individual Report on the United Nations Convention on the Elimination of All Forms of Discrimination against Women*, Report No. 4 (December 2013).

[39] *Individual Report on the United Nations Convention on the Rights of the Child*, Report No. 5 (December 2013).

[40] *Individual Report on the UN General Assembly and the Human Rights Council, including the Universal Periodic Review Process*, Report No. 6 (December 2013).

[41] *Individual Report on the Special Procedures of the United Nations Human Rights Council*, Report No. 7 (December 2013).

[42] *Individual Report on the Rights of Indigenous Peoples*, Report No. 8 (December 2013).

[43] *Individual Report on Global and Regional Environmental Agreements*, Report No. 9 (December 2013).

[44] *Individual Report on Non-Binding International Environmental Instruments*, Report No. 10 (December 2013).

[45] *Individual Report on the Convention on Access to Information, Public*

Participation in Decision-Making and Access to Justice in Environmental Matters (*Aarhus Convention*), Report No. 11 (December 2013).

[46] *Individual Report on the Asia-Pacific, Arab and African Regions as well as the European Social Charter*, Report No. 12 (December 2013).

[47] *Individual Report on the American Declaration of the Rights and Duties of Man, the American Convention on Human Rights, and the Additional Protocol to the American Convention on Human Rights in the Area of Economic, Social and Cultural Rights*, Report No. 13 (December 2013).

[48] *Individual Report on the European Convention on Human Rights and the European Union*, Report No. 14 (December 2013).

[49] Inter-American Commission on Human Rights, *Indigenous and Tribal Peoples' Rights over their Ancestral Lands and Natural Resources: Norms and Jurisprudence of the Inter-American Human Rights System*, doc. OEA/Ser. L/V/II, doc. 56/09, 30 December 2009.

[50] Kiss, A.-C., "Peut-on définir le droit de L'homme à L'environnement?" (1976) 1 *Revue Juridique de L'environnement* 15.

"Le droit à la conservation de L'environnement" (1990) 2*Revue universelle des droits de l'homme* 445.

[51] Knox, J., "Linking Human Rights and Climate Change at the United Nations" (2009) 33 *Harvard Environmental Law Review* 477.

[52] Koch, I. E., "Dichotomies, Trichotomies or Waves of Duties?" (2005) 5 *Human Rights Law Review* 81.

[53] Koivurova, T., "Jurisprudence of the European Court of Human Rights Regarding Indigenous Peoples: Retrospect and Prospects" (2011) 18 *International Journal on Minority and Group Rights* 1.

[54] Kromarek, P., *Le Droit à un Environnement équilibré et Sain, Considéré Comme un Droit de L'homme: sa Mise en Oeuvre Nationale, Européenne et Internationale*, Introductory Report, European Conference on the Environment and Human Rights, Strasbourg 19-20 January 1979.

[55] Langford, M. and A. F. S. Russell (eds.), *The Right to Water. Theory, Practice and Prospects* (Cambridge University Press, 2017).

[56] Limon, M., "Human Rights Obligations and Accountability in the

Face of Climate Change" (2010) 38 *Georgia Journal of International and Comparative Law* 543.

[57] Loucaides, L., "Environmental Protection through the Jurisprudence of the European Convention on Human Rights" (2004) 75 *British Yearbook of International Law* 249.

[58] May, J. R. and E. Daly, *Global Environmental Constitutionalism* (Cambridge University Press, 2014).

[59] Murphy, K., "The Social Pillar of Sustainable Development: A Literature Review and Framework for Policy Analysis" (2012) 8 *Sustainability: Science, Practice, & Policy* 5.

[60] Neumann, R. P., *Imposing Wilderness: Struggles over Livelihood and Nature Preservation in Africa* (Berkeley: University of California Press, 1998).

[61] Office of the High Commissioner for Human Rights, Analytical Study on the Relationship between Human Rights and the Environment, 16 December 2011, UN Doc. A/HRC/19/34.

Analytical Study on the Relationship between Climate Change and the Human Right of Everyone to the Enjoyment of the Highest Attainable Standard of Physical and Mental Health, 6 May 2016, A/HRC/32/23.

[62] Paellemarts, M., "The Human Right to a Healthy Environment as a Substantive Right", in M. Dejeant-Pons and M. Paellemarts (eds.), *Human Rights and the Environment* (Strasbourg: Council of Europe, 2002), pp. 11ff.

[63] Pasqualucci, J., "The Inter-American Human Rights System: Progress Made and Still to Be Made" (2009) 52 *German Yearbook of International Law* 181.

[64] Pavoni, R., *Interesse pubblico e diritti individuali nella giurisprudenza ambientale della Corte europea dei diritti umani* (Naples: Editoriale Scientifica, 2013).

[65] Pentassuglia, G., "Towards a Jurisprudential Articulation of Indigenous Land Rights" (2011) 22 *European Journal of International Law* 165.

"The Strasbourg Court and Minority Groups: Shooting in the Dark or a

New Interpretive Ethos" (2012) 19 *International Journal on Minority and Group Rights* 1.

[66] Perez, B. F. et al., "Rethinking the Role of Development Banks in Climate Finance: Panama's Barro Blanco CDM Project and Human Rights" (2016) 12 *Law, Environment and Development Journal* 1.

[67] Petersmann, M. -C., *Les sources du droit à l'eau en droit international* (Paris: Johanet, 2013).

"The Integration of Environmental Protection Considerations within the Human Rights Law Regime: Which Solutions Have Been Provided by Regional Human Rights Courts?" (2014) 24 *Italian Yearbook of International Law* 191.

"Environmental Protection and Human Rights: When Friends Become Foes-Conflict Management of the CJEU", in C. Voigt and L. J. Kotzé (eds.), *The Environment in International Courts and Tribunals: Questions of Legitimacy* (Cambridge University Press, 2017).

"Narcissus Reflected in the Lake: Anthropocentric Environmental Law and Untold Narratives" (2018) 30 *Journal of Environmental Law* 1.

[68] Report of the Independent Expert on the Issue of Human Rights Obligations Relating to the Enjoyment of a Safe, Clean, Healthy and Sustainable Environment, John H. Knox. Preliminary Report, 24 December 2012, A/HRC/22/43.

[69] Report of the Independent Expert on the Issue of Human Rights Obligations Relating to the Enjoyment of a Safe, Clean, Healthy and Sustainable Environment, John H. Knox. Mapping Report, 30 December 2013, A/HRC/25/53.

[70] Report of the Independent Expert on the Issue of Human Rights Obligations Relating to the Enjoyment of a Safe, Clean, Healthy and Sustainable Environment, John H. Knox. Compilation of good practices, 3 February 2015, A/HRC/28/61.

[71] Report of the Office of the United Nations High Commissioner for Human Rights on the Relationship between Climate Change and Human Rights, 15 January 2009, UN Doc. A/HRC/10/61.

[72] Report of the Special Rapporteur on the Issue of Human Rights Obli-

gations Relating to the Enjoyment of a Safe, Clean, Healthy and Sustainable Environment. Implementation Report, 28 December 2015, A/HRC/31/53.

［73］Report of the Special Rapporteur on the Issue of Human Rights Obligations Relating to the Enjoyment of a Safe, Clean, Healthy and Sustainable Environment, 1 February 2016, A/HRC/31/52.

［74］Saul, B., *Indigenous Peoples and Human Rights. International and Regional Jurisprudence* (Oxford: Hart, 2016).

［75］Schall, C., "Public Interest Litigation Concerning Environmental Matters before the Human Rights Courts: A Promising Future Concept?" (2008) 20 *Journal of Environmental Law* 417.

［76］Shelton, D., "Human Rights, Environmental Rights, and the Right to the Environment" (1991) 28 *Stanford Journal of International Law* 103.

"Human Rights and the Environment: Jurisprudence of Human Rights Bodies" (2002) 32 *Environmental Policy and Law* 158.

"Human Rights, Health and Environmental Protection: Linkages in Law and Practice" (2007) 1 *Human Rights and International Legal Discourse* 9.

"Human Rights Violations and Climate Change: The Last Days of the Inuit People" (2010) 37 *Rutgers Law Record* 182.

"Substantive Rights", in M. Fitzmaurice, D. Ong and P. Merkouris (eds.), *Research Handbook on International Environmental Law* (Cheltenham: Edward Elgar, 2010), pp. 265-283.

"Resolving Conflicts between Human Rights and Environmental Protection: Is There a Hierarchy?", in E. de Wet and J. Vidmar (eds.), *Hierarchy in International Law: The Place of Human Rights* (Oxford University Press, 2012), pp. 206-235.

(ed.), *The Oxford Handbook of International Human Rights Law* (Oxford University Press, 2013).

［77］Sironi, A., "La tutela della persona in conseguenza di danni all'ambiente nella giurisprudenza della Corte europea dei diritti umani" (2011) 5 *Diritti Umani e Diritto Internazionale* 5.

［78］Smith, R., *Textbook on International Human Rights Law* (Oxford

University Press, 2015).

［79］Sohn, L., "The Stockholm Declaration on the Human Environment" (1972) 14 *Harvard International Law Journal* 423.

［80］Stone, C., "Ethics and International Environmental Law", in D. Bodansky, J. Brunnée and E. Hey (eds.), *The Oxford Handbook of International Environmental Law* (Oxford University Press, 2007), pp. 291-312.

［81］Sudre, F., *Droit Européen et International des Droits de L'homme* (Paris: Presses universitaires de France, 2016).

［82］Thielboerger, P., *The Human Right (s) to Water. The Multi-Level Governance of a Unique Human Right* (Berlin: Springer, 2014).

［83］United Nations Development Programme, *Environmental Justice: Comparative Experiences in Legal Empowerment* (June 2014).

［84］United Nations Environment Programme, *Climate Change and Human Rights* (December 2015).

［85］Viñuales, J. E., *Foreign Investment and the Environment in International Law* (Cambridge University Press, 2012).

"The Rise and Fall of Sustainable Development" (2013) 22 *Review of European, Comparative and International Environmental Law* 5.

"A Human Rights Approach to Extraterritorial Environmental Protection? An Assessment", in N. Bhuta (ed.), *The Frontiers of Human Rights. Extraterritoriality and its Challenges* (Oxford University Press, 2016), pp. 177-221.

［86］Virzo, R., "Diritti dei popoli indigeni e conservazione, gestione e commercializzazione di risorse naturali nel diritto internazionale", in M. B. Deli, M. R. Mauro, F. Pernazza and F. P. Traisce (eds.), *Impresa e Diritti Fondamentali Nella Prospettiva Transnazionale* (Naples: Edizioni Scientifiche Italiane, 2012), pp. 341-356.

［87］Weston, B. H. and D. Bollier, "Toward a Recalibrated Human Right to a Clean and Healthy Environment: Making the Conceptual Transition" (2013) 4 *Journal of Human Rights and the Environment* 116.

［88］Winkler, I. T., *The Human Right to Water* (Oxford: Hart, 2012).

第十一章 国际安全的环境维度

第一节 导论

早在1987年,世界环境与发展委员会在《我们共同的未来》(*Our Common Future*)这一报告中便呼吁各国扩大对安全概念的理解以便纳入环境考量:

> 为了打造一个更令人满意的基础来管理安全与可持续发展之间的相互关系,第一步是要拓宽我们的视野。冲突可能不仅源于对国家主权的政治和军事威胁,还可能源于环境退化和对发展选择权的剥夺。[1]

从20世纪90年代[2]开始,特别是在过去十年中,这一核心观点越来越多地体现在环境组织以及旨在维护国际安全的组织所采取的具体举措中。

联合国环境规划署、联合国开发规划署和欧洲安全与合作组织(OSCE)于2002年发起的所谓"东南欧和中亚安全与合作的环境议程"(An Environment Agenda for Security and Co-operation in South Eastern

---

[1] Report of the World Commission on Environment and Development, *Our Common Future*, 10 March 1987 (Our Common Future or Brundtland Report), Chapter 11, para. 37.

[2] On previous efforts to recharacterise the concept of security, see J. Mathews, "Redefining Security" (1989) *Foreign Affairs* 162.

Europe and Central Asia）或 "ENVSEC 倡议"[3] 提供了一个恰当例证。该倡议旨在将环境考量纳入与那些有着重大冲突风险的国家和区域（如巴尔干、高加索或中亚等）有关的安全政策中。该倡议随后扩大到其他三个组织，即北大西洋公约组织（北约）、联合国欧洲经济委员会（UN-ECE）[4] 和中欧和东欧区域环境中心（Regional Environmental Centre for Central and Eastern Europe，REC）。

重新定义安全概念的这种尝试和其他尝试的主要理念在于，有必要去了解环境退化、自然资源的不对称获取或危险物质越境转移等问题对冲突的触发、放大、持续时间或秩序恢复的影响。一般来说，这些尝试突出了环境变化在冲突方面所发挥的积极作用，而不仅仅是被动作用。

本章的目的是分析国际法是如何越来越多地反映出国际安全中的环境问题，无论是保护环境免遭武装冲突破坏，还是应对那些可能引发冲突的环境威胁。第一部分侧重于通过传统上的战时法（本章第二节）来保护环境，战时法既包括针对敌对行动的法律，也包括涉及诉诸武力的法律。第二部分分析了环境退化与安全之间的关系（本章第三节），特别提到了由环境引发的并造成重大安全威胁的两种现象，即环境引发的移民和冲突后重建过程中的环境安全。

第二节 环境和战时法

一 环境和武装冲突

（一）概述

在越南战争期间，美国使用一种化学去叶剂（橙剂）[5] 对环境造成了

---

[3] See www.envsec.org（last visited on 20 April 2017）.

[4] 联合国欧洲经济委员会的参与促进了与联合国欧洲经济委员会环境条约有关的活动的发展。See United Nations Economic Commission for Europe activities in the framework of the Environment and Security Initiative. Note by the secretariat, Information Paper No. 4/Rev. 1（11 January 2017）.

[5] For a concise overview of these developments, see M. N. Schmitt, "War and the Environment: Fault Lines in the Prescriptive Landscape", in J. E. Austin and C. E. Bruch（eds.）, *The Environmental Consequences of War: Legal, Economic and Scientific Perspectives*（Cambridge University Press, 2000）, pp. 87-136, at 87-92.

破坏；随后，武装冲突中的自然环境保护就成为一个主要的法律议题。1990—1991 年的海湾战争[6]以及数年后国际法院发布的《关于核武器合法性的咨询意见》(Advisory Opinion on the Legality of Nuclear Weapons)[7] 再次引发了针对这一议题的争论。长期以来，国际社会主要从三个角度来探讨这一议题。

通常，国际人道主义法学的学术研究对一些战时法 (jus in bello) 文件和规则中的环境规范作了详细的评估（"第一种方法"）。这种方式的要点被《日内瓦公约第一附加议定书》(First Additional Protocol to the Geneva Conventions) 第 35 条第 3 款和第 55 条明确规定[8]，由此波及、影响了有关战争手段的若干法律文件，如《禁止为军事或任何其他敌对目的使用改变环境的技术的公约》(ENMOD Convention)[9]，甚至有可能形成一个"环境的马尔顿斯条款"[10]，即对国际犯罪（指敌对行动期间造成的环境损害）的定义，[11] 甚至还有机会制定以环境保护为重点的《日内瓦第五公约》(Fifth Geneva Convention)。[12]

除这一方式外，自 1992 年地球峰会以来，关于国际环境法"是否"适用于武装冲突时期已经出现了大量论著，重点是习惯法原则（如风险

---

[6] See K. Hulme, "Armed Conflict, Wanton Ecological Devastation and Scorched Earth Policies: How the 1990-91 Gulf Conflict Revealed the Inadequacies of the Current Laws to Ensure Effective Protection and Preservation of the Natural Environment" (1997) 2 *Journal of Armed Conflict Law* 55.

[7] *Legality of the Threat or Use of Nuclear Weapons*, ICJ Reports 1996, p. 226 (*Legality of Nuclear Weapons*), paras. 27-33.

[8] Protocol Additional to the Geneva Conventions of 12 August 1949, and Relating to the Protection of Victims of International Armed Conflicts, 6 August 1977, 1125 UNTS 3 (Additional Protocol I).

[9] Convention for the Prohibition of Military or other Hostile Use of Environmental Modification Techniques, 10 December 1976, 1108 UNTS 151 (ENMOD Convention).

[10] See Report of the Second IUCN World Conservation Congress, 4-11 October 2000, Resolution-CGR2. CNV019 "Martens Clause for Environmental Protection".

[11] See M. Bothe, "Criminal Responsibility for Environmental Damage in Times of Armed Conflict", in R. J. Grunawalt, J. E. King and R. S. McClain (eds.), *Protection of the Environment during Armed Conflict* (Newport, RI: Naval War College, 1996), pp. 473-478. The 1998 Statute of the International Criminal Court (ICC) contains a specific provision (Art. 8 (a) (b) (iv)) establishing criminal responsibility for environmental damage.

[12] See G. Plant (ed.), *Environmental Protection and the Law of War: A "Fifth Geneva" Convention on the Environment in Times of Armed Conflict?* (London: Belhaven Press, 1992).

预防原则）和某些多边环境协定（MEAs）的措辞（"第二种方法"）[13]。除了"是否"适用这一问题外，第二种方法还必须阐释"如何"适用国际环境法，或者换句话说，国际环境规范在此背景下的具体影响是什么？

"第三种方法"侧重于规制某些类型的武器（生物、化学和核武器），但与第一种方法不同，它不仅是规制这些武器的使用，还涉及这类武器生命周期的大部分。从环境角度来看，第三种方法将武器视为"污染物"，必须规制武器的生产、储存、运输、使用和处置，以便有效消除其影响。规制框架的范围和严格程度因武器类型而异，这个问题在核武器问题上引起了激烈的争论。表 11-1 总结了这三种方法。

表 11-1　　　　　　武装冲突中环境保护的法律方法

方法 1	方法 2	方法 3
战时法规范中的环境问题	在武装冲突期间环境法规范是否适用以及如何适用	将武器作为"污染物"予以全程规制

在以下各节中，我们简要讨论了各种方法，重点是最相关的法律文件和规定及其主要局限性。

（二）环境和战时法

1. "特别"规制和"一般"规制

国际人道主义法以两种主要形式来体现对环境的考量。首先，越南战争促成通过了一项条约——《禁止为军事或任何其他敌对目的使用改变环境的技术的公约》，以禁止使用改变环境的技术作为进行战争的手段，并在 1977 年《日内瓦公约第一附加议定书》中列入了两项涉及自然环境保护的具体规定（第 35 条第 3 款和第 55 条）。其次，有大量证据表明，存在着一些包含具体环境保护内容的战时法之习惯法规范。[14]

学者将这部分习惯法规范称为武装冲突中环境保护的"具体的""明确的"或"特别的"规范，以区别于体量更大的国际人道主义法规范，

13　See, e.g., S. Vöneky, "Peacetime Environmental Law as a Basis of State Responsibility for Environmental Damage Caused by War". in Austin and Bruch, supra footnote 5; K. Mollard-Bannelier, *La Protection de L'environnement en Temps de Conflit armé* (Paris: Pédone, 2001).

14　See J.-M. Henckaerts. and L. Doswald-Beck, *Customary International Humanitarian Law* (Cambridge University Press, 2009), Rules 43, 44 and 45.

这些规范虽然没在字面上明说是为了保护环境，但是，还是通过规制作战手段和方法或者通过保护特定目标（例如含有危险物质的军事设施）来实现对自然环境的保护。

2. 特别环境规范

战时法的两项重要文件用相似的措辞对武装冲突期间的环境保护作出了具体规定，但细究后就会发现它们设定了明显不同的门槛。《日内瓦公约第一附加议定书》第35条第3款规定，"禁止使用意图或预期会对自然环境造成广泛、长期和严重损害的战争方法或手段"（强调）。《日内瓦公约第一附加议定书》第55条第1款也采用了同样的限定条件，并附加要求必须是影响人类健康的损害：

> 在战争中应注意保护自然环境，防止其受到广泛、长期和严重的破坏。这种保护包括禁止使用某些战争方法或手段，因为这些战争方法或手段意图或预期会对自然环境造成此类损害，从而损害到人民健康或生存（强调）。

尽管这两项规定相似，但目标并不相同。在《日内瓦公约第一附加议定书》谈判期间曾有人提出这两项规定有点重叠和冗余，但是这一异议最终被抛弃，理由在于，第35条第3款是对进行战争的手段作一般性的限制，而第55条则是力求保护平民免受环境退化造成的伤害。[15]

《禁止为军事或任何其他敌对目的使用改变环境的技术的公约》也面临着内容重复的问题，该公约是于20世纪70年代中期在日内瓦进行的谈判。然而，这一异议最终被抛弃，因为正如美国代表团指出的，《日内瓦公约第一附加议定书》的规定涵盖任何武器，而《禁止为军事或任何其他敌对目的使用改变环境的技术的公约》则只涉及被当作武器使用的环境改造技术。[16]《禁止为军事或任何其他敌对目的使用改变环境的技术的公约》第1条第1款使用连词"或"而不是"和"，因此，用于定性环境

---

15 Y. Sandoz, C. Swinarsky and B. Zimmermann, *Commentary on the Additional Protocols of 8 June 1977 to the Geneva Convention of 12 August 1949* (Leiden/Geneva: Martinus Nijhoff/International Committee of the Red Cross, 1987) (ICRC Commentary), ad Art. 35 (3), para. 1449.

16 Ibid., para. 1450.

损害程度的三个形容词不能被看作叠加的要求：[17]

> 本公约各缔约国均承诺不为军事或任何其他敌对目的使用具有广泛、持久或严重影响的环境改造技术，作为对任何其他缔约国造成破坏、损害或伤害的手段（强调）。

此外，对第 1 条第 1 款使用的每个形容词的解读，与《日内瓦公约第一附加议定书》第 35 条第 3 款和第 55 条第 1 款使用的形容词的含义存在着重大不同。后者被认为比前者的要求要高得多 [例如，"长期"（long-term）是指几十年，[18] 而"持久"（long lasting）则仅要求"数月，最多一个季度的时间"[19]]，一些代表团明确表示，对《日内瓦公约第一附加议定书》在此问题上的解读不应参考其他国际法律文件（如《禁止为军事或任何其他敌对目的使用改变环境的技术的公约》）。[20]

从实践的视角来看，这些差异可产生重大的后果。具体而言，普遍的观点是，第 35 条第 3 款和第 55 条的门槛太高，以至于很少甚至基本没有提供对自然环境的保护。[21] 前南斯拉夫问题国际刑事法庭（ICTY）检察官设立的委员会完成的报告就是一个例证，报告就指控北约（NATO）军队在 1999 年科索沃冲突中使用贫铀弹并导致环境损害的行为向该检察官提供了咨询意见。[22] 委员会在其评估中考虑《日内瓦公约第一附加议定书》第 35 条第 3 款和第 55 条能否为起诉提供法律依据。报告首先承认：

> 第 35 条第 3 款和第 55 条的适用门槛很高。其适用条件极为严

---

[17] Ibid., para. 1457.

[18] Ibid., para. 1454.

[19] ENMOD Convention, supra footnote 9, understandings relating to Art. 1（其他形容词表示的特征如下："广阔"：涵盖数百平方公里；"严重"：涉及对人类生活、自然和经济资源或其他财产的严重或重大破坏或损害）。

[20] See ICRC Commentary, supra footnote 15, ad Art. 35（3），para. 1459.

[21] United Nations Environment Programme, *Protecting the Environment during Armed Conflict. An Inventory and Analysis of International Law* (Nairobi: UNEP, 2009) ("UNEP Report"), p. 11 (and authorities referred to therein).

[22] Final Report to the Prosecutor by the Committee Established to Review the NATO Bombing Campaign against the Federal Republic of Yugoslavia, 13 June 2000 ("Report to the Prosecutor").

格，其适用范围和内容不够精确……例如，据认为，《日内瓦公约第一附加议定书》中的"长期"损害概念需要用数年而不是数月来衡量，因此，第一次世界大战对法国造成的普通战场损害就不在此范围之内。[23]

然后，它得出结论，"基于当前掌握的信息……北约轰炸行动造成的环境损害没有达到《日内瓦公约第一附加议定书》的门槛"。[24] 委员会注意到，在 1990—1991 年海湾战争期间伊拉克造成巨大环境损害的行为是否适用前述条款这一问题上存在分歧，[25] 这进一步证明了《日内瓦公约第一附加议定书》设定的门槛不足以保护自然环境。有可能造成"广泛、长期和严重的"环境破坏的主要情况是核武器的爆炸；然而，在 1996 年的咨询意见中，国际法院无法"在自我防卫的极端情况下，即国家生存受到威胁时"排除核武器的合法性。[26] 委员会报告的另一个值得注意的方面是，它提及了战时法的特别和一般习惯法规则。[27] 这一提法值得注意，因为习惯法适用于所有国家，甚至美国或以色列等这些尚未批准《日内瓦公约第一附加议定书》的国家。

在国际红十字会委员会（ICRC）主持下开展的一项重要研究得出了确定的结论，即国际人道主义习惯法至少以三种方式保护自然环境。[28] 首先，适用于目标保护（军事和非军事目标的区分、军事上的必要性和比例性）的一般原则明确地保护了自然环境：

第 43 条：关于敌对行动的一般原则适用于自然环境：
1. 任何自然环境的一部分不得受到攻击，除非它是军事目标。
2. 禁止破坏自然环境的任何部分，除非存在紧急的军事上的必要性。
3. 如果攻击会对环境造成可预见的、与预期的具体和直接的军

---

[23] Ibid., para. 15.
[24] Ibid., para. 17.
[25] Ibid., para. 15.
[26] *Legality of Nuclear Weapons*, supra footnote 7, operative part, para. 2E.
[27] *Report to the Prosecutor*, supra footnote 22, para. 15.
[28] See Henckaerts and Doswald-Beck, supra footnote 14.

事利益不成比例的附带损害,则应禁止对军事目标发动攻击。[29]

其次,对战争方法和手段的选择和使用也受限于自然环境保护的需要:

> 第44条:战争的方法和手段必须适当考虑自然环境的保护和保全。在军事行动中,必须采取一切可行的风险预防措施,以避免和尽量减少对环境的附带损害。即使某些军事行动对环境的影响还缺乏科学确定性,也不能免除冲突一方采取这种风险预防措施的责任。[30]

本条规定中使用的"风险预防"(precaution)一词最好理解为包括了预防(prevention)原则和风险预防(precautionary)原则(方法)。[31] 实际上,军事行动毫无疑问会对环境造成一个"风险"(即不利后果的可靠概率),因此需要实现评估这一风险。本条规定提到的科学不确定性至少大多数情况下在概念上与和平时期规范所面临的不确定性是不同的,因为在后一种情况下,影响的负面属性尚存疑问,而在前一种情况下,对环境的影响无疑是负面的。因此,"风险预防"(precaution)一词只有在非常特定的情况下,例如所使用的特定武器对环境的影响仍然无法确定,才能被理解为超出了损害预防(prevention)的含义。

最后,根据国际红十字会委员会的研究,《日内瓦公约第一附加议定书》第35条第3款和第55条第1款以及《禁止为军事或任何其他敌对目的使用改变环境的技术的公约》第1条第1款所述的规定已经固化为一项习惯法规则,内容如下:

> 第45条:禁止使用意图或预期对自然环境造成广泛、长期和严重损害的战争方法或手段。对自然环境的破坏不应被当作一个武器。[32]

29　Ibid., p. 143 (and authorities referred to therein).

30　Ibid., p. 147 (and authorities referred to therein).

31　On these principles see Chapter 3.

32　Henckaerts and Doswald-Beck, supra footnote 14, p. 151 (and the authorities referred to therein).

研究结果表明,尽管美国、法国或英国一直反对这一规则,但是充其量也只是它们在使用核武器时可以不适用这一规则,其他情况则都应适用。这是因为,它们的反对实践只有在核武器这一特殊场合下才能保持一致,而在其他场合的反对实践则无法保持一致。一般来讲,它们只能声称在核武器方面受到了"特别影响",而无法说所有武器都受到了"特别影响"。[33] 不论这一具体的习惯法规则是否适用于这些国家,但是"它并不妨碍根据其他规则(例如禁止无差别袭击……以及比例原则)来认定核武器的使用是非法的"。[34] 这一结论源于对第45条和其他一般规则之间关系的正确理解。正如研究结果所示,第45条是绝对的。一旦环境损害的严重程度达到了苛刻的门槛要求,那么军事上的必要性或比例性也不能成为正当理由。相反,由于第43条和第44条并没有规定如此苛刻的门槛要求,那么就可以通过军事上的必要性或者基于履行谨慎注意义务来证明对环境造成的损害是有正当理由的(也就避免了对规则的违反)。这也是为什么不仅要考虑通过战时法的"特别"条款来保护自然环境,还要考虑那些可能适用于这一场景的更"一般的"规则和原则。

3. 战时法的一般规范

无论是基于条约还是习惯法,战时法的许多规范都可以被调动起来为自然环境提供保护。这些规范一般都会涉及特定"目标"的保护(包括平民、平民财产和某些特殊资源/设施)或战争"方法和手段"的规制,尤其是禁止使用某些武器,如果这些武器造成的损害被认定为超出了军事上的必要性。[35] 本书并不打算评论所有的相关规范,[36] 但是,为了理解上一节讨论的具体规范所依据的广义原则和规定,还是有必要简要提及其中一些规范。

只要自然环境可被视为平民财产或对平民的生存而言很重要,区分原则、军事必要性原则和比例性原则就会与环保目的相关。《日内瓦公约第一附加议定书》第48条和第52条阐明了区分原则。后者规定:

---

33 Ibid., p. 154.

34 Ibid., p. 155.

35 See infra section 11.2.1.4.

36 See Mollard-Bannelier, supra footnote 13. For shorter inventories see: UNEP Report, supra footnote 21, pp. 12-21; Schmitt, supra footnote 5, pp. 94-104. The following overview is based on the study by Schmitt, updated when necessary to integrate subsequent developments.

第 52 条 —— 对民用目标的一般保护

1. 民用目标不得成为攻击或报复的对象。民用目标是第二段定义的全部非军事目标。

2. 攻击应严格限于军事目标。就目标而言，军事目标仅限于那些就其性质、地点、目的或用途对军事行动有影响的，并且在当时的情况下，它们的全部或者部分破坏、占据或者中立都会导致确定的军事优势。

早在 1907 年，《关于陆地战时法规和惯例的第四海牙公约》(*IV Hague Convention on the Laws and Customs of War on Land*) 所附的《海牙条例》(*Hague Regulations*) 第 23 条 g 款就阐明了军事必要性原则：

除了特别《公约》规定的禁止外，尤其禁止：……

(g) 摧毁或攫取敌人的财产，除非战争迫切需要摧毁或攫取。[37]

关于比例性，《日内瓦公约第一附加议定书》第 51 条第 5 款 b 项和第 57 条第 2 款 a (iii) 项针对与所寻求的军事优势相比明显过度的任何损害规定了原则：

第 51 条——平民的保护

5. 其中，下列类型的攻击应被视为无差别袭击：……

(b) 攻击可能附带造成的平民丧命、平民受伤、民用目标破坏或兼而有之的损害与预期的具体和直接军事利益相比不成比例。

第 57 条—— 攻击中的风险预防

……

2. 对于攻击，应采取如下预防措施：

(a) 计划或决定攻击的人应：

(iii) 如果攻击可能附带造成的平民丧命、平民受伤、民用目标破坏或兼而有之的损害与预期的具体和直接军事利益相比不成比例，则不应决定发动攻击。

---

[37] Convention (No. IV) respecting the Laws and Customs of War on Land and its Annex: Regulations concerning the Laws and Customs of War on Land, 18 October 1907, 205 CTS 277 (Hague Convention IV).

重要的是，违反了与环保相关的一些规范会导致执法的加重后果，例如，被指控罪犯的所在国有义务进行起诉或者引渡。[38] 举例来讲，违反《日内瓦第四公约》（*IV Geneva Convention*）第 53 条（占领方破坏某些民用财产[39]），在第 147 条所界定的特定情况下，可能构成对公约的一项"严重违反"。同样地，如果出于特定意图或故意违反了《日内瓦公约第一附加议定书》第 56 条（在可能释放出危险力量时，禁止攻击堤坝、水坝或核电厂等设施），也会被认定为一项"严重违反"。[40]

国际（性的）法院已经从个人角度（刑事责任）或国家间角度（国际责任），在一定程度上解决了战时法的一般原则和规则与环境的关联。从刑事责任的角度来看，所谓的"人质案"提供了一个有趣的例证。[41] 该案的被告之一是驻挪威的德国部队司令 Lothar Rendulic，他下令破坏所有避难所和生活资料，当作他从挪威领土进行军事撤退的部分内容。1944 年 10—11 月，由于 Lothar Rendulic（错误地）认为他正在受到俄罗斯军队的追击，这一命令得到了有效执行。然而，Lothar Rendulic 被宣告无罪，理由是他有理由相信他的行为是出于军事需要。法庭认为：

> 证据表明，俄国追击德国人的军队非常出色。他们开通了两条或三条陆上路线，以及在德国防线后方通过海上登陆……所获情报有限，无法摸清俄罗斯人意图……正是面对这种情况，他在挪威芬马克（**Finmark**）省实施了"焦土"政策……破坏程度是一支高效的军队

---

[38] See Geneva Convention (IV) Relative to the Protection of Civilian Persons in Time of War, 12 August 1949, 75 UNTS 287 (IV Geneva Convention), Art. 146; Additional Protocol I, supra footnote 8, Art. 85 (1). The literature on the duty to prosecute or extradite (aut dedere aut judicare) is extensive. seeamong others L. Reydams, *Universal Jurisdiction. International and Municipal Legal Perspectives* (Oxford University Press, 2003); R. O'Keefe, "The Grave Breaches Regime and Universal Jurisdiction" (2009) 7 *Journal of International Criminal Justice* 811.

[39] Article 55 of the Hague Regulations, supra footnote 37, assimilated the duties of the occupying power with respect to the property and resources of the occupied party as those of an usufructuary.

[40] Additional Protocol I, supra footnote 6, Art. 85 (3) (c).

[41] *Hostage Case* (US v. List), 11 TWC 759 (1950). See also *High Command Case* (*US v. Von Leeb*), 11 TWC 462 (1950). The cases were brought before the US authorities in their German occupation zone. Both cases are referred to in Schmitt, supra footnote 5, p. 99.

可以做到的极致……记录中有证据表明，这种毁灭和破坏在军事上没有必要。回顾事实可以很好地支持这一结论。但是，我们必须根据当时被告所感知的情况来进行情况判断。如果经过判断后，事实足以证明行动的正当性，那么在考量到所有因素和现有可能性之后，即使得出的结论可能是错误的，也不能认定是犯罪行为。[42]

本案表明，引用战时法的一般原则存在一定的限制，因为根据这些原则，环境破坏可能因军事需要而具备正当性。然而，自"人质案"以来，有关战争的法律取得了一些进展。在上述北约案件中，委员会确实参照《日内瓦公约第一附加议定书》第52条指出，"即使在针对公认的合法军事目标时，也应避免对经济基础设施和自然环境造成过度的长期损害（因为这种损害会对平民造成后续负面影响）"。[43] 此外，特设的国际刑事法庭和其他特别机制的司法实践对过度损害（包括对目标或生活必需品的损害）的认定持更为开放的态度。[44] 此外，战争罪的环境维度已被明确列入国际刑事法院（International Criminal Court, ICC）检控官2016年9月的《案件选择和优先政策》（*Policy on Case Selection and Prioritisation*）中，[45]

---

[42] Excerpt reproduced in G. D. Solis, *The Law of Armed Conflict: International Humanitarian Law in War* (Cambridge University Press, 2010), p. 289.

[43] *Report to the Prosecutor*, supra footnote 22, para. 18.

[44] See, e.g., *Prosecutor v. Ante Gotovina et al.*, ICTY Trial Chamber, Judgment (Volume II of II), Case No. IT-06-90-T (15 April 2011), paras. 1765-1766; *Prosecutor v. Vlastimir Đorđević*, ICTY Trial Chamber Judgment, Case No. IT-05-87/1-T (23 February 2011), paras. 1597-8; *Prosecutor v. Emmanuel Rukundo*, ICTR Trial Chamber, Judgment, Case No. ICTR-2001-70-T (27 February 2009), paras. 106, 108, 566; *Prosecutor v. Germain Katanga*, ICTR Trial Chamber, Judgment Pursuant to Article 74 of the Statute, Case No. ICC-01/04-01/07 (7 March 2014), paras. 924, 932, 952-953, 1659; *Prosecutor v. Charles Ghankay Taylor*, Special Tribunal for Sierra Leone, Trial Chamber, Judgment, SCSL-03-01-T (18 May 2012), paras. 2006, 2192. These cases are a selection of the more extensive body of jurisprudence surveyed in the second report on the protection of the environment in relation to armed conflicts, submitted by Marie G. Jacobsson, Special Rapporteur, 28 May 2015, A/CN.4/685 (Report II-Jacobsson).

[45] International Criminal Court (Office of the Prosecutor), *Policy on Case Selection and Prioritisation* (15 September 2016), para. 41（办事处将特别考虑起诉因破坏环境、非法开采自然资源或非法剥夺土地等手段或结果所犯的违反《罗马规约》的罪行）。

这表明，这一领域在将来的判例法中将会占据更大的一席之地。[46] 同样在 2016 年 9 月，国际刑事法院根据《罗马规约》（*Rome Statute*）第 8 条第 2 款 e（iv 项）裁判了第一起有关文化遗址破坏的案件。[47]

在国家间层面，国际法院从两个主要案例中分析了军事必要性原则、比例原则与占领方义务的关联。[48] 在上述《关于核武器合法性的咨询意见》中，国际法院强调了环境保护对正确解释必要性和比例原则的影响：

> 各国为了实现合法的军事目标，在评估何种军事行动是必要的和成比例的这一过程中，必须考虑到环境因素。对环境的尊重是评估一项行动是否符合必要性和比例原则的因素之一。[49]

在随后一个案件中，法院认定，乌干达作为刚果民主共和国伊图里区的占领国因为"没有采取适当措施确保其军队不抢劫、侵占和开发刚果民主共和国的自然资源"而违反了其谨慎注意义务。[50] 作为这项义务的基础，法院特别提到了《海牙规则》（*Hague Regulations*）第 43 条和第 47 条以及《日内瓦第四公约》第 33 条。[51] 有意思的是，法院还提及了一个和平时期的条约，即《非洲人权和人民权利宪章》（*African Charter on Human and Peoples' Rights*）第 21 条（对自然资源的集体权利），作为

---

[46] For a recent contribution on this question, see S. Freeland, *Addressing the Intentional Destruction of the Environment during Warfare under the Rome Statute of the International Criminal Court* (Antwerp: Intersentia, 2015).

[47] See *The Prosecutor v. Ahmad Al Faqi Al Mahdi*, ICC Trial Chamber VIII, ICC-01/12-01/15-171, Judgment and Sentence (27 September 2016) (the parties agreed on the characterisation of the act under Article 8 (2) (e) (iv) and the defendant admitted guilt).

[48] Although no clear reference to the environment is made, *Wall Advisory Opinion* is also relevant: *Legal Consequences of the Construction of a Wall in the Occupied Palestinian Territory*, Advisory Opinion, ICJ Reports 2004, p. 136, paras. 133-135 (referring to the duties of the occupying power with regard inter alia to agricultural resources and livelihoods).

[49] *Legality of Nuclear Weapons*, supra footnote 7, para. 30.

[50] *Armed Activities on the Territory of the Congo* (*Democratic Republic of the Congo v. Uganda*), Judgment, ICJ Reports 2005, p. 168 (DRC v. Uganda), para. 246.

[51] Ibid., paras. 245 and 250.

支持其结论的进一步法律依据。[52] 这符合法院以前的做法,认为即使爆发了武装冲突人权条约仍然适用。[53] 如下文所述,关于和平时期的环境条约在战时的适用问题,也提出了同样的问题。

(三) 武装冲突与环境法[54]

1. 概述

国际法院在 1992 年地球峰会召开仅几年后发表的《关于核武器合法性的咨询意见》中,没有明确回答在武装冲突期间"是否"仍然适用环境条约这一问题。取而代之的是,法院将问题重新表述为,"源自这些条约的义务是否意图成为在军事冲突期间完全受限的义务"。[55] 法院认为结论并非如此,同时还强调各国必须根据环境考量来解释其自卫权和战时义务。[56] 自那以后,尚无定论的"是否"适用这一问题就成为热点话题。[57]

在评估环境条约在武装冲突中的适用程度时,除了那些界定条约适用范围的通常标准(属事、属人、属地及临时管辖)之外,还需要考虑到许多挑战,这些挑战是学者和实践工作者针对和平时期条约在战时的适用而提出的。敌对行动的爆发可能直接或间接地对和平时期条约产生三种影响:(1) 影响此类条约是否继续有效或对交战国适用(暂停、退出、终止);(2) 触发一项基于条约的具体回应(部分失效、灵活性处理、增强保护);(3) 引起与其他规范特别是战时法规范的复杂互动。在接下来的部分中,将依次讨论这三种影响。

但在进行分析之前,要弄清两个次序问题。首先,在移至下一种影响之前,必须考虑这三种可能影响的每一个,只有遵循这一逻辑顺序,分析才能继续下去。事实上,如果环境条约在武装冲突中终止或中止,那么审视第二种和第三种可能影响就没有什么意义了。同样,如果某一条约继续生效,但

---

52 Ibid., para. 245.

53 *Legality of Nuclear Weapons*, supra footnote 7, para. 25; *Wall Advisory Opinion*, supra footnote 48, para. 106.

54 This section draws upon M. Kunz and J. E. Viñuales, "Environmental Approaches to Nuclear Weapons", in G. Nystuen, S. Casey-Maslen and A. Golden Bersagel (eds.), *Nuclear Weapons under International Law* (Cambridge University Press, 2014), pp. 269–291.

55 *Legality of Nuclear Weapons*, supra footnote 7, para. 30.

56 Ibid., paras. 30–33.

57 See references mentioned supra footnote 13.

根据条约允许各国在国家紧急情况下违背其核心条款,则没有必要澄清这种规范与战时法义务之间的相互作用。只有某个相关环境条约的义务通过了这些初步检验,它与战时法义务之间的相互作用才需要进一步澄清。这就引发了第二个问题,即按照我们刚才所述的分析步骤再往前进一步,环境规范"是否"适用于武装冲突这一问题就巧妙地成为"如何"适用的问题。

2. 继续适用

条约的终止、废除或某一缔约方退出,以及暂停条约对部分或所有缔约方的效力,只能根据特定条约的规定或根据《维也纳条约法公约》的默认条款。[58]但是,后者在其第 73 条中载有一项一般性保留,根据该保留,公约"不得预判某一条约因为国家间爆发敌对行动而可能产生的任何问题"。2004 年,国际法委员会(ILC)决定解决这一问题,并在 2011 年制定了一套《关于武装冲突对条约的影响的条款草案》。[59]

2011 年条款草案具体涉及第一种影响,即持续适用。国际法委员会所建议的制度是由四个阶段构成的。第一,条款草案指出,武装冲突并不事实上终止或中止交战国之间或与第三国之间的条约的适用(第 3 条)。第二,毫不意外,如果某一条约载有在发生武装冲突时其适用效力的规定,则这些规定适用于这种情况(第 4 条)。第三,当不存在这种规定时,也就是绝大多数环境条约的情况[60],则适用条约解释的国际规则,以

---

58 Vienna Convention on the Law of Treaties, Vienna, 23 May 1969, 1155 UNTS 331 (VCLT), Art. 42 (2).

59 ILC, Draft Articles on the Effects of Armed Conflict on Treaties, 9 December 2011, GA Res. 66/99, UN Doc. A/RES/66/99 (2011 ILC Draft Articles).

60 大多数主要的多边环境条约都没有明确提到它们在敌对行动期间的继续运作问题。Examples include: Convention on International Trade in Endangered Species of Wild Fauna and Flora, Washington, 3 March 1973, 993 UNTS 243 (CITES); Convention on the Conservation of Migratory Species of Wild Animals, Bonn, 23 June 1979, 1651 UNTS 333 (CMS); Montreal Protocol on Substances that Deplete the Ozone Layer, 16 September 1987, 1522 UNTS 3 (Montreal Protocol); Basel Convention on the Control of Transboundary Movements of Hazardous Wastes and their Disposal, 22 March 1989, 1673 UNTS 57 (Basel Convention); Convention on Biological Diversity, 5 June 1992, 1760 UNTS 79 (CBD); United Nations Framework Convention on Climate Change, Rio de Janeiro, 9 May 1992, 1771 UNTS 107 (UNFCCC); Rotterdam Convention on the Prior Informed Consent Procedure for Certain Hazardous Chemicals and Pesticides in International Trade, 10 September 1998, 2244 UNTS 337 (PIC Convention); Stockholm Convention on Persistent Organic Pollutants, Stockholm, 22 May 2001, 2256 UNTS 119 (POP Convention). see UNEP Report, supra footnote 21, pp. 39-40.

确定某一条约是否可以（单方面）中止、终止或退出（第5条）。这种确定不仅必须基于对条约相关条款的解释，而且必须考虑到与武装冲突的特点和该条约的特点有关的各种更广泛的因素（特别是条约的主旨事项），那些事关特定主题的条约，包括涉及环境保护和水体的条约，被假定在武装冲突期间全部或部分继续适用（第6条、第7条和附件）。第四，也是最后一点，条款草案的其余部分对"武装冲突引发的"条约的中止、退出或者终止做出了定性，通过参考适用于条款草案未涉及问题的一般国际法规则，来将《维也纳条约法公约》（VCLT）的条款调整适用于武装冲突这一背景。[61] 这些情况从本质上说明，在战时中止或退出某些条约的权利是对《维也纳条约法公约》所体现的习惯法理论的补充；[62] 这可能不会使侵略国受益，[63] 如果国家明确（或通过其行为）默认了条约的继续适用，[64] 该权利就会被放弃。在这方面，必须指出，事先通知中止或退出条约的意图是一项正式要求，可能会遭到反对，在这种情况下，各国必须寻求和平解决争端的手段。[65] 因此，一般来说，根据2011年国际法委员会条款草案，环境条约在武装冲突期间被假定为继续适用，除非条约另有规定。

这方面的一个重要问题涉及2011年国际法委员会条款草案所制定规则的习惯法地位。"反对条约的自动中止"这一基本原则显然符合国际法院的判例。国际法院在两项咨询意见[66]和一个有争议的案件[67]中处理了与人权条约有关的此类问题。在这些案件中，法院没有参考老的理论（和平时期的条约在战时应自动中止），而是侧重于第二种和第三种影响，下

---

61 2011 ILC Draft Articles, supra footnote 59, Arts. 8–18. The commentary ad Art. 8 explains that the ILC intentionally omitted to treat matters of lawfulness of agreements on modification or suspension, such as the conditions for modification or suspension of a multilateral treaty by certain of the parties only, contained in Arts. 41 and 58 VCLT, "preferring to leave such matters to the operation of general rules of international law, including those reflected in the 1969 Vienna Convention" (para. 5).

62 Ibid., Art. 18.

63 Ibid., Art. 15.

64 Ibid., Art. 12.

65 Ibid., Art. 9.

66 See *Legality of Nuclear Weapons*, supra footnote 7, para. 25; *Wall Advisory Opinion*, supra footnote 48, para. 106.

67 *DRC v. Uganda*, supra footnote 50, paras. 216, 219–220.

文将对此进行讨论。国际法院似乎拒绝承认传统理论（该理论认为，和平时期条约应在武装冲突时实事求是地中止），但这一理论在厄立特里亚—埃塞俄比亚索赔委员会（Eritrea Ethiopia Claims Commission）的一项裁决中得以体现。[68] 委员会认定，在以下情况下：

> 如果条约文本或语境没有明确表示在敌对活动期间也会维持条约的适用……一般认为，应推定缔约国打算至少在敌对行动期间中止此类条约。委员会的结论是，该原则适用于此处。[69]

委员会关于这一点的结论似乎没有考虑到国际法院的有关判例或国际法委员会当时就该主题开展的工作。由于这一原因和本案的其他因素，[70] 裁决不可能反映国际法院实践中采取的现代做法。如前所述，如果考虑到大多数环境条约并未明确处理其在敌对行动期间的适用问题，那么理解这一点就更加重要。

3. 基于条约的回应

多个环境条约确实包含有一些条款，允许在武装冲突等特殊情况下失效，或者通过广义表述赋予各国在履行其实质性义务方面一定的灵活性。相反，有些条约规定在武装冲突期间应不变甚至增强环境保护。我们现在要讨论的是针对条约本身对这种情况的反应。[71]

有一类条约提供最积极的保护，一些环境条约明确规定，它们力求防止其保护的环境进一步恶化，即使在发生武装冲突的情况下也是如此。主要例证是《世界遗产公约》第 11 条第 4 款，[72] 其中规定除应保留正常的

68　Eritrea Ethiopia Claims Commission, *Final Award – Pensions*: *Eritrea's Claims* 15, 19 & 23 (19 December 2005), RIAA, Vol. XXVI, p. 471.

69　Ibid., para. 30.

70　该利害攸关的条约是一项双边条约，它要求埃塞俄比亚在 1993 年正式获得独立后向居住在厄立特里亚的前埃塞俄比亚人支付养恤金，但这只是一项临时安排，而关于永久解决办法的（因武装冲突而中断的）谈判仍在继续，无论如何，该条约可在提前 12 个月通知后由任何一方终止。埃塞俄比亚辩称，条约之所以终止，是因为这两个原因之一，而不是委员会本身在第 31 段承认的条约法下事实上的中止。

71　For an inventory, see UNEP Report, supra footnote 21, pp. 35–39.

72　Convention Concerning the Protection of the World Cultural and Natural Heritage, 16 November 1972, 1037 UNTS 151（WHC）.

《世界遗产名录》外，世界遗产委员会还应保留《濒危世界遗产名录》，其中"只可包括文化和自然遗产中受到严重的特殊危险威胁（例如武装冲突的爆发或威胁）的财产"。《操作指南》还具体规定了将某一遗址列入该清单的标准。[73] 在这种情况下，武装冲突爆发触发了对受影响世界遗产地保护制度的强化，可能是从委员会发出的一个单纯的"关切信息"，也有可能是一套尽可能保护该遗址的国际援助制度。[74] 在这方面，《世界遗产公约》第6条第3款值得一提，根据该条款，缔约国承诺"不得故意采取任何可能直接或间接损害本公约其他缔约国领土内的第1条和第2条中提及的文化和自然遗产的措施"。

其他一些条约则采取相反的立场，它们不但不增强对环境的保护，反而在威胁"紧迫的国家利益"[75] 或者"国家最高利益"[76] 的特殊情况下赋予（缔约国）更多灵活性，或考虑是否减损某些条约义务，或在这种情况下规定不太严格的保护义务。例如，《拉姆萨公约》第4条第2款规定了在此特殊情况下发挥作用的替代性保护制度：

> 当某一缔约国出于紧急国家利益的考虑而取消列入名录的湿地或缩小其边界时，应尽可能弥补湿地资源的任何损失，特别应建立新的自然保护区，以供水禽生存，并在同一地区或其他地区保护原来生境的适当部分。

这项规定的原理不同于《世界遗产公约》第11条第4款的规定。《世界遗产公约》试图尽可能地保护濒危遗址，而《拉姆萨公约》第4条

73　UNESCO World Heritage Committee, *Operational Guidelines for the Implementation of the World Heritage Convention*, 26 October 2016, WHC. 16/01, paras. 177 – 182, available at: http://whc.unesco.org（last visited on 20 April 2017）.

74　Ibid., paras. 183–189.

75　Convention on Wetlands of International Importance especially as Waterfowl Habitat, 2 February 1971, 996 UNTS 245（Ramsar Convention）, Art. 4（2）.

76　African Convention on the Conservation of Nature and Natural Resources, Algiers, 15 September 1968, 1001 UNTS 3, Art. XVII（1）（i）. 2003年7月11日制定了对本公约的一项重要修正案，删除了国家最高利益的例外，并根据国际人道主义法的原则将其替换为针对武装冲突的详细环境保护义务，但该修正案尚未生效。See au. int/en/treaties（last visited on 10 April 2017）.

第 2 款则承认损失,而仅要求采取补偿措施。因此,"紧迫的国家利益"被视为首要考虑因素。然而,在实践中,秘书处保存了一份类似于《濒危世界遗产名录》的清单(《蒙特勒档案》),并在某些情况下进行了干预,以尽可能保护现有遗址。[77]

4. 规范的衔接

即使条约仍在适用,而且在有关条款不受减损的情况下,在武装冲突期间环境规范的适用也必须与其他规范特别是战时法的规范接轨。由此产生的相互作用可能很复杂,但就目前的目的而言,可以从两个主要角度分析这些相互作用,即冲突(即遵守一项适用的规范就会导致违反另一项适用的规范)和协同(即两项规范可以一起适用,一项用于解释或补充另一项)。

国际法委员会在关于国际法碎片化的工作中论及了规范冲突问题,[78]提供了处理此类冲突的相关实践和各种法律手段的有益总结。在国际法广泛认可的一般冲突规范(上位法优于下位法、特别法优于普通法和后法优于前法)中,与环境规范和战时法规范之间的关系最相关的是特别法优于普通法原则。国际法院在其《关于核武器合法性的咨询意见》和《在巴勒斯坦被占领土上修建隔离墙的咨询意见》中提到这一原则,主张战时法规范的适用要优先于人权规范,尽管不排除人权规范的适用。[79] 在"刚果民主共和国诉乌干达案"中,国际法院承认《非洲宪章》第 21 条(人权条款)与战时法同时适用。[80] 这种做法表明,必须将特别法原则当

---

77 在哥斯达黎加和尼加拉瓜之间的边界争端中,哥斯达黎加认为尼加拉瓜正在破坏一块受《拉姆萨公约》保护的湿地,作为运河建设工程的一部分,《拉姆萨公约》秘书处派出了一个特派团,以评估尼加拉瓜行动对相关湿地造成的影响。国际法院鼓励这种干预,在临时措施的命令中指出,哥斯达黎加应当就保护位于有争议领土的湿地问题与《拉姆萨公约》秘书处进行协商。See ICJ, *Certain Activities Carried out by Nicaragua in the Border Area* (*Costa Rica v. Nicaragua*), Request for the indication of provisional measures, Order of 8 March 2011, para. 86 (2).

78 ILC, *Conclusions of the work of the Study Group on the Fragmentation of International Law: Difficulties arising from the Diversification and Expansion of International Law* (2006) (Conclusions). See also the Report of 13 April 2006 (Doc. A/CN. 4/L. 682) on which the Conclusions are based (Report).

79 *Legality of Nuclear Weapons*, supra footnote 7, para. 25; *Wall Advisory Opinion*, supra footnote 48, para. 106.

80 *DRC v. Uganda*, supra footnote 50, para. 245.

作衔接两项可适用规范的一个手段。问题就变成了如何具体衔接不同的可适用规范。

适用于同一情况的两项或多项规范的衔接可以采取不同的形式。如果战时法被视为主导性的特别法，则环境规范可适用于解释目的或通过处理主导性规范未涵盖的方面来补充主导性规范。第一个假设几乎没有争议。国际法院在前面提到的《关于核武器合法性的咨询意见》中确认，在评估威胁使用核武器或者使用核武器的整体合法性时，更明确地说就是在评估调整自卫行为和敌对行为的规范时，必须考虑到损害预防原则。[81] 这种立场可被视为《维也纳条约法公约》第 31 条第 3 款 c 项所规定的广义的系统整合规则的适用，根据该规则，条约的解释者必须结合上下文，考虑"适用于双方之间关系的所有国际法规则"。[82] 第二个假设更为困难。从某种意义上讲，在多大程度上可以依靠环境规范来涵盖特别法没有规定的方面被认为是一个解释的问题，或者，可以理解为在事实上没有特别法规定时直接适用。例如，即使一项行动在不造成过度环境损害的情况下摧毁了合法的军事目标（这是《日内瓦公约第一附加议定书》第 52 条允许的），环境规范也可能对修复受损环境经济负担的分配发挥作用。同样地，《日内瓦公约第一附加议定书》第 57 条第 2 款 a（ⅲ）项规定必须避免发动对平民或平民财产造成过度附带损害的攻击，如果根据习惯环境义务（进行环境影响评价）来解读，该规定就意味着军事行动计划应该具有一些正式的程序性步骤。这种衔接很难抽象地实现，但是，随着环境保护在国际法其他领域日益显现，人们可以期望它对战时法的一般规范的影响也会逐步增加。

（四）作为污染物的武器

1. 概述

关于战争方法和手段，战时法的规范和工具针对的是特定武器的"使用"，因为这些武器会造成不必要的伤害，或者会对平民、平民财产或环境造成无差别的或过度的影响。相比之下，军备控制（或"裁军"）

---

[81] *Legality of Nuclear Weapons*, supra footnote 7, para. 30 read in the context of para. 29.

[82] 国际法院在石油平台案中讨论了这一解释规则（*Islamic Republic of Iran v. United States of America*），ICJ Reports 2003, p. 161, para. 41。

国际法则采取了一个更广泛的视角,对某些被视为"大规模杀伤性武器"[83]的武器类型进行全生命周期规制,从武器的开发直到销毁或转换。规制重点的差异可以通过规制生物武器的两份关键法律文件来举例说明,即禁止生物武器的使用的1925年《日内瓦议定书》(*1925 Geneva Protocol*)[84]和禁止生物武器其他生命周期的1972年《禁止生物武器公约》(*1972 Convention on Biological Weapons*)(也暗含它们的使用)[85]。

就当前目的而言,需要强调的主要特征是这种综合性规制方式与环境条约采用的方法两者间的相似性,例如《蒙特利尔议定书》[86]《持久性有机污染物公约》[87]或《水俣公约》[88],它们规制的是特定污染物的整个生命周期或其中的重要部分。以下各段简要讨论适用于三种主要的大规模杀伤性武器(核武器、生物武器和化学武器)的制度,以便说明前文论及的第三种规制方法在多大程度上已经找到了具体的法律表达。

正如我们将看到的那样,虽然采用这一方法的第一套法律文件针对的是生物武器,但是20年后针对化学武器的文件才是最全面和影响最深远的。关于核武器,若干核国家政治上的强烈反对导致迄今为止仍未产生一项威胁或使用禁止核武器的条约,尽管其生命周期的其他阶段受到了高度规制。然而,正如2017年7月7日通过的(124个国家出席,122票赞成[89])《禁止核武器条约》(TPNW)[90]所表明的那样,越来越多的人支持

---

[83] 虽然"大规模杀伤性武器"一词是联合国委员会在20世纪40年代后期定义的(基于其破坏性和滥杀滥伤效果),但在现代国际法中,它被用来指核武器、生物武器和化学武器,并将这三种武器与"常规"武器进行对比。See H. A. Strydom, "Weapons of Mass Destruction", in *Max Planck Encyclopedia of Public International Law*, available at: www.opil.ouplaw.com (visited on 20 April 2017).

[84] Protocol for the Prohibition of the Use in War of Asphyxiating, Poisonous or Other Gases, and of Bacteriological Methods of Warfare, 17 June 1925, 94 LNTS 65 (1925 Geneva Protocol).

[85] Convention on the Prohibition of the Development, Production and Stockpiling of Bacteriological (Biological) and Toxin Weapons and on their Destruction, 10 April 1972, 1015 UNTS 163 (BWC).

[86] Montreal Protocol, supra footnote 60. On the scope of this treaty, see Chapter 5.

[87] POP Convention, supra footnote 60. On the scope of this treaty see Chapter 7.

[88] Minamata Convention on Mercury, 10 October 2013, available at: www.mercuryconvention.org (visited on 20 April 2017) (Minamata Convention). On the scope of this treaty, see Chapter 7.

[89] See UN Doc. A/CONF. 229/2017/L. 3/Rev. 1.

[90] See Treaty on the Prohibition of Nuclear Weapons, 7 July 2017 (not yet in force).

解决这一差异。该条约是依据 2016 年 12 月联合国大会作出的指令制定的。[91]《禁止核武器条约》一旦得到 50 个国家的批准就会生效，这是迈出的重要一步，尽管目前只是象征性的一步。它对核武器的开发、拥有和使用进行了全面禁止（第 1 条），但没有一个核国家参与《禁止核武器条约》的制定进程。[92]

2. 生物武器

生物（包括细菌）武器是那些旨在散布致病因子（细菌、病毒或者真菌）或毒素来杀人或危害人类或环境的装置。[93] 它们的影响很少立刻呈现，因此它们在战场上可能提供的战争优势不如它们通过长久削弱对手所带来的战略优势重要。[94] 它们对环境的影响有可能是非常重大的，因为从本质上讲，它们需要将有害的病原体释放到环境当中。

控制生物武器使用的努力至少可以追溯到 1899 年和 1907 年的海牙会议。[95] 目前的法律制度以一份陈旧而非常简洁的文件为基础，即上述 1925 年《日内瓦议定书》，该议定书禁止在战争中"使用""有毒的或其他使人窒息的气体，以及所有类似的液体、物质或装置"，并将这一禁令扩大到"细菌战"。[96] 然而，禁止生物武器的主要文件是在 1969—1972 年联合国裁军谈判会议主持下达成的《禁止生物武器公约》（BWC）。根据《禁止生物武器公约》第 1 条：

> 本公约各缔约国均承诺不在任何情况下开发、生产、储存或以其

---

[91] See Resolution 71/258, "Taking forward multilateral nuclear disarmament", 23 December 2016, UN Doc. A/RES/71/258, para. 8.

[92] For an overview of the processes leading to this instrument, see D. Joyner, "The Treaty on the Prohibition of Nuclear Weapons", *EJIL Talk* (26 July 2017), available at: www.ejiltalk.org (visited on 28 July 2017).

[93] See D. Svarc, "Biological Weapons and Warfare", in *Max Planck Encyclopedia of Public International Law* (2011), available at: www.opil.ouplaw.com (visited on 20 April 2017), para. 1; D. H. Joyner, *International Law and the Proliferation of Weapons of Mass Destruction* (Oxford University Press, 2009), chapter 2.

[94] Svarc, supra footnote 93, para. 3.

[95] See Hague Declaration (IV, 2) concerning Asphyxiating Gases, 29 July 1899, 187 CTS 453; Hague Convention IV, supra footnote 37, Regulations, Art. 23 (a).

[96] 1925 Geneva Protocol, supra footnote 84, preamble, para. 1 and declaration, para. 1.

他方式获取或保留：

1. 微生物或其他生物制剂或毒素，不论其来源或生产方法如何、种类和数量，且无正当理由用于预防疾病、保护或其他和平目的；

2. 武器、设备或运载工具，旨在用于敌对目的或武装冲突中使用这种制剂或毒素。

这项禁令是全面的，涉及生物武器的整个生命周期，也隐含生物武器的使用。事实上，1996年在日内瓦举行的《禁止生物武器公约》（BWC）第四次审查会议上，缔约国重申，"根据公约第1条规定，在任何情况下都禁止使用、开发、生产和储存细菌（生物）和毒素武器"。[97] 至于现有的制剂或设备的库存，缔约国必须销毁现有库存的制剂或设备，或将其转用于和平目的，[98] 它们也有义务不向任何接受国转移，或为其他国家或组织提供援助和鼓励去开发此类制剂或设备。[99]《禁止生物武器公约》还对防止恐怖主义组织获取生物武器作了具体规定。[100]

该制度的致命弱点是缺乏适当的核查和实施制度。虽然可以向联合国安全理事会提出申诉（这种可能性迄今尚未使用），[101] 一般认为，核查制度的体制安排尤其薄弱。在1986年采取了多个"建立信任措施"，在2006年设立了一个小型的"履约支持机构"（Implementation Support Unit），但包括一个核查议定书等其他更有意义的步骤都遇到了许多阻力，主要是来自美国和俄罗斯。[102] 还有另一个问题，从裁军的角度来看这一问题可能显得令人费解，但必须从环境的角度来看，这个问题就是制剂的销毁或处置以及设备和设施的停运所造成的影响。正如一位前联合国负责裁军事务的副秘书长指出的那样，"最大的讽刺是，为了和平与安全而必须

---

[97] Fourth Review Conference, Geneva, 25 November – 6 December 1996, Final Declaration, para. 3.

[98] BWC, supra footnote 85, Art. II.

[99] Ibid., Art. III.

[100] Ibid., Art. IV.

[101] Ibid., Art. VI.

[102] On this issue see J. Littlewood, "The Verification Debatein the Biological and Toxin Weapons Convention in 2011" (2010) 3 *Disarmament Forum* 15.

消除此类武器,但是我们却在制造武器的时候搬出了保护环境的理由"。[103]《禁止生物武器公约》第 2 条明确提到这一关切,指出"在执行本条规定时,应遵守一切必要的安全预防措施,以保护人口和环境"。这一挑战也与其他两种大规模杀伤武器有关。[104]

3. 化学武器

1925 年《日内瓦议定书》和《禁止生物武器公约》也与化学武器的规制有关,但这一领域的核心规范是由《禁止化学武器公约》(Chemical Weapons Convention,CWC)提供的,该公约也是在联合国裁军谈判会议主持下谈判达成的,并在 1993 年开放签署。[105] 虽然生物武器和化学武器的概念之间有一些重叠(涉及生物体产生的毒素),但后者被界定为非生物有毒物质。因为化学武器具有无差别的、潜在的大规模影响,所以被认为是大规模杀伤性武器。

《禁止化学武器公约》既是战时法,也是裁军/不扩散条约。公约第 1 条所述的基本义务范围很广,包括:(1)使用;(2)开发、生产、获取、储存、保留和转让;(3)在这方面的协助或鼓励;(4)现有武器和设施的销毁,包括遗弃在另一缔约国领土上的武器和设施。第 2 条对"化学武器"和"化学武器生产设施"进行了具体定性,其依据是它们的用途(允许民用、保护性和国内防暴使用[106])和数量。从环境角度来看,值得注意的是,可能属于"化学武器"的"有毒化学品"是根据其"对生命过程的化学作用(即可能导致人类或动物死亡、暂时丧失行为能力或永

---

[103] J. Dhanapala, "The Environmental Impacts of Manufacturing, Storing, Deploying and Retiring Weapons", in *Symposium*: *Arms and the Environment*: *Preventing the Perils of Disarmament*, National Energy-Environment Law and Energy Policy Institute, The University of Tulsa College of Law Tulsa, Oklahoma, 9 December 1999, available at: www.un.org/disarmament/ (visited on 20 April 2017)。

[104] Similar considerations apply to the destruction of cluster munitions, as stated in the 2015–2020 Dubrovnik Action Plan (Action 2: stockpile destruction) adopted under the Convention on Cluster Munitions, 30 May 2008, 2688 UNTS 39 (CCM).

[105] Convention on the Prohibition of the Development, Production, Stockpiling and Use of Chemical Weapons and on their Destruction, 13 January 1993, 1974 UNTS 45 (CWC). See T. Marauhn, "Chemical Weapons and Warfare", in *Max Planck Encyclopedia of Public International Law* (2010), available at: www.opil.ouplaw.com (visited on 20 April 2017); W. Krutzsch, E. Meijer and R. Trapp (eds.), *The Chemical Weapons Convention. A Commentary* (Oxford University Press, 2014).

[106] CWC, supra footnote 105, Art. II (9).

久伤害）"来定义的。《禁止化学武器公约》序言部分涉及了对非人类和非动物环境造成损害的化学品问题，该序言承认："相关协定和国际法相关原则均体现禁止把除草剂当作一种战争手段来使用。"它参考的是本章前述 1925 年《日内瓦议定书》和《禁止为军事或任何其他敌对目的使用改变环境的技术的公约》等文件，其中为禁止适用设定了一个重要的门槛（尽管低于《日内瓦公约第一附加议定书》）。

与《禁止生物武器公约》不同，《禁止化学武器公约》具有更有力的机构安排，其形式是设在海牙的禁止化学武器组织（OPCW），[107] 以及一个复杂的核查和执行制度。执行制度主要包括缔约国的初次和年度声明，随后禁止化学武器组织秘书处会进行核查。[108] 在怀疑不遵约的情况下还可以临时检查。[109] 还值得注意的是销毁现有化学武器的复杂框架。[110] 与在环境条约中的逐步淘汰一样，《禁止化学武器公约》也有一个"化学品附录"，其中有三个"日程表"，用以区分受规制的化学品，具体取决于它们能否在多大程度上用于军事以外的用途。[111] 销毁这些化学品必须按照"销毁次序"进行销毁，而且必须在《禁止化学武器公约》生效后十年内完成销毁。[112] 可以延期，但只能延长到 2012 年 4 月底这个最晚期限。[113] 虽然在消除储存方面取得了很大进展（已销毁约 80% 已申报的储存），包括

---

[107] Ibid., Art. VIII. See www.opcw.org（visited on 20 April 2017）. On the OPCW, see R. Trapp, "The OPCW in Transition: From Stockpile Elimination to Maintaining a World Free of Chemical Weapons"（2012）1 *Disarmament Forum* 41.

[108] CWC, supra footnote 105, Ars. III and VI.

[109] Ibid., Art. IX（8）-（25）.

[110] Ibid., Art. IV, Annex on Chemicals and Verification Annex.

[111] 日程表一包括沙林、硫黄和氮芥子等化学品，除了军事用途外，很少或根本没有其他用途。日程表二包括神经毒剂阿米顿等化学品，这种化学品基于公约允许的目的而被少量商业化生产。日程表三包括氰化氢等化学品，这些化学品被商业化大量用于金矿和白银开采中，通过它们可以获取其他物质。

[112] Ibid., Art. IV（6）and Verification Annex, part IV（A）, C. 15-19.

[113] CWC, supra footnote105, VerificationAnnex, partIV（A）, C. 24-28（theabsolutelimitissetin paragraph 25 by reference to fifteen years since entry into force of the CWC, which did so on 29 April 1997）.

美国和俄罗斯在内的国家正在销毁其所持有的化学武器库存,[114] 但是在最近的冲突中仍然使用了化学武器(例如在叙利亚内战中)。与《禁止生物武器公约》一样,《禁止化学武器公约》明确要求各国在销毁其所持有的受规制武器时,"将确保人民安全和保护环境作为最高优先事项"。[115]

4. 核武器

规制军事用途核材料的国际规范庞大而复杂,但并不全面。尽管存在大量争议,特别是国际法院在20世纪90年代的《关于核武器合法性的咨询意见》之后,迄今为止,还没有一个全球性的禁令来禁止任何情况下核武器的使用或其生命周期其他阶段的行为(开发、制造、获取、储存等)。[116] 因此,虽然人们可以自信地断言,生物和化学武器是被禁止的,但如果就核武器来说,这种断言将不完全准确。正如国际法院指出的:

> 迄今为止的模式是,由具体文件来宣布大规模杀伤性武器为非法……在过去20年中,就核武器问题进行了许多谈判;它们没有导致一项与全面禁止细菌和化学武器相同的全面禁止核武器条约。[117]

这当然是不符合常理的,因为核武器是迄今为止最危险的大规模杀伤性武器,而且肯定也是对自然环境影响最大的武器。2017年7月通过了《禁止核武器条约》(*Treaty on the Prohibition of Nuclear Weapons*)[118] 是解决这一空白的重要一步,尽管目前所有拥有核武器的国家都缺席该条约,这使其在很大程度上只具有象征意义。然而,国际法并不总是理性的,或者更确切地说,它有时遵循奇特的但政治上强大的理由。本部

---

114 See Report of the OPCW on the Implementation of the Convention on the Prohibition of the Development, Production, Stockpiling and Use of Chemical Weapons and on their Destruction, 4 December 2013, C-18/4, paras. 2-3.

115 CWC, supra footnote 105, Art. IV (10).

116 *Legality of Nuclear Weapons*, supra footnote 7, paras. 53-74(得出的结论是缺乏一个普遍性禁止核武器使用的具体条约或习惯法"规范")。See S. Kadelbach, "Nuclear Weapons and Warfare", in *Max Planck Encyclopedia of Public International Law* (2009), available at: www.opil.ouplaw.com(visited on 20 April 2017); Nystuen, et al., supra footnote 54.

117 *Legality of Nuclear Weapons*, supra footnote 7, paras. 57-58.

118 See supra footnote 90.

分的目的不是重新展开关于核武器合法性的辩论,而只是举例说明核武器生命周期的重要方面是如何被实际规制的,[119] 这就为环境提供了一些保护措施。

除了第七章讨论的有关核能的规范外,数项国际文件还具体调整了核武器生命周期的某些部分。国际法院在其上述咨询意见中为我们提供了各种条约的总览,这些条约规制的是:(1)核武器的获取、制造或拥有;(2)核武器的部署;(3)此类武器的试验;(4)核武器的使用。[120] 这些条约在地理上或实质上都不是全面的。因此,禁止使用的具体承诺适用于某些特定区域(拉丁美洲、南太平洋)[121] 或某些情势(例如,《不扩散核武器条约》的有核武器国家和无核武器缔约国之间,并须遵守例外)。[122] 同样,禁止获取、制造或拥有核武器只适用于特定国家(如德国[123])或类别国家(例如《不扩散核武器条约》中的无核武器国家[124])。关于部署和

---

[119] See Resolution70/47 "Humanitarian consequences of nuclear weapons", 11 December 2015, A/RES/70/47 (calling up on "all States, in their shared responsibility, to prevent the use of nuclear weapons, to prevent their vertical and horizontal proliferation and to achieve nuclear disarmament").

[120] *Legality of Nuclear Weapons*, supra footnote 7, paras. 58-63.

[121] See for Latin America: Treaty for the Prohibition of Nuclear Weapons in Latin America, 14 February 1967, 634 UNTS 281 (Treaty of Tlatelcoco), Art. 1; Additional Protocol I to the Treaty for the Prohibition of Nuclear Weapons in LatinAmerica, 14February1967, 634UNTS 360(向在条约覆盖区域的非拉丁美洲国家开放); Additional Protocol II to the Treaty for the Prohibition of Nuclear Weapons in Latin America, 14 February 1967, 634 UNTS 364(根据这一议定书,《不扩散核武器条约》中的五个核武器国家承诺尊重所涉地区的无核化). For the South Pacific: South Pacific Nuclear Free Zone Treaty, 6 August 1985, 1445 UNTS 177 (Treaty of Rarotonga), Art. 3; Protocol 2 to the South Pacific Nuclear Free Zone Treaty, 1 December 1986, 1971 UNTS 475, Art. 1(《不扩散核武器条约》中的五个核武器国家的其中四个批准了这一议定书). For an overview of these and other areas see S. Szurek, "De Rarotonga à Bangkok et Pelindaba: Note sur les traités constitutifs de nouvelles zones exemptes d'armes nucléaires" (1996) 42 *Annuaire français de droit international* 164.

[122] See Treaty on the Non-Proliferation of Nuclear Weapons, 1 July 1968, 729 UNTS 161 (NPT). 1995年,《不扩散核武器条约》得到延长,《不扩散核武器条约》中的五个核武器国家作出单方声明,承诺不对《不扩散核武器条约》的无核缔约国使用核武器,但有一些有限的例外。

[123] See Treaty on the Final Settlement with Respect to Germany, 12 September 1990, 1696 UNTS 115, Art. 3(1).

[124] NPT, supra footnote 122, Art. 2.

试验的规制，它具有更明确的环境保护影响，例如，通过对南极洲[125]或海底[126]等公共区域的无核化，或禁止大气和水下试验。[127] 总体而言，正如国际法院在 1996 年指出的那样：

"因此，这些条约可被视为预示着今后将普遍禁止使用此类武器"，然而，它立即补充说，"它们本身并不构成这种禁止"。[128]

1996 年以来，又缔结了一些其他相关条约，其中包括在中亚建立"无核武器区"的条约。[129] 尽管此类区域可能会在地理上扩大，但核大国坚决反对全面禁止的原则，这种情况在不远的将来不太可能得到改变。因此，环境保护最好侧重于通过对部署、试验和不扩散的规制来实现，包括不仅禁止核国家"俱乐部"的扩充，还应减少核国家核武器的储存，[130] 并禁止基本污染物（即用于核武器或其他军事装置的裂变材料）的产生。[131]

（五）当前的编纂努力

正如前述和平时期的环境条约与大规模杀伤性武器的规制之间的关联，还存在一种明确情形可以在武装冲突期间实现对环境的保护，这种保护不仅通过战时法的规范，也考虑了一套在敌对行动之前、期间和之后进

125　See Antarctic Treaty, 1 December 1959, 402 UNTS 71, Arts. IandV; Treaty on the Prohibition of the Emplacement of Nuclear Weapons and Other Weapons of Mass Destruction on the SeaBed and the Ocean Floor and in the Subsoil Thereof, 11 February 1971, 955 UNTS 115, Art. I.

126　Treaty on Principles Governing the Activities of States in the Exploration and Use of Outer Space, including the Moon and other Celestial Bodies, 27 January 1967, 610 UNTS 205 (Outer Space Treaty), preamble and Art. IV.

127　See among others the Treaty Banning Nuclear Weapons Tests in the Atmosphere, in Outer Space and under Water, 5 August 1963, 480 UNTS 43 (PNTB).

128　*Legality of Nuclear Weapons*, supra footnote 7, para. 62.

129　Treaty on a Nuclear-Weapon-Free Zone in Central Asia, 8 September 2006, 2212 UNTS 257 (Treaty of Semipalatinsk), followed by a Protocol signed by the five NPT nuclear-weapons States on 6 May 2014.

130　为实现这种削减，已经做出了巨大的努力，特别是美国和苏联（现为俄罗斯）之间。For a concise overview, see Kadelbach, supra footnote 116, paras. 23–27.

131　On the efforts and implications of developing a "Fissile Material Cut-off Treaty", see United Nations Institute for Disarmament Research, *A Fissile Material Cut-off Treaty. Understanding the Critical Issues* (Geneva: UNIDIR, 2010).

行干预的、更广泛的规范。长期以来,(国际社会)已经开展了数次编纂工作,以解决武装冲突对环境的影响[132]或武装冲突对条约的影响等问题。[133]

  2013年,国际法委员会围绕"与武装冲突有关的环境保护"主题开展了相关工作。为了扩大要考虑的规范范围,专门选择了"与……有关"一词。来自瑞典的特别报告员Marie Jacobsson对这项工作在时间上区分为"三个时间段:武装冲突之前、期间和之后(分别为第一阶段、第二阶段和第三阶段)"。[134] 有趣的是,报告员重点关注第一阶段和第三阶段,而这两个阶段在编纂工作中较少受到关注,[135] 并且她在第二阶段的工作中指向了非国际武装冲突。[136] 同时,报告员倾向于不讨论诸如环境造成的冲突、文化财产保护、武器规制以及环境造成的移民等问题。[137]

  关于该主题的工作尚未完成,但产生了多项草案原则。[138] 这些原则仍然按照上述三个阶段进行组织。与第一阶段有关的原则把重点放在预防上面,它们应对的问题包括划定具有自然或文化价值的特别区域、保护土著人民的环境、通过国家和那些开展维和行动的国际组织来防止环境损害等

---

[132] International Committee of the Red Cross (ICRC), *Guidelines for Military Manuals and Instructions on the Protection of the Environment in Times of Armed Conflict*, 1993, available at: www.icrc.org (visited on 20 April 2017). The UN General Assembly encouraged States to incorporate these guidelines into their military manuals. See UN Doc. A/RES/49/50, 17 February 1995, para. 11.

[133] 2011 ILC Draft Articles, supra footnote 59.

[134] Preliminary Report on the Protection of the Environment in Relation to Armed Conflicts. Submitted by Marie G. Jacobsson, Special Rapporteur, 30 May 2014, UN Doc. A/CN. 4/674 ("Preliminary Report-Jacobsson"), para. 58.

[135] See Third report on the protection of the environment in relation to armed conflicts, submitted by Marie G. Jacobsson, Special Rapporteur, 3 June 2016, A/CN. 4/700 (focusing on post-conflict measures) (Report III-Jacobsson).

[136] Report II-Jacobsson, supra footnote 44.

[137] Preliminary Report-Jacobsson, supra footnote 134, paras. 64-67.

[138] Protection of the environment in relation to armed conflict. Text of the draft introductory provisions and draft principles provisionally adopted so far by the Drafting Committee, 22 July 2015, A/CN. 4/L. 870 ("Draft-Introduction"); Protection of the environment in relation to armed conflict. Text of the draft principles provisionally adopted in 2015 and technically revised and renumbered during the present session by the Drafting Committee, 26 July 2016, A/ CN. 4/L. 870/Rev. 1 ("Draft Principles I"); Protection of the environment in relation to armed conflicts. Text of the draft principles provisionally adopted during the present session by the Drafting Committee, 3 August 2016, A/ /CN. 4/L. 876 ("Draft Principles II").

问题。与第二阶段有关的原则是试图阐明一般战时法规范的环境内涵，例如关于区分的规则（自然环境被认为具有民事性质）、比例性、必要性和预防措施（不要与风险预防原则混淆）。关于第三阶段的原则，它们涉及和平谈判中的环境问题、冲突后环境评估、战争遗留物处理和充分的信息提供。

这些原则及其表述有可能被改变，但特别报告员的优点应受到赞扬，因为它从更广的视角来处理环境保护问题，而不仅限于敌对行动中的限制措施。

二 诉诸战争的环境维度

（一）概述

国际法中有关诉诸武力的一系列规则也可能与自然环境的保护有关。可以从三个角度来讨论这一主题。

第一个角度涉及环境保护对武力禁用的两项例外［即《联合国宪章》（United Nations Charter）第 7 章规定的自卫和执行行动］规则的影响。从法律角度来看，这相当于评估这些规范在多大程度上考虑了环境保护。

第二个角度涉及对违反战时法（指武装冲突造成的环境损害）所导致的法律后果，这一问题与联合国安全理事会第 687（1991）号决议［UN Security Council's Resolution 687 （1991）］有关，该决议谴责伊拉克在科威特领土上造成环境破坏。[139]

第三个角度更为宏观，包括环境退化可能造成的新型安全威胁问题。准确地说，产生的问题远远超出了战时法的规范，需要进行更通用的讨论。因此，本节仅讨论前两个角度的问题。本章第三节更详细地讨论了第三个角度的问题。

（二）诉诸战争权和环境保护

国际法院在其《关于核武器合法性的咨询意见》中简要讨论了环境保护对诉诸战争权规则的影响，更具体地说，对自卫权的习惯规则及条约规则的影响。法院得出了结论，认为不能将环境条约解释为"在军事冲突期间完全受限"的义务，法院确认，在评估一项行动是否必要和适当时必须考虑环境保护因素：

---

[139] UN Security Council Resolution 687 （1991）, 8 April 1991, UN Doc. S/RES/687 （1991）.

法院并不认为有关条约会因为一国有保护环境的义务而试图剥夺其在国际法下的自卫权。尽管如此，各国在评估什么样的行动对实现合法军事目标而言是必需的、成比例的时候，必须考虑到环境因素。对环境的尊重是评估一项行动是否符合必要性和比例性原则的要件之一。[140]

必要性和比例性既是诉诸自卫的前提条件，也是规范敌对行动的一般原则。尽管有区别（无论诉诸武力是否合法，这种一般原则都适用），但必要性和比例性这两项义务在一定程度上是相关的，正如法院指出的：

> 自卫法下符合比例的使用武力为了合法，还必须符合适用于武装冲突的法律的要求，特别应包括人道主义法的原则和规则。

因此，环境考量已经介入了对武力使用合法性的评估，这不同于评估敌对行动是否是合法开展。本章第二节第二部分第三点讨论的这一区别的一个含义是，仅仅违反诉诸自卫权的规则就可能导致对环境损害的责任，而无论其是否违反了战时法。

环境的考量也与《联合国宪章》第 7 章规定的执行行动也有关。[141] 一个问题是，环境造成的冲突，或者更广泛地说，自然灾害等环境威胁是否可能触发集体安全机制。从法律上讲，联合国安全理事会可以将此类事件定性为"对国际和平与安全的威胁"，并根据第 7 章通过有约束力的决定，无论这些决定是否涉及使用武力或更温和的干预形式，例如，在没有主权国授权的情况下向受困人民提供援助或进行经济制裁。过去，安全理事会根据《联合国宪章》第 39 条，将侵犯人权、难民潮和人道主义灾难，甚至埃博拉疫情视为对和平的威胁，因此可以适用第 7 章的规定。[142] 然而，安全理事会是否应该参与与维护国际和平安全关联不大的环境造成

---

140 *Legality of Nuclear Weapons*, supra footnote 7, para. 30 (italics added).

141 See C. Gray, "Climate Change and the Law on the Use of Force", in R. Rayfuse and S. V. Scott (eds.), *International Law in the Era of Climate Change* (Cheltenham: Edward Elgar, 2011), pp. 219–240.

142 Ibid., p. 230. On the characterization of the outbreak of Ebola see Security Council, Resolution 2177 (2014), 18 September 2014, UN Doc. S/ RES/2177 (2014).

的问题，还是引发了很多争议。在安全理事会于 2007 年和 2011 年举行的关于气候变化问题的两次辩论中，各国所采取不同的立场就说明了这一点。[143] 主要反对意见来自 77 国集团等，它们不愿意给像安全理事会这样的平台提供扩大其职权范围的额外机会，因为安理会在代表性方面不如联合国大会或经社理事会。

（三）违反诉诸战争规则和环境损害

尽管存在争议，1990—1991 年海湾战争还是可以作为例证说明违反诉诸战争规则的对环境的影响。在伊拉克入侵科威特之后，联合国安理会通过了一系列决议，包括第 687（1991）号决议 [Resolution 687 (1991)]。[144] 该决议第 16 段重申，伊拉克应该：

> 根据国际法，对伊拉克非法入侵和占领科威特所造成的任何直接损失、损害（包括环境损害和自然资源的耗竭）或者对外国政府、国民和企业的损害负责。

为管理索赔事务而设立的机构［即联合国赔偿委员会（UNCC）］的工作前提是，伊拉克应该对与其侵略行为存在因果关系的所有环境损害负责。赔偿委员会不打算对责任原则（其或已包含了对战时法和环境规范的考量）进行法律评估。事实上，为审理不同索赔[145]而设立的专家组经常重申这一前提。例如，关于伊拉克部队在从科威特撤退时纵火引发的"油井井喷失控索赔（WBC 索赔）案"[146]中，专家组回顾说：

---

143 On these debates, see Ibid., pp. 231-233.

144 See supra footnote 139.

145 索赔的结构相当复杂。确定了六大类索赔（A、B、C、D、E and F）。F 类涉及其他国家（例如科威特、沙特阿拉伯、伊朗等）和国际组织提出的索赔，它进一步细分为四个子类别。第四个子类别的索赔涵盖了针对环境损害和自然资源枯竭的索赔。为审理 F4 索赔而设立的小组分五批处理这些索赔。到 2005 年，所有索赔（包括 F 类索赔）都已处理。

146 该索赔主张是由科威特石油公司根据 E 类（公司索赔）提出的。但是，它生动地说明了赔偿委员会小组针对伊拉克赔偿责任的前提所采取的一贯立场。See *Report and Recommendation made by the Panel of Commissioners Appointed to Review the Well Blowout Control Claim（WBC Claim）*, S/AC. 26/1996/5/Annex, 18 December 1996.

安全理事会已经根据《联合国宪章》第 7 章决定，对伊拉克非法入侵和占领科威特所造成的直接损失、损害或伤害，应按照国际法向外国政府、国民和企业提供赔偿，为了恢复国际和平与安全，伊拉克的赔偿责任问题已由安全理事会解决，并构成委员会所能运用的法律的一部分。[147]

因此，赔偿委员会专家组无法——也没有——评估伊拉克在某些情况下造成的损害是否过大，或与其追求的军事利益是否相称，即使通常作为特别法来适用的战时法规则有可能允许这些损害。[148] 安全理事会和赔偿委员会采取的做法受到法学专家的强烈批评，他们认为那是胜利者的司法。[149] 最终，在因环境破坏和资源耗竭而索赔的 850 亿美元中，赔偿委员会裁定赔偿 53 亿美元。[150]

就目前的目的而言，赔偿委员会这一案件说明了诉诸战争规则与环境保护之间的联系，但是，它也强调了违反诉诸战争规则和违反战时法的不同的现实含义，否则这两种违反就只是一种纯理论上的区别。

第三节　国际法上的环境安全

一　避免因环境引发冲突

环境保护与冲突之间的关系是双向的。在前几节中，我们讨论了国际法在多大程度上保护环境免受武装冲突的影响。本节采取相反的做法，研

---

[147] Ibid., para. 68 (emphasis added).

[148] See the discussion in Section 11. 2. 1. 2. 3 in connection with the *Hostages Case* and, more generally, the difference between, on the one hand, the general principles of military necessity and proportionality and, on the other hand, Arts. 35 (3) and 55 (1) of the Additional Protocol I.

[149] See Mollard-Bannelier, supra footnote 13, pp. 417-419; C. Greenwood, "State Responsibility and Civil Liability for Environmental Damage caused by Military Operations", in Grunawalt, supra footnote 11, pp. 397-415, at p. 407.

[150] On the valuation methods used by the F4 panel, see O. Das, *Environmental Protection, Security and Armed Conflict: A Sustainable Development Perspective* (Cheltenham: Edward Elgar, 2013), pp. 200-205.

究如何"保护"和平免受环境的威胁(和避免冲突)。

绝不能低估这种联系的重要性。根据联合国环境规划署2009年的一份报告,自然资源的开采"激化了"至少18次暴力冲突,过去60年中,至少40%的国内冲突可能与自然资源"相关"。[151] 从这个角度看,环境和自然资源变量被认为:(1)助长了冲突的爆发(例如达尔富尔、塞拉利昂和利比里亚);(2)资助或维持了冲突(例如塞拉利昂和利比里亚、安哥拉、柬埔寨);(3)破坏了和平(如科特迪瓦)。[152]

环境—冲突关联的双向性质在政策工具中日益得到体现。[153] 一个例证是《里约宣言》第25条原则,根据这一原则,"和平、发展和环境保护是相互依存和不可分割的"。[154] 最近,联合国采取了一些举措,包括设立国际资源专家组、[155] 建立联合国—欧盟自然资源和预防冲突伙伴关系(UN-EU Partnership on Natural Resources and Conflict Prevention)[156] 以及在环境规划署内设立预警与评估司(Division of Early Warning and Assessment, DEWA)。[157]

然而,这方面的具体法律倡议迄今仍然难以实现。如本章前面所述,联合国安全理事会曾两次讨论气候变化的影响,但并未将任何环境引发的局势当作第39条中的"对和平的威胁"来处理。同样,国际法委员会"武装冲突中保护环境"问题特别报告员明确将环境引发的冲突问题排除在其工作范围之外。[158] 至于条约,虽然一些环境条约(例如《联合国防治

---

[151] See UNEP, *From Conflict to Peacebuilding: The Role of Natural Resources and the Environment* (Geneva: UNEP, 2009) ("UNEP Environmental Conflict Report"), p. 8.

[152] Ibid., pp. 8-14.

[153] For a concise overview, see Das, supra footnote 150, pp. 66-119.

[154] Rio Declaration on Environment and Development, 13 June 1992, UN Doc. A/CONF.151/26 (Rio Declaration).

[155] See www.unep.org/resourcepanel/ (last visited on 20 April 2014). The objective of this panel is to provide reliable policy-relevant information on the use and state of the world's natural resources.

[156] 该伙伴关系汇集了联合国环境署、联合国开发规划署、联合国人居署、联合国政治事务部、联合国经济和社会事务部、联合国建设和平支持办公室和欧盟。关键项目是制定一个"工具包和指南以便预防和管理土地和自然资源冲突"。See www.un.org/en/land-natural-resources-conflict/ (last visited on 20 April 2014).

[157] See www.unep.org/dewa/ (last visited on 20 April 2014). 预警与评估司(DEWA)制定与提供涉及环境威胁的政策类信息和能力建设。

[158] See 2014 Preliminary Report, supra footnote 134, para. 64.

荒漠化公约》[159]）有助于解决那些可能激化冲突的环境根源问题，但迄今为止，尚无一个条约框架来专门应对环境引发的冲突预防。如后文所述，对于诸如环境引起的移民等一些问题，国际法实际上只提供了有限的空间来安置那些近期就会变得日益迫切的问题。

二 环境引发的流离失所

（一）对问题的界定

在过去 20 年中，人们日益关切环境引发的移民，特别是气候变化（诸如飓风等突发事件或海平面上升或荒漠化等缓发事件）引发的移民。[160] 从法律角度来看，这个问题之所以极具挑战性，是因为这一现象的潜在规模（有些预测高达数百万人的迁徙[161]），也是因为现有国际文件的明显不足。也许更根本的是，甚至不清楚如何在法律上界定这一现象，因为环境引发的流离失所只是一个通用术语，包括各种更具体的人口流动类型（临时的或永久的；被迫的或自愿的；环境造成的或环境诱发的；国内的

---

[159] United Nations Convention to Combat Desertification in those Countries Experiencing Serious Drought and/or Desertification, Particularly in Africa, UN Doc. A/AC. 241/15/Rev. 7（1994），17 June 1994, 33 ILM 1328（UNCCD）. This example is referred to in Das, supra footnote 150, p. 112. On this treaty, see Chapter 6.

[160] Aside from some previous occasional uses, the term environmental refugee was introduced in a 1985 UNEP report: E. El-Hinnawi, *Environmental Refugees*（United Nations Environment Programme, 1985）. 然而，当前的辩论是最近才开始的，直到 2005 年前后，主要国际组织才充分认识到它的重要性。See, e. g., Council of Europe Parliamentary Assembly, Committee on Migration, Refugees and Population, *Environmentally Induced Migration and Displacement: A 21st Century Challenge*, COE Doc 11785（23 December 2008）; *Report of the Office of the United Nations High Commissioner for Human Rights on the Relationship between Climate Change and Human Rights*, UN Doc. A/HRC/10/61, 15 January 2009, paras. 55-60; *Climate Change and its Possible Security Implications: Report of the Secretary-General*, UN Doc. A/64/350, 11 September 2009, paras. 54-63; United Nations High Commissioner for Refugees, *Climate Change, Natural Disasters and Human Displacement: A UNHCR Perspective*（14 August 2009）（UNHCR Report）. For a concise overview of the literature, see J. Morrissey, "Rethinking the 'Debate on Environmental Refugees': from 'Maximilists and Minimalists' to 'Proponents and Critics'"（2012）19 *Journal of Political Ecology* 36.

[161] On the limitations of these estimates, see D. Kniveton, K. Schmidt-Verkerk and C. Smith, "Climate Change and Migration: Improving Methodologies to Estimate Flows"（2008）*IOM Migration Research Series* No. 33.

或国际的；等等）。[162]

联合国前秘书长国内流离失所者人权问题代表瓦尔特·卡林（Walter Kölin）对环境引发的流离失所这一概念所涵盖的五种场景做出了有益的描述。[163] 这些场景是根据"迁移的原因"来进行分类的：（1）突发灾害（如飓风、台风、旋风、洪水、泥石流）；（2）缓发的环境恶化（如海平面上升、地下水盐碱化、干旱、荒漠化）；（3）低洼小岛屿国家的缓发环境事件（导致其领土丧失）；（4）禁止人类居住区域的指定（因为它们存在风险，或因为这些区域被分配用于缓解或适应气候变化）；（5）资源紧张引发的动乱、暴力和武装冲突。[164]

这种分类是非常有意义的，因为针对不同迁徙成因的可适用的法律或相关的法律是不一样的。因此，这有助于我们理解国际法是如何应对像环境引发的流离失所这样多面性的客体。

（二）法律应对

关于在国际层面上对这一问题做出的法律回应，争论的焦点在于两条主线。第一个主线是，通过国际难民法来处理环境引发的流离失所在多大程度上是法律上可行的或明智的。如果答案是否定的，正如联合国难民署（United Nations High Commissioner for Refugees，UNHCR）本身和其他人所主张的，第二个争论的焦点在于什么才是最有希望的替代性保护框架。

关于第一个讨论，一个问题是 1951 年《难民公约》（*1951 Refugees*

---

[162] see J. Mc Adam, "Climate Change, Displacement and the Role of International Law and Policy", paper presented at International Dialogue on Migration 2011, Intersessional Workshop on Climate Change, Environmental Degradation and Migration, 29-30 March 2011, p. 1.

[163] "Displacement and Climate Change: Towards Defining Categories of Affected Persons", *Working paper submitted by the Representative of the UN Secretary-General on the Human Rights of Internally Displaced Persons* (25 August 2008). The initial typology (hydrometeorological disasters, areas designated as high-risk zones, environmental degradation and slow onset disasters, sinking islands, armed conflict and violence driven by resource depletion) was subsequently revised in W. Kälin and N. Schrepfer, *Protecting People Crossing Borders in the Context of Climate Change Normative Gaps and Possible Approaches*, UNHCR (PPLA/2012/01), February 2012. We follow the latter.

[164] Kälin and Schrepfer, supra footnote 163, pp. 13-17.

Convention)[165] 是否有可能被用来保护环境难民。在大多数情况下，它不能被用来保护环境难民，因为公约的前提条件是跨越国际边界（从而将本国境内移民的人排除在外，而这其中包括很大部分的环境难民），而且最重要的是，它似乎极难将引发流离失所的环境诱因定性为"迫害"，更难定性为"出于种族、宗教、国籍、某一社会群体的成员或政治见解的原因"进行迫害。[166] 虽然非洲和拉丁美洲有关难民法的区域法律文件[167]包含了广义的难民定义，可能涵盖了逃离自然灾害的人，[168] 但这种定义的扩展最能涵盖的活动也只是突发灾害造成的流动。一般来讲，一般政策的倾向是不愿意将环境引发的流离失所问题置于保护难民的框架之内，以避免模糊一条界线，而这条界线是做出了巨大努力才得以澄清的。联合国难民署在 2009 年关于这一问题的首次报告中表示"对环境难民或气候难民的术语和概念表示严重保留"，并表明立场：

> 这种术语的使用可能会破坏保护难民（这些难民的权利和义务已有明确的定义和理解）的国际法律制度。它似乎暗示气候变化、环境退化和移民与迫害（迫害是难民逃离原籍国和寻求国际保护的根本原因）之间存在一种关联并造成了困惑，这也是无益的。[169]

鉴于通过国际难民法解决这一问题所面临的挑战，国际社会的注意力已转向其他替代性法律框架，包括国际人道主义法、国际人权法（最值得注意的是所谓的"补充保护"）、调整国内流离失所者的法律和国际环

---

[165] Convention relating to the Status of Refugees, 28 July 1951, 189 UNTS 137 ("1951 Refugees Convention"), and Protocol Relating to the Status of Refugees, 31January1967, 606UNTS267 (removing the geographical and time limitations included in the text of the Convention).

[166] 1951 Refugees Convention, supra footnote 165, Art. 1A (2).

[167] Convention Governing the Specific Aspects of Refugee Problems in Africa, 10 September 1969, 1001 UNTS 45, and the Cartagena Declaration on Refugees, 22 November 1984, Annual Report of the Inter-American Commission on Human Rights, OAS Doc. OEA/Ser. L/V/II. 66/ doc. 10, rev. 1, pp. 190-193 (1984-1945).

[168] See W. Kälin, "Conceptualising Climate-Induced Displacement", in J. McAdam (ed.), *Climate Change and Displacement: Multidisciplinary Perspectives* (Oxford: Hart Publishing, 2010), pp. 81-103, at pp. 88-9.

[169] UNHCR Report, supra footnote 160, pp. 8-9.

境法。

在国际环境法的背景下,这个问题在气候谈判中受到了一些关注,特别是在 2010 年《坎昆协议》(2010 Cancun Agreements)之后,该协议建立了一个"坎昆适应框架"(Cancun Adaptation Framework),其中包括"气候变化引起的在国家、区域和国际各级的迁徙、移民和重新安置"。[170] 这一问题也在"损失和损害"[171] 的背景下得到解决,特别是在 2013 年第 19 次缔约方大会设立了"华沙国际损失和损害机制"之后,该机制负责涉及气候变化影响的宽泛任务。在巴黎举行的第 21 次缔约方大会上,在损失和损害主题下专门讨论了气候引发的流离失所问题。虽然《巴黎协定》第 8 条没有提到这个问题,但缔约方大会第 1/21 号决定第 49 段特别要求:

> 华沙国际机制执行委员会应根据其程序和职权范围设立一个特别工作组,以补充、借鉴公约下的现有机构和专家组 [包括适应委员会(Adaptation Committee)和最不发达国家专家组(the Least Developed Countries Expert Group),以及公约以外的有关组织和专家机构] 的工作,并酌情使其参与,提出综合方法的建议,以便避免、尽量减少和解决与气候变化的负面影响相关的流离失所问题。[172]

在此基础上设立了一个"流离失所问题特别工作组",虽然其工作才刚刚开始,但作为其工作范围的一部分,它的职权范围包括确认"法律、政策和体制的挑战、成功实践、经验教训"。[173] 因此,《联合国气候变化框

---

[170] "The Cancun Agreements: Outcome of the Work of the AdHoc Working Group on Long-term Cooperative Action under the Convention", Decision 1/CP. 16, 15 March 2011, Doc. FCCC/ CP/2010/ 7/Add. 1, paras. 13, 14 (f).

[171] On the development of this action area see E. L. Roberts and S. Huq, "Coming Full Circle: The History of Loss and Damage under the UNFCCC" (2015) 8, *International Journal of Global Warming* 141.

[172] See Adoption of he Paris Agreement, Decision 1/CP. 21, 12 December 2015, FCCC/CP/ 2015/ L. 9 ("Paris Decision"). The Paris Agreement is appended as an Annex (Paris Agreement).

[173] "Terms of Reference of the Task Force on Displacement", para. 6 (d), available at: www. unfccc . int (visited on 20 April 2017).

架公约》所采用的方法很可能在很大程度上依赖于那些源自国际法的方法。

从现实的视角来看,关于这一问题的最重要的法律文件是那些有关国内流离失所者的文件。一项有影响力的软法文件,即 1998 年《国内流离失所指导原则》(*1998 Guiding Principles on Internal Displacement*),对所涉人员提供了足够宽泛的定义,即:

> "被迫或不得不逃离或离开其家园或惯常居住地的人或群体,特别是为了避免自然或人为灾害,并尚未跨越国际公认的国家边界"。[174]

这些原则是人权和国际人道主义法[175]的补充,并强调各国有义务向被保护者提供帮助,使其免受流离失所,在涉及迁徙、返回或重新安置问题上为他们提供参与决策的权利,与家人团聚或再团聚的权利,或在该国其他地区寻求安全或离开该国的权利等。虽然指导原则是一项软法,但其内容的很大一部分反映了基本人权和人道主义法义务,并具有习惯法基础。此外,2009 年在乌干达坎帕拉缔结了一项重要条约,处理非洲国内流离失所者的问题。[176] 《坎帕拉公约》(*Kampala Convention*)基本上接受了 1998 年指导原则中使用的措辞,但它在享有免遭任意迁徙的权利[177]和可追责性[178]等领域作了进一步阐述。

基本人权条款与"补充保护"也有关联。[179] 这是基于人权的保护,针对的对象是那些无权根据 1951 年《难民公约》(*1951 Refugees Convention*)受到保护的人,但这些人因为面临严重风险(即可能遭受折磨或残忍的、

---

[174] "Guiding Principles on Internal Displacement", 11 February 1998, UN Doc. E/CN. 4/1998/53/ Add. 2 (1998), Annex, para. 2 (italics added).

[175] Ibid., Principle 2 (2).

[176] African Union Convention for the Protection and Assistance of Internally Displaced Persons in Africa, 23 October 2009, 49 ILM 86 (Kampala Convention).

[177] Ibid., Art. 4.

[178] 值得注意的是,公约第 12 (3) 条规定,"如果缔约国在发生自然灾害时拒绝保护和协助国内流离失所者,则缔约国应有责任向国内流离失所者提供损害赔偿"。

[179] See J. McAdam, *Complementary Protection in International Refugee Law* (Oxford University Press, 2007).

不人道的、侮辱性的对待）而无法返回本国。然而，针对何种风险能够证明补充保护的正当性，现有司法解释为环境威胁提供的适用空间非常有限。[180]

还有一个选择是制定一项新条约或修改现有条约。曾有人提议修改 1951 年《难民公约》以接纳环境难民，[181] 但他们受到许多人的质疑，包括难民署本身。[182] 一些评论员更进一步，提出了一个全新的方案。[183] 在这些努力中，应特别提到 2005 年的"利摩日呼吁"（Appel de Limoges）项目，[184] 在此之后制定了一份详细且定期更新的《环境引发的流离失所者国际地位公约草案》（Draft Convention on the International Status of Environmentally-Displaced Persons）。[185] 草案第 2 条第 2 款将"环境引发的流离失所者"定义为：

> 个人、家庭、族群和民族，他们面临突然或渐进的环境灾难，这种灾难无可避免地影响其生活条件，导致他们一开始就或在整个过程中被迫流离失所。

草案对面临流离失所威胁的人（其权利在第 3 章中述及）和环境引发的流离失所者（他们的权利在第 4 章和第 5 章中作了界定）作了区分，包括承认其地位的权利。尽管针对这一主题想要制定修正案或新的法律文件，必须克服相当大的政治障碍，但"利摩日呼吁"项目提供了一个有用的轮廓来展现在文本的实际起草中如何解决论者提出的诸多难题。

---

[180] For a detailed discussion of the different legal bases that could be used, see J. McAdam, *Climate Change Displacement and International Law: Complementary Protection Standards*, UNHCR (PPLA/2011/03), May 2011, pp. 15-36.

[181] see the proposals of the Mal dives and Bangladesh, reported in E. Piguet et al. (eds.), *Migration and Climate Change* (Cambridge University Press, 2011), p. 103.

[182] UNHCR Report, supra footnote 160, p. 9.

[183] see, e.g., B. Docherty and T. Giannini, "Confronting a Rising Tide: A Proposal for a Convention on Climate Change Refugees" (2009) 33 *Harvard Environmental Law Review* 349.

[184] "Appel de Limoges sur les refugiés écologiques et environnementaux", 23 June 2005, available at: www.cidce.org (last visited on 20 April 2014)

[185] 该草案的第三版于 2013 年 5 月详细制定。See www.cidce.org (last visited on 20 April 2014).

三 后冲突场景下的环境安全

(一) 环境和平建设的兴起

过去几年来，人们日益注意到环境变量在引爆冲突上的作用以及在冲突后场景下的作用，更确切地说，在重燃冲突或帮助建立信任上的作用。[186]

这项工作的重点在于和平建设进程中的经济和政治方面，以及它们如何受到诸如自然资源开发、基本资源和服务（食物和水）提供以及大规模污染的宏观影响等环境变量的正面或负面影响。可以理解的是，环境变量被视为威胁和机会，该工作的大部分是对案例的研究与分析，并以此为基础来汲取政策教训。

在这方面，法律的作用还不太清楚。当然，法律和体制框架的重要性是不容置疑的，因为它们是制订约定的解决方案一个必要部分，方案包括和平协定的谈判[187]到争端的仲裁解决，[188]再到土地所有权制度的实施。[189]但是，国际法的作用，特别是国际环境义务在这方面的作用需要进一步阐明。[190]

---

186 For overviews of this work, see UNEP Environmental Conflict Report, supra footnote 151; Das, supra footnote 150; C. Bruch, D. Jensen, M. Nakayama, J. Unruh, R. Gruby and R. Wolfarth, "Post‐Conflict PeaceBuilding and Natural Resources" (2008) 19*Yearbook of International Environmental Law* 58.

187 See, e.g., section 3.7 of the Comprehensive Peace Agreement between the Government of Nepal and the Communist Party of Nepal (Maoist), which requires the implementation of a land reform programme, referred to in Bruch et al., supra footnote 186, pp. 63-64.

188 see e.g. the allocation of oil resources resulting from the arbitral award in the *Abyei* case: *In the Matter of an Arbitration before a Tribunal Constituted in Accordance with Article 5 of the Arbitration Agreement between the Government of Sudan and the Sudan People's Liberation Movement/Army on Delimiting Abyei Area*, Final Award, 22 July 2009, available at: www.pcacpa.org (last visited on 20 April 2017).

189 See J. Unruh and R. C. Williams, "Land: A Foundation for Peacebuilding", in J. Unruh and R. C. Williams (eds.), *Land and Post‐Conflict Peacebuilding* (London: Earthscan, 2013), pp. 1-20.

190 For a recent contribution to this question see D. Dam-de Jong, *International Law and Governance of Natural Resources in Conflict and Post-Conflict Situations* (Cambridge University Press, 2015).

（二）环境和平建设与环境责任

国际环境义务可能需要适当考虑国际环境和人权原则（例如损害预防、环境影响评估、公众参与、健康权、享有自然资源和整体上令人满意的环境的权利、土著人民的权利），制定国内法律框架来管理高价值资源（如木材、钻石、黄金或石油）和其他类别资源（如土地和水），以防止出现类似于尼日尔三角洲[191]或世界其他多个区域的冲突，这些冲突是由于国家、采掘业和当地社区的利益相互冲突造成的。[192]

国际环境法还有助于将环境考量变成国际组织后冲突活动的主流，可以通过设立"基金"[193]或专门设立"分支机构"，[194]或者通过制定准则以减少组织活动对环境的影响。[195]这种影响也许不太合法但非常重要，因为它为组织提供了法律授权以便将环境考量纳入其工作范畴。自1999年以来，联合国环境规划署后冲突和灾害管理处（UNEP's Post-Conflict and Disaster Management Branch）在巴尔干、阿富汗、被占领巴勒斯坦领土、

---

[191] On the legal dimensions of this conflict from a human rights perspective, see *Social and Economic Rights Action Center (SERAC) and others v. Nigeria*, African Commission Application No. 155/96 (2001-2002) (Ogoni).

[192] For a map of environmental conflicts (including this form of tripartite conflicts) in the world see: www.ejolt.org (last visited on 20 July 2017).

[193] 1997年，世界银行设立了一个冲突后基金，为那些包含环境可持续性成分的方案提供资金。原型碳汇基金参与菲律宾棉兰老地区的恢复计划就是一个例子。See World Bank, *Post-Conflict Fund and Licus Trust Fund. Annual Report* (*fiscal year* 2006), p.5, available at: www.worldbank.org (last visited on 20 April 2017).

[194] 联合国环境规划署于1999年开始其专门方案，成立了位于日内瓦的冲突后和灾害管理处（Post-Conflict and Disaster Management Branch）。See www.unep.org/disastersandconflicts/ (last visited on 20 April 2017). 同样，国际自然保护联盟设立了一个武装冲突和环境专家组主要从事研究和宣传。See www.iucn.org/about/union/commissions/cel/cel_working/cel_wt_sg/cel_sg_armed/ (last visited on 20 April 2017).

[195] 2009年6月，联合国维持和平行动和外勤支持部在环境署的大力支持下，通过了一项"联合国外地特派团的环境政策"，旨在减少维持和平行动的环境痕迹。环境的考量也已被纳入全球外勤支持战略。Report of the Secretary-General, 26 January 2010, UN Doc. A/64/633. Similar steps had previously been taken by the UNHCR. seethe UNHCR's 2005 Environmental Guidelines, available at: www.unhcr.org/3b 03b2a04.html (last visited on 20 April 2017).

尼日利亚或刚果民主共和国等地区进行了几次后危机环境评估。[196] 前述前南斯拉夫问题国际法庭检察官设立的委员会的报告（关于北约轰炸）就例证了这种评估可能在国际诉讼中得以体现。[197]

更具体地说，对自然资源的国际管理或国际化管理可能为冲突各方之间建立信任提供有益的机会。文献中已有案例包括厄瓜多尔和秘鲁共同管理"和平公园"（即跨界生态保育区），并将其当作结束长期边界争端的和平建设努力的一部分，[198] 或以色列和约旦两国在1994年10月达成和平协议之后在水资源方面的合作等。[199]

总体而言，这些努力表明，尽管明确存在国际环境法可能仍然有限，但环境保护考量对国际层面的和平建设活动的影响正与日俱增。

部分参考文献

［1］Austin, J. E. and C. E. Bruch (eds.), *The Environmental Consequences of War: Legal, Economic and Scientific Perspectives* (Cambridge University Press, 2000).

［2］Bardonnet, D., *La Convention sur l'interdiction et l'élimination des armes chimiques* (Dordrecht: Martinus Nijhoff, 1995).

［3］Boelaert-Suominen, S. A. J., *International Environmental Law and Naval War: The Effect of Marine Safety and Pollution Conventions during International Armed Conflict* (Newport, RI: Naval War College, 2000).

［4］Boisson de Chazournes, L. and P. Sands (eds.), *International Law, the International Court of Justice and Nuclear Weapons* (Cambridge Uni-

---

[196] For a concise overview, see K. Concaand J. Wallace, "Environment and Peacebuilding in War Torn Societies: Lessons from the UN Environment Programme's Experience with Post Conflict Assessment", in D. Jensen and S. Lonergan (eds.), *Assessing and Restoring Natural Resources in Post-Conflict Peacebuilding* (London: Earthscan, 2012), pp. 63-84.

[197] See supra footnote 22.

[198] 1998年10月26日签署的《巴西利亚协定》第3条提到了一些双边合作协定，这些协定导致了毗邻自然保护区的建立。The treaty is available at: www.afese.com/img/revistas/revista44/tratadopaz.pdf (visited on 20 April 2017).

[199] Environmental co-operation is specifically addressed in Annex IV (Environment) of the Treaty of Peace between the State of Israel and the Hashemite Kingdom of Jordan, 26 October 1994, referred to in Bruch et al., supra n. 181, pp. 65-66.

versity Press, 1999).

［5］Bothe, M., "Criminal Responsibility for Environmental Damage in Times of Armed Conflict", in R. J. Grunawalt, J. E. King and R. S. McClain (eds.), *Protection of the Environment during Armed Conflict* (Newport, RI: Naval War College, 1996), pp. 473−478.

［6］Bothe, M., C. Bruch, J. Diamond and D. Jensen, "International Law Protecting the Environment during Armed Conflict: Gaps and Opportunities" (2010) 92 *International Review of the Red Cross* 569.

［7］Bruch, C., D. Jensen, M. Nakayama, J. Unruh, R. Gruby and R. Wolfarth, "Post−Conflict Peace Building and Natural Resources" (2008) 19 *Yearbook of International Environmental Law* 58.

［8］Chevrier, M. I., K. Chomiczewski, H. Garrigue, G. Granasztói, M. R. Dando and G. S. Pearson (eds.), *The Implementation of Legally Binding Measures to Strengthen the Biological and Toxin Weapons Convention* (Dordrecht: Kluwer, 2004).

［9］Clapham, A., P. Gaeta and M. Sassoli (eds.), *The 1949 Geneva Conventions. A Commentary* (Oxford University Press, 2015).

［10］Conca, K. and G. Dabelko (eds.), *Environmental Peacemaking* (Princeton, NJ: Woodrow Wilson Center Press, 2002).

［11］Council of Europe Parliamentary Assembly, Committee on Migration, Refugees and Population, *Environmentally Induced Migration and Displacement: A 21st Century Challenge*, COE Doc 11785 (23 December 2008).

［12］Cournil, C. and B. Mayer, *Les migrations environnementales. Enjeux et gouvernance* (Paris: Presses de Sciences Po, 2014).

［13］Dam−de Jong, D., *International Law and Governance of Natural Resources in Conflict and Post−Conflict Situations* (Cambridge University Press, 2015).

［14］Das, O., *Environmental Protection, Security and Armed Conflict: A Sustainable Development Perspective* (Cheltenham: Edward Elgar, 2013).

［15］Freeland, S., *Addressing the Intentional Destruction of the Environment during Warfare under the Rome Statute of the International Criminal Court* (Antwerp: Intersentia, 2015).

[16] Gray, C., "Climate Change and the Law on the Use of Force", in R. Rayfuse and S. V. Scott (eds.), *International Law in the Era of Climate Change* (Cheltenham: Edward Elgar, 2011), pp. 219-240.

[17] Greenwood, C., "State Responsibility and Civil Liability for Environmental Damage Caused by Military Operations", in R. J. Grunawalt, J. E. King and R. S. McClain (eds.), *Protection of the Environment during Armed Conflict* (Newport, RI: Naval War College, 1996), pp. 397-415.

[18] Grunawalt, R. J., J. E. King and R. S. McClain (eds.), *Protection of the Environment during Armed Conflict* (Newport, RI: Naval War College, 1996).

[19] Henckaerts, J. -M. and L. Doswald-Beck, *Customary International Humanitarian Law* (Cambridge University Press, 2009).

[20] Hulme, K., "Armed Conflict, Wanton Ecological Devastation and Scorched Earth Policies: How the 1990-1991 Gulf Conflict Revealed the Inadequacies of the Current Laws to Ensure Effective Protection and Preservation of the Natural Environment" (1997) 2 *Journal of Armed Conflict Law* 55.

[21] Jacobsson, M., Preliminary Report on the Protection of the Environment in Relation to Armed Conflicts. Submitted by Marie G. Jacobsson, Special Rapporteur, 30 May 2014, UN Doc. A/CN. 4/674.

Second Report on the Protection of the Environment in Relation to Armed Conflicts. Submitted by Marie G. Jacobsson, Special Rapporteur, 28 May 2015, A/CN. 4/685.

Third Report on the Protection of the Environment in Relation to Armed Conflicts, Submitted by Marie G. Jacobsson, Special Rapporteur, 3 June 2016, A/CN. 4/700.

[22] Jensen, D. and S. Lonergan (eds.), *Assessing and Restoring Natural Resources in Post-Conflict Peacebuilding* (London: Earthscan, 2012).

[23] Joyner, D. H., *International Law and the Proliferation of Weapons of Mass Destruction* (Oxford University Press, 2009).

[24] Kadelbach, S., "Nuclear Weapons and Warfare", in *Max Planck Encyclopedia of Public International Law* (2009).

[25] Kälin, W., "Conceptualising Climate-Induced Displacement", in

J. McAdam (ed.), *Climate Change and Displacement: Multidisciplinary Perspectives* (Oxford: Hart Publishing, 2010), pp. 81–103.

[26] Kälin, W. and N. Schrepfer, *Protecting People Crossing Borders in the Context of Climate Change Normative Gaps and Possible Approaches*, UNHCR (PPLA/2012/01), February 2012.

[27] Kazazi, M., "Environmental Damage in the Practice of the UN Compensation Commission", in M. Bowman and A. Boyle (eds.), *Environmental Damage in International and Comparative Law* (Oxford University Press, 2002), pp. 111–131. "The UNCC Follow-up Programme for Environmental Awards", in *Law of the Sea, Environmental Law and Settlement of Disputes: Liber Amicorum Judge Thomas A. Mensah* (Leiden: Martinus Nijhoff, 2007), pp. 1109–1129.

[28] Koppe, E., *The Use of Nuclear Weapons and the Protection of the Environment during International Armed Conflict* (Oxford: Hart, 2008).

[29] Krutzsch, W., E. Myjer and R. Trapp (eds.), *The Chemical Weapons Convention. A Commentary* (Oxford University Press, 2014).

[30] Kunz, M. and J. E. Viñuales, "Environmental Approaches to Nuclear Weapons", in G. Nystuen, S. Casey-Maslen and A. Golden Bersagel (eds.), *Nuclear Weapons under International Law* (Cambridge University Press, 2014), pp. 269–291.

[31] Lujala, P. and S. A. Rustad (eds.), *High – Value Natural Resources and Post-Conflict Peacebuilding* (London: Earthscan, 2011).

[32] Marauhn, T., "Chemical Weapons and Warfare", in *Max Planck Encyclopedia of Public International Law* (2010).

[33] McAdam, J., *Complementary Protection in International Refugee Law* (Oxford University Press, 2007).

Climate Change Displacement and International Law: Complementary Protection Standards, UNHCR (PPLA/2011/03), May 2011.

[34] Mollard-Bannelier, K., *La Protection de L'environnement en Temps de Conflit Armé* (Paris: Pédone, 2001).

[35] Morrissey, J., "Rethinking the 'Debate on Environmental Refugees': from 'Maximilists and Minimalists' to 'Proponents and Critics'" (2012) 19 *Journal of Political Ecology* 36.

[36] Nystuen, G., S. Casey-Maslen and A. Golden Bersagel (eds.), *Nuclear Weapons under International Law* (Cambridge University Press, 2014).

[37] Penny, C., "Greening the Security Council: Climate Change as an Emerging 'Threat to International Peace and Security'" (2007) 7 *International Environmental Agreements: Politics, Law, Economics* 35.

[38] Piguet, E., A. Pécoud and P. de Guchteneire (eds.), *Migration and Climate Change* (Cambridge University Press, 2011).

[39] Roberts, E. L. and S. Huq, "Coming Full Circle: The History of Loss and Damage under the UNFCCC" (2015) 8, *International Journal of Global Warming* 141.

[40] Sandoz, Y., C. Swinarsky and B. Zimmermann, *Commentary on the Additional Protocols of 8 June 1977 to the Geneva Convention of 12 August 1949* (Leiden/Geneva: Martinus Nijhoff/International Committee of the Red Cross, 1987).

[41] Schmitt, M. N., "Green War: An Assessment of the Environmental Law of International Armed Conflict" (1997) 22 *Yale Journal of International Law* 1.

"War and the Environment: Fault Lines in the Prescriptive Landscape", in J. E. Austin and C. E. Bruch (eds.), *The Environmental Consequences of War: Legal, Economic and Scientific Perspectives* (Cambridge University Press, 2000), pp. 87–136.

[42] Shelton, D. and A. Kiss, "Martens Clause for Environmental Protection" (2000) 30 *Environmental Policy and Law* 285.

[43] Sindico, F., "Climate Change: A Security (Council) Issue?" (2007) 1 *Carbon and Climate Law Review* 26.

[44] Sur, S. (ed.), *Le droit international des armes nucléaires* (Paris: Pedone, 1998).

[45] Svarc, D., "Biological Weapons and Warfare", in *Max Planck Encyclopedia of Public International Law* (2011).

[46] Szurek, S., "De Rarotonga à Bangkok et Pelindaba: Note sur les traités constitutifs de nouvelles zones exemptes d'armes nucléaires" (1996)

42 *Annuaire Français de Droit International* 164.

[47] Tignino, M., L'eau et la guerre: éléments pour un régime juridique (Brussels: Bruylant, 2011).

[48] United Nations Environment Programme, *From Conflict to Peacebuilding: The Role of Natural Resources and the Environment* (Geneva: UNEP, 2009).

[49] *Protecting the Environment during Armed Conflict. An Inventory and Analysis of International Law* (Nairobi: UNEP, 2009).

[50] United Nations High Commissioner for Refugees, *Climate Change, Natural Disasters and Human Displacement: A UNHCR Perspective* (14 August 2009).

[51] United Nations Institute for Disarmament Research, *A Fissile Material Cut-off Treaty. Understanding the Critical Issues* (Geneva: UNIDIR, 2010).

[52] United Nations Secretary-General, *Climate Change and its Possible Security Implications: Report of the Secretary-General*, UN Doc. A/64/350, 11 September 2009.

[53] Unruh, J. and R. C. Williams (eds.), *Land and Post-Conflict Peacebuilding* (London: Earthscan, 2013).

[54] Vöneky, S., "A New Shield for the Environment: Peacetime Treaties as Legal Restraints of Wartime Damage" (2000) 9 *Review of Community and International Environmental Law* 20.

"Peacetime Environmental Law as a Basis of State Responsibility for Environmental Damage Caused by War", in J. E. Austin and C. E. Bruch (eds.), *The Environmental Consequences of War: Legal, Economic and Scientific Perspectives* (Cambridge University Press, 2000), pp. 190-225.

[55] Weinthal, E., J. Troel and M. Nakayama (eds.), *Water and Post-Conflict Peacebuilding* (London: Earthscan, 2014).

[56] Yee Woon Chin, L., "Nuclear Weapon-Free Zones-A Comparative Analysis of the Basic Undertakings in the SEANWFZ Treaty and their Geographical Scope of Application" (1998) 2 *Singapore Journal of International and Comparative Law* 275.

第十二章　环境保护与国际经济法

第一节　导论

在第十章中，我们分析了人权与环境保护之间的关系，这种关系表现为可持续发展的社会支柱和环境支柱之间的相互作用。本章采取同样的路径来分析环境保护与经济发展之间的联系。在国际层面调整投资、贸易和技术的规范日益变得重要，它们都体现了环境保护与经济发展之间的联系。

与人权和环境之间的关联不同，环境保护与国际经济法之间的联系在很大程度上被认为是相互冲突的关系。环境保护措施被视为变相的贸易保护主义，换言之，环保被当作不再真正注重发展需求的工业化国家的"奢侈品"。与之对应的是，对外国投资、跨界贸易和知识产权（IPRs）的国际保护受到了批评，因为它对国家的监管权力（包括环境保护）施加了限制。

在现实中，环境保护和国际经济法之间可能既有协同也有冲突，这取决于所涉具体问题及其产生的背景。本章讨论了这两个方面的问题，依次集中于投资、贸易和知识产权制度。这一顺序的依据是生产的周期。生产周期一般是从投资开发某些产品开始（本章第二节），然后涉及（除国内销售外）向国外市场出口半成品或者成品（本章第三节），对于技术密集型产品，它力求通过与贸易有关的知识产权制度（本章第四节）确保在国外获得某一确定水平的知识产权保护。当然，我们也可以采用不同的讨论顺序，因为相当一部分的生产过程要使用从国外进口的货物，包括从同一跨国集团内的其他公司进口货物（公司内贸易[1]），或者作为创新驱动器的知识产权要在研发的早期阶段进行干预（这需要投资）。[2] 这些都是重要的问题，本章所采用的投资、贸易和知识产权制度的讨论顺序都会将它们整合进来。

第二节 国际法中的外国投资和环境

一 概览

外国投资是"可持续发展"概念的（经济和社会）"发展"要件急需的，但它与这一概念的其他要件（即"环境保护"）存在着模糊的关系。一方面，外国投资可以利用财政和技术上的资源，通过各种途径（例如提高能源效率、减少温室气体排放、废物处理和其他"清洁"技术）来促进环境保护；另一方面，外国投资可能对东道国的环境产生不利影响（例如生物多样性的破坏、水资源的污染、危险废物的不当处置、在发达国家被禁止或限制的危险化学品的商业化）。

调整外国投资计划的国际法与调整环境保护的国际法之间的关系也变得模糊不清。[3] 国际投资法可通过对外国投资计划的保护［这种保护是依

1　For a concise overview see R. Lanz and S. Miroudot, "Intra－Firm Trade: Patterns, Determinants and Policy Implications" (2011) *OECD Trade Policy Papers*, No. 114, OECD Publishing, available at: last dx. doi. org/10. 1787/5kg9p39lrwnn-en (visited on 20 April 2017).

2　For an early statement of the link IPRs-innovation, see E. Penrose, *The Economics of the International Patent System* (Baltimore, MD: Johns Hopkins Press, 1951). For a contemporary statement, see World Intellectual Property Organisation, *The Changing Face of Innovation* (Geneva: WIPO, 2011). 然而，最近的一些研究表明，这种联系可能不像最初想象的那么牢固。See C. Correa, "Innovation and Technology Transfer of Environmentally Sound Technologies: The Need to Engage in a Substantive Debate" (2013) 22 *Review of European, Comparative and International Environmental Law* 54, 55-57.

3　This section is based on J. E. Viñuales, *Foreign Investment and the Environment in International Law* (Cambridge University Press, 2012); J. E. Viñuales, "Foreign Investment and the Environment in International Law: Current Trends", in K. Miles (ed.), *Research Handbook on Environment and Investment Law* (Cheltenham: Edward Elgar, forthcoming 2018), Chapter 2; P.－M. Dupuy and J. E. Viñuales (eds.), *Harnessing Foreign Investment to Promote Environmental Protection: Incentives and Safeguards* (Cambridge University Press, 2013).

据国际投资协定（International Investment Agreements，IIAs）来开展的]来促进环境目标的实现。除了外国投资者与东道国建立的合同关系外，两种主要类型的条约也被用于促进和保护外国投资。这两种条约即是"双边投资条约"（Bilateral Investment Treaties，BITs）和双边或多边自由贸易协定（Free Trade Agreements，FTAs）当中的有关投资的章节。在这两种条约中，基本的要件从根本上来看是相似的：（1）界定受保护的投资和投资者的条款；（2）必须给予投资者何种待遇的条款（例如关于征收、公平待遇和不歧视的规定）；（3）允许投资者向特设仲裁庭对东道国提出索赔的仲裁条款规定。[4] 虽然环境保护不是此类法律文件的明确目标，但是减少海外投资的风险有利于促进可持续发展，因为投资往往伴随着资本和技术转移。然而，东道国根据国际投资协定所承担的义务，至少在某种程度上，有时可能会与其所担负的国际环境义务发生冲突。一般来讲，投资保护可能与纯国内的环境措施相冲突，越来越多的投资争端便证明了这一点。[5]

在以下各节中，我们将分析环境和投资保护的协同和冲突这两个方面。协同效应（本章第二节第二部分）是通过一些国际政策工具来实现的，这些政策工具能够将外国投资引向提升环境的项目，通常而言，协同效应是通过旨在实现这两个监管领域的更广泛和谐的政策进程来实现的。关于冲突方面（本章第二节第三部分），我们特别关注投资仲裁庭的实践和投资条约制定的趋势。

二 协同

（一）工具

在第九章中，我们讨论了一些政策工具，包括基金和所谓的市场机制，它们被用来促进国际环境法的遵守。本节从一个特别的视角来审视其中一些工具即私营部门作为外国投资者代理人可以在其中扮演的角色。讨论仅限于三个例证，它们阐释了不同类型的工具：环境基金、政府和社会

---

[4] For a concise introduction to international investment law, see R. Dolzer and C. Schreuer, *Principles of International Investment Law* (Oxford University Press, 2013). For an analysis of the most important foundational issues in this field, see Z. Douglas, J. Pauwelyn and J. E. Viñuales (eds.), *The Foundations of International Investment Law* (Oxford University Press, 2014).

[5] See infra section 12.2.3.2.

资本合作模式以及市场机制。

关于第一种工具,迄今为止最重要的例证便是第九章讨论的全球环境基金。从一开始,该基金就意识到了让私营部门参与其活动的重要性。全球环境基金秘书处于 1995 年 10 月编写的一份题为《让私营部门参与其中》(Engaging the Private Sector)的资料文件指出,"全球环境基金面临的挑战是找到有效的模式以便影响('施加影响')……私人……投资以有利于全球环境的方式流动"。[6] 多年来,全球环境基金已经发展了一项"与私营部门接触的战略",这个战略体现在若干文件中。这一战略包括一套"私营部门参与原则"[7] 和"加强"该倡议战略的其他行动。[8] 在这些文件中被全球环境基金采取的参与方式包含不同种类,包括对全球环境基金项目的"间接"参与(即在接受全球环境基金项目的国家为环保公司创造市场条件)或"直接"参与(即向私营公司提供资金以支付项目的增量费用),私营部门对全球环境基金杠杆项目的"共同出资"(全球环境基金的作用是降低私营部门参与的风险),或者为私营部门参与全球环境基金资助的政府项目的公共采购提供便利。2006 年在全球环境基金资源分配框架被确定之后,"直接"参与变得更加困难,因为私营部门的需求在国家调配中并不总会得到充分考虑。[9] 目前私营部门参与的趋势侧重于第一种(间接)和第三种(共同出资)类型的参与。特别是实施机构正在被鼓励去寻找某些能够获得资金和吸引其他出资人共同出资的政府和社会资本合作项目(PPPs)。[10] 如第九章所述,全球环境基金在这方面的做法也被其他基金效仿,[11] 包括绿色气候基金的私营部门基金。

自 2002 年在约翰内斯堡举行的可持续发展世界峰会召开以来,第二

---

   6   GEF, "Engaging the Private Sector", 5 October 1995, GEF/C. 6/Inf. 4, para. 7(Engaging the Private Sector).

   7   GEF, "Principles for Engaging the Private Sector", 16 April 2004, GEF/C. 23/11(GEF Principles).

   8   GEF, "Revised Strategy for Enhancing Engagement with the Private Sector", 7 October 2011, GEF/C. 41/09(GEF Revised Strategy), Annex 1.

   9   Ibid., para. 35

   10   Ibid., para. 32.

   11   See Resolution 70/1, "Transforming our World: The 2030 Agenda for Sustainable Development", 21 October 2015, UN Doc. A/RES/70/1("2030 Agenda"), Declaration, para. 43.

种工具，即 PPPs 作为环境保护的工具日益受到重视。[12] PPPs 可用作项目融资的工具，例如，在全球环境基金的背景下。[13] 利用私营部门的资金资源是 PPPs 的主要功能之一。PPPs 也可以作为现场联合实施项目的一个工具。可持续发展世界峰会的所谓"第二类成果"实际上包括了"由各方行动者联盟（包括私营部门）为了可持续发展的实施而做出的具体目标和目的的承诺"。[14] 多年来，联合国可持续发展委员会（现已不复存在）建立了数百个合作项目，主要集中在水、能源和教育领域，[15] 涵盖了全球、区域或次区域等地理范围。[16] 除了这些 PPPs 之外，一些环境条约的实体机构和一些私营公司还联合发起了一些倡议。[17] 例如，在《拉姆萨公约》[18] 秘书处与达能集团达成协议后在 2002 年设立了"达能—埃维昂水资源基金"，[19]

---

[12] Report of the World Summit on Sustainable Development, A/CONF. 199/20, Part I, item 2: Plan of Implementation of the World Summit on Sustainable Development (Plan of Implementation), paras. 7 (j), 9 (g), 20 (t), 25 (g), 43 (a) or 49. Calls for more private sector involvement in environmental protection can be traced back to at least the 1992 Agenda 21: Report of the United Nations Conference on Environment and Development, A/CONF. 151/ 26/Rev. 1 (Vol. 1), Resolution 1, Annex 2: Agenda 21, 13 June 1992 (Agenda 21), Chapter 30. See also Report of the Secretary-General: Renewing the United Nations: A Programme for Reform, 14 July 1997, UN Doc. A/51/1950, paras. 59-60; Report of the Secretary-General: Enhanced Cooperation between the UN and All Relevant Partners, in particular the Private Sector, 10 August 2005, UN Doc. A/60/214; United Nations Millennium Declaration, UNGA Res 55/2, 8 September 2000, para. 20.

[13] GEF Revised Strategy, supra footnote 8, paras. 28-34, 39.

[14] C. Streck, "The World Summit on Sustainable Development: Partnerships as New Tools in Environmental Governance" (2002) 13 *Yearbook of International Environmental Law* 63, 67.

[15] See webapps01. un. org/dsd/partnerships/public/partnerships/stats/primary_ theme. jpg (last visited on 20 April 2017).

[16] See webapps01. un. org/dsd/partnerships/public/partnerships/stats/geographic_ scope. jpg (last visited on 20 April 2017).

[17] E. Morgera, *Corporate Accountability in International Environmental Law* (Oxford University Press, 2009), pp. 251-254.

[18] Convention on Wetlands of International Importance especially as Waterfowl Habitat, 2 February 1971, 996 UNTS 245 (Ramsar Convention).

[19] Action Programme for Water Resource and Water Quality Protection in Wetlands of International Importance, Memorandum of Understanding, 27 January 1998. The initial instrument has been subsequently completed and amended by a number of other instruments. see www. ramsar. org (last visited on 20 April 2017).

《迁徙物种公约》(*Convention on Migratory Species*, CMS)[20] 与德国汉莎航空公司合作在某些汉莎航空航班宣传公约相关的活动。[21] 此外,《巴塞尔公约》和一些私营公司针对"废旧手机环境无害化处理"而联合开展的"移动电话伙伴关系倡议"(Mobile Phone Partnership Initiative),[22] 即使该公约对废物的定义并未涵盖废旧手机。[23]

  第三种机制,即市场机制,已经在有关《京都议定书》和《巴黎协定》的部分(见第五章)进行了探讨。然而,在这里概括外国投资与环境保护之间的"协同关系"似乎是有益的。与环境基金不同,市场机制既不向国家也不向私营企业提供资金或担保。市场机制的目的是鼓励国家或私营企业开展某些类型的有利于环境的交易。它们通过创造环境的市场来做到这一点。从外国投资者的角度来看,这种激励类型可被认为是全球环境基金赋予"间接参与"这一术语的变体。就《京都议定书》的灵活机制而言,市场的产生是由于某些国家(附件二)的特定温室气体(附件一)的排放有一个总量控制。因此,排放一吨二氧化碳当量的权利对于受总量控制的国家而言是具有价值的,因为这些"排放权"可用于遵守国际义务。在缺乏国际性的总量控制时,这一义务的产生来自各国建立一个碳交易市场的自身决定,如《巴黎协定》的情形。在这两种情形下,该市场体系都由国内或区域立法(例如欧洲《ETS 指令》[24])实施,将排放权市场应用于私营部门当中。就某一私营企业而言,排放权之所以有价值,不仅因为它可以用来遵守法律义务,还可用于其他目的,如品牌宣传、套期保值或只是避免投资与生产方式的重组。同样,某些"生态系统服务"(例如树木造成的碳捕获和储存、水的净化和补充、湿地的防洪

---

  20 Convention on the Conservation of Migratory Species of Wild Animals, 23 June 1979, 1651 UNTS 356 (CMS Convention).

  21 Morgera, supra footnote 17, p. 253.

  22 Sustainable Partnership for the Environmentally Sound Management of End-of-life Mobile Telephones", Decision VI/31, 10 February 2003, UNEP/CHW. 6/40.

  23 On this basis, the Basel Convention Secretariat has developed a "Guidance Document on the Environmentally Sound Management of Used and End-of-life Mobile Phones", 14 July 2011, UNEP/CHW. 10/INF/27.

  24 Directive 2003/87/EC of the European Parliament and of the Council of 13 October 2003 establishing a scheme for greenhouse gas emission allowance trading within the Community and amending Council Directive 96/61/E, OJ 2003 L 0087, 25 June 2009 (consolidated version) (ETS Directive).

功能、热带森林提供的生物多样性保护）可以通过允许它们市场化运营的方式来进行构建。基于这些服务的各自结构，相应的市场也将有不同的特点。一些国家，如巴西和厄瓜多尔，已经设立了基金，公共和私人投资者可以投资于保护热带森林。[25]

（二）政策过程

除了上述具体的工具之外，多个国际组织［包括经济合作与发展组织和联合国贸易和发展委员会（UN Commission on Trade and Development, UNCTAD）］还探讨了更广泛的协同，在《2030年可持续发展议程》的背景下也存在同样的情况。

自20世纪90年代以来，经济合作与发展组织一直在研究外国投资与环境保护在经济方面的联系。[26] 2011年，它将注意力转向这一联系的法律方面，尤其关注国际投资协定和投资仲裁。除了在这方面发表几项有益的研究成果外，该组织各方缔约国的代表们还通过了《经合组织关于利用投资自由促进绿色增长的声明》（*OECD Statement on Harnessing Freedom of Investment for Green Growth*），提出了七个"发现"，并强调以下问题的重要性：

（1）国际环境法和国际投资法的相互支持；（2）监控投资条约有关环境的实践；（3）确保诚信和能力，并提高投资者与国家之间争端解决的透明度；（4）通过事先评估拟议的环境措施并通过有效的环境法和管理实践，增强对国际投资法的遵守；（5）警惕绿色保护主义；（6）鼓励贸易为绿色经济的发展做出贡献；（7）通过外国直接投资（FDI）刺激绿色增长。[27]

这些发现是2011年4月举行的圆桌会议期间代表们经过大量筹备工

---

[25] See www.amazonfund.org and www.sosyasuni.org（last visited on 20 April 2017）.

[26] For a useful survey, see OECD, *FDI and the Environment – An Overview of the Literature*（Paris：OECD, 1997）.

[27] OECD, *Harnessing Freedom of Investment for Green Growth*, Freedom of Investment Roundtable, 14 April 2011, available at：www.oecd.org（last visited on 20 April 2017）.

作、协商和讨论后的结果。它们被视为是经合组织成员国[28]的代表们所支持的共同政策声明,并为我们展示了他们是如何看待这些部门法在将来的互动的。最近,鉴于所谓的"大区域"协定以及这些协定对投资者和国家间争端解决的参考价值还存在争议,经合组织更详细地研究了在贸易和投资协定的文本中为环保提供法定表述的各种形式。后文本章第二节第三部分第三点讨论了这些努力。

联合国贸易和发展委员会(UNCTAD)也做出了类似的努力,由于其职责范围,该委员会更能反映发展中国家的利益。联合国贸易和发展委员会在其《2012年世界投资报告》(*2012 World Investment Report*)中提出了一份《可持续发展投资政策框架》(*Investment Policy Framework for Sustainable Development*,IPFSD),呼吁新一代投资政策(包括投资条约)。[29]《可持续发展投资政策框架》比经合组织的声明更为雄心勃勃,它包括:(1)一套"投资决策的核心原则";(2)一套"国家投资政策准则";(3)投资条约制定中的"政策选项"。投资决策的核心原则被视为"可持续发展投资政策框架"的一个有机组成部分而不是单独的文件。共计有11项核心原则,可分为四类:投资决策的总体目标(原则1);一般决策过程(原则2—4);具体的投资决策过程(原则5—10)和国际合作(原则11)。[30]这些原则中一个值得注意的地方是注重对投资的"促进",以促进"包容性增长和可持续发展",这一特点可能对解释投资保护标准和仲裁条款有特殊的意义。[31] 原则2明确体现了协同增效关系,它规定"所有影响到投

---

28 澳大利亚、奥地利、比利时、加拿大、智利、捷克共和国、丹麦、爱沙尼亚、芬兰、法国、德国、希腊、匈牙利、冰岛、爱尔兰、以色列、意大利、日本、韩国、卢森堡、墨西哥、摩洛哥、荷兰、新西兰、挪威、秘鲁、波兰、葡萄牙、斯洛伐克共和国、斯洛文尼亚、西班牙、瑞典、瑞士、罗马尼亚、土耳其、英国和美国。

29 UNCTAD, *World Investment Report. Towards a New Generation of Investment Policies* (2012), Chapter IV (Investment Policy Framework for Sustainable Development). See also the report specifically on the IPFSD available at: unctad.org/en/Publications Library/diaepcb2012d5_ en.pdf ("IPFSD Report").

30 Ibid. pp. 10-14.

31 围绕外国投资对东道国发展的贡献的广泛讨论通常会涉及仲裁庭[这些仲裁庭是在国际投资争端解决中心(ICSID)下开展工作]的管辖权要求。For an overview of the debate, see J. E. Viñuales, "International Investment Proceedings: Converging Principles?", 2016 Gaetano Morelli Lectures (Rome: La Sapienza, 2017).

资的政策都应在国家和国际两个层面上保持连贯和一致"。[32] 这些原则侧重于准入后待遇，与经合组织的声明不同，虽然该声明也是试图通过提供或促进国外市场来解放投资。谈及《可持续发展投资政策框架》中的"准则"和"政策选项"，它们当然与核心原则是保持连贯和一致的。但是，值得注意的是"就有利于可持续发展的国际投资协定展开谈判"[33] 的呼吁，和关于共同投资条约条款以及如何调整这些条款以便为可持续发展提供适当空间的详细讨论。

对后者的强调源于这样一种认识，即环境规制的变化被广泛认为将导致与现有国际投资协定（尤其是当前投资裁判机构对其语言的宽泛解释）的冲突。这种可能性正越来越多地被意识到，《2030 年可持续发展议程》对此提出了明确构想。该议程在若干方面提到了私营部门的投资。除了在目标 17.3（"从多种渠道为发展中国家动员额外的财政资源"）和目标 17.5（"为最不发达国家制定和实施投资促进体制"）中提及之外，涉及粮食安全、能源和国家间不平等的三项实质性目标都特别地提到了"投资"的促进。[34] 同时，也许是因为有关投资仲裁和规制寒冬的争论热火朝天，议程目标 17.15 特别强调，作为可持续发展目标 17 下的一个"系统性问题"，需要"尊重每个国家制定和执行消除贫困和可持续发展政策的政策空间和领导作用"。[35] 另外，在《2030 年可持续发展议程》的拓展（即议程涵盖的一个文件）中得到体现，这一文件就是 2015 年年初第三次发展筹资问题国际会议（International Conference on Financing for Development）通过的《亚的斯亚贝巴行动议程》（*Addis Ababa Action Agenda*）。[36]《2030 年可持续发展议程》包含了对《亚的斯亚贝巴行动议程》的明确支持，因此该议程被视为"《2030 年可持续发展议程》的一

---

[32] IPFSD Report, supra footnote 29, p. 11

[33] Ibid., p. 39.

[34] 2030 Agenda, supra footnote 11, SDGs, targets 2. a, 7. a, and 10. b.

[35] See also Ibid., 执行手段和《全球伙伴关系》第 63 段在确认必须"尊重每个国家的政策空间和领导力以执行消除贫困和可持续发展的政策"之后，增加了"同时应与相关国际规则和承诺保持一致"这一内容。

[36] Addis Ababa Action Agenda of the Third International Conference on Financing for Development (Addis Ababa Action Agenda), UNGA Resolution 69/313, 27 July 2015, UN Doc A/RES/69/313, Annex.

个组成部分"。[37] 在《亚的斯亚贝巴行动议程》有关私人投资的众多表述中，最重要的一个是专门讨论了"国内和国际私营企业和金融"的"行动领域"。第35段开启了这部分的内容：

> 私人商业活动、投资和创新是生产力、包容性经济增长和创造就业的主要驱动力。我们承认私营部门的多样性，从微型企业到合作社再到跨国集团。我们呼吁所有企业运用它们的创造力和创新来解决可持续发展的挑战。我们请它们作为伙伴参与发展进程，投资于对可持续发展至关重要的领域，并转向更可持续的消费和生产模式。我们欢迎自蒙特雷会议以来国内私营企业活动和国际投资的显著增长。私人国际资本流动，特别是直接投资，以及稳定的国际金融体系，是国家发展努力的重要补充。

该段还有另外两项补充，它们更直接地提到外国投资的法律层面问题：

> 我们承认直接投资，包括外国直接投资，能够对可持续发展作出重要贡献，特别是当项目符合国家和区域可持续发展战略时。我们将鼓励投资促进和其他相关机构重点做好项目储备。我们将优先安排最有潜力促进充分的生产性就业、所有人都能体面工作的、生产和消费模式可持续发展的、结构转型和可持续工业化的、生产多样性的或者农业的项目。在国际上，我们将通过财政和技术援助、能力建设以及原籍国和东道国机构之间更密切的合作来支持这些努力。我们将考虑使用保险、投资担保，包括通过多边投资担保机构，以及新的金融工具，来激励对发展中国家（特别是最不发达国家、内陆发展中国家、小岛屿发展中国家和处于冲突和冲突后中的国家）的直接投资。我们关注到，尽管许多最不发达国家的投资环境有所改善，但它们仍然在很大程度上被外国直接投资排除在外，而这些外国直接投资本可以帮助使其实现经济多样化。我们决心制定和实施针对最不发达国家的

---

[37] 2030 Agenda, supra footnote 11, Means of implementation and the Global Partnership para. 62.

投资促进体制。我们还将为项目储备和合同谈判提供财政和技术支持,为解决投资相关争议提供咨询支持,提供有关投资便利和风险保障的信息,以及应最不发达国家的要求提供担保,例如通过多边投资担保机构提供。[38]

这明确承认了外国投资与可持续发展(包括环境保护)之间可能存在的协同增效关系。这也许是迄今为止在可持续发展文件中对这种协同增效作用的最重要的承认。

三 冲突

(一)规范性冲突与合法性冲突

在过去几年里,包含环境要件的投资争端的数量急剧上升。1990年以前只有两件此类诉请被提出,但1990—2000年案件数量有所上升(11件),2001—2011年数量进一步增加(44件,有些在审理中),尤其是自2012年以来数量明显增加(2012—2015年年末有60件,许多仍在审理中)。[39]这些数字只是一个保守的估计,因为它们没有考虑到未公开的争端(相信是众多的)或向其他司法机关(如国内法院或人权法院)提交的诉求。这些争端中的焦点问题包括因环境原因(例如保护自然或文化场所)而征收投资者财产,推迟颁发/暂停/撤销经营许可证(例如废物处理设施、发电、某些化学物质的生产和商业化等),追究环境损害的责任(例如场地净化),采取卫生或健康措施,设计和管理上网电价政策(例如在参与可再生能源补贴计划时要求"当地购买")。至于案件所涉金额,从几百万美元到一些天文数字不等(例如,雪佛龙公司对厄瓜多尔共和国提起的诉讼所涉案件争议金额达180亿美元)。

在这一背景下,便产生了一个重要的法律问题,即国际环境法与这些投资争端的解决之间存在多大的关联度。尽管在这些案件中,被质疑的环境措施本质上是属于国内措施,但是,投资所在国依据国际环境法所承担的义务明确或隐含地引发了这些措施或者证明了其正当性。在实践中,投资裁判机构对纯粹的国内措施和国际法引发的措施是一并处理的。因此,

---

38 Addis Ababa Action Agenda, supra footnote 36, paras. 45-46.
39 These estimations are based on a set of 117 decisions compiled in Viñuales (2017), supra footnote 3.

国际法两种规范之间的冲突（"规范性冲突"）已经被合并成国内（环境）措施与国际（投资）规范之间的冲突（"合法性冲突"）。

界定问题的方式的不同是具有法律意义的，因为适用于解决潜在冲突的规则与适用于解决广义纠纷的规则在这两种场景下是不一样的。具体而言，按照国际法的一般规则（国际裁判机构遵循了这一规则），国际法优先于国内法，[40] 这样就把国内环境措施（即使是履行环境条约的措施）置于投资条约的从属地位。一般来讲，国内环境措施与环境条约之间明显的脱节，可能会损害投资裁判机构赋予此类措施的合法性。

因此，很难确定环境条约对外国投资纠纷的影响。一般来说，投资裁判机构在这方面可以采用三种不同的方法。

（二）投资裁判机构的实践[41]

"传统的方法"是将所有冲突视为合法性冲突。因此，东道国采取的环境措施被视为"可疑的"（变相的单方面保护主义），在所有的情况下都应当"服从于"国际（投资）法（作为前面提到的国际法优于国内法的结果）。这种观点可能反映了一些早期案例（例如"S. D. Myers 诉加拿大案"[42] "Metalclade 诉墨西哥案"[43] "CDSE 诉哥斯达黎加案"[44] "Tecmed 诉墨西哥案"[45]）的具体

40　See, e.g., *Southern Pacific Properties (Middle East) Limited (SPP) v. Arab Republic of Egypt*, ICSID Case No. ARB/84/3, Award (20 May 1992) (*SPP v. Egypt*), paras. 75-76; *Compañía del Desarrollo de Santa Elena SA v. Republic of Costa Rica*, ICSID Case No. ARB/96/1, Award (17 February 2000) (*CDSE v. Costa Rica*), paras. 64-65.

41　For a detailed analysis of the issues discussed in this section, see J. E. Viñuales, "The Environmental Regulation of Foreign Investment Schemes under International Law", in Dupuy and Viñuales, supra footnote 3, pp. 273-320.

42　*S. D. Myers Inc. v . Canada*, NAFTA Arbitration (UNCITRAL Rules), Partial Award (13 November 2000) (*S. D. Myers v. Canada*). 该案的证据得出的结论是：美国投资者所质疑的危险废物出口禁令实际上是用于偏袒加拿大籍竞争对手。

43　*Metalclad Corp. v. United Mexican States*, ICSID Case No. ARB (AF) /97/1, Award (25 August 2000) (*Metalclad v. Mexico*). 该争端涉及出于非真正的环境原因拒绝颁发建造垃圾填埋场的许可，为保护仙人掌而建立自然保护区的法令在争端后期才颁布。

44　*CDSE v. Costa Rica*, supra footnote 40. 正式征用投资者拥有的土地的法令未提及任何可能适用的环境条约。

45　*Técnicas Medioambientales Tecmed S. A. v. United Mexican States*, ICSID Case No. ARB (AF) /00/2, Award (29 May 2003) (*Tecmed v. Mexico*). 由于公众对该计划的反对声日益高涨，投资者更新其废物处理设施的运营许可证的要求被拒绝。

事实情况。这一观点有时候被用于评估真正的环境措施甚至是国际引发的措施，不幸的结果是，环境因素的考量在法律上仍然要服从于纯粹的经济因素考量。

另外，还有可能将冲突视为"规范性冲突"。根据这一观点，大多数国内环境措施将被视为国际条约引发的（与诸如投资规则等其他国际法规范是平等的关系），并反映了多边行动（从而挫败了单边保护主义的怀疑）。这一观点实际上是想对不同类型的冲突（"合法性"和"规范性"冲突）[46] 适用不同的冲突规则，从而消除一些裁判机构仍然存在的怀疑和不信任（尽管国际层面上环境意识正在形成），并将其当作分析环境规范的起点。从严格的法律视角来看这一方法更为精确，但它在实践中面临着巨大的挑战。首先，正如我们在第4—7章中所看到的，国际环境规范的表述往往相当宽泛，因此很难在国内环境措施和国际环境义务之间建立清晰的联系。欧盟法院（Court of Justice of the European Union，CJEU）的"航空案"和"Bonaire 案"提供了两个截然不同的例证，在航空案中《京都议定书》第2条被认定为要求采取行动以限制排放而并未要求采取任何具体措施；[47] 而在"Bonaire 案"中，荷兰法院判决认为，像《拉姆萨公约》第3条那样被宽泛表述的规范是可以直接适用的，因而荷兰当局拒绝授权是合法的。[48] 其次，在所有事件中，这种联系都必须得到为处理投资（而非环境）争端而专门设立的仲裁庭的承认。尽管针对此类裁

---

[46] 在"S. D. Myers 诉加拿大"一案中，仲裁庭考虑了加拿大的论点，即受到质疑的措施是根据《巴塞尔公约》制定的，该公约优先于《北美自由贸易协定》第104条冲突规范所产生的义务。由于美国尚未批准《巴塞尔公约》，该冲突规范在技术上并未得到应用。See *S. D. Myers v. Canada*，supra footnote 42，para. 150（Canadian argument）and 213-215（tribunal's rejection of the argument）.

[47] 该案涉及对欧盟《碳排放交易指令》（*ETS Directive*）（前注24）的拓展适用（扩大到航空领域）的质疑。法院认为，议定书允许当事各方以他们认为最适当的方式和节奏来履行目标，并补充说不能直接援引不够精确的第2条第2款。*Air Transport Association of America and others v. Secretary of State for Energy and Climate Change*，CJEU Case C-366/10（21 December 2011），paras. 76-77.

[48] *Netherlands Crown Decision (in Dutch) in the case lodged by the Competent Authority for the Island of Bonaire on the annulment of two of its decisions on the Lac wetland by the Governor of the Netherlands Antilles*，11 September 2007，Staatsblad 2007，347（*Bonaire*）. 具体而言，荷兰国务委员会裁定第3条在国内可直接施行，并据此维持一项行政决定，即撤销在拉姆萨保护区周围的缓冲区内建造度假胜地的行政许可。See M. Bowman，P. Davies and C. Redgwell，*Lyster's International Wildlife Law*（Cambridge University Press，2nd edn，2010），p. 419.

判机构是否会偏袒投资者利益还存在很大争议，但似乎很清楚的是，除了极少数例外，⁴⁹ 它们尚未准备好将国际环境法与投资条约同等看待。用一个比喻来说，国际环境法充其量只能是国际投资法领域的"移民"，这与本章后面讨论的世贸组织争端解决方案大致相同。在这两种情况下，国际环境法的存在空间只是投资法或贸易法专门给它分配的。

然而，随着时间的推移，在不适当的传统观点和不现实的激进观点之间产生了一种替代方法。事实上，通过对一些法律概念的解释，如警察权力原则、"类似情形"的定义、投资者所提要求的合理性程度或者危急情况和紧急避险条款的适用等，环境考量在外国投资纠纷中找到了越来越大的空间。因此，在"Chemtura 诉加拿大案"中，法庭认为：禁止一种对环境有害的农药的生产和商业化措施是加拿大警察权力的有效行使，因此驳回了投资者关于赔偿的诉求。⁵⁰ 在"Parkerings 诉立陶宛案"中，裁判机构驳回了关于违反最惠国待遇条款（一项非歧视标准）的申诉，理由是原告的项目对联合国教科文组织保护下的一个遗址产生了不利影响，因此，它不属于其他投资者的某个项目（指在本案中被确定为参照物的其他项目）的"类似情形"。⁵¹ 在"Plama 诉保加利亚案"中，裁判机构认为，国内环境法将净化场地的财政负担修改交给投资者，并不违反所适用的投资协议，因为投资者如果做到了该有的谨慎注意就应该会知道，在它进行投资时，保加利亚议会正在讨论这样的规制变化。⁵² 最后，在一些针对阿根廷的案件中，特别是在 LG&E 提出的案件中，裁判机构认为，阿根

49　在"SPP 诉埃及"一案中，由国际法院前院长主持的仲裁庭得出结论认为，埃及违反了其投资义务（根据国内法和一项合同），但补充指出，在金字塔遗址列入《世界遗产名录》后的这段时期内可不承担任何赔偿。因为从那时起，根据《世界遗产公约》这项国际法，该投资是非法的。See *SPP v. Egypt*, supra footnote 40, para. 191.

50　*Chemtura Corporation (formerly Crompton Corporation) v. Government of Canada*, UNCITRAL, Award (2 August 2010) (*"Chemtura v. Canada"*), para. 266. The tribunal referred to its analysis of the claim under Art. 1105, which explained that the measure adopted by Canada was consistent with its obligations under international environmental law (the POP Protocol to the LRTAP Convention and the POP Convention, discussed in Chapters 5 and 7).

51　*Parkerings-Compagniet AS v. Republic of Lithuania*, ICSID Case No. ARB/05/8, Award (11 September 2007) (*Parkerings v. Lithuania*), para. 392.

52　*Plama Consortium Ltd v. Republic of Bulgaria*, ICSID Case No. ARB/03/24, Award (27 August 2008), paras. 219-221.

廷违反投资条约是合法的，因为需要确保公众能够在经济和社会危机中负担得起某些基本公共服务。[53] 表12-1概括了以上讨论的三种方法。

表 12-1　　处理投资与环境关联的判例法方法

	环境措施是否被视为：			
	隐秘的贸易保护主义	真正的规制	本质上属于国内措施	国际因素引发
传统的方法	√		√	
渐进的方法		√		√
升级的方法		√	√	

"升级的"方法已经得到最近发展动态的证实。重要的是，投资裁判机构的推理已经以日益明确和公开的形式将环境因素纳入其中，即使相关环境措施违反了投资法。将最近的一些进展联系起来就可以划出一条判例的路线，这些进展包括"Unglaube诉哥斯达黎加案"[54]"克莱顿案和比尔康诉加拿大案"[55]"黄金储备诉委内瑞拉案"[56]"佩伦科诉厄瓜多尔案"[57]

---

[53] *LG&E v. Argentina*，ICSID Case No. ARB/02/1，Decision on Liability（13 October 2006）（*LG&E v. Argentina*），paras. 234-237，245. 在另外两起案件中，仲裁庭认为，水和卫生服务的提供是联合国国际法委员会于2001年通过的《国家对国际不法行为的责任条款草案》中必须规则条款下的国家的一个"核心利益"。See *Suez, Sociedad General de Aguas de Barcelona S. A. and Inter-Aguas Servicios Integrales del Agua SA v. The Argentine Republic*，ICSID Case No. ARB/03/17，Decision on Liability（30 July 2010），para. 238；*Suez, Sociedad General de Aguas de Barcelona, SA and Vivendi Universal, SA v. The Argentine Republic*，ICSID Case No. ARB/03/19，Decision on Liability（30 July 2010），para. 260.

[54] *Marion Unglaube v. Republic of Costa Rica*，ICSID Case No. ARB/08/1 and *Reinhard Unglaube v. Republic of Costa Rica*，ICSID Case No. ARB/09/20，Award（16 May 2012）（*Unglaube v. Costa Rica*）.

[55] *William Ralph Clayton, William Richard Clayton, Douglas Clayton, Daniel Clayton, and Bilcon of Delaware, Inc. v. Government of Canada*，NAFTA（UNCITRAL），Award（17 March 2015）（*Clayton and Bilcon v. Canada*）.

[56] *Gold Reserve Inc. v. Bolivarian Republic of Venezuela*，ICSID Case No. ARB（AF）/09/1，Award（22 September 2014）.

[57] *Perenco Ecuador Ltd v. The Republic of Ecuador and Empresa Estatal Petróleos del Ecuador*（*Petroecuador*），ICSID Case No. ARB/08/6，Interim Decision on the Environmental Counterclaim（11 August 2015）.

和"Al Tamimi 诉阿曼案"[58] 的裁决。这一路线突出表明，环境推理已经日益成为投资类判例理论的主流；更重要的是，它标志着投资案例中举证和裁决的思维模式转变。这种变化的"轨迹"有三种主要形式。第一，在讨论外国投资法中共同法律概念的运用时，理所当然地将环境考量作为一个明显的参照点。第二，是在裁决的附带意见中突出强调环境考量的重要性。第三，使用一些专门为应对环境争端的特殊性而制定的技术，同样，在没有太多特别理由的情况下，强调采用此类技术的规范性。

对两个关联案件作出的第一份裁决似乎并没有对"CDSE 诉哥斯达黎加案"中的传统做法进行补充。从表面上看，"Unglaube 诉哥斯达黎加案"的事实构成确实与"CDSE 诉哥斯达黎加案"的情况相当类似。这两起案件都涉及环境保护（建立自然保护区）与旅游地产开发之间的冲突，在这两起案件中，裁判机构都认定哥斯达黎加对原告财产予以征收的做法违反了所适用的投资条约。然而，通过进一步的审视，除了每个争端案件的具体事实存在许多不同之处以外，裁判机构对待环境保护的方式也存在明显差异。在"CDSE 诉哥斯达黎加案"中，法庭对环境考量缺乏重视，基本上限于两段话和一个脚注，[59] 尽管被告在进行辩护时强调了这些考量。[60] 相比之下，在"Unglaube 诉哥斯达黎加案"中，裁判机构给予环境影响以具体的实际效果。在原告方专家的促进下，当裁判机构借鉴"最高和最佳用途"这些标准来评估财产的公平市场价值时，在定性这些标准时参照了环境考量。[61] 在此可以尝试与"SPP 诉埃及案"[62] 裁判机构所采取的方法作一个对比，根据这一方法，对被征用财产的估价必须考虑到这样一个事实，即一旦金字塔遗址被列入《世界遗产名录》，原告项目的相关活动将是非法的。此外，在"Unglaube 诉哥斯达黎加案"中，裁判

58　*Adel A Hamadi Al Tamimi v. Sultanate of Oman*，ICSID Case No. ARB/11/33，Award（3 November 2015）.

59　*CDSE v. Costa Rica*，supra footnote 40，paras. 71-72 and footnote 32.

60　See C. Brower and J. Wong, "General Valuation Principles: The Case of Santa Elena", in T. Weiler (ed.) *International Investment Law and Arbitration: Leading Cases from the ICSID, NAFTA, Bilateral Treaties and Customary International Law* (2005) 764.

61　*Unglaube v. Costa Rica*，supra footnote 54，para. 309.

62　*SPP v. Egypt*，supra footnote 40，para. 191.

机构的心态也更偏向于当前的环保需要，包括参考投资者所应尽到的谨慎[63]和对国家规制活动（包括征收以外的活动）的遵从，[64] 特别重要的是，还要参考在给予不同实体差别待遇时，在多大程度上与环境考量相关。[65]

其他投资裁判机构的推理更明确地处理了对国内规制的遵从这些问题。"Clayton 和 Bilcon 诉加拿大案"的裁决引起了许多争议。该案涉及的是，根据环境审查小组的建议，（主管部门）拒绝在新斯科舍省颁发采矿许可证。裁判机构的多数观点是，审查小组的行为违反了加拿大环境法，进而违反了《北美自由贸易协定》（NAFTA）第 1105 条所载的国际最低待遇标准。这是有问题的，因为加拿大法院并没有查明对加拿大环境法的违反，而且一般而言，包括三个北美自由贸易协定缔约方也那样认为，仅仅是违反国内法（何况此种违反尚未被恰当地查明），不足以达到违反《北美自由贸易协定》第 1105 条的苛刻门槛。[66] 然而，就当前目的而言"Clayton 和 Bilcon 诉加拿大案"的重要意义在于，裁判机构多数方做出了巨大努力，试图使这项裁决看起来像是对环境负责的和尊重的。这些努力体现在各个方面，例如该裁决包含了多个特别重要的附带意见。例如，在第 531 段中，在判定环境审查小组使用的"社区核心价值"标准是不恰当的之后，裁判机构补充说，它"绝对毫无疑问的是，社区成员对各种可估价要件的估值可以被看作环境评估的完全合法的一部分"。后来，在分析对第 1105 条的违反这一诉求时，裁判机构做出了冗长的附带意见，这清楚地传达了裁判机构多数方的看法，即想要证明裁决的正当性，除了仅仅依靠法律，还需要其他方面。[67] 在裁决的结尾，还给出了附带意见，这次明确回应了少数法官的不同意见。[68] 不同意见强调了多个问题，其中包括该裁决的两个深远影响，一个是环境审查方式的潜在变化，如今的审查方式更多地关注本身是否合法（也就是所谓的"规制寒冬"的变量）

63　*Unglaube v. Costa Rica*, supra footnote 54, para. 258.

64　Ibid., paras. 246–247.

65　Ibid., para. 264.

66　See *Clayton and Bilcon v. Canada*, supra footnote 55. Dissenting Opinion of Professor Donald McRae, para. 40.

67　*Clayton and Bilcon v. Canada*, supra footnote 55, paras. 595–601.

68　Ibid., paras. 735–738.

而较少关注事实,另一个是高估了技术因素(特别是减缓措施)而低估了公众对环境使用的偏好。[69] 两者都是重要的观点。但是,为了使裁决从一个公共政策的视角来看是可接受的,裁判机构的大多数法官还是经历了巨大的烦恼。这种努力可以与"Gold Reserve 诉委内瑞拉案"所采取的更自信的做法形成对比,在此案中,裁判机构就保护环境的必要性作出了更短的附带意见,[70] 因为证据记录清楚表明,环境保护不是导致争议措施的主要推动因素。[71] 因此,"Clayton 和 Bilcon 诉加拿大案"的裁决是史无前例的,尽管裁判机构的多数方认为存在违约行为,但是它仍然试图(在附带意见中)强调环境保护在投资争端解决中的重要性。

要从对环保的抽象赞扬转向环保在外国投资争端中所能发挥的实际作用,我们必须把注意力转向另外两个方面的进展。一个涉及投资协议中环境条款的运作("分割"),而另一个涉及外国投资者环境管理不善的影响,更具体地说,由此导致的责任。环境条款的操作是"Al Tamimi 诉阿曼案"中的一个主要问题,这是由《美国—阿曼自由贸易协定》引起的争端。在本案中,涉及对石灰石采石场投资执行环境法,裁判机构既提及了第 10 条第 10 款(一项保留了环境规制的条款),也提到了第 17 章(该条约的环境章节),将其作为一种手段来解释第 10 条第 5 款规定的国际最低待遇标准。重要的是,它指出,当判断是否违反了第 10 条第 5 款规定的最低待遇标准的时候,裁判机构必须遵从条约明文规定的环境规制和保护所提供的有力辩护。[72] 这种考量帮助裁判机构裁定驳回针对第 10 条第 5 款的诉求。第二个值得注意的进展是在"(法国)Perenco 石油公司诉厄瓜多尔案"中针对被告提出的环境反诉的裁决。[73] 该案涉及法国 Perenco 石油公司在亚马孙雨林厄瓜多尔部分的石油开采活动对环境的影响。裁判机构根据厄瓜多尔法律规定的严格责任和过错责任制度评估了 Perenco 石油公司对环境造成损害的赔偿责任,并纳入了可适用的合同法框架。裁判机构远非采取"绿色"立场,只是冷静地评估了国内环境法

69　Dissenting opinion McRae, supra footnote 66, paras. 44-51.

70　*Gold Reserve v. Venezuela*, supra footnote 56, para. 595.

71　Ibid., para. 580.

72　*Al Tamimi v. Oman*, supra footnote 58, para. 389 (italics added).

73　*Perenco v. Ecuador*, supra footnote 57.

以及一些有关投资者过失的案例。裁判机构避免使用那种在"Clayton 和 Bilcon 诉加拿大案"的裁决中体现出来的抱歉语气。它坚决适用环境法，在某些情况下，它求助于特殊的环境技巧（例如，所谓的环境友好型推理、[74] 对裁判机构专家的指定[75]以及鼓励各方就赔偿金额达成和解[76]）。因此，我们可以将这一裁定理解为朝着心态改变迈出的又一步，或者更确切地说，是所谓的正常化的足迹。环境因素并不是作为一个外部因素或某一激进观点的一个要件而被整合到推理中。它们只是被当作采掘业正常运营的一项要求。这种做法并未呈现"绿色"的痕迹。环境考量似乎是裁判机构推理中一个正常的（甚至是显眼的）要件，不需要额外的理由。

当然，每一项措施和每个案件都有其特定的法律和政治背景，裁判机构必须在此基础上作出裁决。表 12-1 概括的三种方法只是为了描述那些可能共存的趋势或方法及其随着时间迁移而改变的相应权重或影响，以便反映出对环保这样一个日益重要的监管客体的认知的变化。"升级的"方法无疑是最务实的，投资条约制定中的当前做法符合为环境监管提供更明确的政策空间这一需要，因此这种做法就不足为奇了。

（三）投资条约的实践

在过去 20 年中，双边投资条约和自由贸易协定（这两类共同称为国际投资协定）给予环境考量的空间已大为扩大。根据经合组织针对 1623 项国际投资协定（约占当时国际投资协定的 50%）于 2011 年发表的一份报告指出，所分析国际投资协定中只有 8.2%明确提及环境问题。[77] 但是，如果添加了时间维度，则全貌将发生巨大变化。事实上，经合组织的报告表明，自 20 世纪 90 年代中期以来：

> 新缔结的包含环境术语的国际投资协定的比例开始慢慢增加，并且从 2002 年开始，急剧上升……2008 年达到高峰，当时新缔结的 89 项条约都提到了环境问题。[78]

---

[74] Ibid., paras. 361, 470-473 and 495.

[75] Ibid., paras. 569, 587-588, 611（8）and（17）.

[76] Ibid., paras. 593 and 611（9）.

[77] K. Gordon and J. Pohl, "Environmental Concerns in International Investment Agreements: A Survey"（2011）*OECD Working Papers on International Investment* No. 2011/1（OECD Report）, p. 8.

[78] Ibid., p. 8.

这些条约提及环境因素的方式各有不同。报告指出了在国际投资协定中反复出现的七类环境条款:

1. 序言中提及环境问题和将保护环境作为条约缔约方关切事项的一般性表述……
2. 为环境监管保留政策空间……
3. 为更具体、更有限的环境主题（绩效要求和国民待遇）的规制保留政策空间……
4. 明确缔约方的共识（即非歧视性环境规制不构成"间接征收"）的规定……
5. 防止为吸引投资而放松环境规制的规定……
6. 涉及仲裁机构诉诸环境专家的规定……
7. 鼓励加强环境规制与合作的规定。[79]

这些规定出现的频率因国而异，并随时间而变化。最常见的条款类别（含有环境术语的 133 个国际投资协定的 62%）是为环境规制保留政策空间（第 2 类），它实际上具有潜在的许可效力。更具体的条款（第 3 类和第 4 类）和更激进的条款（第 7 类）则比较少（第 3 类为 14%；第 4 类为 9%；第 7 类为 18%）。

2014 年发表的另外两份报告[80]证实了这一趋势，它们集中在以下两点：(1) 自由贸易协定和所谓"大区域"协定等条约实践的贡献；(2) 环境考量逐步融合的主要驱动因素。关于第一点，2013 年贸发会议的一份报告对 18 项国际投资协定（11 项双边投资协定和 7 项自由贸易协定）作了分析，该报告显示，大多数条约是以序言或者与《关贸总协定》（GATT）类似的例外规定来表述环境问题，或者仍然使用反对环境标准竞次（anti-race-to-the-bottom）条款。少数（5/18）也以单独条款或序

---

[79] Ibid., p. 11 (the numbering has been added and italics omitted).

[80] See UNCTAD, *World Investment Report* 2014. *Investing in the SDGs* (2014) (UNCTAD 2014), available at: www.unctad.org (visited on 2 April 2017); C. George, "Environment and Regional Trade Agreements: Emerging Trends and Policy Drivers", *OECD Trade and Environment Working Papers*, 2014/02 (OECD 2014), available at: http://dx.doi.org/10.1787/5jz0v4q45g6h – en (visited on 2 April 2017).

言的形式提到了公司和社会责任标准。重要的是,多个条款和机制也是进行中的大区域协定谈判的一部分。其中,贸发会议的上述报告除了提及常用的类似于《关贸总协定》的例外规定外,还提及企业社会责任促进条款和监管合作机制,涉及法律/法规草案的交换和贸易/投资合格评估。另一项更为详细的研究[81][这项研究是基于2006年《全球欧洲通讯》(Global Europe Communication)[82]和2006年《更新的可持续发展战略》(SDS)[83]的授权]讨论了从2007年起开始制定的《欧盟自由贸易协定》(EU FTAs)中的可持续发展条款/章节。这些条款/章节体现在多个欧盟经济伙伴协定中,包括与加勒比论坛国家(加勒比非洲、加勒比和太平洋国家集团论坛)、韩国、中美洲、哥伦比亚和秘鲁等的协定,这些条款/章节有几个共同点,特别是都提及了"背景和目标",以及针对规制权、多边环境协定的作用,不降低环境规制以吸引贸易和投资的义务,绿色贸易和投资的促进,合作和实施机制等条款。[84]

关于第二点,经合组织2014年一份专门讨论自由贸易协定(因此不是专门针对投资)中的环境考量的报告揭示了将环境考量融入条约实践的理由。其中一个原因是,一些国家或贸易集团在国内立法或政策文件中承诺将环境因素纳入其贸易谈判。2006年《可持续发展战略》和《全球欧洲通讯》在欧盟背景下所给予的推动就是一个很好的例证。2014年经合组织报告审查了澳大利亚、加拿大、智利、欧洲自由贸易联盟、日本、新西兰、瑞士或美国等国家或贸易区的其他类似承诺。[85]但是,这些承诺其实是基于更重要的政策目标,而这些政策目标可被视为环境整合的真正驱动因素。报告指出了四个目标:(1)促进可持续发展这一首要目标;

---

[81] R. Zvelc, "Environmental Integration in EU Trade Policy: The Generalised System of Preferences, Trade Sustainability Impact Assessments and Free Trade Agreements", in E. Morgera (ed.), *The External Environmental Policy of the European Union EU and International Law Perspectives* (Cambridge University Press, 2012), pp. 174-203.

[82] Commission, "Communication-Global Europe: Competing in the World: A Contribution to the EU's Growth and Jobs Strategy", COM (2006) 567.

[83] Council, "Review of the EU Sustainable Development Strategy (EU SDS) - Renewed Strategy", 26 June 2006, p. 21 available at: http://register.consilium.europa.eu (visited on 3 April 2017).

[84] Zvelc, supra footnote 81, pp. 195-200.

[85] OECD 2014, supra footnote 80, pp. 14-19.

(2) 确保协定缔约方之间有一个公平的竞争环境;(3) 在共同关心的环境问题上加强合作;(4) 达成国际环境议程。[86] 有趣的是,但也许毫不奇怪,所追求的政策目标通常是"确保协定缔约方之间有一个公平的竞争环境",换言之,出于工具性(竞争)的原因保护环境。这就是经合组织贸易与环境联合工作项目(OECD Joint Working Programme on Trade and Environment)的10个代表团(代表31个国家)对报告作者所分发的调查问卷的答复。[87] 对可持续发展的促进排在第二位,仅次于竞争力政策理由。想要定量分析政策理由对某些条款的支撑力度或者其与上述驱动因素的关联度,是一项微妙的工作,它可能会导致不同的解释。也就是说,2014年经合组织报告提供了重要证据,表明在自由贸易协定中纳入环境条款不仅仅是一个绿色意识形态问题。恰恰相反,一个关键的政策驱动力是经济自由化。

总体而言,这些结果表明,国际投资协定对环境考量越来越敏感,但目前的做法倾向于宽泛甚至不确定的条款。就当前的目的而言,主要信息是,投资条约制定的实践所体现的趋势与投资裁判机构的判例和前述政策进程相同,即环保规范与外国投资的保护和促进规范之间的日益互动。如后文所述,贸易与环境规制之间的联系也走上了类似的道路(其实从20世纪90年代就已经开始了),主要是由推动1992年地球峰会和1994年乌拉圭回合的贸易谈判的平行谈判进程造成的。[88]

第三节 环境保护与国际贸易法

一 概述

与投资/环境之间的联系一样,贸易自由化对环境保护的影响也是模棱两可的,因为它可能导致更有效地利用自然资源(由于生产者之间的全球竞争),或导致环境友好型商品和技术的更大范围的流通,但它也可

---

86 Ibid., p. 14.
87 Ibid., pp. 11-12.
88 On this connection, see K. von Moltke, "The Last Round: The General Agreement on Tariffs and Trade in Light of the Earth Summit" (1993) 23 *Environmental Law* 519.

能限制合法的环境规制,或导致污染物的更大范围的流通。[89] 然而,与投资/环境的联系不同,贸易/环境的联系至少 20 年来一直受到法律评论员的注意。[90]

事实上,在贸易规制的历史上,(人们)很早就认识到了调和这两个部门法的重要性。1948 年失败的《哈瓦那宪章》(*1948 Havana Charter*)[91] 及其前身 1927 年的《废除进出口禁令和限制公约》(*1927 Convention for the Abolition of Import and Export Prohibitions and Restrictions*)[92] 都载有明确的例外,以适应今天所谓的环境措施。[93] 这个问题在斯德哥尔摩会议召开之前再次出现,以至于在 1971 年《关贸总协定》缔约国成立了一个环境措施与国际贸易工作组(Working Group on Environmental Measures and International Trade, EMIT Group),但是该工作组直到 1992 年地球峰会才开

---

[89] On this debate see e. g. J. Frankel and A. Rose, "Is Trade Good or Bad for the Environment? Sorting out the Causality" (2005) 87 *Review of Economics and Statistics* 85 (发现贸易倾向于减少空气污染,并且一般对其他环境指标没有负面影响); J. Frankel, *Environmental Effects of International Trade*, Expert Report No. 301, commissioned by Sweden's Globalisation Council (2008), available at: www. hks. harvard. edu (last visited on 20 April 2017).

[90] Some of the seminal work on this connection includes D. Zaelke, R. Housman and P. Orbach (eds.), *Trade and the Environment: Law, Economics and Policy* (Washington, DC: Island Press, 1993); D. Esty, *Greening the GATT: Trade, Environment, and the Future* (Washington, DC: Institute for International Economics, 1994); E. U. Petersmann, *International and European Trade and Environmental Law after the Uruguay Round* (The Hague: Kluwer, 1995); E. Brown Weiss and J. Jackson (eds.), *Reconciling Environment and Trade* (Ardsley, NY: Transnational Publishers, 2001). For two more recent studies, see E. Vranes, *Trade and the Environment. Fundamental Issues in International Law, WTO Law, and Legal Theory* (Oxford University Press, 2009); J. Watson, *The WTO and the Environment* (London: Routledge, 2013). For concise overviews, see S. Charnovitz, "The WTO's Environmental Progress", in W. J. Davey and J. Jackson (eds.), *The Future of International Economic Law* (Oxford University Press, 2008), pp. 247 – 268; D. Bodansky and J. Lawrence, "Trade and Environment", in D. Bethlehem, D. McRae, R. Neufeld and I. Van Damme (eds.), *The Oxford Handbook of International Trade Law* (Oxford University Press, 2009), pp. 505 – 538.

[91] Havana Charter for an International Trade Organization, 24 March 1948, UN Doc. E/Conf. 2178, Art. 45 (1) (a) (x).

[92] Convention for the Abolition of Import and Export Prohibitions and Restrictions, 8 November 1927, 97 LNTS 391, Art. 4.

[93] Both instruments are referred to in Charnovitz, supra footnote 90, pp. 247-248.

始工作。[94] 事实上，直到 20 世纪 90 年代初，多个相互关联的进程［包括墨西哥和美国之间关于金枪鱼进口的争端，[95]《北美自由贸易协定》（North American Free Trade Agreement，NAFTA）的谈判，[96] 导致地球峰会的谈判以及 1994 年结束的乌拉圭回合的谈判[97]］才导致这一议题重新启动。

世界贸易组织的成立带来了许多环境方面的重大进展，包括在《马拉喀什协定》（*Marrakesh Agreement*）[98] 序言中提及可持续发展，以及通过了一项《关于贸易与环境的部长级决定》［设立贸易与环境委员会（Committee on Trade and Environment，CTE）以取代休眠的环境措施与国际贸易工作组］。[99] 贸易与环境委员会通过讨论和研究，为明确贸易/环境的接口做出了贡献，并促进了国家和国际层面上贸易与环境官员之间的互动。随着时间的推移，环境考量在世贸组织背景下的重要性日益增加，2001 年《部长宣言》（*2001 Ministerial Declaration*）（该宣言启动了多哈回合的贸易谈判）所设想的"贸易与环境"工作计划也承认了这一点。[100] 这方面的谈判委托给贸易委员会或其特别会议，重点讨论贸易法与环境条约之间的联系以及环境商品和服务（Environmental Goods and Services，EGS）的贸易的便利化。然而，从法律角度来看，多哈回合这些项目的进步非常有限。

然而，多哈《部长宣言》仍然是一个有益的标志，它指明了可以在哪些领域探索协同效应（主要是通过"相互支持"和环境商品和服务），同时，它还界定了潜在冲突（即贸易法与环境条约的冲突和贸易法中的环境差异），以便避免这些冲突或使其最小化。图 12-1 概括了以下各节中讨论的领域。

94　See Bodansky and Lawrence, supra footnote 90, p. 514.

95　*United States-Restrictions on Imports of Tuna*, Panel Report, DS21/R-39S/155（3 September 1991）（*Tuna-Dolphin I*）.

96　North American Free Trade Agreement, 17 December 1992, 32 ILM 296（NAFTA）. Together with the NAFTA, the parties concluded a parallel North American Agreement on Environmental Cooperation, 17 September 1992, 32 ILM 1519（NAAEC）.

97　See von Moltke, supra footnote 88.

98　Agreement establishing the World Trade Organization, 15 April 1994, 1867 UNTS 154.

99　Marrakesh Ministerial Decision on Trade and Environment, 14 April 1994, MTN. TNC/45MIN.

100　WTO Ministerial Conference Fourth Session, Ministerial Declaration, WT/MIN（01）/DEC/1（20 November 2001）（Doha Declaration）, paras. 28, 31-33, 51.

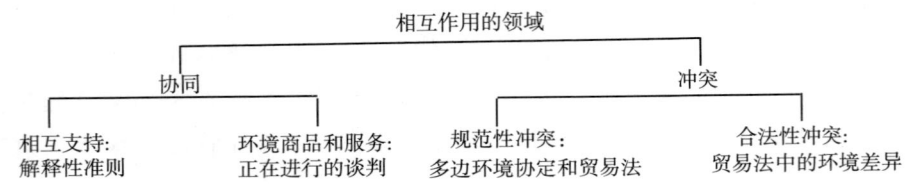

```
                        相互作用的领域
                    ┌─────────┴─────────┐
                   协同                 冲突
              ┌─────┴─────┐         ┌─────┴─────┐
           相互支持:    环境商品和服务:   规范性冲突:      合法性冲突:
          解释性准则    正在进行的谈判   多边环境协定和贸易法  贸易法中的环境差异
```

图 12-1　贸易与环境关系的法律问题

这些领域之间存在重要的联系，有时也存在部分重叠。对潜在冲突的一些解决办法（例如相互支持的解释）实际上可以视为协同方法。然而，协同和冲突之间的区分，有助于将贸易置于相同的概念图中来评估环境保护与投资或者人权法之间的联系。

二　协同效应

（一）相互支持

在促成 1992 年地球峰会的谈判进程中，与贸易规制有关的环境保护受到很大关注。地球峰会的成果，特别是《里约宣言》原则 12[101] 和《21 世纪议程》第 2 章[102]都表达了发展中国家的一个关切，即环境规制会被用于限制其出口产品进入市场。《21 世纪议程》强调，必须使贸易与环境"相互支持"。[103] 类似的考量也促成《世贸组织协定》（*WTO Agreement*）序言第一段提及可持续发展，尽管这里的重点是自然资源的有效利用。

在随后的 20 年中，"相互支持"这一概念与"可持续发展"这一概念一样，在多个国际文件中，从协同（而非冲突）的角度来阐明环境条约与贸易规则之间的关系。[104] 例如，1998 年《持久性有机污染物公约》、[105]

---

[101]　"Rio Declaration on Environment and Development", 13 June 1992, UN Doc. A/CONF. 151/26. Rev. 1 （《里约宣言》）.

[102]　Agenda 21, supra footnote 12

[103]　Ibid., paras. 2.3 (b) and 2.9 (d).

[104]　See R. Pavoni, "Mutual Supportiveness as a Principle of Interpretation and Law-Making: A Watershed for the 'WTO-and-Competing-Regimes' Debate?" (2010) 3 *European Journal of International Law* 649, 654-655 （指《生物多样性公约》第 22 条第 1 款的"冲突条款"。《北美自由贸易协定》第 104 条也可以用来例证这一方法）.

[105]　Rotterdam Convention on the Prior Informed Consent Procedure for Certain Hazardous Chemicals and Pesticides in International Trade, 10 September 1998, 2244 UNTS 337, preamble, paras. 8-10.

2000 年《生物安全议定书》、[106] 2001 年《植物遗传资源条约》、[107] 2001 年《持久性有机污染物公约》[108] 的序言，或最近的 2005 年《教科文组织文化多样性公约》（UNESCO Convention on Cultural Diversity）第 20 条[109]和 2010 年《名古屋议定书》第 4 条[110]。

在此背景下产生的一个重要的法律问题涉及"相互支持"的影响。这些影响的范围可能是一项单纯的政策声明，一项解释性准则（或一些评论员所称的"原则"），一项划分层级的冲突条款，甚至一项"立法"原则。[111] 在判例法中，这个问题并没有被明确地提及，更不用说得到解决了，但有一些权威的说法是，相互支持至少可以在贸易争端中发挥解释作用。直到目前为止，这方面的标志性成果仍然是 1998 年世贸组织上诉机构（Appellate Body, AB）针对"海虾和海龟案"的报告。[112] 该案涉及美国采取的国内环境措施，影响某些海虾的进口（如果在捕捞这些海虾时没有充分保护到海龟）。作为辩护的一部分，美国援引了《关贸总协定》第 20 条 g 款中关于保护不可再生自然资源的一般例外。尽管世贸组织上诉机构最后得出结论，美国的措施并无法依据第 20 条获得正当性（因为它违反了第 20 条的引言部分），但它还是提及《世贸组织协定》的序言和两项环境条约，即《联合国海洋法公约》[113] 和《濒危野生动植物种国际

---

[106] Cartagena Protocol on Biosafety to the Convention on Biological Diversity, 29 January 2000, 39 ILM 1027, preamble, paras. 9-11.

[107] International Treatyon Plant GeneticResourcesfor Food and Agriculture, 3 November 2001, 2400 UNTS 379, preamble, paras. 9-11.

[108] Stockholm Convention on Persistent Organic Pollutants, 22 May 2001, 40 ILM 532 (2001), preamble, para. 9.

[109] Convention on the Protection and Promotion of the Diversity of Cultural Expressions, 20 October 2005, 2440 UNTS 311.

[110] Nagoya Protocol on Access to Genetic Resources and the Fair and Equitable Sharing of the Benefits Arising from their Utilization to the Convention on Biological Diversity, 29 October 2010, available at: www.cbd.int/abs/doc/protocol/nagoya-protocol-en.pdf (last visited on 20 April 2017).

[111] See Pavoni, supra n. 104, who argues that the principle requires good faith negotiations to amend, as necessary, the relevant treaties so as to achieve mutual supportiveness.

[112] United States-Import Prohibition of Certain Shrimp and Shrimp Products, Report of the Appellate Body, 12 October 1998, WT/DS58/AB/R (Shrimp-Turtle).

[113] United Nations Convention on the Law of the Sea, 10 December 1982, 1833 UNTS 397.

贸易公约》[114],用于解释第 20 条 g 款。上述机构认为,对第 20 条 g 款中的"不可再生的自然资源"一词的解释必须"参照国际社会当前对环境保护和保全的关切"。[115]

这种解释方法可被视为对《维也纳条约法公约》第 31 条第 3 款 c 项[116]规定的系统整合的习惯规则的一般适用,但世贸组织争端解决机构并未一贯地遵循这一方法。在专家组 2006 年关于"欧共体生物技术案"的报告中,采用了对系统整合的限制性解读,抵消了《生物多样性公约》和《卡塔赫纳生物安全议定书》在解释可适用贸易规则上可能发挥的作用。[117]

随后,在"中国原材料案"中,中国提到了相互支持和对自然资源的永久主权,以证明根据第 20 条 g 款它对某些原材料实行的出口限制是合理的。[118] 在一项争论不休的裁决中,专家小组和后来的上诉机构认为,中国不能依据第 20 条作为违反中国《入世议定书》(Protocol of Accession)的理由,但他们还是从争议性以及违反《关贸总协定》两个角度讨论了第 20 条的可适用性。专家小组还提到了多项环境条约(包括《生物多样性公约》)对"保护"这一术语的定性,以便阐明第 20 条 g 款的一般含义。[119] 然后,它提到了上诉机构在"海虾和海龟案"中的报告,特别是《世贸组织协定》的序言及其关于可持续发展的提法。[120] 值得注意的是,专家小组明确承认,在解释第 20 条时,必须考虑到那些适用于世贸组织成员的一般国际法原则,但它援引了专家小组在"欧共体生物技术案"中的报告作为这一断言的权威依据。[121] 同理,对第 20 条 g 款的解释还应考虑到自

114　Convention on International Trade in Endangered Species of Wild Fauna and Flora, 3 March 1973, 983 UNTS 243.

115　*Shrimp-Turtle*, supra footnote 112, paras. 129–132.

116　Vienna Convention on the Law of Treaties, 23 May 1969, 1155 UNTS 331 (VCLT). See *Oil Platforms case* (*Islamic Republic of Iran v. United States of America*), ICJ Reports 2003, p. 161, para. 41.

117　*European Communities-Measures affecting the Approval and Marketing of Biotech Products*, WT/DS291/R, WT/DS292/R, WT/DS293/R (29 September 2006), paras. 7.74 and 7.75.

118　*China-Measures related to the Exportation of Various Raw Materials*, Panel Reports, WT/DS394/R;WT/DS395/R;WT/DS398/R(5 July 2011)[*China-Raw Materials*(*Panel*)], para. 7.364.

119　Ibid., para. 7.372, footnote 594.

120　Ibid., para. 7.373.

121　Ibid., para. 7.377.

然资源主权的习惯法原则。这一原则的习惯法性质就克服了"欧共体生物技术案"对系统整合的狭义解读所导致的困难。就目前的目的而言，需要强调的要点是，专家小组明确承认了相互支持："环境保护和经济发展不一定是相互排斥的政策目标，它们可以和谐地共存"。[122]

（二）环境商品和服务

《多哈授权》（Doha Mandate）第 31 段将关于环境商品和服务的谈判委托给贸易与环境委员会。对环境商品和服务贸易的促进可以服务于若干目的，包括激励世界各地的绿色工业，创造"绿色就业机会"和增加绿色产品的传播。然而，作为实现"三赢"成果（即有利于贸易、环境和发展）的领域之一，关于环境商品和服务的谈判在世贸组织层面陷入了僵局。主要原因在于，对于什么样的商品或服务才能被视为"环境商品"或相关环境服务没有达成一致意见。当然，也有一些指导性定义，例如欧盟委员会提供并由经合组织接受的定义：

> 能够测量、预防、限制或矫正环境损害（如水、空气、土壤的污染，以及涉及废物和噪声的问题）的商品和服务。它们包括清洁技术，使得污染和原材料的使用最小化。[123]

然而，正如 2014 年联合国环境规划署《贸易和绿色经济手册》（UNEP's Handbook on Trade and Green Economy）[124] 所指出的，这一贸易体制可能涵盖的每一类商品或服务的界定都面临着艰巨的挑战。

第一类将涵盖那些可用于预防、监测和治理环境影响的商品。然而，其中许多商品具有"双重用途"（例如恒温器），因此，它们与这种具体环

---

[122] Ibid., para. 7. 381.

[123] OECD, *The Global Environmental Goods and Services Industry* (Paris: OECD, 1994), p. 4. For more recent overviews of characterisations see: A. Viklhyaev, "Environmental Goods and Services: Defining Negotiations or Negotiating Definitions?" (2004) *UNCTAD Trade and Environment Review*, available at: unctad.org/en/docs/ditcted20034a2_ en.pdf (last visited on 20 April 2014); World Bank, *Inclusive Green Growth: The Pathway to Sustainable Development* (Washington, DC: World Bank, 2012), pp. 92-93.

[124] UNEP, *Trade and Green Economy: A Handbook* (Geneva: UNEP, 3rd edn) ("Handbook"), pp. 111-112.

境用途的联系可能变成利于其他用途的交易的借口。第二类涉及那些环境色彩不太浓的商品。这一类别面临一个主要的问题是可比性和分级。举例来讲，省油的燃油车应该如何与耗油的生物燃料车相比，特别是当我们不仅考虑到排放，而且考虑到对土地用途变化和用水效率的影响？具有讽刺意味的是，第三类由于工艺和生产方法（Processes and Production Methods，PPM），被认为更"环保"。正如本章后面讨论的那样，这个问题在贸易方面非常具有争议性，由于它们的生产方式的不同（造成污染的多少），它会导致对两种"类似"甚至相同商品的区别对待。因此，如果不充分强调需要把重点放在产品特性（而非生产过程）上，那么关于环境商品和服务的辩论则有可能成为世贸组织内部的环境"特洛伊木马"。

尽管存在这些障碍，但在地区层面取得了重大进展。2012 年 9 月，亚太经济合作组织（APEC）的 21 个国家达成协议，将 54 种环境商品清单[125]上的关税降至 5% 的上限，这就处理了世界贸易中的绝大多数份额。体现了这一协议的"宣言"明确指出，它们的削减承诺"不影响亚太经合组织国家在世界贸易组织中的立场"。在多边层面也发起了一个仅以商品为重点的类似倡议，它涉及来自不同地区的世贸组织成员，包括澳大利亚、加拿大、中国、欧盟、日本、韩国、新西兰、挪威、新加坡、瑞士和美国等。这个想法出现于 2014 年达沃斯论坛，并在 2014 年 7 月正式被提出。[126] 它很快扩展到 40 多个国家，目标是在 2016 年年底前缔结一项"环境商品协定"（Environmental Goods Agreement，EGA）。但是，此目标可能无法实现。2016 年 12 月，由于有的国家在最后一刻试图在环境商品清单中加入一些内容，谈判陷入僵局。关键的挑战仍然是确定何种商品或服务将会受益于环境商品协定（或环境商品和服务协定）的优惠待遇。

正如这些例证所示，在贸易/环境的联系中存在着具体协同的巨大空间。虽然迄今为止的协同大多具有原则性属性（竞争加剧导致的资源效率的提升和贸易引发的技术转让），但是区域性的亚太经合组织倡议和潜

---

[125] See "20th APEC Economic Leaders' Declaration", Vladivostok, Russia, 9 September 2012, Annex C：APEC List of Environmental Goods, available at：www. apec. org（last visited on 20 April 2017）.

[126] See " Group of WTO Members Launch Talks on ' Green Goods ' ", available at：www. twnside. org . sg/ title2/ wto. info/2014/ti140706. htm（last visited on 20 April 2017）. see further "Progress made on Environmental Goods Agreement, setting stage for further talks", WTO News item（4 December 2016）, available at：www. wto. org（last visited on 20 April 2017）.

在的多边环境商品协定表明,可以以各种方式具体利用贸易法以促进环境保护。然而,还是必须预防和最小化贸易与环境法之间的摩擦,这一必要性不应被协同的可能性所掩盖。

三 冲突

(一) 规范性冲突和合法性冲突

本章前面介绍的规范性冲突(涉及两个或两个以上国际法规范的冲突)和合法性冲突(涉及一项国际义务和一项国内措施的冲突)之间的区别有助于界定贸易与投资监管之间的相互作用。与投资法一样,国际环境法对贸易法的影响仍不清楚。

虽然贸易规制的历史早已承认了它们之间的潜在摩擦,[127] 而且国际社会还采取了若干举措(包括《多哈授权》的部分内容[128])来明确这一点,但开发某种形式的"激进"方法的尝试并不成功。然而,正如将要讨论的,随着时间的推移,贸易小组越来越重视环境保护,从"传统的"方法(有时称为"内向型审视",这一方法将环境措施视为保护主义并应从属于贸易规则)转变为"升级的"的方法(有时称为"外向型审视",[129] 这是一种公开化的方法,它在解释贸易法时会考虑到环境因素和国际环境法)。

然而,贸易法留给环境差别化的空间仍然是有限的,它主要体现在次级规范这一层级,或者更具体地说,仅限于很少被承认的个别"例外"。随着时间的推移,人们可能会期望这个空间应该逐步增加;最初,是在例外这一层级,有更大的可行性来应对环境考量;然后,谨慎地从次级规范层级转向初级规范层级,特别是通过"部分废除"(或"拆分",即限制贸易规则的适用范围),或通过对环境标准的宽松认定(在涉及贸易的技术壁垒或卫生和植物检疫措施时);最后,通过泛化贸易规则的核心概念,如"相同性"或补贴中的"收益"概念。这些步骤不会遵循线性时

---

127 See supra footnote 92.

128 See supra footnote 100, para. 31.

129 A famous passage of the AB Report in *US-Reformulated Gasoline* is often referred to as the beginning of this openness process. The AB noted that the GATT was "not to be read in clinical isolation from public international law", *United States - Standards for Reformulated and Conventional Gasoline*, AB Report (29 April 1996), WT/DS2/AB/R ("*US-Reformulated Gasoline*"), p. 17.

间轨迹。更有可能的是,它们将根据每个争端的实际情况来逐个展开。此外,它们将采用新条约(如环境商品协定)或(自由贸易协定或大区域条约的)条约条款这两种途径,以复杂的方式开展互动并体现环境问题上的差异化处理,这两种途径有时会交叉在一起,有时会相互配合(例如,当条约谈判进展缓慢或遭遇瓶颈时重新解释核心概念)。但是,对环境考量的逐步开放这一趋势看起来是清晰的。

这在实践中尤其重要,因为在转向以低碳能源为基础的"包容性的绿色经济"的背景下,许多国家正在推行"绿色产业政策",这些政策的目标是在涉及环境的部门(如可再生能源)中发展强大和有竞争力的工业。除非贸易法发生演变,否则这些行业可能会受到国际贸易和投资规则的阻碍。[130] 这些摩擦已经成为现实。一些例证包括中国和欧盟之间由于一些欧洲国家可再生能源政策中针对当地成分的要求[131]、日本与加拿大[132]或美国与印度之间发生的类似摩擦,[133] 以及阿根廷和印度尼西亚针对欧盟对生物燃料采取的反倾销措施所提起的申诉。[134]

(二)多边环境条约和贸易规制

贸易条约与环境条约之间潜在的规范性冲突大多与所谓的"与贸易有关的环境措施"(Trade-Related Environmental Measures,TREMs)相关。

---

[130] See M. Wu and J. Salzman, "The Next Generation of Trade and Environment Conflicts: The Rise of Green Industrial Policy"(2014) 108 *Northwestern University Law Review* 401.

[131] See *European Union and certain Member States-Certain Measures Affecting the Renewable Energy Generation Sector-Request for Consultations by China*(7 November 2012), WT/ DS452/1, G/L/1008, G/SCM/D95/1, G/TRIMS/D/34. 争议在 2013 年 7 月下旬得到解决,尽管太阳能电池板更具体的组件已经进行了几次迭代。

[132] See *Canada-Certain Measures Affecting the Renewable Energy Generation Sector*, Panel Report(19 December 2012), WT/DS412/R and *Canada-Measures Relating to the Feed in Tariff Program*, WT/DS426/R, AB Report(6 May 2013), WT/DS412/AB/R and WT/DS426/ AB/R(*Canada-Renewables*).

[133] *India-Certain Measures Relating to Solar Cells and Solar Modules*, AB Report(16 September 2016), WT-DS456/AB/R(*India-Solar Cells*).

[134] See *European Union and certain Member States - Certain Measures on the Importation and Marketing of Biodiesel and Measures Supporting the Biodiesel Industry - Request for Consultations by Argentina*(23 May 2013), WT/DS459/1, G/L/1027, G/SCM/D97/1, G/ TRIMS/D/36, G/TBT/D/44(在本书创作时仍然处于磋商中);*European Union-Anti-Dumping Measures on Biodiesel from Indonesia-Request for consultations by Indonesia*(17 June 2014), WT/DS480/1, G/L/1071, G/ADP/D104/1(专家组在 2015 年 11 月 4 日组成,在本书创作时这一争议仍在审理中)。

事实上，数个重要的环境条约对某些物质实行贸易限制，甚至禁止贸易。

从广义上讲，可以把这些条约做一个区分，有些条约的主要目的是实行贸易限制，而另一些条约则将贸易限制当作实施工具的一种。第一类包括那些明确表述了事先知情同意原则（详见第三章）的条约，如《巴塞尔公约》[135]《事先知情同意公约》[136] 或《卡塔赫纳生物安全议定书》[137] 以及其他一些条约，例如《濒危野生动植物种国际贸易公约》就是通过控制（来自发达国家的）需求来保护（大多位于发展中国家的）濒危物种。[138] 第二类包括《蒙特利尔议定书》[139] 或《持久性有机污染物公约》[140] 等条约，其中贸易措施（通常是禁止向非缔约国转让）有助于避免将受规制物质的生产或消费转移到非条约缔约国。当然，由于大多数条约都会使用各种不同的规范手段，因此这种贸易禁令也见于第一类条约，例如《巴塞尔公约》，该公约禁止与非缔约国开展贸易，除非它们有管理危险废物的类似保护制度。[141]

贸易界针对与贸易有关的环境措施进行了一些详细的分析。例如，世贸组织秘书处编制了一份环境条约的"方阵"，其中包括与贸易有关的环境措施，[142] 而且《多哈授权》委托贸易与环境委员会的一个特别小组负责阐释与贸易有关的环境措施与《世贸组织协定》之间的关系。[143] 尽管这些努力的成功有限，但不可低估这些努力对拓宽贸易的"思维模式"的价值。也就是说，重要的是，这种分析不应局限于那些与贸易有关的环境措施对冲突和摩擦的狭义认识。

事实上，与贸易有关的环境措施并不是环境条约要求或授权下的唯一

---

[135] Basel Convention on the Control of Transboundary Movements of Hazardous Wastes and their Disposal, 22 March 1989, 1673 UNTS 57 (Basel Convention).

[136] See supra footnote 105.

[137] See supra footnote 106.

[138] See supra footnote 76.

[139] Montreal Protocol on Substances that Deplete the Ozone Layer, 16 September 1987, 1522 UNTS 28 (Montreal Protocol), Arts. 4 and 4A.

[140] POP Convention, supra footnote 108, Art. 3 (1) (a) (ii) and 3 (2).

[141] Basel Convention, supra footnote 135, Arts. 4 (5) and 11 (1).

[142] WTO/CTE, Matrix on Trade Measures pursuant to Selected Multilateral Environmental Agreements, 14 March 2007, WT/CTE/W/160/Rev. 4, TN/TE/S/5/Rev. 2.

[143] Doha Declaration, supra footnote 100, para. 31.

可能与贸易规则相冲突的措施。一项没有明确要求采取与贸易有关的环境措施的条约（例如《联合国气候变化框架公约》）可被解释为授权采取与贸易有关的环境措施或者涉及贸易的其他（非 TREM）措施（例如，对某种产品的生产采取绿色产业政策措施，从而降低该行业对本地和国外生产的某些其他商品的需求）。关于所谓"边境碳调节"（border carbon adjustments）（即进口国对在国外生产的排放量较高的进口产品征收关税，或者向本国生产商提供补贴，以便与外国产品竞争的辩论）的讨论则忽略了这一维度。问题在于这些调节措施的正当性能否被《关贸总协定》的一般例外（第 20 条）确认，它是否符合《补贴与反补贴措施协定》（SCM Agreement），[144] 即是否符合贸易法，而不在于这些调节措施是否是环境条约要求的或有理由采取的。这两个问题都很重要，但关注第一个问题不能过分掩盖第二个问题的相关性。广义表述的环境规范不具有"约束力"或只是"软法"这一误解，在法律上是完全错误的。宽泛的规范，如"各国应给予公平和平等的待遇"（在国际投资法中）或"国会应有权规制与外国和若干州之间的商业关系"（美国宪法中的商业条款）已被解释和应用得非常详细。同样的逻辑也适用于有适当授权的法院对宽泛的环境规范的适用。某项措施是否得到这些宽泛的规范的授权或禁止确实是相关的，因为其可适用的冲突规则或者至少是解释方法（《维也纳条约法公约》第 31 条第 3 款 c 项），与纯贸易争端所采用的规则和方法是不同的。

"印度太阳能电池案"为我们提供了适当的案例来说明贸易界普遍存在的误解。[145] 在本案中，一个含有当地含量要求的可再生能源支持计划被认定违反了《关贸总协定》第 3 条第 4 款的国民待遇条款和《与贸易有关的知识产权协定》（TRIMs Agreement）第 2 条第 1 款。[146] 专家小组和随后的上诉机构分析了《关贸总协定》（GATT）第 20 条 d 款（涉及"为确保遵守法律法规"而必须采取的措施，这也是印度的抗辩理由）能否确认这项措施的正当性，并驳回了印度的主张。重要的是，印度还特别指出，为了确保对《联合国气候变化框架公约》的遵约，受质疑的措施是

---

[144] Agreement on Subsidies and Countervailing Measures, 15 April 1994, 1867 UNTS 14 (SCM Agreement).

[145] *India-Solar Cells*, supra footnote 133.

[146] Agreement on Trade-Related Investment Measures, 15 April 1994, 1868 UNTS 186.

必需的。上诉机构回顾了在此前一个案件中对"法律法规"一词的定义,[147] 它包含了"那些属于世贸组织成员国国内法律制度组成部分的规则,包括那些源自国际协定并被融入世贸组织成员的国内法律的规则,或依据国内法律制度而具有直接效力的规则"。它通过借鉴另一个案件进一步指出,如果某项措施的设计显示出它确保了对某些法律或法规规定的具体规则、义务或要求的遵守,那么这项措施就可以被认定是为了确保这些法律或法规的遵守。[148] 然后,上诉机构重申被告有举证义务去证明此类要求的存在,[149] 并确定了一系列标准以评估某一法律或法规的规范性程度,[150] 一般认为,规范性程度越高,措施的正当性被确认的可能性就越大。应用此测试时,问题产生了。事实上,专家小组和上诉机构认为,根据某一立法文件的授权而制订的计划并没有足够的规范性效力来强制要求遵守。它表明,针对环境政策在全世界绝大多数国家的运作方式,存在着深刻的误解,换言之,各国采取了一种过分谨慎的做法,即限制第 20 条 d 款的适用,从而排除了大量环境政策的适用。更成问题的是对国际环境法(特别是《联合国气候变化框架公约》)的运行的认识。专家小组和上诉机构都认为,该文件的规范性程度不足以使其构成第 20 条 d 款规定的"法律或法规"。尽管事实上他们承认政府行政部门可以直接根据这一文件制定条例。如果遵循这一逻辑,那么立法部门制定的某个立法也不属于"法律或法规"的定义范畴,因为正如绝大多数的立法法案一样,这一立法的实际执行是要依靠法规的。如前所述,这表明对环境法在国内和国际两个层面的运行方式存在着有缺陷的了解。针对它们所处理问题的特性,环境法和条约采用了宽泛的措辞,以便将权力授权给行政部门(及其机

---

147 *India-Solar Cells*, supra footnote133, para. 5. 106 [referring to *Mexico-Tax Measures on Soft Drinks and Other Beverages*, AB Report (6 March 2006), WT/DS308/AB/R, para. 79].

148 Ibid., para. 5. 110 [referring to *Argentina-Measures Relating to Trade in Goods and Services*, AB Report (14 April 2016), WT/DS453/AB/R, para. 6. 203].

149 Ibid., para. 5. 111.

150 Ibid., para. 5. 113 [该测试标准包括:(1)文书的规范程度,以及文书在何种程度上建立了成员国国内法律制度所应遵守的行为规则或行动方针;(2)相关规则的具体程度;(3)该规则是否在法律上可强制执行的,包括用于法庭;(4)该规则是否已被主管当局(指根据成员国国内法律制度拥有必要权力的主管当局)制定或承认;(5)赋予成员国国内法律制度中任何文书的形式和名称;(6)相关规则可能附带的处罚或制裁]。

构),行政部门(及其机构)就能更好地具体运用规制框架来适应不断演变的环境问题。

因此,"印度太阳能电池案"的主要问题,首先在于它是以一个过度专业化的贸易思维模式来展示的,其次在于它的狭义结论(即当地含量要求等同于歧视)。如果各国对朝向低碳经济的转型是认真的,显然世界上三个主要碳排放国中的两个——中国和印度——将需要大规模转向可再生能源。从政治角度来看,这种做法是完全不现实的,对当地工业也没有好处。根据贸易法,这种好处可能是非法的,但问题是贸易法是促进还是阻碍向低碳经济过渡。这并不是说,对当地含量要求进行笼统授权是可取的(即使实践中会经常这样做)。但是,如果一个小突破[例如例外条款(第20条d款)的适用,并由被告承担举证责任]也因对环境政策的理解不足(或者对相关例外条款的过于谨慎的解释)而被排除,那么这一问题就更为根本了。在不久的将来,需要适应环境的差别对待。对此关闭大门只会凸显一个事实,即贸易制度已经与现实脱节。

(三)实践中的环境保护

1. 加工和生产方法(PPMs)

在国际贸易裁决中,环境保护措施迄今仍然局限于贸易法"例外"允许的一种法律可能性,作用并不大。即使这样,如前文所述,期望专家小组或上诉机构将环境法与贸易法同等对待(一种"渐进的"方法),通过"例外"(次级规范)而非"拆分"或其他蕴含重大法律后果的初级规范来对待环境法,这也是不现实的,这不仅仅是涉及关于加工和生产方法的关键辩论。从这个角度来看,目前在贸易裁决中采用的方法可以看作前述"升级的方法"的一个谨慎变种。

事实上,贸易法禁止基于加工和生产方法的环保影响对两种"相同产品"进行区别对待。为了理解这一点,最好回顾上诉机构在"欧共体石棉案"中对"相同产品"的定性。上诉机构认为必须考虑到四组特征:

(1)产品的物理特性;(2)产品能在多大程度上用于相同或类似的终端用途;(3)消费者在多大程度上把产品当作发挥特定功能

以满足特定需要或需求的替代手段；(4) 产品基于关税目的的国际分类。[151]

因此，加拿大对法国禁止进口含石棉产品的措施提出了质疑。一个关键问题在于，温石棉纤维和可替代它们的纤维是否是《关贸总协定》第3条第4款规定的"相同产品"。专家小组的结论认为它们是，但根据《关贸总协定》第20条b款（"保护人类、动物或植物生命或健康所必需的"），这项措施是合理的。在上诉时，上诉机构推翻了专家小组的结论，指出这两种产品不是相同产品，因为两种产品的不同成分对健康有重要影响。上诉机构确认，无论如何，根据第20条b款，这项措施是正当的。因此，该案支持这一主张，即两种产品的不同构成不仅可能会被允许获得"例外"对待（其先决条件是构成违约并将举证责任转移给被告），还要求对"相同产品"这一含义做一个调整，以便一开始（在初级规范层级）就可以排除违约。另一个问题是，如果两种产品的构成没有差别，仅仅是生产方法有所不同（与产品特征无关的生产加工方法），是否能够通过上述两个观点中的一个来作法律上的区别对待。从环境角度来看，这一点很重要，因为不同的生产加工方法的环境印迹很少体现在产品的构成中。

对这一问题的"传统"或"内向型审视"的做法认为这种区分是歧视性的，甚至第20条一般例外条款的规定也不能为其提供合法的基础。在众所周知的"金枪鱼和海豚案"中，专家小组得出结论，美国对金枪鱼进口施加的限制（理由是在捕捞这些金枪鱼时对海豚造成了极高的误伤）违反了《关贸总协定》第11条（该条禁止对贸易予以数量限制），《关贸总协定》第20条的一般例外条款［特别是第20条b款（见前文）］和第20条g款（关于不可再生自然资源的保护）也无法证明其正当性。[152] 随着WTO体系的出现，一种谨慎的"升级的"方法（有时称为

---

[151] *European Communities-Measures Affecting Asbestos and Products Containing Asbestos*, AB Report (12 March 2001), WT/DS135/AB/R, para. 101.

[152] See *Tuna - Dolphin I*, supra footnote 95, and *United States - Measures Concerning the Importation, Marketing and Sale of Tuna and Tuna Products*, Panel report (16 June 1994), DS29/R (Tuna-Dolphin II).

"外向型审视"方法)首次出现于上诉机构在"美国精炼汽油案"中的报告,[153] 随后在"海虾与海龟案"中得到确认。[154] 根据这种方法,基于生产加工方法的差别化对待是歧视性的(因此,尽管生产加工方法的环境影响不同,但这两种产品还是会被认定为"相同产品"),但是,如果能满足第 20 条(包括其起首语)的要求,那么差别化对待的正当性还是有可能被确认的。与投资法中采用的"升级的"方法相比,这种方法在两个主要方面都是"谨慎的"。首先,生产加工方法并没有被理解成是对某个贸易规则(例如"相同产品"这一术语)的解释的改变。[155] 其次,虽然在证明基于例外条款所采取的某项措施的合理性时可以参考生产加工方法,但迄今为止,这种可能性在实践中从未被承认。

2. 一般例外的适用

除了生产加工方法的问题外,适用例外条款是目前在贸易法下开展环境保护的主要途径。《关贸总协定》第 20 条 a、b、d、g 和 j 款曾经被用于证明诸如翻新轮胎[156]或海豹产品[157]的进口禁令或某些原材料[158]的出口限制的正当性,或用于证明以环境为由对国内太阳能电池板生产商给予优惠待遇[159]的正当性。但是,在所有案件中,基于第 20 条的抗辩均告失败,要么是因为一般例外条款被认为不适用,要么是因为受到质疑的措施不符合起首语的严格要求,即:

> 对情况相同的各国,实施的措施不得构成武断的或不合理的差别

---

[153] *US-Reformulated Gasoline*, supra footnote 129, p. 17.

[154] *Shrimp-Turtle*, supra footnote 112, paras. 129-132.

[155] See by contrast the analysis of likeness in *Parkerings v. Lithuania*, supra footnote 51.

[156] *Brazil-Measures Affecting Imports of Retreaded Tyres*, AB Report (3 December 2007), WT/DS332/AB/R (*Brazil-Retreaded Tyres*).

[157] *European Communities-Measures Prohibiting the Importation and Marketing of Seal Products*, AB Report (22 May 2014), WT/DS400/AB/R, WT/DS401/AB/R (*EC-Seal Products*).

[158] *China - Raw Materials (Panel)*, supra footnote 118; *China - Measures Relating to the Exportation of Rare Earths, Tungsten, and Molybdenum*, AB Report (7 August 2014), WT/DS431/AB/R, WT/DS432/AB/R, and WT/DS433/AB/R (*China-Rare Earths*), paras. 2.28-2.29.

[159] *India-Solar Cells*, supra footnote 133, paras. 5.51-5.52 [regarding XX (j)], 5.92-5.93 [regarding XX (d)]. None of the exceptions was deemed to be available so the analysis did not reach the level of Article XX's chapeau.

待遇，或构成对国际贸易的变相限制。[160]

然而，这些案件大大有助于了解第 20 条及其在环境保护方面的潜力。

例如，在"巴西翻新轮胎案"中，上诉机构特别讨论了第 20 条 b 款下的为保障人民、动植物的生命和健康"所必需"的措施的具体含义。它的结论是，这项措施不仅应"足以为目标的实现提供实质帮助"，[161] 又必须是成比例的，因为它必须比追求同一目标的其他实际可用的措施具有较少的贸易限制。[162] 重要的是，上诉机构认识到：

> 某些复杂的公共卫生或环境问题只能通过包含多种相互作用的措施的综合政策来解决。在短期内，可能难以将某一具体措施对公共卫生或环境目标的贡献与其他同属于综合政策的措施的贡献进行区分。此外，某些行动（例如，为减缓全球变暖和气候变化而采取的措施，或为减少疾病发病率而采取的某些预防行动）所获取的成果有赖于时间来证明。[163]

这一认识随后在"中国原材料案"中得到确认。[164] 该案以及具有类似事实的另一个案例，即"中国稀土案"[165] 有助于我们了解第 20 条 g 款中例外条款在环境背景下的适用情况。"中国稀土案"上诉机构的说理在这方面特别有启发性，因为它对第 20 条 g 款的讨论借鉴了第 20 条下的其他例外。上诉机构依据其先前在"美国海虾案"和"中国原材料案"的裁决，确认"自然资源"一词不是静态的，可以同时包括矿物和生物资源，而"保护"一词是指"对环境特别是自然资源的保护"。[166] 此外，它重申，涉及不可再生资源保护的措施"在措施和保护目标之间必须有一个

---

160 For an overview of the WTO jurisprudence on the chapeau, see *EC–Seal Products*, supra footnote 157, paras. 5.296–5.306.

161 *Brazil–Retreaded Tyres*, supra footnote 156, para. 150.

162 Ibid., para. 156.

163 Ibid., para. 151.

164 *China–Raw Materials (Panel)*, supra footnote 118, paras. 7.481, 7.485.

165 *China–Rare Earths*, supra footnote 158.

166 Ibid., para. 5.89.

紧密关系（目的和手段的关系）"。[167] 对第 20 条 g 款之要求的评估必须依据措施的"设计和结构"（它为措施所追求的真实目标提供了一个更可信赖的基准）[168] 以及相关市场的主要特征。[169] 因此，有的国家的措施未能达到这些要求和第 20 条 g 款的其他要求，对《关贸总协定》规则的违反也是缺乏正当性的。

在最近的"欧共体海豹产品案"中，根据第 20 条 a 款，针对海豹产品的进口禁令被认为是"保护公共道德所必需的"，尽管受到质疑的措施不符合起首语的要求。这是第一宗将动物福利等环境问题列为第 20 条 a 款中公共道德保护范畴的个案。"公共道德"的内容可能随时间而改变，以便反映某个国家人民的逐渐提升的环境意识。在此背景下，专家小组和上诉机构确认了早先在一起非环境案件中的结论，该结论认为：

> 公共道德的内容的定性可以有一定程度的差异，因此，应该给予成员国一定的空间，根据自己的制度和价值尺度，自行界定和运用公共道德这一概念。[170]

尽管出现了这些令人鼓舞的发展，但人们可能会质疑，想要在贸易法中融入环境保护，一般例外的运用是否是一种适当的方法（更不用说是否是最合适的方法）。如果环境法得到了适当的解释和适用，则没有理由将它的适用局限于引发例外。依据缔约国之间适用的其他国际法规则（由《维也纳条约法公约》第 31 条第 3 款 c 项规定）来解释《关贸总协定》第 1 条、第 3 条或第 21 条等贸易规则，可能需要对"相同产品"这一术语（或初级规范的其他相关表述）的含义进行一个调整，或者广义地利用条约的"部分废除"（或拆分）这一手段（例如第 20 条第 8 款之规定）。确立一个术语的适当含义并不等同于证明狭义例外的可用性。在第二个案件中，被告已经被发现违反条约，它将负有举证责任去证明，根

167　Ibid., para. 5. 90.
168　Ibid., para. 5. 96.
169　Ibid., para. 5. 97.
170　*EC-Seal Products*, supra footnote 157, para. 5. 199.

据一个现有的例外该措施是合理的。[171] 迄今为止，第 20 条的起首语的要求已被证明是环境措施合法性的重大障碍。

3. 具体的贸易协定：《卫生与植物检疫措施协议》（SPS）和《技术性贸易壁垒协议》（TBT）

国家采取保护人类、动物或植物健康所必需的贸易限制措施的权力不仅符合第 20 条的例外规定，而且它还体现在贸易规则（初级规范）层面。事实上，除了《关贸总协定》第 1 条、第 3 条和第 11 条所载的一般规则外，《卫生与植物检疫措施协议》（SPS）[172] 规定，此类措施的采取必须服从一些具体要求，这些要求的目的是确保透明度（通过针对通知的要求）、[173] 行政正当程序（通过检查程序中针对便利性和合理性的要求），[174] 以及某种国际协调措施（通过参考对等物和国际标准）。[175] 重要的是，相关措施必须以科学证据和一个风险评估为基础。[176]

从环境角度来看，这项条约可被视为试图界定贸易法中损害预防的范围。除了预防（即超越风险），基于风险预防（即存在不确定性时）而采取的措施的范围是被严格界定的。《卫生与植物检疫措施协议》（SPS）第 5 条第 7 款规定：

> 在相关科学证据不足的情况下，成员国可根据现有相关信息（包括来自有关国际组织的信息以及来自其他成员所采取的卫生或植物检疫措施）有条件地采取卫生或动植物检疫措施。在这种情况下，成员国应设法在合理时期内获得补充信息以便更客观地评估风险并检讨卫生或植物检疫措施。

---

171 除了证明是否存在例外情况外，还要证明是否满足了前言的要求。See *ibid.*, para. 5. 297. see further *China-Rare Earths*, supra footnote 158, para. 5. 99（我们还注意到，根据第 20 条 g 款有正当理由采取的措施是那些已被发现不符合 1994 年《关贸总协定》所载义务的措施。这些措施本身可能对市场产生了扭曲作用。在我们看来，它使得因果关系问题更加复杂，需要依据第 20 条 g 款中的"实证效应检验"采取更谨慎的态度）。

172 Agreement on the Application of Sanitary and Phytosanitary Measures, 15 April 1994, 1867 UNTS 493（SPS Agreement）.

173 Ibid., Art. 7 and Annex B.

174 Ibid., Art. 8 and Annex C.

175 Ibid., Art. 3 and 4 and Annex A.

176 Ibid., Art. 2（2）and 5.

《卫生与植物检疫措施协议》为基于风险预防所采取的环境措施预留的空间受到了热议，特别涉及两个案例，即"欧共体荷尔蒙案"[177]和"欧共体生物技术案"。[178] 在这两个案件中，欧共体都试图参照第三章讨论的风险预防原则来为贸易限制性措施辩护。欧共体的主张并未成功。在"欧共体荷尔蒙案"中，上诉机构拒绝以风险预防原则的习惯法基础来采取一般性立场，并指出，无论如何，"风险预防原则"[179]都已被纳入《卫生与植物检疫措施协议》第 5 条第 7 款并被赋予了具体的含义。[180] 同样，在"欧共体生物技术案"中，专家小组认为，风险预防原则的法律地位在一般国际法[181]中仍未确定，因此，该原则与《卫生与植物检疫措施协议》的解释无关。[182]

另一个重要的问题是国际标准问题。这一问题源自《卫生与植物检疫措施协议》和《技术性贸易壁垒协议》[183]的文本，后者界定了那些调整技术壁垒（如各种环境和效率标准）制定的贸易规则。这两项协议都力求通过一个可反驳的推定来协调相关措施的实施基础。根据《卫生与植物检疫措施协议》，[184] 依据公认的国际标准所采取的措施被视为成比例的（对贸易的限制程度不超过达成目标所必需的），而根据《卫生与植物检疫措施协议》，这些措施也被视为科学上合理的和必要的。[185] 这一推定存在的基础取决于"国际标准"的定义。《卫生与植物检疫措施协议》和《技术性贸易壁垒协议》都为适当标准的确定提供了一些指导。《卫生与植物检疫措施协议》附件 A 第 3 节参考了食品法典委员会（Codex Alimentarius Commission）（食品安全）、国际动物疫病办公室

---

[177] *European Communities-Measures concerning Meat and Meat Products*（*Hormones*），AB Report（16 January 1998），WT/DS26/AB/R，WT/DS48/AB/R（"EC-Hormones"）.

[178] *EC-Biotech*，supra footnote 117.

[179] It noted that "it is unnecessary, and probably imprudent, for the Appellate Body in this appeal to take a position on this important, but abstract, question", *EC-Hormones*, supra n. 177, para. 123.

[180] Ibid., para. 120.

[181] *EC-Biotech*, supra footnote 117, para. 7.88.

[182] Ibid., paras. 7.89 and 7.90.

[183] Agreement on Technical Barriers to Trade, 15 April 1994, 1868 UNTS 120（TBT Agreement）.

[184] Ibid., Art. 2（5）.

[185] See SPS Agreement, supra footnote 172, Arts. 2（2）（for the requirement）and 3（2）（for the presumption）.

（International Office for Epizootics）（动物健康）或《国际植物公约》（*International Plant Convention*）秘书处（植物健康）的标准、准则和建议。对于未涵盖的问题，第3节（d）参考了"全面开放的其他相关国际组织"。《技术性贸易壁垒协定》没有明确规定"国际标准"一词，但它参考了国际标准化组织（International Standardization Organization, ISO），并指出，国际标准是向所有世贸组织成员国的相关组织开放的机构以协商一致方式通过的。[186]

对这一术语含义的进一步阐明可以从上诉机构对重启的"金枪鱼海豚案"的裁决中得出。[187] 在该案中，墨西哥控诉美国《海豚保护消费者信息法》（*Dolphin Protection Consumer Information Act*, DPCIA）所施加的要求（随后美国法院进行了司法解释），即进口的金枪鱼必须贴上"海豚安全"的标签。根据美国法规，针对墨西哥船队在太平洋地区捕捞的金枪鱼，"海豚安全"标签授予取决于所使用的捕捞方法［具体来说，通过设置围网捕捞的金枪鱼不能被授予"海豚安全"标签，如果这些围网同时可以捕捞该地区（而非其他地区）的海豚］。值得注意的是，墨西哥和美国都加入的《国际海豚保育计划协议》（AIDCP）规定，授予"海豚安全"标签的前提条件是其他数量标准（海豚的死亡率和严重伤害水平，而不是捕捞方法）。这一争端最后被裁决违反了《技术性贸易壁垒协定》第2条第1款，但就当前目的而言，最相关的部分是针对何种标准才能构成该协议第2条第4款中"一个相关的国际标准"的讨论。专家小组认为，《国际海豚保育计划协议》可以设定相关的国际标准，但上诉机构推翻了这一结论，理由是《国际海豚保育计划协议》不是一个《技术性贸易壁垒协定》项下的国际标准化组织，因为它不向任何世贸组织成员自动开放加入。这一裁决设立了一个很高的门槛，来评估环境条约机构是否有能力采取那些符合《技术性贸易壁垒协定》的标准。

---

[186] TBT Agreement, supra footnote 183, Annex 1, Sections 2 and 4.

[187] *United States—Measures Concerning the Importation, Marketing and Sale of Tuna and Tuna Products*, AB Report (16 May 2012), WT/DS381/AB/R.

第四节　环境保护与知识产权

一　概述

阿马蒂亚·森（Amartya Sen）曾经指出，为了预防饥荒，必须解决的问题不一定是粮食的可用性，而是使有需要的人可以获得粮食。[188] 对于技术而言，也可以提出类似的观点。然而，与粮食不同，用于引导技术创新的战略（特别是知识产权或 IPRs）对此类技术的后续获取产生了影响。这是因为知识产权赋予发明人垄断地位，导致更高的价格，在某些情况下，还会导致其拒绝将技术许可给潜在的竞争公司。因此，发展无害化环境技术不仅是一个技术挑战，而且是一个政策挑战（如何促进创新）和法律挑战（不严格限制技术的获取）。[189]

我们已经在前面的章节中讨论了这个问题的某些方面。在第九章中，我们介绍了关于技术转让的争论，这是共同但有区别的责任原则的重要组成部分。在第六章中，我们分析了在所谓的"种子战争"的具体背景下，对遗传资源、传统知识和植物品种主张财产权所造成的影响。这些只是本节所述更广泛问题的两种表现：如何促进无害化环境技术的传播而又不阻碍它们的发展。如第九章所述，从法律角度来看，争议体现在技术转让可能采取的形式上。经济理论所确定的主要"形式"，即（被制造的产品或含有特定技术的产品的）贸易、许可（授权在特定条件下使用某一技术或其一部分）和外国直接投资（在东道国设立一个能够获得相关技术的实体），[190] 具有大不相同的政治和法律影响。

出于各种原因，知识产权的国际保护在三种情况下是非常关键的。确

---

[188] See A. Sen, *Poverty and Famines. An Essay on Entitlement and Deprivation*（Oxford University Press，1981）.

[189] For two recent surveys of legal techniques that may help to strike a balance, see S. Chuffart, *Optimising Environmental Technology Diffusion under Intellectual Property Constraints: A Legal Analysis*（Zurich: Schulthess，2016）; Zhuang Wei, *Intellectual Property Rights and Climate Change. Interpreting the TRIPS Agreement for Environmentally Sound Technologies*（Cambridge University Press，2017）.

[190] See K. Keller, "International Technology Diffusion"（2004）42 *Journal of Economic Literature* 752.

保知识产权保护的基本标准，特别是专利（授予发明人的对发明的生产、使用和商业化的临时法律垄断），对于保护出口产品中嵌入的技术至关重要。许可的基本思想是建立在尊重知识产权的基础之上的。至于外国直接投资，根据投资的具体构成方式，知识产权保护的运作方式将有所不同。专利保护是保持投资工具在东道国的市场地位的关键，这种工具通常都会积极地推进受专利保护的产品的商业化，或者积极地组装甚至生产产品。如果含有技术的部件是在东道国制造的，则必须将技术和诀窍转移到投资工具中，知识产权保护将会发挥作用，以保护子公司免受竞争对手或东道国的侵害。

在这三种假设中，知识产权保护不仅有利于技术的发展，而且有利于促进技术的传播。然而，只有权利所有者享有更好的发明保护，这种传播才会得到促进。但是，如果拥有了某项垄断，权利所有者就可以大幅提高其产品的价格，甚至拒绝签订许可协议。这种力量可能成为技术传播的重要障碍，从而阻止发展中国家出现类似的产业。它还可能阻碍创新，因为它限制了技术的获取，而这些技术是开发其他相关技术的必要基石，对技术初创公司和市场"颠覆者"而言更是如此。因此，与投资和贸易一样，可以从协同和冲突的视角来分析环境保护与知识产权之间的关系。

二　协同效应

（一）国际专利保护的方式

上述看法有助于了解国际法在保护知识产权方面的作用。虽然有大量的多边条约涉及知识产权的各个方面，[191] 但目前最相关的条约是《与贸易有关的知识产权协定》（*Agreement on Trade-Related Aspects of Intellectual Property Rights*, TRIPS）、[192]《保护工业产权巴黎公约》（*Paris Convention for the Protection of Industrial Property*, Paris Convention）[193] 和《专利合作条

---

[191] For an introduction, see F. M. Abbott, T. Cottier and F. Gurry, *International Intellectual Property in an Integrated World Economy* (New York: Wolters Kluwer, 2011).

[192] Agreement on Trade-Related Aspects of Intellectual Property Rights, 15 April 1994, 1869 UNTS 299. On this treaty, see C. Correa, *Trade-Related Aspects of Intellectual Property Rights. A Commentary on the TRIPs Agreement* (Oxford University Press, 2007).

[193] Paris Convention for the Protection of Industrial Property, 20 March 1883, available at: www.wipo.org (last visited on 20 May 2017).

约》(Patent Cooperation Treaty, PCT)。[194]

后两者专门致力于扩大专利保护的地理范围,尽管程度有限。虽然这种保护仍然是地域性的,但这些文件为那些在缔约国提交的专利申请赋予了一定的国际效力。因此,根据《巴黎公约》,第一次提交之日将会计入其他缔约国在 12 个月内提交的所有其他申请。更重要的是,根据《专利合作条约》,只要满足某些条件,某个国际申请可以被视为在所有缔约国的同时申请。因此,这一制度试图促进创新,包括环境方面的创新,因为它大大降低了许多国家寻求专利保护的交易成本。

《与贸易有关的知识产权协定》采取了一个不同的方法。它要求世贸组织成员在其立法中提供知识产权的基本保护。协定特别制定了专利保护标准(第 27—34 条)。与以往专利保护的国际努力相比,该协定更加广泛和深入,协定还为国内执法(第三部分)设定了参照物,并提供了诉诸 WTO 争端解决机构的机会(第 64 条)。这种保护为创新提供了一个明确的激励,因为它大大提升了权利所有人的地位。此外,《与贸易有关的知识产权协定》特别提到了技术转让问题。第 7 条明确规定:

> 知识产权的保护和实施应当对促进技术革新以及技术转让和传播作出贡献,对技术知识的生产者和使用者的共同利益作出贡献,并应当以一种有助于社会和经济福利以及有助于权利与义务平衡的方式进行。

第 66 条第 2 款涉及这一义务,该条要求发达国家鼓励本国公司向最不发达国家转让技术。然而,除了一些象征性的步骤,例如建立一个"机制"来监控这项规定的执行情况外,[195] 几乎没有采取具体的行动。

除了这些条约提供的一般激励措施之外,最近几年国际社会还探讨了其他方法,以特别鼓励与环境有关的技术创新。在以下各节中,我们将讨论其中的两个,即环境专利快速通道和建立知识产权市场的努力。

---

[194] Patent Cooperation Treaty, 19 June 1970, 1160 UNTS 231 (PCT).

[195] See TRIPs Council, Implementation of Article 66 (2) of the TRIPs Agreement, 20 February 2003, IP/C/28 [this decision requires the submission of reports by developed countries detailing steps taken to comply with Art. 66 (2)].

(二) 环境专利快速通道

近年来，英国、中国、韩国、美国、澳大利亚等国的国家专利局对涉及环境创新技术的专利申请给予了优惠待遇。[196] 这些申请大多涉及可再生能源技术，快速通道方案可以大大加快审查速度，将获得专利所需的时间缩短一半甚至更多。

国内的经验引发了一个讨论，即是否可能通过修订《专利合作条约》来推广这种优惠待遇。[197] 可供选择的方案包括加快申请流程、降低费用和加强绿色申请的传播。因此，所寻求的协同效应类型是进一步降低提交专利申请所需的交易成本。这一申请不仅将通过《专利合作条约》同时提交给所有成员国办事处，还可以在所有成员国中得到优惠待遇。然而，迄今为止，这一方面的进展在国际层面上较为缓慢，这主要是因为这种制度在国内专利法中需要进行重大改革，而且与环境商品协定一样，在确定符合条件的专利类型方面遇到了挑战。

(三) 知识产权市场

在保护知识产权和加强知识产权传播之间取得平衡的一个创新工具是知识产权市场的利用。[198] 这种市场可以采取不同的形式，从仅仅将技术提供者和接受者联系起来，到有组织地销售专利（例如通过拍卖），到建立不同程度自由交换许可证权利的市场。

第一种手段可以参照世界知识产权组织（WIPO）绿色平台[199]加以说明，该平台实际上是一个绿色技术数据库，经提供者同意后发布，并提供给有兴趣获得该技术的各种参与者进行搜索。此平台的目的是提供一个撮合供需方的市场，而不干预后续交易（例如技术许可）。该工具的优点（和缺点）是可以维护技术提供者的权利，包括有权向潜在收购方授予或不授予许可证或协商其条款。

---

[196] See A. Dechezleprêtre, "Fast-tracking Green Patent Applications: An Empirical Analysis, ICTSD Programme on Innovation, Technology and Intellectual Property: Issue Paper No. 37" (2013).

[197] See Meeting of International Authorities under the Patent Cooperation Treaty, *Preferential Treatment for International Applications Relating to "Green" Technologies*, 21 January 2010, Doc. PCT/MIA/17/5.

[198] See A. H. B. Monk, "The Emerging Market for Intellectual Property: Drivers, Restrainers, and Implications" (2009) 9 *Journal of Economic Geography* 469.

[199] See webaccess.wipo.int/green/ (last visited on 15 May 2017).

第二种手段是通过拍卖程序有组织地出售知识产权,特别是专利。例如,2005年和2006年在加利福尼亚州举行的专利拍卖,专利组合以数百万美元的价格售出。[200] 这一手段的目的是在知识产权保护与技术传播之间实现一个平衡,但是这一目的有时无法实现,因为如果出卖人(例如已破产的公司)丧失其知识产权的所有权,收购方就必须支付专利的市场价格。

第三种手段更为复杂。与第一种手段一样,它为满足供应和需求提供了一个正规的市场;而且,它和第二种手段一样,还可以处理知识产权的转让。然而,在这些市场交换的对象不是专利,而是使用某一专利或某个基于多项专利的技术的"许可"权。例如,2010年在达沃斯推出的"绿色交易所"(GreenXchange)项目,[201] 卖方可以选择是否将该技术许可给潜在的收购者。因此,交易成本的降低主要来自流程的标准化。然而,在另一个案例中,IPXI[202] 在市场上交换的许可权("单位许可权")是在一个非歧视的基础上提供的;因此,技术提供商不能参与市场,除非他同意将技术许可给参与市场的所有收购方。虽然 IPXI 并不特别涉及无害化环境技术,但它确实包括其中一些技术,例如节能电器。IPXI 是一个短暂的实验,在开放后不久就停止了运行。但它仍然很好地说明了不仅需要"硬"技术的创新,而且需要"软"(法律或金融)技术的创新。

三 冲突

(一)《与贸易有关的知识产权协定》和环境保护

《与贸易有关的知识产权协定》对各国限定知识产权保护的能力予以限制以促进技术传播,特别是通过它的专利保护标准。但是,它规定了一些严格的例外情形,根据这些例外,一国可以排除一项发明的可专利性或限制其保护范围。其中以下三个方面与环境保护有关。

首先,当保护公共秩序或道德(包括保护人类、动物或植物生命或健康或避免对环境的严重损害)所必需的时候,国家可以排除发明的可专利性(第27条第2款)。其次,各国还可以排除"除微生物以外的植

---

[200] See Chuffart, supra footnote 189, pp. 134–135.

[201] Ibid., pp. 135–136.

[202] Ibid., pp. 137–139.

物和动物的可专利性,以及除生产非生物和微生物过程以外的植物或动物的生物学过程",但仅限于通过专利或"有效的独特制度或其任何组合"保护植物品种的情况下(第 27 条第 3 款 b 项)。最后,专利权人享有的排他性或垄断权,在一定条件下可以受到限制;这为发展某些技术的所谓的"强制许可"铺平了道路(第 30—31 条)。

这一制度因其对公共卫生政策[203]以及气候变化技术的传播的影响而受到批评。[204] 随着时间的推移,《与贸易有关的知识产权协定》相关条款被解释,以便向发展中国家提供一些灵活性(本章第四节第三部分第二点)。然而,在修订《与贸易有关的知识产权协定》和其他法律文件以平衡专利保护与遗传资源和传统知识权利的保护的过程中,仍然存在着许多问题(本章第四节第二部分第三点)。

(二)《与贸易有关的知识产权协定》的解读

1. 强制许可和公共卫生

如上一节所述,《与贸易有关的知识产权协定》允许其专利授予和保护的规范性标准具有一定的灵活性。第 31 条允许各国在其立法中列入在某些情况下不经权利人授权就可以授权第三方使用专利。通常,只有在第三方已经尝试从权利人那里获得许可证时,才可能被授予此类授权。但是,"在发生全国性紧急状态或其他极端紧急状态或为公共的非商业性目的而使用的情况下"可免除这一要求(第 31 条 b 款)。

在一些国家,这种被称为"强制许可"的例外用于生产非专利药品(用于 HIV/AIDS 和其他疾病)。《2001 年与贸易有关的知识产权协定和公共卫生宣言》(*2001 Declaration on the TRIPS Agreement and Public Health*)特别认可了这种可能性,根据该宣言,"协定的解释和执行方式可以而且必须支持世贸组织成员的保护公共卫生的权利",因此:

> 每个成员都有权确定何种情况能构成国家紧急情况或其他极端紧

---

[203] For an overview of the debate, see R. Love, "Corporate Wealth or Public Health? WTO/TRIPS Flexibilities and Access to HIV/AIDS Antiretroviral Drugs by Developing Countries" (2007) 17 *Development in Practice* 208.

[204] *Contribution of Intellectual Property to Facilitating the Transfer of Environmentally Rational Technology. Communication from Ecuador*, 27 February 2013, IP/C/W/585.

急情况,据了解,公共卫生危机,包括与艾滋病毒/艾滋病、结核病、疟疾和其他流行病有关的危机,可构成国家紧急情况或其他极端紧急情况。[205]

2003年,总理事会的一项决定承认,可以将通用药品出口至那些有需要的国家(前提是当地没有能力生产),这就部分解决了《与贸易有关的知识产权协定》第31条f款(规定强制许可下的生产主要用于国内消费)造成的第二个障碍。[206] 2005年12月制定了有关的修正案(引入第31条),[207] 2017年1月,最终达成生效所需的世贸组织成员2/3多数的支持,从而将公共卫生这一强制性许可例外植入了《与贸易有关的知识产权协定》的文本。这一发展特别值得注意,因为这是自1995年世贸组织开始运行以来,世贸组织的一项多边协定首次被正式修订,而且修正案追求的目标不同于单纯的贸易自由化。

这种强制许可制度很好地说明了,当潜在冲突得到公开承认和界定时,可以通过权威的解释得到有效解决,而且当公众压力足够大时,还可以通过一个实际的修正案得到有效解决。

2. 对植物品种的专门保护

《与贸易有关的知识产权协定》第27条第3款b项赋予各国在植物品种的可专利性方面一定的灵活性。如第六章所述,对植物品种的保护是有争议的,因为许多发展中国家和土著群体认为,这是正式承认"被盗的"遗传资源或传统农业知识。在这方面,《与贸易有关的知识产权协定》对育种者有利(对农民相对不利),要求各国通过专利或其他专门的手段保护植物品种。

第27条第3款b项所允许的灵活性程度完全取决于"有效的专门制度"(effective sui generis sysems)一词的含义。尽管进行了几次尝试,但《与贸易有关的知识产权协定》理事会仍在讨论这一问题,对于何种制度

---

[205] "Declaration on the TRIPs Agreement and Public Health", 14 November 2011, WT/MIN (01) / DEC/2, paras. 4 and 5.

[206] "Implementation of paragraph 6oftheDohaDeclarationonthe TRIPS Agreement and public health", 1 September 2003, WT/L/540 and Corr. 1.

[207] "Amendment of the TRIPS Agreement", 6 December 2005, WT/L/641.

有资格成为一个可接受的制度,存在较大分歧。问题的根源在于,育种者在植物品种保护上的权利在多大程度上可以与农民的权利(特别是农民再植所收获的部分种子或将其投入流通的权利)相平衡。

根据联合国环境规划署的《贸易和绿色经济手册》(Handbook on Trade and Green Economy)、[208]《保护植物新品种国际公约》(International Convention for the Protection of New Varieties of Plants,UPOV Convention)[209]所建立的制度正是这种有效的专门制度。与《与贸易有关的知识产权协定》一样,《保护植物新品种国际公约》主要是为了保护育种者的权利,它因此受到了批评,包括联合国食品权特别报告员(UN Special Rapporteur on the Right to Food)的批评,因为它对种子保存和流通的传统制度的生存以及生物多样性保护产生了不利影响。[210] 另一个问题就是,一些发展中国家目前正在拟订的国内计划或区域计划(这些计划旨在为农民权利提供额外的保护)是否也会受益于第 27 条第 3 款 b 项的例外情形。[211]

(三)遗传资源和传统知识:拟议的修正案

第六章对遗传资源和传统知识的讨论介绍了《与贸易有关的知识产权协定》的修订尝试应当在何种背景下进行评估。发展中国家(也是绝大多数生物多样性的发现地)在制定《生物多样性公约》[212]和《名古屋议定书》[213]时所追求的一个目标是规制遗传资源和传统知识的获取。一般认为,这种规制对于防止跨国公司利用这些资源开发药物和植物品种并申请专利而又不进行惠益分享十分重要。[214] 这个问题已经提交至两个主要

---

[208] Handbook, supra footnote 124, pp. 91-92.

[209] International Convention for the Protection of New Varieties of Plants, 2 December 1961, 815 UNTS 89 (subsequently revised, particularly in 1991).

[210] See Seed Policies and the Right to Food: Enhancing Agrobiodiversity and Encouraging Innovation. Report presented to the UN General Assembly, 23 July 2009, UN Doc. A/64/170.

[211] Handbook, supra footnote 124, section 4.5.2.

[212] Convention on Biological Diversity, 5 June 1992, 1760 UNTS 79 (CBD).

[213] See supra footnote 110.

[214] See S. Safrin, "Hyper ownership in a Time of Biotechnological Promise: The International Conflict" (2004) 98 *American Journal of International Law* 641; J. Curci, *The Protection of Biodiversity and Traditional Knowledge in International Law of Intellectual Property* (Cambridge University Press, 2009).

论坛。

讨论的一部分是在《与贸易有关的知识产权协定》理事会这一背景下进行的。《多哈宣言》（*Doha Declaration*）第19段委托理事会阐明《与贸易有关的知识产权协定》与《生物多样性公约》之间的关系。理事会秘书处编写了简报，概述了谈判的主要步骤。[215] 迄今的主要举措是数个发展中国家于2006年提出的关于修订《与贸易有关的知识产权协定》的提案，以便在专利条例中增加一个信息披露的要求。具体而言，各国应规定一项要求，即当专利涉及生物材料或传统知识时，专利申请人必须披露所用材料的来源，并提供合法获取材料的证据（即符合事先知情同意和惠益分享要求）。[216] 拟议的修正可采用不同的法律形式，例如第27条中可专利性（可专利标的）的一个附加例外、第29条中的附加段落（关于专利申请人的条件）或一项全新的规定（第29条的重塑）。[217] 违反拟议的信息披露要求可能会产生严重后果，甚至可能被撤销专利。[218] 然而，迄今为止，这些努力没有成功。如果欧盟等重要集团支持修正案提案，情况可能会改变。目前看来这并未完全不可能，因为欧洲议会通过了一项决议，要求欧盟委员会指示其谈判人员将《名古屋议定书》作为引入披露要求的出发点。[219]

在世界知识产权组织（WIPO），特别是2000年9月成立的知识产权和遗传资源、传统知识和民间文学艺术政府间委员会［Intergovernmental Committee (IGC) on Intellectual Property and Genetic Resources, Traditional Knowledge and Folklore］，也进行了相关讨论。在过去几年中，委员会议定了三份文本（虽然在很大程度上是雷同的），构成了关于遗传资源、[220]

---

[215] The Relationship between the TRIPs Agreement and the Convention on Biological Diversity: Summary of Issues Raised and Points Made, 8 February 2006, IP/C/W/368/Rev. 1. (Summary Note).

[216] Ibid., para. 71.

[217] Ibid., para. 79.

[218] Ibid., para. 75.

[219] European Parliament Resolution of 15 January 2013 on Development Aspects of Intellectual Property Rights on Genetic Resources: The Impact on Poverty Reduction in Developing Countries, 2012/2135 (INI), paras. 32-34, available at: www.europarl.europa.eu (last visited on 20 April 2017).

[220] Consolidated Document Relating to Intellectual Property and Genetic Resources, WIPO/GRTKF/IC/34/4 (15 March 2017), available at: www.wipo.org (last visited on 10 April 2017).

传统知识[221]和传统文化展示[222]的披露要求的完整草案。第一稿（遗传资源）还特别针对《专利合作条约》和《专利法条约》设计了一个修订,[223]要求或授权各国在其立法中引入信息披露要求。然而，谈判已经进行了数年，取得正式结果的前景仍不明朗。

部分参考文献

[1] Abbott, F. M., T. Cottier, and F. Gurry, *International Intellectual Property in an Integrated World Economy* (New York: Wolters Kluwer, 2011).

[2] Asteriti, A., *Greening Investment Law* (PhD dissertation, Glasgow, 2011).

[3] Bodansky, D. and J. Lawrence, "Trade and Environment", in D. Bethlehem, D. McRae, R. Neufeld and I. Van Damme (eds.), *The Oxford Handbook of International Trade Law* (Oxford University Press, 2009), pp. 505–538.

[4] Boisson de Chazournes, L. and M. Mbengue, "A propos du principe de soutien mutual. Les relations entre le Protocole de Cartagena et les Accords de l'OMC" (2007) 111 *Revue Générale de Droit International Public* 829.

[5] Brown Weiss, E. and J. Jackson (eds.), *Reconciling Environment and Trade* (Ardsley NY: Transnational Publishers, 2001).

[6] Charnovitz, S., "The WTO's Environmental Progress", in W. J. Davey and J. Jackson (eds.), *The Future of International Economic Law* (Oxford University Press, 2008), pp. 247–268.

[7] Chuffart, S., *Optimising Environmental Technology Diffusion under Intellectual Property Constraints: A Legal Analysis* (Zurich: Schulthess, 2016).

---

[221] The Protection of Traditional Knowledge: Draft Articles, WIPO/GRTKF/IC/34/5 (15 March 2017), available at: www.wipo.org (last visited on 10 April 2017).

[222] The Protection of Traditional Cultural Expressions: Draft Articles, WIPO/GRTKF/IC/34/6 (14 March 2017), available at: www.wipo.org (last visited on 10 April 2017).

[223] Patent Law Treaty, 19 June 1070, 39 ILM 1047.

[8] Cordonnier Segger, M. - C., M. W. Gehring and A. Newcombe (eds.), *Sustainable Development in World Investment Law* (Alphen aan den Rijn: Wolters Kluwer, 2011).

[9] Correa, C., *Trade-Related Aspects of Intellectual Property Rights. A Commentary on the TRIPs Agreement* (Oxford University Press, 2007).

"Innovation and Technology Transfer of Environmentally Sound Technologies: The Need to Engage in a Substantive Debate" (2013) 22 *Review of European, Comparative and International Environmental Law* 54.

[10] Curci, J., *The Protection of Biodiversity and Traditional Knowledge in International Law of Intellectual Property* (Cambridge University Press, 2009).

[11] Dechezleprêtre, A., *Fast-tracking Green Patent Applications: An Empirical Analysis*, ICTSD Programme on Innovation, Technology and Intellectual Property: Issue Paper No. 37 (2013).

[12] Di Benedetto, S., *International Investment Law and the Environment* (Cheltenham: Edward Elgar, 2013).

[13] Dolzer, R. and C. Schreuer, *Principles of International Investment Law* (Oxford University Press, 2013).

[14] Douglas, Z., J. Pauwelyn and J. E. Viñuales (eds.), *The Foundations of International Investment Law: Bringing Theory into Practice* (Oxford University Press, 2014).

[15] Dupuy, P. -M. and J. E. Viñuales (eds.), *Harnessing Foreign Investment to Promote Environmental Protection: Incentives and Safeguards* (Cambridge University Press, 2013).

[16] Esty, D., *Greening the GATT: Trade, Environment, and the Future* (Washington, DC: Institute for International Economics, 1994).

[17] Frankel, J. and A. Rose, "Is Trade Good or Bad for the Environment? Sorting out the Causality" (2005) 87 *Review of Economics and Statistics* 85.

[18] George, C., "Environment and Regional Trade Agreements: Emerging Trends and Policy Drivers", *OECD Trade and Environment Working Papers*, 2014/02, available at: http://dx.doi.org/10.1787/5jz0v4q45g6

h-en (visited on 2 April 2017).

[19] Gordon, K. and J. Pohl, "Environmental Concerns in International Investment Agreements: A Survey" (2011) *OECD Working Papers on International Investment* No. 2011/1.

[20] Henry, G., *Technologies vertes et propriete intellectuelle* (Paris: Lexis Nexis, 2013).

[21] Love, R., "Corporate Wealth or Public Health? WTO/TRIPS Flexibilities and Access to HIV/AIDS Antiretroviral Drugs by Developing Countries" (2007) 17 *Development in Practice* 208.

[22] Miles, K., *The Origins of International Investment Law* (Cambridge University Press, 2013).

[23] Monk, A. H. B., "The Emerging Market for Intellectual Property: Drivers, Restrainers, and Implications" (2009) 9 *Journal of Economic Geography* 469.

[24] Mortenson, J. D., "Meaning of 'Investment': ICSID *Travaux* and the Domain of International Investment Law" (2010) 51 *Harvard International Law Journal* 257.

[25] Pavoni, R., "Mutual Supportiveness as a Principle of Interpretation and Law-Making: A Watershed for the 'WTO-and-Competing-Regimes' Debate?" (2010) 3 *European Journal of International Law* 649.

[26] Petersmann, E. U., *International and European Trade and Environmental Law after the Uruguay Round* (The Hague: Kluwer, 1995).

[27] Robert-Cuendet, S., *Droits de L'investisseur Étranger et Protection de L'environnement: Contribution à L'analyse de L'expropriation Indirecte* (Leiden: Martinus Nijhoff, 2010).

[28] Romson, A., *Environmental Policy Space and International Investment Law* (PhD dissertation, Stockholm, 2012).

[29] Safrin, S., "Hyperownership in a Time of Biotechnological Promise: The International Conflict" (2004) 98 *American Journal of International Law* 641.

[30] Streck, C., "The World Summit on Sustainable Development: Partnerships as New Tools in Environmental Governance" (2002) 13 *Yearbook*

of International Environmental Law 63.

[31] United Nations Commission on Trade and Development, *World Investment Report* 2014. *Investing in the SDGs* (2014), available at: www.unctad.org (visited on 2 April 2017).

[32] United Nations Environment Programme, *Trade and Green Economy: A Handbook* (Geneva: UNEP, 3rd edn 2014).

[33] Viñuales, J. E., *Foreign Investment and the Environment in International Law* (Cambridge University Press, 2012).

"Foreign Investment and the Environment in International Law: Current Trends", in K. Miles (ed.), *Research Handbook on Environment and Investment Law* (Cheltenham: Edward Elgar, 2018), chapter 2.

[34] Von Moltke, K., "The Last Round: The General Agreement on Tariffs and Trade in Light of the Earth Summit" (1993) 23 *Environmental Law* 519.

[35] Vranes, E., *Trade and the Environment. Fundamental Issues in International Law, WTO Law, and Legal Theory* (Oxford University Press, 2009).

[36] Watson, J., *The WTO and the Environment* (London: Routledge, 2013).

[37] Wu, M. and J. Salzman, "The Next Generation of Trade and Environment Conflicts: The Rise of Green Industrial Policy" (2014) 108 *Northwestern University Law Review* 401.

[38] Zaelke, D., R. Housman and P. Orbach (eds.), *Trade and the Environment: Law, Economics and Policy* (Washington, DC: Island Press, 1993).

[39] Zhuang Wei, *Intellectual Property Rights and Climate Change. Interpreting the TRIPS Agreement for Environmentally Sound Technologies* (Cambridge University Press, 2017).

[40] Zvelc, R., "Environmental Integration in EU Trade Policy: The Generalised System of Preferences, Trade Sustainability Impact Assessments and Free Trade Agreements", in E. Morgera (ed.), *The External Environmental Policy of the European Union EU and International Law Perspectives* (Cambridge University Press, 2012), pp. 174–203.